THE
CAREER
DIRECTORY

1999 EDITION

Edited by:
Richard W. Yerema

MEDIACORP CANADA INC.
TORONTO

SOME PAST REVIEWS...

"The Career Directory is an excellent resource for first-time job seekers
and those looking for entry-level positions.
Well indexed by company name and functional speciality"
Canada Employment Weekly

"A valuable reference guide for job seekers"
The Toronto Star

"The Career Directory is a user-friendly resource,
easy to use and informative. It is an excellent career search resource"
Guidance & Counselling

"The Directory is an affordable and essential
book for job hunting and career planning in Canada"
The Aquinian, St. Thomas University

"It is easy-to-use, an excellent source, and is necessary
for anyone who wants to break into the job market"
The Underground, University of Toronto

"While written for new graduates seeking employment, it is useful for
career-changers or students considering educational programs who want
to foresee potential areas and types of employment.
Also new Canadians with training from foreign institutions have found this book useful"
Career Action News, Toronto Centre for Career Action

"Students intending to look for summer or full-time work
later this year will find a valuable resource in The Career Directory"
The Toronto Star

"For those looking for that first job upon graduation
or even a summer job, this book could prove invaluable"
The Lance, University of Windsor

"Finding a job is the formidable hurdle facing university graduates
and others these days. These books offer information and advice that could help"
The Star Phoenix, Saskatoon

"It can also help you determine whether a company is right for you even
before you walk in the door"
Eye On Toronto, CFTO - CTV

"An excellent source of pertinent information"
Toronto Career Directory User

"A truly informative directory"
London Career Directory User

"Helps one make sense of what occupations are available for what degrees,
what prospective companies are actually looking for,
and valuable contact names within various corporations"
The Lexicon, York University •

ABOUT THE CREATION OF THIS BOOK...

The Career Directory is the result of the experiences of two University of Toronto graduates. Frustrated in their own job searches by the lack of accessible and up-to-date information, they endeavoured to develop an information source that would provide relevant information to match each individual's qualifications to the requirements of individual employers. This publication is a result of those early efforts.

One of the most difficult tasks you will face in your job search is obtaining recruitment information about potential employers. This process can be time-consuming and expensive. However, possessing the right information about employers remains critical for organizing an intelligent and well-targeted job search.

Within the pages of this directory, you will find valuable and unique information about employers that will help focus your job search efforts and allow you to tap the potential of the hidden job market. All the information in this book is presented in an easily-read and understood format. There are no tables, abbreviations or code deciphering required.

This year's Directory is the eighth annual edition and represents a significant expansion in the book's coverage. In addition to updated and expanded listings for returning employers, this year's edition includes more new employers than ever before.

I hope that you will find my book useful in your job search.

Richard Yerema
ry@mediacorp2.com

Thoughts and Thanks

Of the definitions listed in the dictionary for the word change, the one that best suits this story is "to move from one phase to another". The evidence is in your hands, the directory and yours truly have moved from one phase to another.

Many thanks to all who have supported the directory as an independent undertaking for the past seven years, and thanks to Tony and company for helping in the transformation, and for leaving enough white space for this note.

The Career Directory
Mediacorp Canada Inc.
15 Madison Avenue
Toronto, Ontario
M5R 2S2

Telephone   (416) 964-6069
Fax   (416) 964-3202

E-mail   info@mediacorp2.com
Web Site   http://www.mediacorp2.com

To purchase the information in this directory on disk or in label format, telephone (416) 964-6069.

ISBN 0-9681447-5-6. 8th Edition. First edition: 1992.

Printed in Canada by Webcom.

TABLE OF CONTENTS

HOW TO USE THIS DIRECTORY

This directory is a guide for job-seekers interested in finding Canadian employers that recruit people with particular educational backgrounds. You can use this book to find:

- Employers that recruit full-time employees with your educational background;

- Employers in a particular industry;

- Employers in a particular region of the country;

- Employers that participate in co-op work/study programs; and

- Employers that offer summer jobs.

The information in this directory is compiled from thousands of listing forms sent to employers and interviews conducted with human resource managers and recruiters.

To use this directory, start with the **Educational Index**. Locate your degree or diploma (e.g. Bachelor of Arts, Bachelor of Engineering, Community College Diploma) in the Table of Contents (p. 9). Then turn to that section and find the particular field of study that applies to you (e.g. Bachelor of Arts in Journalism, Bachelor of Engineering in Aerospace, Community CollegeDiploma in Nursing). The companies listed below your degree or diploma are your primary targets for full-time employment.

Next, go back to the starting point for your degree or diploma. At the top of each section are employers that hire people with your degree or diploma, but have not specified a field of study. (Their field of study is listed as "General".) These employers are your secondary targets for full-time employment.

Once you have identified your primary and secondary targets, go the **Employer Listings** to find out more information on the employers. Each employer listing provides:

- A brief overview of the company's operations, including the number of employees.

- Full contact information, including the employer's human resources contact, mailing address, telephone and fax numbers, email address and website.

- The average starting salary, and whether benefits are offered.

- A rating on the company's potential for career advancement.

- A rating on the benefits offered.

- The academic qualifications desired, including degree, diploma and field of study.

- The non-academic skills desired.

- Information on whether co-op or summer employment opportunities are available.

- The preferred method for initial contact by job-seekers (e.g. send resume, call, apply online).

The information in each listing will allow you to make informed decisions about which employers are best suited to your qualifications and career objectives.

Besides the Educational Index, there are four useful topical indexes located after the employer listings. The **Industry Index** lets you find all the employers in a particular business or line of work that may interest you. The **Geographic Index** lists the employers by province. The **Co-Op** Index shows all the employers that participate in co-op work/study programs. And the **Summer Job Index** lists all the employers that traditionally offer summer positions for students.

A final word is in order about the scope of this directory. Don't be disheartened if you have qualifications that are superior to those listed by employers, or are not exactly what the employer has specified. Always write the employer and inquire whether positions for people with your particular qualifications are available. This directory should be seen as a starting point for your job search, not a replacement for your own hard work and research. The aim of this book is to point you in the right direction, but the journey is up to you.

Education Index

BACHELOR OF ARCHITECTURE

BACHELOR OF LANDSCAPE ARCHITECTURE

BACHELOR OF ARTS - GENERAL

BACHELOR OF ARTS - ARCHEOLOGY

BACHELOR OF ARTS - BUSINESS

BACHELOR OF ARTS - CRIMINOLOGY

BACHELOR OF ARTS - ECONOMICS

BACHELOR OF ARTS - ENGLISH

BACHELOR OF ARTS - FRENCH

BACHELOR OF ARTS - GEOGRAPHY

BACHELOR OF ARTS - GRAPHIC/FINE ARTS

BACHELOR OF ARTS - HISTORY

BACHELOR OF ARTS - POLITICAL SCIENCE

BACHELOR OF ARTS - PSYCHOLOGY

BACHELOR OF ARTS - PUBLIC RELATIONS

BACHELOR OF ARTS - RECREATION STUDIES

BACHELOR OF ARTS - SOCIOLOGY/SOCIAL WORK

BACHELOR OF ARTS - URBAN GEOGRAPHY / PLANNING

BACHELOR OF COMMERCE/BUSINESS ADMINISTRATION - GENERAL

BACHELOR OF COMMERCE/BUSINESS ADMINISTRATION - ACCOUNTING

BACHELOR OF COMMERCE/BUSINESS ADMINISTRATION - FINANCE

BACHELOR OF COMMERCE/BUSINESS ADMINISTRATION - HOTEL/FOOD

BACHELOR OF COMMERCE/BUSINESS ADMINISTRATION - HUMAN RESOURCES

BACHELOR OF COMMERCE/BUSINESS ADMINISTRATION - INFORMATION SYSTEMS/MIS

BACHELOR OF COMMERCE/BUSINESS ADMINISTRATION - MARKETING

BACHELOR OF COMMERCE/BUSINESS ADMINISTRATION - PUBLIC ADMINISTRATION

BACHELOR OF EDUCATION - ADULT

BACHELOR OF EDUCATION - GENERAL

BACHELOR OF EDUCATION - EARLY CHILDHOOD (ECE)

BACHELOR OF EDUCATION - INTERMEDIATE SENIOR (7-12)

BACHELOR OF EDUCATION - JUNIOR INTERMEDIATE (4-10)

BACHELOR OF EDUCATION - PHYSICAL AND HEALTH

BACHELOR OF EDUCATION - PRIMARY JUNIOR (0-6)

BACHELOR OF EDUCATION - SPECIAL NEEDS

BACHELOR OF ENGINEERING - GENERAL

BACHELOR OF ENGINEERING - AEROSPACE

BACHELOR OF ENGINEERING - AGRICULTURAL ENGINEERING

BACHELOR OF ENGINEERING - ARCHITECTURAL/BUILDING

BACHELOR OF ENGINEERING - AUTOMATION/ROBOTICS

BACHELOR OF ENGINEERING - BIOMEDICAL ELECTRONICS

BACHELOR OF ENGINEERING - BIOTECHNOLOGY

BACHELOR OF ENGINEERING - CHEMICAL

BACHELOR OF ENGINEERING - CIVIL

BACELOR OF ENGINEERING - COMPUTER SYSTEMS

BACHELOR OF ENGINEERING - ELECTRICAL

BACHELOR OF ENGINEERING - ENGINEERING PHYSICS

BACHELOR OF ENGINEERING - ENVIRONMENTAL/RESOURCES

BACHELOR OF ENGINEERING - FOOD PROCESSING

BACHELOR OF ENGINEERING - FOREST RESOURCES

BACHELOR OF ENGINEERING - GEOLOGICAL ENGINEERING

BACHELOR OF ENGINEERING - INDUSTRIAL CHEMISTRY

BACHELOR OF ENGINEERING - INDUSTRIAL DESIGN

BACHELOR OF ENGINEERING - INDUS-
TRIAL ENGINEERING

BACHELOR OF ENGINEERING - INDUS-
TRIAL PRODUCTION/MANUFACTURING

BACHELOR OF ENGINEERING - INSTRUMENTATION

BACHELOR OF ENGINEERING - MARINE

BACHELOR OF ENGINEERING - MATERIALS SCIENCE

BACHELOR OF ENGINEERING - MECHANICAL

BACHELOR OF ENGINEERING - METALLURGY

BACHELOR OF ENGINEERING - MICROELECTRONICS

BACHELOR OF ENGINEERING - MINING

BACHELOR OF ENGINEERING - PETRO-LEUM/FUELS

BACHELOR OF ENGINEERING - POLLUTION TREATMENT

BACHELOR OF ENGINEERING - POWER/HYDRO

BACHELOR OF ENGINEERING - PULP & PAPER

BACHELOR OF ENGINEERING - SURVEYING

BACHELOR OF ENGINEERING - TELECOMMUNICATIONS

BACHELOR OF ENGINEERING - TRANS-PORTATION

BACHELOR OF ENGINEERING - WATER RESOURCES

BACHELOR OF ENGINEERING - WELDING

BACHELOR OF LAWS - GENERAL

BACHELOR OF LAWS - CORPORATE

BACHELOR OF LAWS - ENVIRONMENTAL

BACHELOR OF LAWS - LABOUR

BACHELOR OF SCIENCE - GENERAL

BACHELOR OF SCIENCE - ACTUARIAL

BACHELOR OF SCIENCE - AGRICULTURE/ HORTICULTURE

BACHELOR OF SCIENCE - AUDIOLOGY

BACHELOR OF SCIENCE - BIOLOGY

BACHELOR OF SCIENCE - CHEMISTRY

BACHELOR OF SCIENCE - COMPUTER SCIENCE

BACHELOR OF SCIENCE - DENTISTRY

BACHELOR OF SCIENCE - ECOLOGY

BACHELOR OF SCIENCE - ENVIRONMEN-TAL STUDIES

BACHELOR OF SCIENCE - FORESTRY

BACHELOR OF SCIENCE - GEOGRAPHY

BACHELOR OF SCIENCE - GEOLOGY

BACHELOR OF SCIENCE - HEALTH SCIENCES

BACHELOR OF SCIENCE - IMMUNOLOGY

BACHELOR OF SCIENCE - MATERIALS SCIENCE

BACHELOR OF SCIENCE - MATHEMATICS

BACHELOR OF SCIENCE - METALLURGY

BACHELOR OF SCIENCE - METEOROLOGY

BACHELOR OF SCIENCE - MICROBIOLOGY

BACHELOR OF SCIENCE - NURSING

BACHELOR OF SCIENCE - NUTRITIONAL SCIENCES

BACHELOR OF SCIENCE - OCCUPATIONAL THERAPY

BACHELOR OF SCIENCE - OCEANOGRAPHY

BACHELOR OF SCIENCE - OPTOMETRY

BACHELOR OF SCIENCE - PHARMACY

BACHELOR OF SCIENCE - PHYSICAL THERAPY/PHYSIOTHERAPY

BACHELOR OF SCIENCE - PHYSICS

BACHELOR OF SCIENCE - PSYCHOLOGY

BACHELOR OF SCIENCE - SPEECH PATHOLOGY

BACHELOR OF SCIENCE - TEXTILES

BACHELOR OF SCIENCE - ZOOLOGY

CHARTERED ACCOUNTANT - GENERAL

CHARTERED ACCOUNTANT - FINANCE

CERTIFIED GENERAL ACCOUNTANT - GENERAL

CERTIFIED GENERAL ACCOUNTANT - FINANCE

CERTIFIED MANAGEMENT ACCOUNTANT - GENERAL

CERTIFIED MANAGEMENT ACCOUNTANT - FINANCE

COMMUNITY COLLEGE - GENERAL

COMMUNITY COLLEGE - ACCOUNTING

COMMUNITY COLLEGE - ADMINISTRATION

COMMUNITY COLLEGE - ADVERTISING

COMMUNITY COLLEGE - AGRICULTURE/ HORTICULTURE

COMMUNITY COLLEGE - AIRCRAFT MAINTENANCE

COMMUNITY COLLEGE - AMBULANCE/ EMERGENCY CARE

COMMUNITY COLLEGE - ANIMAL HEALTH

COMMUNITY COLLEGE - ANIMATION

COMMUNITY COLLEGE - ARCHITECTURAL TECHNICIAN

COMMUNITY COLLEGE - AUDIO/VISUAL TECHNICIAN

COMMUNITY COLLEGE - AUTOMOTIVE MECHANIC

COMMUNITY COLLEGE - BUSINESS

COMMUNITY COLLEGE - CAD/CAM/ AUTOCAD

COMMUNITY COLLEGE - CARPENTRY

COMMUNITY COLLEGE - COMMUNICA-TIONS/PUBLIC RELATIONS

COMMUNITY COLLEGE - COMPUTER SCIENCE

COMMUNITY COLLEGE - COOKING/CHEF TRAINING

COMMUNITY COLLEGE - DENTAL ASSISTANT

COMMUNITY COLLEGE - DENTAL HYGIENIST

COMMUNITY COLLEGE - DIETICIAN/ NUTRITION

COMMUNITY COLLEGE - ELECTRONICS TECHNICIAN

COMMUNITY COLLEGE - ENGINEERING TECHNICIAN

COMMUNITY COLLEGE - FACILITY MANAGEMENT

COMMUNITY COLLEGE - FASHION ARTS/ DESIGN

COMMUNITY COLLEGE - FINANCIAL PLANNING

COMMUNITY COLLEGE - FORESTRY

COMMUNITY COLLEGE - FUNERAL SERV- ICES

COMMUNITY COLLEGE - GRAPHIC ARTS/ DESIGN

COMMUNITY COLLEGE - HEALTH/HOME CARE AIDE

COMMUNITY COLLEGE - HOSPITALITY

COMMUNITY COLLEGE - HUMAN RE-SOURCES

COMMUNITY COLLEGE - HVAC SYSTEMS

COMMUNITY COLLEGE - INFORMATION SYSTEMS

COMMUNITY COLLEGE - INSURANCE

COMMUNITY COLLEGE - JOURNALISM

COMMUNITY COLLEGE - LABORATORY TECHNICIAN

COMMUNITY COLLEGE - LEGAL ASSISTANT

COMMUNITY COLLEGE - MARINE ENGINEERING

COMMUNITY COLLEGE - MARKETING/ SALES

COMMUNITY COLLEGE - MASSAGE THERAPY

COMMUNITY COLLEGE - MUSIC

COMMUNITY COLLEGE - NUCLEAR MEDICINE

COMMUNITY COLLEGE - NURSING RN

COMMUNITY COLLEGE - NURSING RNA

COMMUNITY COLLEGE - ORTHOTICS/ PROSTHETICS

COMMUNITY COLLEGE - PHOTOGRAPHY

COMMUNITY COLLEGE - PLUMBER

COMMUNITY COLLEGE - PODIATRY

COMMUNITY COLLEGE - PURCHASING/ LOGISTICS

COMMUNITY COLLEGE - RADIOLOGY

COMMUNITY COLLEGE - REAL ESTATE SALES

COMMUNITY COLLEGE - RECREATION STUDIES

COMMUNITY COLLEGE - REHABILITATION THERAPY

COMMUNITY COLLEGE - RESPIRATORY THERAPY

COMMUNITY COLLEGE - SECRETARIAL

COMMUNITY COLLEGE - SECURITY/ ENFORCEMENT

COMMUNITY COLLEGE - SOCIAL WORKER/ DSW

COMMUNITY COLLEGE - TOOL & DIE/ MACHINIST

COMMUNITY COLLEGE - TRAVEL/TOURISM

COMMUNITY COLLEGE - TELEVISION/ RADIO ARTS/BROADCASTING

COMMUNITY COLLEGE - ULTRASOUND TECHNICIAN •

COMMUNITY COLLEGE - UPHOLSTERY

COMMUNITY COLLEGE - URBAN PLANNING

COMMUNITY COLLEGE - WELDING

MASTER OF ARTS - GENERAL

MASTER OF ARTS - CRIMINOLOGY

MASTER OF ARTS - ECONOMICS

MASTER OF ARTS - ENGLISH

MASTER OF ARTS - GEOGRAPHY

MASTER OF ARTS - GRAPHIC ARTS

MASTER OF ARTS - HUMAN RESOURCES

MASTER OF ARTS - INDUSTRIAL RELA-TIONS

MASTER OF ARTS - JOURNALISM

MASTER OF ARTS - MUSIC

MASTER OF ARTS - POLITICAL SCIENCE

MASTER OF ARTS - PSYCHOLOGY

MASTER OF ARTS - RECREATION STUDIES

MASTER OF ARTS - SOCIOLOGY/SOCIAL WORK

MASTER OF ARTS - URBAN GEOGRAPHY/ PLANNING

MASTER OF BUSINESS ADMINISTRATION - GENERAL

MASTER OF BUSINESS ADMINISTRATION - ACCOUNTING

MASTER OF BUSINESS ADMINISTRATION - FINANCE

MASTER OF BUSINESS ADMINISTRATION - HUMAN RESOURCES

MASTER OF BUSINESS ADMINISTRATION - INFORMATION SYSTEMS/MIS

MASTER OF BUSINESS ADMINISTRATION - MARKETING

MASTER OF BUSINESS ADMINISTRATION - PUBLIC ADMINISTRATION

MASTER OF EDUCATION - GENERAL

MASTER OF EDUCATION - ADULT

MASTER OF EDUCATION - PHYSICAL AND HEALTH

MASTER OF EDUCATION - SPECIAL NEEDS

MASTER OF ENGINEERING - GENERAL

MASTER OF ENGINEERING - AEROSPACE

MASTER OF ENGINEERING - ARCHITECTURAL/BUILDING

MASTER OF ENGINEERING - BIOMEDICAL ELECTRONICS

MASTER OF ENGINEERING - BIOTECHNOLOGY

MASTER OF ENGINEERING - CHEMICAL

MASTER OF ENGINEERING - CIVIL

MASTER OF ENGINEERING - COMPUTER SYSTEMS

MASTER OF ENGINEERING - ELECTRICAL

MASTER OF ENGINEERING - ENGINEERING PHYSICS

MASTER OF ENGINEERING - ENVIRONMENTAL/RESOURCES

MASTER OF ENGINEERING - FOOD PROCESSING

MASTER OF ENGINEERING - FOREST RESOURCES

MASTER OF ENGINEERING - GEOLOGICAL ENGINEERING

MASTER OF ENGINEERING - INDUSTRIAL CHEMISTRY

MASTER OF ENGINEERING - INDUSTRIAL DESIGN

MASTER OF ENGINEERING - INDUSTRIAL ENGINEERING

MASTER OF ENGINEERING - TELECOMMU-NICATIONS

MASTER OF ENGINEERING - TRANSPORTA-TION

MASTER OF ENGINEERING - WATER RESOURCES

MASTER OF LIBRARY SCIENCE

MASTER OF SCIENCE - GENERAL

MASTER OF SCIENCE - ACTUARIAL

MASTER OF SCIENCE - AGRICULTURE/ HORTICULTURE

MASTER OF SCIENCE - AUDIOLOGY

MASTER OF SCIENCE - BIOCHEMISTRY

MASTER OF SCIENCE - BIOLOGY

MASTER OF SCIENCE - CHEMISTRY

MASTER OF SCIENCE - COMPUTER SCIENCE

MASTER OF SCIENCE - ECOLOGY

MASTER OF SCIENCE - ENVIRONMENTAL

MASTER OF SCIENCE - EPIDIMIOLOGY

MASTER OF SCIENCE - FORESTRY

MASTER OF SCIENCE - GEOGRAPHY

MASTER OF SCIENCE - GEOLOGY

MASTER OF SCIENCE - HEALTH SCIENCES (ALL AREAS)

MASTER OF SCIENCE - MATERIALS SCIENCE

MASTER OF SCIENCE - MATHEMATICS

MASTER OF SCIENCE - METALLURGY

MASTER OF SCIENCE - METEOROLOGY/ CLIMATE

MASTER OF SCIENCE - MICROBIOLOGY

MASTER OF SCIENCE - NURSING

MASTER OF SCIENCE - NUTRITIONAL SCIENCES

MASTER OF SCIENCE - OCCUPATIONAL THERAPY

MASTER OF SCIENCE - PHARMACY

MASTER OF SCIENCE - PHYSICAL THERAPY

MASTER OF SCIENCE - PHYSICS

MASTER OF SCIENCE - PSYCHOLOGY

MASTER OF SCIENCE - SPEECH PATHOL- OGY

DOCTORATE (ARTS) - GENERAL

DOCTORATE (ARTS) - GEOGRAPHY

DOCTORATE (ARTS) - PSYCHOLOGY

DOCTORATE (ARTS) - URBAN GEOGRA-PHY/PLANNING

DOCTORATE (EDUCATION) - GENERAL

DOCTORATE (ENGINEERING) - GENERAL

DOCTORATE (ENGINEERING) - CHEMICAL

DOCTORATE (ENGINEERING) - CIVIL

DOCTORATE (ENGINEERING) - COMPUTER SYSTEMS

DOCTORATE (ENGINEERING) - ELECTRICAL

DOCTORATE (ENGINEERING) - ENGINEERING PHYSICS

DOCTORATE (ENGINEERING) - GEOLOGICAL ENGINEERING

DOCTORATE (ENGINEERING) - INDUSTRIAL CHEMISTRY

DOCTORATE (ENGINEERING) - INDUSTRIAL DESIGN

DOCTORATE (ENGINEERING) - INDUSTRIAL

DOCTORATE (ENGINEERING) - INDUSTRIAL PRODUCTION/MANUFACTURING

DOCTORATE (ENGINEERING) - MATERIALS SCIENCE

DOCTORATE (ENGINEERING) - MECHANICAL

DOCTORATE (ENGINEERING) - MICROELECTRONICS

DOCTORATE (ENGINEERING) - TELECOMMUNICATIONS

DOCTORATE (SCIENCE) - GENERAL

DOCTORATE (SCIENCE) - ANIMAL SCIENCES/VETERINARY

DOCTORATE (SCIENCE) - BIOCHEMISTRY

DOCTORATE (SCIENCE) - BIOLOGY

DOCTORATE (SCIENCE) - CHEMISTRY

DOCTORATE (SCIENCE) - COMPUTER SCIENCE

DOCTORATE (SCIENCE) - FORESTRY

DOCTORATE (SCIENCE) - GEOGRAPHY

DOCTORATE (SCIENCE) - GEOLOGY

DOCTORATE (SCIENCE) - GERONTOLOGY

DOCTORATE (SCIENCE) - HEALTH SCIENCES

DOCTORATE (SCIENCE) - IMMUNOLOGY

DOCTORATE (SCIENCE) - MATERIALS SCIENCE

HIGH SCHOOL DIPLOMA

Employer Listings

3M CANADA INC.
P.O. Box 5757
London, ON N6A 4T1

Tel. 519-451-2500
Fax 519-452-6502

3M Canada Inc. is involved in manufacturing of a variety of consumer products. There are more than 1,000 employees at this location. Graduates most likely to be hired come from the following academic areas: Bachelor of Arts (General), Bachelor of Science (Chemistry, Mathematics, Pharmacy), Bachelor of Engineering (Chemical, Electrical, Mechanical), Bachelor of Commerce/Business Administration (Marketing), and Master of Business Administration. Graduates are hired to occupy Engineer, Sales Representative, and Technical Representative positions. Highly motivated, and excellent interpersonal and communication skills are listed as desirable non-academic qualifications. Company benefits and the potential for advancement are both rated as excellent. The average annual starting salary falls within the $30,000 to $35,000 range. The most suitable method for initial contact by those seeking employment is to mail a resume with a covering letter. 3M Canada Inc. does hire a limited number of summer students annually. Contact: K.F. Schmidt, Manager, Human Resources Operations.

A.G. SIMPSON CO. LTD.
675 Progress Avenue
Toronto, ON M1H 2W9

Tel. 416-438-6650
Fax 416-431-8766

A.G. Simpson Co. Ltd. is a OEM supplier of automotive stampings and assemblies. The company employs 500 people at this location, and a total of 3,500 employees across Canada. Graduates most likely to be hired come from the following academic areas: Bachelor of Arts (Economics, Psychology), Bachelor of Science (Computer Science, Environmental, Metallurgy), Bachelor of Engineering (General, Chemical, Materials Science, Metallurgy, Pollution Treatment, Automation/Robotics, Computer Systems, Instrumentation, Microelectronics, Mechanical, Industrial Design, Industrial Production, Welding, Resources/Environmental), Bachelor of Commerce/Business Administration (Accounting, Finance, Human Resources, Information Systems, Marketing), Chartered Accountant, Certified Management Accountant, Certified General Accountant, Master of Business Administration (Accounting, Finance, Human Resources, Information Systems, Marketing), Community College Diploma (Accounting, Business, Communications, Facility Management, Financial Planning, Human Resources, Marketing/Sales, Purchasing/Logistics, Secretarial, Security, CAD/CAM/Autocad, Computer Science, Electronics Technician, Engineering Technician, Laboratory Technician, Nursing RN), and High School Diploma. Graduates would occupy Process Engineer, Q.C. Technician, Production Planning, Tooling Engineer, etc. positions. Previous work experience in automotive stamping and QS9000 work

environments are both listed as desirable non-academic qualifications. Company benefits are rated as excellent. The potential for advancement is listed as being good. The average annual starting salary falls within the $35,000 to $40,000 range. The most suitable method for initial contact by those seeking employment is to mail a resume with a covering letter. Contacts: Diane Martin, Manager, Human Resources, Corporate Office or Steve W. Bray, Manager, Human Resources, Plant #1.

ABB, GUELPH DIVISION
201 Woodlawn Road West
Guelph, ON N1H 1B8

Tel. 519-822-2120
Fax 519-837-4625

ABB, Guelph Division is a manufacturer of small and specialty power transformers, as well as operating a transformer repair facility for the utilities and industrial markets. ABB is ISO 9001 registered company, employing 260 people at this location, a total of 2,000 people in Canada, and 220,000 people worldwide. Graduates most likely to be hired come from the following academic areas: Bachelor of Engineering (Electrical, Mechanical), Community College Diploma (CAD/CAM/Autocad, Carpentry, Engineering Technician), and High School Diploma. Graduates would occupy Design Engineer, Drafting Designer, Insulation Manufacturer, and Power Transformer Winder, Assembler, and Tanker positions. Innovative, initiative, team work and good customer service skills are all listed as desirable non-academic qualifications. Company benefits are rated above average. The potential for advancement is listed as excellent. The average annual starting salary falls within the $45,000 to $50,000 range. The most suitable method for initial contact by those seeking employment is to fax a resume with a covering letter. Contact: Ken Dietz, Human Resources Manager.

ABC GROUP
110 Ronson Drive
Rexdale, ON M9W 1B6

Tel. 416-246-1782
Fax 416-246-1780

ABC Group is a major Tier 1 supplier of plastic injection moulded and blow moulded products to General Motors, Ford and Chrysler. The company has enjoyed 25 years of success within the automotive industry, supplying the highest quality plastic products to their customers. ABC Group operates worldwide with subsidiaries in Germany, Spain, Japan, Mexico, the United States, and Canada. There are 150 employees at this location, a total of 3,500 employees in Canada, and a total of 5,000 employees worldwide. The Company boasts one of the most diverse product lines in the automotive industry, including fuel tanks, spoilers, interior/exterior trim and many custom accessories. Graduates most likely to be hired come from the following academic areas: Bachelor of Engineering (General, Chemical, Electrical, Mechanical, Automation/Robotics, Industrial

Design, Industrial Engineering, Industrial Production, Instrumentation), Bachelor of Commerce/Business Administration (General, Accounting, Finance, Human Resources), Certified Management Accountant, Certified General Accountant, Master of Business Administration (General, Accounting, Finance, Human Resources), Master of Engineering (Mechanical), and Community College Diploma (Accounting, Business, Human Resources, Secretarial, CAD/CAM/Autocad, Engineering Technician, Tool and Die, Machinist, Welding, Laboratory Technician). Graduates would occupy Project Engineer, Process Engineer, Program Manager, Plant Manager, Design Engineer, Robotic Engineer, Quality Engineer, Controls Engineer, CAD Operators, Plant Controllers, and Accounting Coordinator positions. A willingness to learn and perform duties as required are both listed as desirable non-academic qualifications. Company benefits are rated as industry standard. The potential for advancement is listed as excellent. The average annual starting salary falls within the $40,000 to $45,000 range. The most suitable methods for initial contact by those seeking employment are to mail or fax a resume with a covering letter, or through on-campus recruitment programs (see your campus career centre for details). ABC Group does hire summer and co-op work term students. *Contact:* Scott Smith, Recruiter, Human Resources Department.

ACCUCAPS INDUSTRIES LIMITED
2125 Ambassador Drive
Windsor, ON N9C 3R5

Tel. 519-969-5404
Fax 519-969-5022
Email .... jrad@accucaps.com

Accucaps Industries Limited is a progressive manufacturer of soft gelatin capsules for the pharmaceutical, health and nutrition, and cosmetic and recreation markets. The company has experienced rapid growth and is recognized as one of "Canada's 50 Best Managed Private Companies". Accucaps employs a total of 280 personnel. Graduates most likely to be hired come from the following academic areas: Bachelor of Science (Chemistry, Computer Science, Microbiology), Bachelor of Engineering (Chemical, Mechanical), Bachelor of Commerce/Business Administration (General, Accounting, Finance, Human Resources, Information Systems, Marketing), Certified Management Accountant, Community College Diploma (Accounting, Administration, Business, Human Resources, Information Systems, Marketing/Sales, Purchasing/Logistics, Computer Science, Engineering Technician, Tool and Die, Machinist, Laboratory Technician), and High School Diploma. Innovative, strong team skills, and good communication skills are listed as desirable non-academic qualifications. Company benefits are rated above average. The potential for advancement is listed as excellent. The average annual starting salary falls within the $30,000 to $35,000 range. The most suitable method for initial contact by those seeking employment is to mail a resume with a covering letter. Accucaps Industries Limited does hire summer and

co-op work term students. *Contact:* Human Resources Department.

AD OPT TECHNOLOGIES INC.
3535 Queen Mary Road, Suite 650
Montreal, QC H3V 1H8

Tel. 514-345-0580
Fax 514-345-0422
Email .... hum-res@adopt.qc.ca
Website .... www.adopt.qc.ca

AD OPT Technologies Inc. develops and markets state of the art software for the decision-making and optimization of human and material resources in the airline industry. As a leading provider of advanced software in the industry, the company's client list includes Air Canada, Air Transat, Delta Airlines, Federal Express, Northwest Airlines, the Federal Aviation Administration (FAA) in New York, U.P.S., Sabena, TWA, Canadian Regional, and NAV Canada. AD OPT employs a total of 60 people. Graduates most likely to be hired come from the following academic areas: Bachelor of Science (Computer Science), Bachelor of Engineering (Computer Systems), and Bachelor of Commerce/Business Administration (Marketing). Graduates would occupy Programmer, Analyst, Software Developer, Project Manager, Account Manager, Sales and Marketing Manager, and Sales and Marketing Assistant positions. Bilingual (French/English), team player, fast learner, and initiative are all listed as desirable non-academic qualifications. Company benefits are rated above average. The most suitable methods for initial contact by those seeking employment are to e-mail a resume with a covering letter, or by applying through AD OPT's website at www.adopt.qc.ca. *Contact:* Domenica Fiori, Recruiting Manager.

ADDICTIONS FOUNDATION OF MANITOBA, THE
1031 Portage Avenue
Winnipeg, MB R3G 0R8

Tel. 204-944-6200
Fax 204-786-7768

The Addictions Foundation of Manitoba (AFM) is a provincial crown agency providing a a broad range of services relating to alcohol, drug and gambling problems. Substance abuse and gambling prevention, education and treatment programs, and impaired driver services are available across the province through AFM. The agency also provides many youth programs in accordance with its mandate to provide counselling, education, prevention and research with regards to the problems associated with addictions. Graduates most likely to be hired come from the following academic areas: Bachelor of Arts (Psychology, Social Work), Bachelor of Education (Adult), Bachelor of Commerce/Business Administration (Accounting), and Community College Diploma (Accounting). Graduates would occupy Rehabilitation Counsellor and Secretarial positions. Adaptable, confident, enthusiastic, leadership skills, patient, productive, professional, good writing skills, analytical, dependable, flexible, logical, personable, communicative, responsible, persuasive, organized, innovative, and diplomatic are all listed as desirable non-academic qualifications. Company benefits and the potential for advancement are both rated as excellent. The average annual starting salary falls within the $25,000 to $30,000 range. The most suitable method for initial contact by those seeking employment is to mail a resume with a covering letter. The Addictions Foundation of Manitoba occasionally hires students for summer and co-op work terms. *Contact:* Personnel Manager.

ADDISON WESLEY LONGMAN
26 Prince Andrew Place, P.O. Box 580
Don Mills, ON M3C 2T8

Tel.	416-447-5101
Fax	416-443-0948

Addison Wesley Longman is a publisher of Canadian educational materials, and distributor of educational and professional publications. The company employs a total of 180 people across Canada. Graduates most likely to be hired come from the following academic areas: Bachelor of Arts (English, French, Journalism), Bachelor of Science (Mathematics), Bachelor of Education (Early Childhood, Primary Junior, Junior Intermediate, Intermediate Senior, Adult), Bachelor of Commerce/Business Administration (Accounting, Finance, Human Resources, Marketing), Master of Business Administration, Master of Arts (English), and Community College Diploma (Accounting, Administration, Business, Human Resources, Marketing/Sales, Secretarial, Journalism). Graduates would occupy Editorial Assistant, Editor, Marketing Assistant, Sales Representative, Desktop Designer, Sales Assistant, Accounts Receivable Clerk, Accounts Payable Clerk, and Warehouse positions. Excellent communication and interpersonal skills, a basic understanding of computers, demonstrated team player, creativity, and self motivated are all listed as desirable non-academic qualifications. Company benefits are rated as excellent. The potential for advancement is listed as being good. The most suitable method for initial contact by those seeking employment is to mail a resume with a covering letter. Addison Wesley Longman does hire summer students. *Contact:* Director, Human Resources - Human Resources Department.

ADM MILLING COMPANY
950 Mill Street
Montreal, QC H3C 1Y4

Tel.	514-846-8500
Fax	514-933-3802

ADM Milling Company is involved in the milling of wheat into flour and is a division of Archer Daniels Midland Company. ADM Milling Company maintains five manufacturing facilities in Canada, and many more in the United States. Graduates most likely to be hired come from the following academic areas: Bachelor of Science (Chemistry), Bachelor of Engineering (Electrical, Mechanical), Bachelor of Commerce/Business Administration (Accounting,

Finance, Marketing), Certified Management Accountant, Certified General Accountant, and Community College Diploma (Accounting, Administration, Business, Marketing/Sales, Secretarial, Electronics Technician, Engineering Technician, Mechanic, Laboratory Technician). Graduates would occupy R&D Technician, QC Technician, Junior Engineer, Accountant, and Sales and Marketing Representative positions. Enthusiasm, flexibility, adaptability, and a desire to learn are all listed as desirable non-academic qualifications. Company benefits are rated above average. The potential for advancement is listed as average. The average annual starting salary falls within the $20,000 to $25,000 range. The most suitable method for initial contact by those seeking employment is to mail a resume with a covering letter. *Contact:* Human Resources.

ADP CANADA
2150 Islington Avenue
Toronto, ON M9P 3V4

Tel.	416-248-3200
Fax	416-248-3326

ADP Canada is a rapidly growing payroll service bureau providing payroll and related services. There are more than 400 employees at this Canadian head office location, a total of 1,200 across Canada, and 30,000 employees worldwide. Other Canadian locations include Halifax, Montreal, Winnipeg, Regina, Edmonton, Calgary, and Vancouver. The parent company, ADP is based in Roseland, New Jersey. Graduates most likely to be hired come from the following academic areas: Bachelor of Science (Computer Science), and Bachelor of Commerce/Business Administration (Accounting, Finance, Human Resources, Information Systems, Marketing), Chartered Accountant, Certified Management Accountant, Certified General Accountant, Master of Business Administration (Accounting, Finance, Human Resources, Information Systems, Marketing), and Community College Diploma (Accounting, Administration, Business, Communications, Financial Planning, Human Resources, Marketing/Sales, Secretarial). Graduates would occupy Accountant, Sales, Information Systems, Client Services, Computer Operations, PC Support, Applications Development, Programming, and Administrative Assistant positions. Applicants should possess a client service orientation. Company benefits are rated above average. The potential for advancement is listed as excellent. The average annual starting salary falls within the $25,000 to $30,000 range. The most suitable method for initial contact by those seeking employment is to mail a resume with a covering letter. ADP Canada has temporary work available through their busy season, between November and February. *Contact:* Human Resources Consultant.

ADVANCED CONCEPTS CENTER (ACC), LOCKHEED MARTIN CORPORATION
3001 Solandt Road
Kanata, ON K2K 2M8

Tel. 613-599-3280
Fax 613-592-4111
Email .... acc.solutions@lmco.com
Website .... www.lmco.com/acc

Advanced Concepts Center (ACC) is part of Integrated Business Solutions (IBS), the commercial IT services arm of Lockheed Martin Corporation, an international professional services organization that partners with customers to develop and deploy business process and information technology solutions. ACC helps their customers use current leading-edge information technologies to achieve their particular business goals faster and more efficiently. ACC has helped its customers from industries such as manufacturing, telecommunications, insurance, banking, finance and retail, leverage ACC's capabilities in object technology, data warehousing, enterprise-wide work flow solutions, imaging, internet technologies, and project management, to strengthen their business strategy through their technology investment. With more than 200 instructor-led training courses available in on-site forums or public/open enrollment courses throughout North America and around the world, the ACC has developed an evolved approach that guarantees that every program is focused, effective and enjoyable. There are 9 professionals at this location, a total of 15 in Canada, and more than 200 worldwide. Graduates most likely to be hired come from the following academic areas: Bachelor of Science (Computer Science, Mathematics), Bachelor of Engineering (Computer Science), Master of Science (Computer Science, Information Technology), Master of Engineering (Computer Science, Computer Systems, Information Technology), and Doctorate (Information Technology). These graduates would occupy positions as Instructors, Consultants, and Mentors with 10 plus years industry experience. Entrepreneurial and self-motivated are listed as desirable non-academic qualifications. Company benefits are rated above average. The potential for advancement is listed as excellent. The average annual starting salary falls in the $60,000 plus range. The most suitable method for initial contact by those seeking employment is to fax a resume with a covering letter. *Contact:* Check Web Site at www.lmco.com/acc.

ADVANTECH, ADVANCED MICROWAVE TECHNOLOGIES INC.
657 Orly Avenue
Dorval, QC H9P 1G1

Tel. 514-420-0045
Fax 514-420-0055
Email .... nebeng@advantech.ca
Website .... www.advantech.ca

ADVANTECH, Advanced Microwave Technologies Inc. is a Montreal based company that specializes in the design, manufacturing and marketing of leading-edge solid state power amplifiers (SSPAs) and related subsystems (eg. converters, filters, synthesizers) for the telecommunications industry. ADVANTECH's products are used worldwide in point-to-point microwave systems, satellite earth-stations, VSAT terminals as well as for PCS, MMDS and LMCS/LMDS applications. The company has a total of 105 employees. Graduates most likely to be hired come from the following academic areas: Bachelor of Engineering (Electrical, Industrial Engineering, Microwave Telecommunications), Bachelor of Commerce/Business Administration (Marketing), Master of Engineering (Microwave Telecommunications), Doctorate of Engineering (Microwave Telecommunications), and Community College Diploma (Electronics Technician). Graduates would occupy Radio Frequency Engineer, Industrial Engineer, Components Engineer, Project Manager (with a military background), Digital Signal Processing Engineer, Manufacturing Manager, Product Manager, Technical Sales Representative, Radio Frequency Technician, and Technical Writer (with a military background) positions. Team player, creative, self motivated, results oriented, and able to work in a deadline driven environment are all listed as desirable non-academic qualifications. Company benefits are rated as industry standard. The potential for advancement is listed as excellent. The average annual starting salary falls within the $30,000 to $35,000 range. The most suitable methods for initial contact by those seeking employment are to fax or e-mail a resume with a covering letter. *Contacts:* Gabrielle Neben, Human Resources or Stella Gelerman, VP Human Resources.

ÆTERNA LABORATORIES INC.
456 Marconi Street
Sainte-Foy, QC G1N 4A8

Tel. 418-527-8525
Fax 418-527-0881
Email .... aeterna@aeterna.com
Website .... www.aeterna.com

Æterna Laboratories Inc. is the third largest medical biotechnological company in Quebec and one of the ten largest in Canada. The company conducts research to develop and market innovative products that contribute to the well-being of the population. Æterna operates on a worldwide scale by establishing strategic alliances, at selected times in product development, with companies in the pharmaceutical, nutritional and cosmetic fields. The activities of Æterna Laboratories are concentrated into two divisions, the Biopharmaceutical Division and the Cosmetics and Nutrition Division. The Biopharmaceutical Division has a diversified program to develop a new class of treatments to control a number of diseases complicated by the formation of new blood vessels. The products developed by Æterna based on the angiogenesis inhibitor Æ-941 target such diseases as solid tumor cancers, psoriasis, age-related muscular degeneration (AMD), rheumatoid arthritis and osteoarthritis. The Cosmetics and Nutrition Division supports Æterna's distinct positioning as a profitable biotechnology corporation. By marketing nutritional supplements and active ingredients for cosmetics, this division helps Æterna finance part of the development of antiangionenic therapies. Æterna employs approximately 100 people at this location. Graduates most likely to be hired come from the following academic areas: Bachelor of Science (Biology, Chemistry, Computer Science, Microbiology, Nursing, Pharmacy), Bachelor of Engineering (Chemical, Civil, Industrial Engineering, Instrumentation), Bachelor of Commerce/Business Administration (Accounting, Finance, Human Resources, Marketing), Chartered Accountant, Certified Management Accountant, Master of Business Administration (General, Finance, Human Resources, Marketing), Master of Science (Biology, Biochemistry, Microbiology, Chemistry, Biotechnology, Cellular Biology, Molecular Biology, Pharmacology, Nutrition/Dietetic), Doctorate (Pharmacology, Immunology, Virology, Biochemistry, Endocrinology), Community College Diploma (Human Resources, Marketing/Sales, Secretarial, Computer Science, Laboratory Technician, Nursing RN), and High School Diploma. Leadership skills, a high level of motivation, autonomy, and a scientific spirit are all listed as desirable non-academic qualifications. Company benefits and the potential for advancement are both rated as excellent. The most suitable method for initial contact by those seeking employment is to fax or e-mail a resume with a covering letter. Æterna Laboratories Inc. does hire summer students. *Contacts:* Yvon Carrier, Human Resources Department or Richard Bordeleau, Vice President, Corporate Development.

AETNA LIFE INSURANCE COMPANY OF CANADA
79 Wellington Street West
P.O. Box 120, Aetna Tower, TD Centre
Toronto, ON M5K 1N9

Tel. 416-864-8000
Fax 416-864-8549
Website .... www.aetna.ca

For more than a century Aetna Life Insurance Company of Canada has been offering Canadians financial security through superior insurance products and related services. Among the company's products and services are group life insurance, group health insurance, individual life insurance, and individual disability insurance. Graduates most likely to be hired come from the following academic areas: Bachelor of Science (Actuarial, Computer Science, Health Sciences, Mathematics, Nursing, Psychology), Bachelor of Commerce/Business Administration (Accounting, Finance, Marketing, Information Systems), Chartered Accountant, Certified Management Accountant, Certified General Accountant, Master of Business Administration (Accounting, Finance, Marketing, Information Systems), Community College (Accounting, Administration, Advertising, Business, Communications, Facility Management, Insurance, Marketing, Purchasing/Logistics, Secretarial, Human Resources, Journalism, Law Clerk, Security/Law Enforcement, Computer Science, Dental Assistant, Nursing RN/RNA), and High School Diploma. Graduates would occupy a wide variety of positions in many functional areas. Team player, customer service oriented, computer skills, integrity, and excellent verbal and communication skills are all listed as desirable non-academic qualifications. Company benefits are rated as excellent. The potential for advancement is listed as being good. The most suitable methods for initial contact by those seeking employment are to mail, fax or e-mail a resume with a covering letter, or through the company's website at www.aetna.ca. Aetna Life Insurance Company of Canada does hire summer and co-op work term students. *Contact:* Human Resource Services.

AGF MANAGEMENT LIMITED
TD Bank Tower, P.O. Box 50
Toronto, ON M5K 1E9

Tel. 416-367-1900
Fax 416-865-4189
Email .... resume@agf.com
Website .... www.agf.com

Founded in 1957, AGF Management Limited is one of Canada's oldest and most broadly diversified wealth management companies, with assets under management in excess of $5 billion. AGF Management Limited is an independent Canadian-owned company, listed on the Toronto Stock Exchange, headquartered in Toronto, with offices in Oakville, Montreal, Vancouver and Halifax. AGF employs 400 people at the Toronto location, and a total of 650 people in Canada. Graduates most likely to be hired come from the following academic areas: Bachelor of Arts (English, French, Journalism, Languages), Bachelor of Science (Actuarial, Computer Science, Mathematics), Bachelor of Engineering (Electrical, Computer Systems), Bachelor of Commerce/Business Administration (General, Accounting, Finance, Information Systems), Chartered Accountant, Certified Management Accountant, Certified General Accountant, Master of Business Administration (Accounting, Finance, Information Systems, Marketing), and Community College Diploma (Accounting, Administration, Business, Human Resources, Information Systems, Secretarial, Journalism). Graduates would occupy Financial Analyst, Client Administration Representative, Client Service Representative, Marketing Coordinator, Systems Administrator, Application Developer, Accountant, and Copywriter positions. Customer service skills, team player, flexible, computer skills, analytical, and excellent communication skills are all listed as desirable non-academic qualifications. Company benefits and the potential for advancement are both rated as excellent. The average annual starting salary falls within the $25,000 to $30,000 range. The most suitable methods for initial contact by those seeking employment are to mail, fax or e-mail a resume with a covering letter. AGF Management Limited does hire summer and co-op work term students. Most hiring for work terms occurs between October and April. *Contact:* Manager, Recruitment and Development.

AGRA INC.

335 - 8th Avenue SW, Suite 1900
Calgary, AB T2P 1C9

Tel. 403-263-9606
Fax 403-263-9676

AGRA Inc. is an international engineering, construction, environment and technology corporation. The company employs approximately 4,500 people in 150 offices in 25 countries. This location is the corporate head office and employs approximately 30 people. Positions relating to AGRA's activities (other than those specified in this listing) are not available through this location. To inquire about other positions you must contact each subsidiary company directly (research at your campus placement centre and see next listing). Graduates hired for positions at this location come from the following academic areas: Bachelor of Laws, Bachelor of Commerce/Business Administration (Accounting, Finance, Marketing), Chartered Accountant (Finance), Certified Management Accountant (Finance), Certified General Accountant (Finance), Community College Diploma (Administration, Secretarial), and High School graduates for support staff functions. Relevant work experience, a high energy level, excellent communication skills, outside interests, and computer skills (Windows) are all listed as desirable non-academic qualifications. Company benefits are rated above average. The potential for advancement is listed as average. The average annual starting salary is dependent upon the position being considered. The most suitable method for initial contact by those seeking employment is to mail a resume with a covering letter. AGRA Inc. occasionally hires summer students at this location. *Contact:* Director of Human Resources.

AGRA MONENCO INC.

2010 Winston Park Drive
Oakville, ON L6H 6A3

Tel. 905-829-5400
Fax 905-829-5625
Email .... hr.corp@monenco.agra.com

AGRA Monenco Inc. is an international engineering, procurement and construction management company and a leader in technologies related to infrastructure, power, process industries and systems. AGRA Monenco provides its clients with integrated project solutions, offering a complete range of professional engineering, project development and financing, systems, project execution, operation and maintenance services. AGRA Monenco is a wholly-owned subsidiary of AGRA Inc., headquartered in Calgary (see previous listing). There are approximately 325 employees at this location, and a total of 2,000 employees in Canada. Graduates most likely to be hired come from the following academic areas: Bachelor of Science (Computer Science, Environmental, Metallurgy), Bachelor of Engineering (General, Chemical, Civil, Electrical, Mechanical, Resources/Environmental), Bachelor of Commerce/Business Administration (Accounting, Information Systems), Master of Business Administration (Finance), and Community College Diploma (Administration, Human Resources, Purchasing/Logistics, Architecture/Drafting, CAD/CAM/Autocad, Computer Science, Engineering Technician, HVAC Systems). Graduates are hired for various positions relating to their academic backgrounds. Company benefits are rated above average. The potential for advancement is listed as being good. The average annual starting salary falls within the $30,000 to $35,000 range. The most suitable methods for initial contact by graduates seeking employment are to mail a resume with a covering letter, or through employee referrals. AGRA Monenco Inc. does hire summer and co-op work term students. *Contact:* Max Bonanno, Employment Manager.

AIR CANADA

Case Postale 14,000
Saint-Laurent, QC H4Y 1H4

Tel. 514-422-5641
Fax 514-422-5650
Website .... www.aircanada.ca

Air Canada is a full service international air carrier. Graduates most likely to be hired come from the following academic areas: Bachelor of Science (Computer Science), Bachelor of Engineering (Aerospace), Bachelor of Commerce/Business Administration (Accounting, Finance, Information Systems, Marketing), Certified General Accounting, and Master of Business Administration (Finance, Human Resources, Information Systems, Marketing). Good customer service skills, team player, positive attitude, flexibility, and excellent communication and interpersonal skills are all listed as desirable non-academic qualifications. Company benefits are rated above average. The potential for advancement is listed as being good. The average annual starting salary falls within the $25,000 to $30,000 range. The most suitable method for initial contact by those seeking employment is to mail a resume with a covering letter. Air Canada does hire summer students on occasion. *Contact:* Carol Enright, Manager Staffing, Employment & Human Resource Programs.

AIR ONTARIO INC.

1 Air Ontario Drive
London, ON N5V 3S4

Tel. 519-453-8440
Fax 519-453-8470

Air Ontario Inc. is a commercial airline providing regional service to destinations in Ontario, Quebec and the northeastern United States, primarily servicing business customers. There are 150 employees at this location, and a total of 595 employees in Canada. Graduates most likely to be hired come from the following academic areas: Bachelor of Science (Computer Science), Bachelor of Engineering (Computer Systems), Bachelor of Commerce/Business Administration (Accounting, Finance, Human Resources, Information Systems, Marketing), Certified General Accountant, Master of Business Administration, Community College Diploma (Accounting, Advertising, Financial Planning, Human Resources, Marketing/Sales, Purchasing/Logistics, Secretarial, Travel/Tourism, Aircraft Maintenance, and High School Diploma. Graduates would occupy PC Support Trainer, Executive Secretary, Receptionist, Human Resources Officer, Payroll Assistant, Revenue Accounting Clerk, Accounts Payable Clerk, Assistant Controller, Supervisor Revenue Accounting, AME, AME Apprentice, and Maintenance Supervisor positions. Customer service skills, positive attitude, enthusiasm, technical knowledge relating to job skills, good job fit/qualifications, flexibility, and good communication skills are all listed as desirable non-academic qualifications. Company benefits are rated as excellent. The potential for advancement is listed as being good. The most suitable method for initial contact by those seeking employment is to mail a resume with a covering letter. Summer students are hired as required. This may not be every year however, and is usually only 1 or 2 students per season. *Contact:* Human Resources.

AIR PRODUCTS CANADA LTD.

2090 Steeles Avenue East
Brampton, ON L6T 1A7

Tel. 905-791-2530
Fax 905-791-6797

Air Products Canada Ltd. is an industrial gas company concerned with the manufacture, sale and distribution of industrial gas products. These include liquid products (LOX, LIN, LAR) used in their merchant business; cylinder products, used primarily in their welding products supply and specialty gas business; and onsite generation. There are 75 employees at this location, a total of 375 in Canada, and 12,000 employees worldwide. Graduates most likely to be hired come from the following academic areas: Bachelor of Science (Chemistry), Bachelor of Engineering (Chemical, Metallurgy, Civil, Mechanical, Welding), Bachelor of Commerce/Business Administration, Certified Management Accountant, Certified General Accountant, Master of Business Administration, Community College Diploma (Business, Secretarial, Welding), and High School Diploma. Graduates would occupy Applied Research Engineer, Development Engineer, Specialty Gas Sales, Welding Products Sales, Sales Representative, Inside Sales Representative, Clerk/Secretary, and Customer Service Representative positions. Good interpersonal and communication skills, business aptitude, bilingual, flexible, and computer literacy are all listed as desirable non-academic qualifications. Company benefits are rated above average. The potential for advancement is listed as being good. The

average annual starting salary falls within the $30,000 to $35,000 range. The most suitable method for initial contact by those seeking employment is to mail a resume with a covering letter. *Contact:* Helene Bourdages, Human Resources.

AIT CORPORATION

1545 Carling Avenue, Suite 700
Ottawa, ON K1Z 8P9

Tel. 613-722-2070
Fax 613-722-2063
Email .... jobs@ait.ca
Website .... www.ait.ca

AIT Corporation in involved in the design and development of identification and security systems, including secure travel documents, passport issuance systems, and passport readers. In addition, AIT designed and developed a remote telesurveillance system - Rapid Eye. The company employs approximately 85 employees at this location, and a total of 100 employees worldwide. Graduates most likely to be hired come from the following academic areas: Bachelor of Science (Computer Science), Bachelor of Engineering (Electrical, Computer Systems), Certified General Accountant, Master of Science (Computer Science), Master of Engineering (Electrical), and Community College Diploma (Information Systems, Computer Science, Electronics Technician, Engineering Technician). Graduates would occupy Programmer, Technical Support, Electromechanical Draftsperson, Hardware Developer, and Software Designer positions. The ability to work independently, good communication skills, relevant work experience, co-op work term experience, team player, and good problem solving skills are all listed as desirable non-academic qualifications. Company benefits are rated as excellent. The potential for advancement is listed as being good. The average annual starting salary falls within the $40,000 to $45,000 range, depending upon experience. The most suitable method for initial contact by those seeking employment is to e-mail a resume with a covering letter. AIT Corporation does hire summer students, and co-op students throughout the year. *Contact:* Donna Burnett, Manager, Human Resources.

AJAX, PICKERING & WHITBY ASSOCIATION FOR COMMUNITY LIVING

36 Emperor Street
Ajax, ON L1S 1M7

Tel. 905-427-3300
Fax 905-427-3310

The functions of The Association for Community Living staff and services are that of supporting the participation of individuals in the life of the community who are disadvantaged by an impairment in ability to learn, generalize what is learned, and transfer learning from one specific context to another. Support to an individual with such an impairment means the promotion of circumstances and conditions which: minimize restrictions on people's lives, enhance their life long opportunities for effective, rewarding participation; enable people to gain more control over their own lives; enable people to build their own career and lifestyle at home and in leisure pursuits; and ensure security of the person in his/her home, and protect against imposed discontinuity of relationships with family and chosen people. The Association employs 150 people. Graduates most likely to be hired come from the following academic areas: Bachelor of Arts (Psychology, Recreation Studies), Bachelor of Science (Nursing, Psychology), Bachelor Education (Special Needs), Community College Diploma (Nursing RNA), and Developmental Service Worker. Graduates would occupy the following positions: Counsellor, and Support Worker (for developmentally delayed adult individuals), and Contract Support Worker (providing support to families and their handicapped family member). Excellent communication skills, maturity, commitment to the principles of the Association, experience, flexible regarding work hours, able to work independently, able to handle emergencies, and a knowledge of community resources are all listed as desirable non-academic qualifications. Company benefits are rated above average. The potential for advancement is listed as average. The average annual starting salary falls within the $25,000 to $35,000 range. The most suitable method for initial contact by those seeking employment is to mail a resume with a covering letter. The Association for Community Living does hire summer students. *Contacts:* Human Resources Department or Residential Services Department or A.R.C. Industries (Vocational Department).

ALBERTA ALCOHOL AND DRUG ABUSE COMMISSION
10909 Jasper Avenue, 6th Floor
Edmonton, AB T5J 3M9

Tel. 403-427-7935
Fax 403-427-1436

The Alberta Alcohol and Drug Abuse Commission (AADAC) is an agency funded by the government of Alberta to help Albertans achieve lives free from the abuse of alcohol, other drugs and gambling. AADAC's role is to promote people's independence and well being through increasing use of social, emotional, spiritual and physical resources, and to provide cost-effective, holistic alternatives to hospital-based and medical services. Founded in 1951 as the Alcoholism Foundation of Alberta to treat drinking problems, AADAC's name and mandate expanded to include other drugs in 1970. In 1994, AADAC also became responsible for addressing problem gambling. The Commission delivers services in four areas: Community Outpatient and Prevention Services, Crisis Services, Residential Treatment Services, and Research Information and Monitoring Services. Currently, AADAC employs 500 people in the province of Alberta. Graduates most likely to be hired come from the following academic areas: Bachelor of Arts (Psychology, Sociology/Social Work), Bachelor of Science (Nursing, Psychology), and Community College Diploma (Social Work/DSW, Nursing RN). Graduates would occupy Nurse or Addictions Counsellor positions. Company benefits are rated

as industry standard. The potential for advancement is listed as being good. The average annual starting salary falls within the $35,000 to $40,000 range. The most suitable method for initial contact by those seeking employment is to telephone the Commission directly. AADAC does hire summer students. *Contact:* Human Resource Consultants.

ALBERTA JUSTICE, HUMAN RESOURCES
9833 - 109 Street
Edmonton, AB T5K 2E8

Tel. 403-427-4978
Fax 403-422-1330

Alberta Justice is the province of Alberta's provincial department of justice. The department employs 4,000 people. Graduates most likely to be hired come from the following academic areas: Bachelor of Arts (Criminology, Economics, Psychology, Sociology), Bachelor of Science (Chemistry, Computer Science, Nursing, Occupational Therapy), Bachelor of Laws, Bachelor of Commerce/Business Administration (Accounting, Finance, Human Resources, Information Systems), Chartered Accountant, Certified Management Accountant, Certified General Accountant, Doctorate (Medical Doctor), and Community College Diploma (Accounting, Administration, Business, Financial Planning, Human Resources, Secretarial, Legal Assistant, Law Enforcement, Corrections Worker, Computer Science, Laboratory Technician, Nursing RN, Radiology Technician). Graduates would occupy Clerical, Professional, Technical, Medical, Legal, and Administrative positions. Related work experience, team player, enthusiasm, and good organization skills are all listed as desirable non-academic qualifications. Departmental benefits are rated above average. The potential for advancement is listed as being good. The average annual starting salary ranges widely, depending upon the class of position. The most suitable method for initial contact by those seeking employment is to mail a resume with a covering letter. Alberta Justice does hire summer students. *Contact:* Brian Sveinbjornson, Manager, Recruitment Classification and Employee Relations.

ALBERTA POWER LIMITED
10035 - 105 Street
Edmonton, AB T5J 2V6

Tel. 403-420-4189
Fax 403-420-3847

Alberta Power Limited supplies electrical power to the people of Alberta. Graduates most likely to be hired come from the following academic areas: Bachelor of Engineering (Electrical, Power, Mechanical, Industrial Design), Bachelor of Commerce/Business Administration (Accounting, Finance, Human Resources, Information Systems), Certified Management Accountant, Master of Business Administration (General, Finance, Human Resources), Master of Engineering (Mechanical, Electrical), and Community College Diploma (Accounting, Human Resources, Purchasing/Logistics, CAD/CAM/Autocad,

Engineering Technician, Health Nurse/Wellness). The most suitable method for initial contact by those seeking employment is to mail a resume with a covering letter. *Contact:* Human Resources.

ALBERTO-CULVER CANADA INC.
506 Kipling Avenue
Toronto, ON M8Z 5E2

Tel. 416-251-3741
Fax 416-251-3062
Website .... www.alberto.com

Alberto-Culver Canada Inc. employs more than 100 people in the manufacture of toiletries and household products. Products include Alberto European, and VO5 hair care products, and Sugar Twin, Molly McButter and Mrs. Dash food products. Graduates most likely to be hired come from the following academic areas: Bachelor of Arts (Business), Bachelor of Commerce/Business Administration (Marketing, Finance), Certified Management Accountant (Finance, Accounting), Certified General Accountant, Master of Business Administration, and Community College Diploma (Accounting). Employment opportunities for graduates exist as Assistant Product Managers, Sales Representatives, Accounting Clerks and General Office positions. Computer literacy is listed as a desirable non-academic qualification. Company benefits are rated as excellent. The potential for advancement is listed as being good. The average annual starting salary falls within the $20,000 to $25,000 range. The most suitable method for initial contact by those seeking employment is to mail a resume with a covering letter. Alberto-Culver does hire summer students occasionally. *Contact:* Joan Madden, Administrator, Human Resources.

ALCATEL CANADA WIRE INC.
140 Allstate Parkway
Markham, ON L3R 0Z7

Tel. 905-944-4300

Alcatel Canada Wire Inc. is the largest manufacturer of wire and cable in Canada. There are approximately 100 employees at this location. Graduates most likely to be hired come from the following academic areas: Bachelor of Engineering (Computer Systems, Manufacturing), Chartered Accountant (Finance), Master of Business Administration (Accounting, Finance, Information Systems). Good communication skills, straight dealing, task oriented, and a high energy level are all listed as desirable non-academic qualifications. Company benefits are rated above average. The potential for advancement is listed as being good. The average annual starting salary falls within the $25,000 to $35,000 range and ultimately depends upon qualifications and previous experience. The most suitable method for initial contact by those seeking employment is to mail a resume with a covering letter. Alcatel Canada Wire Inc. does hire summer students. *Contact:* Human Resources.

ALLAN CRAWFORD ASSOCIATES LTD.
5835 Coopers Avenue
Mississauga, ON L4Z 1Y2

Tel. 905-890-2010
Fax 905-890-1959

Allan Crawford Associates Ltd. is a high technology sales agent involved in the selling of test and measurement OEM components, and computer networks. There are more than 50 employees at this location. Graduates most likely to be hired come from the following academic areas: Bachelor of Arts (General), Bachelor of Science (Chemistry, Computer Science, Physics), Bachelor of Engineering (General, Chemical, Civil, Systems, Environmental, Electrical, Industrial, Materials Science, Mechanical), Bachelor of Commerce/Business Administration (Accounting, Finance, Marketing, Information Systems), Master of Business Administration (Information Systems), and Community College Diploma (Computer Science, Electronic Technician, Engineering Technician, Mechanic). Graduates would occupy the position of Sales Engineer of Sales Agent. Accordingly, possessing a sales aptitude is listed as a desirable non-academic qualification. Company benefits are rated above average. The potential for advancement is listed as being good. The average annual starting salary falls within the $25,000 to $30,000 range. The most suitable method for initial contact by graduates seeking employment is to mail a resume with a covering letter. Allan Crawford Associates Ltd. does hire summer students on a regular basis. *Contact:* Operations Manager.

ALLCOLOUR PAINT LTD.
1257 Speers Road
Oakville, ON L6L 2X5

Tel. 905-827-4173
Fax 905-827-6487
Email .... mauro25@ibm.net

Allcolour Paint Ltd. is involved in the manufacture of industrial paint and paint related products. There are 80 employees at this location, and a total of 84 employees in Canada. Graduates most likely to be hired come from the following academic areas: Community College Diploma (Administration, Secretarial), and High School Diploma. Graduates would occupy Clerical positions. Company benefits are rated above average. The potential for advancement is listed as average. The average annual starting salary falls within the $25,000 to $30,000 range. The most suitable methods for initial contact by those seeking employment are to mail, fax, or e-mail a resume with a covering letter. Allcolour Paint Ltd. does hire summer students. *Contact:* Mauro LoRusso, B.B.M., CMA, Controller.

ALLELIX BIOPHARMACEUTICALS INC.
6850 Goreway Drive
Mississauga, ON L4V 1V7

Tel. 905-677-0831
Fax 905-677-9595
Website .... www.allelix.com

Allelix Biopharmaceuticals Inc. is a leading Canadian biotechnology company which focuses on the discovery and development of biopharmaceutical products for tissue repair, immunological and inflammatory diseases. The company applies the latest advances in the scientific understanding of molecular and cellular biology to discover new approaches for the development of therapeutic products for these conditions. A subsidiary division focuses on bioinformatics, and a sister company works in radiopharmaceutical research. Currently the company employs 180 people and continues to grow steadily. Graduates most likely to be hired come from the following academic areas: Bachelor of Science (General, Biology, Chemistry, Computer Science, Health Sciences, Microbiology, Pharmacy), Bachelor of Engineering (Chemical), Bachelor of Commerce/Business Administration (Finance, Marketing), Master of Business Administration (Finance, Marketing), Master of Science (Molecular Biology, Chemistry, Pharmacy), Doctorate (Molecular Biology, Biochemistry, Pharmacy), and Community College Diploma (Laboratory Technician). Graduates are hired to occupy positions in Research and Development, Business Development, Finance and General Administration. Initiative, drive, a strong work ethic, creativity, research oriented, and excellent communication skills are all listed as desirable non-academic qualifications. Company benefits are rated as excellent. The potential for advancement is listed as being good. The most suitable method for initial contact by those seeking employment is to mail a resume with a covering letter. Contact: Human Resources Department.

ALLIANZ CANADA
425 Bloor Street East, Suite 200
Toronto, ON M4W 3R5

Tel. 416-961-5015
Fax 416-961-3088
Email .... kabbott@Allianz.ca

Allianz Canada is the 3rd largest insurance company in the world. The company employs 250 people at this location and a total of 450 people in Canada. Graduates most likely to be hired come from the following academic areas: Bachelor of Arts (General, Economics), Bachelor of Science (General, Actuarial, Computer Science, Mathematics), Bachelor of Commerce/Business Administration (Accounting, Finance, Human Resources, Information Systems, Marketing), Chartered Accountant, Certified Management Accountant, Certified General Accountant, Master of Business Administration (Accounting, Finance, Human Resources, Information Systems, Marketing), and Community College Diploma (Accounting, Administration, Business, Human Resources, Information Systems, Insurance, Secretarial, Computer Science). Graduates would occupy entry level positions such as, Claims Clerk, Underwriting Clerk, and Accounting Clerk. Team player, insurance experience, and good communication skills are all listed as desirable non-academic qualifications. Company benefits and the potential for advancement are both rated as excellent. The average annual start-

ing salary falls within the $20,000 to $25,000 range. The most suitable method for initial contact by those seeking employment is to mail a resume with a covering letter. Contact: Kerry Abbott, Human Resources Consultant.

ALLIED INTERNATIONAL CREDIT CORP.
11 Allstate Parkway, Suite 500
Markham, ON L3R 9T8

Tel. 905-513-3504
Fax 905-470-8155

Allied International Credit Corp. is a third party debt collections company. There are approximately 240 employees at this location, a total of 310 in Canada, and 420 employees worldwide. Graduates most likely to be hired come from the following academic areas: Bachelor of Arts (Psychology), Bachelor of Commerce/Business Administration (Finance), Community College Diploma (Business, Financial Planning, Secretarial, Legal Assistant), and High School Diploma. Graduates would occupy Collections Officer, Financial Negotiator, Secretary, Data Entry Clerk, Customer Service Representative, Payroll Clerk, and Human Resources Assistant positions. Company benefits are rated as industry standard. The potential for advancement is listed as being good. The average annual starting salary falls within the $20,000 to $25,000 range. The most suitable method for initial contact by those seeking employment is to mail a resume with a covering letter. Allied International Credit Corp. does hire summer students. Contact: Carole Geroux, Consultant, Human Resources.

ALLSTATE INSURANCE COMPANY OF CANADA
10 Allstate Parkway
Markham, ON L3R 5P8

Tel. 905-475-4322
Fax 905-475-4924
Website .... www.allstate.ca

Allstate Insurance Company of Canada is a property and casualty insurance company, employing approximately 400 people at this location, and a total of 1,200 people across Canada. Activities include policy sales, claims administration, administration of current/renewal policies, writing new policies/processing, accounting/collections and the development of new products. Graduates most likely to be hired come from the following academic areas: Bachelor of Arts (Economics), Bachelor of Science (Actuarial, Computer Science, Mathematics), Bachelor of Commerce/Business Administration (Accounting, Finance, Marketing), Chartered Accountant, Certified General Accountant, Master of Business Administration (General, Accounting, Finance), and Community College Diploma (Accounting, Business, Communications, Financial Planning, Insurance). Graduates would occupy positions as Accountants, Underwriters, Programmers, and Supervisory and Customer Service positions. Initiative, team player, and good communication and problem solving skills are listed as desirable non-academic qualifications. Company benefits are rated above average. The potential for advancement is listed as being good. The average annual starting salary falls within the $25,000 to $30,000 range. The most suitable methods for initial contact by those seeking employment are to mail a resume with a covering letter, or by responding to positions advertised in major newspapers. *Contacts:* Ms. Tricia Biglow, Human Resources Manager or Ms. Mary Collins, Sr. Human Resources Representative.

AMDAHL CANADA LIMITED
12 Concorde Place, Suite 300
Toronto, ON M3C 3R8

Tel. 416-510-3111
Fax 416-510-2296

This location of Amdahl Canada Limited is primarily involved in the sales and service of large, mainframe computers. Located in downtown Toronto, there are more than 100 people employed at this location. Graduates most likely to be hired come from Bachelor of Commerce/Business Administration (General, Finance) programs. Graduates would be hired to occupy the position of Associate Account Executive. Company benefits are rated as excellent. The potential for advancement is listed as being good. The average annual starting salary falls within the $30,000 to $35,000 range. The most suitable method for initial contact by those seeking employment is to mail a resume with a covering letter. Amdahl Canada Limited does hire summer students, primarily for mail room positions. *Contact:* Charles Charzan, Human Resources Manager.

AMERICAN AIRLINES INC.
P.O. Box 6005, L.B. Pearson International Airport
Malton, ON L5P 1B6

Fax 905-612-0144

American Airlines Inc. is an international scheduled airline transportation company, serving over 300 destinations worldwide. There are 125 employees at this location, a total of 500 in Canada, and 100,000 employees worldwide. Graduates most likely to be hired come from the following academic areas: Bachelor of Arts (General), Bachelor of Commerce/Business Administration (General, Accounting, Marketing), Master of Business Administration (General, Marketing), and Community College Diploma (Administration, Business, Marketing/Sales). At this location, graduates would occupy entry level positions as Airport Passenger/Cargo Service Agents, as well as Passenger Sales and Marketing positions. Team player, flexible, enthusiastic, and responsible are all listed as desirable non-academic qualifications. Company benefits are rated as industry standard. The potential for advancement is listed as average. The average annual starting salary for entry level positions falls within the $15,000 to $20,000 range. The most suitable method for initial contact by those seeking employment is to mail a resume with a covering letter. *Contact:* Human Resources/Administration.

AMERICAN EXPRESS CANADA INC.
101 McNabb Street
Markham, ON L3R 4H8

Tel. 905-474-8000
Fax 905-474-8004

American Express Canada Inc. provides Financial Services such as credit cards and travellers cheques, and Banking Services such as asset management and lines of credit, and Insurance and Travel Services. There are more than 1,000 employees at this location. Graduates most likely to be hired come from the following academic areas: Bachelor of Arts, Bachelor of Science, Bachelor of Laws, Bachelor of Commerce/Business Administration, Master of Business Administration (Marketing, Finance), Masters (General/Related) and Community College Diploma (Business/Finance). Graduates would occupy entry level positions in Marketing, Systems, Finance, Customer Service and Administration. Company benefits and the potential for advancement are both rated as excellent. The average annual starting salary falls within the $25,000 to $30,000 range. The most suitable method for initial contact by graduates seeking employment is to mail a resume with a covering letter. American Express Canada Inc. does hire summer students on a limited basis. *Contact:* Human Resources.

AMERICAN STANDARD INC.
1401 Dupont Street
Toronto, ON M6H 2B1

Tel. 416-536-1078
Fax 416-535-9760

American-Standard Inc. is a major manufacturer of plumbing fixtures, fittings, and bathroom accessories. The company employs more than 250 people at this location. Graduates most likely to be hired come from the following academic areas: Bachelor of Engineering (General), and Community College Diploma (General/Related). Company benefits are rated as excellent. The potential for advancement is listed as being good. The average annual starting salary is dependent upon the level of position. The most suitable method for initial contact by graduates seeking employment is to mail a resume with a covering letter. *Contact:* Employee Relations.

AMJ CAMPBELL VAN LINES
1190 Meyerside Drive
Mississauga, ON L5T 1R7

Tel. 905-670-7111
Fax 905-795-3455

AMJ Campbell Van Lines is the largest member of Atlas Van Lines, active in the transportation of household goods and commercial products. Divisions include domestic and overseas moving, trade show division, and office moving division. There are approximately 350 employees at this location and more than 2,000 employees across Canada, including branches and franchises. Graduates most likely to be hired come from the following academic areas:

Bachelor of Commerce/Business Administration, Master of Business Administration, and Community College Diploma (Accounting, Administration, Business, Facility Management, Marketing/Sales, Secretarial). Hard working, team player, and a great attitude are all listed as desirable non-academic qualifications. Company benefits are rated above average. The potential for advancement is listed as excellent. The average annual starting salary falls within the $25,000 to $30,000 range. The most suitable methods for initial contact by those seeking employment are to mail a resume with a covering letter, or via telephone. Summer students are always in demand for moving positions. *Contact:* Marilyn Ogston, Human Resources.

AML WIRELESS SYSTEMS INC.
260 Saulteaux Crescent
Winnipeg, MB R3J 3T2

Tel. 204-949-2400
Fax 204-889-1268
Email .... lrosney@amlwireless.com

AML Wireless Systems Inc. designs and manufactures telecommunications equipment. The company employs approximately 38 people. Graduates most likely to be hired come from the following academic areas: Bachelor of Science (Computer Science, Physics), Bachelor of Engineering (Electrical, Telecommunications), Bachelor of Commerce/Business Administration (Marketing), Master of Engineering (Electronics, Electrical), and Community College Diploma (Administration, Marketing/Sales, CAD/CAM/Autocad, Computer Science, Electronics Technician, Engineering Technician). Graduates would occupy Applications Engineer, Sales/Marketing Representative, Test Technician, and Documentation Clerk (Autocad) positions. Company benefits are rated as excellent. The potential for advancement is listed as being good. The most suitable methods for initial contact by those seeking employment are to mail, fax or e-mail a resume with a covering letter. AML Wireless Systems Inc. does hire summer students. *Contact:* Lisa Rosney, Human Resources.

AMP OF CANADA LTD.
20 Esna Park Drive
Markham, ON L3R 1E1

Tel. 905-475-6222
Fax 905-474-5525

AMP of Canada Ltd. is involved in the manufacture and sale of electrical connectors and connector systems. There are approximately 275 employees at this location and a total of 330 employees across Canada. Graduates most likely to be hired come from the following academic areas: Bachelor of Science (Computer Science), Bachelor of Engineering (Metallurgy, Mechanical), Bachelor of Commerce/Business Administration (Finance), and Master of Business Administration (Marketing). Graduates would occupy Sales Trainee, Administrative Trainee, and Manufacturing Engineer positions. Team oriented, and good communication skills are both listed as desirable non-academic qualifications. Company benefits are rated as excellent. The potential for advancement is listed as being good. The average annual starting salary falls within the $30,000 to $35,000 range. The most suitable method for initial contact by those seeking employment is to mail a resume with a covering letter. AMP of Canada Ltd. does hire a limited number of summer students. *Contact:* Human Resources Department.

AMS MANAGEMENT SYSTEMS CANADA INC. (MONTREAL)
1250 Rene Levesque Blvd West, Suite 4500
Montreal, QC H3B 4W8

Tel. 514-939-4662
Fax 514-939-6015
Website .... www.amsinc.com

AMS Management Systems Canada, Inc. is a subsidiary of one of the world's leading business and information technology consulting firms, American Management Systems, Inc., headquartered in Fairfax, Virginia. Founded in 1970, AMS has over 8,500 employees in 55 offices throughout North America and Europe. AMS Management Systems Canada, Inc. was established in 1985, and has grown to over 200 employees supporting clients in Ottawa (see next listing), Toronto and Montreal. AMS Canada partners with clients in the financial, telecommunications and government sectors to achieve breakthrough performance through the intelligent use of information technology. AMS provides a full range of consulting services, from business re-engineering, change management, systems integration, and systems development and implementation. There are 26 employees at this location. Graduates most likely to be hired come from the following academic areas: Bachelor of Science (Computer Science), Bachelor of Engineering (Computer Systems), Bachelor of Commerce/Business Administration (Information Systems), Master of Business Administration (Information Systems), and Community College Diploma (Information Systems). Graduates would occupy Programmer Analyst and Business Analyst positions. Team oriented, effective speaker, good judgment skills, and previous IT experience are all listed as desirable non-academic qualifications. Company benefits and the potential for advancement are both rated as excellent. The average annual starting salary falls within the $35,000 to $40,000 range. The most suitable method for initial contact by those seeking employment is to mail a resume with a covering letter. *Contacts:* Antonio Petruccelli or Andrew Gates.

AMS MANAGEMENT SYSTEMS CANADA INC. (OTTAWA)
180 Elgin Sttreet, Suite 700
Ottawa, ON K2P 2K3

Tel. 613-232-7400
Fax 613-232-0324
Website .... www.amsinc.com

AMS Management Systems Canada, Inc. is a subsidiary of one of the world's leading business and information technology consulting firms, American Management Systems, Inc., headquartered in Fairfax, Virginia. Founded in 1970, AMS has over 8,500 employees in 55 offices throughout North America and Europe. AMS Management Systems Canada, Inc. was established in 1985, and has grown to over 200 employees supporting clients in Ottawa, Toronto and Montreal (see previous listing). AMS Canada partners with clients in the financial, telecommunications and government sectors to achieve breakthrough performance through the intelligent use of information technology. AMS provides a full range of consulting services, from defining strategy to implementing solutions. Graduates most likely to be hired come from the following academic areas: Bachelor of Science (Computer Science), Bachelor of Engineering (Electrical, Computer Systems), Bachelor of Commerce/Business Administration (Information Systems), and Master of Business Administration (Information Systems). Graduates would occupy IT Consultant positions, fulfilling a variety of roles such as Systems Analyst and Applications Developer. Strong oral and written communication skills, team player, and previous exposure to IT are all listed as desirable non-academic qualifications. Company benefits are rated above average. The potential for advancement is listed as excellent. The most suitable method for initial contact by those seeking employment is through on-campus recruitment initiatives (visit your campus career centre for details). AMS Management Systems Canada Inc. (Ottawa Location) does hire students for summer and co-op work terms. *Contact:* Recruiting - Human Resources.

ANDERSEN CONSULTING
185 The West Mall, Suite 500
Toronto, ON M9C 5L5

Tel. 416-695-5050
Fax 416-695-5074
Website .... www.ac.com

Andersen Consulting is a $7.2 billion global management and technology consulting organization whose mission is to help its clients from a wide range of industries link their people, processes and technologies to their strategies. Andersen Consulting employs nearly 49,000 persons in 47 countries. The Canadian practice of Andersen Consulting maintains offices across Canada in Vancouver, Toronto, Etobicoke, Ottawa and Montreal. The Canadian practice employs over 1,100 talented professionals with skills in Strategy, Change Management, Process, and Technology consulting. Andersen's Canadian practice provides consulting services to clients in the Communications, Government, Products, Resources, and Financial Services industries. Graduates most likely to be hired come from the following

academic areas: Bachelor of Arts (Economics, Psychology), Bachelor of Science (Computer Science, Mathematics), Bachelor of Engineering (General, Chemical, Civil, Electrical, Mechanical, Aerospace, Automation/Robotics, Computer Systems, Engineering Physics, Environmental/Resources, Food Processing, Industrial Design, Industrial Engineering, Industrial Production/Manufacturing, Microelectronics, Power/Hydro, Pulp and Paper), Bachelor of Commerce/Business Administration (General, Accounting, Finance, Human Resources, Information Systems, Marketing, Public Administration), Master of Business Administration (General, Accounting, Finance, Human Resources, Information Systems, Marketing, Public Administration), Master of Arts (Psychology, Industrial Relations), Master of Science, and Master of Engineering. Graduates would occupy Analyst positions in Technology, Process and Change Management. Team player, good problem solving skills, well rounded interests, strong communication skills, an ability to work hard, and an interest in travel are listed as desirable non-academic qualifications. Andersen Consulting offers a total engineering environment, in which applicants are challenged to learn on their own, on the job in one of the industry's best training programs. Accordingly, company benefits are rated above average and the potential for advancement is listed as excellent. The most suitable method for initial contact by those seeking employment is to apply through on-campus recruitment initiatives (see your campus career centre for details). *Contact:* Charmaine Denton, Recruiting.

AON CONSULTING
145 Wellington Street West, Suite 500
Toronto, ON M5J 1H8

Tel. 416-542-5531
Fax 416-542-5501
Email ...... joanne.campbell@aonconsulting.aon.ca

Aon Consulting, through its integrated consulting approach provides innovative solutions to assist clients in linking human resource strategies with business strategies, in the areas of health and benefits, retirement, human resources, change management, compensation and workers compensation. Aon Consulting is part of Aon Consulting Worldwide Inc., a subsidiary of the Aon Group, a global organization serving clients through 400 owned offices in 60 countries. The Canadian organization has 12 offices nationally and operates as Aon MLH Martineau Provencher in Quebec, and Aon Consulting in the rest of Canada. There are 150 employees at this location, and a total of 540 employees in Canada. Graduates most likely to be hired come from the following academic areas: Bachelor of Arts (General), Bachelor of Science (Actuarial, Mathematics, Nursing, Occupational Therapy, Physical Therapy), Bachelor of Laws, Bachelor of Commerce/Business Administration (Accounting, Finance, Human Resources, Information Systems), Chartered Accountant, Certified Management Accountant, Certified General Accountant, Master of Business Administration (Accounting, Finance, Human Resources,

Information Systems), and Community College Diploma (Accounting, Administration, Human Resources, Secretarial). Graduates would occupy Pension Administrator, Secretary, Actuarial Analyst, Research Analyst, Financial Analyst, Accountant, Programmer, Pension Analyst, Benefits Analyst, and Human Resources Analyst positions. Computer literacy, customer service skills, strong communication and organization skills, team player, and previous consulting experience are all listed as desirable non-academic qualifications. The average annual starting salary falls within the $25,000 to $30,000 range. The most suitable methods for initial contact by those seeking employment are to mail or fax a resume with a covering letter. Aon Consulting occasionally hires summer students. Actuarial students are hired for co-op work term placements. *Contacts:* Shelly Nielsen, Director, Human Resources (shelly_nielsen@aonconsulting.aon.ca) or Joanne Campbell, Manager, Human Resources.

APOTEX INC.
150 Signet Drive
Toronto, ON M9L 1T9

Tel.	416-749-9300
Fax	416-401-3828
Email	recruit@apotex.ca

Apotex Inc. is the largest vertically integrated Canadian owned pharmaceutical company, with over 2,500 employees in the group across Canada. The company researches, develops, manufactures and distributes 165 quality medicines which also are exported to 110 countries. With a research budget of $72.9 million in 1997, Apotex was the 17th largest R&D spender for all companies in Canada. Graduates most likely to be hired come from the following academic areas: Bachelor of Science (Chemistry, Computer Science, Microbiology), Bachelor of Engineering (Chemical, Civil, Electrical, Mechanical, Computer Systems, Industrial Chemistry, Industrial Engineering, Industrial Production/Manufacturing, Instrumentation, Telecommunications), Bachelor of Commerce/Business Administration (Accounting, Finance, Human Resources, Information Systems, Marketing), Chartered Accountant, Certified Management Accountant, Certified General Accountant, Master of Business Administration (General, Human Resources, Information Systems), Master/Doctorate of Science (Chemistry), and Community College Diploma (Accounting, Human Resources, Information Systems, Secretarial, Computer Science, Electronics Technician, Engineering Technician, HVAC Systems, Plumber). Graduates would occupy Office Clerk, Administration, Accounting, Human Resource, Chemist, Biochemist, Microbiologist, Clinical Research, and Industrial Engineer positions. Excellent communication and interpersonal skills, flexibility, and the ability to work in a team are all listed as desirable non-academic qualifications. Company benefits and the potential for advancement are both rated as excellent. The average annual starting salary is dependent upon the position being considered. The most suitable methods for initial contact by those seeking employment are to mail or fax a resume with a covering letter. Apotex Inc. does hire students for co-op work terms. *Contact:* Human Resources - Recruiter.

APPLE CANADA INC.
7495 Birchmount Road
Markham, ON L3R 5G2

Tel.	905-513-5800
Fax	905-513-4291

Apple Canada Inc. is the Canadian sales and marketing subsidiary of Apple Computer Inc. based in Cupertino, California. Apple employs approximately 100 people in 12 offices across Canada. The head office is the Markham location employing approximately 60 people. Graduates most likely to be hired come from the following academic areas: Bachelor of Science (Computer Science), Bachelor of Commerce/Business Administration (Accounting, Finance, Marketing), Master of Business Administration (General, Accounting, Finance, Marketing), and Community College Diploma (Marketing/Sales). Recent post-secondary graduates without job-related experience are not generally hired. Company benefits are rated as excellent. The potential for advancement is listed as being good. The most suitable method for initial contact by those seeking employment is to mail a resume with a covering letter. Apple Canada Inc. does hire summer students. *Contacts:* Lynne Jarjour, Human Resources Manager or Bethany Kopstick, Human Resources Specialist.

APPLIED DIGITAL ACCESS CANADA INC.
8644 Commerce Court, Imperial Square
Burnaby, BC V5A 4N6

Tel.	604-415-5917
Fax	604-415-5900
Email	bcg_careers@ada.com
Website	www.ada.com

Applied Digital Access Canada Inc. (ADA) is a leading provider of systems, software and services that manage the performance, quality, reliability and availability of telecommunications service provider's networks. Telecommunications service providers demand powerful network management tools to help them effectively compete in the marketplace. Benefits, which can be realized by deployment of ADA products, include improved quality of service, increased productivity, and lower operating expenses. ADA targets all types of network operators, telecommunications service providers, internet service providers (ISPs), cable, cellular, and wireless providers. ADA's goal is to consistently meet and frequently exceed customer expectations, continually striving to improve the capability, quality and reliability of its products and services. The company employs 90 people in Canada, and a total of 300 people worldwide. ADA's headquarters is located in San Diego, California. Graduates most likely to be hired come from the following academic areas: Bachelor of Science (Computer Science, Mathematics), Bachelor of Engineering (Electrical), Bachelor of Commerce/Business Administration (Information Systems), Master of Science, Master of Engineering, and Community College Diploma (Administration, Communications/Public Relations, Human Resources, Information Systems, Computer Science, Electronics Technician). Graduates would occupy Verification and Software Developer positions. Team player, require minimal guidance, enthusiastic, and able to work on own initiative are all listed as desirable non-academic qualifications. Company benefits are rated above average. The potential for advancement is listed as being good. The average annual starting salary falls within the $40,000 to $45,000 range. The most suitable methods for initial contact by those seeking employment are to e-mail a resume with a covering letter, or by applying through the company's website at www.ada.com. Applied Digital Access Canada Inc. does hire students for summer and co-op work terms. *Contact:* Jennifer Rigal, Technical Recruiter.

AQUALTA

10065 Jasper Avenue, 20th Floor Capitol Square
Edmonton, AB T5J 3B1

Tel. 403-412-3054
Fax 403-412-7888
Email .... lgeorge@aqualta.com
Website .... www.aqualta.com

Aqualta is a member of the EPCOR group of companies. EPCOR, based out of Edmonton, is the parent company of Edmonton Power, Aqualta and Eltec. EPCOR is governed by an independent Board of Directors and Management Team. The City of Edmonton is the sole shareholder of the EPCOR group. Incorporated May 1, 1996, Aqualta is the third largest water distributor in Canada, with pipelines spanning 2,800 kilometers. Aqualta's main responsibility is to provide high quality water to the citizens of Edmonton and 40 surrounding communities in Alberta. As part of this responsibility, the company manages two water treatment plants and the distribution system within the city boundaries. In order to maintain the infrastructure, Aqualta also manages capital projects which ensures that service disruptions are kept to a minimum and allow Aqualta to maintain a very strong technological edge with its competitors. The company also runs a full scale laboratory to ensure that water quality remains at its peak while researching the newest water treatment technologies. Aqualta has entered into private and public partnerships in building and operating systems in other parts of western Canada. Presently, Aqualta employs 273 permanent and 40 temporary (mostly seasonal) employees. Graduates most likely to be hired come from the following academic areas: Bachelor of Science (Chemistry), Bachelor of Engineering (Civil, Environmental/Resources, Water Resources), Chartered Accountant, Certified Management Accountant, Master of Engineering (Environmental Sciences), and Community College Diploma (CAD/CAM/Autocad, Electrician, Engineering Technician, Instrumentation Technician, Laboratory Technician. Graduates would occupy Water Plant Director, Controller, Drafting Technician, Junior Engineer, Accountant, Engineering Technologist, Contract Inspector, Project Coordinator, and Project Manager positions. Leadership skills, initiative, empowering of others, teamwork skills, adaptive to change, and open communication skills are all listed as desirable non-academic qualifications. Company benefits are rated as industry standard. The potential for advancement is listed as being good. The average annual starting salary falls within the $25,000 to $30,000 range for Clerical positions, $30,000 to $35,000 range for Technical positions, and $45,000 to $50,000 range for Professional positions. The most suitable method for initial contact by those seeking employment is via telephone. Aqualta does hire students for summer and co-op work terms. *Contact:* Céline-Lise George, Director, Human Resources.

ARBOR MEMORIAL SERVICES INC.

2 Jane Street
Toronto, ON M6S 4W8

Tel. 416-763-4531
Fax 416-763-8714
Email .... hrarbor@arbormemorial.com

Arbor Memorial Services Inc. owns cemetery properties, funeral homes and crematoria across Canada. The company employs over 1,600 people in Canada. Graduates most likely to be hired come from the following academic areas: Bachelor of Arts (General), Bachelor of Science (General, Horticulture), Bachelor of Engineering (Civil), Bachelor of Landscape Architecture, Bachelor of Commerce/Business Administration (Accounting, Human Resources, Information Systems, Marketing), Chartered Accountant, Certified Management Accountant, Certified General Accountant, and Community College Diploma (Accounting, Administration, Business, Human Resources, Marketing/Sales, Secretarial, Architecture/Drafting, Horticulture, Computer Science, Funeral Services). Graduates would be hired to occupy Administrative Assistant/Clerical, Marketing Coordinator, Accounting Clerk, Property Manager, Sales Representative, and Funeral Director positions. An adaptable and flexible approach to working, team player, problem solving abilities, and entrepreneurial skills are all listed as desirable non-academic qualifications. Company benefits are rated above average. The potential for advancement is listed as being good. The average annual starting salary falls within the $25,000 to $35,000 range, and is commission based for sales positions. The most suitable methods for initial contact by those seeking employment are to mail, fax or e-mail a resume with a covering letter. Arbor Memorial Services Inc. does hire summer students to work primarily on the cemetery properties. Co-op work term students are hired occasionally. *Contacts:* Michelle Gibbons, Human Resources or Dana Dramnitzke, Human Resources.

ARCHITECTS CRANG AND BOAKE INC.
1 Valleybrook Drive
Toronto, ON M3B 2S7

Tel. 416-449-1203
Fax 416-449-4063
Email .... acbi@interlog.com

Architects Crang and Boake Inc. is an architectural design firm providing contract documents for construction purposes. The firm maintains offices in China, the U.A.E., and in Toronto. There are 50 employees at this location, a total of 70 employees worldwide. Graduates most likely to be hired come from the following academic areas: Bachelor of Engineering (Architectural/Building), Bachelor of Architecture, Community College Diploma (CAD/CAM/Autocad), and High School Diploma. Recent graduates would occupy CADD Drafting Technician (architectural) and CADD Designer positions. Self-starter, able to travel, team player, and cooperative are listed as desirable non-academic qualifications. Company benefits are rated as industry standard. The potential for advancement is listed as being good. The average annual starting salary falls within the $25,000 to $45,000 plus range, depending upon the experience of the applicant, and the position being considered. The most suitable methods for initial contact by graduates seeking employment are to mail a resume with a covering letter, or via telephone. Architects Crang and Boake Inc. does hire summer students. *Contact:* Sheldon Ublansky.

ARCTIC CO-OPERATIVES LIMITED
1645 Inkster Boulevard
Winnipeg, MB R2X 2W7

Tel. 204-697-1625
Fax 204-697-1880

Arctic Co-operatives Limited is owned and controlled by 42 member co-ops in Canada's north. The co-operative provides accounting services, merchandise procurement services, construction services, management advice and direction, and recruitment and benefits administration. Member co-ops are aboriginally owned. There are a 55 employees at this location, and a total of 90 employees in the co-operative. Graduates most likely to be hired come from the following academic areas: Bachelor of Commerce/Business Administration (Accounting, Finance, Human Resources, Information Systems, Marketing), and Certified General Accountant. Graduates would occupy Auditor, Area Manager, and Merchandise Manager positions. Knowledge of Aboriginal cultures is listed as a desirable non-academic qualification. Company benefits are rated above average. The potential for advancement is listed as average. The average annual starting salary falls within the $15,000 to $20,000 range. The most suitable method for initial contact by those seeking employment is to mail a resume with a covering letter. Arctic Co-operatives Limited does hire summer students. *Contact:* James Kaassen, Division Manager, Human Resources.

ARMTEC
P.O. Box 3000
Guelph, ON N1H 6P2

Tel. 519-822-0210
Fax 519-822-1160

Armtec engineers, manufactures, and markets products used in municipal, highway, industrial, mining, and water resource construction products. Products include corrugated steel drainage pipes, guard rails for highways, retaining walls, field-assembled under passes and bridges, metal grating, water control gates, and distribution of geotextiles. Armtec maintains Branch Office, Sales Office and Plant locations across Canada. There are approximately 250 employees across Canada. Graduates most likely to be hired come from the following academic areas: Bachelor of Engineering (Civil, Mechanical), Bachelor of Commerce/Business Administration (Accounting), and Community College Diploma (Accounting, Engineering). Graduates would occupy Junior Engineer, Engineering Technologist, and Cost Accounting Clerk positions. Computer software knowledge, good verbal and written communications skills, interpersonal skills, and relevant work experience are all listed as desirable non-academic qualifications. Company benefits are rated as excellent. The potential for advancement is listed as average. The average annual starting salary depends upon the position being considered. The most suitable method for initial contact by those seeking employment is to mail a resume with a covering letter. Armtec does hire a limited number of summer students, primarily for clerical and plant positions. In addition, Armtec occasionally hires engineering students for co-op work terms. *Contact:* Jan McEwin, Human Resources.

ARNOLD BROTHERS TRANSPORT LTD.
739 Lagimodiere Boulevard
Winnipeg, MB R2J 0T8

Tel. 204-257-6666
Fax 204-257-2213

Arnold Brothers Transport Ltd. is a line haul transportation company, providing full load service throughout Canada and the United States. Established in 1958, the company employs approximately 300 people at this location, and a total of 500 people in Canada. Graduates most likely to be hired come from the following academic areas: Bachelor of Commerce/Business Administration (General, Marketing), Chartered Accountant, Certified Management Accountant, Certified General Accountant, and Community College Diploma (Accounting, Computer Science). Graduates would occupy accounting management/supervision, general accounting, computer programming, computer systems maintenance, and sales and marketing representative/management positions. Past work experience, transportation background, self and time management skills, team oriented, detail and deadline oriented, pro-active approach, reliable, dependable, and problem solving skills are all listed as desirable non-academic qualifications. Company benefits are rated as industry standard. The potential for advancement is listed as being good. The average annual starting salary is dependent upon the position being considered. The most suitable method for initial contact by those seeking employment is to mail a resume with a covering letter. Arnold Brothers Transport Ltd. does hire summer students. *Contacts:* Sandy Ryder, Vice President, Human Resources or Ross Arnold, Vice President.

ART GALLERY OF ONTARIO
317 Dundas Street West
Toronto, ON M5T 1G4

Tel. 416-977-0414
Fax 416-979-6646

The Art Gallery of Ontario is Ontario's main art gallery. Employing approximately 300 people, gallery activities include the displaying of art and all associated administrative functions. Graduates most likely to be hired come from the following academic areas: Bachelor of Arts (Fine Art, History) and Community College Diploma (Food/Nutrition, Administration, Secretarial). Graduates would occupy clerical, secretarial, food service and educational positions. Company benefits are rated above average. The potential for advancement is listed as average. The average annual starting salary falls within the $25,000 to $30,000 range. The most suitable method for initial contact by those seeking employment is to mail a resume with a covering letter. The Art Gallery of Ontario does hire summer students through government programs. *Contact:* Director of Human Resources.

ARTSMARKETING SERVICES INC.
260 King Street East, Suite 500
Toronto, ON M5A 1K3

Tel. 416-941-9000
Fax 416-941-8989

Artsmarketing Services Inc. (AMS) is an international marketing company that works exclusively with non-profit organizations throughout North America. Clients include major symphonies, theatres, operas, and ballet companies, as well as museums and public television stations. Graduates most likely to be hired come from the following academic areas: Bachelor of Arts (General, Economics, English, Fine Arts, Journalism, Music, Psychology, Arts Management, Theatre, Communications), Bachelor of Science, Bachelor of Education, Bachelor of Commerce/Business Administration (Finance, Public Administration, Marketing, Information Systems), Master of Business Administration (Accounting, Finance, Marketing, Information Systems), Master of Arts (Arts Management), and Community College Diploma (Administration, Advertising, Business, Communications, Marketing, Graphic Arts, Human Resources, Photography, Television/Radio Arts). Graduates who are hired will enter an extensive hands-on management training program. Following the successful completion of the training program, they are made Campaign Managers whose responsibilities include hiring, training and motivating a sales staff of 12 to 15 people. Listening skills, sense of humour, interpersonal and communication skills, problem solving abilities, leadership qualities, an arts background, ability to relocate, sales, telemarketing, managerial and fundraising experience are all listed as desirable non-academic qualifications. The potential for advancement is listed as excellent. Remuneration is commission based and may vary between $18,000 and $30,000 for the first year. The most suitable methods for initial contact by those seeking employment are to mail or fax a resume with a covering letter, or via telephone. *Contacts:* Ken Lampe, Director, Human Resources (x 226) or David Macdonald, Manager, Human Resources (x 239).

ASCENT POWER TECHNOLOGY INC.
146 Adesso Drive
Concord, ON L4K 3C3

Tel. 905-660-9819
Fax 905-660-9567
Email .... kenl@ascent.ca
Website .... www.ascentpower.com

Ascent Power Technology Inc. is involved in the production of power supply units for commercial (fax machines, photocopiers) and medical (ultrasound equipment) markets. The company designs units to customer specifications and provides complete customer service. Ascent Power Technology employs 300 people at this location, and a total of 850 people worldwide. Graduates most likely to be hired come from the following academic areas: Bachelor of Engineering (Electrical, Mechanical, Industrial Engineering, Industrial Production/Manufacturing), Bachelor of Commerce/Business Administration (Accounting, Finance), and Community College Diploma (Accounting, Business). Team player and good problem skills are both listed as desirable non-academic qualifications. Company benefits are rated above average. The potential for advancement is listed as being good. The most suitable methods for initial contact by those seeking employment are to mail or fax a resume with a covering letter. Ascent Power Technology Inc. does hire summer students (sometimes), and co-op work term students. *Contacts:* Dora Malizia, Human Resources Assistant or Ken Lawrence, Human Resources Manager.

ASEA BROWN BOVERI INC. (ABB)
200 Chisholm Drive
Milton, ON L9T 5E7

Tel. 905-875-4500
Fax 905-875-4602

Asea Brown Boveri Inc. is involved in the manufacturing of Switchgear equipment. Asea Brown Boveri Inc. is ISO 9001 registered company, employing 100 people at this location, a total of 2,000 people in Canada, and 220,000 people worldwide. Graduates most likely to be hired come from the following academic areas: Bachelor of Engineering, Bachelor of Commerce/Business Administration, Chartered Accountant, and Community College Diploma (General/Related). Graduates would occupy Engineering Technologist, Production Planner, and Accountant positions. Company benefits are rated as industry standard. The potential for advancement is listed as excellent. The average annual starting salary is competitive within the industry. The most suitable method for initial contact by graduates seeking employment is to mail a resume with a covering letter. Asea Brown Boveri Inc. does hire summer students on a regular basis. *Contact:* Human Resources Manager.

ASECO INTEGRATED SYSTEMS LTD.
635 Fourth Line, Unit 16
Oakville, ON L6L 5B3

Tel. 905-339-0059
Fax 905-339-3857
Email .... aseco@istar.ca
Website .... www.aseco.net

ASECO Integrated Systems Ltd. is an employee owned provider of consulting and systems integration services. The company's expertise is in providing manufacturing information and control systems, management information systems and their connectivity. Over the last ten years, ASECO has rapidly emerged as a leader in computer and control systems integration, manufacturing execution systems, control systems engineering, and custom software development. ASECO has been providing high quality consulting and integration services to clients such as Nabisco Ltd., Heinz USA, Ford Motor Company, DuPont, General Electric and Glaxo/Wellcome Pharmaceuticals throughout North America and Europe. Graduates most likely to be hired come from the following academic areas: Bachelor of Science (Computer Science), Bachelor of Engineering (Electrical, Computer Systems, Industrial Engineering, Industrial Production), Bachelor of Commerce/Business Administration (Information Systems), and Community College Diploma (Computer Science, Engineering Technician). Graduates would occupy Engineer-in-Training, and Programmer Analyst positions. Previous co-op work experience, excellent written and oral communication skills, and a willingness to travel are all listed as desirable non-academic qualifications. Company benefits are rated as industry standard. The potential for advancement is listed as excellent. The average annual starting salary falls within the $45,000 to $55,000 range. The most suitable methods for initial contact by those seeking employment are to mail, fax or e-mail a resume with a covering letter, or by applying via the company's website at www.aseco.net. ASECO Integrated Systems Ltd. does hire summer and co-op work term students. *Contacts:* Diane Filippin, Human Resources or Robert Peters, President.

ASSOCIATED BRANDS
335 Judson Street
Toronto, ON M8Z 1B2

Tel. 416-259-5658

Associated Brands employs more than 100 people in the manufacture and wholesale of ingredients for baking. Graduates most likely to be hired come from the following academic areas: Bachelor of Science (Technical Services), Certified Management Accountant (Finance), Community College Diploma (General/Related), and graduates with a M.C.I. accreditation (Credit Institute). Graduates should be personable, possessing a record of reliability and honesty. Company benefits are rated above average. The potential for advancement is listed as being good. The average annual starting salary for the majority of positions falls within the $25,000 to $30,000 range, while it may vary beyond this range for certain positions. The most suitable method for initial contact by graduates seeking employment is to mail a resume with a covering letter. Associated Brands occasionally hires summers students. *Contact:* Personnel Officer.

ASSOCIATES FINANCIAL SERVICES OF CANADA LTD., THE
8500 Leslie Street, Suite 600
Thornhill, ON L3T 7P1

Tel. 905-882-5050
Fax 905-882-5142

The Associates is a consumer loan company providing personal loans, mortgages, sales finance, and private label credit cards. There are approximately 35 employees at this location, a total of 700 across Canada, and 6,000 employees worldwide. Graduates most likely to be hired come from the following academic areas: Bachelor of Arts (General), Bachelor of Commerce/Business Administration, and High School Diploma. Graduates would occupy Management Trainee, Customer Service Representative, Account Executive, Sales Representative, and Clerical positions. Good organization and interpersonal skills, energy, initiative, leadership skills, flexibility, and good oral and written communication skills are all listed as desirable non-academic qualifications. Company benefits are rated above average. The potential for advancement is listed as excellent. The average annual starting salary falls within the $20,000 to $25,000 range. The most suitable method for initial contact by those seeking employment is to mail a resume with a covering letter. The Associates does hire summer students on occasion. *Contacts:* Wm. P. Campbell, Director of Human Resources or Bruce Clooten, Human Resources Manager.

ASSUMPTION LIFE
P.O. Box 160
Moncton, NB E1C 8L1

Tel. 506-853-6040
Fax 506-853-5428

Assumption Life is a mutual life insurance company which provides life insurance, disability insurance and annuity products, as well as pension plans and mortgage loans to clients in the four Atlantic provinces, Quebec and Ontario. The company's products are distributed through career officers, as well as brokers and general agents. This location is the head office location for Assumption Life. The company employs a total of 200 people in Canada. Graduates most likely to be hired come from the following academic areas: Bachelor of Science (Actuarial, Computer Science, Nursing), Bachelor of Laws (Corporate), Bachelor of Commerce/Business Administration (General, Accounting, Finance, Information Systems, Marketing), Chartered Accountant, Certified General Accountant, Master of Business Administration (General), and Community College Diploma (Accounting, Communications/Public Relations, Information Systems, Insurance, Marketing/Sales, Secretarial, Nursing RN). Adaptable, creative, enthusiastic, leadership skills, professional, analytical, communicative, flexible, organized, dependable, initiative, and good writing skills are all listed as desirable non-academic qualifications. Company benefits are rated above average. The average annual starting salary falls within the $20,000 to $30,000 range. The most suitable methods for initial contact by those seeking employment are to mail or fax a resume with a covering letter. Assumption Life does hire summer and co-op work term students. *Contact:* Rachelle Gagnon, Human Resources Consultant.

ATLANTIC PACKAGING PRODUCTS LTD.
111 Progress Avenue
Toronto, ON M1P 2Y9

Tel. 416-298-5410
Fax 416-297-2264

Atlantic Packaging Products Ltd. employs more than 100 people in the manufacture of paper and plastic packaging products. Atlantic Packaging is also involved in the manufacture of recycled paper products. Graduates most likely to be hired come from the following academic areas: Bachelor of Science (Chemistry), Bachelor of Engineering (Mechanical, Electrical), Bachelor of Commerce/Business Administration, Chartered Accountant, Certified Management Accountant, and Community College Diploma (General/Related). Graduates would occupy Junior Engineering and Clerk positions. Graduates should possess good verbal and written communication skills as well as possessing initiative. Company benefits are rated above average. The potential for advancement is listed as being good. The average annual starting salary falls within the $20,000 to $25,000 range. The most suitable methods for initial contact by those seeking employment are to mail or fax a resume with a covering letter, or via telephone. Atlantic Packaging Products Ltd. does hire summer students. *Contact:* Recruiter, Personnel.

ATLANTIS AEROSPACE CORPORATION
1 Kenview Boulevard
Brampton, ON L6T 5E6

Tel. 905-792-1981
Email .... positions@atlantis.com
Website .... www.atlantis.com

Founded in 1978, Atlantis Aerospace Corporation is a leading Canadian design and engineering firm specializing in training and performance enhancement products for industry and government. Atlantis is a international leader in the development of simulation and training devices, performance support software systems, and avionics testing equipment. The company employs more than 200 people. Graduates most likely to be hired come from the following academic areas: Bachelor of Science (Computer Science, Physics), Bachelor of Engineering (General, Aeronautical), and Community College Diploma (Aircraft Maintenance, Computer Science, Electronics Technician). Graduates would occupy Simulation and Software Designer/Developer positions. Good communication skills, the ability to work in a team environment, and a proven ability to plan for and meet deadlines are all listed as desirable non-academic qualifications. Company benefits are rated above average. The potential for advancement is listed as being good. The average annual starting salary falls within the $35,000 to $40,000 range. The most suitable methods for initial contact by those seeking employment are to mail or e-mail a resume with a covering letter. Atlantis Aerospace Corporation does hire summer students. *Contact:* Human Resources.

ATOMIC ENERGY CONTROL BOARD
280 Slater Street, P.O. Box 1064, Station B
Ottawa, ON K1P 5S9

Tel. 613-992-7229
Fax 613-995-0390
Email .... Thibert.J@Atomcon.ga.ca
Website www.cbsc.org/fedbis/bis/2298.html

The mission of the Atomic Energy Control Board (AECB) is to ensure that the use of nuclear energy in Canada does not pose undue risk to health, safety, security and the environment. This is accomplished by controlling the development, application and use of nuclear energy in Canada, and by participating on behalf of Canada in international measures of control. Established in 1946, the AECB reports to Parliament through the Minister of Natural Resources. There are approximately 360 employees at this location, and a total of 416 across Canada. Graduates most likely to be hired come from the following academic areas: Bachelor of Science (Computer Science, Mathematics), Bachelor of Engineering (Electrical, Mechanical), Bachelor of Commerce/Business Administration (Accounting, Finance, Human Resources, Information Systems), Master of Science (Health Physicist), Master of Engineering (Nuclear Engineering), and Community College Diploma (Human Resources, Secretarial, Computer Science). Graduates would occupy Health Physicist, Reactor Physicist, Program Officer, Project Officer - at Nuclear Sites, and various professional and administrative positions in Finance, Human Resources, Information Systems and Training. At the Research Office graduates would occupy Scientific positions to regulate disposal of radioactive waste, Transport positions to regulate the transportation of radioactive materials, and Inspector positions. Leadership ability, interpersonal skills, good communication skills, customer service skills, and an ability to work independently and within groups are all listed as desirable non-academic qualifications. The most suitable method for initial contact by those seeking employment is to mail a resume and covering letter. AECB does hire summer students. *Contact:* Jacques Thibert, Head, Resourcing, Planning & Official Languages Services.

AVALON EAST SCHOOL BOARD
215 Water Street, Suite 601, Atlantic Place
St. John's, NF A1C 6C9

Tel. 709-758-2372

Avalon East School Board employs approximately 750 people. Graduates most likely to be hired come from the following academic areas: Bachelor of Arts (English, French, Geography, Graphic Arts, History, Languages, Music), Bachelor of Science (Biology, Chemistry, Computer Science, Geology, Geography, Mathematics, Physics), Bachelor of Education (General, Early Childhood, Primary Junior, Junior Intermediate, Intermediate Senior, Special Needs), Master of Arts (English, French, Geography, Graphic Arts, History, Languages, Music), Master of Science (Biology, Chemistry, Computer Science, Geology, Geography, Mathematics, Physics), Master of Education, and Community College Diploma (Accounting, Secretarial). Graduates would be hired to occupy Teacher, School Administrator, Student Assistant, and Secretarial positions. Child centred, and excellent interpersonal and communication skills are listed as desirable non-academic qualifications. The average annual starting salary falls within the $25,000 to $30,000 range. The most suitable method for initial contact by those seeking employment is to mail a resume with a covering letter. The Avalon East School Board hires summer students in specialized areas (eg. French Immersion). *Contacts:* Thelma Whalen, Assistant Director of Personnel or Bob Johnston, Business Manager.

AVCO FINANCIAL SERVICES CANADA LIMITED
201 Queens Avenue
London, ON N6A 1J1

Tel. 519-672-4220
Fax 519-660-2637

Avco Financial Services Canada Limited maintains over 225 branch locations across Canada, providing a variety of financial services, including loans, mortgages, revolving charges, and sales contracts. Avco employs about 1,200 persons across Canada. The head office, located in London, Ontario, provides human resources, marketing, product development, accounting, audit, legal, communication, and insurance services to the field. The company's international headquarters are located in Costa Mesa, California. Graduates most likely to be hired come from the following academic areas: Bachelor of Arts (Marketing), Bachelor of Commerce/Business Administration (Finance, Marketing), and Community College Diploma programs. Graduates would be hired to occupy related entry-level positions. Finance or marketing experience as well as sales or customer

service experience are all listed as desirable assets. Company benefits are rated as excellent. The potential for advancement is listed as being good. The average annual starting salary depends upon the position being considered. The most suitable method for initial contact by graduates seeking employment is to mail a resume with a covering letter. *Contact:* Human Resources.

AVENOR, INC., DRYDEN MILL
Duke Street
Dryden, ON P8N 2Z7

Tel. 807-223-2323
Fax 807-223-9388
Website .... www.avenor.com

Avenor Inc. is a pulp and paper manufacturer. The Dryden Mill produces white papers, while other company mills manufacture newsprint. There are approximately 1,000 employees at the Dryden Mill, while Avenor Inc. employs a total of 5,200 people across Canada and a total of 6,000 people worldwide. Graduates most likely to be hired come from the following academic areas: Bachelor of Engineering (Chemical, Pulp and Paper, Architectural/Building, Instrumentation, Mechanical, Resources/Environmental), Bachelor of Commerce/Business Administration (Human Resources, Information Systems), and Certified General Accountant. Graduates would occupy professional positions in engineering, accounting, information systems, or other office positions. An ability to work hard and use common sense, and a proven work history are listed as desirable non-academic qualifications. Company benefits are rated above average. The potential for advancement is listed as excellent. The average annual starting salary falls within the $40,000 to $45,000 plus range. The most suitable method for initial contact by those seeking employment is to mail a resume with a covering letter. Avenor Inc., Dryden Mill does hire summer students. *Contact:* Art Dykstra, Employment Coordinator.

AVESTA SHEFFIELD INC.
2140 Meadowpine Boulevard
Mississauga, ON L5N 6H6

Tel. 905-567-9900
Fax 905-567-3300
Website .... www.avestasheffield.com/na

Avesta Sheffield AB, based in Stockholm, Sweden, is one of the world's largest stainless steel producers. The North American Division of Avesta Sheffield offers the widest range of premium-quality standard and special grade stainless steel product forms to the domestic and international market. The North American Division includes a division headquarters in Shaumburg, Illinois, four mills in the United States, the Canadian operation (based at this location), and a welding products subsidiary in New York. Stainless steel is Avesta's only product, therefore the company is committed to promoting and supporting its use, as well as being committed to long term mutually beneficial partnerships with more than

200 authorized stock distributors in the United States. In addition, Avesta serves a limited number of fabricators and end users in a wide variety of industries in the United States, Canada and Mexico. Avesta Sheffield employs 73 people at this location, a total of 143 people in Canada, and 7,500 people worldwide. Graduates most likely to be hired come from the following academic areas: Bachelor of Science (Chemistry, Computer Science, Metallurgy), Bachelor of Engineering (Industrial Chemistry, Metallurgy, Pulp and Paper, Water Resources), Bachelor of Commerce/Business Administration (Accounting, Finance, Marketing), Master of Engineering (Metallurgy), and Community College Diploma (Marketing/Sales, Purchasing/Logistics, CAD/CAM/Autocad). Graduates would occupy Inside Sales, Warehouse, Materials Processing, and Management positions in Sales, Finance and Purchasing. Team player, leadership skills, initiative, creativity, sales experience, an ability to learn, relationship building, and negotiation skills are all listed as desirable non-academic qualifications. Company benefits are rated above average. The potential for advancement is listed as being good. The average annual starting salary falls within the $25,000 to $30,000 range. The most suitable method for initial contact by those seeking employment is to mail a resume with a covering letter. Avesta Sheffield Inc. does hire summer and occasionally co-op work term students. *Contact:* Victoria Stamper, Manager, Training & Development.

AVNET INTERNATIONAL (CANADA) LTD.
6705 Millcreek Drive, Suite #1
Mississauga, ON L5N 5R9

Tel. 905-812-4400

Avnet International (Canada) Ltd. is a Fortune 100 company involved in the distribution of electronic components, computers and peripherals. The majority of Avnet's staff are sales people. There are 80 employees at this location, a total of 160 across Canada, and approximately 6,000 employees worldwide. Graduates most likely to be hired come from the following academic areas: Bachelor of Engineering (Computer Systems, Microelectronics), Bachelor of Commerce/Business Administration (Accounting, Human Resources, Marketing), and Community College Diploma (Administration, Business, Human Resources, Marketing/Sales, Computer Science, Electronics Technician, Engineering Technician). Graduates would occupy Inside Sales Representative, Administrative Assistant, Product Integration Technician, Human Resources Generalist, Credit and Collections Representative, and Customer Service Representative positions. Previous work experience in distribution (specifically electronics and computers), a pro-active approach and a willingness to learn are all listed as desirable non-academic qualifications. Company benefits are rated above average. The potential for advancement is listed as excellent. The average annual starting salary varies with the position. The most suitable method for initial contact by those seeking employment is to mail a resume with a covering letter. *Contact:* Ms. Kerry Clinton, Human Resources Manager.

AVON CANADA INC.
5500 Trans Canada Highway
Pointe-Claire, QC H9R 1B6

Tel. 514-630-5482
Fax 514-630-5480

Avon Canada Inc. is involved in the manufacturing and direct selling of a wide range of consumer products. The company employs approximately 600 employees at this location and a total of 1,000 employees across Canada. Graduates most likely to be hired come from the following academic areas: Bachelor of Arts (Graphic Arts), Bachelor of Science (Computer Science), Bachelor of Engineering (Computer Systems, Industrial Production), Bachelor of Laws, Bachelor of Commerce/Business Administration (Finance, Human Resources, Marketing), Master of Business Administration, Community College Diploma (Administration), and High School Diploma. Graduates would occupy Marketing Assistant, Industrial Engineer, Systems Analyst, and Financial Analyst positions. Bilingualism, team player and flexibility are listed as desirable non-academic qualifications. Company benefits are rated above average. The potential for advancement is listed as excellent. The average annual starting salary falls within the $25,000 to $30,000 range. The most suitable method for initial contact by those seeking employment is to mail a resume with a covering letter. Avon Canada Inc. does hire summer students. *Contact:* Line Charette, Human Resources.

AXA INSURANCE (CANADA)
5700 Yonge Street, Suite 1400
Toronto, ON M2M 4K2

Tel. 416-250-1992
Fax 416-218-4174
Email .... hr@axa-insurance.ca
Website .... www.axa-insurance.ca

AXA Insurance (Canada) is part of the France Based AXA Group, the second largest insurer in the world, and active in over 60 countries on five continents. In 1996, AXA posted revenues of $89 billion. AXA Insurance (Canada) serves Ontario, the Atlantic and Prairie provinces. The company markets a broad range of property/casualty insurance products through independent brokers. There are 215 employees at this location, and a total of 500 employees in Canada. The AXA Group employs 100,000 people worldwide. Graduates most likely to be hired come from the following academic areas: Bachelor of Arts (General), Bachelor of Science (Actuarial, Computer Science), Bachelor of Commerce/Business Administration (Accounting, Finance, Human Resources, Information Systems), Chartered Accountant, Certified Management Accountant, Certified General Accountant, Community College Diploma (Accounting, Business, Insurance), AIIC/FIIC designations, and High School Diploma. Graduates would occupy Customer Service Representative, Claims Representative, Personal Lines Underwriter, Portfolio Analyst, Junior Accountant, and various clerical and support positions. Team player, initiative, customer relations skills, organized, excellent interpersonal skills, and an ability to adapt quickly to change are all listed as desirable non-academic qualifications. The most suitable methods for initial contact by those seeking employment are to mail, fax or e-mail a resume with a covering letter, or via the company's website at www.axa-insurance.ca. AXA Insurance (Canada) does hire a limited number of summer students. In addition, AXA also hires co-op work term students. *Contact:* Recruiter.

B.A. BANKNOTE, DIVISION OF QUEBECOR PRINTING INC.

P.O. Box 399, Station A
Ottawa, ON K1N 8V4

Tel. 613-728-5854

B. A. Banknote is a printer of securities products. There are 155 employees at this location, a total of 310 employees in Canada, and 320 employees worldwide. Graduates most likely to be hired come from the following academic areas: Bachelor of Arts (Economics, Graphic Arts), Bachelor of Science (Chemistry), Bachelor of Engineering (Pollution Treatment, Pulp and Paper), Bachelor of Commerce/Business Administration (General, Accounting, Finance, Human Resources, Information Systems, Marketing, Public Administration), Certified Management Accountant, Certified General Accountant, Master of Business Administration (Marketing, Public Administration), and Community College Diploma (Accounting, Administration, Business, Communications, Human Resources, Graphic Arts, HVAC Systems). Graduates would occupy Customer Service Representative, International Sales Representative, Laboratory Technician, Manager, and Printing positions. Team player, flexible, creative, and innovative are all listed as desirable non-academic qualifications. Company benefits and the potential for advancement are both rated as excellent. The average annual starting salary falls within the $20,000 to $25,000 range. The most suitable method for initial contact by those seeking employment is to mail a resume with a covering letter. *Contact:* Manager, Human Resources.

BABCOCK & WILCOX CANADA

581 Coronation Boulevard
Cambridge, ON N1R 5V3

Tel. 519-621-2130
Fax 519-621-2310
Email .... majichg@pgg.mcdermott.com
Website .... www.babcock.com

Based in Cambridge, Ontario, Babcock & Wilcox is Canada's largest manufacturer of steam generation products and services. Steam generation products convert water into steam using a variety of heat sources. The resulting steam is used by utilities to drive the generators that produce electricity. Steam also produces power for industry and is used in many industrial processes. Babcock & Wilcox Canada is a division of The Babcock & Wilcox Company, a wholly owned subsidiary of McDermott International, Inc. Based in New Orleans, McDermott is a multinational corporation specializing in energy-related industries, such as offshore oil technology, marine construction and power generation. Babcock & Wilcox Canada employs 900 people at this location and a total of 950 in Canada. Graduates most likely to be hired come from the following academic areas: Bachelor of Arts (General, Economics, Journalism), Bachelor of Science (General), Bachelor of Engineering (Mechanical, Industrial Engineering, Metallurgy), Bachelor of Commerce/Business Administration (Accounting, Finance, Human Resources), Chartered Accountant, Certified Management Accountant, Certified General Accountant, Master of Business Administration (General), Community College Diploma (Accounting, Administration, Business, Communications, Human Resources, Purchasing/Logistics, Secretarial, Journalism, Legal Assistant, CAD/CAM/Autocad, Computer Science, Electronics Technician, Engineering Technician, Tool and Die, Machinist, Welding, Nursing RN/RNA), and High School Diploma. Graduates would occupy Trainee, Clerk, Technician, Engineering, Drafting, Marketing, Communications, Industrial, Personnel, Co-op, Accountant, Analyst, Proposal/Project Manager, and Construction Site Manager positions. Good communication, negotiation, computer, team player, leadership, and people management skills are all listed as desirable non-academic qualifications. Company benefits are rated above average. The potential for advancement is listed as excellent. The average annual starting salary falls within the $30,000 to $35,000 range. The most suitable methods for initial contact by those seeking employment are to mail or fax a resume with a covering letter. Summer students are hired, primarily co-op placements with high schools, colleges, and universities. *Contacts:* Gloria Majich, Manager, Staff Relations and Employment or Tom Thomas, Personnel Officer, Human Resources.

BAFFIN DIVISIONAL BOARD OF EDUCATION

P.O. Box 1330
Iqaluit, NT X0A 0H0

Tel. 867-979-5236
Fax 867-979-4868

Baffin Divisional Board of Education is the school board for Baffin Region in Northwest Territories, operating 21 schools (Grades from K-6, 7-9, 10-12) in 14 communities. Graduates most likely to be hired are Bachelor of Education graduates specializing in the following areas: Early Childhood ECE, Primary Junior, Junior Intermediate, Intermediate Senior, Special Needs, and General. Graduates would occupy Teacher, Consultant, Program Support Teacher, Assistant Principal, and Principal positions. Previous experience in isolated communities, team player, and cross-cultural experience are all listed as desirable non-academic qualifications. The most suitable method for initial contact by those seeking employment is to mail a resume with a covering letter. *Contacts:* Lorne Levy, Assistant Director or Sherri Dubeau, Human Resource Officer.

ᒥᐳ ᓴᑉᑉᓯᐨᒡᒃᒡ ᐊᖕᐊᓴᑉᑲᐸᐃᓄᐨᓄᓴᑉᐧ,
ᐃᓄᐨᓄᓴᑉᐨᒡᐧ ᑲᖕᐸᐃᑦ
Baffin Regional Health
and Social Services Board

BAFFIN REGIONAL HEALTH AND SOCIAL SERVICES BOARD

P.O. Box 200
Iqaluit, NT X0A 0H0

Tel.	867-979-7610
Fax	867-979-7404
Website	www.nunanet.com/~brhbfin

Baffin Regional Health and Social Service Board represents the interests of the people (predominately Inuit) served in the region. It operates and controls programs established and funded by the government of the Northwest Territories. In addition to a 34 bed acute care hospital with diagnostic and support services in Iqaluit, the Baffin Regional Health and Social Services Board operates 12 community health centres, provides Regional Health Programs (Dental, Health, Promotion, Nutrition, Environmental Health), Medivac Services (Air Ambulance) and Social Services Programs. The Board employs a total of 300 people throughout the Region. In addition to eligibility for NWTRNA registration, significant directly related nursing experience is vital for success. A Nursing Degree or advanced Nursing Diploma qualification are required for OR, Public and Community Health Assignments. Equivalencies are always considered. Graduates would occupy professional nursing opportunities in the hospital, urban public health office and home care service, and remote community health centres. Self-reliance, and a sense of adventure would be desirable character attributes. Baffin Regional Health and Social Services Board offers a competitive salary, Northern and other allowances, relocation and rental assistance (and the chance to find out all about amoutis and muktuk!). Accordingly, employee benefits are rated above average. The potential for advancement is listed as being good. The most suitable method for initial contact by those seeking employment is to fax a resume with a covering letter, or for further information visit the Board's website at www.nunanet.com/~brhbfin, or phone toll free at 1-800-663-5738. Baffin Regional Health Board does hire co-op work term students. *Contact:* Keith Dennison, Director, Human Resources.

BAIN AND COMPANY

162 Cumberland Street, Suite 300
Toronto, ON M5R 3N5

Tel.	416-929-1888
Fax	416-929-3470

Bain and Company provides strategic management consulting services. There are more than 25 employees at this location. Graduates most likely to be hired come from the following academic areas: Bachelor of Commerce/Business Administration (General, Finance), and Master of Business Administration. Bachelor of Commerce/Business Administration graduates would occupy Associate Consultant positions, and Master of Business Administration graduates would occupy Consultant positions. Graduates should possess a strong record of achievement. Company benefits and potential for advancement are both rated as excellent. The most suitable method for initial contact by those seeking employment is to mail a resume, covering letter, and a copy of academic transcripts. Bain and Company does hire summer students, primarily Masters of Business Administration students from Harvard University, Stanford, and the University of Pennsylvania. *Contact:* Recruiting Coordinator.

BALLARD POWER SYSTEMS

9000 Glenlyon Parkway
Burnaby, BC V5J 5J9

Tel.	604-454-0900
Fax	604-412-4747
Email	careers@ballard.com
Website	www.ballard.com

Ballard Power Systems is at the forefront of research, development and manufacture of the Proton Exchange Membrane (PEM) fuel cell. There are 300 employees at this location, a total of 425 in Canada, and a total of 475 employees worldwide. Graduates most likely to be hired come from the following academic areas: Bachelor/Master/Doctorate of Science (Chemistry, Computer Science, Physics), Bachelor/Master/Doctorate of Engineering (Chemical, Electrical, Mechanical, Computer Systems, Engineering Physics, Industrial Chemistry, Industrial Design, Industrial Engineering, Industrial Production/Manufacturing, Materials Science), Bachelor of Commerce/Business Administration (General, Accounting, Finance, Marketing), Chartered Accountant, Certified Management Accountant, Certified General Accountant, Master of Business Administration (General, Marketing), and Community College Diploma (Accounting, Human Resources, Purchasing/Logistics, CAD/CAM/Autocad, Computer Science, Engineering Technician). Graduates would occupy Junior Engineer, Test Technician, Administrative Assistant, and Clerk positions. Team player, proactive, enthusiastic, and flexible are all listed as desirable non-academic qualifications. In addition, work term or co-op experience is regarded highly. Company benefits and the potential for advancement are both rated as excellent. The average annual starting salary is dependent upon the position and the department (Please note: Ballard participates in numerous surveys to ensure that wages are competitive). The most suitable methods for initial contact by those seeking employment are to mail or e-mail a resume with a covering letter, or by applying through Ballard's website at www.ballard.com. Ballard Power Systems does hire summer and co-op work term students. *Contacts:* Ken Cooper, Human Resources Specialist or Kae Innes, Human Resources Specialist (Co-op Students).

BANFF CENTRE FOR CONTINUING EDUCATION, THE

P.O. Box 1020, Station 19
Banff, AB T0L 0C0

Tel.	403-762-6173
Fax	403-762-6677
Email	Lisa_Flierjans@banffcentre.ab.ca
Website	www.banffcentre.ab.ca

The Banff Centre for Continuing Education is an unique Canadian institution playing a special role in the advancement of cultural and professional life. Internationally recognized for its advanced work in the arts and management, and for developing and hosting conferences on contemporary issues. The Banff Centre employs approximately 529 people, and is divided into four main divisions: Centre for the Arts, Centre for Management, Centre for Conferences, and Centre for Mountain Culture. Graduates most likely to be hired come from the following academic areas: Bachelor of Arts (General, Journalism, Music), Bachelor of Engineering (Computer Systems), Bachelor of Education (Adult), Bachelor of Commerce/Business Administration, Master of Business Administration, Master of Arts (Music, Dance, Visual Arts, Theatre Arts, Media), Master of Education (Adult, Career Development), and Community College Diploma (Accounting, Administration, Communications, Marketing/Sales, Cooking, Graphic Arts, Hospitality, Human Resources, Journalism, Photography, Recreation, Security/Enforcement, Computer Science). These graduates are hired for a broad range of positions, from entry level guest service positions, to administrative and clerical, to program coordinators and supervisors, and finally to management levels. Team player, strong customer service orientation, creative, hard working, and innovative are all listed as desirable non-academic qualifications. The average annual starting salary falls within the $15,000 to $20,000 range for junior level positions. Company benefits and the potential for advancement are both rated as excellent. The most suitable methods for initial contact by those seeking employment are to mail a resume with covering letter, or via telephone. The Banff Centre may or may not have summer job opportunities available, it varies from year to year. *Contacts:* Lisa Flierjans, Recruiting & Training Coordinator or Jenn Bain, Administrative Assistant, Recruiting.

BANK OF MONTREAL

55 Bloor Street West, 5th Floor
Toronto, ON M4W 3N5

Tel.	416-944-7258
Fax	416-927-5772
Website	www.bmo.com

The Bank of Montreal provides a full range of financial products and services from locations throughout Canada. Founded in 1817, Bank of Montreal is Canada's first bank, and today employs 30,000 people across Canada, with 7,000 employed at this location. Graduates most likely to be hired come from the following academic areas: Bachelor of Arts (General, Economics), Bachelor of Science (Computer Science, Mathematics), Bachelor of Engineering (Electrical, Computer Systems, Telecommunications), Bachelor of Commerce/Business Administration (Accounting, Finance, Human Resources, Information Systems, Marketing), Chartered Accountant, Master of Business Administration (Accounting, Finance, Human Resources, Information Systems, Marketing, Pubic Administration), Master of Arts (Economics), Master of Science (Computer Science), Master of Engineering (Computer Systems), and Community College Diploma (Accounting, Administration, Business, Human Resources). Graduates would occupy Account Manager Trainee, Associate Development Program Trainee, Treasury Development Program Trainee, Customer Service Representative, Financial Services Officer, Assistant Branch Manager Trainee, and Systems Analyst positions. Customer service orientation, team-building, leadership skills, motivation to excel, risk management, and a dedication to continuous improvement are all listed as desirable non-academic attributes. Company benefits are rated above average. The potential for advancement is listed as being good. The most suitable methods for initial contact by those seeking employment are to mail a resume with a covering letter, or via on-campus recruitment initiatives (visit your campus career centre for details). The Bank of Montreal does hire summer students. *Contacts:* Chris Chapman, Sytems Operations; Sheilah Butler, MBanx; Brigit Sergis, Global Treasury; Tom Case, Corporate Services; Donald R. Katz, University Relations or Lynda Keating, Personal and Commercial Financial Services.

BANKERS TRUST, BT ALEX BROWN

Royal Bank Plaza, North Tower, Suite 1700
Toronto, ON M5J 2J2

Tel.	416-865-2206
Fax	416-865-1346

Bankers Trust, BT Alex Brown is a corporate investment banking firm providing global banking services. The company employs 70 people at this location, a total of 75 people in Canada, and 26,000 people worldwide. Graduates most likely to be hired come from the following academic areas: Bachelor of Science (Actuarial, Mathematics), Bachelor of Engineering (General, Civil, Electrical, Environmental/Resources, Industrial Chemistry, Industrial Engineering), Bachelor of Commerce/Business Administration (Accounting, Finance, Marketing), Chartered Accountant, Certified General Accountant, and Master of Business Administration (Finance). Graduates would occupy Corporate Financial Analyst, Credit Analyst, and Controller Analyst positions. Company benefits are rated as excellent. The average annual starting salary is dependent upon the position being considered. The most suitable methods for initial contact by those seeking employment are to mail or fax a resume with a covering letter. Bankers Trust, BT Alex Brown does hire summer and co-op work term students. *Contact:* Kathryn Wash, Human Resources Manager.

BARR SHELLEY STUART - CHARTERED ACCOUNTANTS

808 - 4 Avenue SW, Suite 600
Calgary, AB T2P 3E8

Tel. 403-269-1320
Fax 403-269-3573

There are three companies at this location: Barr Shelley Stuart - Chartered Accountants, involved in accounting, audit and tax accounting; Barr Shelley Stuart Consultants, involved in human resources, marketing, and business strategy development; and Tamarack Group - Corporate Finance, involved in mergers and acquisitions, business valuations, investor relations, financing, and venture capital. Graduates most likely to be hired come from the following academic areas: Bachelor of Arts (Economics, English, Journalism), Bachelor of Science (Computer Science), Bachelor of Laws (Corporate), Bachelor of Commerce/Business Administration (Accounting, Finance, Human Resources, Information Systems, Marketing), Chartered Accountant, Certified Management Accountant, Certified General Accountant, Community College Diploma (Accounting, Administration, Business, Facility Management, Human Resources, Marketing/Sales, Secretarial, Graphic Arts, Journalism, Legal Assistant), and High School Diploma. Graduates would occupy Chartered Accountant, CA Student, Junior/Intermediate/Senior Accountant, Staff Accountant, Human Resources Manager, Accounting Technician, General Counsel, Marketing Manager, Administrative Assistant, Clerk and Administrative positions. Team player, flexible, strong written and verbal communication skills, related work experience, and excellent interpersonal skills are all listed as desirable non-academic qualifications. Company benefits are rated above average. The potential for advancement is listed as average. The average annual starting salary falls within the $20,000 to $25,000 range, depending upon position, skills, and experience. The most suitable method for initial contact by those seeking employment is to mail a resume with a covering letter. Summer students are hired occasionally, depending upon the workload. *Contact:* Jane Grant, Human Resources Manager.

BAYCREST CENTRE FOR GERIATRIC CARE

3560 Bathurst Street
Toronto, ON M6A 2E1

Tel. 416-785-2500
Fax 416-785-2490

The Baycrest Centre for Geriatric Care is a large chronic care, geriatric hospital and home for the aged The centre employs more than 1,000 people. Graduates most likely to be hired come from the following academic areas: Bachelor of Science (Nursing RN), Chartered Accountant, Master of Social Work, Master of Science (Nursing Administration), and Community College Diploma (Secretarial, Administration, Food/Nutrition Sciences). Company benefits are rated above average. The potential for advancement is listed as average. The average annual starting salary falls within the $20,000 to $25,000 range.

The most suitable method for initial contact by graduates seeking employment is to mail a resume with a covering letter. The Baycrest Centre for Geriatric Care does hire summer students through government grant programs. *Contacts:* Mitzi Harris, Employee Relations or Margaret Wharton, Employee Relations.

BAYER INC.

77 Belfield Road
Toronto, ON M9W 1G6

Tel. 416-248-0771

Bayer Inc. is a major pharmaceutical manufacturer, employing approximately 2,300 people in Canada, and 150,000 people worldwide. Graduates most likely to be hired come from the following academic areas: Bachelor of Arts (Economics, French, Graphic Arts, Languages, Political Science, Psychology), Bachelor of Science (Actuarial, Agriculture, Biology, Chemistry, Computer Science, Environmental, Mathematics, Microbiology, Pharmacy, Psychology), Bachelor of Engineering (Chemical, Industrial Chemistry, Pulp and Paper, Computer Systems, Telecommunications), Bachelor of Commerce/Business Administration (Accounting, Finance, Human Resources, Information Systems, Marketing), Chartered Accountant, Certified Management Accountant, Certified General Accountant, Master of Business Administration (Accounting, Finance, Human Resources, Information Systems, Marketing), Master of Science (General, Health Sciences), and Community College Diploma (Accounting, Administration, Business, Communications, Financial Planning, Human Resources, Marketing/Sales, Purchasing/Logistics, Graphic Arts, Legal Assistant, Photography, Computer Science, Animal Health, Radiology Technician). The most suitable method for initial contact by those seeking employment is to mail a resume with a covering letter. Bayer Inc. does hire summer students. *Contact:* Human Resources Department.

BAZAAR & NOVELTY

301 Louth Street
St. Catharines, ON L2S 3V6

Tel. 905-687-1700
Fax 905-984-6377

Bazaar & Novelty is involved in the manufacture, wholesale and retail of specialty paper and printed products. Graduates most likely to be hired come from the following academic areas: Bachelor of Science (Computer Science), Bachelor of Engineering (Industrial Production), Bachelor of Commerce/Business Administration (Accounting, Finance, Human Resources, Marketing), Chartered Accountant, and Community College Diploma (Accounting, Administration, Advertising, Business, Purchasing/Logistics, Graphic Arts, Electronics Technician). Company benefits are rated above average. The potential for advancement is listed as being good. The average annual starting salary depends upon the position being considered. The most suitable methods for initial contact by those seeking employment are to mail or fax a resume with a covering letter. *Contact:* Human Resources Manager.

BDH INC.
350 Evans Avenue
Toronto, ON M8Z 1K5

Tel. 416-255-8521
Fax 416-255-5985

BDH Inc. is involved in the manufacturing and distribution of chemical and pharmaceutical products. The company employs approximately 120 people. Graduates most likely to be hired come from the following academic areas: Bachelor of Science (Chemistry, Microbiology), Certified Management Accountant, and Community College Diploma (Business, Sciences). Graduates would occupy Laboratory Technician, Accounting Clerk, and Customer Service Representative positions. Previous experience in this industry is listed as a definite asset. Company benefits are rated as excellent. The potential for advancement is listed as being good. The most suitable method for initial contact by graduates seeking employment is to mail a resume with a covering letter. BDH Inc. does hire summer and co-op work term students. *Contact:* Human Resources Department.

BDO DUNWOODY - CHARTERED ACCOUNTANTS
Royal Bank Plaza, P.O. Box 32
Toronto, ON M5J 2J8

Tel. 416-865-0200
Fax 416-865-0887

BDO Dunwoody is a public accounting and business consulting firm employing approximately 800 employees in 76 offices across Canada. BDO ranks as the eighth largest firm in the country as well as a member of the tenth largest international firm. Activities include Audit, Accounting, Tax, Insolvency, Corporate Recovery, Merger and Acquisitions, Valuations, Mediation and Arbitration, Litigation Support, and Forensic Accounting. Graduates most likely to be hired come from the following academic areas: Bachelor of Commerce/Business Administration (Accounting), Master of Business Administration (Accounting), and Community College Diploma (Accounting). Graduates would occupy C.A. Student, Accounting Technician, and Insolvency Technician positions. Company benefits and the potential for advancement are both rated as excellent. The average annual salary for an entry level position falls within the $25,000 to $32,000 range. The most suitable method for initial contact by those seeking employment in any Toronto region office is to mail a resume with a covering letter to the Toronto office (check your yellow/white pages for the office location nearest your). BDO Dunwoody does hire third year students majoring in accounting for summer positions at some office locations. *Contact:* Gary Wasylow.

BEARDEN ENGINEERING CONSULTANTS LTD.
4646 Riverside Drive, Unit #1
Red Deer, AB T4N 6Y5

Tel. 403-343-6858
Fax 403-343-2122
Email .... bearden@telusplanet.net

Bearden Engineering Consultants Ltd. is an engineering firm involved in the complete planning, design and detailing of commercial buildings, community centres, curling and ice arenas, churches and funeral homes, restaurant and lounges, office buildings, apartments and row housing, motels and hotels, warehouses and industrial buildings, and custom homes. In addition, the company is also involved in structural analysis, design and inspection of new and existing buildings or structures, frames, trusses, cranes and industrial applications, preserved wood foundations, and building science studies. The company has a total of 12 employees. Graduates most likely to be hired come from the following academic areas: Bachelor of Engineering (Civil, Architectural/Building), Master of Engineering (Project Management), and Community College Diploma (Accounting, Administration, Secretarial, Architecture/Drafting, CAD/CAM/Autocad, Engineering Technician). Engineering and Technical graduates would occupy Structural Engineer, Architectural Technologist, Project Manager, and Inspector positions. Team player, wide interests, and clear long-term goals are listed as desirable non-academic qualifications. Company benefits are rated as industry standard. The potential for advancement is listed as average. The average annual starting salary falls within the $25,000 to $45,000 range. The most suitable method for initial contact by those seeking employment is to mail a resume with a covering letter. Bearden Engineering Consultants Ltd. does hire summer students. *Contacts:* Terry Bearden, President or Steve Chow, Secretary.

BEAVER FOODS LIMITED
493 Dundas Street, P.O. Box 5644, Station A
London, ON N6A 5M9

Tel. 519-679-2661
Fax 519-679-3268

Beaver Foods Limited, a wholly owned division of Cara Operations Ltd., is the largest and fastest growing, Canadian owned contract food service management company. The company currently employs over 6,000 people and has over 1,000 food service units across Canada. This location is the Home Office, and the company maintains 11 other office locations across Canada. Graduates most likely to be hired come from the following academic areas: Bachelor of Science (Computer Science, Health Sciences), Certified General Accountant, and Community College Diploma (Accounting, Marketing, Secretarial, Human Resources, Computer Science, Industrial Design, Cooking, Hospitality, Food/Nutrition). Graduates would be hired to occupy Level 1 Programmer Analyst Trainee, Level 1 I.C. Support Analyst Trainee, Level 1 Technical Support Analyst Trainee, Administrative Dietitian, Therapeutic Dietitian, Baker, District Accountant, Unit Manager Trainee, Unit Cook, Unit Chef, CAD Operator/Design Layout, Secretary, and Data Entry Operator positions. Able to work in a team environment, strong interpersonal and organizational skills, a degree of mobility, creative, adaptive and pro-active are all listed as desirable non-academic qualifications. Company benefits and the potential for advancement are both rated as excellent. The average annual starting salary depends upon the position being considered and the applicant's field of study. The most suitable method for initial contact by those seeking employment is to mail a resume with a covering letter. Beaver Foods Limited does hire summer students, with the number varying from year to year. *Contact:* John Hodgson, Director, Training and Development.

BECKER MILK COMPANY LIMITED, THE
671 Warden Avenue
Toronto, ON M1L 3Z7

Tel. 416-698-2591
Fax 416-698-2907

The Becker Milk Company Limited is involved in the manufacturing and retailing of milk and fresh/ready food products. Graduates most likely to be hired come from the following academic areas: Bachelor of Science (Biology, Chemistry, Computer Science, Health Sciences, Microbiology), Bachelor of Commerce/Business Administration (Accounting, Finance, Marketing, Information Systems, Public Administration), Chartered Accountant, Certified Management Accountant, Community College Diploma (Accounting, Administration, Advertising, Marketing/Sales, Purchasing/Logistics, Computer Science) and High School Diploma. Graduates are hired to occupy Accounting Clerk, Laboratory Technician, and general Clerk positions. Strong written and oral communication skills, and a professional manner and appearance are listed as desirable non-academic qualifications. Company benefits are rated as excellent. The potential for advancement is listed as being good. The average annual starting salary falls within the $20,000 to $25,000 range. The most suitable method for initial contact by those seeking employment is to mail a resume with a covering letter. The Becker Milk Company Limited does hire summer students for plant positions. *Contact:* Ms. C. Vani, Human Resources Manager.

BECKMAN INSTRUMENTS (CANADA) INC.
6733 Mississauga Road
Mississauga, ON L5M 6J5

Tel. 905-819-1234

Beckman Instruments (Canada) Inc. is involved in the sales and service of life sciences and diagnostic instrumentation to research laboratories and diagnostic laboratories. There are more than 50 people employed at this location. Graduates most likely to be hired come from the following academic areas: Bachelor of Science (Life Sciences - Chemistry, Biology, Physics), Bachelor of Engineering (Electrical), Master of Science (Chemistry, Biology), and Community College Diploma (Electronics Technician). Graduates would occupy Sales Representative, Customer Service Representative and Service Technician positions. Laboratory experience and experience in the selling of lab equipment are listed as desirable non-academic qualifications. Company benefits are rated above average. The most suitable method for initial contact by graduates seeking employment is to mail a resume with a covering letter. Beckman Instruments (Canada) Inc. does hire summer students. *Contact:* Human Resources.

BELL CANADA
C.P. 11-471, Downtown Branch
Montreal, QC H3C 5N1

Email .... bell-hr@sympatico.ca
Website .... www.bell.ca

Bell Canada, the largest Canadian telecommunications operating company, markets a world class portfolio of products and services to more than seven million business and residence customers in Ontario and Quebec. The skilled and committed Bell team is comprised of approximately 38,000 employees on a corporate mission TO BE A WORLD LEADER IN HELPING PEOPLE COMMUNICATE AND MANAGE INFORMATION. Bell is looking for forward thinking graduates of Computer Science, Mathematics, Electrical Engineering and Business programs who have a good academic record, have demonstrated leadership in extra curricular activities or through job experiences, who can excel in a competitive environment characterized by constant change, function effectively as a team player and focus on exceeding customers' needs and expectations. Typical permanent and contract positions in the Toronto, Montreal and Ottawa areas include: Project Manager, Communications Systems Specialist, Applications Programmer and Customer Systems Associate. Bell offers a competitive benefits package, comprehensive employee development programs and exciting career opportunities. The most suitable methods for initial contact by those seeking employment are to send a resume with a covering letter, or through on-campus recruitment initiatives (see your campus career centre for details). Bell Canada is an equal opportunity employer. *Contact:* Management Recruiting-Resume Processing Centre.

BELL MOBILITY INC.
2920 Matheson Boulevard East
Mississauga, ON L4W 5J4

Tel. 905-282-4499
Fax 905-282-3290
Website .... www.bellmobility.ca

As part of BCE Mobile Communications, Bell Mobility Inc. delivers wireless communication services, any time, any place. Graduates are hired from the following academic areas: Bachelor of Arts (General), Bachelor of Science (General), Bachelor of Engineering (RF Technology), Bachelor of Commerce/Business Administration (Accounting, Finance, Information Systems, Marketing), and Community College Diploma (Accounting, Administration, Advertising, Business, Communications, Marketing/Sales, Secretarial, Computer Science, Engineering Technician). Highly motivated, team spirited, results oriented, and possessing a customer service orientation are all listed as desirable non-academic qualifications. Company benefits and the potential for advancement are both rated as excellent. The average annual starting salary is dependent upon the position being considered. The most suitable methods for initial contact by those seeking employment are to mail or fax a resume with a covering letter (no phone calls please). *Contact:* Staffing Co-ordinator.

BENCHMARK TECHNOLOGIES INC.

1682 West 7th Avenue, Suite 310
Vancouver, BC   V6J 4S6

Tel. 604-731-8584
Fax 604-738-8625
Email .... brianh@benchtech.com
Website .... www.benchtech.com

Benchmark Technologies Inc. develops custom software solutions for mostly Fortune 5000 sized companies. The company consults and advises clients on appropriate technology, coding standards, database selection (as well as modeling and administration), tools selections, and systems configuration. Benchmark employs a total of 25 people. Graduates most likely to be hired come from the following academic areas: Bachelor of Science (Computer Science, Mathematics), Bachelor of Engineering (Computer Systems, Telecommunications), Bachelor of Commerce/Business Administration (Information Systems), Master of Business Administration (Information Systems), Master of Science (Computer Science), Master of Engineering (Computer Systems, Telecommunications), and Community College Diploma (Computer Science). Graduates would occupy Software Programmer, Programmer/Analyst, Software Engineer, and Network Specialist positions. High intelligence, creativity, flexibility, team player, love for learning, quick learner, and relevant work experience are all listed as desirable non-academic qualifications. Company benefits are rated above average. The potential for advancement is listed as being good. The average annual starting salary falls within the $30,000 to $35,000 range, depending upon the experience of the applicant and the position being considered. The most suitable method for initial contact by those seeking employment is to mail a resume with a covering letter. *Contacts:* Brian Haley, President or Peter Humphrys, Managing Partner.

BEST WESTERN WHEELS INN

615 Richmond Street, P.O. Box 637
Chatham, ON   N7M 5J7

Tel. 519-436-5501
Fax 519-436-5541

Best Western Wheels Inn provides hospitality, restaurant, fitness and entertainment facilities. There are approximately 420 employees at this location.

Graduates most likely to be hired come from the following academic areas: Bachelor of Arts (General, Recreation), Bachelor of Science (General), Bachelor of Engineering (General, Mechanical), Certified General Accountant, Community College Diploma (Accounting, Administration, Advertising, Business, Facility Management, Human Resources, Marketing/Sales, Secretarial, Cooking, Hospitality, Travel/Tourism, Massage Therapy), and High School Diploma. Customer service skills, related work experience, team player, loyalty, dependable, and a positive attitude are all listed as desirable non-academic qualifications. Company benefits are rated as industry standard. The potential for advancement is listed as being good. The average annual starting salary falls in the $15,000 plus range, depending upon the position being considered. The most suitable methods for initial contact by those seeking employment are to mail a resume with a covering letter, via telephone, or by appointment for network purposes. Best Western Wheels Inn does hire summer students. *Contacts:* Ross Barnwell, Director, Human Resources or Jeanette Pake, Payroll.

BETHANY CARE SOCIETY

1001 - 17 Street NW
Calgary, AB   T2N 2E5

Tel. 403-284-0161
Fax 403-284-1232

Bethany Care Society is in the business of providing innovative delivery of health care, housing and lifestyle services to seniors and persons with disabilities. The Society's leadership strength is founded on a rich history in the community since 1947, and a philosophy of care that emphasizes wellness, choice and independence. Bethany Care Society employs over 1,000 people in its facilities throughout southern Alberta. Graduates most likely to be hired come from the following academic areas: Bachelor of Arts (Recreation Studies), Bachelor of Science (Computer Science, Nursing, Occupational Therapy, Pharmacy, Physio/Physical Therapy), Certified Management Accountant, Certified General Accountant, and Community College Diploma (Accounting, Communications/Public Relations, Facility Management, Human Resources, Information Systems, Secretarial, Cook/Chef Training, Recreation Studies, Social Work/DSW, Dietitian/Nutrition, Nursing RN/RNA/NA/LPN). Graduates would occupy various healthcare positions relating directly to their designated professions. Good problem solving skills, energetic, team player, self-motivated, excellent communication skills, and a desire to make a positive difference in someone's life are all listed as desirable non-academic qualifications. Full time employees are offered a comprehensive benefits package that is competitive in the health care industry. The potential for advancement is rated as average. The most suitable method for initial contact by those seeking employment is to mail a resume with a covering letter. Bethany Care Society does hire summer and co-op practicum students. *Contact:* Michael Stuart, Human Resources Advisor of Employment.

BIC INC.
155 Oakdale Road
Downsview, ON M3N 1W2

Tel. 416-742-9173
Fax 416-741-4965
Website .... www.bicworld.com

BIC Inc. is involved in the manufacturing and distribution of writing instruments, lighters and razors. There are approximately 65 employees at this location, a total of 100 employees in Canada, and 10,000 employees worldwide. Graduates most likely to be hired come from the following academic areas: Bachelor of Commerce/Business Administration (Accounting, Finance, Human Resources, Information Systems, Marketing), Chartered Accountant, Certified Management Accountant, Certified General Accountant, and Community College Diploma (Accounting, Business, Human Resources, Marketing/Sales, Purchasing/Logistics, Secretarial, Engineering Technician). Graduates would occupy Clerk, Secretary, Computer Programmer, Trade Analyst, Product Manager, Cost Analyst, Customer Service Representative, Inventory/Purchasing, Account Manager, and Accounts Payable/Receivable positions. Adaptable, creative, responsible, analytical, personable, enthusiastic, professional, customer service focussed, team players, out-of-the-box thinker, an aptitude to learn other languages, and adaptability are all listed as desirable non-academic qualifications. Company benefits are listed as excellent. The potential for advancement is rated as average. The average annual starting salary for entry level positions falls within the $25,000 to $30,000 range. The most suitable method for initial contact by those seeking employment is to mail a resume with a covering letter. BIC Inc. does hire summer students, and co-op work term students for positions in Human Resources, Marketing, and Information Systems. Contact: Monica Parenti, Human Resources Manager.

BIOMIRA INC.
2011 - 94th Street
Edmonton, AB T6N 1H1

Tel. .... 403-450 3761 x 251
Fax 403-463-0871

Biomira Inc. is a biotechnology firm dedicated to the development and commercialization of products to benefit patients with cancer. Products in development for cancer management include blood tests, imaging agents, and innovative, non-toxic approaches to therapy. The company employs approximately 164 people at this location, and a total of 234 people in Canada. Graduates most likely to be hired come from the following academic areas: Bachelor of Science (Chemistry, Microbiology, Medical Laboratory Sciences, Immunology, Pharmacology), Bachelor of Engineering (Biotechnology), Master of Science (Chemistry, Microbiology, Immunology, Pharmacology), Master of Engineering (Biotechnology), Doctorate (Chemistry, Microbiology, Immunology, Pharmacology), and Community College Diploma (Biological Sciences - Lab Option). Graduates would occupy Technician, Research Scientist, and Bioprocess Engineer positions. Previous lab experience, able to work under direction, attention to detail, and good communication skills are all listed as desirable non-academic qualifications. Company benefits are rated as excellent. The potential for advancement is listed as being good. The average annual starting salary depends upon the candidate. The most suitable method for initial contact by those seeking employment is to mail a resume with a covering letter. Biomira Inc. hires summer students, generally from the province of Alberta. Contact: Irene Watson, Human Resources Advisor.

BIRKS JEWELLERS INC.
1240 Phillips Square
Montreal, QC H3B 3H4

Tel. 514-397-2526
Fax 514-397-2455

Birks Jewellers Inc. has been a retail industry leader and a provider of high-end jewellery and luxury gift items for over a century. The company's aim is to offer its customers across Canada a superior quality of service and merchandise. Presently, the company employs 200 people at this location and a total of 800 people across Canada. Graduates most likely to be hired come from the following academic areas: Bachelor of Commerce/Business Administration (General, Accounting, Finance, Human Resources, Information Systems, Marketing), Community College Diploma (Accounting, Administration, Business, Human Resources, Marketing/Sales), and High School Diploma. Graduates would be hired as trainees for store management positions and sales associate positions. Self motivated, enthusiastic, customer service driven, team player and good communication skills are all listed as desirable non-academic qualifications. The most suitable method for initial contact by those seeking employment is to mail a resume with a covering letter. Birks Jewellers Inc. does hire summer students. Contacts: Mrs. A. Attalla, Manager, Human Resources or Mrs. M. Borsellino, Administrative Assistant, Human Resources.

BIWAY, A DIVISION OF DYLEX LIMITED
637 Lakeshore Boulevard West, Suite 330
Toronto, ON M5V 3L6

Tel. 416-586-1212
Fax 416-586-6948

BiWay, a Division of Dylex Ltd. is Canada's leading community discount retailer. BiWay employs approximately 5,000 people in stores located in Ontario, New Brunswick, Nova Scotia, Newfoundland, and Prince Edward Island. Graduates most likely to be hired should possess a High School Diploma, while some level of post-secondary education is preferred for Management positions. Graduates would occupy Management Trainee and Sales Associate positions. Excellent communication skills, dynamic, driven, dedicated, thrive on challenges, previous retail experience, including fashion retailing, and good organizational and problem solving skills are all listed as desirable non-academic qualifications. Company benefits are rated above average. The potential for advancement is listed as excellent. The average annual starting salary is dependent upon the experience of the applicant and the position being considered. The most suitable methods for initial contact by those seeking employment are to mail or fax a resume with a covering letter to the Recruiting Manager at the head office, or the Store Manager at the desired Store location (check yellow/white pages for location nearest you). *Contacts:* Recruiting Manager (head office) or Store Manager (store locations).

BLAKE, CASSELS & GRAYDON

Commerce Court West, Box 25
Toronto, ON M5L 1A9

Tel. 416-863-2400
Fax 416-863-2653

Blake, Cassels & Graydon is a full-service, international law firm employing approximately 700 people at this location. Graduates most likely to be hired come from the following academic areas: Bachelor of Laws, and Community College Diploma (Legal Secretary, Law Clerk). Graduates would occupy Associate, Legal Secretary, Law Clerk, Accounting, and Computer Systems positions. Highly motivated, positive attitude, and excellent communication skills are listed as desirable non-academic qualifications. Company benefits are rated above average. The potential for advancement is listed as being good. The average annual starting salary falls within the $20,000 to $25,000 range. The most suitable methods for initial contact by those seeking employment are to mail a resume with a covering letter, or via telephone. Blake, Cassels & Graydon does hire summer students for Secretarial, Reception and Clerical help positions. *Contacts:* Mary Giles, Training and Development Co-ordinator or Sue Gagliardi, Recruitment Co-ordinator.

BLOORVIEW MACMILLAN CENTRE

25 Buchan Court
Willowdale, ON M2J 4S9

Tel. 416-494-2222
Fax 416-494-9985

The Bloorview MacMillan Centre (formerly Bloorview Children's Hospital) provides children's health care and related services. Graduates most likely to be hired come from the following academic areas: Bachelor of Arts (Recreation Studies), Bachelor Science (Nursing, Nutritional Sciences, Occupational Therapy, Pharmacy, Physical Therapy), Bachelor of Education (Early Childhood ECE), Bachelor of Commerce/Business Administration (Accounting, Finance, Human Resources, Information Systems), Certified Management Accountant, Certified General Accountant, Master of Business Administration (Finance, Human Resources), Master of Arts (Journalism) Master of Social Work, Master of Science (Nursing, Health Administration, Speech Pathology), Master of Library Science, Doctorate (Psychology), and Community College Diploma (Human Resources, Secretarial, Nursing RPN, Respiratory Therapy). The most suitable method for initial contact by those seeking employment is to mail a resume with a covering letter. *Contact:* Human Resources.

BLOORVIEW MACMILLAN CENTRE

350 Rumsey Road
Toronto, ON M4G 1R8

Tel. 416-424-3824

The Bloorview MacMillan Centre (formerly Hugh MacMillan Rehabilitation Centre) provides rehabilitation services for children and young adults with physical disabilities. Children and young adults are medically referred for in-patient or out-patient services. The centre employs more than 250 people at this location. Graduates most likely to be hired come from the following academic areas: Bachelor of Arts (Physiotherapy, Occupational Therapy), Bachelor of Science (Physiotherapy, Psychology, Nursing RN), Bachelor of Engineering (Mechanical, Electrical, Biomedical), Bachelor of Education, Chartered Accountant (Finance), Masters (Social Work, Speech Pathology), Doctorate (Psychology), and Community College Diploma (Recreation, Nursing RN/RNA, Dental Assistant). Previous related work experience, reliability, dedication and sensitivity are all listed as desirable non-academic qualifications. Company benefits are rated above average. The potential for advancement is listed as average. The most suitable method for initial contact by those seeking employment is to mail a resume with a covering letter. The Bloorview MacMillan Centre does hire summer students for mostly recreation and pool positions. *Contact:* Human Resources.

BLUE CROSS OF QUEBEC

550, rue Sherbrooke ouest, Office 160
Montreal, QC H3A 1B9

Tel. 514-286-8471
Fax 514-286-8475
Email .... resshum@qc.croixbleue.ca

Blue Cross of Quebec provides health insurance, travel insurance, and related assistance products and services. There are 300 employees at this location. Graduates most likely to be hired come from the following academic areas: Bachelor of Science (Actuarial, Computer Science, Mathematics, Nursing), Bachelor of Commerce/Business Administration (Accounting, Marketing), Chartered Accountant, Certified Management Accountant, Certified General Accountant, and Community College Diploma (Accounting, Administration, Communications, Insurance, Secretarial, Hospitality, Travel/Tourism, Nursing RN). Graduates would occupy Customer Service Agent, Actuary, Claims Agent, and Underwriter positions. Team player, a dynamic person, customer service oriented, and previous work experience are all listed as desirable non-academic qualifications. The average annual starting salary falls within the $20,000 to $30,000 range. The most suitable method for initial contact by those seeking employment is to mail a resume with a covering letter. Blue Cross of Quebec does hire summer students.

Contacts: Mr. Claude Soucy, Human Resources Director or Ms. Denise Gagnon, Human Resources Advisor.

BOILER INSPECTION & INSURANCE CO. OF CANADA, THE
18 King Street East
Toronto, ON M5C 1C4

Tel. 416-363-5491
Fax 416-363-0538
Website .... www.biico.com

The Boiler Inspection & Insurance Co. of Canada is a specialized market leader in boiler and machinery insurance, believing in the value added concept of engineering and technical expertise in insuring risks. The company underwrites, inspects, advises, engineers, adjudicates claims, and assists customers in preventing losses. There are 87 employees at this location, and a total of 210 employees in Canada. Graduates most likely to be hired come from the following academic areas: Bachelor of Engineering (Mechanical), Bachelor of Commerce/Business Administration, and Community College Diploma (Insurance). Graduates would occupy Customer Service Representative, Marketing Representative, Inspection Trainee, and Claims Trainee positions. Computer interest and literacy, a transferable skill set, maturity, and dependability are all listed as desirable non-academic qualifications. Company benefits are rated as excellent. The potential for advancement is listed as being good. The most suitable method for initial contact by those seeking employment is to mail a resume with a covering letter. The Boiler Inspection & Insurance Co. of Canada does hire summer students. *Contact:* Teresa Tos, Director, Human Resources & Public Relations.

BOMBARDIER REGIONAL AIRCRAFT
Garratt Boulevard
Downsview, ON M3K 1Y5

Tel. 416-375-3976

Bombardier Regional Aircraft is Canada's largest aircraft manufacturer employing approximately 5,000 people at this location. Graduates most likely to be hired come from the following academic areas: Bachelor of Arts, Bachelor of Science, Bachelor of Engineering, Bachelor of Laws, Bachelor of Education, Bachelor of Commerce/Business Administration, Chartered Accountant, Master of Business Administration, and Community College Diploma (General/Related). The most suitable method for initial contact by graduates seeking employment is to mail a resume with a covering letter. *Contact:* Anna Maria Andreucci.

BONAR INC.
2360 McDowell Road
Burlington, ON L7R 4A1

Tel. 905-637-5611
Fax 905-637-9954

Bonar Inc. is involved in the manufacture and sale of packaging materials of paper and plastic film and rigid plastic containers. There are approximately 300 employees at this location, 750 in Canada, and a total of 1,200 employees in Canada and the United States. Graduates most likely to be hired come from the following academic areas: Bachelor of Engineering (Pulp and Paper, Mechanical, Industrial Production), Bachelor of Commerce/Business Administration (Accounting, Finance, Marketing), Master of Business Administration (Accounting, Finance, Marketing), and Community College Diploma (Accounting, Administration, Business, Marketing/Sales). Graduates would occupy Engineer Technician (QC), Sales and Service Coordinator, Sales Representative, Sales Trainee, Accounting Clerk, Junior Accountant, Secretary, and Production Control positions. Company benefits are rated above average. The potential for advancement is listed as being good. The average annual starting depends upon the position and the applicant's experience. The most suitable method for initial contact by those seeking employment is to mail a resume with a covering letter. Bonar Inc. does hire summer students at some locations. *Contact:* Human Resources.

BONUS RESOURCE SERVICES CORP.
7506 - 43 Street, Suite #1
Leduc, AB T9E 7E8

Tel. 403-986-3070
Fax 403-986-8810

Bonus Resource Services Corp. provides oil well services, including well workover's and completion's. There are approximately 200 employees at this location, a total 1,000 in Canada and a total of 1,100 employees worldwide. Graduates most likely to be hired come from the following academic areas: Bachelor of Commerce/Business Administration (Accounting, Finance), Certified Management Accountant, Master of Business Administration (Accounting, Finance), Community College Diploma (Accounting, Human Resources, Marketing/Sales, Purchasing/Logistics, Secretarial, Auto Mechanic, Electronics Technician, Welding), and High School Diploma. Graduates would occupy Clerk, Middle Management, and a variety of Support positions. Previous work experience, team player, self-motivated, flexible, and a good attitude are all listed as desirable non-academic qualifications. Company benefits are rated as excellent. The potential for advancement is listed as being good. The most suitable methods for initial contact by those seeking employment are to mail or fax a resume with a covering letter. Bonus Resource Services Corp. occasionally hires summer students. *Contact:* Janice L. Escaravage, Manager Human Resources.

BOT CONSTRUCTION LIMITED
1224 Speers Road
Oakville, ON L6L 2X4

Tel. 905-827-4167
Fax 905-827-0458

Bot Construction Limited is active in heavy civil engineering construction and development projects. This includes bridges, roadways, sewers, watermains, and major rock and earth excavations. There are 17 employees at this location and a total of 300 employees in Ontario. Graduates most likely to be hired come from the following academic areas: Bachelor of Engineering (Civil), and Community College Diploma (Engineering Technician). Graduates would occupy Contracts Co-ordinator, Estimator, Project Administrator, Project Engineer, and Project Manager positions. A proven, solid work ethic, good references, and an ability and ambition to learn are all listed as desirable non-academic qualifications. Company benefits are rated as industry standard. The potential for advancement is listed as being good. The average annual starting salary falls within the $30,000 to $35,000 range. The most suitable method for initial contact by those seeking employment is to mail a resume with a covering letter. Bot Construction Limited does hire summer students. *Contact:* Human Resources.

BOWLERAMA LIMITED
28 Cecil Street
Toronto, ON M5T 1N3

Tel. 416-979-2142
Fax 416-979-0119

Bowlerama Limited operates 17 bowling centres in southern Ontario (8 in Metropolitan Toronto). There are 15 Bowlerama employees at its head office with 125 permanent employees in the bowling centres. It also employs approximately 300 part-time workers during the bowling season. Operational activities include bowling sales and services. Post-secondary education is not required for employment application. Graduates and non-graduates would apply for bowling centre Manager and Assistant Manager positions. The most suitable method for initial contact by graduates and non-graduates seeking employment is to mail a resume with a covering letter. Bowlerama Limited does hire summer students. *Contacts:* Harry Fine, Vice President or Ali Qureshi, Vice President, Finance.

BRAEMAR
637 Lakeshore Boulevard West
Toronto, ON M5V 3J7

Tel. 416-586-7338
Fax 416-586-7087

Braemar, The Wardrobing Experts, are involved in the retail of ladies clothing. In addition to the company's head office at this address, Braemar employs a total of 1,200 people across Canada in retail operations. Graduates most likely to be hired come from the following academic areas: Bachelor of Arts (General), Bachelor of Commerce/Business Administration (General, Accounting, Marketing, Public Administration), and Community College Diploma (Administration, Advertising, Business, Communications, Human Resources, Marketing/Sales, Hospitality). Graduates would occupy Administrative, Store Management, Financial, Sales Associates, and Planning/ Merchandise Assistant positions. Team oriented, initiative, enthusiastic, good communication skills, receptive to change, thorough, retail experience, computer skills, and leadership skills (for management positions) are all listed as desirable non-academic qualifications. Company benefits are rated above average. The potential for advancement is listed as excellent. The average annual starting salary falls within the $20,000 to $30,000 range. The most suitable method for initial contact by those seeking employment is to mail a resume with a covering letter. *Contact:* Christine Leskovar, Human Resources Co-ordinator.

BRANDON UNIVERSITY
270 - 18th Street
Brandon, MB R7A 6A9

Tel. 204-728-9520
Fax 204-726-4573

Located in Manitoba's second largest city, Brandon University employs approximately 400 people in the provision of quality post-secondary education. Graduates most likely to be hired come from the following academic areas: Bachelor of Arts (General, Criminology, Economics, English, French, Geography, History, Journalism, Languages, Music, Philosophy, Political Science, Psychology, Recreation Studies, Sociology), Bachelor of Science (General, Biology, Chemistry, Computer Science, Geology, Geography, Mathematics, Physics, Zoology, Nursing, Psychology), Bachelor of Education (General, Early Childhood, Primary Junior, Junior Intermediate, Intermediate Senior, Physical/Health), Bachelor of Commerce/Business Administration, Chartered Accountant, Certified Management Accountant, Certified General Accountant, Master of Business Administration, Master of Arts, Master of Science, Master of Health Science, Doctorate, and Community College Diploma (Business). Depending upon academic background and experience, graduates would occupy Lecturer, Assistant Professor, Professional Associate, Administrative Associate, Instructional Associate, Library Assistant, Technician, Computer Programmer, and Accountant positions. Relevant work experience, particularly in an academic environment is a definite asset. Company benefits are rated above average. The potential for advancement is listed as being good. The average annual starting salary falls within the $30,000 to $35,000 range. The most suitable method for initial contact by those seeking employment is to mail a resume with a covering letter. Brandon University does hire summer students. *Contacts:* Mrs. Barbara M. Smith, Director, Human Resources or Mrs. Brenda Bull, Assistant, Human Resources.

BREWERS RETAIL INC.
1 City Centre Drive
Mississauga, ON L5B 4A6

Tel. 905-277-7526
Fax 905-277-7533

Brewers Retail Inc. operates 440 Beer Store retail outlets and commercial delivery depots throughout Ontario. There are approximately 130 employees at this location and a total of 6,000 employees across the province. Graduates most likely to be hired come from the following academic areas: Bachelor of Arts (General, Economics, Urban Geography/Planning), Bachelor of Science (Computer Science), Bachelor of Commerce/Business Administration and Community College Diploma (Accounting, Administration, Advertising, Business, Human Resources, Marketing/Sales, Secretarial, Computer Science). Graduates would be hired to occupy a limited number of clerk or trainee positions in one of the company's field operations offices, located in major cities across Ontario, with the opportunity to become Store Manager within approximately two to three years from starting. A positive attitude, good work ethic, management potential, and strong interpersonal skills are all listed as desirable non-academic qualifications. Company benefits are rated above average. The potential for advancement is listed as average. The most suitable methods for initial contact by graduates seeking employment are to mail or fax a resume with a covering letter. Brewers Retail Inc. does hire part-time staff in retail stores throughout the province. *Contact:* Recruiting & Personnel Services.

BRIGGS & STRATTON CANADA INC.
301 Ambassador Drive
Mississauga, ON L5T 2J3

Tel.	905-795-2632
Fax	905-795-8768

Briggs & Stratton Canada Inc. employs approximately 35 people in the distribution of small engines and small engine parts. Graduates most likely to be hired come from the following academic areas: Bachelor of Commerce/Business Administration (Accounting, Marketing), Chartered Accountant (Finance), Certified Management Accountant (Finance), and Community College Diploma (Accounting, Business, Marketing/Sales, Purchasing/Logistics, Secretarial). Graduates would occupy accounting, clerical, and secretarial positions. Good interpersonal and communication skills, and hands-on mechanical abilities are listed as desirable non-academic qualifications. Company benefits are rated as excellent. The average annual starting salary falls within the $25,000 to $30,000 range. The most suitable method for initial contact by graduates seeking employment is to mail a resume with a covering letter. Briggs & Stratton Canada Inc. does hire summer students. *Contact:* Al Lehrner, Controller.

BRISTOL AEROSPACE LIMITED
660 Berry Street, P.O. Box 874
Winnipeg, MB R3C 2S4

Tel.	204-775-8331
Fax	204-774-0195

Bristol Aerospace Limited is Western Canada's largest aerospace company. The company has over a half century of experience in design, development, and manufacture for the world aerospace community, providing Aeroengine component and Aerostructure fabrication using CAD-CAM and Flexible Machining; Military Fighter Aircraft and Helicopter Life Cycle Management, Avionics Update, and Repair and Overhaul; Jet Engine Afterburner Restoration; Research and Defence Rockets and Missiles; and Electronics for Space and Military applications. Graduates most likely to be hired come from the following academic areas: Bachelor of Science (Metallurgy), Bachelor of Engineering (Metallurgy, Electrical, Mechanical, Aerospace), Bachelor of Commerce/Business Administration (Finance), Chartered Accountant, Certified General Accountant, and Community College Diploma (Aircraft Maintenance, Engineering Technician). Graduates would occupy Accounting Clerk, Design Engineer, Metallurgy Engineer, Electrical Engineer, Avionics Engineer, Production Planner, Avionics Technician/Mechanic, Aircraft Technician/Mechanic, and Engineering Technologist positions. Company benefits are rated as excellent. The potential for advancement is listed as being good. The most suitable method for initial contact by those seeking employment is to mail a resume with a covering letter. *Contact:* Human Resources.

BRITISH COLUMBIA INSTITUTE OF TECHNOLOGY (BCIT)
3700 Willingdon Avenue
Burnaby, BC V5G 3H2

Tel.	604-451-6909
Fax	604-434-8462
Email	byu@bcit.bc.ca
Website	www.bcit.bc.ca/~hr/

British Columbia Institute of Technology (BCIT) is a post-secondary education provider in the province of British Columbia. BCIT employs 1,400 people and offers a wide variety of career programs from pre-apprenticeship to degree levels. Program profiles include Vocational Trades, Business, Computing and Academic Studies, Construction, Electrical and Electronic Technology, Health Sciences, Manufacturing, Mechanical and Industrial Technologies; Processing, Energy and Natural Resources; and Transportation. Graduates are hired from a broad range of academic disciplines for Managerial and Supervisory, Instructional, Instructional Support, Technical and Administrative Support, Miscellaneous and International opportunities. Company benefits are rated as excellent. The potential for advancement is listed as being good. The average annual starting salary falls within the $30,000 to $55,000 range, depending on the position being considered. The most suitable methods for initial contact by those seeking employment are to mail, fax or e-mail a resume with a covering letter, by applying in person, or through the institute's website at www.bcit.bc.ca/~hr/. BCIT does hire summer students. British Columbia Institute of Technology is an equal opportunity employer and invites applications from all qualified men and women, persons with disabilities, aboriginals, and members of visible minority groups. *Contact:* Human Resources.

BRITISH COLUMBIA REHABILITATION SOCIETY
4255 Laurel Street
Vancouver, BC V5Z 2G9

Tel. 604-737-6350
Fax 604-737-6494
Website .... www.bcrehab.bc.ca

The British Columbia Rehabilitation Society is a free standing, tertiary rehabilitation centre for severely, physically disabled adults. The Society employs approximately 1,050 people, and also maintains an on-site integrated daycare facility. Graduates most likely to be hired come from the following academic areas: Bachelor of Arts (Recreation Studies), Bachelor of Science (Audiology, Nursing, Nutritional Sciences, Occupational Therapy, Pharmacy, Physical Therapy, Psychology, Speech Pathology), Bachelor of Education (Early Childhood, Special Needs), Bachelor of Commerce/Business Administration (Accounting, Finance, Human Resources, Information Systems, Public Administration), Master of Business Administration (Accounting, Finance, Human Resources, Information Systems, Public Administration), Master of Arts (Social Work), Master of Science (Nursing, Counselling Psychology, Speech Pathology, Physical Therapy), Master of Education (Adult, Special Needs), Medical Doctor (Psychologist, Physical/Rehabilitative Medicine), and Community College Diploma (Accounting, Administration, Business, Communications, Facility Management, Human Resources, Purchasing/Logistics, Secretarial, Recreation Studies, Computer Science, Electronics Technician, Dietician, Emergency Technician, Nursing RN/RNA, Radiology Technician, Respiratory Therapy, Social Work, Rehabilitation Assistant, Orthotics, Prosthetics). Graduates would occupy positions directly related to their academic backgrounds. Recent, related experience in discipline, experience working in a multidisciplinary team, and effective communication skills are all listed as desirable non-academic qualifications. Company benefits are rated above average. The potential for advancement is listed as average. The average annual starting salary falls within the $30,000 to $35,000 range. The most suitable method for initial contact by those seeking employment is to mail a resume with a covering letter. The British Columbia Rehabilitation Society does support numerous academic practicums and internship programs. Contact: Human Resources.

BRITISH COLUMBIA TELEPHONE COMPANY (BC TEL)
3777 Kingsway Avenue
Burnaby, BC V5H 1H5

Tel. 604-432-2796
Fax 604-436-1352
Website .... www.bctel.com

The British Columbia Telephone Company (BC TEL) provides telecommunication services to the residents of British Columbia. BC TEL employs a total of 14,000 people. Graduates most likely to be hired come from the following academic areas: Bachelor of Science (Computer Science), Bachelor of Engineering (Electrical, Computer Systems, Telecommunications), and Bachelor of Commerce/Business Administration (General, Accounting, Finance, Marketing). Graduates would occupy Clerk, Trainee, Technician, and Customer Service positions. Possessing previous work experience in a related field is a definite asset. The most suitable method for initial contact by those seeking employment is to mail a resume with a covering letter. BC TEL does hire summer students. Contact: Employment Centre.

BRITISH COLUMBIA TRANSIT
13401 - 108th Avenue, Unit C650
Surrey, BC V3T 5T4

Tel. 604-540-3010
Fax 604-540-3005

British Columbia Transit provides public transit services. There are approximately 400 employees at this location and a total of 4,000 employees in British Columbia. The company reviews applications from individuals from all degree and diploma areas, depending upon the position under consideration. There is a general equivalency for all positions. Entry level positions include Customer Information Clerk, Farebox Attendant, Farebox Receipts Attendant, Traffic Checker - all casual. Company benefits are rated as excellent. The average annual starting salary falls within the $25,000 to $30,000 range. The most suitable method for initial contact by those seeking employment is to mail a resume with a covering letter. British Columbia Transit does hire summer students. Applications for summer positions are accepted starting in January, with most of the positions filled by April. British Columbia Transit is committed to employment equity. Contact: Employment Services Advisor, Employment Services.

BRITISH COLUMBIA'S WOMEN'S HOSPITAL & HEALTH CENTRE SOCIETY
4490 Oak Street
Vancouver, BC V6H 3V5

Tel. 604-875-2722
Fax 604-875-2599

The British Columbia Women's Hospital & Health Centre Society is a maternity hospital and women's health centre. Programs include sexual assault, PMS, osteoporosis, HIV program, and menopause. The hospital and health centre employ a total of 975 people. Graduates most likely to be hired come from the following academic areas: Bachelor of Arts (General), Bachelor of Science (General, Health Sciences), Bachelor of Commerce/Business Administration (Accounting, Finance, Human Resources, Information Systems, Marketing, Public Administration), Certified Management Accountant, Certified General Accountant, Master of Business Administration (Accounting, Finance, Information Systems, Marketing, Public Administration), Master of Arts (Social Work), Community College Diploma (Accounting, Administration, Advertising, Business, Communications, Financial Planning, Human Resources, Purchasing/Logistics, Secretarial, Social Work, Laboratory Technician, Nursing RN), and High School

Diploma. Graduates would occupy RN, Clerical, Social Worker, Physiotherapist, Accounting, Counsellor, and Housekeeping, etc. positions. Previous work experience, good work ethic, team player, good attendance record, and a high level of motivation are all listed as desirable non-academic qualifications. The potential for advancement is rated as being good. The average annual starting salary falls within the $25,000 to $40,000 range, varying with the position being considered. The most suitable method for initial contact by those seeking employment is to mail a resume with a covering letter. The British Columbia Women's Hospital & Health Centre Society does hire summer students (eg. housekeeping, clerical, etc.). *Contacts:* Linda J. Hand, Human Resource Consultant or Joan McAlary, Human Resource Consultant.

BURGER KING RESTAURANTS OF CANADA INC.

401 The West Mall, 7th Floor
Toronto, ON M9C 5J4

Tel. 416-626-7412
Fax 416-626-6696

Burger King Restaurants of Canada Inc. operates fast food restaurants. Locations are throughout Canada with each location employing approximately 40 people, including 3 managers per restaurant. Burger King seeks qualified candidates for Restaurant Management positions, which involve the following responsibilities: cost control, administration, training, food quality control, communications and scheduling. Graduates most likely to be hired come from the following academic areas: Bachelor of Arts (General), Bachelor of Commerce/Business Administration (Accounting, Finance, Human Resources, Information Systems, Marketing, Public Administration), Community College Diploma (Cooking, Hospitality), and High School Diploma. Applicants should possess experience in retail or the food industry, preferably in a management capacity. Company benefits are rated above average. The potential for advancement is listed as excellent. The average annual starting salary is dependent upon the position being considered, and the experience and education of the applicant. The most suitable method for initial contact by graduates seeking employment is to mail a resume with a covering letter to this address. Burger King Restaurants of Canada Inc. does hire summer students for general restaurant help only (contact individual Restaurant Manager). *Contacts:* Chantal Gignac, Regional Human Resources Manager or Brenda Marlowe, Regional Human Resources Manager.

BURGESS WHOLESALE LTD.

1172 Davis Drive
Newmarket, ON L3Y 4X7

Tel. 905-853-6544
Fax 905-853-5682

Burgess Wholesale Ltd. is a food service distributor involved in the selling of products to restaurants, hospitals, institutions etc. The company employs approximately 200 people at this location and a total of 400 people in Canada. Graduates most likely to be hired come from the following academic areas: Bachelor of Commerce/Business Administration (Finance, Human Resources, Information Systems, Marketing), and Community College Diploma (Business, Marketing/Sales, Purchasing/Logistics, Hospitality). Graduates would be hired to occupy entry level positions in Sales, Purchasing, Finance and Administration, Warehouse and Delivery, Information Systems, and Human Resources. Ambition, solid work ethic, positive attitude, and a willingness to offer long term commitment through advancement, and relocation are all listed as desirable non-academic qualifications. Company benefits and the potential for advancement are both rated as excellent. The average annual starting salary falls within the $20,000 to $25,000 range. The most suitable method for initial contact by those seeking employment is to mail a resume with a covering letter. Burgess Wholesale Ltd. does hire summer students. *Contact:* Daryn Smith, Employee Relations Manager.

BUSINESS DEPOT LTD.

30 Centurian Drive, Suite 106
Markham, ON L3R 8B9

Tel. 905-513-6116
Fax 905-513-7194
Email .... careers@business-depot.com
Website .... www.businessdepot.com

Business Depot Ltd. is one of Canada's fastest growing retailers, operating 117 locations from coast to coast, employing over 5,000 people. Partnered with its parent company Staples, the Company has 720 stores and growing. In 1998 Business Depot Canada will open a new store every 13 days. Business Depot's first store was opened in 1991 in Concord, Ontario, and since then has become Canada's leading retailer in office supply products. Stores average 30 thousand square feet, carry over 7,000 brand name products, and are conveniently located in high traffic areas. Graduates most likely to be hired come from the following academic areas: Bachelor of Arts (General, Economics, Political Science, Psychology, Recreation Studies, Sociology/Social Work), Bachelor of Engineering (Computer Systems), Bachelor of Commerce/Business Administration (General, Accounting, Finance, Human Resources, Information Systems, Marketing, Public Administration, Hospitality), Chartered Accountant, Certified Management Accountant, Certified General Accountant, and Community College Diploma (Accounting, Administration, Advertising, Business, Communications/Public Administration, Facility Management, Human Resources, Information Systems, Marketing/Sales, Recreation Studies, Travel/Tourism). Graduates would occupy Executive Assistant, Category Specialist, Junior Technical Systems Analyst, Help

Desk Support, Entry Level Human Resource, Graphic Artist, Programmer/Analyst, CAD Operator, and Management positions. Retail or service related experience, team player, goal oriented, self-starter, quick learner, energetic, entrepreneurial spirit, leadership and excellent communication skills are all listed as desirable non-academic qualifications. With projected growth of 30 stores per year, Business Depot offers current and future associates excellent opportunities for personal and professional growth. Associates would utilize their management skills almost immediately, have the option to travel in Canada, apply their education and enhance their skills. Career positions offer an attractive and competitive compensation (the average annual starting salary falls within the $25,000 to $30,000 range) and benefits package. The most suitable methods for initial contact by those seeking employment are to mail, fax or e-mail a resume with a covering letter, quoting reference number CD-001. Business Depot Ltd. does hire co-op work term students. *Contacts:* Christine Arruda - Store Management Positions or Joanne Taylor - Home Office Positions.

BUSINESS EXPRESS
1140 Sheppard Avenue West, Unit 12B
Downsview, ON M3K 2A2

Tel. 416-638-2075

Business Express operates retail outlets, providing copying, computing, and communications services. Graduates most likely to be hired are Computer Science graduates from Community College programs. Graduates would occupy Computer Advisor positions. Working in a retail environment, these graduates would assist customers with computer software and hardware issues. Team player, enthusiasm, self-motivated, energetic, sales skills, and a willingness to learn are all listed as desirable non-academic qualifications. Company benefits and the potential for advancement are both rated as excellent. The average annual starting salary is dependent upon applicant's experience. The most suitable method for initial contact by those seeking employment is to mail a resume with a covering letter. *Contact:* Human Resources Department.

C-FER TECHNOLOGIES INC.
200 Karl Clark Road
Edmonton, AB T6N 1H2

Tel. 403-450-3300
Fax 403-450-3700
Email .... d.zurawell@cfertech.com
Website .... www.cfertech.com

For over 15 years, C-FER Technologies Inc. has developed new technologies and processes in the energy industry that have reduced costs, increased revenues, reduced risk, increased safety, and extended the life of wells and equipment in the field. The company holds patents and intellectual property rights to dozens of products and processes, including revolutionary Downhole Oil/Water Separation technology, PC-PUMP software, PIRAMID software and more. C-FER offers engineering expertise from the ground up, including project management, engineering economics, experimental design, risk and reliability engineering, limit states design, failure analysis/structural testing, investigative engineering, software development, computer modeling, solid mechanics, materials engineering, and prototype design and manufacture. C-FER's world class laboratory services offer a powerful combination of testing and analysis tools designed to accommodate a vast range of research and testing requirements. With extensive review and development, testing and refining, the company has the know how to make solutions work in the real world. C-FER employs 46 full-time and 10 part-time (summer, contract, co-op) employees at this location. The company also maintains an office location in Calgary, Alberta. Graduates most likely to be hired come from the following academic areas: Bachelor of Science (Computer Science), Bachelor of Engineering (Civil, Electrical, Mechanical), Bachelor of Commerce/Business Administration (Accounting, Finance, Human Resources, Information Systems, Marketing), Master of Engineering, Doctorate of Engineering, and Community College Diploma (Accounting, Business, Human Resources, Marketing/Sales, Secretarial, Electronics Technician, Engineering Technician). Graduates would occupy Engineer, Marketing, Salesperson, Secretary, Software Developer, Technologist, Accountant, and Human Resource positions. Team player, self-motivated, initiative, and excellent communication skills are all listed as desirable non-academic qualifications. Company benefits are rated as excellent. The potential for advancement is listed as average. The average annual starting salary is dependent upon the position being considered. The most suitable method for initial contact by those seeking employment is to mail a resume with a covering letter. C-FER Technologies Inc. does hire co-op work term students. High School graduates are hired for summer positions, usually only one student per summer season. *Contact:* Diane Zurawell, Human Resources.

CAA TORONTO
60 Commerce Valley Drive East
Markham, ON L3T 7P9

Tel. 905-771-3111
Fax 905-771-3101

CAA Toronto employs more than 100 people in three main operational areas: Auto Club, Travel Agency, and Insurance Company. Post-secondary education is not a prerequisite for employment application. Most entry-level positions are clerical and customer service in nature, requiring good customer service skills, knowledge of the city and a basic knowledge of North American geography. Company benefits are rated as excellent. The potential for advancement is listed as average. The average annual starting salary falls within the $15,000 to $20,000 range. The most suitable method for initial contact regarding employment opportunities is to mail a resume with a covering letter. CAA Toronto does employ summer students to work from May to September. *Contact:* Stephanie Pavlich, Recruiter.

CADABRA

1 Antares Drive, Suite 300
Nepean, ON K2E 8C4

Tel.	613-226-7046
Fax	613-226-5276
Email	info@cadabratech.com
Website	www.cadabratech.com

CADABRA is a leader in the development of physical synthesis tools, stretching the boundaries of automated design. Graduates working in the company's R&D Group, develop state of the art IC design automation tools. These graduates have experience in UNIX, C++, object oriented design methodologies, and in developing user friendly, intuitive GUI's. Graduates working with the company's Customer Team, design custom IC solutions and perform architectural optimization analysis on customer driven programs. In addition, these graduates participate in core product development, are lead users providing direct input into the tool design, aid customers in developing custom cell libraries, act as the front line in customer support, provide a liaison between customers and CADABRA, and actively participate in defining the product feature set. Graduates most likely to be hired come from the following academic areas: Bachelor of Science (Computer Science, Combinatories & Optimization, Mathematics), and Bachelor of Engineering (Electrical, Computer Systems, Systems Design, Engineering Physics). Graduates would occupy Software Designer/Developer, and Applications Engineer positions. Fast, smart, flexible, an ability to drive creative solutions to complex engineering problems, and strong technical and interpersonal skills are all listed as desirable non-academic qualifications. The most suitable methods for initial contact by those seeking employment are to mail or e-mail (hrmgr@cadabratech.com) a resume with a covering letter. CADABRA does hire summer and co-op work term students. *Contact:* Human Resources Manager.

CADILLAC FAIRVIEW CORPORATION LIMITED, THE

20 Queen Street West
Toronto, ON M5H 3R4

Tel.	416-598-8407
Fax	416-598-8578

The Cadillac Fairview Corporation Limited is one of Canada's premier owners and operators of commercial real estate properties. Employed at this location are more than 250 people involved in the development of new projects through all phases of planning, financing, construction, leasing and management of completed properties. Graduates most likely to be hired come from the following academic areas: Bachelor of Arts (General, Economics, Urban Geography), Bachelor of Science (General, Computer Science, Mathematics), Bachelor of Commerce/Business Administration (Accounting, Finance, Marketing), Certified Management Accountant (Finance), Certified General Accountant (Finance), Master of Business Administration (Accounting, Finance, Marketing, Information Systems), and Community College Diploma (Architecture/Drafting, Computer Science, HVAC Systems). A positive attitude, team player and possessing related background experience are all listed as desirable non-academic qualifications. Graduates would occupy entry level clerk, analyst positions, etc. Company benefits and the potential for advancement are both rated as excellent. The most suitable method for initial contact by those seeking employment is to mail a resume with a covering letter identifying the type of position being sought. The Cadillac Fairview Corporation Limited does hire a limited number of summer students annually (approximately 6 to 12 students). *Contact:* Susan Henderson, Recruitment Coordinator, Personnel/Human Resources.

CADMAN GROUP CONSULTING INC., THE

666 Burrard Street, Suite 1300
Vancouver, BC V6C 3J8

Tel.	604-689-4345
Fax	604-689-4348
Email	kwilder@cadman.ca
Website	www.cadman.ca

The Cadman Consulting Group Inc. is a wholly owned Canadian company incorporated in British Columbia in 1993. The group provides services in the area of information technology consulting. Service offerings include programming and analysis, system analysis and design, project management and end-user technical support and training. The Cadman Group currently employs 30 professionals whose expertise is being used by a broad spectrum of clients in most vertical markets including the telephony, R&D, commercial and government sectors. Graduates most likely to be hired come from the following academic areas: Bachelor of Science (Computer Science), Bachelor of Engineering (Computer Systems, Telecommunications), Bachelor of Commerce/Business Administration (Information Systems), Master of Business Administration (Information Systems), and Community College Diploma (Information Systems, Computer Science). Company benefits are rated as industry standard. The potential for advancement is listed as being good. The most suitable methods for initial contact by those seeking employment are to e-mail or fax a resume with a covering letter. *Contact:* Kathryn Wilder, Account Manager.

CAE ELECTRONICS LTD.

C.P. 1800
Saint-Laurent, QC H4L 4X4

Tel.	514-341-6780
Fax	514-340-5335
Email	hr@cae.ca
Website	www.cae.ca

CAE Electronics Ltd. is one of the world's leading advanced technology companies and Canada's foremost scientific systems and software enterprise. CAE applies sophisticated real-time computer based technology to large complex simulation, training, control and monitoring tasks across a broad spectrum of civil and military aviation, hydro and thermal power generation, transmission and distribution, air traffic management, maritime operations, space exploration and submarine detection systems. There are 3,600 employees at this location, a total of 4,000 in Canada, and approximately 6,000 employees worldwide. Graduates most likely to be hired come from the following academic areas: Bachelor of Arts (Languages), Bachelor of Science (Mathematics, Physics), Bachelor of Engineering (Chemical, Electrical, Automation/Robotics, Computer Systems, Power, Telecommunications, Mechanical, Aeronautical, Marine), Bachelor of Commerce/Business Administration (Accounting, Finance, Human Resources, Information Systems, Marketing), Chartered Accountant, Certified Management Accountant, Certified General Accountant, Master of Business Administration (Accounting, Finance, Human Resources, Information Systems, Marketing), Master of Science, Master of Engineering, Community College Diploma (Accounting, Administration, Business, Marketing/Sales, Secretarial, Aircraft Maintenance, CAD/CAM/Autocad, Computer Science, Electronics, Engineering, HVAC Systems, Marine Engineering), and High School Diploma. Good communication skills, a willingness to learn, adaptability, flexibility, team player, innovative and creative are all listed as desirable non-academic qualifications. Company benefits are rated as excellent. The potential for advancement is listed as being good. The average annual starting salary falls within the $30,000 to $35,000 range. The most suitable methods for initial contact by those seeking employment are to mail, fax or e-mail a resume with a covering letter. CAE Electronics Ltd. does hire summer students. *Contacts:* Julie Phaneuf, Staffing Manager or Aurora Pietianiro, Group Leader.

CALGARY CENTRE FOR PERFORMING ARTS, THE

205 - 8th Avenue SE
Calgary, AB T2G 0K9

Tel. 403-294-7455
Fax 403-294-7457

The Calgary Centre for Performing Arts is an arts centre with a concert hall, four theatres, banquet and retail space. The company administrates the building, and operates as the landlord to the other resident companies. The centre's operations are divided into the following departments: Executive, Facility Management, Stage Production, Reception/Security, and Public Information and Programming. The centre employs 34 full-time and 100 part-time employees. Graduates most likely to be hired come from the following areas: Bachelor of Arts (General, Criminology, Economics, English, Journalism, Languages, Music), Bachelor of Science (General, Computer Science), Bachelor of Engineering (General, Computer Systems), Bachelor of Commerce/Business Administration (Accounting, Finance, Marketing, Information Systems, Public Administration), Chartered Accountant, Certified Management Accountant, Master of Business Administration (Accounting, Finance, Marketing, Information Systems, Public Administration), and Community College Diploma (Accounting, Administration, Advertising,

Business, Communications, Facility Management, Financial Planning, Human Resources, Marketing, Secretarial, Engineering Technician, HVAC Systems). Applicants would be considered for Director of Facilities, Director of Programming, Controller, Accounting Clerk, Stage Technician, Administrative Assistant, Front of House Coordinator, Building Operating Engineer, Utility Person, Catering Sales, Catering Coordinator, Communications Manager, and Contract Administrator positions. Team player, a love of the arts, and three to five years work experience are listed as desirable non-academic qualifications. Company benefits are rated as excellent. The potential for advancement is listed as average. The average annual starting salary falls within the $20,000 to $25,000 range. The most suitable method for initial contact by those seeking employment is to mail a resume with a covering letter. *Contact:* Cheryl Craiggs, Controller, Finance Department.

CAMBIOR INC.

800, boul René-Levesque ouest, Bureau 850
Montreal, QC H3B 1X9

Tel. 514-878-3166
Fax 514-878-0635

Cambior Inc. is an international diversified gold producer with operations, advanced development projects, and exploration activities in both North and South America. The company has more than 2,300 full time employees. Cambior hires university and college graduates with a Degree or Diploma in Science and Engineering (Mining, Geology, Metallurgy, Industrial Production, Instrumentation, Environment and Pollution Treatment), Commerce and Business Administration (Accounting, Finance, Human Resources and Actuarial Sciences) and Corporate and International Law. Successful candidates occupy positions as engineers, geologists, technicians, legal advisors and supervisors. Previous work experience, team player, and dedication are listed as desirable non-academic qualifications. The average annual starting salary ranges between $35,000 and $40,000. Company benefits and the potential for advancement are considered excellent. Graduates interested in seeking permanent employment with the company should mail a resume or curriculum vitae and a covering letter to the Human Resources Department. Cambior Inc. also hires summer students. *Contact:* Roxanne Hugron.

CAMBRIDGE MEMORIAL HOSPITAL

700 Coronation Boulevard
Cambridge, ON N1R 3G2

Tel. 519-621-2330

Cambridge Memorial Hospital is a major health care institution employing approximately 1,200 people. Graduates most likely to be hired come from the following academic areas: Bachelor of Science (Nursing, Nutritional Sciences, Occupational Therapy, Pharmacy, Physical Therapy, Speech Pathology), Bachelor of Engineering (Biomedical Electronics), and Community College Diploma (Human Resources, Social Work, Dietician, Emergency Technician, Laboratory Technician, Nuclear Medicine Technician, Nursing RN/RNA, Radiology Technician, Respiratory Therapy, Ultra-Sound Technician). Company benefits are rated above average. The potential for advancement is listed as average. The average annual starting salary varies depending on the position being considered. The most suitable methods for initial contact by those seeking employment are to mail a resume with a covering letter, or via telephone. Cambridge Memorial Hospital does hire summer students, but not every year. *Contact:* Susan Toth, Human Resources.

CAMECO CORPORATION
2121 - 11th Street West
Saskatoon, SK   S7M 1J3

Tel. 306-956-6371
Fax 306-956-6539

Cameco Corporation operates and owns two-thirds of the world's two largest, high-grade uranium mines at Key Lake and Rabbit Lake in northern Saskatchewan. The company also obtains a share of production from the Crow Butte mine in Nebraska, and recently purchased about three-quarters of the Wyoming based, Highland operation. Cameco also maintains a controlling interest in both McArthur River and Cigar Lake, the two largest uranium projects under development in the world, located in northern Saskatchewan. The company also has refining and conversion plants in Ontario, at Blind River and Port Hope respectively. In addition, the company also mines gold in Saskatchewan as well as operates and owns one-third of the Kumtor gold project located in Kyrgyzstan in Central Asia. There are 250 employees at this location, a total of 1,450 employees in Canada, and a total of 1,800 employees worldwide. Graduates most likely to be hired come from the following academic areas: Bachelor of Science (Chemistry, Computer Science, Environmental, Geology, Metallurgy, Nursing), Bachelor of Engineering (Chemical, Industrial Chemistry, Metallurgy, Automation, Computer Systems, Instrumentation, Industrial Design, Fish/Wildlife, Mining, Water Resources), Bachelor of Commerce/Business Administration (Accounting, Finance, Human Resources, Information Systems, Marketing), Chartered Accountant, Certified Management Accountant, Certified General Accountant, Master of Business Administration (General, Finance), Master of Science (Chemistry), Master of Engineering (Chemical, Mechanical, Mining), Community College Diploma (Accounting, CAD/CAM/Autocad, Computer Science, Electronics, Engineering, Chemical Technician, Safety and Radiation Technician, Welding), and High School Diploma. Team player, adaptability, self-starter, previous work experience, adaptability, and good communication, problem-solving, decision making and leadership skills are all listed as desirable non-academic qualifications. Company benefits are rated as excellent. The potential for advancement is listed as being good. The most suitable method for initial contact for those seeking employment is to mail a resume with a covering letter.

Cameco Corporation does hire summer students. *Contact:* A. Scott Tuttle, Supervisor, Staffing & Recruitment.

CAMPBELL SOUP COMPANY LIMITED
60 Birmingham Street
Toronto, ON   M8V 2B8

Tel. 416-251-1131
Fax 416-255-3815

Campbell Soup Company Limited is involved in the processing and marketing of food products. There are over 500 employees at this location. Graduates most likely to be hired come from the following academic areas: Bachelor of Science (General, Chemistry, Computer Science, Microbiology), Bachelor of Engineering (Civil, Industrial), Bachelor of Commerce/Business Administration (Finance, Marketing), Chartered Accountant, and Master of Business Administration (Marketing). Graduates would occupy Marketing Assistant, Research Assistant (Research and Development), Accountant, Computer Programmer, and Systems Analyst positions. A compatibility with the organization, creative, personable, innovative, ambitious, team oriented, and initiative are all listed as desirable non-academic qualifications. Company benefits are rated above average. The potential for advancement is listed as excellent. The average annual starting salary falls within the $35,000 plus range. The most suitable methods for initial contact by those seeking employment are to mail a resume with a covering letter, or via telephone. Campbell Soup Company Limited does hire summer students, depending upon the current need of the company. *Contact:* Susan Dufresne.

CANADA 3000 AIRLINES LIMITED
27 Fasken Drive
Toronto, ON   M9W 1K6

Tel. 416-674-0257
Fax 416-674-7225
Website www.canada3000.com

Canada 3000 Airlines Limited provides reliable, affordable, air travel based on the needs of the leisure traveller. Founded in Toronto in 1988, the airline now has operating bases from coast to coast in all of Canada's major cities. Since its inception, Canada 3000 has demonstrated a steady growth and built a solid reputation, in both Canada and the many overseas markets in which it serves. The Airline employs 2,000 people worldwide. Graduates most likely to be hired come from the following academic areas: Bachelor of Commerce/Business Administration (General, Accounting, Finance), and Community College Diploma (Accounting, Information Systems, Marketing/Sales, Hospitality, Travel/Tourism, Aircraft Maintenance, Engineering Technician). Graduates would occupy Junior Clerk, Intermediate Accountant, Administrator, Sales Assistant, Reservation Sales Agent, Passenger Service Agent, Flight Attendant, Aircraft Maintenance Engineer/Technician, and Information Systems Analyst positions. Motivated, task oriented, committed, flexible, travel familiarity, and work experience are all listed as desirable non-academic qualifications. Company benefits are rated above average. The potential for advancement is listed as being good. The average annual starting salary falls within the $20,000 to $25,000 range. The most suitable method for initial contact by those seeking employment is to mail a resume with a covering letter. *Contact:* Director, Human Resources.

CANADA LIFE ASSURANCE COMPANY
330 University Avenue
Toronto, ON M5G 1R8

Tel. 416-597-1456
Fax 416-597-3892

The Canada Life Assurance Company, with assets of over $23 Billion, is ranked among the top four insurance companies in Canada. The company has operations in four countries - the United States, Ireland, Great Britain and Canada. Canada Life also has a number of subsidiaries that specialize in specific product lines, such as INDAGO Investments, Canada Life Casualty Insurance Company, Canada Life Mortgage Services and Adason Properties. Leadership and people are the foundation of Canada Life's strategic plan of bold growth and expansion. The corporate culture is characterized by the fact that Canada Life is a learning organization and a performance driven organization. There are 1,700 employees at this location, 2,300 employees in Canada, and a total of 5,000 employees worldwide. Graduates most likely to be hired come from the following academic areas: Bachelor of Arts (General), Bachelor of Science (General, Actuarial, Computer Science, Nursing, Occupational Therapy), Bachelor of Engineering (Computer Science), Bachelor of Commerce/ Business Administration (General), Chartered Accountant, Master of Business Administration (Accounting, Finance, Investments), and Community College Diploma (Accounting, Administration, Business, Human Resources, Information Systems, Insurance, Secretarial, Legal Assistant, Computer Science, Dental Assistant, Dental Hygiene, Nursing RN/ RNA). Graduates would occupy Actuarial Student, Portfolio Management Trainee, Health/Dental Claims Analyst, Pension Administration Clerk, Business Analyst, Underwriter, Programmer/Analyst, and Auditor positions. Integrity, partnership, customer commitment, leadership skills, continuous learning, entrepreneurial, and community involvement are all listed as desirable non-academic qualifications. Company benefits and the potential for advancement are both rated as excellent. The most suitable method for initial contact by those seeking employment is to mail a resume with a covering letter. The Canada Life Assurance Company does hire summer and co-op work term students. *Contact:* Human Resources Department.

CANADA MARKET RESEARCH LIMITED
1235 Bay Street, Suite 600
Toronto, ON M5R 2A9

Tel. 416-964-9222
Fax 416-964-3937

Canada Market Research Limited provides social research, marketing and advertising services to both the private and public sector. There are over 25 employees at this location. Post-secondary graduates are hired, but they are hired only on a part-time basis as Market Research Interviewers. As Market Research Interviewers graduates work by telephone, door-to-door or through scheduled interviews with business executives. Applicants should possess a strong command of the English language, pleasant voice and an outgoing personality. All work is hourly paid, with rates varying. The majority of the work is in the evenings and on weekends. The most suitable method for initial contact by those seeking employment is to mail a resume with a covering letter. *Contact:* Fieldwork Director.

CANADA POST CORPORATION
1 Dundas Street West, Suite 700
Toronto, ON M5G 2L5

Tel. 416-204-4115
Fax 416-204-4115
Website .... www.mailposte.ca

Canada Post Corporation is the Canadian postal service responsible for the delivery and receipt of mail across Canada. Canada Post employs more 65,000 people across Canada. Graduates most likely to be hired come from the following academic areas: Bachelor of Engineering (Industrial), Bachelor of Commerce/Business Administration (Accounting, Finance, Human Resources, Marketing), Chartered Accountant, Certified Management Accountant, Certified General Accountant, Master of Business Administration (Accounting, Finance, Human Resources, Marketing), Community College Diploma (Administration, Business, Human Resources, Marketing/Sales, Secretarial, Legal Assistant), and High School Diploma. Graduates would occupy Engineer, Technician, Mechanic, Human Resource, Finance, etc. positions. Company benefits are rated above average. The potential for advancement is listed as being good. The average annual starting salary falls within the $25,000 to $30,000 range. The most suitable method for initial contact by graduates seeking employment is to mail a resume with a covering letter. Canada Post Corporation does hire summer students. *Contact:* Staffing Officer.

CANADA TRUST
275 Dundas Street, P.O. Box 5703
London, ON N6A 4S4

Tel. 519-663-1977
Fax 519-663-1967
Website .... www.canadatrust.com

Canada Trust is one of the Nation's largest financial institutions. Assets under administration are in excess of $150 billion. With head office in London,

Ontario, and Executive Offices and Corporate Operations in both London and Toronto, Canada Trust serves millions of Canadians in Retail Banking Services, Trust Services and Investment Services through a coast-to-coast branch network. Graduates most likely to be hired come from the following academic areas: Bachelor of Arts (Journalism), Bachelor of Science (Computer Science, Mathematics), Bachelor of Commerce/Business Administration (Accounting, Finance), Chartered Accountant, Certified Management Accountant, Certified General Accountant, and Community College Diploma (Accounting, Business, Data Processing, Computer Science). Commitment, teamwork, service orientation, and strong communication and interpersonal skills are all listed as desirable non-academic qualifications. Company benefits and the potential for advancement are both rated as excellent. The average annual starting salary is dependent upon the position being considered. The most suitable method for initial contact by graduates seeking employment is to mail a resume with a covering letter. *Contacts:* Personnel (Head Office Positions - Fax & Phone Above) or Southwestern Ontario Region Office (Branch Positions).

CANADIAN AIRLINES INTERNATIONAL LTD.
6001 Grant McConachie Way
Richmond, BC V7B 1K3

Tel. 905-270-5211
Fax 905-270-5848
Website .... www.cdnair.ca

Canadian Airlines International Ltd. is an international airline flying to five continents. Service includes business and pleasure travel, airfreight shipments and cargo services. Over 5,000 people are employed at locations in Vancouver, Toronto and Calgary (head office), with support offices in most Canadian cities. Graduates most likely to be hired come from the following academic areas: Bachelor of Commerce/Business Administration, and Community College Diploma (Accounting, Travel/Tourism, Marketing/Sales, Aircraft/Vehicle Mechanic). Graduates would occupy Customer Service Agent, Sales and Marketing Representative, Engineer, Technician (Avionics), Clerical and Secretarial positions, and a wide spectrum of Supervisory and Management positions. Flexible, dependable and excellent interpersonal skills are listed as desirable non-academic qualifications. Company benefits are rated as excellent. The potential for advancement is listed as being good. The average annual starting salary falls within the $15,000 to $25,000 range. The most suitable method for initial contact by graduates seeking employment is to contact the Company's automated Employment Information Line at (416) 207-0247, or mail a resume with a covering letter to the Vancouver Office, quoting the competition of interest. Please note, Canadian Airlines International uses an automated resume tracking system, and for this reason the resume format used should be simple and content specific. *Contact:* Employment Services.

CANADIAN ARMED FORCES
National Defence Headquarters (Attn DRS)
Ottawa, ON K1A 0K2

Tel. 613-992-6259
Fax 613-995-0786

The Canadian Armed Forces employs University and Community College graduates from the full academic spectrum, as well as employing High School graduates. The Canadian Armed Forces employs a total of 76,000 people. Specific employment will depend on educational qualifications and other factors as determined during recruitment processing. Applicants may discuss, without obligation, individual particulars with staff at the nearest recruiting centre. Employment opportunities include the following: uniformed personnel of the Canadian Armed Forces, entry level and skilled entry level positions, and part-time employment with the Reserve Force. Employee benefits are rated above average. The potential for advancement is listed as being good. The most suitable methods for initial contact by those interested in a career with The Canadian Armed Forces are to visit, call, or write the local Canadian Forces Recruiting Centre (listed in the Yellow Pages under Recruiting). *Contact:* Canadian Forces Recruiting Centre, listed in the Yellow Pages.

CANADIAN BROADCASTING CORPORATION - RADIO CANADA
P.O. Box 500, Station A
Toronto, ON M5W 1E6

Tel. 416-205-3311
Fax 416-205-5622

The Canadian Broadcasting Corporation - Radio Canada operates Canada's national and international television and radio networks. In Toronto this involves the operation of television stations CBLFT (French) and CBLT (English), and radio stations CJBC 860 (French) and CBL 740 (English). Also, Midday, The National, and The Journal are all national programs which are produced at Toronto facilities. For other facility locations, check your local telephone white pages. Graduates most likely to be hired come from the following academic areas: Bachelor of Arts, Bachelor of Science, Bachelor of Engineering, Bachelor of Laws, Bachelor of Commerce/Business Administration, Master of Business Administration, Master of Arts (Political Science), and Community College Diploma (General/Related). Graduates would occupy a wide variety of positions in Sales, Broadcasting, Technical, and Production. Company benefits and the potential for advancement are both rated as excellent. The average annual starting salary falls with the $15,000 to $20,000 range, but varies widely with position and experience. The most suitable method for initial contact by those seeking employment is to visit the Job Shop at 25 John Street, between 10:30 to 1:30 weekdays only. Applicants are invited to apply for available positions that are a match to their qualifications (please, no unsolicited resumes). The CBC - Radio Canada does hire summer students for short term positions. *Contact:* Human Resources.

CANADIAN CENTRE FOR OCCUPATIONAL HEALTH & SAFETY
250 Main Street East
Hamilton, ON L8N 1H6

Tel.	905-572-2981
Fax	905-572-4419
Email	custserv@ccohs.ca
Website	www.ccohs.ca

The Canadian Centre for Occupational Health & Safety is the national resource for occupational health and safety information, operating a worldwide electronic service as well as an inquiries service. The centre employs 72 full time staff and approximately three term staff. Graduates most likely to be hired come from the following academic areas: Bachelor of Science (Biology, Chemistry, Ergonomics, Toxicology, Information Science, Computer Science), Certified Management Accountant, Certified General Accountant, Master of Business Administration (Accounting, Information Systems), Master of Science (General), Master of Engineering (General), Community College Diploma (Accounting, Secretarial, Graphic Arts, Computer Science), and High School Diploma. Graduates would occupy Programmer, Analyst, System Analyst, Technical Illustrator, Scientist/Subject Specialist, Marketing Officer, Technical Specialist, Information Specialist, Data Entry Technician, Clerk, and Secretarial positions. Work experience, project management experience, attentive to details, team player, flexible, excellent interpersonal, communication and organizational skills are all listed as desirable non-academic qualifications. Company benefits are rated above average. The potential for advancement is listed as average. The average annual starting salary falls within the $30,000 to $35,000 range. The most suitable methods for initial contact by those seeking employment are to mail, fax or e-mail a resume with a covering letter. The Canadian Centre for Occupational Health & Safety hires summer students on a limited basis. *Contacts:* Louise Henderson, Manager, Human Resources or Lynn Walker, Human Resources Officer.

CANADIAN DEPOSITORY FOR SECURITIES LTD., THE
85 Richmond Street West
Toronto, ON M5H 2C9

Tel.	416-365-8612
Fax	416-365-0758
Website	www.positionwatch.com

The Canadian Depository For Securities Ltd. provides post-trading services to the securities industry. The services provided include, clearing, custody and settlement of transactions. There are over 250 employees at this location. Graduates most likely to be hired come from the following areas: Bachelor of Arts (Economics), Bachelor of Science (Computer Science), Bachelor of Commerce/Business Administration (Finance), Chartered Accountant, Certified Management Accountant, and Community College Diploma (Finance, Business, Secretarial). The types of positions vary, most are clerical and analytical in nature. Applicants should be outgoing, self motivated and "able to see the broad picture". Knowledge of spreadsheet, word processing and database applications is listed as definite asset. Company benefits are rated as excellent. The potential for advancement is listed as being good. The average annual starting salary falls within the $20,000 to $25,000 range. The most suitable method for initial contact by graduates seeking employment is to mail a resume with a covering letter. The Canadian Depository For Securities Ltd. does hire summer students. *Contact:* Anne Shields, Personnel Representative, Human Resources.

CANADIAN FREIGHTWAYS LIMITED
4041A - 6th Street, P.O. Box 1108, Station T
Calgary, AB T2H 2J1

Tel.	403-287-4368
Fax	403-287-3030

Canadian Freightways Limited is a federally regulated freight transportation company, normally a LTL (Less Than Truckload) carrier. The company also provides logistic solutions for cross border transportation and customs clearance. There are 90 employees at the head office location in Calgary, and a total of 900 employees across Western Canada. Graduates most likely to be hired come from the following academic areas: Bachelor of Arts (General, Psychology), Bachelor of Science (Computer Science), Bachelor of Engineering (Industrial Production), Bachelor of Commerce/Business Administration (General, Accounting, Human Resources, Information Systems, Marketing, Operations Management, Transportation and Logistics), Certified Management Accountant, Certified General Accountant, Community College Diploma (Accounting, Administration, Business, Human Resources, Marketing/Sales, Purchasing/Logistics, Secretarial), and High School Diploma. Graduates would occupy Technician, Computer Operator, Management/Information Systems Trainee, and Sales/Marketing or Operations Trainee positions. Previous summer work experience, good organizational and planning skills, time management skills, team player and good communication skills are all listed as desirable non-academic qualifications. Company benefits are rated above average. The potential for advancement is listed as excellent. The average annual starting salary falls within the $32,000 to $38,000 range, depending upon the position being considered. The most suitable method for initial contact by those seeking employment is to mail a resume with a covering letter. Canadian Freightways Limited does hire co-op and summer students. Summer students are hired primarily for unionized dock operation positions. *Contacts:* Bruce Ogilvie, Manager, Human Resource Services or Ken Czech, Director, Human Resource Services.

CANADIAN GENERAL INSURANCE GROUP LTD.
2206 Eglinton Avenue East
Toronto, ON M1L 4S8

Tel.	416-288-5230
Fax	416-288-3199

Since 1907, Canadian General Insurance Group Ltd. has marketed its products through a family of companies and a network of independent insurance brokers. The company is one of the 15 largest property and casualty insurance companies in Canada, and is comprised of four Canadian based insurance companies (The Assumed Reinsurance Division, Traders General Insurance Company, Scottish & York Insurance Company Ltd., Victoria Insurance Company), each functioning independently. These companies are serviced by a centralized claims department. There are approximately 400 employees at this location and a total of 700 employees across Canada. Graduates most likely to be hired come from the following academic areas: Bachelor of Arts (General, Criminology, Economics), Bachelor of Science (Actuarial), Chartered Accountant, Certified Management Accountant, Certified General Accountant, Master of Business Administration, Community College Diploma (Accounting, Business, Insurance), AIIC/FIIC/RIBO Designations, and High School Diploma. Graduates would occupy Claims Adjuster Trainee, Junior Underwriter Trainee, Reinsurance Analyst Trainee, Junior Accountant, Actuarial Analyst Trainee, and a variety of clerical positions. Good communication and customer relations skills, reliable, initiative, team player, and good time management skills are all listed as desirable non-academic qualifications. Company benefits are rated above average. The potential for advancement is listed as being good. The most suitable methods for initial contact by those seeking employment are to mail or fax a resume with a covering letter. Canadian General Insurance Group Ltd. does hire summer students, however, there are very few openings. *Contact:* Shawna Findlay-Thompson, Human Resources Generalist.

CANADIAN HEARING SOCIETY, THE

271 Spadina Road
Toronto, ON M5R 2V3

Tel. 416-964-9595
Fax 416-928-2517
Website .... www.chs.ca

The Canadian Hearing Society (CHS) is a non-profit organization involved in the provision of services and counselling for deaf, deafened and hard of hearing individuals and their families. CHS also provides products and support services to these individuals. There are approximately 100 employees at this location and a total of 275 employees in Ontario. Graduates most likely to be hired come from the following academic areas: Bachelor of Arts (Psychology, Social Work), Bachelor of Science (Speech Pathology), Bachelor of Education (Adult, Special Needs), Master of Science (Audiology, Speech Pathology), and Community College Diploma (Social Work). Graduates would occupy General Social Services Counsellor, Employment Counsellor, V.R. Counsellor, Sign Language Interpreter, Audiologist, Speech Therapist, Hearing Instrument Dispenser, and Clinical Psychologist positions. Fluency in ASL, or a willingness to learn is required. In addition, computer skills, team player and an awareness of deaf culture are all listed as desirable non-academic qualifications. Company benefits are rated as industry standard. The potential for advancement is listed as average. The average annual starting salary falls within the $25,000 to $35,000 range, depending upon the position being considered. The most suitable methods for initial contact by those seeking employment are to mail, fax or e-mail a resume with a covering letter, stating the area of employment or the position being sought. Applicants may also view current vacancies online at the CHS's website at www.chs.ca. The Canadian Hearing Society does hire summer and co-op work term students, as government funding permits. *Contact:* Human Resources.

CANADIAN MEDICAL LABORATORIES LTD.

1644 Aimco Boulevard
Mississauga, ON L4W 1V1

Tel. 905-624-0440
Fax 905-624-4433

Canadian Medical Laboratories Ltd. consists of a network of laboratories serving Metro Toronto and the Golden Horseshoe area of Ontario. Canadian Medical Laboratories provides physicians, hospitals, and long-term care facilities with today's best in diagnostic laboratory capabilities. Since the company's beginning in 1976, it has expanded to offer a wide range of specialized services for the medical professions. Today, Canadian Medical Laboratories offers diverse consulting capabilities in such areas as diagnostics, medical computer systems, and medical building development. Graduates most likely to be hired come from the following academic areas: Bachelor of Science (Chemistry, Microbiology), and Community College Diploma (Laboratory Technician). Graduates would occupy Registered Technologist, Laboratory Technician, and Laboratory Assistant positions. Good communication skills, a sense of business maturity, an ability to take on responsibility, and a familiarity with mainframe terminals and personal computers are all listed as desirable non-academic qualifications. Company benefits are rated above average. The potential for advancement is listed as average. The average annual starting salary at the new graduate level for a Laboratory Assistant or Technician falls within the $20,000 to $25,000 range. The most suitable method for initial contact by those seeking employment is to mail a resume with a covering letter. Canadian Medical Laboratories does hire summer students (typically these are required "work assignments" necessary to graduate, 5 to 10 work days). *Contact:* Human Resources.

CANADIAN MEMORIAL CHIROPRACTIC COLLEGE

1900 Bayview Avenue
Toronto, ON M4G 3E6

Tel. 416-482-2340
Fax 416-482-9745

Canadian Memorial Chiropractic College's mission is to advance the art, science and philosophy of chiropractic medicine, educate chiropractors to further the development of the chiropractic profession, and to improve the health of the society as a whole. The College employs approximately 180 employees, both full and part-time faculty and administrative staff. Faculty most likely to be hired will have a related health sciences background and are a Doctor of Chiropractic, with a minimum of five years experience. Applicants applying for positions in the areas of accounting and administration must have related experience, and strong interpersonal and communication skills. Benefits and the potential for advancement are both rated as excellent. The average annual starting salary varies depending upon the position being considered. The most suitable method for initial contact by those seeking employment is to mail a resume with a covering letter. Students enrolled at Canadian Memorial Chiropractic College are selected for summer job opportunities when available. *Contact:* Susan Sanderson, Director, Human Resources.

CANADIAN NATIONAL INSTITUTE FOR THE BLIND, THE

1929 Bayview Avenue
Toronto, ON M4G 3E8

Tel. 416-486-2500

The Canadian National Institute for the Blind (CNIB) is a non-profit organization providing services to blind, visually impaired and deaf blind individuals. This includes low vision assessment, rehabilitation teaching, mobility training, and vocational assessment and teaching. There are approximately 200 employees at this location and over 1,200 employees across Canada. Graduates most likely to be hired come from the following academic areas: Bachelor of Arts (General, Gerontology/Sociology, Psychology), Bachelor of Science (Nursing RN), Bachelor of Education (Special Needs Education), Bachelor of Commerce/Business Administration (Accounting, Human Resources), Community College Diploma (Accounting, Human Resources, Secretarial, Nursing, Orientation and Mobility Rehabilitation), and High School Diploma. Graduates would occupy Rehabilitation Teacher, Low Vision Nurse, Orientation and Mobility Instructor, Deaf-Blind Intervener, Clerical, Secretarial, Accounting, and Management positions. Two to five years work experience (preferably in the not-for-profit sector), team player, detail oriented, and empathetic to disabled individuals are all listed as desirable non-academic qualifications. Company benefits are rated above average. The potential for advancement is listed as being good. The average annual starting salary falls within the $25,000 to $30,000 range. The most suitable method for initial contact by those seeking employment is to mail a resume with a covering letter. The CNIB does hire summer students. *Contact:* Fran Gard, Human Resources.

CANADIAN OCCIDENTAL PETROLEUM LTD.

635 - 8th Avenue S.W., Suite 1500
Calgary, AB T2P 3Z1

Tel. 403-234-6700
Fax 403-234-1050
Email .... hr_staffing@cdnoxy.com
Website .... www.cdnoxy.com

Canadian Occidental Petroleum Ltd. (COPL/CanadianOxy) is a global oil and gas exploration and production company, as well as a low cost producer and marketer of industrial bleaching chemical products in North America. The company's diversified business interests are managed through a number of wholly owned subsidiaries. These are as follows: Wascana Energy (manages Canadian oil and gas assets and operations), Canadian Petroleum Ltd. (manages international oil and gas assets and activities), CXY Chemical (manufactures and markets chemical products in Canada and the United States), CXY Energy (manages U.S. oil and gas assets and operations), CXY Energy Marketing (Canadian, U.S., and international marketing activities of oil and gas products). The corporate functions that support CanadianOxy as a whole are based in Calgary, Alberta. These include Human Resources, Procurement, Security, Legal, Corporate Affairs, Environment, Health and Safety, Investor Relations, and Finance and Treasury. There is often operational representation of these functions within the subsidiaries with policies and procedures established corporately. CanadianOxy employs 745 people at this location, a total of 1,532 in Canada, and a total of 1,710 employees worldwide. Graduates most likely to be hired come from the following academic areas: Bachelor of Arts (Economics), Bachelor of Science (Computer Science, Geology), Bachelor of Engineering (General, Civil, Mechanical, Computer Systems, Geological Engineering), Bachelor of Commerce/Business Administration (General, Accounting, Finance, Human Resources), Chartered Accountant, Certified Management Accountant, Certified General Accountant, Master of Business Administration (General, Accounting, Finance, Human Resources), and Community College Diploma (Accounting, Administration, Business, Human Resources, Information Systems, Legal Assistant, Computer Science). Graduates would occupy Analyst, Clerk, Junior Accountant, Engineer, Geologist, Geophysicist, Legal Administrator Assistant, Administrative Assistant, and Computer Operator positions. Adaptable to change, excellent interpersonal and communication skills, team player, culturally sensitive, and an understanding of the oil and gas business are all listed as desirable non-academic qualifications. Company benefits are rated as excellent. The potential for advancement is listed as being good. The average annual starting salary falls within the $35,000 to $40,000 range, and varies depending on discipline. Initial contact is best made by mailing, faxing or e-mailing a resume with a cover letter, or by applying through the company's website at www.cdnoxy.com. CanadianOxy does hire summer and co-op students. *Contacts:* Staffing & Corporate Resources (Domestic) or International Human Resources (International).

CANADIAN PACIFIC HOTELS
1 University Avenue, Suite 1400
Toronto, ON M5J 2P1

Tel. 416-367-7111
Fax 416-863-6097

Canadian Pacific Hotels operates full service hotels, offering accommodation, food and beverage, banquet and conference facilities, and recreational facilities in the company's resort properties. Canadian Pacific Hotels is Canada's oldest hotel company, employing approximately 10,000 people across the country. Graduates most likely to be hired come from the following academic areas: Bachelor of Arts (English), Bachelor of Science (Forestry), Bachelor of Commerce/Business Administration (Accounting, Finance, Human Resources, Information Systems, Marketing, Public Administration), Chartered Accountant, Certified Management Accountant, Certified General Accountant, Master of Business Administration (Accounting, Finance, Human Resources, Information Systems, Marketing, Public Administration), Community College Diploma (Accounting, Administration, Business, Communications, Human Resources, Marketing/Sales, Purchasing/Logistics, Secretarial, Cooking, Hospitality, Security/Enforcement, Travel/Tourism, HVAC Systems, Massage Therapy), and High School Diploma. Graduates would occupy Front Office Clerk, Accounting Clerk, Cook, Server, Massage Therapist, Room Attendant, and Concierge positions. Strong interpersonal and problem solving skills, empathy, intuition, and good verbal and written communication skills are all listed as desirable non-academic qualifications. Company benefits are rated as excellent. The potential for advancement is listed as being good. The average annual starting salary falls within the $20,000 to $25,000 range. The most suitable method for initial contact by those seeking employment is to mail a resume with a covering letter. Canadian Pacific Hotels does hire summer students. *Contacts:* Supervisor, Human Resources (Corporate Office) or Human Resources Department (Individual Property Locations).

CANADIAN PACIFIC HOTELS, THE LODGE AT KANANASKIS
Kananaskis Village
Kananaskis, AB T0L 2H0

Tel. 403-591-6223
Fax 403-591-7269
Email .... rohearn@lak.mhs.compuserv.com

The Lodge at Kananaskis is a Canadian Pacific Hotel employing 315 people, dedicated to providing uniquely satisfying guest experiences and consistently exceeding guest expectations. Graduates most likely to be hired come from the following academic areas: Bachelor of Commerce/Business Administration (General, Hospitality/Food and Beverage Management), Community College Diploma (Hospitality, Travel/Tourism), High School Diploma, and Bachelor of Arts (General). Graduates are hired to occupy a variety of positions from entry level to management, depending upon experience. Team

player, dedicated, customer service oriented, positive attitude, and able to work in and enjoy a constantly changing environment are all listed as desirable non-academic qualifications. Company benefits are rated as excellent. Canadian Pacific Hotels is dedicated to promoting from within and has a successful internal promotion program in place called, The Pathfinder Program. Accordingly, the potential for advancement is also rated as excellent. The average annual starting salary is dependent upon the position being considered. The most suitable methods for initial contact by those seeking employment are to mail or fax a resume with a covering letter. Summer students are hired, primarily through hospitality management co-op placement programs. *Contacts:* Kim Van Pelt, Director, Human Resources or Robin O'Hearn, Assistant Director, Human Resources.

CANADIAN STANDARDS ASSOCIATION (CSA)
178 Rexdale Boulevard
Toronto, ON M9W 1R3

Tel. 416-747-4018
Fax 416-747-4169

The Canadian Standards Association (CSA) is a standards writing organization, undertaking testing and certification of commercial products. There are more than 500 people employed within the organization. Graduates most likely to be hired come from the following academic areas: Bachelor of Engineering (Electrical, Mechanical), and Community College Diploma (Electrical Technician, Mechanical Technician). These graduates are hired as Engineers and Engineering Technologists respectively. Strong interpersonal skills, team player, and good communication skills are listed as desirable non-academic qualifications. Company benefits and the potential for advancement are both rated as excellent. The average annual starting salary falls within the $25,000 to $35,000 range, depending upon the position being considered. The most suitable method for initial contact by graduates seeking employment is to mail a resume with a covering letter. The Canadian Standards Association does hire summer students. *Contact:* Human Resources.

CANADIAN THERMOS PRODUCTS INC.
2040 Eglinton Avenue East
Toronto, ON M1L 2M8

Tel. 416-757-6231
Fax 416-757-6230

Canadian Thermos Products Inc. is involved in the manufacturing of miscellaneous plastic products. Activities include Accounting, Maintenance, Marketing/Sales, Data Processing, and Shipping/Receiving. There are more than 100 employees at this location. Graduates most likely to be hired come from the following academic areas: Bachelor of Science (Chemistry, Computer Science), Bachelor of Engineering (Chemical, Robotics), Bachelor of Commerce/Business Administration (Accounting, Finance, Human Resources, Marketing), Chartered Accountant, and

Community College Diploma (Accounting, Business, Marketing/Sales, CAD/CAM/Autocad, Computer Science). Initiative, excellent communication skills, team player and team building skills are all listed as desirable non-academic qualifications. Company benefits are rated above average. The potential for advancement is listed as average. The average annual starting salary falls within the $25,000 to $30,000 range. The most suitable method for initial contact by graduates seeking employment is to mail a resume with a covering letter. Canadian Thermos Products Inc. does hire summer students. *Contact:* Janice Cameron, Human Resources Manager.

CANBRA FOODS LTD.
Box 99
Lethbridge, AB T1J 3Y4

Tel. 403-329-5573
Fax 403-328-7933

Canbra Foods Ltd. is a fully integrated Canola processing plant. Activities range from seed procurement, to refining, to packaging of both edible and non-edible products. There are more than 250 employees at this location. Graduates most likely to be hired come from the following academic areas: Bachelor of Science (Chemistry), Bachelor of Engineering (Industrial, Mechanical), Bachelor of Commerce/Business Administration (Finance), Certified Management Accountant, Certified General Accountant, and Community College Diploma (Accounting, Human Resources, Architecture/Drafting, Engineering, Industrial Design, Mechanic). Graduates would occupy Engineering Manager, Q.C. Manager, Operations Manager, Package Products Manager, Draftsperson, Maintenance Supervisor, Human Resources Assistant, Accounts Payable Manager, and Accounts Receivable Manager positions. Company benefits are rated above average. The potential for advancement is listed as being good. The average annual starting salary falls within the $35,000 to $40,000 range. The most suitable method for initial contact by those seeking employment is to mail a resume with a covering letter. *Contacts:* Keith L. Beerling, Vice President, Human Resources & Corporate Secretary or Jason T. Elliott, Supervisor, Human Resources.

CANGENE CORPORATION
104 Chancellor Matheson Road
Winnipeg, MB R3T 5Y3

Tel. 204-989-6895
Fax 204-269-7003

Cangene Corporation is a world leader in the development, manufacture, and distribution of specialty hyperimmune plasma and biotechnology products. Cangene's research collaborations and marketing efforts span the globe. The company has over 160 employees, with manufacturing and research facilities across Canada. Graduates most likely to be hired come from the following academic areas: Bachelor of Science (Biology, Chemistry, Computer Science, Microbiology, Immunology, Nursing, Pharmacy),

Bachelor of Engineering (Chemical, Biotechnology, Industrial Chemistry, Biomedical Electronics, Computer Systems), Bachelor of Commerce/Business Administration (Accounting, Finance, Human Resources, Information Systems, Marketing), Certified Management Accountant, Certified General Accountant, Master of Business Administration (Accounting, Finance, Human Resources, Information Systems, Marketing), Master/Doctorate of Science, Community College Diploma (Accounting, Human Resources, Marketing/Sales, Computer Science, Electronics Technician, Engineering Technician, Laboratory Technician), and High School Diploma. Graduates would occupy Clerk, Laboratory Technician, Associate, Administrator, Assistant, and Coordinator, etc. positions. Good verbal and written communication skills, manual dexterity, and team player are listed as desirable non-academic qualifications. Company benefits are rated as excellent. The potential for advancement is listed as being good. The average annual starting salary falls within the $25,000 to $35,000 range. The most suitable method for initial contact by those seeking employment is to mail a resume with a covering letter. Cangene Corporation does hire summer students. *Contact:* Gisèle Marks, Human Resources.

Canon

CANON CANADA INC.
6390 Dixie Road
Mississauga, ON L5T 1P7

Tel. 905-795-2107
Fax 905-795-2046
Email .... hrmississauga@canada.canon.com
Website .... www.usa.canon.com

Canon Canada Inc., headquartered in Mississauga, Ontario with branch offices across Canada, is an industry leader in professional and consumer imaging equipment and information systems. Canon's extensive product line enables businesses and consumers worldwide to capture, store and distribute visual information. Canon products include digital, analogue and full-color copiers, laser printers, color Bubble Jet printers, digital imaging systems, facsimile machines, calculators, video camcorders, cameras and lenses, semiconductors, broadcast and optical equipment and other specialized industrial products. Canon Canada Inc. offers many challenging and rewarding career opportunities for graduates. Graduates are hired to join one of Canon's professional teams in sales, sales support, marketing, service technology, accounting, advertising, computer networking, administration and operations. Canon, including its business to business sales division OE (see OE's listing), offers excellent career growth potential and mobility, supported by the stability of a globally successful company. Canon offers comprehensive rewards designed to meet the needs of their employees today and throughout their careers. The most suitable methods to inquire about job opportunities at Canon Canada Inc. are to mail or e-mail a resume with covering letter to the above address, or via the Job Line at (905) 795-2107. *Contact:* Human Resources.

CANTEL AT&T
1 Mount Pleasant Road
Toronto, ON M4Y 2Y5

Tel. 416-935-1100
Website .... www.rogers.com

Cantel AT&T, formed through an alliance between Rogers Cantel Inc. and AT&T, combines the reliable customer service, quality and innovation of Canada's national cellular service, with the global reach of one of the world's preeminent names in telecommunications. Graduates most likely to be hired come from the following academic areas: Bachelor of Arts (General), Bachelor of Science (Computer Science), Bachelor of Engineering (Civil, Electrical, Industrial), Bachelor of Commerce/Business Administration, Chartered Accountant, Certified Management Accountant, Master of Business Administration, and Community College Diploma (Engineering Technician, Electrical Technician, Radio Technician). Graduates would be hired to occupy positions in the following operational areas: Human Resources, Finance and Administration, Sales and Marketing, Customer Service, Treasury, PCS and Cellular, Paging, Treasury, Wireless Data, and in eight interrelated branches within the Engineering Division. Previous and related work experience is listed as a definite asset. Company benefits and the potential for advancement are both rated as excellent. The most suitable method for initial contact by graduates seeking employment is to mail a resume with a covering letter. Cantel AT&T does hire summer students. *Contact:* Recruiter, Human Resources.

CARBONE OF AMERICA (LCL) LTD.
496 Evans Avenue
Toronto, ON M8W 2T7

Tel. 416-251-2334
Fax 416-252-1742

Carbone of America (LCL) Ltd. manufactures carbon brushes for electric motors. The company employs a total of 115 people. Graduates most likely to be hired come from the following academic areas: Bachelor of Arts (General), Bachelor of Engineering (Electrical, Mechanical), Bachelor of Commerce/Business Administration (General, Accounting, Finance, Human Resources, Marketing), Master of Business Administration (Finance), Community College Diploma (Accounting, Administration, Business, Human Resources, Marketing/Sales, Purchasing/Logistics, Engineering Technician), and High School Diploma. Team player, a good attitude, and previous work experience are all listed as desirable non-academic qualifications. Company benefits and the potential for advancement are both rated as excellent. The most suitable method for initial contact by those seeking employment is to mail a resume with a covering letter. Carbone of America (LCL)

Ltd. does hire summer students. *Contact:* Nancy DiBernardo, Human Resources.

CARGILL LIMITED
300 - 240 Graham Avenue
Winnipeg, MB R3C 4C5

Tel. 204-947-6251
Fax 204-947-6222

Cargill Limited operates in the agricultural sector and was established in Canada over 60 years ago. Canadian businesses include, grain merchandising, grain handling, farm supplies, feed manufacturing, beef processing, and fertilizer manufacturing. There are 210 employees at this location, approximately 3,800 employees across Canada, and 70,000 employees worldwide. Graduates most likely to be hired come from the following academic areas: Bachelor of Science (General, Agriculture, Computer Science), Bachelor of Commerce/Business Administration (Accounting, Information Systems, Marketing), Certified Management Accountant, Certified General Accountant, and Community College Diploma (Accounting, Administration, Business, Computer Science). All positions start at the trainee level. Within the Elevator/Farm Supply division, transferability is required with initial assignments possibly being located in farm communities. Highly motivated, team player, computer literacy, and good communication skills are all listed as desirable non-academic qualifications. Company benefits are rated above average. The potential for advancement is listed as excellent. The average annual starting salary falls within the $25,000 to $35,000 range. The most suitable method for initial contact by graduates seeking employment is to mail a resume with a covering letter. Cargill Limited occasionally hires summer students. *Contact:* Bob Johnson, Director, Human Resources.

CARLINGVIEW AIRPORT INN
221 Carlingview Drive
Rexdale, ON M9W 5E8

Tel. 416-675-3303

Carlingview Airport Inn in full service hotel/restaurant employing approximately 50 people. Post-secondary education is not listed as a prerequisite for employment application. Graduates would occupy entry-level Front Desk Clerk, Night Audit Clerk, and Housekeeping positions. Previous hotel work experience is listed as a desirable non-academic qualifications. Company benefits are rated above average. The potential for advancement is listed as being good. The average annual starting salary falls in the $15,000 plus range. The most suitable method for initial contact regarding employment opportunities is to mail a resume with a covering letter. The Carlingview Airport Inn does hire summer students. *Contacts:* Mr. Paul Lira, Comptroller or Mr. Verge Jacobelli, Managing Director.

CARLSON MARKETING GROUP LTD.

3300 Bloor Street West, Centre Tower, 15th Floor
Toronto, ON M8X 2Y2

Tel. 416-236-1991
Fax 416-236-9915
Email .... hr@carlson-marketing.ca

Carlson Marketing Group provides integrated marketing solutions designed to improve employee, dealer and distributor productivity and enhance customer loyalty for their clients' products and services. Award programs could be incentive travel or catalogue merchandise programs, business meeting and event marketing, promotional premiums, program management, sales promotion, customer loyalty programs and database marketing. There are 350 employees at this location and a total of 410 in Canada. Carlson is part of an international company that employs more than 180,000 people worldwide. The company does not seek individuals who have a particular academic background, instead, they are more interested in eager individuals who possess the following non-academic qualifications: good personal presentation, computer software/operating skills, people oriented, willing to accept customer service positions or entry level positions at reasonable salaries. Bilingual (French/English) is a big plus. Acceptable academic backgrounds include Bachelor of Arts (General, English, French), Bachelor of Commerce/Business Administration (Marketing), Community College Diploma (Administration, Advertising), and High School Diploma. Company benefits are rated as industry standard. The potential for advancement is listed as being good. The average annual starting salary falls within the $21,000 to $25,000 range. The most suitable methods for initial contact by those seeking employment are to fax or e-mail a resume with a covering letter. *Contact:* Human Resources Department.

CARRIER CANADA LIMITED

1515 Drew Road
Mississauga, ON L5S 1Y8

Tel. 905-672-0606
Fax 905-405-4003
Email .... cathy.sciberras@carrier.utc.com
Website .... www.carrier.com

Carrier Canada Limited is involved in the distribution, sales and service of HVAC equipment across Canada. The company employs approximately 120 people at this location and a total of 475 people across Canada. Graduates most likely to be hired come from the following academic areas: Bachelor of Arts (General), Bachelor of Engineering (Mechanical), Bachelor of Commerce/Business Administration (Accounting, Finance), Certified Management Accountant, Certified General Accountant, Master of Business Administration (Finance), and Community College Diploma (Accounting, Engineering Technician, HVAC Systems). Graduates would occupy Accountant, Accounting Clerk, Customer Service Representative, Finance and Budget Managers, Counter Sales Representative, Inside Sales Representative, and Technical Representative positions. Computer literate, working knowledge of HVAC industry, excellent communication and interpersonal skills, team player, and fluency in the French language are all listed as desirable non-academic qualifications. Company benefits are rated as excellent. The potential for advancement is listed as being good. The average annual starting salary depends upon the position being considered, and the previous work experience and educational background of the applicant. The most suitable methods for initial contact by those seeking employment are to mail or fax a resume with a covering letter. Carrier Canada Limited hires summer students for clerical positions, and some warehouse/shipping positions in other branches. Co-op work term students are also hired. Carrier Canada Limited is dedicated to employment equity. *Contact:* Cathy Sciberras, Human Resources.

CARSEN GROUP INC.

151 Telson Road
Markham, ON L3R 1E7

Tel. 905-479-4100
Fax 905-479-2595

Carsen Group Inc. is a National distributor employing approximately 110 people. There are 4 major divisions: Medical Instruments Division, Precision Instruments, Industrial Technology and Consumer Products Group. Graduates most likely to be hired come from the following academic areas: Bachelor of Arts (General), Bachelor of Science (General), and Bachelor of Commerce/Business Administration (General, Information Systems). Graduates would occupy Customer Service Representative, Sales Representative, Technical Service Representative, Sales Coordinator, and Product Manager positions. Excellent communication and interpersonal skills, team player and computer literacy are all listed as desirable non-academic qualifications. Company benefits are rated as excellent. The potential for advancement is listed as being good. The average annual starting salary depends upon the position being considered, and the previous work experience of the applicant. The most suitable methods for initial contact by those seeking employment are to mail or fax a resume with a covering letter. Carsen Group Inc. does hire summer students. Carson Group Inc. supports employment equity. *Contact:* Gladys Soer, Human Resources Manager.

CAUGHT IN THE WEB, INC.

40 King Street West, Suite 3310, Scotia Plaza
Toronto, ON M5H 3Y2

Tel. 416-941-9340
Fax 416-941-9183
Email .... careers@citw.com
Website .... www.citw.com

Caught in the Web, Inc. sets people up on the web. This includes designing websites and web pages for clients. The company employs approximately 25 people. Graduates most likely to be hired come from the following academic areas: Bachelor of Science (Computer Science), Bachelor of Engineering (Computer Systems), Bachelor of Commerce/Business Administration (Accounting), and Community College Diploma (Accounting, Administration, Communications/Public Relations, Marketing/Sales, Secretarial, Graphic Arts, Computer Science). Graduates would occupy Computer Technical Development, Computer/Graphic Designer, Marketing/Sales Trainee, Accounting Assistant, and Public Relations positions. Team player, enthusiastic, friendly, and multi-tasking abilities are all listed as desirable non-academic qualifications. Company benefits are rated above average. The potential for advancement is listed as being good. The average annual starting salary falls within the $25,000 to $30,000 range. The most suitable methods for initial contact by those seeking employment are to fax or e-mail a resume with a covering letter. Caught in the Web, Inc. does hire summer and co-op work term students. *Contact:* Colomba Vani.

CAVENDISH FARMS
P.O. Box 3500
Summerside, PE C1N 5J5

Tel. 902-836-5555
Fax 902-836-3299

Cavendish Farms employs 900 people in the production of frozen potato food products. Graduates most likely to be hired come from the following academic areas: Bachelor of Science (Agriculture, Biology, Chemistry, Computer Science, Environmental), Bachelor of Engineering (Food Processing, Pollution Treatment, Electrical, Instrumentation, Mechanical, Industrial Production), Bachelor of Architecture, Bachelor of Commerce/Business Administration (General, Accounting, Finance, Human Resources, Information Systems, Marketing), Community College Diploma (Accounting, Administration, Business, Financial Planning, Human Resources, Computer Science, Electronics Technician, Engineering Technician), and High School Diploma. Graduates would occupy Clerk, Maintenance, Managerial and Supervisory etc. positions. Previous work experience, leadership skills, facilitator, team player, adaptability, and good communication skills are all listed as desirable non-academic qualifications. The most suitable method for initial contact by those seeking employment is to mail a resume with a covering letter. Cavendish Farms does hire summer students. *Contact:* Daniel Hughes, Human Resource Manager.

CENTENARY HEALTH CENTRE
2867 Ellesmere Road
Toronto, ON M1E 4B9

Tel. 416-281-7271
Fax 416-281-7417

Centenary Health Centre is an accredited 500 bed hospital dedicated to providing quality health care to the community. There are more than 1,000 people employed at the health centre. Graduates most likely to be hired come from the following academic areas: Bachelor of Arts (Labour Studies), Bachelor of Science (Nursing, Pharmacy), Master of Social Work, and Community College Diploma (Laboratory Technician, Radiology Technician, Respiratory Technician, Medical Secretary, and Nursing). Excellent organizational, communication and interpersonal skills, and an ability to work within a team, in a hectic environment. Computer skills (eg. WordPerfect, Lotus 123, etc.) and previous experience in a health care or hospital setting are listed as desirable non-academic qualifications. Company benefits are rated as excellent. The potential for advancement is listed as being good. The average annual starting salary is dependent upon the position being considered. The most suitable method for initial contact by graduates seeking employment is to mail a resume with a covering letter. Centenary Health Centre does hire summer students occasionally. *Contact:* Angela deJonge, Manager, Employment Services.

CENTRAL PARK LODGES LTD.
175 Bloor Street East, Suite 601, South Tower
Toronto, ON M4W 3R8

Tel. 416-929-5450
Fax 416-929-1339

Established in 1961, Central Park Lodges Ltd. founded the first chain of retirement lodges and nursing homes in Canada. Today, the company has expanded its operations to 27 facilities covering a geographic base which includes the provinces of British Columbia, Alberta, Manitoba, Ontario, and Quebec. There are approximately 50 employees at this location and more than 2,500 employees in Canada. Graduates most likely to be hired come from the following academic areas: Bachelor of Arts (General, Economics, Psychology, Recreation, Sociology/Social Work), Bachelor of Science (Nursing), Bachelor of Commerce/Business Administration (Accounting, Finance, Human Resources, Information Systems, Marketing), Chartered Accountant (Finance), Certified Management Accountant (Finance), Certified General Accountant (Finance), and Community College Diploma (Accounting, Administration, Business, Facility Management, Human Resources, Marketing, Secretarial, HVAC Systems, Dietician/Nutrition, Nursing RN/RNA). Graduates would occupy RN, RNA, Health Care Aide, Dietary Aide, Cook, Janitor, Activity Aide, Food Service Supervisor, Maintenance Supervisor, Activity Director, and Accounting positions. Good communication, organization, marketing, critical thinking skills, patience, flexibility, and comfort with seniors are all listed as desirable non-academic qualifications. Company benefits are rated as industry standard. The potential for advancement is listed as being good. The most suitable method for initial contact by those seeking employment is to mail a resume with a covering letter. Central Park Lodges Ltd. does hire summer students. *Contacts:* Sandy Lauder, Director, Human Resources, Retirement Division or Elaine Lau, Human Resources Officer.

CENTRAL PROJECTS GROUP INC.
250 Shields Court, Unit #15
Markham, ON L3R 9W7

Tel. 905-470-6570
Fax 905-470-0958
Email .... rdevries@ibm.net
Website .... www.cpg.ca

Central Projects Group Inc. is an engineering firm involved in environmental audits and assessments, emergency response, project management, environmental remediation, and engineering design. There are 20 employees at this location, and a total of 25 employees in Canada. Graduates most likely to be hired come from the following academic areas: Bachelor of Science (Environmental), Bachelor of Engineering (Pollution Treatment, Civil, Resources/Environmental), Master of Science (Environmental), Master of Engineering (Environmental), and Community College Diploma (Engineering Technician). Graduates would occupy Technician and Project Manager positions. Excellent verbal and written communication skills, and work experience in site assessment/remediation are listed as desirable non-academic qualifications. Company benefits and potential for advancement are both rated as excellent. The average annual starting salary falls within the $25,000 to $30,000 range. The most suitable method for initial contact by those seeking employment is to mail a resume with a covering letter. Central Projects Group Inc. does hire summer students. Contacts: Mr. Harry Kim or Mr. René De Vries.

CENTRES JEUNESSE DE MONTRÉAL, LES
9335, rue St-Hubert
Montreal, QC H2M 1Y7

Tel. 514-858-3903
Fax 514-858-3914

Les Centres Jeunesse de Montréal provides social services and rehabilitation counselling in a youth protection centre. There are approximately 4,000 employees throughout the organization. Graduates most likely to be hired come from the following academic areas: Bachelor of Arts (Criminology, Psychology, Social Work), Bachelor of Science (Computer Science, Nursing), Bachelor of Engineering (Civil), Bachelor of Education (Special Needs), Bachelor of Laws (Rehabilitation Law), Bachelor of Commerce/Business Administration (General, Accounting, Finance, Human Resources, Information Systems, Public Administration), Chartered Accountant, Certified General Accountant, Master of Business Administration (General, Public Administration), and Community College Diploma (Accounting, Administration, Human Resources, Secretarial, Recreation Studies, Social Work, Rehabilitation Therapy). The average annual starting salary falls within the $20,000 to $25,000 range. The most suitable method for initial contact by those seeking employment is to mail a resume with a covering letter. Les Centres Jeunesse de Montréal does hire summer students. Contact: Nicole Godfroy, technicienne en administration, Direction des ressources humaines.

CENTRIFUGAL COATERS INC.
1317 Speers Road
Oakville, ON L6L 2X5

Tel. 905-827-1156
Fax 905-827-0868

Centrifugal Coaters Inc. is a Tier 2 Supplier and custom coater (paint) of decorative trim parts supplied to the automotive industry. The company employs a total of 130 people. Graduates most likely to be hired come from the following academic areas: Bachelor of Arts (General), Bachelor of Engineering (Chemical, Automation/Robotics), Doctorate (Engineering), and Community College Diploma (Engineering Technician, Quality Management). Graduates would occupy Process Engineer/Technician, Quality Auditor, Scheduler/Purchaser, and Data Entry Clerk positions. Team player, good interpersonal skills, ability to self-motivate and take initiative, and good organization skills are all listed as desirable non-academic qualifications. Company benefits are rated above average. The potential for advancement is listed as average. The average annual starting salary falls within the $25,000 to $30,000 range. The most suitable method for initial contact by those seeking employment is to mail a resume with a covering letter. Contact: Karen Blake Carnevale, Director, Corporate Affaires & Human Resources.

CFMT-TV (ROGERS BROADCASTING LTD.)
545 Lakeshore Boulevard West
Toronto, ON M5V 1A3

Tel. 416-260-0047
Fax 416-260-3615
Website .... www.rogers.com

CFMT-TV is a television broadcasting station owned by Rogers Broadcasting Limited. Programming activities involve purchased programming and in-house production. The station employs between 180 and 200 people. Graduates most likely to be hired come from the following academic areas: Bachelor of Arts (General, Journalism, Languages), Bachelor of Engineering (Electrical, Mechanical, Telecommunications), Bachelor of Commerce/Business Administration (General, Accounting, Finance, Human Resources, Information Systems, Marketing), Chartered Accountant, Certified General Accountant, Master of Business Administration (Marketing), Community College Diploma (Accounting, Administration, Business, Communications/Public Relations, Human Resources, Information Systems, Marketing/Sales, Secretarial, Graphic Arts, Journalism, Television/Radio Arts, Broadcasting, Electronics Technician, Engineering Technician), and High School Diploma. Graduates would occupy Production Assistant, Junior Writer, Clerk, Accountant, and Sales Representative positions. Possessing a high level of maturity, good judgment, a positive attitude, and related work experience are all listed as desirable non-academic qualifications. Company benefits and the potential for advancement are both rated as excellent. The average annual starting salary falls within the $25,000 to $30,000 range, and for certain positions it is commission based. The most suitable methods for initial contact by graduates seeking employment are to mail or fax a resume with a covering letter. CFMT-TV does hire summer students on a volunteer basis, as well as hiring co-op work term students. *Contact:* Marisa Tenuta, Human Resource Manager.

CGI GROUP INC.
275 Slater Street,
14th Floor
Ottawa, ON K1P 5H9

Tel.	613-234-2155
Fax	613-234-6934
Email	sharon.bruyere@cgi.ca
Website	www.cgi.ca

CGI Group Inc. provides information systems and management consulting services. The company employs 200 people at this location and over 2,700 people across Canada. Graduates most likely to be hired come from the following academic areas: Bachelor of Science (Computer Science), Bachelor of Engineering (Electrical, Telecommunications), Bachelor of Commerce/Business Administration (Information Systems), Master of Business Administration (Information Systems), and Community College Diploma (Facility Management, Financial Planning, Computer Science). Graduates would be hired to occupy Programmer and Systems Analyst positions. The most suitable methods for initial contact by those seeking employment are to mail or e-mail a resume. CGI Group Inc. does hire summer students, depending upon the contracts the company has at that particular time. *Contacts:* Sharon Bruyere, Manager Human Resources or Tammy Scrivener, Human Resources Officer.

CH2M GORE & STORRIE LTD.
255 Consumers Road
Toronto, ON M2J 5B6

Tel.	416-499-9000
Fax	416-499-4687

CH2M Gore & Storrie Ltd. is a leading Canadian consulting engineering company, providing environmental engineering and scientific services for industries and municipalities in Canada and abroad. There are approximately 350 employees in 5 Ontario locations, Calgary and Vancouver. Graduates most likely to be hired come from the following academic areas: Bachelor of Arts (Urban Geography), Bachelor of Science (Biology, Computer Science, Environmental), Bachelor of Engineering (Chemical, Metallurgy, Architectural/Building, Surveying, Electrical, Instrumentation, Mechanical, Aeronautical), Bachelor of Commerce/Administration (Accounting, Finance, Human Resources, Information, Systems), Master of Business Administration (Accounting, Finance, Human Resources), and Community College Diploma (Accounting, Architecture/Drafting, CAD/CAM/Autocad, HVAC Systems). Graduates would occupy Engineering, Process, Building Services, Environmental Planning, Contaminant Sciences, and Administration positions. Quality conscious, flexible, technically sound, team players, maintain a professional approach and presentation, and excellent verbal and written communication skills are all listed as desirable non-academic qualifications. Company benefits are rated above average. The average annual starting salary falls within the $20,000 to $45,000 range, depending upon the position and the applicant's qualifications. The most suitable method for initial contact by those seeking employment is to mail a resume with a covering letter. *Contact:* Wendy Jones, HR Specialist, Human Resources.

CHAMPION ROAD MACHINERY LIMITED
P.O. Box 10,
Maitland Road
Goderich, ON N7A 3Y6

Tel.	519-524-2601
Fax	519-524-3013

Champion Road Machinery Limited is one of the world's leading manufacturers of graders and related equipment used in the construction and maintenance of roads. Champion's products are sold primarily through 170 independent dealers who operate approximately 300 sales and service outlets throughout the U.S., Canada, and 96 other countries, and through four company-owned retail outlets in Ontario. There are approximately 590 employees at this location and a total of 700 employees in Canada. Graduates most likely to be hired come from the following academic areas: Bachelor of Arts (Economics), Bachelor of Science (Computer Science, Mathematics), Bachelor of Engineering (General, Electrical, Mechanical, Industrial Design, Industrial Production, Welding), Bachelor of Commerce/Business Administration (Accounting, Finance, Human Resources, Information Systems, Marketing), Chartered Accountant, Certified Management Accountant, Certified General Accountant, Master of Business Administration (Accounting, Finance, Information Systems, Marketing), and Community College Diploma (Accounting, Business, Human Resources, Purchasing/Logistics, CAD/CAM/Autocad, Computer Science, Engineering Technician, Welding). Graduates would occupy Junior Engineer, Marketing Management Trainee, Systems Analyst, Financial Analyst, Draftsperson, Welding Technician, and Planner positions. Company benefits are rated as excellent. The potential for advancement is listed as being good. The average annual starting salary falls within the $30,000 to $35,000 range. The most suitable method for initial contact by those seeking employment is to mail a resume with a covering letter. Engineering, Finance, Information Systems, Industrial Engineering, and Marketing students are hired for summer positions. *Contact:* James G. E. Paterson, Human Resources Manager.

Great Books Are Just The Beginning

CHAPTERS INC.
90 Ronson Drive
Toronto, ON M9W 1C1

Tel.	416-243-3138
Fax	416-243-5420

Chapters Inc. was created in 1995 from the merger of Canada's two leading book retailers, Coles and SmithBooks. With the merger, Chapters has more than 340 mall-based and high-street bookstores with representation in every province. There are 180 employees here at the head office location, and over 4,200 employees across Canada. In addition to books and magazines, the SmithBooks and Coles stores carry related multi-media products such as audio tapes and books on CD-ROM. Launched in the fall of 1995, the Chapters Superstores carry more than 100,000 titles and offer learning and play areas for children, comfortable armchairs for curling up with a favourite selection and a coffee bar for customers. Graduates most likely to be hired come from the following academic areas: Bachelor of Arts (General), Bachelor of Commerce/Business Administration, and Community College Diploma (Business). Graduates are hired to occupy Retail Management, and Sales and Merchandising positions. Entrepreneurial spirit, sales building, strong work ethic, persuasiveness, dependability, a passion for retail and a love of books are all listed as desirable non-academic qualifications. Company benefits are rated above average. The potential for advancement is listed as excellent. The average annual starting salary falls within the $25,000 to $30,000 range. The most suitable methods for initial contact by those seeking employment are to mail of fax a resume with a covering letter. Summer students are hired at retail store locations (check white/yellow pages for the nearest location). *Contact:* Human Resources Department.

CHARTERWAYS TRANSPORTATION LIMITED
35 Crockford Boulevard
Toronto, ON M1R 3B7

Tel.	416-752-6120
Fax	416-752-4641

Charterways Transportation Limited is involved in the operation of school bus services for a variety of individual school boards. This also involves transporting physically disabled children and children requiring special education services. Graduates most likely to be hired come from the following academic areas: Bachelor of Commerce/Business Administration, and Community College Diploma (General). Graduates would occupy Management, Accounting, Secretarial and Clerical positions. Possessing a positive attitude and previous work experience are both listed as desirable non-academic qualifications. Company benefits are rated above average. The potential for advancement is listed as being good. The average annual starting salary falls within the $20,000 to $25,000 range. The most suitable method for initial contact by those seeking employment is to mail a resume with a covering letter. Charterways Transportation Limited does hire summer students on a regular basis. *Contact:* Recruiting Department.

CHEVRON CANADA RESOURCES
500 - 5th Avenue SW
Calgary, AB T2P 0L7

Tel.	403-234-5000
Fax	403-234-5947

Chevron Canada Resources is involved in the exploration, production, and marketing of oil and gas. The company employs 500 people at this location and a total of 800 people across Canada. Graduates most likely to be hired come from the following academic areas: Bachelor of Science (Computer Science, Geology), and Bachelor of Engineering (General, Chemical, Industrial Chemistry, Civil, Electrical, Instrumentation, Mechanical, Resources/Environmental, Petroleum). Graduates would begin as a trainee in their chosen field and progress to a fully trained professional in their field of specialization. Good communication skills, and being a demonstrated team player are both listed as desirable non-academic qualifications. Company benefits and the potential for advancement are both rated as excellent. The average annual starting salary falls within the $30,000 to $35,000 range, and is dependent upon the position being filled and the qualifications of the individual applicant. The most suitable method for initial contact by those seeking employment is to mail a resume with a covering letter. Chevron Canada Resources does hire summer students. *Contact:* Jim Causgrove, Manager, Strategy, People and Technology Development.

CHILDREN'S AID SOCIETY OF THE REGION OF PEEL
8 Nelson Street West, Suite 204
Brampton, ON L6X 4J2

Tel.	905-796-2121
Fax	905-796-2293

The Children's Aid Society of the Region of Peel is involved in child protection work, mandated by the Child and Family Services Act. This involves investigations and assessments of children at risk from harm, and placement and family court involvement for children (and families) in need of protection. Graduates most likely to be hired come from the following academic areas: Bachelor of Arts (Social Work), and Master of Arts (Social Work). Graduates would occupy Front-Line Social Worker, and°

Intake or Family Worker positions. Applicants should possess child welfare or children's aid society work experience. Employee benefits are rated as excellent. The potential for advancement is listed as average. The average annual starting salary falls within the $34,000 to $37,000 range. The most suitable method for initial contact by those seeking employment is to mail a resume with a covering letter. The Children's Aid Society of the Region of Peel does hire approximately three summer students annually as recreation aids. *Contact:* Human Resources.

CHILDREN'S AID SOCIETY OF TORONTO
33 Charles Street East
Toronto, ON M4Y 1R9

Tel. 416-924-4646
Fax 416-324-2502
Website .... www.casmt.on.ca

The Children's Aid Society of Toronto is the largest Board operated Child Welfare Agency in North America. There are 500 full-time staff in six branches, and in partnership with foster parents and volunteers, a range of protection and prevention services are provided. Graduates most likely to be hired come from the following academic areas: Bachelor of Arts (Social Work/BSW), Master of Arts (Social Work/MSW), and Community College Diploma (Child and Youth Worker). Graduates would occupy positions as a Social Worker, and Residential Child and Youth Care Worker. Applicants should have related experience with children and families, a driver's license, and access to an automobile. Employee benefits are rated above average. The potential for advancement is listed as being good. The average annual starting salary for a Child and Youth Worker is $30,700, and for a Social Worker it is $35,000. The most suitable method for initial contact by those seeking employment is to mail a resume with a covering letter. *Contacts:* Corinne McDonald, Human Resources or Donna Duke, Human Resources.

CHILDREN'S HOSPITAL OF EASTERN ONTARIO
401 Smyth Road
Ottawa, ON K1H 8L1

Tel. 613-737-2681
Fax 613-738-4803

The Children's Hospital of Eastern Ontario (CHEO) is an acute care, teaching hospital employing approximately 2,000 people. Graduates most likely to be hired come from the following academic areas: Bachelor of Science (Nursing, Occupational Therapy, Dietician, Pharmacy), Masters (Social Work, Speech Pathology, Audiology), and Community College Diploma (Laboratory Technologist, Radiology Technologist, RN, RPN). Company benefits are rated above average. The potential for advancement is listed as average. The average annual starting salary falls within the $30,000 to $35,000 range. The most suitable method for initial contact by those seeking employment is to mail a resume with a covering letter. The Children's Hospital of Eastern Ontario does hire a limited number of summer students annually. *Contact:* Managing Director, Patient Support Units.

CHOREO SYSTEMS INC.
1300 - 112 Kent Street
Ottawa, ON K1P 5P2

Tel. 613-238-1050
Fax 613-238-4453
Email .... jenmw@choreosystems.com
Website .... www.choreosystems.com

Choreo Systems Inc. is a network integration company providing a comprehensive suite of interoperability, intranet and communication security software and technical services. There are 33 employees at this location, and a total of 41 employees in Canada. Graduates most likely to be hired come from the following academic areas: Bachelor of Science (Computer Science), Master of Science (Computer Science), and Community College Diploma (Computer Science, Engineering Technician). Graduates would occupy Product Support Specialist - Response Services, Project Specialist - Engineering Services, Inside Sales Representative, and Account Executive positions. Team player, good interpersonal skills, ambitious, driven, organized, and good communication skills are all listed as desirable non-academic qualifications. Company benefits are rated above average. The potential for advancement is listed as being good. The most suitable method for initial contact by those seeking employment is to mail a resume with a covering letter. *Contact:* Jennifer Wishart, Human Resources Specialist.

CHRISTIAN HORIZONS
384 Arthur Street South
Elmira, ON N3B 2P4

Tel. 519-669-1571
Fax 519-669-1574
Website .... www.domino.christian-horizons.org

Christian Horizons is a non-denominational evangelical not-for-profit organization supporting individuals with developmental disabilities across Ontario through the provision of residential and other support services. The Organization employs approximately 1,500 people throughout Ontario, including full-time, part-time, and relief staff. Graduates most likely to be hired come from the following academic areas: Bachelor of Arts (General, Psychology, Recreation Studies, Sociology/Social Work), Bachelor of Science (Computer Science), Bachelor of Education (Special Needs), Community College Diploma (Accounting, Business, Social Work/DSW, Health/Home Care Aide, Nursing RN), and High School Diploma. Graduates would occupy Residential Counsellor, Relief Counsellor, Program Manager, and Administrative Support positions in Accounting, Human Resources and Administration. Leadership skills, patient, dependable, responsible, professional, organized, diligent, flexible, adaptable, confident, and good oral and written communication skills are all listed as desirable non-academic qualifications. Company benefits are rated as industry standard. The potential for advancement is listed as being good. The average annual starting salary falls within the $20,000 to $25,000 range. The most suitable method for initial contact by those seeking employment is to mail a resume with a covering letter. Christian Horizons does hire summer students. *Contacts:* Coordinator of Services and Supports, Human Resources or Human Resources Generalist.

CHRYSLER CANADA LTD. - ETOBICOKE CASTING PLANT
15 Browns Line
Toronto, ON M8W 3S3

Tel. 416-253-2310
Fax 416-253-2317

The Chrysler Canada Ltd. - Etobicoke Casting Plant is an aluminum casting plant for automotive castings. There are more than 250 people employed at this location. Graduates most likely to be hired come from the following academic areas: Bachelor of Science (Chemistry, Metallurgy), Bachelor of Engineering (Mechanical, Electrical), Bachelor of Commerce/Business Administration (Accounting), Certified Management Accountant, and Master of Business Administration (Information Systems). Graduates would occupy supervisory production and maintenance positions for engineering projects, and a variety of staff positions. Applicants should not mind working on the production floor. Company benefits and the potential for advancement are both rated as excellent. The average annual starting salary falls within the $25,000 to $30,000 range. The most suitable method for initial contact by graduates seeking employment is to mail a resume with a covering letter. The Etobicoke Casting Plant does hire summer students on a limited basis. *Contact:* Personnel Manager.

CHUBB SECURITY CANADA INC.
5201 Explorer Drive
Mississauga, ON L4W 4H1

Tel. 905-629-2600
Fax 905-206-8480
Website .... www.chubbsecurity.com

Chubb Security Canada Inc. is involved in the design, development and manufacture of security related products. Products include Alarm, Access Control, and Software Security systems. There are more than 250 employees at this location. Graduates most likely to be hired come from the following academic areas: Bachelor of Arts (General), Bachelor of Science (Computer Science), Bachelor of Engineering (Computer Systems), Bachelor of Commerce/Business Administration (Accounting, Marketing, Finance), Certified Management Accountant (Finance), Certified General Accountant (Finance), Master of Business Administration, and Community College Diploma (Marketing/Sales, Secretarial, Security/Enforcement, Computer Science, Electronics). Graduates are hired for entry level positions in Sales, Marketing, Finance, Systems Design, Administration, and Support. A sales focus, customer orientation, creativity and flexibility are all listed as desirable non-academic qualifications. Company benefits are rated above average. The potential for advancement is listed as being good. The average annual

starting salary falls within the $25,000 to $40,000 range. The most suitable method for initial contact by those seeking employment is to mail a resume with a covering letter. Chubb Security Canada Inc. does hire summer and co-op work term students. *Contact:* Human Resources Group - Recruitment.

CIBC WORLD MARKETS - CIBC WOOD GUNDY
181 Bay Street, Suite 3800
Toronto, ON M5J 2J3

Tel. 416-307-3204
Fax 416-368-0859
Website .... www.cibcwm.com

CIBC Wood Gundy is the Canadian operation of CIBC World Markets, the global investment banking arm of the Canadian Imperial Bank of Commerce (CIBC). CIBC Wood Gundy provides clients with advice and capital from an integrated platform of product and industry groups. In recent years, the company has dramatically enhanced its capabilities through the strategic acquisition of companies and talent. CIBC World Markets employs over 8,000 people worldwide. Graduates most likely to be hired come from the following academic areas: Bachelor of Arts (Economics), Bachelor of Science (Computer Science, Mathematics), Bachelor of Engineering (Computer Systems, Telecommunications, Forest Resources, Mining, Petroleum), Bachelor of Laws (Corporate), Bachelor of Commerce/Business Administration (Accounting, Finance, Marketing), Chartered Accountant, Certified Management Accountant, Certified General Accountant, Master of Business Administration (Finance), and CSC and CPH designations. Strong analytical and effective interpersonal skills are listed as desirable non-academic qualifications. Company benefits are rated above average. The potential for advancement is listed as being good. The most suitable method for initial contact by graduates seeking employment is to mail a resume with a covering letter. CIBC Wood Gundy does hire summer students. Resumes for summer positions are accepted beginning in February. *Contacts:* Bella Chow, Staffing Consultant or Sandra Smit, Staffing Consultant.

CIGNA INSURANCE COMPANY OF CANADA
2 First Canadian Place
Exchange Tower, 12th Floor, P.O. Box 18
Toronto, ON M5X 1A8

Tel. 416-368-2911

CIGNA Insurance Company of Canada is a large commercial insurance company employing more than 100 people at this location. It is part of CIGNA Corporation, with assets in excess of $58 billion. Graduates most likely to be hired come from the following academic areas: Bachelor of Commerce/Business Administration, Chartered Accountant, Certified Management Accountant, and Community College Diploma (General,Insurance). Graduates would occupy positions Accounting, Underwriting and Administration positions. Applicants should be bright, willing and able to work under pressure. Company benefits are rated as excellent. The potential for advancement is listed as being good. The average annual starting salary falls within the $15,000 to $20,000 range, and is dependent upon the position being considered. The most suitable method for initial contact by graduates seeking employment is to mail a resume with a covering letter. CIGNA Insurance Company of Canada does hire summer students. *Contact:* Human Resources.

CIMMETRY SYSTEMS, INC.
6700 Cote-de-Liesse, Suite 206
St-Laurent, QC H4T 2B5

Tel.	514-735-3219
Fax	514-735-6440
Email	resumes@cimmetry.com
Website	www.cimmetry.com

Cimmetry Systems, Inc. (CSI) is a world leader in the development of Viewing and Mark-up software. CSI targets worldwide markets in CAD, Document Management, Engineering, Imaging, and Workflow. Products are available in several languages to corporate customers in over 50 countries. Graduates most likely to be hired come from the following academic areas: Bachelor of Arts (General), Bachelor of Engineering (General, Electrical, Computer Systems), Bachelor of Commerce/Business Administration (Marketing), Master of Business Administration (Marketing), Community College Diploma (Administration, Business, Marketing/Sales, Secretarial, Computer Science), and High School Diploma. Graduates would occupy Software Developer, Technical Support, Inside Sales, Marketing, and General Office Clerk positions. Autonomous, organized, proficiency in English, previous work experience in the computer/software industry, and interested in a dynamic, challenging and fast paced career are all listed as desirable non-academic qualifications. Company benefits are rated as industry standard. The potential for advancement is listed as average. The average annual starting salary falls within the $20,000 to $45,000 range, depending on the position being considered. The most suitable methods for initial contact by those seeking employment are to mail or fax a resume with a covering letter. Cimmetry Systems, Inc. does hire summer students. *Contact:* Gabriel Takacs, Personnel Manager.

CINRAM VIDEO CENTRE
5590 Finch Avenue East
Toronto, ON M1B 1T1

Tel.	416-332-9000
Fax	416-332-9018
Website	www.cinram.ca

Cinram Video Centre is a high tech manufacturer of compact discs CD's, CD ROM's, video and audio tapes. The company employs 400 people at this location, a total of 900 people in Canada, and 2,800 people worldwide. Graduates most likely to be hired come from the following academic areas: Bachelor of Commerce/Business Administration (Accounting, Human Resources), Certified General Accountant,

Community College Diploma (CAD/CAM/Autocad, Engineering Technician), and High School Diploma. Dedication and stability are both listed as desirable non-academic qualifications. Company benefits are rated above average. The potential for advancement is listed as being good. The average annual starting salary falls within the $25,000 to $30,000 range. The most suitable method for initial contact by those seeking employment is to mail a resume with a covering letter. Cinram Video Centre does hire summer students. *Contact:* Cheryl Givelas, Manager, Human Resources.

CIRCON TECHNOLOGY CORPORATION
1503 Cliveden Avenue
Delta, BC V3M 6P7

Tel.	604-521-9162
Fax	604-521-9168

Circon Technology Corporation is involved in the development and marketing of building automation systems. Circon's mission is to apply the latest technologies to help building owners, managers and systems integrators cost-effectively meet the demands of modern building automation. The company employs approximately 20 people. Graduates most likely to be hired come from the following academic areas: Bachelor of Science (Computer Science), Bachelor of Engineering (Architectural/Building, Computer Systems, Telecommunications, Industrial Design, Industrial Production), Master of Engineering (Building Automation), and Community College Diploma (Facility Management, CAD/CAM/ Autocad, Computer Science, Engineering Technician, HVAC Systems). Work experience with a start-up company, dynamic, multi-tasking capabilities, and able to work well in a team environment are listed as desirable non-academic qualifications. Company benefits are rated as excellent. The potential for advancement is listed as being good. The most suitable method for initial contact by those seeking employment is to mail a resume with a covering letter. Circon Technology Corporation does hire summer students. *Contact:* Nicola Mancey, Controller.

the citadel

CITADEL GENERAL ASSURANCE COMPANY, THE
1075 Bay Street
Toronto, ON M5S 2W5

Tel.	416-928-5586
Fax	416-928-1553

The Citadel General Assurance Company employs more than 250 people in the provision of commercial and personal automobile and property insurance, as well as special risk insurance. Graduates most likely to be hired come from the following academic areas: Bachelor of Arts (General), Bachelor of Commerce/Business Administration, and Community College Diploma (Accounting, Administration, Business, Insurance, Secretarial, Human Resources). Preference is given to graduates who possess or are working toward the AIIC designation. Graduates would occupy Claims Adjuster Trainee, Underwriter Trainee, and Accounting Clerk positions. Flexible, an ability to think independently, good problem solving and communication skills, able to work well with others, and committed to life long learning are all listed as desirable non-academic qualifications. Company benefits are rated above average. The potential for advancement is listed as being good. The average annual starting salary falls within the $20,000 to $25,000 range. The most suitable method for initial contact by those seeking employment is to mail a resume with a covering letter. The Citadel General Assurance Company does hire summer students, preferring repeat students from previous years. *Contact:* Yvonne Smith, Human Resources Specialist.

CLEARNET COMMUNICATIONS INC.

300 Consilium Place, 9th Floor
Toronto, ON M1H 3G2

Tel.	416-296-7836
Fax	416-296-7835
Email	shirleenw@clearnetbc.com
Website	www.clearnet.com

Clearnet Communications Inc. is a leading Canadian wireless communications company. Clearnet is unique in offering Canadians two state-of-the-art digital wireless communications services, Mike for business people, and Clearnet PCS for consumers. Mike is a fully digital service that offers business workgroups the ability to save time and money by integrating Mike's Direct Connect two-way radio mobile digital phone, text messaging with acknowledgment (paging) and internet communications - all in a single handset operating on a single wireless network. Clearnet PCS offers Canadian consumers the easiest-to-use and easiest-to-buy digital wireless communications product in the country. Utilizing a dual-mode, dual-band digital PCS/analogue cellular phone that works everywhere in Canada that cellular does, Clearnet PCS offers affordable talktime plans, fair per second billing and extra calling features included without additional charge. Clearnet employs 1,120 people at this location, and more than 2,000 people in Canada. Graduates most likely to be hired come from the following academic areas: Bachelor of Arts (French, Languages), Bachelor of Science (Computer Science), Bachelor of Engineering (General, Electrical, Computer Systems, Engineering Physics, Industrial Engineering, Telecommunications), Bachelor of Education (Adult), Bachelor of Laws, Bachelor of Commerce/Business Administration (General, Accounting, Finance, Human Resources, Information Systems, Marketing), Chartered Accountant, Certified Management Accountant, Certified General Accountant, Master of Business Administration (General, Accounting, Finance, Human Resources, Information Systems, Marketing), and Community College Diploma (Accounting, Administration, Advertising, Business, Communications/

Public Relations, Facility Management, Financial Planning, Human Resources, Information Systems, Marketing/Sales, Purchasing/Logistics, Secretarial, Electronics Technician, Engineering Technician). Graduates would occupy SAP Analyst, Accounts Receivable, Computing Support Team Leader, Information Resources Manager, Account Executive, Channel Business Analyst, Client Business Analyst, Bilingual Internet Communications Specialist, and Network Engineer positions. Strong communication skills, team player, bilingual (French, Mandarin, Cantonese), computer literacy (eg. Windows environment, Word, Excel, PowerPoint), organized, and strong interpersonal skills are all listed as desirable non-academic qualifications. Company benefits are rated as excellent. The potential for advancement is listed as being good. The most suitable method for initial contact by those seeking employment is through the company's website at www.clearnet.com. Clearnet Communications Inc. does hire students for summer and co-op work terms. *Contact:* Human Resources.

CLOSER TO HOME COMMUNITY SERVICES

1610 - 37th Street S.W., Suite 206
Calgary, AB T3C 3P1

Tel.	403-543-0550
Fax	403-246-6406

Closer To Home Community Services is a non-profit organization which provides counselling, training and placement services for children with behavioral and emotional problems. The agency operates family support programs, family resource centres, group homes, foster care and a semi-independent living program. Closer To Home Community Services employs 70 individuals. Graduates most likely to be hired come from the following academic areas: Bachelor of Arts (Psychology, Social Work), Bachelor of Science (Psychology), Bachelor of Education (Special Needs), Master of Arts (Psychology, Social Work), Master of Science (Psychology), and Community College Diploma (Social Work/DSW). Graduates would occupy Counsellor, Family Counsellor, Social Worker, and Case worker positions. A good attitude towards learning and performance evaluations, optimistic, and flexible are all listed as desirable non-academic qualifications. Company benefits are rated above average. The potential for advancement is listed as excellent. The average annual starting salary falls within the $25,000 to $30,000 range. The most suitable method for initial contact by those seeking employment is to mail a resume with a covering letter. Closer To Home Community Services does hire summer students. *Contact:* Larry Mathieson, MBA, Operations Director.

CLUB MONACO INTERNATIONAL

430 King Street West
Toronto, ON M5V 1L5

Tel.	416-585-4896
Fax	416-585-4176
Email	recruitment@clubmonaco.com
Website	www.clubmonaco.com

Club Monaco is a brand of fresh, modern products for men, women, boys and girls, sold exclusively in 115 Club Monaco stores worldwide. The Club Monaco brand encompasses products ranging from clothing and accessories to eyewear, watches, cosmetics, silver jewellry and items for the home. Based in Toronto, the Club Monaco World Headquarters employs more than 100 people in the design, development and marketing of the Club Monaco brand internationally. Graduates most likely to be hired come from the following academic areas: Bachelor of Arts (Journalism), Bachelor of Commerce/Business Administration (Accounting, Finance, Human Resources, Information Systems, Marketing), and Community College Diploma (Accounting, Administration, Communications/Public Relations, Human Resources, Information Systems, Marketing/Sales, Real Estate Sales, Secretarial, Fashion Arts, Graphic Arts, Journalism). At the World Headquarters, graduates would occupy Accounting and Finance, Advertising and Marketing, Buying and Product Development, Communications, Design Team, Distribution and Traffic, Franchise, Human Resources, Information Technology, Loss Prevention, Merchandise Planning and Analysis, Real Estate and Leasing, Technical and Quality Control, and Visual Merchandising and Presentation positions. At Store locations, graduates would occupy Sales Associate, Stock Person, Cashier, In-Store Visual Presentation Technician, Make-up Specialist, Assistant Store Manager, Store Manager, Product Manager, Sales and Resource Manager, General Manager, District Manager, and Regional Manager positions. Company benefits are rated as industry standard and include a discount on Club Monaco merchandise, bonuses that reward outstanding performance, employee referral bonuses, group insurance benefits and more. The potential for advancement is listed as excellent. The average annual starting salary varies according to the position being considered. For opportunities at the Club Monaco Headquarters, the most suitable methods for initial contact by those seeking employment are to mail or fax a resume with a covering letter. For a list of current job opportunities at the Toronto Headquarters, applicants should visit the company's website at www.clubmonaco.com. For Store opportunities candidates should apply directly to the store of their choice, see website for the nearest location. Club Monaco International does hire students for summer and co-op work terms. *Contact:* The Recruitment Team.

CML TECHNOLOGIES
75 Boul. de la Technologie
Hull, QC J8Z 3G4

Tel. 819-778-2053
Fax 819-778-3408
Email .... cmlhr@cmltech.com
Website .... www.cmltech.com

Since 1979, CML has evolved into a recognized leader in specialized areas of the international telecommunications industry. CML has steadily grown into a multi-million dollar enterprise, and employs a staff of over 150, and growing. Headquarters within North America are found in Hull, Quebec, and Atlanta, Georgia, while numerous office are throughout the United States. CML's exceptional product lines include mobile radio consoles, enhanced 911 emergency calling systems, and other specialized switching systems for customized computer telephony applications. Products and services are sold through major organizations in the telecommunications industry, as well as directly through CML's own sales network. Graduates most likely to be hired come from the following academic areas: Bachelor of Science (Computer Science), Bachelor of Engineering (Electrical), Bachelor of Commerce/Business Administration (Finance, Marketing), Master of Business Administration (Finance, Marketing), Bachelor of Arts (Technical Writing), and Community College Diploma (Accounting, Administration, Computer Science, Electronics Technician, Engineering Technician, Technical Writing). Graduates would occupy software Designer, Hardware Designer, Technician, Market Specialist, Project Coordinator (Technical), and Technical Writer positions. Team player, good work ethic, and initiative are listed as desirable non-academic qualifications. Company benefits are rated as industry standard. The potential for advancement is listed as excellent. The average annual starting salary falls within the $35,000 to $40,000 range. The most suitable methods for initial contact by those seeking employment are to mail, fax, or e-mail a resume with a covering letter, or by applying through the company's website at www.cmltech.com. CML Technologies does hire summer and co-op work term students. *Contact:* Human Resources Department.

CO-OP ATLANTIC
123 Halifax Street, P.O. Box 750
Moncton, NB E1C 8N5

Tel. 506-858-6028
Fax 506-858-6473

Co-op Atlantic is a regional co-operative wholesaler and supplier of farm inputs, providing services and products to its member owned co-ops in the Atlantic provinces and the Magdalen Islands. Co-op Atlantic supplies 160 retail and agricultural co-ops, buying clubs, and agricultural societies. In addition, 25 other associated co-operatives are also members of Co-op Atlantic. Co-op Atlantic employs approximately 700 people throughout the Maritime region. Graduates most likely to be hired come from the following academic areas: Bachelor of Arts (Graphic Arts, Journalism, Languages), Bachelor of Science (Computer Science), Bachelor of Engineering (Environmental), Bachelor of Commerce/Business Administration (General, Accounting, Finance, Human Resources, Information Systems, Marketing), Chartered Accountant, Certified Management Accountant, Certified General Accountant, Master of Business Administration (Accounting, Finance, Human Resources, Information Systems, Marketing), Community College Diploma (Accounting, Administration, Advertising, Business, Communications, Facility Management, Financial Planning, Human Resources, Marketing, Purchasing/Logistics, Secretarial, Graphic Arts, Journalism, Computer Science), and High School Diploma. Graduates would occupy Communications Officer, Typesetter, Member Relations Officer, Analyst Programmer, Engineering Technologist, Accountant, Mechanic, Distribution, Administration, and various Retail positions. Good communication and interpersonal skills, team player, analytical, organized and good supervisory skills are all listed as desirable non-academic skills. Company benefits are rated as excellent. The potential for advancement is listed as being good. The average annual starting salary falls within the $25,000 to $35,000 range, depending on the position being considered. The most suitable method for initial contact by those seeking employment is to mail a resume with a covering letter. Co-op Atlantic does hire summer students. *Contact:* Angela Vautour, Human Resources Area Manager.

CO-OPERATIVE TRUST CO. OF CANADA
333 - 3rd Avenue North
Saskatoon, SK   S7K 2M2

Tel.	306-956-1800
Fax	306-244-1704

Co-operative Trust Co. of Canada provides financial services and products such as mortgages, deferred income products, deposits, estate planning and administration. There are 125 employees at this location, and a total of 200 employees in Canada. Graduates most likely to be hired come from the following academic areas: Bachelor of Commerce/Business Administration (Accounting, Finance, Human Resources, Information Systems, Marketing, Public Administration), Chartered Accountant, Certified Management Accountant, Certified General Accountant, Master of Business Administration, and Community College Diploma (Accounting, Administration, Advertising, Business, Communications, Financial Planning, Human Resources, Marketing/Sales, Secretarial). Initiative and strong interpersonal skills are both listed as desirable non-academic qualifications. Company benefits are rated as excellent. The potential for advancement is listed as being good. The average annual starting salary falls within the $20,000 to $25,000 range. The most suitable method for initial contact by those seeking employment is to mail a resume with a covering letter. Co-operative Trust Co. of Canada does hire summer students. *Contact:* Maryann Deutscher, Manager, Human Resources.

COATS PATONS
1001 Roselawn Avenue
Toronto, ON   M6B 1B8

Tel.	416-782-4481
Fax	416-782-8982

Coats Patons is a manufacturer and distributor of hand knitting yarns and sewing aids. There are approximately 240 employees at this location, 300 employees across Canada, and over 60,000 employees worldwide. Graduates most likely to be hired come from the following academic areas: Bachelor of Engineering (Electrical, Computer Systems, Mechanical, Industrial), Bachelor of Commerce/Business Administration (Finance, Marketing), and Community College Diploma (Marketing/Sales, Purchasing/Logistics, Welding). Graduates would occupy Management Trainee positions. Excellent communication skills, motivation, drive, team player and the flexibility to fit into a multicultural work environment are all listed as desirable non-academic qualifications. Company benefits are rated above average. The potential for advancement is listed as being good. The average annual starting salary falls within the $25,000 to $30,000 range. The most suitable method for initial contact by those seeking employment is to mail a resume with a covering letter. Coats Patons does hire summer students, usually I.E. and third year Electrical and Mechanical Engineering students. *Contacts:* Silvana Morra or Josie Ricci.

COCHRANE GROUP
1230 Blackfoot Drive, Suite 200
Regina, SK   S4S 7G4

Tel.	306-585-1990
Fax	306-586-1560

Cochrane Group provides various engineering services, and is associated with SNC-Lavalin Inc. Cochrane Group employs 70 people at this location, 104 people across Canada, and 156 people worldwide. Graduates most likely to be hired come from the following academic areas: Bachelor of Science (Agriculture, Computer Science), Bachelor of Engineering (Architectural/Building, Surveying, Electrical, Instrumentation, Power, Mechanical, Industrial Design, Environmental, Water Resources), and Community College Diploma (Accounting, Secretarial, Architecture/Drafting, CAD/CAM/Autocad, Computer Science, HVAC Systems). Graduates would occupy Engineer and Technologist positions. An entrepreneurial spirit, initiative, and previous work experience are all listed as desirable non-academic qualifications. Company benefits are rated as excellent. The potential for advancement is listed as being good. The average annual starting salary is dependent upon the position being considered and the applicants qualifications. The most suitable method for initial contact by those seeking employment is to mail a resume with a covering letter. The Cochrane Group does hire a limited number of summer students annually. *Contact:* Human Resources Manager.

COGNOS INCORPORATED
3755 Riverside Drive, P.O. Box 9707
Ottawa, ON   K1G 4K9

Tel.	613-738-1440
Fax	613-738-0002
Email	jobs@cognos.com
Website	www.cognos.com

Cognos is active in developing, marketing and supporting advanced application development tools and reporting applications that run on a wide range of proprietary and industry standard platforms, providing end users with direct access to the critical business information they need. The company employs approximately 466 people at this location, a total of 562 in Canada, and 1,010 people worldwide. Graduates most likely to be hired come from the following academic areas: Bachelor of Arts (Graphic Arts), Bachelor of Science (Computer Science, Mathematics), Bachelor of Engineering (Electrical, Computer Systems), Bachelor of Commerce/Business Administration (Accounting, Finance, Human Resources, Information Systems, Marketing), Chartered Accountant, Certified Management Accountant, Certified General Accountant, Master of Business Administration (Finance, Information Systems, Marketing), Master of Science (Computer Science), and Community College Diploma (Accounting, Financial Planning, Human Resources, Marketing/Sales, Computer Science, Engineering Technician). Graduates would occupy Software Engineer, Technical Analyst, Programmer Analyst, Software Architect, Computer Operator, Quality Control Analyst, Marketing Specialist, Accountant, Writer, Editor, Customer Support, Education Specialist, Marketing Specialist, Sales Representative, Public Relations Specialist, and Translator positions. An ability to work in a team environment, positive attitude, good verbal and written communication skills, love of learning, and demonstrated prior success are all listed as desirable non-academic qualifications. Company benefits and the potential for advancement are both rated as excellent. The average annual starting salary falls within the $25,000 to $35,000 range. The most suitable methods for initial contact by those seeking employment are to mail or e-mail a resume with a covering letter. Cognos does hire summer students, mainly those enrolled in university and college. *Contact:* Human Resoucers (Corporate).

COLE, SHERMAN & ASSOCIATES LTD.
75 Commerce Valley Drive East
Thornhill, ON L3T 7N9

Tel. 905-882-4401
Fax 905-882-4399

Cole, Sherman & Associates Ltd. employs 125 people in the provision of consulting engineering, architectural and planning services. In addition, there are 10 employees located outside of Canada. Graduates most likely to be hired come from the following academic areas: Bachelor of Arts (Graphic Arts), Bachelor of Science (Computer Science), Bachelor of Engineering (Civil, Architectural/Building), Bachelor of Architecture, Bachelor of Landscape Architecture, Master of Engineering (Structural, Transportation), Doctorate (Structural Engineering), and Community College Diploma (Computer Science, HVAC Systems). Company benefits and the potential for advancement are both rated as excellent. The average annual starting salary falls within the $25,000 to $35,000 range. The most suitable method for initial contact by graduates seeking employment is to mail a resume with a covering letter. Cole, Sherman & Associates Ltd. does hire a limited number of summer students annually. *Contact:* Paul N. Kikot, Personnel Manager.

CP COLGATE-PALMOLIVE CANADA INC.
TORONTO, CANADA M4G 2H6

COLGATE-PALMOLIVE CANADA INC.
99 Vanderhoof Avenue
Toronto, ON M4G 2H6

Tel. 416-421-6000
Fax 416-421-0286

Colgate-Palmolive Canada Inc. is a major manufacturer of household goods such as soaps, cleaners, detergents, toiletries, etc. The company employs 150 people at this location, and a total of 500 people in Canada. Graduates most likely to be hired come from the following academic areas: Bachelor of Science (Chemistry), Bachelor of Engineering (Chemical), Bachelor of Commerce/Business Administration (Accounting, Information Systems), Chartered Accountant, Certified Management Accountant, Certified General Accountant, Master of Business Administration (Finance, Marketing), and Community College Diploma (Human Resources, Secretarial, Laboratory Technician). Graduates would occupy Product Assistant (Marketing), Laboratory Technician, and Clerical (Finance) positions. Previous work experience, team player, and leadership skills are listed as desirable non-academic qualifications. The most suitable method for initial contact by those seeking employment is to mail a resume with a covering letter. *Contact:* Rob Madeley, Manager Human Resources.

COLONIA LIFE INSURANCE COMPANY
2 St. Clair Avenue East, Suite 6/F
Toronto, ON M4T 2V6

Tel. 416-960-3601
Fax 416-960-5291

COLONIA Life Insurance Company is involved in the sale of individual life insurance, annuities and segregated funds through brokers and independent agents from coast to coast. The company currently employs a total of 95 people. Graduates most likely to be hired come from the following academic areas: Bachelor of Science (Actuarial, Computer Science, Mathematics), Bachelor of Commerce/Business Administration (Accounting, Finance, Information Systems, Marketing), Master of Business Administration (Marketing), Community College Diploma (Administration, Business, Secretarial), and High School Diploma. Graduates would occupy Technician, Administrator, Analyst, Coordinator, and Assistant positions. Previous work experience, self-starters, good oral and written communication skills, excellent interpersonal skills, working knowledge of the French language, and life insurance experience are all listed as desirable non-academic qualifications. Company benefits are rated above average. The potential for advancement is listed as average. The average annual starting salary falls within the $20,000 to $25,000 range, depending upon qualifications. The most suitable method for initial contact by those seeking employment is to mail a resume with a covering letter. COLONIA Life Insurance Company does hire a limited number of summer students annually. *Contact:* Susan Fors, Human Resources Manager.

COLUMBIA HOUSE COMPANY, THE
5900 Finch Avenue East
Toronto, ON M1B 5X7

Tel. 416-299-9400
Fax 416-299-7491
Website .... www.columbiahouse.com

The Columbia House Company is involved in direct mail order marketing of music and video entertainment products. The company employs approximately 420 people at this location, and a total of 5,000 employees worldwide. Operational activities include repertoire selection for new releases, marketing, and distribution. Graduates most likely to be hired come from the following academic areas: Bachelor of Arts (Journalism, Music), Bachelor of Commerce/Business Administration (Accounting, Marketing), Chartered Accountant (Finance), Certified General Accountant, Community College Diploma (Accounting, Business, Marketing/Sales, Purchasing/Logistics, Secretarial, Graphic Design), and High School Diploma. Graduates would occupy positions in Customer Service, Purchasing/Order Inventory, Graphic Arts, Desk-Top Publishing, Marketing, and Distribution. Strong verbal and written communication skills, familiarity with Lotus 123, music background and musical interests are all listed as desirable non-academic qualifications. Company benefits are rated above average. The potential for advancement is listed as average. The average annual starting salary falls within the $22,000 to $25,000 range for clerical positions, and within the $25,000 to $30,000 range for management positions. The most suitable method for initial contact by those seeking employment is to mail a resume with a covering letter. *Contacts:* Jan Thompson, CHRP, Director of Personnel or Michelle Lobez, Recruitment Manager.

COM DEV
155 Sheldon Drive
Cambridge, ON N1R 7H6

Tel. 519-622-2300
Fax 519-622-5543

COM DEV is a Canadian company, and world leader in satellite communications, and remote sensing technology. There are more than 400 employees at this location. Graduates most likely to be hired come from the following academic areas: Bachelor of Science (Computer Science, Mathematics, Physics), Bachelor of Engineering (Computer Systems, Electrical, Industrial, Mechanical), Master of Engineering (Mechanical, Electrical, Aeronautics), and Community College Diploma (Administration, Purchasing/Logistics, Secretarial, Electronics). Graduates would occupy Engineer, Technologist, Secretary, Programmer, and Systems Analyst positions. Possessing good, relevant work experience is a definite asset. Company benefits are rated above average. The potential for advancement is listed as being good. The most suitable method for initial contact by those

seeking employment is to mail a resume with a covering letter. COM DEV does hire a few summer students annually. *Contact:* Recruitment Specialist.

COMCARE/MED-CARE HEALTH SERVICES
2300 Yonge Street, Suite 904, P.O. Box 2341
Toronto, ON M4P 1E4

Tel. 416-484-4433
Fax 416-484-4636

Comcare/Med-Care Health Services is a Canadian leader in delivering innovative health care services. The company offers a comprehensive range of services provided 24 hours a day, 7 days a week including nursing visits, foot care services, occupational nursing, palliative care, home support services, occupational and physiotherapy services. There are approximately 250 employees at this location and 1,500 employees across Canada. Graduates most likely to be hired come from the following academic areas: Bachelor of Arts (General), Bachelor of Science (Nursing, Occupational Therapy, Physical Therapy), Bachelor of Education (Special Needs), and Community College Diploma (Business, Nursing RN, Nursing RNA). Graduates would occupy supervisor, field staff, and marketing positions. Team player, highly motivated, creative, and excellent organizational skills are all listed as desirable non-academic qualifications. Company benefits are rated as industry standard. The potential for advancement is listed as average. The most suitable methods for initial contact by those seeking employment are to mail or fax a resume with a covering letter. Comcare/Med-Care Health Services does hire summer students. (Other Locations: Comcare/Med-Care Health Services, 2130 Lawrence Avenue East, Suite 404, Scarborough, ON, M1R 3A6, Phone 416-759-8242, Fax 416-759-9677; Comcare/Med-Care Health Services, 720 Spadina Avenue, Suite 409, Toronto, ON, M5S 2T9, Phone 416-929-3364, Fax 416-929-1738). *Contact:* Human Resources.

COMINCO LTD.
200 Burrard Street
Vancouver, BC V6C 3L7

Tel. 604-682-0611
Fax 604-685-3019
Website .... www.cominco.com

Cominco Ltd. is an integrated natural resource company whose principle activities are mineral exploration, mining, smelting, and refining. Cominco Ltd. employs approximately 100 employees at this location, a total of 4,000 across Canada, and 5,500 employees worldwide. Graduates most likely to be hired come from the following academic areas: Bachelor of Science (Geology), and Bachelor of Engineering (Chemical, Materials Science, Metallurgy, Mining). Graduates are hired for Geologist and Engineer-in-training positions. Enthusiasm, flexibility, a strong work ethic, and related work experience are all listed as desirable non-academic qualifications. Company benefits and the potential for advancement are both listed as excellent. The average annual starting salary falls within the $35,000 to $40,000 range. The most suitable method for initial contact by those seeking employment is to mail a resume with a covering letter. Cominco Ltd. does hire summer students. *Contact:* Human Resources.

COMMUNITY CARE ACCESS CENTRE OF PEEL
2227 South Millway, Suite 202
Mississauga, ON L5L 3R6

Tel.	905-628-1177
Fax	905-820-3368

The Community Care Access Centre of Peel is a new and exciting not-for-profit organization which plays a leading role in managing and providing community based healthcare and long term care services in the Region of Peel. The centre employs a total of 200 people. Graduates most likely to be hired come from the following academic areas: Bachelor of Arts (Communications, Journalism), Bachelor of Science (Nursing), Bachelor of Commerce/Business Administration (Human Resources, Information Systems), Certified Management Accountant, Certified General Accountant, and Community College Diploma (Accounting, Human Resources, Information Systems, Secretarial, Public Health Nurse). Graduates would occupy Case Manager, Accounting, Communications, and Administrative Support positions. Team player, community nursing experience, an ability to manage multiple priorities, and good communication skills are all listed as desirable non-academic qualifications. Company benefits are rated above average. The potential for advancement is listed as average. The average annual starting salary falls within the $30,000 to $35,000 range. The most suitable method for initial contact by those seeking employment is to mail a resume with a covering letter. *Contact:* Human Resources Associate.

COMMUNITY LIVING LONDON
190 Adelaide Street South
London, ON N5Z 3L1

Tel.	519-686-3000
Fax	519-686-5490

Community Living London is active in supporting persons with developmental challenges within the community. Support services include accommodations, vocational, employment, leisure, nursery school, and senior's support services. Community Living London employs 380 people. Graduates most likely to be hired come from the following academic areas: Bachelor of Arts (General, Psychology, Sociology), Bachelor of Science (Psychology), Bachelor of Education (Early Childhood ECE, Special Needs), and Developmental Service Worker. Graduates would occupy the following positions: Support Worker (to work with developmentally challenged children and adults), and Family Support Worker (to work with families). Previous experience with developmentally challenged individuals, team player, and excellent communication skills are listed as desirable non-academic qualifications. Company benefits are rated above average. The potential for advancement is listed as average. The average annual starting salary for full time staff falls within the $25,000 to $30,000 range (staff generally must work part time initially). The most suitable method for initial contact by those seeking employment is to mail a resume with a covering letter. *Contact:* Human Resources.

COMMUNITY LIVING MISSISSAUGA
755 The Queensway East
Mississauga, ON L4Y 4C5

Tel.	905-275-4705
Fax	905-566-1365

Community Living Mississauga is a non profit organization providing services and support to people who have an intellectual handicap, assisting them to live and participate in community life. Support services include, group homes, supported employment, preschool, independent living, sheltered work shops, associate families, respite, and leisure. Community Living employs approximately 300 people in Mississauga. Graduates most likely to be hired come from the following academic areas: Bachelor of Arts (General, Psychology, Social Work), Bachelor of Science (Nursing, Occupational Therapy, Physical Therapy, Psychology), Bachelor of Education (Early Childhood, Adult, Physical and Health, Special Needs), Bachelor of Commerce/Business Administration (General, Accounting, Human Resources, Information Systems), Certified Management Accountant (Non-Profit), Certified General Accountant (Non-Profit), and Community College Diploma (Accounting, Business, Human Resources, Recreation Studies, Social Work, Developmental Service Worker, Nursing RN/RNA). Graduates would occupy Support Worker (assisting those who have an intellectual handicap), Management (most positions are often filled from within), and Administrative support positions. An ability to communicate with ease, empathetic, caring, considerate to people's needs, team player, enthusiastic, organized, leadership skills, flexible, and strong communication skills are all listed as desirable non-academic qualifications. Company benefits are rated as excellent. The potential for advancement is listed as average. The average annual starting salary falls within the $25,000 to $30,000 range. The most suitable method for initial contact by those seeking employment is to mail a resume with a covering letter. Summer students are hired for leisure activities. This is usually done through Support Services (905) 615-1630, and is usually completed by the end of May. *Contact:* Maria Delfino, Human Resources.

COMPAGNIE MINIERE QUÉBEC CARTIER
Route 138
Port Cartier, QC G5B 2H3

Tel.	418-768-2269
Fax	418-768-2105

Compagnie Miniere Québec Cartier operates the iron ore mine and the associated pellet plant in Port Cartier. In addition, the company is responsible for the management of the town, railway, port, etc. The company employs approximately 2,000 people. Graduates most likely to be hired come from the following academic areas: Bachelor of Science (Computer Science, Metallurgy), Bachelor of Engineering (Industrial Chemistry, Metallurgy, Electrical, Computer Systems, Instrumentation, Power, Industrial Design, Industrial Production, Marine, Welding, Mining), Bachelor of Commerce/Business Administration (Accounting, Finance, Human Resources), Master of Business Administration (Accounting, Finance), and Community College Diploma (Business, Financial Planning, Human Resources, Aircraft Maintenance, Auto Mechanic, Computer Science, Electronics Technician, Marine Engineering Technician). Previous related work experience, team player, and able to live and work in an isolated area are listed as desirable non-academic qualifications. Company benefits are rated as excellent. The potential for advancement is listed as average. The average annual starting salary falls within the $45,000 to $50,000 range. The most suitable method for initial contact by those seeking employment is via telephone. Compagnie Miniere Québec Cartier does hire summer students. *Contact:* Adelard Robicaud, Director of Employment.

COMPUSEARCH MICROMARKETING DATA AND SYSTEMS
330 Front Street West, Suite 1100
Toronto, ON M5V 3B7

Tel. 416-348-9180
Fax 416-348-9195

Compusearch Micromarketing Data and Systems conducts research and analytical studies, and is involved in the sales and marketing of demographic information as well as the development of software packages. Graduates most likely to be hired come from the following academic areas: Bachelor of Arts (Geography, Psychology), Bachelor of Science (Computer Science), Bachelor of Commerce/Business Administration (Marketing), Master of Business Administration, Masters (Geography, Statistics), Doctorate (Geography, Statistics), and Community College Diploma (Statistics/Research). Graduates would occupy Researcher, Marketing Representative, Programmer/Analyst, Product Manager, and Administrative positions. Sales ability, self-starting, management experience, analytical skills, good organizational and communication skills are all listed as desirable qualifications. Company benefits are rated above average. The potential for advancement is listed as average. The average annual starting salary falls within the $20,000 to $30,000 range. The most suitable method for initial contact by those seeking employment is to mail a resume with a covering letter. Compusearch Micromarketing Data and Systems does hire summer students. *Contact:* Administration.

COMPUTER TASK GROUP (CTG)
184 Front Street East, Suite 602
Toronto, ON M5A 4N3

Tel. 416-360-3756
Fax 416-360-3773
Email .... linda.fuhro@ctg.com
Website .... www.ctg.com

Computer Task Group (CTG) is an information technology consulting firm providing variable workforce solutions to business clients. Services provided range from high level consulting to providing technical resources with skills in both the mainframe and client server area. CTG employs 50 people across Canada, and a total of 5,000 people worldwide. Graduates most likely to be hired come from the following academic areas: Bachelor of Science (Computer Science), and Community College Diploma (Computer Science). Graduates would occupy Junior Software Engineer positions. Team player, willing to learn, and an ability to feel comfortable meeting new people and entering into new situations are all listed as desirable non-academic qualifications. Company benefits are rated above average. The potential for advancement is listed as being good. The average annual starting salary falls within the $30,000 to $35,000 range. The most suitable method for initial contact by those seeking employment is to mail a resume with a covering letter. *Contact:* Linda Fuhro, Resource Manager.

COMPUTERTIME NETWORK CORPORATION
10340, Côte de Liesse
Lachine, QC H8T 1A3

Tel. 514-633-9900

Computertime Network Corporation develops and markets software products aligned with multi-vendor Open Systems computing, 4GL and SQL relational database technologies through two major product divisions. One division specializes in systems management software products while the other specializes in packaged application software. The company was founded in 1979 and has been publicly listed in Canada (Montreal Stock Exchange) since 1986. The company employs more than 25 people at this location. Graduates most likely to be hired come from the following academic areas: Bachelor of Science (Computer Science), Bachelor of Commerce/Business Administration (Accounting, Marketing), Chartered Accountant (Finance), Certified General Accountant (Finance), Master of Business Administration (Accounting, Marketing), and Master of Science (Computer Science). Business graduates would occupy positions in Sales and Marketing, and Customer Implementation. Computer Science graduates would occupy positions as Junior Programmers, Analysts, and Designers. Company benefits are rated above average. The potential for advancement is listed as excellent. The average annual starting salary falls within the $20,000 to $25,000 range. The most suitable method for initial contact by graduates is to mail a resume with a covering letter. *Contact:* Human Resources.

COMPUTING DEVICES CANADA LTD.
3785 Richmond Road
Nepean, ON K2H 5B7

Tel. 613-596-7194
Fax 613-596-7637
Email .... doreen.pasternack@cdott.com
Website .... www.computingdevices.com

Computing Devices Canada Ltd. is one of Canada's largest hi-tech employers, with 800 employees at this location and a total of 1,500 employees in the country. The company is involved in the design and manufacturing of systems for the defense industry. This requires expertise in the areas of electrical, mechanical, and software engineering. Graduates most likely to be hired come from the following academic areas: Bachelor of Science (Computer Science), Bachelor of Engineering (Electrical, Mechanical, Computer Systems, Industrial Engineering), and Community College Diploma (Information Systems, Electronics Technician, Engineering Technician, Nursing RN). Graduates would occupy Junior Software Engineer, Junior Hardware Engineer, Manufacturing Engineer, and Technician positions. Team Player, and excellent interpersonal and communication skills are all listed as desirable non-academic qualifications. Company benefits are rated as industry standard. The potential for advancement is listed as being good. The average annual starting salary falls within the $40,000 to $45,000 range. The most suitable method for initial contact by those seeking employment is through the company's website at www.computingdevices.com. Computing Devices Canada Ltd. does hire students for summer and co-op work terms. Contact: Doreen Pasternack, Human Resources Advisor.

COMSHARE LTD.
3045 South Creek Road, Unit #10
Mississauga, ON L4X 2X6

Tel. 905-212-7700

Comshare Ltd. is involved in the development and sales of computer software. Comshare Ltd. employs more than 10 people at this location. Graduates most likely to be hired come from the following academic areas: Bachelor of Arts (Business), Bachelor of Science (General, Computer Science), Bachelor of Engineering (Computer Systems), Bachelor of Commerce/Business Administration (Finance, Marketing, Information Systems), and Master of Business Administration (Accounting, Finance, Marketing, Information Systems). Graduates are hired to occupy Associate Applications Consultant, Assistant Applications Consultant, and Sales Executive positions. Outgoing, analytical, and driven are listed as desirable non-academic qualifications. Company benefits are rated above average. The potential for advancement is listed as being good. The average annual starting salary falls within the $20,000 to $25,000 range. The most suitable method for initial contact by those seeking employment is to mail a resume with a covering letter. Contacts: Sales Director or Client Service Manager.

COMSTOCK CANADA LTD.
3455 Landmark Road
Burlington, ON L7M 1T4

Tel. 905-335-3333
Fax 905-335-4265

Comstock Canada Ltd. is involved in the full range of mechanical and electrical construction, building maintenance, power production and electrical transmission. There are approximately 700 employees at this location, a total of 1,500 in Canada, and 12,000 employees worldwide. Graduates most likely to be hired come from the following academic areas: Bachelor of Engineering (General, Chemical, Pollution Treatment, Pulp and Paper, Electrical, Automation/Robotics, Power, Mechanical, Industrial Design, Industrial Production, Welding), Bachelor of Commerce/Business Administration (General, Marketing), Master of Engineering (Electrical, Mechanical), Community College Diploma (Accounting, Administration, Business, Secretarial, Architecture/Drafting, CAD/CAM/Autocad, Engineering Technician, Welding), and High School Diploma. Graduates would occupy Estimator, Project Engineer, Project Manager, Technician, Trainee, Clerk, Accounting, and Administration positions. An insistence on quality, devotion to work, and an interest in advancement are all listed as desirable non-academic qualifications. Company benefits and the potential for advancement are both rated as excellent. The average annual starting salary falls within the $30,000 to $35,000 range, depending upon the applicants experience and ability. The most suitable method for initial contact by those seeking employment is to mail a resume with a covering letter. Comstock Canada Ltd. does hire co-op work term students. Contact: Denis Flynn, Vice President.

CON-DRAIN COMPANY (1983) LTD.
30 Floral Parkway
Concord, ON L4K 4R1

Tel. 905-669-5400
Fax 905-669-2296

Con-Drain Company (1983) Ltd. is a sewer and water main general contractor. The company employs more than 250 people. Graduates most likely to be hired come from the following academic areas: Bachelor of Engineering (Civil), Bachelor of Commerce/Business Administration (Finance, Accounting), Certified Management Accountant, and Community College Diploma (Civil Engineering). Graduates would be hired to occupy Supervisor, Project Manager, Estimator, Foreman, Controller and Purchasing Agent positions. Company benefits are rated as excellent. The potential for advancement is listed as being good. The average annual starting salary falls within the $25,000 to $30,000 range. The most suitable method for initial contact by graduates seeking employment is to mail a resume with a covering letter. Con-Drain Company (1983) Ltd. does hire summer students. Contact: Nunzio Bitondi, CMA, Controller.

CONAIR AVIATION LTD.
P.O. Box 220
Abbotsford, BC V2S 4N9

Tel.	250-855-1171
Fax	250-855-1017
Email	work@conair.ca
Website	www.conair.ca

Conair Aviation Ltd. is a privately owned company headquartered in Abbotsford, British Columbia. The 30 year old company has two key areas of business. The first area is aircraft maintenance, repair and overhaul services for commuter aircraft and narrow body jets. Conair also provides aeronautical engineering services (design, analysis, certification) and services for corporate aircraft refurbishment (paint, interiors, avionics). The second area is aircraft operations with a large fleet of airplanes and helicopters, providing specialty services such as aerial fire control, forest fertilization, oil and gas seismic exploration. Conair employs approximately 330 people. Graduates most likely to be hired come from the following academic areas: Bachelor of Engineering (Aerospace), and Community College Diploma (Aircraft Maintenance). Graduates would occupy Aircraft Maintenance Engineer positions. Team player and previous work experience are both listed as desirable non-academic qualifications. Conair is a dynamic, flexible workplace, with competitive starting salaries ($40,000 to $45,000 range) and a full benefits package. The company offers a challenging and interesting work environment, and a corporate commitment to employee training and development. Accordingly, company benefits are rated as industry standard and the potential for advancement is listed as being good. The most suitable method for initial contact by those seeking employment is to mail a resume with a covering letter. Conair Aviation Ltd. occasionally hires co-op work term students. *Contact:* Human Resources Department.

CONCORD ELEVATOR INC.
107 Alfred Kuehne Boulevard
Brampton, ON L6T 4K3

Tel.	905-791-5555
Fax	905-791-2222

Concord Elevator Inc. is involved in the manufacture of commercial and residential handicap accessibility equipment and lifts. The company has approximately 180 employees at this location and a total of 220 employees in Canada. Graduates most likely to be hired come from the following academic areas: Bachelor of Engineering (Civil, Architectural/Building, Electrical, Mechanical, Industrial Design, Industrial Production), Bachelor of Commerce/Business Administration (General, Accounting, Finance, Marketing), Master of Business Administration (General, Accounting, Finance, Marketing), and Community College Diploma (Accounting, Administration, Advertising, Business, Marketing/Sales, Purchasing/Logistics). Graduates would occupy Production Engineer, R & D Engineer, Sales and Marketing, Personnel, and Purchasing positions. Personable, ambitious, confident, team player, and good communication skills are all listed as desirable non-academic qualifications. Company benefits are rated as industry standard. The potential for advancement is listed as being good. The average annual starting salary falls within the $25,000 to $30,000 range. The most suitable method for initial contact by those seeking employment is to mail a resume with a covering letter. Concord Elevator Inc. does hire summer students for Junior Engineering positions and special projects. *Contact:* Human Resources Manager.

CONESTOGA ROVERS & ASSOCIATES
651 Colby Drive
Waterloo, ON N2V 1G2

Tel.	519-725-3313
Fax	519-725-5240
Email	phutcheson@rovers.com
Website	www.rovers.com

Conestoga Rovers & Associates is an Engineering firm specializing in the following areas: hazardous waste remediation, environmental assessment, hydrogeology, municipal infrastructure, water supply and treatment, waste water treatment, water resources, site remediation, sold waste management, air quality, and design and construction. There are approximately 280 employees at this location, a total of 300 within Canada, and a total of 880 employees worldwide. Graduates most likely to be hired come from the following academic areas: Bachelor of Science (Computer Science, Geology, Mathematic), Bachelor of Engineering (General, Chemical, Civil, Electrical, Mechanical, Environmental/Resources, Geological Engineering, Industrial Chemistry, Pollution Treatment, Water Resources), and Community College Diploma (Information Systems, CAD-CAM/Autocad, Engineering Technician). Graduates would occupy Professional Engineer, Analytical Chemist, Environmental Scientist, Environmental Planner, Geologist, Hydrogeologist, Industrial/Occupational Hygienist, Technician and Technologist positions. Previous work experience, leadership skills, initiative, growth potential, strong interpersonal skills, and good work habits are all listed as desirable non-academic qualifications. Company benefits and the potential for advancement are both rated as excellent. The starting annual salary for a new engineering graduate is $33,500. The most suitable methods for initial contact by those seeking employment are to mail, fax or e-mail a resume with a covering letter. Conestoga Rovers & Associates uses the University of Waterloo's Co-op Program for student and part-time needs throughout the year. *Contact:* Paul Hutcheson, Human Resources Manager.

CONNAUGHT LABORATORIES LIMITED
1755 Steeles Avenue West
Willowdale, ON M2R 3T4

Tel. 416-667-2944
Fax 416-667-2659

Connaught Laboratories Limited is Canada's largest producer of biological products for health care, this being primarily vaccines for human use. Connaught's operations are fully integrated and include research and development, manufacturing and Canadian marketing. Connaught Laboratories Limited employs more than 500 people. Graduates most likely to be hired come from the following academic areas: Bachelor of Science, Bachelor of Engineering (Chemical), Master of Science, and Community College Diploma (Life Sciences/Science, Animal Health-Care). Graduates would occupy Advanced Technician and Technologist positions. Company benefits are rated above average. The potential for advancement is listed as being good. The average annual starting salary falls within the $20,000 to $30,000 range. The most suitable methods for initial contact by those seeking employment are to mail a resume with a covering letter, or through on-campus recruitment programs (see your campus career centre for details). Connaught Laboratories Limited does hire summer students. *Contact:* Employment Office - Human Resources.

CONSUMERS GAS COMPANY LTD., THE
P.O. Box 650
Toronto, ON M1K 5E3

Tel. 416-495-5459
Fax 416-495-5739

The Consumers Gas Company Ltd. is involved in the distribution of natural gas throughout specific geographic areas. There are more than 1,000 people employed at this location. Graduates most likely to be hired come from the following academic areas: Bachelor of Arts (General), Bachelor of Engineering (Civil, Electrical, Mechanical), Bachelor of Laws, and Master of Business Administration (Finance). Graduates would occupy entry-level Clerical, Operations Engineer, Associate Corporate Solicitor, and Financial Analyst positions. Customer service and computer skills are both listed as desirable non-academic qualifications. Company benefits are rated as industry standard. The potential for advancement is listed as being good. The average annual starting salary falls within the $30,000 to $35,000 range. The most suitable method for initial contact by those seeking employment is to mail a resume with a covering letter. The Consumers Gas Company Ltd. does hire summer students. *Contact:* Employee Relations.

COOPER INDUSTRIES (CANADA) INC.
336 Courtland Avenue
Vaughan, ON L4K 4Y1

Tel. 905-761-5400
Fax 905-761-5600

Cooper Industries (Canada) Inc. is involved in the sale and distribution of aftermarket automotive products across Canada. The company employs 120 people at this location and a total of 200 people in Canada. Graduates most likely to be hired come from the following academic areas: Bachelor of Arts (Economics), Bachelor of Commerce/Business Administration (General, Accounting, Finance, Information Systems, Marketing), Certified Management Accountant, Certified General Accountant, and Community College Diploma (Accounting, Advertising, Business, Marketing/Sales). Graduates would occupy Marketing Co-ordinator, Product Manager, and Customer Service Representative positions. Computer skills, and excellent communication skills are both listed as desirable non-academic qualifications. Company benefits are rated as excellent. The potential for advancement is listed as being good. The average annual starting salary falls within the $25,000 to $30,000 range. The most suitable method for initial contact by those seeking employment is to mail a resume with a covering letter. Cooper Industries does hire summer students. *Contact:* Mary Jones, Director of Human Resources.

COOPÉRATIVE FÉDÉRÉE DE QUÉBEC, LA
9001, boul l'Acadie, bureau 200
Montreal, QC H4N 3H7

Tel. 514-858-2013
Fax 514-385-1041

La Coopérative Fédérée de Québec is an agriculture cooperative. There are 300 employees at this location, and a total of 5,000 employees in the cooperative. Graduates most likely to be hired come from the following academic areas: Bachelor of Science (Agriculture), Bachelor of Commerce/Business Administration (Accounting, Human Resources), Chartered Accountant, Certified Management Accountant, Certified General Accountant, and Community College Diploma (Accounting, Human Resources, Information Systems, Agriculture/Horticulture, Animal Health). Graduates would occupy Secretarial, Clerk, Technician, Representative, and Management positions. Team player, autonomy, initiative, and previous work experience are all listed as desirable non-academic qualifications. Company benefits are rated above average. The potential for advancement is listed as being good. The average annual starting salary falls within the $20,000 to $25,000 range. The most suitable method for initial contact by those seeking employment is to mail a resume with a covering letter. La Coopérative Fédérée de Québec does hire summer and co-op work term students. *Contacts:* Lise Arsenault or Yuan de La Cheurotière.

CORADIX TECHNOLOGY CONSULTING LTD.
2500 Don Reid Drive
Ottawa, ON K1H 1E1

Tel. 613-737-9800
Fax 613-739-9721
Email .... hr@coradix.com
Website .... www.coradix.com

Coradix Technology Consulting Ltd. provides informatics consulting services in three strategic areas, including, application development, network services, and management consulting. The company employs a total of 80 people. Graduates most likely to be hired come from the following academic areas: Bachelor of Science (Computer Science), and Bachelor of Commerce/Business Administration (Information Systems). Graduates would occupy Programmer Analyst, and Network Administrator positions. Good communication skills, professional appearance and presentation, a positive attitude, and a focus on quality are all listed as desirable non-academic qualifications. The average annual starting salary falls within the $35,000 to $40,000 range. The most suitable methods for initial contact by those seeking employment are to mail or e-mail a resume with a covering letter. *Contacts:* Tony Carmanico, Director of Professional Services or Jean Beaulieu, Director of Business Development.

CORECO INC.
6969 Trans Canada Highway, Suite 142
St-Laurent, QC H4T 1V8

Tel. 514-333-1301
Fax 514-333-1388
Email .... info@coreco.com
Website .... www.coreco.com

Coreco Inc. employs 67 people in the design and manufacture of high end image processing BDS and DSP engines for the machine vision, medical, and scientific imaging markets. Graduates most likely to be hired come from the following academic areas: Bachelor of Engineering (Automation/Robotics, Computer Systems, Microelectronics), and Community College Diploma (Electronics Technician, Engineering Technician). Graduates would occupy Research and Development, Hardware Engineer, and Test Technician positions. Enthusiasm, a willingness to learn, motivated, team player, self-starter, and interested in challenges are all listed as desirable non-academic qualifications. Company benefits are rated above average. The potential for advancement is listed as being good. The average annual starting salary falls within the $25,000 to $30,000 range. The most suitable method for initial contact by those seeking employment is to mail a resume with a covering letter. *Contact:* Human Resources Department.

COREL CORPORATION
1600 Carling Avenue
Ottawa, ON K1Z 8R7

Tel. 613-728-8200
Fax 613-761-9176
Email .... hr@corel.com
Website .... www.corel.com

Corel Corporation is a major Canadian computer software development company (visit Corel's home page at www.corel.com for detailed information). The company employs approximately 950 people at this location and a total of 1,500 worldwide. Graduates most likely to be hired come from the following academic areas: Bachelor of Arts (General, Economics, Graphic Arts, Journalism), Bachelor of Science (Computer Science, Mathematics), Bachelor of Engineering (Computer Systems), Bachelor of Laws, Bachelor of Commerce/Business Administration (General, Accounting, Human Resources, Information Systems, Marketing), Chartered Accountant, Master of Business Administration (Marketing), Master of Science (Computer Science), Doctorate (Computer Science), and Community College Diploma (Accounting, Administration, Advertising, Business, Communications, Human Resources, Marketing/Sales, Journalism, Legal Assistant, CAD/CAM/Autocad, Computer Science, Electronics Technician, Engineering Technician). Graduates would occupy Sales and Marketing Account Manager, Accountant, Software Developer, Quality Assurance Technician, Technical Support, Inside Sales, Project Manager, Human Resources Generalist, Advertising, and Graphic Designer positions. Organized, team player, open minded, enthusiastic, and a willingness to learn are all listed as desirable non-academic qualifications. Company benefits and the potential for advancement are both rated as excellent. The average annual starting salary falls within the $35,000 to $40,000 range. The most suitable methods for initial contact by those seeking employment are to mail or e-mail (hr@corel.com) your resume with a covering letter. Corel Corporation does hire summer students. *Contact:* Human Resources.

CORRECTIONAL SERVICE OF CANADA
3 Place Laval, 2e étage
Laval, QC H7N 1A2

Tel. 450-967-3333
Fax 450-967-3337

The Correctional Service of Canada, as part of the criminal justice system, contributes to the public safety, through the rehabilitation of criminal offenders, seeking to integrate those individuals into the community as law abiding citizens, while exercising reasonable supervision and control to ensure public safety. The Correctional Service of Canada employs approximately 3,140 people in the Quebec region, and a total of 11,300 people across Canada. Graduates most likely to be hired come from the following academic areas: Bachelor of Arts (Criminology, Psychology, Sociology/Social Work), Bachelor of Science (Nursing, Psychology), Bachelor of Engineering (Computer Systems), Bachelor of Commerce/Business Administration (Human Resources), Master of Business Administration (Finance), Master of Arts (Psychology), Community College Diploma (Accounting, Cooking, Security/Police/Enforcement, Social Worker, Corrections Worker, Computer Science, Nursing RN), and High School Diploma. Graduates would occupy Corrections Officer, Case Administrator, Psychologist, Nurse, Human Resources Counsellor, Financial Controller, Financial Services Manager, Cook, Information Services Analyst, Administration, Secretarial, and Warehouse positions. Employee benefits are rated as excellent. The potential for advancement is rated as being good. The most suitable method for initial contact by those seeking employment is to mail a resume with a covering letter. The Correctional Service of Canada does hire summer students. *Contacts:* Human Resources Division or Regional Manager, Human Resources.

COSYN TECHNOLOGY

9405 - 50 Street, Suite 101
Edmonton, AB T6B 2T4

Tel. 403-440-7000
Fax 403-462-3897
Website .... www.cosyn.ab.ca

CoSyn Technology is a division of Colt Engineering Corporation and was established in 1991 to provide engineering, procurement and construction management services to Syncrude through an alliance partnering relationship. The alliance is a long term commitment to achieve specific business objectives. The resources of both alliance partners are focused on improving the core business. The scope of the work includes preliminary engineering work, preparation of basic engineering packages, the preparation of cost estimates, planning and scheduling, and project management for large and small projects. Staff are employed in a multidisciplinary environment including mechanical, process, electrical, civil/structural, piping, instrumentation controls, extraction, project services, office services and financial services. CoSyn has a structured quality system that is registered to the ISO 9000 Standard. CoSyn does high quality work for Syncrude and is committed to continuous improvement. There are 230 employees at this location, and a total of 260 employees in Canada. Graduates most likely to be hired come from the following academic areas: Bachelor of Science (Computer Science), Bachelor/Master of Engineering (General, Chemical, Civil, Electrical, Mechanical, Environmental/Resources, Petroleum/Fuels, Process), and Community College Diploma (Information Systems, Purchasing/Logistics, Secretarial, CAD/CAM/Autocad, Computer Science, Engineering Technician). Graduates would occupy Engineer, Project Engineer, Project Manager, Technologist, Designer, CAD Operator, Estimator, Purchaser/Buyer, Expeditor, and Secretarial positions. Decision making abilities, team orientation, good interpersonal and communication skills, flexibility, and a customer service orientation are all listed as desirable non-academic qualifications. Company benefits are rated above average. The potential for advancement is listed as being good. The most suitable methods for initial contact by those seeking employment are to mail or fax a resume with a covering letter. CoSyn Technology does hire summer and co-op work term students. *Contact:* Susan Tanghe, Human Resources Leader.

COTTER CANADA HARDWARE AND VARIETY COOPERATIVE INC.

P.O. Box 6800
Winnipeg, MB R3C 3A9

Tel. 204-453-9560
Fax 204-452-6615

Cotter Canada is an expanding wholesale distributor of hardware and general merchandise, serving a national chain of over 500 stores. The company, based in Winnipeg, is a cooperative owned by Canadian independent retailers. Cotter Canada employs a total of 350 people. Graduates most likely to be hired come from the following academic areas: Bachelor of Science (Computer Science), Bachelor of Commerce/Business Administration (Accounting, Finance, Human Resources, Information Systems), Chartered Accountant, Certified Management Accountant, Certified General Accountant, Master of Science (Computer Science), Community College Diploma (Accounting, Advertising, Human Resources, Purchasing/Logistics, Secretarial, CAD/CAM/Autocad, Computer Science), and High School Diploma. Graduates would occupy Programmer/Analyst, Technical Support (Retail Systems), Communications/Network Support, Controller, Assistant Controller, Human Resources Manager, Human Resources Administrator, Desk-Top Publishing, Accounting Clerk, and General Clerical positions. Previous work experience, outside activities/hobbies, and possessing future goals are all listed as desirable non-academic qualifications. Company benefits are rated above average. The potential for advancement is listed as average. The average annual starting salary for entry level clerical jobs falls within the $15,000 to $20,000 range. For other areas, the average annual starting salary depends upon the position being considered. The most suitable method for initial contact by those seeking employment is to mail a resume with a covering letter. Cotter Canada hires summer students for entry level accounting and summer receptionist positions. *Contacts:* Karen Froese or Cathy Gamby.

CRAMER NURSERY INC.

1002 St-Dominique Road
Les Cedres, QC J7T 3A1

Tel. 450-452-2121
Fax 450-452-4053

Cramer Nursery Inc. is a production nursery operating 1,500 acres of ornamental nursery stock. Also, as a secondary activity, the company operates three garden centres in the Montreal region. Production activities range from growing seedlings to specimen plants. The main market areas served are in Canada and the United States with some in Europe. There are approximately 125 employees at this location and a total of 175 employees within Canada. Graduates most likely to be hired come from the following academic areas: Bachelor of Science (Agriculture, Biology, Forestry, Horticulture), Bachelor of Engineering (Forest Resources), Bachelor of Landscape Architecture, Bachelor of Commerce/Business Administration, and Community College Diploma (Accounting, Administration, Business, Marketing/Sales, Secretarial, Agriculture, Forestry, Horticulture). In horticultural activities, graduates would occupy Propagation, Pruning, Harvesting, and Maintenance positions. In administration, graduates would occupy Sales, Office, and Clerical positions. Company benefits are rated above average. The potential for advancement is listed as excellent. The average annual starting salary is dependent upon the position being considered. The most suitable methods for initial contact by those seeking employment are to mail or fax a resume with a covering letter. Cramer Nursery Inc. does hire co-op work term students, and summer students to work in the garden centres and at the production nursery, where on-site lodging is available (Toll Free Number 1-888-8CRAMER). *Contacts:* Walter Cramerstetter, Sales, Administration & Research or Mario Cramerstetter, Production, General Labour.

CRAWFORD & CO. INSURANCE ADJUSTERS/ THG
185 The West Mall, Suite 1200
Toronto, ON M9C 5L5

Tel.	416-620-7248 x 302
Fax	416-620-7046

Crawford & Co. Insurance Adjusters/THG provides insurance adjusting services, health, and risk management services. There are more than 25 employees at this location, and more than 250 employees across Canada. Graduates most likely to be hired come from the following academic areas: Bachelor of Arts (General), Bachelor of Science (General, Computer Science, Forestry, Geography, Geology, Health Sciences, Nursing, Psychology), Bachelor of Engineering (General, Environmental, Materials Science), Bachelor of Commerce/Business Administration (Marketing), and Community College Diploma (Accounting, Administration, Business, Communications, Insurance, Marketing/Sales, Secretarial, Human Resources, Computer Science, Nursing RN). Graduates would occupy Insurance Adjuster, Secretary, Administrative Assistant, Data Entry Clerk, Receptionist, Computer System Coordinator, Medical/Vocational and Employment Consultant positions. Previous work experience in Adjusting (claims), and Appraising are both listed as desirable non-academic qualifications. Company benefits and the potential for advancement are both rated as excellent. The average annual starting salary falls within the $15,000 to $20,000 range. The most suitable method for initial contact by those seeking employment is to mail a resume with a covering letter. Crawford & Co. Insurance Adjusters/THG does hire summer students. *Contact:* Tina Du, Human Resources Advisor.

CRESTAR ENERGY INC.
333 - 7th Avenue SW, P.O. Box 888
Calgary, AB T2P 4M8

Tel.	403-231-3868
Fax	403-231-6811
Email	robert.nadon@crestar-energy.com
Website	www.crestarenergy.com

Crestar Energy Inc. is an oil and gas exploration and production company. There are approximately 270 employees at this location and a total of 450 employees in Canada. Graduates most likely to be hired come from the following academic areas: Bachelor of Science (Chemistry, Computer Science, Geology), Bachelor of Engineering (Chemical, Civil, Electrical, Instrumentation, Resources/Environmental, Petroleum), Bachelor of Commerce/Business Administration (Accounting, Finance, Marketing), Certified Management Accountant, and Community College

Diploma (Accounting, Administration, Human Resources). Graduates would occupy Engineer, Geologist, Geophysicist, Accountant, and Marketing positions. Team player, innovative, and risk taker are listed as desirable non-academic qualifications. Company benefits are rated as excellent. The potential for advancement is listed as average. The most suitable method for initial contact by those seeking employment is to mail a resume with a covering letter. Crestar Energy Inc. does hire summer students. *Contact:* Bob Nadon, Human Resources.

CRILA PLASTIC INDUSTRIES LTD.
979 Gana Court
Mississauga, ON L5S 1N9

Tel.	416-798-9333 x 232
Fax	416-798-9229

Crila Plastic Industries Ltd. is a manufacturer of plastic extrusions/plastic decorative trim. Manufacturing divisions include appliances, automotive, and industrial. The company employs approximately 120 people at this location and a total of 250 people in Canada. Graduates most likely to be hired come from the following academic areas: Bachelor of Arts (General), Bachelor of Science (General), Bachelor of Engineering (General, Mechanical, Industrial Design, Industrial Production), Bachelor of Commerce/Business Administration (General, Accounting, Finance, Human Resources), Community College Diploma (Accounting, Administration, Business, Human Resources, Marketing/Sales, CAD/CAM/Autocad), and High School Diploma. Graduates would occupy Engineer (Cost Estimator, CAD Designer), Quality Control Inspector, Accounts Payable Clerk, Accounts Receivable Clerk, Inside Sales/Customer Service Representative, Secretary, Receptionist, Data Entry Clerk, and Marketing Assistant positions. Previous work experience, a positive attitude, team player, developed skill sets, ambition, and enthusiasm are all listed as desirable non-academic qualifications. The most suitable methods for initial contact by those seeking employment are to mail or fax a resume with a covering letter. Crila Plastic Industries Ltd. does hire summer students. *Contact:* Leonard Starrett, Human Resources Manager.

CROSSKEYS SYSTEMS CORPORATION
350 Terry Fox Drive
Kanata, ON K2K 2W5

Tel.	613-591-1600
Fax	613-599-2310
Email	careers@crosskeys.com
Website	www.crosskeys.com

Founded in 1992, CrossKeys Systems Corporation is an independent software vendor that develops, markets and supports telecommunications-management software products and services for telecommunications service providers around the world. CrossKeys software products and associated services meet the needs of service providers who require open, scaleable products that operate on multiple software platforms and integrate equipment from multiple vendors. The company's core competency is delivering Element, Network and Service management applications, primarily in the areas of performance, accounting and configuration management. CrossKeys also offers professional services and customer support, including customization, project management, training, installation and post-warranty support. Graduates most likely to be hired come from the following academic areas: Bachelor of Science (Computer Science), and Bachelor of Engineering (Computer Systems). Graduates would occupy Software Developer and Product Verification Engineer positions. Previous telecommunications experience, self-motivated, team player, and strong communication skills are all listed as desirable non-academic qualifications. Company benefits and the potential for advancement are both rated as excellent. The average annual starting salary is dependent upon the position being considered. The most suitable methods for initial contact by those seeking employment are to fax a resume with a covering letter, or by applying through the company's website at www.crosskeys.com. CrossKeys Systems Corporation does hire summer and co-op work term students. *Contact:* Human Resources.

CROWN LIFE INSURANCE COMPANY
1901 Scarth Street, P.O. Box 827
Regina, SK S4P 3B1

Tel. 306-751-6050
Fax 306-751-6051

Founded in 1900, Crown Life Insurance Company is an international leader in providing personal and corporate financial services. Crown Life markets a wide range of life and health insurance annuities and pension products to individuals and groups. The company also provides reinsurance services to other insurance companies and investment management services to external clients. The company employs approximately 1,062 people at this location, a total of 1,305 across Canada, and 1,400 people worldwide. Graduates most likely to be hired come from the following academic areas: Bachelor of Arts (Economics, French), Bachelor of Science (Actuarial, Computer Science, Mathematics, Nursing), Bachelor of Engineering (Computer Systems), Bachelor of Education (Adult), Bachelor of Commerce/Business Administration (Accounting, Finance, Human Resources, Information Systems, Marketing), Chartered Accountant, Certified Management Accountant, Certified General Accountant, Master of Business Administration (Accounting, Finance, Human Resources, Information Systems, Marketing), and Community College Diploma (Accounting, Administration, Business, Communications, Financial Planning, Human Resources, Insurance, Marketing, Purchasing, Secretarial, Graphic Arts, Legal Assistant, Photography, CAD/CAM/Autocad, Computer Science, Electronics Technician). Initiative, good judgment, logical thinking, sense of responsibility, positive attitude, team player, strong interpersonal and communication skills, and a demonstrated desire for continuous learning are all listed as desirable non-academic qualifications. Company benefits are rated as

excellent. The most suitable methods for initial contact by those seeking employment are to mail a resume with a covering letter, or via telephone. Crown Life does hire summer students. *Contacts:* Erin Wendel, Human Resources or Angela Ricci, Human Resources.

CROWNE PLAZA CHATEAU LACOMBE
10111 Bellamy Hill
Edmonton, AB T5J 1N7

Tel. 403-428-6611
Fax 403-420-8378

The Crowne Plaza Chateau Lacombe is a beautifully renovated 24 floor, luxury hotel overlooking Edmonton's river valley. For over 30 years the Hotel has distinguished itself by offering hospitality that is highly competent, yet genuine and warm. Today, the Crowne Plaza Chateau Lacombe employs 240 people, and is always on the look out for enthusiastic, friendly, high-energy people with a desire to exceed guest expectations. Graduates most likely to be hired come from Community College Diploma Programs in Accounting, Administration, Business, Marketing/Sales, Cook/Chef Training, Hospitality, and Travel/Tourism. Graduates would occupy Administrative Assistant, Front Desk Agent, Reservations Agent, Sous Chefs, Apprentice Cooks, Sales Management, Catering Coordinator, Night Audit, Food and Beverage Servers, and Management positions. Customer service oriented, team player, strong interpersonal and communication skills, enthusiasm, excellent organizational abilities, a high energy level, and good verbal and written communication skills are all listed as desirable non-academic qualifications. The Hotel provides competitive starting salaries ($20,00 to $30,000 range), great employee benefits, advancement opportunities, and a team oriented fun atmosphere. The most suitable methods for initial contact by those seeking employment are to mail or fax a resume with a covering letter, or by applying in person at the Hotel. The Crowne Plaza Chateau Lacombe does hire a limited number of summer students and co-op work term students. *Contact:* Sherry Mattson, Human Resources.

CROWNE PLAZA TORONTO CENTRE
225 Front Street West
Toronto, ON M5V 2X3

Tel. 416-597-1400
Fax 416-597-8164

Crowne Plaza Toronto Centre is a busy 587 guest room hotel located in downtown Toronto. There are 15 meeting rooms, 4 food and beverage outlets, and 2 levels of service. The hotel employs more than 250 people. Graduates most likely to be hired come from the following Community College programs: Marketing/Sales, Cooking, Hospitality, Recreation, Security/Enforcement, and Travel/Tourism. Graduates would occupy Front Desk Receptionist, Console Operator, Reservation Clerk, Waitress, 1st - 2nd - 3rd Cook, Recreation Club Attendant, Housekeeper, and Busperson positions. Outgoing, organized, honest, reliable, dependable, and people oriented are all listed as desirable non-academic qualifications. Company benefits are listed as excellent. The average annual starting salary falls within the $15,000 to $25,000 range. The most suitable method for initial contact by those seeking employment is to mail a resume with a covering letter. *Contact:* Human Resources.

CRYOVAC CANADA INC.
2365 Dixie Road
Mississauga, ON L4Y 2A2

Tel. 905-273-5656
Fax 905-273-3572

Cryovac Canada Inc. is a "Fortune 100" company employing more than 250 people in the manufacture of flexible plastic packaging products, packaging machines and art services. Graduates most likely to be hired come from the following academic areas: Bachelor of Arts (General, Economics, Fine Arts, Psychology, Sociology), Bachelor of Science (Biology, Chemistry, Computer Science, Mathematics, Physics, Psychology), Bachelor of Engineering (General, Chemical, Environmental, Electrical, Industrial, Mechanical), Bachelor of Commerce/Business Administration (Accounting), Master of Business Administration (General), Master of Science (Chemistry), Master of Engineering (Chemical, Electrical, Mechanical), and Community College Diploma (Accounting, Administration, Business, Purchasing/Logistics, Graphic Arts, Human Resources, Computer Science, Electronics Technician, Engineering Technician, Mechanic, Laboratory Technician). Graduates would occupy Technician, Technologist, Junior Engineer, Production Planner, Junior Buyer, Customer Service Representative, Credit Analyst, and Office Clerk positions. Enthusiasm, creativity, a positive attitude, flexibility, patience and persistence are all listed as desirable non-academic qualifications. Company benefits are rated as excellent. The potential for advancement is listed as good. The average annual starting salary falls within the $25,000 to $35,000 range. The most suitable method for initial contact by graduates seeking employment is to mail a resume with a covering letter. Cryovac Canada Inc. does hire a limited number of summer students. *Contact:* Dick Irvine, Employee Development Manager.

CTC COMPUTER-TECH CONSULTANTS LTD.
240 Graham Avenue, Suite 824
Winnipeg, MB R3C 0J7

Tel. 204-942-6699
Fax 204-942-8833
Email .... rsierra@ctctech.com
Website .... www.ctctech.com

CTC Computer-Tech Consultants Ltd. is one of Western Canada's largest providers of information technology resources, including software development, programming and analysis, and project management. CTC has six offices across Canada including Calgary, Edmonton, Vancouver, Victoria, Regina, and Winni-

peg. There are 8 employees at this location and a total of 190 employees in Canada. Graduates most likely to be hired come from the following academic areas: Bachelor of Science (Computer Science), Bachelor of Commerce/Business Administration (Information Systems), Master of Business Administration (Information Systems), Master of Science (Computer Science), and Community College Diploma (Computer Science). Graduates would occupy Programmer/Analyst, Systems Analyst, Senior Analyst, Team Leader, Project Manager, Network Administrator/Implementation, and Software Developer positions. Team player, good attitude, well-balanced, willing to learn and grow, thrive on challenges, and excellent communication skills are all listed as desirable non-academic qualifications. Company benefits are rated above average. The potential for advancement is listed as excellent. The average annual starting salary falls within the $15,000 to $45,000 plus range, depending on the position being considered. The most suitable methods for initial contact by those seeking employment are to mail, fax or e-mail a resume with a covering letter. CTC Computer-Tech Consultants Ltd. does hire summer students. *Contacts:* Renée Sierra, Manager or Human Resources.

CTV TELEVISION NETWORK LTD.
250 Yonge Street, Suite 1800
Toronto, ON M5B 2N8

Tel. 416-595-4100
Fax 416-595-1036

CTV Television Network Ltd. is a national television broadcaster. There are 210 employees at this location, a total of 300 employees in Canada, and a total of 360 employees worldwide. Graduates most likely to be hired come from the following academic areas: Bachelor of Arts (Economics, English, Graphic Arts, Journalism, Languages, Political Science), Bachelor of Science (General, Computer Science) Bachelor of Engineering (General, Automation/Robotics, Computer Systems, Telecommunications), Bachelor of Laws, Bachelor of Commerce/Business Administration (General, Accounting, Finance), Chartered Accountant, Certified General Accountant, Master of Business Administration (General, Accounting, Marketing), Master of Arts, Community College Diploma (Accounting, Administration, Business, Communications, Marketing/Sales, Graphic Arts, Journalism, Legal Assistant, Television/Radio Arts, CAD/CAM/Autocad, Computer Science, Engineering Technician), and High School Diploma. Company benefits are rated as excellent. The potential for advancement is listed as average. The average annual starting salary falls within the $30,000 to $35,000 range. The most suitable methods for initial contact by those seeking employment are to contact the Job Line at (416) 595-4475, to listen to current opportunities, or to mail a resume with a covering letter. CTV Television Network Ltd. does hire summer students. *Contact:* Theresa Bradshaw, Human Resource Coordinator.

CUSTOMER CARE INSURANCE AGENCY LTD.
3 Robert Speck Parkway, 4th Floor
Mississauga, ON L4Z 3Z9

Tel. 905-306-3900
Fax 905-306-3131

Customer Care Insurance Agency Ltd. is a wholly owned subsidiary of TeleTech Holdings Incorporated, a leading global provider of customer care solutions to Fortune 500 and international business. The company helps clients acquire, service and retain customers by managing their telephone, internet, and multimedia inquiries. Customer Care's business is in providing the highest level of customer care for the life of each customer and for the life of each business. Through the integration of talented people, ISO Processes, and leading technology, TeleTech handles over 400,000 interactions for clients every day. There are 400 employees at this location, and a total of 10,000 employees worldwide. Graduates most likely to be hired come from the following academic areas: Bachelor of Arts (General), Bachelor of Science (General, Actuarial, Computer Science), Bachelor of Education (General, Adult), Bachelor of Commerce/Business Administration (General, Human Resources), Master of Business Administration (General, Human Resources), and Community College Diploma (Administration, Business, Facility Management, Human Resources, Information Systems, Insurance, Marketing/Sales, Secretarial). Qualified applicants are hired for positions in Customer Service, Sales, Quality Assurance, Operations, Technology, Human Resources, Training and Administration. Creativity, initiative, team player, and customer sensitive are listed as desirable non-academic qualifications. Customer Care offers employees viable career opportunities, an exciting environment, generous benefits and extensive training. The average annual starting salary falls within the $30,000 to $35,000 range. The most suitable method for initial contact by those seeking employment is to fax a resume with a covering letter. *Contacts:* Stan Arnold, Human Resources Manager or Sandra Melanson, Human Resources Generalist.

DAEDALIAN SYSTEMS GROUP INC.
34 King Street East, Floor 8
Toronto, ON M5C 1E5

Tel. 416-862-1401
Fax 416-862-2656
Email .... jobs@daedalian.com
Website .... www.daedalian.com/bmain.html

Daedalian Systems Group Inc. is a rapidly expanding systems development and integration firm specializing in client/server and internet projects. Daedalian's technological expertise and superior client relations have earned it a reputation for outstanding service. The company offers extensive training in software applications, and seeks candidates with Bachelor, Master, or Doctorate degrees in Engineering, Science, or Mathematics. Graduates would occupy the full-time positions of Programmer/Analyst and Systems Integrator. Team player, good communication skills, and strong analytical and problem solving skills are all listed as desirable non-academic qualifications. Company benefits and the potential for advancement are both rated as excellent. The average annual entry-level salary falls within the $35,000 to $40,000 range. The most suitable method for initial contact by those seeking employment is to fax a resume with a covering letter. Daedalian Systems Group Inc. does hire summer and co-op students. *Contact:* Ms. Miriam Rubin.

World-class products. World-class service.

DANKA CANADA
13351 Commerce Parkway, Suite 1163
Richmond, BC V6V 2X7

Tel. 604-273-3224
Fax 604-273-3839
Website .... www.dankaoi.com

Danka is one of the World's largest independent suppliers of office imaging equipment and related services, parts, and supplies. Danka's strategy is to become the preferred source for document solutions by acting as an advocate for its customers. The company's vision extends beyond copiers and network printers. In order to deliver value to its customers, Danka considers their organizational culture, that being the people, processes and technologies involved in how they use information. Danka is a worldwide corporation with over 20,000 employees in 700 office locations in 30 countries. There are 70 employees at this location. Graduates most likely to be hired come from the following academic areas: Bachelor of Arts (General, Economics), Bachelor of Engineering (Electrical, Mechanical, Computer Systems), Bachelor of Commerce/Business Administration (General, Marketing), and Community College Diploma (Marketing/Sales, Secretarial). Graduates would occupy Field Technician, Systems Engineer, Clerk, Receptionist, and Sales Representative positions. Self-starter and team player are both listed as desirable non-academic qualifications. Company benefits are rated above average. The potential for advancement is listed as being good. The average annual starting salary falls within the $25,000 to $30,000 range, and is salary plus commission based for marketing positions. The most suitable methods for initial contact by those seeking employment are to mail or fax a resume with a covering letter. *Contacts:* Cliff Leduc, Service Department; John Saleski, Sales Department or Mollie Joestl, Administration Department.

DATALINK SYSTEMS CORPORATION
1500 West Georgia Street, Suite 1590
Vancouver, BC V6G 2Z6

Tel. 604-257-2700
Fax 604-602-0817
Email .... hresources@datalink.net
Website .... www.datalink.net

DataLink Systems Corporation provides powerful, ubiquitous information services geared to the needs of people on-the-go. Those enabled with wireless (PCS phones and pagers) and internet technology (PC's with browsers and e-mail) would benefit most directly from DataLink's innovative services. At the confluence of the internet and wireless worlds, Datalink's "MessageX" site is a universal portal that provides both messaging services and information services to its users. Via the internet, messages (pages) can be sent from virtually any location in the world to any user with a PCS phone or pager. At the same time, financial, news, sports and other lifestyle information services are provided at the user's fingertips wherever and whenever required. Datalink's information services are provided on both a "push" and "pull" basis. Users specify their information needs and preferences on DataLink's website. DataLink's information system, drawing on a wide variety of information feeds, delivers relevant messages (even e-mail) in real time directly to the users' wireless devices. This information may also be accessed on demand with a two-way pager or a smart phone. Using the home or office PC and its browser, this information can be retrieved from DataLink's website. The user can even dial a telephone number and listen to e-mail or other text messages converted to speech or can have these messages sent to a fax machine close at hand. Graduates most likely to be hired at DataLink come from the following academic areas: Bachelor of Science (Computer Science), Bachelor of Engineering (Electrical, Computer Systems), and Community College Diploma (Computer Science). Graduates would occupy Software Engineer and Software Developer positions. Company benefits are rated above average. The potential for advancement is listed as excellent. The average annual starting salary falls within the $40,000 to $45,000 range. The most suitable method for initial contact by those seeking employment is to e-mail a resume with a covering letter. DataLink Systems Corporation does hire co-op work term students. *Contacts:* Kal Toth, Vice President, Engineering or Cornel Fota, Director, Software Development.

DDM PLASTICS INC.
P.O. Box 574
Tillsonburg, ON N4G 4J1

Tel. 519-688-1060
Fax 519-688-1052

DDM Plastics Inc. is involved in plastic injection moulding, painting and light assembly work. The company operates large tonnage (1300 - 3000 ton) mould machines, and 2K paint systems with robotics. The company employs a total of 700 people. Graduates most likely to be hired come from the following academic areas: Bachelor of Science (General, Computer Science, Mathematics), Bachelor of Engineering (General, Chemical, Industrial Chemistry, Electrical, Automation/Robotics, Instrumentation, Mechanical, Industrial Design, Industrial Production), Bachelor of Commerce/Business Administration (Accounting, Finance, Human Resources, Information Systems, Marketing), Certified General

Accountant, Master of Business Administration (Accounting, Finance, Human Resources), and Community College Diploma (Business, Facility Management, Financial Planning, Human Resources, Marketing/Sales, Purchasing/Logistics, CAD/CAM/Autocad, Computer Science, Electronics Technician, Engineering Technician, Nursing RNA). Graduates would occupy Production Supervisor, Production Engineer, Process Engineer, Chemical Engineer, Cost Accountant, Controller, and Sales Representative positions. Good organizational, leadership and problem solving skills, and two to four years manufacturing experience are all listed as desirable non-academic qualifications. Company benefits are rated above average. The potential for advancement is listed as excellent. The most suitable method for initial contact by those seeking employment is to mail a resume with a covering letter. DDM Plastics Inc. does hire summer students. *Contacts:* Rita Scott, Manager, Human Resources or General Affairs Department.

DELFOUR CORPORATION
140 Renfrew Drive, Suite 101
Markham, ON L3R 6B3

Tel. 905-415-9779
Fax 905-415-9778
Email .... llawson@delfour.com
Website .... www.delfour.com

Delfour Corporation was incorporated in 1988. The company was established by four partners who had a vision of creating a software system that would be leading edge in warehouse management systems. Delfour Corporation has been a pioneer in using relational database management systems for the warehousing industry, in addition to developing unique features which are now commonly used by other software companies. Today, Delfour offers a complete set of software systems designed specifically for the contract logistics industry. There are 89 employees at this location and a total of 117 employees worldwide. In addition to the Markham location, Delfour is incorporated in Atlanta, Memphis, England, Argentina, and Brazil. Graduates most likely to be hired come from the following academic areas: Bachelor of Science (Computer Science), Bachelor of Engineering (Computer Systems, Industrial Engineering), Bachelor of Commerce (General, Accounting, Finance, Human Resources, Information Systems, Marketing), Certified General Accountant, and Community College Diploma (Information Systems, Marketing/Sales, Computer Science). Graduates would occupy Development Specialist, Systems Design, Business Analyst, Implementation Specialist, Account Manager, Accounting, Customer Support, Human Resource, and Sales and Marketing positions. Leadership skills, team player, strategic thinking skills, and dynamic software skills are all listed as desirable non-academic qualifications. Company benefits and the potential for advancement are both rated as excellent. The average annual starting salary falls within the $45,000 to $50,000 range. The most suitable methods for initial contact by those seeking employment are to fax or e-mail a resume with a covering letter, or by applying through the company's website at www.delfour.com. Delfour Corporation does hire co-op work term students. *Contacts:* Leslie Lawson, Manager of Human Resources or Dave Carrick, General Manager.

DELOITTE & TOUCHE
181 Bay Street, BCE Place, Suite 1400
Toronto, ON M5J 2V1

Tel. 416-601-6150
Fax 416-601-6151

Deloitte & Touche is a major chartered accountancy firm employing approximately 5,000 people in over seventy Canadian centres. Graduates most likely to be hired come from the following academic areas: Bachelor of Arts (Economics), Bachelor of Commerce/Business Administration (General, Accounting, Finance), Master of Business Administration (General, Accounting, Finance, Information Systems), and Community College Diploma (Computer Science). Graduates would occupy the position of Staff Accountant. Leadership, team building and entrepreneurial skills combined with a strong academic standing are listed as desirable qualifications. The potential for advancement is listed as being excellent. The most suitable method for initial contact by graduates seeking employment is through on-campus recruitment programs (see your campus career centre for details). Deloitte & Touche does hire summer students on a regular basis. *Contact:* Human Resources Department.

DELTA HOTELS & RESORTS
350 Bloor Street East, Suite 300
Toronto, ON M4W 1H4

Tel. 416-926-7800
Fax 416-926-7809
Website .... www.deltahotels.com

Delta Hotels and Resorts is a management company providing hotel management services. The company operates hotels and resorts across Canada, Florida, the Caribbean, Thailand, Philippines, Vietnam, and Malaysia. The company employs 60 people at the corporate office, a total of 4,500 across Canada, and 7,000 people worldwide. Graduates most likely to be hired come from the following academic areas: Bachelor of Commerce/Business Administration (Accounting, Human Resources, Information Systems), Community College Diploma (Accounting, Administration, Human Resources, Secretarial, Hospitality, Travel and Tourism), and High School Diploma. Graduates would occupy Hospitality positions within the Hotels, including Food and Beverage, Front Office, and Housekeeping positions, as well as Engineering, Human Resources, and Finance positions. Initiative, team oriented, very personable and approachable, and a willingness to do that "extra-mile" for the customer are all listed as desirable non-academic qualifications. Company benefits and the potential for advancement are both listed as excellent. The average annual starting salary falls within the $20,000 to $25,000 range for entry level positions. The most suitable method for initial contact by those seeking employment is to mail a resume with a covering letter to the hotel of their choice. Delta Hotels and Resorts does hire summer students at the hotel level but not at the corporate office. *Contacts:* Human Resources Director (at each Hotel location) or Human Resources Coordinator (Corporate Office).

DELTA HUDSON ENGINEERING LTD.
P.O. Box 5244, Station A
Calgary, AB T2H 2N7

Tel. 403-258-6494
Fax 403-258-6645
Email .... resume.hr@mcdermott.com
Website .... www.deltahudson.com

Delta Hudson Engineering Ltd. provides engineering, procurement, construction, construction management, and contract maintenance services. There are 230 employees at this location, and a total of 430 employees across Canada. Graduates most likely to be hired come from the following academic areas: Bachelor of Science (General, Chemistry, Computer Science), Bachelor of Engineering (General, Chemical, Pollution Treatment, Pulp and Paper, Civil, Electrical, Instrumentation, Power, Mechanical, Industrial Design), Bachelor of Commerce/Business Administration (Accounting, Information Systems), Master of Business Administration (Accounting, Information Systems), Community College Diploma (Accounting, Human Resources, Secretarial, Architecture/Drafting, CAD/CAM/Autocad, Computer Science, Engineering Technician), and High School Diploma. Graduates would occupy Clerk, Secretary, Document Control, Data Entry, Administrative Assistant, Drafter, Designer/Checkers, Design Specialist, Sub-Contract Specialist, Technician/Specialist, Engineer, Buyer, Expeditor, Project Control (Planner/Scheduler), Programmer/Analyst, Hardware/Software Support Technician, and QA/QC Inspector positions. Previous work experience, strong communication skills, self starter, results oriented, and an ability to work effectively with others and independently are all listed as desirable non-academic qualifications. Company benefits are rated above average. The potential for advancement is listed as being good. The average annual starting salary falls within the $30,000 to $35,000 range. The most suitable method for initial contact by those seeking employment is to apply through the company's website at www.deltahudson.com. Delta Hudson Engineering Ltd. does hire co-op work term students. *Contacts:* S. Boland, Manager, Staff Human Resources or J. Cox, Principal Human Resources Representative, Human Resources.

DELTA MEADOWVALE RESORT & CONFERENCE CENTRE
6750 Mississauga Road
Mississauga, ON L5N 2L3

Tel. 905-542-6726
Fax 905-542-6757

The Delta Meadowvale Resort & Conference Centre of Mississauga is a full service hotel providing accommodation, restaurant, conference and resort facilities. The hotel employs more than 350 people. Graduates most likely to be hired come from the following academic areas: Bachelor of Arts (General), Bachelor of Commerce/Business Administration and Community College Diploma (Hospitality, Hotel/Restaurant Management). Graduates would occupy Entry-Level Supervisory positions. The exact type and level of position is determined upon the experience of the applicant. Initiative, team player, self-motivated, and strong customer service skills are all listed as desirable non-academic qualifications. Company benefits and the potential for advancement are both rated as excellent. The average annual starting salary falls within the $20,000 to $25,000 range. The most suitable method for initial contact by those seeking employment is to fax a resume with a covering letter. The Delta Meadowvale Resort & Conference Centre does offer co-op work term placements in the majority of its departments. *Contacts:* Nancy McTeague, Director of Human Resources or Reni Kalirai-Chakal, Human Resources Coordinator.

DEPARTMENT OF THE SOLICITOR GENERAL, NEW BRUNSWICK

P.O. Box 6000
Fredericton, NB E3B 5H1

Tel. 506-453-3992
Fax 506-453-7481

The overall objective of the Department of the Solicitor General is to ensure the administration of justice through the enforcement of criminal law, the delivery of correctional services, the delivery of services to victims of crime, and the delivery of Sheriff/Coroner services in the province of New Brunswick. The department employs approximately 700 people. Graduates most likely to be hired come from the following academic areas: Bachelor of Arts (Criminology, Political Science, Psychology, Sociology), Bachelor of Science (Computer Science), Bachelor of Education (Intermediate Senior, Adult, Special Needs), Bachelor of Laws, Bachelor of Commerce/Business Administration (Accounting, Finance, Human Resources, Information Systems, Public Administration), Master of Business Administration (Finance, Public Administration), Master of Arts (Criminology), Master of Science (Clinical Psychology), and Community College Diploma (Secretarial, Cooking, Security/Law Enforcement, Computer Science). Graduates would occupy Accounting Officer, Human Resources Officer, Information Systems, Research and Planning Officer, Correctional Services Supervisor, Correctional Institutions Superintendent, Nurse, Social Worker, Correctional Officer, Youth Counsellor, Probation Officer, Parole Officer, Clinical Psychologist, Victim Services Coordinator, Inspector, Sheriff/Coroner, and Commercial Vehicle Enforcement positions. The most suitable methods for initial contact by those seeking employment are to mail a resume with a covering letter, or through job fair competitions (visit your campus career cen-

tre for details). The Department of the Solicitor General hires summer students through Job Creation Programs. *Contacts:* John Oxner, Corrections / Ed Peterson, Law Enforcement or Sandra Cameron/ Jerry Fife, Sheriff/Coroner Policing.

DEPARTMENT OF TRANSPORTATION, NORTHWEST TERRITORIES

P.O. Box 1320
Yellowknife, NT X1A 2L9

Tel. 867-920-3459
Fax 867-873-0283
Email .... shupen@internorth.com

The Department of Transportation is responsible for planning, designing, constructing, reconstructing, acquiring, operating, and maintaining the public transportation infrastructure in Northwest Territories. This includes community airports, docks, and the highway system. The department also regulates and licences individuals and vehicles operating in NWT. The Department employs 315 people throughout NWT. Graduates most likely to be hired come from the following academic areas: Bachelor of Engineering (Civil), Bachelor of Commerce/Business Administration (Accounting, Finance, Human Resources, Information Systems, Public Administration), Chartered Accountant, Certified Management Accountant, Certified General Accountant, Master of Business Administration (Accounting, Finance, Human Resources, Information Systems, Public Administration), Master of Engineering, Community College Diploma (Accounting, Administration, Engineering Technician), and High School Diploma. Graduates would occupy Project Technician, Highway Technician, Design Engineer, Structural Technician, Soils Technician, and Drafting Technician positions. A willingness to work in remote and isolated areas, team player, and able to work in cross-cultural settings are all listed as desirable non-academic qualifications. The most suitable methods for initial contact by those seeking employment are to mail, fax or e-mail a resume with a covering letter. The Department of Transportation does hire summer students, primarily NWT students. *Contacts:* Colleen Kilty, Manager, Human Resources or Neal Shupe, Human Resources Specialist; Dale Dean, Human Resources Specialist.

DH HOWDEN DIVISION

3232 White Oak Road, P.O. Box 5485
London, ON N6A 4G8

Tel. 519-686-2200
Fax 519-686-2333

DH Howden Division is a wholesaler of hardware and renovation products. The company employs approximately 275 people at this location, and a total of 300 people. Graduates most likely to be hired come from the following academic areas: Bachelor of Arts (General), Bachelor of Commerce/Business Administration (General), Community College Diploma (Advertising, Information Systems, Marketing/Sales, CAD/CAM/Autocad), and High School Diploma. Graduates would occupy Clerk, Coordinator, and Analyst positions. Flexibility and the ability to react quickly to changing market conditions are both listed as desirable non-academic qualifications. Company benefits are rated as industry standard. The potential for advancement is listed as average. The average annual starting salary falls within the $20,000 to $25,000 range. The most suitable method for initial contact by those seeking employment is to mail a resume with a covering letter. DH Howden Division does hire summer and co-op work term students. *Contact:* Marc Fraser, Manager, Human Resources.

DIANA SWEETS LTD.
75 The Donway West
Toronto, ON M3C 2E9

Tel. 416-441-6380
Fax 416-441-6376

Diana Sweets Ltd. is a licensed, full-service restaurant chain with 3 locations in Greater Toronto. It has been in operation since 1912 and is the longest established restaurant chain that is still under the ownership of the original operating family. Each location employs more than 25 people. Graduates most likely to be hired come from Community College programs in Hotel and Restaurant Management. Graduates are hired as Junior/Assistant Managers or for Kitchen Staff positions. Good communication and interpersonal skills, flexible, sound judgment, common sense, a good work ethic, team player initiative, and an eagerness and ability to learn quickly are all listed as desirable non-academic qualifications. Company benefits are rated above average. The potential for advancement is listed as being good. The most suitable method for initial contact by graduates seeking employment is to mail a resume with a covering letter. Diana Sweets Ltd. does hire summer students when positions are available. *Contact:* Diane Bolgyesi, Vice President Personnel.

DIMPLEX NORTH AMERICA LIMITED
1367 Industrial Road, P.O. Box 1726
Cambridge, ON N1R 7G8

Tel. 519-650-3630

Dimplex North America Limited employs more than 250 people in the manufacture of electrical heating products. Operations involve dealing with distributors, manufacturers and contractors. The product line includes industrial, commercial and space heating products. Graduates most likely to be hired come from the following academic areas: Bachelor of Arts (Social Sciences), Bachelor of Engineering (Mechanical, Electrical), Bachelor of Commerce/Business Administration, Certified Management Accountant, and Community College Diploma (Accounting, Electrical Technician, Computer Science). Graduates would occupy Human Resources, Engineering, Accounting, Information Systems, and Technical Sales positions. Good problem solving and decision making abilities, computer literacy, and strong verbal and written communication skills are all listed as desirable non-academic qualifications. Company

benefits are rated as excellent. The potential for advancement is listed as average. The average annual starting salary falls within the $30,000 to $35,000 range. The most suitable method for initial contact by those seeking employment is to mail a resume with a covering letter. *Contact:* Human Resources.

DINECORP HOSPITALITY INC.
1 Concorde Gate, Suite 400
Toronto, ON M3C 3N6

Tel. 416-449-1999
Fax 416-449-1972

Dinecorp Hospitality Inc. (founded 1981), is a dynamic Canadian company with restaurant complexes in seven Canadian provinces. Dinecorp is the largest holder of Swiss Chalet and Harvey's franchises and currently operates 27 Swiss Chalet and 16 Harvey's restaurants which generate annual sales of $75 million and employ more than 2,000 Team Members in total. Dinecorp is committed to professional management in the food service industry. Graduates most likely to be hired in restaurant operations come from the following academic areas: Bachelor of Arts (General, Economics, English), Bachelor of Commerce/Business Administration (Commerce, Accounting, Finance, Marketing), Certified Management Accountant, Certified General Accountant, Community College Diploma (Accounting, Administration, Business, Cooking, Hospitality), and High School Diploma. Personable, sales oriented, and good communication skills are listed as desirable non-academic qualifications. Company benefits and the potential for advancement are both rated as excellent, since Dinecorp strongly believes in promotion from within and in people development. The average starting salary falls within the $24,000 to $34,000 range. The most suitable method for initial contact by those seeking employment is to mail a resume with a covering letter. Summer students are hired at the restaurant level for entry level positions. *Contact:* Mr. P. Metelski.

DISCOUNT CAR AND TRUCK RENTALS
720 Arrow Road
Toronto, ON M9M 2M1

Tel. 416-744-0123
Fax 416-744-9829
Email .... hr@discountcar.com
Website .... www.discountcar.com

Discount Car and Truck Rentals is at the forefront of the automobile rental industry with locations across Canada and many more opening in the United States and around the world. Discount's spectacular growth has created many opportunities for ambitious and hard-working individuals who are interested in long-term growth and a dynamic work environment. Graduates most likely to be hired come from the following academic areas: Bachelor of Arts (General), Bachelor of Science (General), Bachelor of Commerce/Business Administration (General, Marketing), and Community College Diploma (Business). Graduates would occupy Management Trainee positions. Team player, outgoing, a strong desire to rise to the top, and previous sales experience are all listed as desirable non-academic qualifications. Company benefits are rated above average. The potential for advancement is listed as excellent. The average annual starting salary falls within the $20,000 to $25,000 range. The most suitable methods for initial contact by those seeking employment are to mail, fax or e-mail a resume with a covering letter. Discount Car and Truck Rentals does hire summer students. *Contacts:* Joanne Fessenden, Recruiter or Monica Nagasuye, Human Resources Coordinator.

DIVERSEY INC.
2645 Royal Windsor Drive
Mississauga, ON L5J 1L1

Tel.	905-822-3511
Fax	905-822-3797

Diversey Inc. employs 550 people in the manufacturing, marketing and selling of specialized chemicals used for cleaning and sanitation purposes. Graduates most likely to be hired come from the following academic areas: Bachelor of Science (Chemistry, Microbiology), Bachelor of Engineering (Chemical, Environmental, Mechanical), Bachelor of Commerce/Business Administration (Accounting, Information Systems), Certified Management Accountant, Certified General Accountant, Master of Science (Chemistry), Doctorate of Science (Chemistry), and Community College Diploma (Accounting, Administration, Marketing/Sales, Computer Science, Engineering, Industrial Design). Related work experience, computer skills (spreadsheet and word processing applications) and good communication skills are listed as desirable non-academic qualifications. Company benefits are rated above average. The potential for advancement is listed as being good. The average annual starting salary falls within the $30,000 to $35,000 range. The most suitable method for initial contact by those seeking employment is to mail a resume with a covering letter. Diversey Inc. does hire summer students. *Contact:* Michael Wityk, Employee Relations Manager.

DMR CONSULTING GROUP INC.
252 Adelaide Street East
Toronto, ON M5A 1N1

Tel.	416-594-2000
Fax	416-363-4739
Email	dmr_recruiting@dmr.com
Website	www.dmr.com

DMR Consulting Group Inc., Amdahl's professional services company, is a leading international provider of information technology services to private and public sector enterprises. Founded in Montreal in 1973, DMR has a reputation for providing integrated business and IT solutions that enable clients to increase their competitive position, market share and productivity. To date, the company has served thousands of businesses and public enterprises internationally, accumulating experience in managing large-scale systems development and integration projects, combined with expertise in management consulting, an unique ability to engineer solutions, and a suite of proven methods. DMR employs 2,000 professionals in Canada, and a total of 6,000 people in Canada, the U.S., Asia-Pacific, and Europe. Graduates most likely to be hired come from the following academic areas: Bachelor of Science (Computer Science, Mathematics), Bachelor of Engineering (Computer Systems), Bachelor of Commerce/Business Administration (Information Systems), Master of Business Administration (Accounting, Finance, Human Resources, Information Systems, Marketing), Master of Science (Computer Science), and Community College Diploma (Computer Science). Graduates would occupy Programmer/Analyst and Consultant positions. Team player and mobility are both listed as desirable non-academic qualifications. Company benefits are rated above average. The potential for advancement is listed as excellent. The average annual starting salary falls within the $40,000 to $45,000 range, depending upon location of employment. The most suitable methods for initial contact by those seeking employment are to mail or e-mail a resume with a covering letter. DMR Consulting Group Inc. hires co-op students from computer science programs. *Contact:* Resources Manager.

DMS MARKET SERVICES
112 Merton Street, 2nd Floor
Toronto, ON M4S 2Z8

Tel.	416-481-8838
Fax	416-481-0688

DMS Market Services is the largest full-service communications company in Canada, operating throughout the country and employing approximately 1,700 people. Since 1972, DMS has been active in planning and executing telemarketing, and field marketing programs in the areas of sales, customer service, promotions and research. The company provides both business to consumer, and business to business outbound telephone communication services, as well as inbound telephone communication services. DMS seeks highly motivated individuals from all academic areas. Outgoing, team player, previous customer service experience, excellent communication skills, basic keyboarding skills, and excellent listening and probing skills are all listed as desirable non-academic qualifications. Bilingualism (French/English) is a definite asset. Applicants are hired to occupy Customer Service Representative, Telephone Sales Representative, and In-Store Promotion positions. Full or part time, daytime and evening shift work hours are available. The average starting wage range is $7.50 to $10.00 per hour, depending upon the position and the applicant's skill set. In addition to a guaranteed hourly wage and employee training, the company offers a generous benefits package. The most suitable method for initial contact by those seeking employment is via telephone, Monday through Friday, 9:00am to 5:00pm. DMS Market Services does have summer and part-time positions available. *Contact:* Human Resources Department.

DOMINION COMPANY, THE
555 Burrard Street, Suite 300
Two Bentall Centre
Vancouver, BC V7X 1S9

Tel. 604-631-1000
Fax.. 604-631-1100

The Dominion Company is one of western Canada's leading development, design, and construction companies with offices in Vancouver, Calgary, Edmonton, Regina, Winnipeg, and Santa Ana, California. Over the past 84 years, The Dominion Company has established itself as a design-builder of some of the most prominent commercial, industrial, and retail properties in western Canada. The company employs 100 people at this location, an additional 50 people in Canada, and 21 employees in the United States. Graduates most likely to be hired come from the following academic areas: Bachelor of Engineering (Civil, Architectural/Building, Surveying, Electrical, Mechanical, Industrial Design), Bachelor of Architecture, Bachelor of Commerce/Business Administration (Accounting, Information Systems), Certified Management Accountant, Certified General Accountant, and Community College Diploma (Accounting, CAD/CAM/Autocad, Engineering Technician). Graduates would occupy Junior Mechanical Engineer, Junior Structural Engineer, Junior Electrical Engineer, Architectural Technologist, Project Assistant, and Accounting Clerk positions. A commitment to leaning, resource management, innovative, achievement oriented, teamwork, customer focus, leadership and problem solving skills are all listed as desirable non-academic qualifications. Company benefits are rated above average. The potential for advancement is listed as being good. The most suitable methods for initial contact by those seeking employment are to mail or fax a resume with a covering letter. The Dominion Company does hire summer students. Contact: Deborah Louvier, Vice President, Human Resources.

DOMINION OF CANADA GENERAL INSURANCE COMPANY, THE
165 University Avenue
Toronto, ON M5H 3B9

Tel. 416-350-3740
Fax.. 416-362-1602
Email .... careers@thedominion.ca

The Dominion of Canada General Insurance Company is a Canadian owned and operated general insurance company which has been serving Canadians since 1887. Today, The Dominion is one of Canada's largest property and casualty insurance companies. The company is committed to providing high quality home, automobile and business insurance products through the independent brokerage system. With offices in Halifax, Ottawa, Scarborough, Toronto, Oakville, London, Calgary, Edmonton, and Vancouver, The Dominion has over 900 employees. This location employs 250 people. Graduates most likely to be hired come from the following academic areas: Bachelor of Arts (General, Economics, Political Science, Psychology, Sociology), Bachelor of Science (General, Actuarial, Computer Science, Mathematics), Bachelor of Commerce/Business Administration (Accounting, Finance, Human Resources, Information Systems, Marketing), Chartered Accountant, Certified Management Accountant, Certified General Accountant, Master of Business Administration (Accounting, Finance, Information Systems, Marketing), and Community College Diploma (Administration, Business, Insurance, Marketing/Sales, Secretarial). Graduates would occupy Commercial Lines Underwriter Trainee, Personal Lines Underwriter Trainee, Claims Service Representative Trainee, Actuarial Analyst, Programmer/Analyst, Financial Analyst, Accounting Clerk, and Customer Service Representative positions. Good customer service skills, team player, results oriented, initiative, excellent problem solving and decision making skills, good communication skills, and an ability to learn are all listed as desirable non-academic qualifications. Company benefits are rated above average. The potential for advancement is listed as being good. The average annual starting salary falls within the $25,000 to $30,000 range. The most suitable methods for initial contact by those seeking employment are to mail, fax or e-mail a resume with a covering letter. The Dominion does hire summer and co-op work term students. Contact: Employee Services Coordinator, Human Resources.

DOMTAR PAPERS
800 Second Street West
Cornwall, ON K6J 1H6

Tel. 613-932-6620
Fax.. 613-938-4567

Domtar Papers, Cornwall Plant is an integrated pulp mill with four paper machines and a finishing department producing fine grade paper. There are 1,100 employees at this location, while Domtar employs a total of 9,000 people in Canada, and a total of 9,200 people worldwide. Graduates most likely to be hired come from the following academic areas: Bachelor of Science (Chemistry, Computer Science, Environmental), Bachelor of Engineering (Chemical, Industrial Chemistry, Pollution Treatment, Pulp and Paper, Architectural/Building, Instrumentation, Industrial Design, Industrial Production, Water Resources), Bachelor of Commerce/Business Administration (Finance, Human Resources, Information Systems), Chartered Accountant, Certified Management Accountant, Certified General Accountant, Master of Business Administration (Accounting, Finance, Human Resources, Information Systems), Master of Engineering (Mechanical, Electrical, Pulp and Paper), and Community College Diploma (Accounting, Administration, Business, Purchasing/Logistics, Secretarial, Security/Enforcement, Computer Science, Welding). Graduates would occupy a variety of entry level jobs based upon each candidate's education and experience. Customer oriented, team player, follow-up skills, flexibility, and computer skills are all listed as desirable non-academic qualifications. Company benefits and the potential for advancement are both rated as excellent. The average annual starting salary is dependent upon the position being considered. The most suitable method for initial contact by those seeking employment is to mail a resume with a covering letter. Domtar Papers does hire summer students. *Contact:* Human Resources Department.

DRUMMOND WELDING & STEEL WORKS INC.
700 Talon
Longueuil, QC J4G 1P7

Tel. 514-526-4411
Fax 514-679-1686

Drummond Welding & Steel Works Inc. is involved in the manufacturing of steel tanks and pressure vessels. There are 95 employees at this location and a total of 100 employees in the Company. Graduates most likely to be hired come from the following academic areas: Bachelor of Science (Computer Science, Metallurgy), Bachelor of Engineering (Civil, Architectural/Building, Industrial Design, Industrial Production, Mechanical, Metallurgy, Welding, Petroleum), Bachelor of Commerce/Business Administration (Accounting, Human Resources, Marketing), Community College Diploma (Accounting, Marketing/Sales, Purchasing/Logistics, Secretarial, CAD/CAM/Autocad, Engineering Technician, Welding), and High School Diploma. Graduates would occupy Draftsperson, Inside Sales Representative, Design Engineer, Production Planner, Estimator, Buyer, Inspector, and Accountant positions. Initiative, dynamic, and a working knowledge of French and English are all listed as desirable non-academic qualifications. Company benefits are rated as industry standard. The potential for advancement is listed as being good. The average annual starting salary falls within the $20,000 to $25,000 range. The most suitable method for initial contact by those seeking employment is to mail a resume with a covering letter. *Contacts:* Christine Bellefeuille, Human Resources Manager or Louis Caissie, Human Resources Manager.

DUCKS UNLIMITED CANADA
P.O. Box 1160,
Oak Hammock Marsh
Stonewall, MB R0C 2C0

Tel. 204-467-3209
Fax 204-467-9028
Email .... c_barber@ducks.ca

Ducks Unlimited Canada is a non-profit, private company dedicated to the preservation of breeding habitat in Canada for waterfowl, providing assistance to farmers in land use which benefits the environment and provides water for agriculture, domestic and recreational uses. There are approximately 120 employees at this location and a total of 500 employees across Canada. Graduates most likely to be hired come from the following academic areas: Bachelor of Arts (History), Bachelor of Science (Agriculture, Biology, Computer Science, Wetland and Marsh Management), Bachelor of Engineering (Environmental/Resources, Water Resources), Bachelor of Commerce/Business Administration (Accounting, Finance, Information Systems, Marketing), Chartered Accountant (Finance), Certified Management Accountant (Finance), Certified General Accountant (Finance), Master of Business Administration (Accounting, Finance, Information Systems, Marketing), Master of Science (Wetland and Marsh Management), and Community College Diploma (Accounting, Communications/Public Relations, Human Resources, Information Systems, Secretarial, Audio/Visual Technician, Journalism, Recreation Studies, Travel/Tourism, Agriculture/Horticulture, CAD-CAM/Autocad, Computer Science). Graduates would occupy Biologist, Agrologist, Research Biologist, Interpreter, Fund Raiser, Administrative Assistant, Writer, G.I.S. Specialist, I.S. Developer, I.S. Analyst, Engineer, Computer Technician and Computer Operator positions. Initiative, team player, risk taker, quality and goal oriented are all listed as desirable nonacademic qualifications. In addition, most positions call for two to five years related work experience. Company benefits are rated above average. The potential for advancement is listed as average. The most suitable method for initial contact by those seeking employment is to mail a resume with a covering letter. Ducks Unlimited Canada does hire local summer students for the interpretive program, from history (history of Oak Hammond Marsh) and biology (waterfowl and plants) programs. *Contacts:* Ms. C. Barber, Personnel or For other Provinces contact the Manager of Field Operations.

DUN & BRADSTREET CANADA
5770 Hurontario Street
Mississauga, ON L5R 3G5

Tel. 905-568-6350
Fax 905-568-6360

Dun & Bradstreet Canada provides a host of business information services to support companies in making business to business decisions. In addition to credit reports, marketing services and collection services, Dun & Bradstreet conducts education seminars. The company employs 300 people at this location, a total of 560 in Canada, and 16,000 people worldwide. Graduates most likely to be hired come from the following academic areas: Bachelor of Arts (General), Bachelor of Commerce/Business Administration (General, Accounting, Finance, Human Resources, information Systems, Marketing), Master of Business Administration (General), and Community College Diploma (Accounting, Administration, Advertising, Human Resources, Information Systems, Insurance, Marketing/Sales, Secretarial, Graphic Arts). Graduates would occupy Business Analyst, Accountant, Programmer, and Collections Officer positions. Initiative, drive, creativity, and self-starter are all listed as desirable non-academic qualifications. The most suitable methods for initial contact by those seeking employment are to mail or fax a resume with a covering letter. Dun & Bradstreet Canada does hire summer and co-op work term students. *Contact:* Cathy Partridge.

DuPont Canada

DUPONT CANADA INC.
P.O. Box 2200, Streetsville
Mississauga, ON L5M 2H3

Tel. 905-821-3300
Fax 905-821-5592

DuPont Canada Inc. is a diversified industrial chemical manufacturing company. The wide range of DuPont products sold include: synthetic fibres, polymer resins, packaging films, automotive finishes, agricultural and industrial chemicals. There are 350 employees at the head office in Mississauga, and a total of 3,200 employees in five manufacturing facilities located in Ontario. These include, Ajax, Corunna, Kingston, Maitland and Whitby. Graduates most likely to be hired come from the following academic areas: Bachelor Science (Chemistry, Computer Science), Bachelor of Engineering (Chemical, Mechanical, Electrical), Bachelor of Commerce/Business Administration, Master/Doctorate of Science (Chemistry, Computer Science), and Master/Doctorate of Engineering (Chemical, Mechanical, Electrical). Company benefits and the potential for advancement are both rated as very good. DuPont Canada is committed to setting and meeting high safety, health and environmental standards. The most suitable methods for initial contact by graduates seeking employment are to mail a resume with a covering letter to The Staffing Team of DuPont Canada, or through your campus career centre, please indicate preferred field of work (eg. accounting, chemical engineering, administration, etc). *Contact:* The Staffing Team, Human Resources & Communications.

D Y N A P R O

DYNAPRO
800 Carleton Court, Annacis Island
New Westminster, BC V3M 6L3

Tel. 604-521-3962
Fax 604-521-8474
Email .... debbie_paulsen@dynapro.com
Website .... www.dynapro.com

Dynapro simplifies interaction by designing and manufacturing world class hardware, software, and touch screen solutions. Dynapro's products include touch computers, terminals, monitors, touch screens, software, and related components for the industrial and non-industrial marketplace. Dynapro employs over 500 people, approximately 280 at its main facility in Vancouver and approximately 220 in Milwaukee, Wisconsin. Graduates most likely to be hired come from the following academic areas: Bachelor of Engineering (Computer Science, Mathematics, Physics), Bachelor of Engineering (Chemical, Electrical, Mechanical, Computer Systems, Engineering Physics, Industrial Production/Manufacturing, Materials Science), Bachelor of Commerce/Business Administration (Accounting, Finance, Information Systems, Marketing), Certified Management Accountant, Master of Business Administration (General, Finance, Marketing), Master/Doctorate of Science (Computer Science), Master/Doctorate of Engineering (Electrical, Chemical, Mechanical), and Community College Diploma (Accounting, Administration, Human Resources, Information Systems, Marketing/Sales, CAD/CAM/Autocad, Electronics Technician, Engineering Technician). Graduates would occupy Engineer, Technologist, Technician, Management, Support and Accounting positions. Good verbal and written communication skills, previous work experience, team player, and PC skills are all listed as desirable non-academic qualifications. Company benefits are rated as excellent. The potential for advancement is listed as average. The most suitable methods for initial contact by those seeking employment are to mail or e-mail a resume with a covering letter, or by applying through the company's website at www.dynapro.com. Dynapro does hire summer students. *Contacts:* Debbie Paulsen, Human Resources Director or Cheryl Charron, Human Resources Administrator.

EAST YORK PLANNING DEPARTMENT
850 Coxwell Avenue
Toronto, ON M4C 5R1

Tel. 416-778-2040

The East York Planning Department employs fewer than 10 people in municipal planning activities. These activities include policy development, development control and the Committee of Adjustment. Graduates most likely to be hired come from the following academic areas: Bachelor of Arts (Urban Planning), Master of Arts (Urban Planning), and Community College Diploma (Architecture/Drafting). Graduates would occupy Planning Technician, Planner, Intermediate Planner, and Senior Planner positions. Ethical, outstanding written and communication skills, intellectual discipline, and excellent organizational skills are all listed as desirable non-academic qualifications. Company benefits are rated as excellent. The potential for advancement is listed as being good. The most suitable method for initial contact by graduates seeking employment is to mail a resume with a covering letter. The East York Planning Department is part of the new City of Toronto Urban Planning and Development Services Department. *Contact:* Commissioner of Planning.

EAST YORK WORKS AND ENVIRONMENT DEPARTMENT
850 Coxwell Avenue
Toronto, ON M4C 5R1

Tel.	416-778-2000
Fax	416-466-9877

The East York Works and Environment Department is responsible for the infrastructure of the community. This involves activities ranging from installation of new sewer systems to providing garbage collection and water supply. The department employs more than 250 people. Graduates most likely to be hired come from the following academic areas: Bachelor of Engineering (Civil, Environmental) and Community College Diploma (Engineering Technicians). In addition to employing Engineers and Engineering Technicians the Department employs clerical, support staff, labourers and skilled tradespeople in the Operations Division. Graduates should possess computer skills and a driver's license. Employee benefits are rated above average. The potential for advancement is listed as being good. The average annual starting salary is dependent upon the level of position. The most suitable method for initial contact by graduates seeking employment is to mail a resume with a covering letter. The department hires summer students for Relief Labour and Technical Help positions. East York Works and Environment Department is part of the new City of Toronto Works and Emergency Services Department. *Contact:* Personnel Department.

EATON, T. COMPANY LIMITED, THE
290 Yonge Street, 7th Floor
Toronto, ON M5B 1C8

Tel.	416-349-7111
Fax	416-349-7115
Website	www.eatons.com

The T. Eaton Company Limited (Eaton's) is one of Canada's major department store retailers. Eaton's operates approximately 60 stores across Canada, with its corporate offices located in Toronto. Eaton's has been at the forefront of Canadian retail for more than 125 years, and is known for quality, service and the Eaton guarantee. Graduates most likely to be hired come from the following academic areas: Bachelor of Arts (Graphic Arts), Bachelor of Commerce/Business Administration (Human Resources, Information Systems, Marketing), Master of Business Administration (Human Resources, Information Systems, Marketing), and Community College Diploma (Fashion Merchandising). Company benefits and the potential for advancement are both rated as excellent. The average annual starting salary falls within the $15,000 to $20,000 range. The most suitable method for initial contact by those seeking employment is to fax a resume. *Contacts:* Heather Howard, Manager, Recruitment or Human Resources Department.

ECE GROUP LTD., THE
205 Lesmill Road
Don Mills, ON M3B 2V1

Tel.	416-449-1030
Fax	416-449-2876

The ECE Group Ltd., founded in 1955, provides consulting and engineering services in electrical and mechanical engineering. In addition, the company provides services in specialty disciplines of communication, security and associated environmental engineering needs. ECE's experience has been gathered in the design of a wide range of commercial, institutional, public and special-purpose buildings. The company's range of services includes investigations, reports, research, design and inspection. Through a wholly owned subsidiary, the Company also provides facility management services. ECE employs 64 people at this location. Graduates most likely to be hired come from the following academic areas: Bachelor of Engineering (Electrical, Mechanical, Computer Systems, Industrial Design), and Community College Diploma (Architectural Technician, CAD/CAM/Autocad, Engineering Technician, HVAC Systems). Graduates would occupy Mechanical and Electrical CAD Designer, Technician, and Engineering positions. Energetic, hardworking, self-directed, able to work well with others, and good oral and verbal communication skills are all listed as desirable non-academic qualifications. Company benefits and the potential for advancement are both rated as excellent. The average annual starting salary falls within the $32,000 to $38,000 range. The most suitable method for initial contact by graduates seeking employment is to mail a resume with a covering letter. The ECE Group Ltd. does hire summer and co-op work term students. *Contact:* Marianne Villa, Manager, Human Resources.

ECOLAB LTD.
5105 Tomken Road
Mississauga, ON L4W 2X5

Tel.	905-238-0171
Fax	905-238-2006
Website	www.ecolab.com

Ecolab Ltd. is involved in the manufacture and marketing of cleaning and sanitizing chemical products. Products are sold worldwide via a direct sales force. In Canada, Ecolab Ltd. employs 400 people and maintains one manufacturing plant. Graduates most likely to be hired come from the following academic areas: Bachelor of Science (General, Biology, Chemistry, Microbiology), Bachelor of Engineering (General, Environmental, Chemical), Bachelor of Commerce/Business Administration, and Community College Diploma (Accounting, Administration, Secretarial, Engineering, Mechanic). Graduates would to occupy Territory Manager Trainee, Engineer, and Production Supervisor positions. Sales ability, good organizational skills, and a strong sense of urgency are listed as desirable non-academic qualifications. Company benefits are rated as industry standard. The potential for advancement is listed as excellent. The average annual starting salary falls within the $30,000 to $35,000 range, and is commission based for some positions. The most suitable method for initial contact by those seeking employment is to mail a resume with a covering letter. Ecolab Ltd. does hire summer students. *Contact:* Jan Moody, Human Resources Coordinator.

ECONOMICAL INSURANCE GROUP, THE

111 Westmount Road South, P.O. Box 2000
Waterloo, ON N2J 4S4

Tel. 519-570-8200
Fax 519-570-8239
Email .... hrd@economicalinsurance.com

The Economical Insurance Group is a top 10, Canadian owned, property and casualty insurer with a track record of success spanning over 125 years. Economical is expanding its products, services and technology to meet the challenges of the new millennium, and is committed to working with its business partners to meet these goals. The company is a recognized market leader in interface technology and in its ability to succeed in new product markets. Presently, there are 420 employees at this location and a total of 1,200 employees in Canada. Economical believes in recruiting, training and rewarding dedicated people who believe in their ability to achieve. Graduates most likely to be hired come from the following academic areas: Bachelor of Arts (General, Economics, English, Geography), Bachelor of Science (General, Actuarial, Computer Science, Mathematics), Bachelor of Commerce (General, Accounting, Finance, Human Resources, Information Systems), Chartered Accountant, Certified Management Accountant, Certified General Accountant, Master of Business Administration (General), and Community College Diploma (Accounting, Administration, Business, Human Resources, Information Systems, Insurance, Secretarial). Graduates would occupy Administrative Assistant, Accounting Clerk, Computer Programmer/Analyst, Financial Analyst, Claims Trainee, and Underwriter Trainee positions. Good written and oral communication skills, organized, teamwork, flexibility, demonstrated performance to rise above and beyond that expected, and a willingness to seek skills and knowledge through the challenge of continuous learning are all listed as desirable non-academic qualifications. Company benefits are rated above average. The potential for advancement is listed as being good. The average annual starting salary falls within the $20,000 to $25,000 range. The most suitable methods for initial contact by those seeking employment are to mail, fax or e-mail a resume with a covering letter. The Economical Insurance Group does hire summer and co-op work term students. *Contact:* Carol Boss, Specialist - Staffing, Human Resources.

EDELSTEIN DIVERSIFIED COMPANY

21 Mount Vernon
Montreal, QC H8R 1J9

Tel. 514-489-8689
Fax 514-489-9707
Email .... info@edelstein.com
Website .... www.edelstein.com

Edelstein Diversified Company Limited, established in 1973, is a leading supplier of specialty pressure sensitive tapes. The corporate headquarters is located in Montreal, with sales and warehousing facilities maintained and operated in Chicago, Los Angeles, Norfolk, Toronto and Vancouver. The company employs approximately 60 people at this location, a total of 75 in Canada, and a total of 90 people worldwide. Edelstein supplies pressure sensitive tapes to every segment of industry including the leading paper, food, tobacco, metal and plastic manufacturers. The company's research and development facilities work to provide the most technically advanced products at competitive pricing. Graduates most likely to be hired come from the following academic areas: Bachelor of Arts (Economics, Psychology), Bachelor of Engineering (General, Forest Resources, Industrial Engineering, Industrial Production/Manufacturing, Materials Science, Pulp and Paper), Bachelor of Commerce/Business Administration (General, Finance, Marketing), Master of Business Administration (Marketing), and Community College Diploma (Business, Marketing/Sales). Edelstein continually seeks graduates for Sales positions. Team player, initiative, drive, enthusiasm, problem solving skills, computer literacy, and sales experience are all listed as desirable non-academic qualifications. Company benefits are rated above average. The most suitable methods for initial contact by those seeking employment are to mail or fax a resume with a covering letter. Edelstein Diversified Company Limited does hire summer students. *Contact:* Human Resource Department.

EDS CANADA

33 Yonge Street, Suite 810
Toronto, ON M5E 1G4

Tel. 1-800-263-3840
Website .... www.eds.com

EDS Canada has been active in the Canadian marketplace since 1985 and has quickly evolved into a leading provider of information technology services. From offices in 21 Canadian cities, more than 2,000 highly skilled employees provide a broad range of professional services that are used to enhance business systems and processes for more than 50 private and public sector client organizations. Graduates are hired from the following academic areas: Bachelor of Science (General, Computer Science, Mathematics), Bachelor of Engineering (General, Systems, Electrical, Mechanical), Bachelor of Commerce/Business Administration (Information Systems), and Community College Diploma (Business Administration, Information Systems, Computer Programming, Electronics Technology). EDS is interested in well rounded individuals who possess a variety of skills such as leadership ability, a high level of professionalism and technical aptitude. Good communication and customer relation skills are also requirements. Rewards are based on performance, creativity, and contribution to the organization. Promotions at EDS occur from within, allowing the best qualified and available employees the opportunities for advancement. EDS is committed to an equal employment opportunity policy in all its operations and in all employment practices. Interested applicants should mail a resume and covering letter to Staffing Services. Summer students are encouraged to apply by January 15th. *Contact:* Staffing Services.

EDSCHA OF CANADA

P.O. Box 660
Niagara Falls, ON L2E 6V5

Tel. 905-374-3400
Fax 905-374-3614

Edscha of Canada is involved in the manufacturing of auto parts, primarily door hinges and checks. There are approximately 230 employees at this location. Graduates most likely to be hired come from the following academic areas: Bachelor of Engineering (General, Electrical, Automation/Robotics, Computer Systems, Mechanical, Industrial Design, Industrial Production), Bachelor of Commerce/Business Administration (General, Accounting, Finance, Human Resources, Information Systems, Marketing), Chartered Accountant (Auto Manufacturing), Certified Management Accountant (Auto Manufacturing), Certified General Accountant (Auto Manufacturing), Master of Business Administration (Accounting, Finance, Human Resources, Information Systems, Marketing), Community College Diploma (Accounting, Administration, Business, Financial Planning, Human Resources, Marketing/Sales, Purchasing/ Logistics, Secretarial, CAD/CAM/Autocad Computer Science, Engineering Technician), and High School Diploma. Graduates would occupy Accounting Clerk, Engineer and Trainee positions. Previous work experience, team player, and good communication skills are listed as desirable non-academic qualifications. Company benefits are rated above average. The potential for advancement is listed as average. The average annual starting salary depends upon the position being considered, ranging from $30,000 to $35,000 for administrative positions, and $40,000 to $45,000 for technical positions. The most suitable methods for initial contact by those seeking employment are to mail a resume with a covering letter, or through job placement agencies. Edscha of Canada does hire summer students, although not every summer. *Contact:* Connie MacDonald, Payroll and Benefits Administration.

Edward Jones®

Serving Individual Investors

EDWARD JONES

90 Burnhamthorpe Road West, Suite 902
Sussex Centre
Mississauga, ON L5B 3C3

Tel. 905-275-4525
Fax 905-306-8624
Email .... careeropcan@edwardjones.com
Website .... www.edwardjones.com

Edward Jones is a full-service financial services firm that serves the long-term investment needs of individuals. Edward Jones pioneered the concept of single-broker, community-oriented branch offices, and has built the largest brokerage office network throughout the United States, Canada and the United Kingdom. The cornerstone of Edward Jones' heritage is its face-to-face investment approach that serves the individual conservative investor. This approach is essential to the company's ongoing success and plans. Presently, Edward Jones employs 300 people in Canada, and a total of 10,500 people worldwide. Graduates most likely to be hired come from the following academic areas: Bachelor of Arts (Economics), Bachelor of Commerce/Business Administration (General, Accounting, Finance, Marketing), Chartered Accountant, Certified Management Accountant, Certified General Accountant, Master of Business Administration (General, Accounting, Finance, Marketing), and Community College Diploma (Accounting, Business, Financial Planning, Insurance, Marketing/Sales, Real Estate Sales). Graduates are hired as Investment Representatives. As an Investment Representative, graduates start at the top, getting right to work building a business and running their own Edward Jones branch office. Edward Jones provides training and a fully equipped and furnished office, which includes a full-time assistant, advanced computer and satellite video technology, and much more. The company seeks self-reliant, highly ambitious, energetic, committed, hard working, and highly successful people who are determined to build and manage their own profitable business without the cash investment that usually accompanies a startup. Applicants should be acutely aware of the entrepreneurial opportunities that exist in the growth environment of Edward Jones. The company is an equal opportunity employer and offers a competitive salary and benefits package. Accordingly, company benefits and the potential for advancement are both rated as excellent. The average annual starting salary falls within the $50,000 to $55,000 range. The most suitable methods for initial contact by those seeking employment with Edward Jones, are to call 1-800-380-4517 (extensions 38632 or 38693), or through the company's website at www.edwardjones.com. *Contacts:* Ilona Gonsalves, Sales Hiring Specialist or Mina Modarelli, Sales Hiring Specialist.

EFA SOFTWARE SERVICES LTD.

605 - 5th Avenue SW, Suite 800
Calgary, AB T2P 3H5

Tel. 403-265-6131
Fax 403-265-2893
Email .... gthompson@efasoftware.ab.ca

EFA Software Services Ltd. is a computer software company employing approximately 72 people. Graduates most likely to be hired come from the following academic areas: Bachelor of Science (Computer Science), Bachelor of Commerce/Business Administration (Information Systems), and Community College Diploma (Journalism, Computer Science). The average annual starting salary is currently being reviewed. The most suitable method for initial contact by those seeking employment is to mail a resume with a covering letter. *Contacts:* Geoff Thompson, Vice President or Jim Bird, Manager.

EG & G OPTOELECTRONICS CANADA

22001 Dumberry Road
Vaudreuil, QC J7V 8P7

Tel.	514-424-3300
Fax	514-424-3413

EG & G Inc. was founded over 45 years ago by H. Edgerton, K.F. Germeshausen and H.E. Grier, whose initials form the company name. Today, EG & G Inc., headquartered in Wellesley, Massachusetts, is a diversified high-tech company with over 14,000 employees. EG & G Optoelectronics Canada's principle focus is on optoelectronic products and applications such as emitters, photocells, lasers, detectors and electronic imaging devices. Our customer base includes companies who manufacture fibre optics and communication systems, medical and analytical instruments, automobiles, smoke alarms, etc. There are approximately 213 employees at this location. Graduates most likely to be hired come from the following academic areas: Bachelor of Science (Chemistry, Physics), Bachelor of Engineering (Chemical, Industrial Chemistry, Electrical, Microelectronics, Telecommunications), Bachelor of Commerce/Business Administration (Accounting, Finance, Human Resources, Information Systems, Marketing), Certified Management Accountant, Master of Science (Chemistry, Physics), Master of Engineering (Chemistry, Electrical), and Community College Diploma (Accounting, Administration, Business, Marketing/Sales, Purchasing/Logistics, Secretarial, Electronics Technician, Engineering Technician, HVAC Systems). Graduates would occupy Engineer, member of Technical Staff, Technician, Technician Assistant, Clerk, Secretary, and Administrator positions. Bilingualism, mobility, available to work on shifts (Technicians), and experience in a manufacturing environment are all listed as desirable non-academic qualifications. The average annual starting salary falls within the $30,000 to $35,000 range. The most suitable method for initial contact by those seeking employment is to mail a resume with a covering letter. *Contacts:* Barbara Blair or Lucie Giguère.

is vendor independent, and therefore can work objectively in a multi-vendor environment to design and implement technology solutions that best meet the needs of its clients. Whether it is network and systems integration services, software development, resource and project management or technical support, Ehvert Engineering is able to provide professional services that complement an organization's own technical resources. The company strives to provide the highest quality of service and support for corporations that are implementing or supporting technology infrastructures. Ehvert Engineering's specialized engineers and technicians form a team that can provide a complete technology solution, and are certified by a broad range of vendors. Graduates most likely to be hired come from the following academic areas: Bachelor of Science (Computer Science), Bachelor of Engineering (General, Civil, Electrical, Mechanical, Architectural/Building, Computer Systems, Engineering Physics, Telecommunications), Bachelor of Commerce/Business Administration (Accounting, Finance, Information Systems, Marketing), Chartered Accountant, Master of Business Administration (Accounting, Finance, Marketing), and Community College Diploma (Information Systems, CAD/CAM/Autocad, Computer Science, Engineering Technician). Graduates would occupy Infrastructure/Site Engineering Specialist, Senior Systems Consultant, Network and Systems Engineer, Technical Support Specialist, Software Developer, Controller, Marketing and Sales Representative positions. Good interpersonal and communication skills, self-starter, team player, strong technical abilities, good presentation skills, and previous work experience are all listed as desirable non-academic qualifications. The most suitable methods for initial contact by those seeking employment are to fax or e-mail a resume with a covering letter, or by applying through the company's website at www.ehvert.com. Ehvert Engineering does hire co-op work term students. *Contact:* Debra Zanon, Human Resources.

EHVERT ENGINEERING
Professional Technology Services

EHVERT ENGINEERING

1 University Avenue, Suite 604
Toronto, ON M5J 2P1

Tel.	416-868-1933
Fax	416-868-6229
Email	recruiting@ehvert.com
Website	www.ehvert.com

Ehvert Engineering is a multi-faceted technology services firm and Microsoft Certified Solution Provider. The Company's specialized team offers superior professional technical services and expertise in several diverse fields to large organizations. Ehvert

electro sonic

ELECTRO SONIC INC.

1100 Gordon Baker Road
Willowdale, ON M2H 3B3

Tel.	416-494-1666
Fax	416-496-3030
Website	www.e-sonic.com

Electro Sonic, an ISO 9002 registered company, is one of Canada's largest distributors of electronic components and parts. Electro Sonic is a supplier of both the repair and maintenance, as well as the original equipment manufacturers' markets. The company employs a total of 373 people in Canada. Graduates most likely to be hired come from the following academic areas: Bachelor of Arts (General, Economics, Philosophy, Political Science, Psychology), Bachelor of Science (Computer Science, Mathematics, Psychology), Bachelor of Engineering

(Electrical, Computer Systems, Environmental/Resources, Industrial Design, Industrial Engineering, Microelectronics, Telecommunications), Bachelor of Commerce/Business Administration (General, Accounting, Finance, Human Resources, Information Systems, Marketing), Chartered Accountant, Certified Management Accountant, Certified General Accountant, Master of Business Administration (Finance, Human Resources, Marketing), Master of Engineering (Industrial Design), Community College Diploma (Accounting, Administration, Advertising, Business, Communications/Public Relations, Human Resources, Information Systems, Marketing/Sales, Purchasing/Logistics, Secretarial, Computer Science, Electronics Technician, Engineering Technician), High School Diploma, those with CMP, APRC, PMAC, CHRP, CHRY designations, and graduates from the Canadian Securities Course. Graduates would occupy Trainee, Technician, Product Manager, Account Manager, Inside Sales Representative, A/P Coordinator, Financial Analyst, and Customer Service Representative. Strong interpersonal skills, detail oriented, good organizational skills, technical, results oriented, and the ability to deal and work with tight deadlines are all listed as desirable non-academic qualifications. Company benefits are rated above average. The potential for advancement is listed as being good. The average annual starting salary falls within the $30,000 to $35,000 range. The most suitable method for initial contact by those seeking employment is to mail a resume with a covering letter. Electro Sonic does hire summer and co-op students. *Contact:* Marilyn Gary, Training and Recruitment.

ELECTRONIC DIRECT MARKETING LTD.
39 Casebridge Court
Toronto, ON M1B 5N4

Tel. 416-282-1201
Fax 416-282-1897
Website .... www.edm-ltd.com

Electronic Direct Marketing Ltd. (EDM) is a state-of-the-art call centre and fulfillment company. EDM provides all levels of inbound and outbound services including customer/technical support, order taking and telesales. EDM's clients include various Fortune 500 companies. EDM employs over 800 people in Canada. Graduates most likely to be hired come from the following academic areas: Bachelor of Arts (General, English, French, Languages), Bachelor of Commerce/Business Administration (General, Human Resources, Information Systems, Marketing), Master of Business Administration (General, Accounting, Information Systems), and Community College Diploma (Administration, Business, Communications/Public Relations, Human Resources, Information Systems, Marketing/Sales). Graduates would occupy Call Centre Associate, Programmer, Systems Administrator, Billing Clerk, Recruiter, and Trainer positions. Team player, excellent communication skills, drive to succeed, and adaptability are all listed as desirable non-academic qualifications. Company benefits are rated as industry standard. The potential for advancement is listed as excellent. The

average annual starting salary falls within the $20,000 to $25,000 range. The most suitable method for initial contact by those seeking employment is to fax a resume with a covering letter. Electronic Direct Marketing Ltd. does hire summer students. (Other Toronto Location: Electronic Direct Marketing Ltd., 100 Sheppard Avenue East, Toronto, ON, M2N 6N5, Phone 416-226-1076). *Contact:* Jamie Allison, Manager, Human Resources.

ELECTROPHOTONICS CORPORATION
7941 Jane Street, Unit 200
Concord, ON L4K 4L6

Tel. 905-669-4660
Fax 905-669-3722
Email .... careers@electrophotonics.com
Website .... www.electrophotonics.com

ElectroPhotonics Corporation was formed in 1993 as a spin-off from the University of Toronto Fiber Optic Smart Structures Laboratory. Innovation is the key to the success of ElectroPhotonics in the development of products in fiber optic sensing systems and fiber optic telecommunication devices. The company has demonstrated a strong ability to take novel technological concepts through to product development and commercial reality both in the telecommunication and sensing arenas. A critical factor in this regard is the ability to attract and motivate a highly skilled group of individuals. The company's early success has been in pioneering the development of fiber optic Bragg grating sensing technology and a line of commercial sensing systems. The engineering team's knowledge and experience have been essential to the development of the novel concepts and devices integral to the ElectroPhotonics' novel telecom products. ElectroPhotonics' proprietary technology is poised to provide solutions to significant needs in the burgeoning market for high capacity fiber transmission systems. The company was formed by professionals with a strong and unique blend of backgrounds in research and product development. The company's staff consists of highly skilled individuals with complimentary background and experience. The disciplines represented include electronics, fiber optics, mechanics and materials, and physics. This make-up provides ElectroPhotonics with a unique spectrum of knowledge and skill with which to pursue its highly interdisciplinary product development program. Graduates most likely to be hired come from the following academic areas: Bachelor of Science (Physics), Bachelor of Engineering (General, Electrical, Mechanical, Computer Systems, Engineering Physics, Instrumentation, Microelectronics, Telecommunications), Bachelor of Commerce/Business Administration (General), Master of Science, Master of Engineering, and Community College Diploma (CAD/CAM/Autocad, Electronics Technician, Engineering Technician). Innovative, team player, expertise, initiative, self-motivated and flexibility are all listed as desirable non-academic qualifications. Company benefits are rated above average. The potential for advancement is listed as excellent. The average annual starting salary falls within the $35,000 to $40,000 range. The most suitable methods for initial contact by those seeking employment are to mail a resume with a covering letter, or by applying through the company's website at www.electrophotonics.com. ElectroPhotonics Corporation does hire summer and co-op work term students. *Contact:* Human Resources.

ELI LILLY CANADA INC.
3650 Danforth Avenue
Toronto, ON M1N 2E8

Tel.	416-694-3221
Fax	416-699-7241
Website	www.lilly.com

Eli Lilly Canada Inc. employs more than 400 people at this address and across Canada in the areas of research and development, sales and marketing, and corporate services focused towards the promotion of ethical pharmaceutical products. Graduates most likely to be hired come from the following academic areas: Bachelor of Science, Bachelor of Engineering, Bachelor of Commerce/Business Administration, Chartered Accountant, Certified Management Accountant, Master of Business Administration, Masters (Science/General), and Community College Diploma (Business, Operations Management). Graduates would occupy Sales Representative, Financial Analyst, and Clinical Research Associate position. Company benefits are rated above average. The potential for advancement is listed as being good. The average annual starting salary is dependent upon the level of the position. The most suitable method for initial contact by graduates seeking employment is to mail a resume with a covering letter. Eli Lilly Canada Inc. does hire summer and co-op work term students. *Contacts:* Marie Walton, Recruitment & Relocation Co-ordinator or Human Resources.

ELSAG BAILEY (CANADA) INC.
860 Harrington Court
Burlington, ON L7N 3N4

Tel.	905-639-8840
Fax	905-639-8639
Email	patterson@bailey.ca
Website	www.bailey.ca

Elsag Bailey (Canada) Inc. is a supplier of process control systems, services and instrumentation products to a broad section of the industrial process and utility markets in Canada and overseas. Product lines include INFI 90 Strategic Process Management, Information Systems, and stand-alone products, including transmitters, analyzers, control drives, recorders, etc. Markets served include chemical and petroleum, pulp and paper, mining and metals, water and waste, food and beverage, and utility sectors. There are 300 employees at this location, and a total of 550 employees in Canada. Elsag Bailey (Canada) Inc. is a unit of Elsag Bailey Process Automation N.V., which in turn is a division of Finmeccanica of Italy, employing 12,000 people worldwide. Graduates most likely to be hired come from the following academic areas: Bachelor of Science (Computer Science, Mathematics), Bachelor of Engineering (General, Chemi-

cal, Pulp and Paper, Electrical, Computer Systems, Instrumentation, Mechanical, Petroleum), Bachelor of Commerce/Business Administration (Accounting, Finance), and Community College Diploma (Accounting, Business, CAD/CAM/Autocad, Computer Science, Electronics Technician). Graduates would occupy Technician - Sales and Service, and Engineering - Sales, Engineering, and Marketing positions. Team player, strong communication skills, good negotiating skills, well organized, customer focused, and an ability to meet deadlines are all listed as desirable non-academic qualifications. The most suitable method for initial contact by those seeking employment is to mail a resume with a covering letter. *Contacts:* Sharon Patterson or Bernice Dworak.

ENERTEC GEOPHYSICAL SERVICES LIMITED
615 Macleod Trail SE, Suite 900
Calgary, AB T2G 4T8

Tel.	403-233-7830
Fax	403-233-9368

Enertec Geophysical Services Limited provides land and marine geophysical seismic survey and processing services to the oil and gas industry. The company currently operates out of Calgary, Houston and Baton Rouge. Enertec is a public company, traded on the Toronto Stock Exchange as ERS. There are 50 employees at the Calgary head office, a total of 400 employees in Canada, and a total of 500 employees worldwide. Graduates most likely to be hired come from the following academic areas: Bachelor of Science (Computer Science), and Bachelor of Engineering (Computer Systems, Engineering Physics, Geological Engineering). Graduates would occupy Junior Processing Geophysicist, Junior Systems/Applications Programmer, and Junior Sales Representative positions. Dedicated, solid work ethic, team player, active and healthy lifestyle, and a positive attitude are all listed as desirable non-academic qualifications. Company benefits are rated as excellent. The potential for advancement is listed as being good. The average annual starting salary falls within the $30,000 to $35,000 range, with a performance bonus for experienced employees in most departments. The most suitable method for initial contact by those seeking employment is to mail a resume with a covering letter. Enertec Geophysical Services Limited does hire summer students, occasionally. *Contact:* Dave Martin, General Manager.

ENGINEERED FOAM PRODUCTS CANADA LTD.
12 Kenhar Drive
Weston, ON M9L 1N1

Tel.	416-746-7334
Fax	416-746-7831

Engineered Foam Products Canada Ltd. employs more than 25 people in the manufacture of flexible foam products. Post-secondary graduates are hired. The specific academic areas recruited from is dependent upon the position to be filled. To inquire about employment opportunities and the qualifications required for available positions, please telephone the company directly at 416-746-7334. *Contact:* Reg Sloan, Human Resources (630-6633 Head Office).

EOS BUSINESS SYSTEMS INC.
521 - 3rd Avenue SW, Suite 500
Calgary, AB T2P 3T3

Tel. 403-266-7262
Fax 403-266-7522

EOS Business Systems Inc. employs 35 people in the development of computer program applications. Graduates most likely to be hired come from Bachelor of Engineering (Computer Systems) programs. A willingness to listen and learn, team player, and able to make decisions are all listed as desirable non-academic qualifications. Company benefits and the potential for advancement are both rated as excellent. The average annual starting salary falls within the $35,000 to $40,000 range. The most suitable methods for initial contact by those seeking employment are to mail or fax a resume with a covering letter. EOS Business Systems Inc. does hire summer students, applicants must have strong computer skills. *Contacts:* Catherine Langstaff or Bruce Brennan.

EQUINOX ENGINEERING LTD.
640 - 12 Avenue SW, Suite 472
Calgary, AB T2R 0H2

Tel. 403-205-3833
Fax 403-205-3818
Email .... equinox@cadvision.com

Equinox Engineering Ltd. is a dynamic engineering consulting firm specializing in facilities design, implementation, and operation assistance for the oil and gas industry. The company has in-depth knowledge of oil and gas production and processing, oil and gas pipelines, oil refining and chemical industry projects. Equinox provides over 80 years of expertise in preliminary and detailed engineering services in natural gas gathering systems and pipelines, compressor stations, natural gas treatment, LPG separation, underground storage of hydrocarbons and oil battery design. The company provides ongoing involvement with its clients' facilities in the areas of troubleshooting, facility operations assistance and upgrading for revised feedstock and market conditions. Equinox employs 21 people at this location. Graduates most likely to be hired come from the following academic areas: Bachelor of Engineering (General, Chemical, Electrical, Mechanical, Instrumentation, Petroleum/Fuels). Graduates would occupy E.I.T.'s and Technologist positions. Team player (very important), innovative, organized, and motivated are all listed as desirable non-academic qualifications. Company benefits are rated as industry standard. The potential for advancement is listed as being good. The average annual starting salary falls within the $35,000 to $40,000 range. The most suitable method for initial contact by those seeking employment is to mail a resume with a covering letter. *Contact:* Carey Haarmann.

EQUION SECURITIES
320 Bay Street, Suite 1100, P.O. Box 15
Toronto, ON M5H 9A6

Tel. 416-216-6500
Fax 416-216-6510
Website .... www.equion.com

The Equion Group is a partnership of financial service professionals who have become Canada's premier financial planning and money management organization. The Equion Group specializes in helping clients identify and achieve their financial goals in a manner which is consistent with their personal lifestyle and level of comfort. The goal of Equion is to help clients achieve and maintain financial independence and the peace of mind that comes from knowing that they have an effective long-term plan in place. Equion is committed to providing clients with the best in financial advice, products and service. There are 85 employees at this location, and a total of 270 employees in Canada. Graduates most likely to be hired come from the following academic areas: Bachelor of Arts (General, Economics, English, Psychology), Bachelor of Commerce/Business Administration (Accounting, Finance, Information Systems), Chartered Accountant, Certified Management Accountant, Master of Business Administration (Accounting, Finance), and Community College Diploma (Business). Graduates would occupy Sales Assistant, Marketing Assistant, Administrative Assistant, Client Service Representative, and Administrator positions. Excellent verbal and written communication skills, professional, minimum six months work experience - preferably in financial services, and strong computer software skills are all listed as desirable non-academic qualifications. Company benefits are rated above average. The potential for advancement is listed as being good. The average annual starting salary falls within the $25,000 to $30,000 range, depending upon experience. The most suitable method for initial contact by those seeking employment is to mail a resume with a covering letter. The Equion Group does hire summer students, on occasion. *Contacts:* Cindy Grant, Manager, Equion University or Allyson Newburg, Administrator, Equion University.

EQUIPEMENT LABRIE LTÉE
175, route Du Pont, CP 37
St-Nicolas, QC G7A 2T3

Tel. 418-831-8250
Fax 418-831-4052

Equipement Labrie Ltée employs approximately 230 people in the manufacture of garbage and recycling trucks. Graduates most likely to be hired come from the following academic areas: Bachelor of Science (Mathematics, Metallurgy), Bachelor of Engineering (Metallurgy, Mechanical, Industrial Production, Welding), Bachelor of Commerce/Business Administration (Accounting, Human Resources, Marketing), Master of Business Administration (Finance), and Community College Diploma (Accounting, Administration, Purchasing/Logistics, Secretarial, Welding, Mechanic). Company benefits are rated as industry standard. The potential for advancement is listed as being good. The average annual starting salary falls within the $25,000 to $30,000 range, depending upon the position being considered. The most suitable method for initial contact by those seeking employment is to mail a resume with a covering letter. Equipement Labrie Ltée does hire summer students. *Contact:* Joseé Morin, Human Resources Manager.

ERNST & YOUNG - MISSISSAUGA
90 Burnhamthorpe Road West, Suite 1100
Mississauga, ON L5B 3C3

Tel. 905-270-2121
Fax 905-270-9984

Ernst & Young is a chartered accountancy and management consultant firm. The practice areas in the Mississauga and Brampton office include: audit, entrepreneurial services, tax (corporate and personal), insolvency, actuarial benefits consulting, compensation and pay equity consulting, executive search and general management consulting. There are more than 100 employees at this location. Graduates most likely to be hired come from the following academic areas: Bachelor of Arts (General, Economics), Bachelor of Science (General), Bachelor of Engineering (General), Bachelor of Commerce/Business Administration (Accounting, Finance), Chartered Accountant (Finance), and Master of Business Administration (Accounting, Finance). Graduates would start as CA students in the audit and entrepreneurial services practice area. Having obtained leadership positions in extracurricular activities, and possessing excellent interpersonal and communications skills are listed as desirable non-academic qualifications. Company benefits are rated as industry standard. The potential for advancement is listed as being good. The average annual starting salary falls within the $25,000 to $30,000 range. The most suitable method for initial contact by graduates seeking employment is to mail a resume, cover letter, and a copy of a university transcript. This Ernst & Young location does hire summer students occasionally. *Contact:* Office Managing Partner.

ERNST & YOUNG - TORONTO
Ernst & Young Tower, P.O. Box 251, TD Centre
Toronto, ON M5K 1J7

Tel. 416-864-1234
Fax 416-864-1174

Ernst & Young is an international professional services firm, providing expert counsel in auditing and accounting, tax, general management and IT consulting, actual, benefits, compensation and human resources consulting. Ernst & Young employs approximately 765 people at this location and a total of 3,490 people across Canada. Graduates most likely to be hired come from the following academic areas: Bachelor of Science (Actuarial), Bachelor of Engineering (General), Bachelor of Commerce/Business Administration (Accounting, Finance, Information Systems), Chartered Accountant, Certified Management

Accountant, Certified General Accountant, Master of Business Administration (Accounting, Finance, Marketing), Master of Health Administration, Master of Engineering, Master of Science (Computer Science), and Community College Diploma (Accounting, Administration, Advertising, Communications, Facility Management, Human Resources, Purchasing/Logistics, Secretarial, Graphic Arts, Legal Assistant). Company benefits are rated above average. The potential for advancement is listed as good. The most suitable method for initial contact by those seeking employment is to mail a resume with a covering letter. Ernst & Young does hire summer students. *Contacts:* Jack Taylor, Director - Toronto Human Resources or Shelley Pearlman, Principal - Management Consulting.

ETOBICOKE FINANCIAL SERVICES DIVISION
399 The West Mall
Toronto, ON M9C 2Y2

Tel. 416-394-8168

The Etobicoke Financial Services employs approximately 18 people, providing a variety of financial services for the city of Etobicoke. These include; Accounts Payable, Investments, Long Term Financing, Current Budget, Capital Budget, and Insurance. Graduates most likely to be hired come from the following academic areas: Chartered Accountant, Certified Management Accountant, and Master of Business Administration. Positions occupied would correspond directly with the qualifications of the applicant. Employee benefits are listed as excellent. The potential for advancement is listed as being good. The average annual starting salary falls within the $25,000 to $30,000 range. The most suitable method for initial contact by graduates seeking employment is to mail a resume with a covering letter to the City of Toronto Human Resources Department. The Etobicoke Financial Services Division is part of the Finance Department in the new City of Toronto. *Contact:* Human Resources Department.

ETOBICOKE PARKS AND RECREATION SERVICES DEPARTMENT
399 The West Mall
Toronto, ON M9C 2Y2

Tel. 416-394-8510
Fax 416-394-8935

The Etobicoke's Parks and Recreation Services Department employs more than 250 people in the managing of 3,700 acres of parkland and 130 recreational buildings. The department also offers recreation programs to all ages in physical, cultural, social and educational activities. Graduates most likely to be hired come from the following academic areas: Bachelor of Arts (Fine Arts, Sociology, Recreation, Gerontology), Bachelor of Science (Forestry), Bachelor of Engineering (Civil), Bachelor of Architecture, Bachelor of Landscape Architecture, Bachelor of Commerce/Business Administration (Public Administration), Master of Business Administration (Public Administration), Master of Arts (Recreation), and

Community College Diploma (Recreation, Parks, Forestry, Facility Management). Good interpersonal and communication skills are both listed as desirable non-academic qualifications. Employee benefits and the potential for advancement are both rated as excellent. The average annual starting salary falls within the $30,000 to $35,000 range. The most suitable methods for initial contact by those seeking employment are to mail a resume with a covering letter, or via telephone. The Parks and Recreation Services Department requires part-time student employees on a year round basis for a variety of positions. The Parks and Recreation Services Department is the largest employer of students in Etobicoke. The Etobicoke's Parks and Recreation Services Department is part of the new City of Toronto Economic Development, Culture and Tourism Department. *Contacts:* Executive Director of Recreation or Executive Director of Parks.

ETOBICOKE PLANNING DEPARTMENT
399 The West Mall, Etobicoke City Hall
Toronto, ON M9C 2Y2

Tel. 416-394-8215
Fax 416-394-6063

The Etobicoke Planning Department is responsible for urban development, official plan amendments, zoning code amendments, site control agreements, special studies, gathering of statistical data, and maintaining computerized data bases for Etobicoke. The department employs more than 25 people. Graduates most likely to be hired come from the following academic areas: Bachelor of Arts (Urban Geography/Planning), Bachelor of Engineering (Environmental), Bachelor of Architecture, Bachelor of Landscape Architecture, Bachelor of Commerce/Business Administration (Public Administration), and Community College Diploma (Urban Planning, Architecture/Drafting, Computer Science). A solid employment record, and previous work experience in municipal fields are listed as desirable non-academic qualifications. Employee benefits are listed as good. The potential for advancement is listed as average. The average annual starting salary falls within the $35,000 to $40,000 range. The most suitable method for initial contact by graduates seeking employment is to mail a resume with a covering letter. The Planning Department does hire summer students. The Etobicoke Planning Department is part of the new City of Toronto Urban Planning and Development Services Department. *Contact:* Planning Commissioner.

ETOBICOKE PUBLIC WORKS DEPARTMENT
399 The West Mall, 3rd Floor, South Block
Toronto, ON M9C 2Y2

Tel. 416-394-8350
Fax 416-394-8942

The Etobicoke Public Works Department employs more than 150 people in the development and maintenance of municipal services (eg. water, sewers). Graduates most likely to be hired come from the following academic areas: Bachelor of Engineering (Civil) and Community College Diploma (CAD/CAM/Autocad, Engineering Technician). Graduates would occupy Engineer or Engineering Technician positions. Employee benefits are listed as excellent. The potential for advancement is listed as being good. The average annual starting salary falls within the $35,000 to $40,000 range. The most suitable method for initial contact by graduates seeking employment is to mail a resume with a covering letter. The Public Works Department does hire summer students. The Etobicoke Public Works Department is part of the new City of Toronto Works and Emergency Services Department. *Contacts:* J.S. Yee, Executive Director, Engineering or Robert Corazzola, Acting Director, Systems & Administration.

EUCLID-HITACHI HEAVY EQUIPMENT, LTD.
200 Woodlawn Road West
Guelph, ON N1H 1B6

Tel. 519-823-2000
Fax 519-837-4220

Euclid-Hitachi Heavy Equipment, Ltd. is involved in the manufacturing of off-highway and mining rigid hauler trucks. There are approximately 300 employees at this location and a total of 500 employees worldwide. Graduates most likely to be hired come from the following academic areas: Bachelor of Engineering (Industrial Design, Industrial Production, Welding), Bachelor of Commerce/Business Administration (Accounting, Finance, Human Resources, Information Systems, Marketing), and Community College Diploma (Engineering Technician, Welding). Able to accomplish goals on a timely basis, and a high energy level are both listed as desirable non-academic qualifications. Company benefits are rated above average. The potential for advancement is listed as being good. The most suitable method for initial contact by those seeking employment is to mail a resume with a covering letter. *Contact:* Mr. F. J. Leone, Manager Human Resources.

EVEREST & JENNINGS CANADIAN LIMITED
111 Snidercroft Road
Concord, ON L4K 2J8

Tel. 905-669-2381
Fax 905-660-7875

Everest & Jennings Canadian Limited is involved in the manufacture of metal folding wheelchairs, hospital and sick room equipment, and other invalid aids. Production facilities were first established in 1962 in Don Mills, Ontario. Since 1970, Everest & Jennings has been involved with products that include folding, non-folding, manual and battery powered wheelchairs; distributors of patient lifters, institutional beds, commodes, cushions and seating systems. The company employs a total of 165 people. Graduates most likely to be hired come from the following academic areas: Bachelor of Engineering (Mechanical, Industrial Design), Bachelor of Commerce/Business Administration (Accounting, Human Resources, Marketing), Certified Management Accountant, Certified General Accountant, Master of Science, Community College Diploma (Accounting, Administration, Business, Marketing, Purchasing/Logistics, Secretarial, CAD/CAM/ Autocad, Computer Science, Electronics Technician, Engineering Technician), CHRM, PAAC, CEBS, and High School Diploma. Graduates would occupy Accounting, Accounting Clerk, Accounts Receivable/ Payable Clerk, CAD Operator, Customer Service Representative, General Labourer, Marketing Manager, Mechanical Engineer, Mechanical Design Engineer, Engineering Technologist, Programmer, Sales Representative, Purchasing/Logistics Administrator, Secretary, and Skilled Trades positions. Results oriented, excellent interpersonal and communications skills, customer focussed, innovative, self-directed, continuous learner, excellent computer skills, and good organizational and analytical skills are all listed as desirable non-academic qualifications. Company benefits are rated as industry standard. The potential for advancement is listed as excellent. The average starting salary falls within the $30,000 to $35,000 range. The most suitable method for initial contact by those seeking employment is to mail a resume with a covering letter. Everest & Jennings Canadian Limited does hire summer students for general office help and general labourer positions. *Contacts:* Dwayne Webster, Manager, Manufacturing or Drew Gibney, Manager, Engineering & Product Development.

EVI OIL TOOLS-COROD

2801 - 84 Avenue
Edmonton, AB T6P 1K1

Tel. 403-417-4800
Fax 403-464-5189

EVI Oil Tools-Corod is a leading world class manufacturer and marketer of quality oil lifting equipment. The Company has manufacturing facilities in Edmonton, producing Progressive Cavity Pumps and Drives, and a new plant producing Continuous Sucker Rods. In addition, the company operates a fleet of 37 Co Rigs throughout Western Canada and the United States, and several more in Venezuela. There are 150 employees at this location, and a total of 400 employees in Canada. Graduates most likely to be hired come from the following academic areas: Bachelor of Science (Computer Science, Metallurgy), Bachelor of Engineering (Materials Science, Metallurgy, Computer Systems, Instrumentation, Mechanical, Welding), Chartered Accountant, Certified Management Accountant, Certified General Accountant, Master of Business Administration (Accounting, Finance, Human Resources), Master of Engineering (Mechanical, Computer Systems), Community College Diploma (Accounting, Secretarial, CAD/CAM/ Autocad, Computer Science, Electronics Technician, Engineering Technician, Welding), and High School Diploma. Graduates would occupy Product Development Engineer/Technologist, Applications Engineer, Accountant, Controller, Payable/Receivable Representative, Administrative Assistant, Welder, Millwright, Heavy Duty Technician, Plant Operator, Test Bench Technician, Assembler, and Warehouse

positions. Team player, good verbal and written communication skills, initiative, strong work ethic, punctual, excellent attendance record, able to work safely and add value, reliable, and efficient are all listed as desirable non-academic qualifications. Company benefits are rated above average. The potential for advancement is listed as excellent. The average annual starting salary falls within the $40,000 to $45,000 range. The most suitable method for initial contact by those seeking employment is to mail a resume with a covering letter. EVI Oil Tools-Corod does hire engineering students for summer and co-op work terms. *Contact:* Mike Hebert, Human Resources Advisor.

EXECUTRAIN OF TORONTO

5140 Yonge Street, Suite 800
Toronto, ON M2N 6L7

Tel. 416-221-5353
Fax 416-221-5352
Email .... saumureb@etcanada.com
Website .... www.executrain.ca

ExecuTrain is a global training organization offering training in computer applications as well as certification programs for Microsoft, Novell, and Lotus. The company employs 22 people at this location, 75 people in Canada, and a total of 1,235 people worldwide. Graduates most likely to be hired come from the following academic areas: Bachelor of Arts (General), Bachelor of Science (Computer Science), Bachelor of Education (Adult), Bachelor of Commerce (General, Information Systems), and Community College Diploma (Information Systems, Marketing/Sales, Computer Science). Graduates would occupy Sales and Marketing, Instructor, and Operational positions. Team player, motivated, positive attitude, willing to learn, and flexible are all listed as desirable non-academic qualifications. Company benefits are rated above average. The potential for advancement is listed as excellent. The average annual starting salary falls within the $30,000 to $35,000 range. The most suitable methods for initial contact by those seeking employment are to fax or e-mail a resume with a covering letter. ExecuTrain of Toronto does hire summer and co-op work term students. *Contacts:* Bruce Saumure, Manager of Technology & Training or Pam White, Manager of Operations.

EXFO ELECTRO-OPTICAL ENGINEERING INC.

465 Godin Avenue
Vanier, QC G1M 3G7

Tel. 418-683-0211
Fax 418-683-2170
Email .... resume@exfo.com
Website .... www.exfo.com/carrieres

EXFO Electro-Optical Engineering Inc. designs and manufactures fiber-optic test and measurement equipment. Fiber optics is a high technology field that is rapidly growing due to the importance of information technologies and the undeniable advantages of fiber-optic networks over traditional communication networks. With 350 employees in

Canada and a total of 400 employees worldwide, EXFO ranks fourth in its category on a worldwide scale. The company exports over 95% of its products to more than 100 countries throughout the world. Its main customers are telephone and cable service providers, as well as research and development laboratories. EXFO Europe in Versailles, France, EXFO America in Dallas, Texas, and sales offices in Montreal, Toronto, Vancouver, Chicago, Atlanta, Denver, Harrisburg, San Jose, and Hungary constitute the EXFO sales network around the globe. EXFO has set out to become the world's number one fiber-optic test equipment manufacturer, and has recently bought a Swiss firm (GAP Optique), and the optoelectronics division of a French company (Froilabo). Graduates most likely to be hired come from the following academic areas: Bachelor of Engineering (Electrical, Mechanical, Engineering Physics, Microelectronics, Telecommunications), Master of Engineering, and Community College Diploma (Electronics Technician). Graduates would occupy Researcher, Engineer, and Technician positions. Team player, dynamism, bilingual (French/English), and good communication skills are all listed as desirable non-academic qualifications. Company benefits are rated above average. The potential for advancement is listed as being good. The average annual starting salary falls within the $35,000 to $40,000 range. The most suitable method for initial contact by those seeking employment is through the company's website at www.efco.com/carrieres. EXFO does hire summer and co-op work term students. *Contacts:* Human Resources Depatment or Isabelle de Cournuaud, Recruitment Specialist.

EXOCOM SYSTEMS CORP.

45 O'Connor Street, Suite 1400
World Exchange Plaza
Ottawa, ON K1P 1A4

Tel. 613-237-0257
Fax 613-237-0314
Email .... hr@exocom.com
Website .... www.exocom.com

EXOCOM is a leading provider of successful and innovative strategic information technology (IT) solutions. Since 1982, EXOCOM has achieved a cumulative growth rate in excess of 30 per cent per year and employs over 130 of the highest calibre IT professionals in the industry. Canadian owned, EXOCOM maintains offices in Ottawa, Toronto, and Calgary. The company's clients are comprised of both federal and provincial government clients, and a solid corporate client base including prominent corporations such as Sprint Canada, NBTel, the Bank of Nova Scotia and Petro Canada. EXOCOM's fully integrated suite of IT offerings include Strategic Information Management and Planning, Business Process Design, Change and Performance Management, Enterprise Networking, Client/Server and Internet/Intranet Applications Development, Secure Network Solutions, and Document Management Solutions. Current IT business partners include Microsoft, Cisco, Cognos, Oracle, Entrust Technologies, Mobius, ICL, KyberPass, Cyberguard and the

Gartner Group. Graduates most likely to be hired come from the following academic areas: Bachelor of Science (Computer Science, Mathematics, Bachelor of Engineering (General, Electrical, Computer Systems, Telecommunications), Bachelor of Commerce/Business Administration (Information Systems), Certified Management Accountant, Master of Business Administration (General, Information Systems), and Community College Diploma (Information Systems, Computer Science). Graduates would occupy Junior Consultant positions. EXOCOM only hires full-time employees who are career oriented and who possess a high level of initiative. Company benefits and the potential for advancement are both rated as excellent. The average annual starting salary falls within the $30,000 to $40,000 range. The most suitable methods for initial contact by those seeking employment are to e-mail a resume with a covering letter, or by applying through the company's website at www.exocom.com. EXOCOM does hire summer and co-op work term students. *Contacts:* Pierre Côté, Human Resources Specialist - IT Division or Allison Seymour-Swim, Human Resources.

EXPLORER HOTEL, THE

Postal Service 7000
Yellowknife, NT X1A 2R3

Tel. 867-873-3531
Fax 867-873-2789
Email .... explorer@internorth.com
Website .... www.explorerhotel.nt.ca

The Explorer Hotel is a 128 bedroom, full service luxury hotel, located just steps away from the commercial and government centre of Yellowknife. In addition to a warm welcome, the Hotel provides facilities for pleasure and business travellers alike. The Explorer Hotel employs approximately 100 people. Graduates most likely to be hired come from the following academic areas: Bachelor of Arts (General), Bachelor of Engineering (General, Electrical, Mechanical), Bachelor of Commerce/Business Administration (General, Accounting, Finance, Human Resources, Marketing), and Community College Diploma (Accounting, Administration, Advertising, Business, Communications/Public Relations, Facility Management, Human Resources, Marketing/Sales, Secretarial, Cook/Chef Training, Hospitality, Travel/Tourism, Carpentry, Plumber). Graduates would occupy Cook, Waitperson, Maintenance, Front Desk, Housekeeper and Junior Manager positions. Adaptable, efficient, leadership skills, personable, responsible, decisive, organized, flexible, productive, confident, and professional are all listed as desirable non-academic qualifications. Company benefits and the potential for advancement are both rated as excellent. The average annual starting salary falls within the $15,000 to $25,000 range. The most suitable methods for initial contact by those seeking employment are to mail or fax a resume with a covering letter, or by applying in person at the Hotel. The Explorer Hotel does hire summer and co-op work term students. *Contact:* General Manager, Regency International Hotels.

EXPRESS INFORMATION TECHNOLOGY CORPORATION
101 - 6 Avenue SW, Suite 1220
Calgary, AB T2P 3P4

Tel.	403-215-3800
Fax	403-215-3803
Email	eitc@expressit.ab.ca
Website	www.expressmicrostore.com

Express Information Technology Corporation is a total IT solution provider and a Top 100 Value Added Reseller of hardware and software in Canada. The company employs approximately 30 people in the provision of both quality products and services to corporations, ranging from home based businesses to Fortune 100 companies. Its' group of companies provide Microsoft certified professional services, Novell services and supports, as well as HP Unix systems support and outsourcing functions of IT departments. The company is also a ValueNet Partner of FileNet Corporation, the largest integrated document management corporation in the world. Express Information Technology Corporation is a fast growing technology company that strives for excellence and complete customer satisfaction as its top priority. Graduates most likely to be hired come from the following academic areas: Bachelor of Science (Computer Science), Bachelor of Engineering (Electrical, Computer Systems, Telecommunications), Bachelor of Commerce/Business Administration (Accounting, Human Resources, Information Systems, Marketing), Certified Management Accountant, Master of Business Administration (Human Resources, Information Systems, Marketing), and Community College Diploma (Administration, Communications/Public Relations, Information Systems, Marketing/Sales, Purchasing/Logistics, CAD/CAM/Autocad, Computer Science, Electronics Technician). Graduates would occupy Computer Systems Engineer, Computer Systems Consultant, Marketing and Promotions Manager, Office Administrator, and Financial Controller positions. Excellent communication and organization skills, strong work ethic, team player, and strong leadership skills are all listed as desirable non-academic qualifications. Company benefits are rated above average. The potential for advancement is listed as excellent. The average annual starting salary falls within the $25,000 to $30,000 range. The most suitable method for initial contact by those seeking employment is to e-mail a resume with a covering letter. Express Information Technology Corporation does hire summer and co-op work term students. *Contacts:* Winston Chow, General Manager or Polinda So, IT Administrator.

EXTENDICARE (CANADA) INC.
3000 Steeles Avenue East, Suite 700
Markham, ON L3R 9W2

Tel.	905-470-5623
Fax	905-470-5588

Extendicare (Canada) Inc. owns and operates approximately 50 nursing homes across Canada. The company also provides home-care service and hospital management services. Graduates most likely to be hired come from the following academic areas: Bachelor of Arts (General, Recreation), Bachelor of Science (Mathematics, Nursing), Bachelor of Commerce/Business Administration (Accounting, Finance, Marketing), Chartered Accountant (Finance), Certified Management Accountant (Finance), Certified General Accountant (Finance), Master of Business Administration (Accounting, Finance, Marketing), and Community College Diploma (Accounting, Administration, Advertising, Business, Communications, Purchasing/Logistics, Secretarial, Human Resources, Journalism, Recreation, Computer Science, Food/Nutrition, Nursing RN/RNA). This is the head office location, employing more than 100 people in largely accounting and administrative functions. Graduates would occupy Senior Analyst, Accounts Receivable Clerk, Accounts Payable Clerk, General Accounting Clerk, Secretarial and Office Clerk positions. Good communication, organization and analytic skills are all listed as desirable non-academic qualifications. Company benefits and the potential for advancement are both rated as excellent. The most suitable method for initial contact by graduates seeking employment is to mail a resume with a covering letter. Extendicare (Canada) Inc. does hire summer students. *Contact:* Director, Employment Services, Human Resources Department.

FALCONBRIDGE

FALCONBRIDGE LIMITED
95 Wellington Street West, Suite 1200
Toronto, ON M5J 2V4

Tel.	416-956-5700
Fax	416-956-5869
Website	www.falconbridge.com

Falconbridge Limited is an international resource company engaged in the exploration, development, mining, processing and marketing of metals and minerals. Falconbridge employs approximately 6,800 people in locations across Canada and around the globe. There are approximately 100 employees at this location, which is the Corporate Office, and includes the Administration, Finance, Sales, and Marketing departments. Graduates most likely to be hired come from the following academic areas: Bachelor of Arts (General), Bachelor of Science (Computer Science, Geology, Mathematics, Metallurgy), Bachelor of Engineering (Chemical, Civil, Environmental, Materials Science, Metallurgy, Mining), Bachelor of Commerce/Business Administration (Accounting, Finance, Marketing), Chartered Accountant, Certified Management Accountant, Certified General Accountant, Master of Business Administration (Finance, Marketing), Master of Engineering (Chemical, Mining, Metallurgy), Doctorate of Engineering, and Community College Diploma (Business, Marketing/Sales, Secretarial, Human Resources, Journalism, Engineering). Team player, and excellent interpersonal and communication skills are listed as desirable non-academic qualifications. The most suitable methods for initial contact by those seeking employment are to mail or fax a resume with a covering letter. *Contact:* Paula Petrie, Manager, Recruiting.

FAMILY AND CHILDREN'S SERVICES OF THE WATERLOO REGION
200 Ardelt Avenue
Kitchener, ON N2C 2L9

Tel. 519-576-0540
Fax 519-570-0160

Family and Children's Services is the children's aid society for the Region of Waterloo. It is incorporated as a charitable, non-profit social service agency working under the authority of Ontario child welfare legislation. Family and Children's Services provides protection and preventative service as mandated under the Child and Family Services Act to families and children. The Service employs a total of 160 people in the Region of Waterloo. Graduates most likely to be hired come from the following academic areas: Bachelor of Arts (Social Work), Master of Arts (Social Work), and Community College Diploma (Social Work/DSW). Bachelor and Master of Social Work graduates would occupy Family Service Worker and Intake Worker positions. Proven oral and written communication skills, willing to work as an integral member of a team, and strong time management skills are all listed as desirable non-academic qualifications. Company benefits are rated above average. The potential for advancement is listed as being good. The average annual starting salary falls within the $40,000 to $45,000 range. The most suitable method for initial contact by those seeking employment is to mail or fax a resume with a covering letter. Family and Children's Services does hire summer students. *Contact:* Lynn Taylor Miceli, Supervisor, Human Resource Administration.

FAMILY SERVICE ASSOCIATION OF TORONTO
355 Church Street
Toronto, ON M5B 1Z8

Tel. 416-595-9230
Email .... hrdep@fsamt.on.ca

The Family Service Association of Toronto is a nonprofit social service agency providing a range of services to individuals and families who are vulnerable and/or in distress. Services offered include counselling, family life education, community development, etc. The Association employs approximately 160 people across Metropolitan Toronto. Graduates most likely to be hired are Master of Social Work MSW graduates. These graduates would occupy Social Worker positions. Relevant work experience, and experience in cross-cultural counselling are both

listed as desirable non-academic qualifications. The average annual starting salary falls within the $35,000 to $40,000 range. The most suitable method for initial contact by those seeking employment is to mail a resume with a covering letter. The Family Service Association of Toronto does hire a number of summer students to work in their Residential Children's Summer Camp which is located in Bolton, Ontario. *Contact:* Human Resource Services.

FARM BOY INC.
2255 St. Laurent Boulevard, Suite 300
Ottawa, ON K1G 4K3

Tel. 613-247-1007
Fax 613-247-8731
Email .... fbmail@farmboy.on.ca
Website .... www.farmboy.on.ca

Farm Boy Inc. is a family run retail business specializing in fresh food (especially produce) with 5 stores in Eastern Ontario (Cornwall and Ottawa) employing a total of 600 people. Graduates most likely to be hired come from the following academic areas: Bachelor of Arts (Economics), Bachelor of Commerce/Business Administration (General, Accounting, Finance, Human Resources, Information Systems, Marketing), Chartered Accountant, Master of Business Administration (General, Accounting, Finance, Human Resources, Information Systems, Marketing), Community College Diploma (Accounting, Administration, Advertising, Business, Communications, Human Resources, Marketing/Sales, Secretarial, Computer Science), and High School Diploma. Graduates would occupy Financial Manager/Analyst, Controller, Human Resources Coordinator, Payroll Clerk, Accountant, Store Manager, Department Manager, Computer Technician, Executive Secretary, Executive Assistant, Administrative Assistant, and Retail Operations Analyst positions. Food retail experience, good communication and entrepreneurial skills, people oriented, team builder and an ability to delegate are all listed as desirable non-academic qualifications. Company benefits are rated as industry standard. The potential for advancement is listed as being excellent. The average annual starting salary falls within the $35,000 to $40,000 range. The most suitable method for initial contact by those seeking employment is to mail a resume with a covering letter. *Contact:* Daniel Bellemare, Director of Human Resources.

FARM CREDIT CORPORATION
1800 Hamilton, P.O. Box 4320
Regina, SK S4P 4L3

Tel. 306-780-8100
Fax 306-780-5508

Farm Credit Corporation is a Federal Crown Corporation which provides financial services, and the lending of monies to the agricultural/agribusiness community on a Canada wide basis. The corporation employs 250 people at this location and a total of 800 people in Canada. Graduates most likely to be hired come from the following academic areas: Bachelor of Arts (Economics, French, Journalism), Bachelor of Science (Agriculture, Computer Science), Bachelor of Education (Adult), Bachelor of Commerce/Business Administration (Accounting, Finance, Human Resources, Information Systems, Marketing, Public Administration), Chartered Accountant, Certified Management Accountant, Certified General Accountant, Master of Business Administration (Accounting, Finance, Human Resources, Information Systems, Marketing, Public Administration), and Community College Diploma (Accounting, Administration, Business, Communications, Human Resources). Graduates would occupy Accounting Clerk, Finance Clerk, Management, Lending Officer, Research Officer, Administrative Officer, Credit Advisor, Treasury Analyst, Financial Officer, Human Resources Clerk/Officer/Manager, Communications Officer, Translation Officer, Marketing Officer, Programmer, Business Systems Analyst, and Computer Operator positions. Company benefits are rated above average. The potential for advancement is listed as being good. The average starting salary is very competitive and depends upon the level of the position being considered. The most suitable method for initial contact by those seeking employment is to mail a resume with a covering letter. Farm Credit Corporation does hire summer students at this location and at the individual regional offices (check your local white/yellow pages for the nearest location). *Contact:* Karen Bright, Manager, Staffing & Employee Relations.

FARMERS CO-OP SEEDS LTD.
Box 579
Rivers, MB R0K 1X0

Tel. 204-328-5346
Fax 204-328-7400

Farmers Co-Op Seeds Ltd. is a dynamic, growth oriented agricultural seed company, involved in all areas of seed production, processing, conditioning, warehousing, and distribution at retail and wholesale levels. The company is also involved in field production of pedigree seeds, performs seed quality testing, and seed coatings of fungicides and insecticides. The company employs 22 people. Graduates most likely to be hired come from the following academic areas: Bachelor of Science (Agriculture, Computer Science), Bachelor of Commerce/Business Administration (Accounting, Human Resources, Marketing), Master of Business Administration (Accounting, Human Resources, Marketing), and Community College Diploma (Accounting, Administration, Advertising, Human Resources, Marketing/Sales, Secretarial). Graduates would occupy Clerical, Management, Production, and Technical positions. Quality oriented, self motivated, above average abilities within specific field of expertise, driven, and aggressive team player are all listed as desirable non-academic qualifications. Company benefits and the potential for advancement are both rated as excellent. The average annual starting salary falls within the $20,000 to $25,000 range. The most suitable method for initial contact by those seeking employment is to mail a resume with a covering letter.

Farmers Co-Op Seeds Ltd. hires summer students occasionally, on a part-time basis. *Contacts:* Donald G. Kostesky, CEO or Glen Jardine, Sales Manager.

FARMERS COOPERATIVE DAIRY LTD.
P.O. Box 8118, Station A
Halifax, NS B3K 5Y6

Tel. .... 902-835-4005 x 135
Fax 902-835-4015

Farmers Cooperative Dairy Ltd. manufactures and distributes dairy and related products, in Atlantic Canada. Production facilities are located in Bedford and Truro, Nova Scotia, St. Johns and Deerlake, Newfoundland, and Hunter River, Prince Edward Island. There are 400 employees at this location, and a total of 500 employees in Atlantic Canada. Graduates most likely to be hired come from the following academic areas: Bachelor of Science (Agriculture, Biology, Computer Science), Bachelor of Engineering (General, Chemical, Mechanical, Agricultural, Food Processing, Industrial Engineering, Industrial Production/Manufacturing), Bachelor of Commerce/Business Administration (General, Accounting, Finance, Human Resources, Information Systems, Marketing), Chartered Accountant, Certified Management Accountant, Master of Business Administration, and Community College Diploma (Accounting, Human Resources, Information Systems, Marketing/Sales, Purchasing/Logistics, Industrial Mechanic, Computer Science, Welding). Graduates would occupy Sales Representative, Accounting Clerk, Computer Programmer, Industrial Mechanic, Electrician, Operations Management (eg. Plant or Distribution Supervisor), Purchasing (Buyer or Releaser), and Human Resource Administrator positions. Team player, initiative, problem solving skills, specialized knowledge, and good interpersonal skills are all listed as desirable non-academic qualifications. Company benefits are rated above average. The potential for advancement is listed as being good. The average annual starting salary falls within the $30,000 to $35,000 range. The most suitable method for initial contact by those seeking employment is to mail a resume with a covering letter. Farmers Cooperative Dairy Ltd. hires summer and co-op work term students for a variety of positions, including Accounting, Human Resources, Sales, and Plant positions. *Contacts:* Joanne Brown, Human Resources Manager, Human Resources Department or Kellie Hogan, Human Resources Administrator, Human Resources Department.

FCB RONALDS-REYNOLDS LTD.
245 Eglinton Avenue East, Suite 300
Toronto, ON M4P 3C2

Tel. 416-483-3600
Fax 416-489-8782

FCB Ronalds-Reynolds Ltd. is a full-service advertising agency employing more than 100 people. They are involved in all aspects of the advertising process, including costing, development of marketing strategies, research and strategic planning, marketing, creative development and the development of advertising copy. Graduates most likely to be hired come from the following academic areas: Bachelor of Arts (General/Related), Bachelor of Science, Bachelor of Commerce/Business Administration, Chartered Accountant, Certified Management Accountant, Master of Business Administration, Masters (Related/General), and Community College Diploma (Marketing, Advertising). The ability to handle a variety of responsibilities, leadership qualities demonstrated through extra-curricular activities, and good communication skills are all listed as desirable non-academic qualifications. Also, summer/part-time positions and academic grades are reviewed upon application. Company benefits and the potential for advancement are both rated as excellent. The average annual starting salary falls within the $15,000 to $20,000 range. The most suitable method for initial contact by graduates seeking employment is to mail a resume with a covering letter. Summer students are hired for clerical positions. *Contact:* Maureen Jones, Vice President, Director of Human Resources.

FGI
10 Commerce Valley Drive E., Suite 200
Thornhill, ON L3T 7N7

Tel. 905-886-2157
Fax 905-886-4337
Website .... www.fgiworld.com

FGI offers world-class professional services in the areas of Employee Assistance Programs, Global Relocation Support Programs, Work Ability (psychological counselling service for disability management), and Community Based Services. FGI employs 75 people at this location, a total of 170 people in Canada, and an additional 10 people outside of Canada. Graduates most likely to be hired come from the following academic areas: Bachelor of Arts (Psychology, Social Work), Bachelor of Science (Psychology), Master of Arts (Psychology), and Master of Social Work. Graduates would occupy EAP and International Service Co-ordinator positions. Previous crises counselling experience and bilingualism (French/English) are both listed as desirable non-academic qualifications. Company benefits are rated above average. The potential for advancement is listed as average. The average annual starting salary falls within the $30,000 to $35,000 range. The most suitable methods for initial contact by those seeking employment are to mail a resume with a covering letter, or by applying through the company's website www.fgiworld.com. FGI does hire summer and co-op work term students. *Contact:* Supervisor of Service Co-ordinators.

FIDELITY INVESTMENTS CANADA LIMITED
222 Bay Street, Suite 900
TD Centre, Ernst & Young Tower, PO Box 90
Toronto, ON M5K 1P1

Tel. 416-307-5300
Fax 416-307-5520
Website .... www.fidelity.ca

Fidelity Investments is the world's largest mutual fund company with more than $648 billion under management on behalf of over 11 million investors. Fidelity serves Canadians through Fidelity Investments Canada Limited and Fidelity Group Pensions Canada in managing over 25 mutual funds and more than $10.5 billion. Fidelity mutual funds are sold by independent investment professionals. There are 425 employees at this location, and a total of 450 employees in Canada. Fidelity considers graduates whose academic credentials include: Bachelor of Arts (General, Economics, English, French, Political Science, Psychology), Bachelor of Education (Adult), Bachelor of Commerce/Business Administration (General, Accounting), Chartered Accountant, Certified Management Accountant, Certified General Accountant, Master of Business Administration (General, Accounting), Community College Diploma (Accounting, Administration, Business, Secretarial, Graphic Arts, Computer Science), High School Diploma, and CSC and IFIC courses. Graduates would occupy positions in Sales and Marketing, Client Services, Corporate Services, Fund Operations, Transfer Agency, Information Systems, and other Fidelity business units. Applicants should posses a strong customer service orientation. Fidelity offers substantial company benefits and the Position Yourself Program to promote employee advancement. Both full time and contract work are offered. The most suitable methods for initial contact by those seeking employment are to mail or fax a resume with a covering letter. Fidelity Investments hires college and university students for summer positions. *Contact:* Human Resources.

FINANCIAL MODELS COMPANY INC.
2355 Skymark Avenue
Mississauga, ON L4W 4Y6

Tel. 905-629-8000
Fax 905-629-0022
Email .... careers@fmco.com
Website .... www.fmco.com

Financial Models Company Inc. (FMC) was established in 1976 and is an award winning and innovative software development company. The company develops, sells and supports systems for all aspects of the investment management process, and serves many of the largest, most advanced organizations in the world, such as the Bank of New York and United Bank of Switzerland. FMC's clients include banks, investment counsel, pension funds, mutual funds and government agencies. FMC offers a full suite of products including, portfolio management, performance measurement, electronic trading and settlement, investment accounting, reconciliation, 'what if' analysis, financial data interchange and client reporting. With it systems managing over $1 trillion in assets, FMC is one of Canada's top 15 software companies and growing rapidly. Presently, there are 222 employees at this location, a total of 257 employees in Canada, and 332 employees worldwide. In addition to the Mississauga head office, Financial Models has offices in the United Kingdom, New York, Montreal, Chicago and San Diego. FMC is listed on the Toronto Stock Exchange. Graduates most likely to be hired come from the following academic areas: Bachelor of Arts (Economics), Bachelor of Science (Computer Science, Mathematics), Bachelor of Engineering (Computer Systems), Bachelor of Commerce/Business Administration (Accounting, Finance, Information Systems), Master of Business Administration (Finance, Information Systems), Master of Science (Computer Science), Master of Engineering (Computer Systems/Science), and Canadian Securities Course graduates. Graduates would occupy Software Developer, Systems Implementation, Client Services, Business Analyst, P.O. Support, and LAN/WAN Specialist positions. Adaptable, team player, a desire to learn, and able to work independently are all listed as desirable non-academic qualifications. Company benefits and the potential for advancement are both rated as being excellent. FMC offers a comprehensive incentive package for recent graduates. The package includes a signing bonus, confirmation bonus and student loan repayment program. In addition, FMC offers an excellent health benefits package and education allowance. The average annual starting salary is dependent upon the applicant's experience, and the position being considered. The most suitable method for initial contact by those seeking employment is to fax a resume with a covering letter. Financial Models Company Inc. does hire co-op work term students. *Contact:* Human Resources.

FISCHER & PORTER (CANADA) LIMITED

134 Norfinch Drive
Toronto, ON M3N 1X7

Tel. 416-667-9800
Fax 416-667-8469

Fischer & Porter (Canada) Limited employs more than 50 people in the manufacture and sale of industrial measuring and control instruments. Graduates most likely to be hired come from the following academic areas: Bachelor of Engineering (Mechanical, Chemical, Electrical), and Community College Diploma (Instrumentation Electronics). Graduates would occupy Service Technician, Sales Engineer, Systems Engineer, Calibration Technician, and Project Manager positions. Reliable, dependable, ingenuity, a sense of urgency, and a good work attitude are all listed as desirable non-academic qualifications. Company benefits are rated above average. The potential for advancement is listed as excellent. The average annual starting salary falls within the $25,000 to $30,000 range. The most suitable method for initial contact by graduates seeking employment is to mail a resume with a covering letter. Fischer & Porter (Canada) Limited does hire summer students, depending on the workload at that particular time (inquire first). *Contact:* Human Resources.

FISHERY PRODUCTS INTERNATIONAL LTD. (FPI)

70 O'Leary Avenue, P.O. Box 550
St. John's, NF A1C 5L1

Tel. 709-570-0000
Fax 709-570-0209

Fishery Products International Ltd. (FPI) is a global seafood enterprise with Canadian sales offices in St. John's, Montreal, Toronto, and Vancouver; United States sales offices in Danvers MA, and Seattle WA; and European sales offices in Reading, England and Cuxhaven, Germany. FPI produces and markets a full range of seafood products, and through the company's seafood sourcing network, provides its customers with a variety of seafood items from throughout North America, Southeast Asia, South America, and Europe. The company's harvesting and processing operations include eight deep-sea trawlers, five scallop draggers, a shrimp freezer trawler, three value-added processing plants, four primary groundfish processing plants, a shrimp processing plant, and a crab processing plant. There are 90 employees at this location, approximately 2,600 across Canada, and a total of 3,000 employees worldwide. Graduates most likely to be hired come from the following academic areas: Bachelor of Arts (Economics), Bachelor of Science (Chemistry, Computer Science, Nursing), Bachelor of Engineering (Computer Systems, Mechanical), Bachelor of Commerce/Business Administration (Accounting, Finance, Human Resources, Information Systems, Marketing), Master of Business Administration (Accounting, Finance, Human Resources, Information Systems, Marketing), Master of Science (Biochemistry, Biology), Community College Diploma (Accounting, Administration, Human Resources, Insurance, Marketing/Sales, Purchasing/Logistics, Secretarial, Cooking, Computer Science, Electronics Technician, Marine Engineering, Nursing RN), and High School Diploma. Team player, initiative, analytical, good communication and interpersonal skills, and adaptive to change are all listed as desirable non-academic qualifications. Company benefits are rated above average. The potential for advancement is listed as being good. The average annual starting salary falls within the $25,000 to $30,000 range. The most suitable methods for initial contact by those seeking employment are to mail a resume with a covering letter, or via telephone. Fishery Products International Ltd. does hire summer students. *Contact:* Donna M. Crockwell, Personnel Supervisor.

FLOW AUTOMATION

970 Syscon Road
Burlington, ON L7L 5S2

Tel. 905-681-8575
Fax 905-681-8580
Website .... www.flowcorp.com

Flow Automation is a progressive leader in the design and manufacture of specialized automation equipment, robotic work cells, and vibratory feeder systems. Flow International, the parent company, operates out of Kent, Washington, and designs, develops, manufactures, markets and services ultra high pressure water-jet cutting and cleaning systems. Graduates most likely to be hired come from the following academic areas: Bachelor of Engineering (Electrical, Mechanical, Automation/Robotics, Industrial Engineering), Bachelor of Commerce/Business Administration (Accounting, Information Systems), and Community College Diploma (Administration, Business, Communications/Public Relations, Purchasing/Logistics, Secretarial, CAD/CAM/Autocad, Electronics Technician, Tool and Die, Machinist, Welding). Graduates would occupy Electrical Designer, Mechanical Designer, Machinist, Junior Machine Builder, Purchasing Clerk, Receptionist, and Sales Assistant positions. A willingness to travel, team player, and able to work flexible hours are all listed as desirable nonacademic qualifications. Company benefits are rated above average. The potential for advancement is listed as being good. The average annual starting salary depends upon the position being considered. The most suitable methods for initial contact by those seeking employment are to mail or fax a resume with a covering letter. Flow Automation does hire summer and co-op work term students. *Contacts:* Laura Gibson, Human Resources Manager or Sara Birdsell, Human Resources Assistant.

FOCUS CORPORATION LTD., THE
7605 - 50 Street
Edmonton, AB T6B 2W9

Tel. 403-466-6555
Fax 403-466-8200
Email .... edmonton@focus.ca
Website .... www.focus.ca

The Focus Corporation Ltd. provides quality geomatics and engineering services to clients throughout Canada and around the world. Focus and its group of companies have nearly fifty years of geomatics experience and currently offer Surveying, Engineering, Mapping, Geographic Information Systems (GIS), Global Positioning Systems (GPS), Land Administration, Consulting and Project Management services to the resource, infrastructure and land development sectors worldwide. Services are offered to private industry, First nations and all levels of government in Canada. Focus is an employee-owned organization with offices in major centres throughout British Columbia, Alberta, and Saskatchewan. The company is one of Canada's largest geomatics companies, employing more than 250 people. Graduates most likely to be hired come from the following academic areas: Bachelor of Arts (Geography, Urban Geography), Bachelor of Science (Computer Science, Forestry, Geology, Geography, Metallurgy), Bachelor of Engineering (General, Chemical, Civil, Computer Systems, Engineering Physics, Environmental/Resources, Forest Resources, Geological Engineering, Industrial Chemistry, Industrial Design, Industrial Engineering, Instrumentation, Materials Science, Metallurgy, Mining, Petroleum/Fuels, Pulp and Paper, Surveying, Telecommunications), Bachelor of Landscape Architecture, Bachelor of Commerce/Business Administration (General, Accounting, Finance, Human Resources, Information Sys-

tems, Marketing, Public Administration), Chartered Accountant, Certified Management Accountant, Master of Business Administration (General, Accounting, Finance, Human Resources, Information Systems, Marketing, Public Administration), Community College Diploma (Accounting, Administration, Business, Communications/Public Relations, Financial Planning, Human Resources, Information Systems, Marketing/Sales, Purchasing/Logistics, Secretarial, Graphic Arts, Photography, Urban Planning, Architectural Technician, CAD/CAM/Autocad, Computer Science, Engineering Technician, Forestry), and High School Diploma. Graduates would occupy Technician and Engineer-in-Training positions. Team player, positive attitude and strong interpersonal skills are listed as desirable non-academic qualifications. Company benefits are rated as excellent. The potential for advancement is listed as being good. The most suitable methods for initial contact by those seeking employment are to mail, fax or e-mail a resume with a covering letter, or by applying through the company's website at www.focus.ca. The Focus Corporation Ltd. does hire summer and co-op work term students. *Contact:* Brenda Moren, Manager, Human Resources.

FORVEST BROADCASTING CORPORATION
345 - 4th Avenue South
Saskatoon, SK S7K 5S5

Tel. 306-244-1975
Fax 306-665-7730

Forvest Broadcasting Corporation is a privately owned radio station, CJWW/Hot 93 FM. The Station has been Saskatchewan's country music station of the year for the past five consecutive years, maintaining a high profile community involvement. Forvest Broadcasting employs approximately 50 people. Graduates most likely to be hired come from the following academic areas: Bachelor of Arts (Journalism), Bachelor of Engineering (General, Electrical, Computer Systems), Bachelor of Commerce/Business Administration (General, Accounting, Finance, Human Resources, Information Systems, Public Administration, Marketing), Certified Management Accountant, Certified General Accountant, Master of Business Administration, Community College Diploma (Accounting, Administration, Advertising, Communications, Human Resources, Marketing/Sales, Secretarial, Journalism, Television/Radio Arts, Electronics Technician, Engineering Technician, Broadcasting), and High School Diploma. Graduates would occupy Accounting, Secretarial, Creative Writing, Production, On-Air Staff/Announcing, News, Sales and Marketing, and Promotion positions. A willingness to learn and take on new tasks, team player, good attitude, and flexibility are all listed as desirable non-academic qualifications. For certain positions, applicants should possess related work experience. Company benefits are rated as excellent. The potential for advancement is listed as being good. The average annual starting salary falls within the $15,000 to $20,000 range. The most suitable method for initial contact by those seeking employment is to mail a resume with a covering letter.

Contacts: Vic Dubois, Senior V.P. and G.M. (Technical/On Air Positions) or Irene Osborn, Chief Accountant (Administrative Positions).

FORZANI GROUP LTD., THE
824 - 41st Avenue NE
Calgary, AB T2E 3R3

Tel. 403-230-8200
Fax 403-230-8370

The Forzani Group Ltd. (FGL) is the leading national sporting goods retailer providing customers with a vast selection of merchandise ranging from clothing to sporting equipment. FGL operates under the banners of Sport Chek, Forzani's Locker Room, RnR Walking Store and Sports Experts. The company has over 4,000 employees in its corporate stores and Calgary Corporate Office locations. FGL has a separate office in Laval, to oversee its 140 franchise stores across Canada, operating under the banners of Podium, Zone Athletik, Jersey City and Sports Experts. Graduates most likely to be hired come from the following academic areas: Bachelor of Commerce/Business Administration (Accounting, Finance, Human Resources, Information Systems, Marketing), Certified General Accountant, and Community College Diploma (Accounting, Advertising, Human Resources, Information Systems, Purchasing/Logistics, Secretarial). Graduates would occupy IS Support, General Accounting, Graphic Design, Desktop Publishing, Financial Analyst, and Administrative Assistant positions. Good communication skills, initiative, team player, self-motivated, and strong interpersonal skills are all listed as desirable non-academic qualifications. Company benefits are rated above average. The potential for advancement is listed as being good. The average annual starting salary falls within the $20,000 to $25,000 range. The most suitable method for initial contact by those seeking employment is to mail a resume with a covering letter. The Forzani Group Ltd. does hire summer and co-op work term students. *Contact:* Human Resources Department.

FOUR SEASONS HOTEL - TORONTO
21 Avenue Road
Toronto, ON M5R 2G1

Tel. 416-964-0411
Fax 416-964-6152

The Four Seasons Hotel - Toronto, is a full-service, 380 guestroom hotel, located in the heart of the fashionable Yorkville district. The Hotel employs approximately 500 people. Graduates most likely to be hired come from the following academic areas: Bachelor of Arts, Bachelor of Commerce/Business Administration, Chartered Accountant, Certified Management Accountant, Certified General Accountant, Master of Business Administration, and Community College Diploma (Hospitality, Travel/Tourism). The types of positions occupied by graduates varies with academic qualifications accordingly. They may be service oriented, administrative or junior management positions. An excellent attitude, and directly or indirectly related work experiences are listed as desirable non-academic qualifications. Company benefits and the potential for advancement are both rated as excellent. The most suitable methods for initial contact by those seeking employment are to visit the Human Resources Department from Monday to Friday, 9:00am to 5:00pm, telephone call, or mail a resume with covering letter. The Four Seasons Hotel does hire summer students when suitable positions are available. *Contacts:* Catherine Caven, Director of Human Resources or Zane DeSerrano, Assistant Director of Human Resources.

FREDERICTON, CITY OF
P.O. Box 130, Station A
Fredericton, NB E3B 4Y7

Tel. 506-452-9502
Fax 506-452-9509

The City of Fredericton employs 560 people in the provision of municipal services, including planning and development, public works, recreation, police, fire, transit, human resources, treasury, purchasing, and legal services. Graduates most likely to be hired come from the following academic areas: Bachelor of Arts (English, Psychology, Recreation Studies, Urban Geography), Bachelor of Science (Computer Science, Environmental, Forestry, Geology, Geography, Psychology), Bachelor of Engineering (Architectural/Building, Surveying, Computer Systems, Environmental, Water Resources), Bachelor of Laws, Bachelor of Commerce/Business Administration (Accounting, Finance, Human Resources, Information Systems, Marketing, Public Administration), Chartered Accountant, Certified Management Accountant, Certified General Accountant, Master of Business Administration (General, Human Resources), Master of Health Sciences, Community College Diploma (Accounting, Administration, Facility Management, Financial Planning, Human Resources, Secretarial, Hospitality, Journalism, Legal Assistant, Recreation Studies, Security/Enforcement, Urban Planning, Auto Mechanic, CAD/CAM/Autocad, Computer Science, Electronics Technician, Engineering Technician, Forestry, HVAC Systems, Welding), and High School Diploma. Graduates would occupy a wide variety of positions in all city departments. Previous related work experience, computer skills, management or supervisory skills (where applicable), team player, good attitude, initiative, motivated and good interpersonal and communication skills are all listed as desirable non-academic qualifications. Company benefits and the potential for advancement are both rated as excellent. The average annual starting salary falls within the $25,000 to $30,000 range. The most suitable methods for initial contact by those seeking employment are to mail a resume with a covering letter, apply in person, or via telephone. The City of Fredericton does hire summer students. *Contacts:* Meghan Briggs, Human Resource Officer or J. David King, Director of Human Resources.

FREISEN CORP.
Box 720
Altona, MB R0G 0B0

Tel. 204-324-6401
Fax 204-324-1227

Freisen Corp. is a full service printing and book binding company, including desk top publishing. There
are 350 employees at this location, and a total of 500
employees across Canada. Graduates most likely to
be hired come from the following academic areas:
Bachelor of Arts (Graphic Arts), Bachelor of Engineering (Telecommunications, Electrical), and Community College Diploma (Business, Graphic Arts,
Electronics Technician). Graduates would occupy
Technician and Trainee positions. A positive attitude, team player and a willingness to work shift work
are listed as desirable non-academic qualifications.
Company benefits are rated as excellent. The potential for advancement is listed as being good. The
most suitable method for initial contact by those seeking employment is to mail a resume with a covering
letter. Freisen Corp. does hire summer students.
Contacts: Ria Kuhn, Human Resources Manager or
Ike Braun, Plant Manager.

FRIGIDAIRE EUREKA
866 Langs Drive
Cambridge, ON N3H 2N7

Tel. 519-653-8880
Fax 519-653-3189

Frigidaire Eureka is a household appliance company.
This location is involved in the assembly, sales and
marketing, and related administrative operations.
Frigidaire Eureka has 160 employees at this location, a total of 1,000 employees in Canada, and a
total of 20,000 employees worldwide. Graduates
most likely to be hired come from the following academic areas: Bachelor of Arts (Economics), Bachelor of Commerce/Business Administration (Marketing), Certified Management Accountant, Community
College Diploma (Accounting, Advertising, Human
Resources, Marketing/Sales, Secretarial), and High
School Diploma. Graduates would occupy Administrative Assistant, Marketing Coordinator, Sales
Administrator, Financial Analyst, and Accounting
Clerk positions. Team player and professionalism
are both listed as desirable non-academic qualifications. Company benefits are rated as industry standard. The potential for advancement is listed as average. The average annual starting salary falls within
the $20,000 to $25,000 range. The most suitable
method for initial contact by those seeking employment is to mail a resume with a covering letter.
Frigidaire Eureka does hire summer students. Contacts: Marie Murphy, Human Resources Coordinator
or Liz MacAlpine, Human Resources Coordinator.

G.F.I. CONTROL SYSTEMS INC.
100 Hollinger Crescent
Kitchener, ON N2K 2Z3

Tel. 519-576-4270
Fax 519-576-7045
Email .... sheldman@wchat.on.ca

G.F.I. Control Systems Inc. develops natural gas and
propane fuel delivery systems for the Ford Engineering, Development and Production company. The
company employs 110 people at this location and a
total of 130 people worldwide. G.F.I. is a division
of Devtek, a $400 million Canadian company in-
volved in the development of new fuel injection technology, software (Intel and Motorola) development,
and computer hardware engineering. Devtek is part
of a 50% joint venture with Stuart Stevenson USA,
involving international sales and marketing, research
and development and production activities. Graduates most likely to be hired at G.F.I. Control Systems come from the following academic areas: Bachelor of Science (Computer Science), Bachelor of
Engineering (Chemical, Electrical, Mechanical, Au-
tomation/Robotics, Computer Systems, Industrial
Engineering, Industrial Production/Manufacturing,
Microelectronics, Petroleum/Fuels), Chartered Accountant, Master of Business Administration (Marketing), and Community College Diploma (Accounting, Facility Management, Information Systems,
Purchasing/Logistics, Automotive Mechanic, CAD/
CAM/Autocad, Computer Science, Electronics Technician, Engineering Technician, Tool and Die, Machinist). Graduates would occupy Junior Chemical
Engineer, Junior Mechanical Engineer, Electronics
Technician, Mechanical Technician, Electrical Technician, Software Developer, Buyer, Industrial Engineer, Process Planner, and Master Scheduler positions. Flexibility, team skills, personality, and good
problem solving skills are all listed as desirable non-
academic qualifications. Company benefits are rated
as industry standard. The potential for advancement
is listed as excellent. The average annual starting
salary falls within the $30,000 to $35,000 range. The
most suitable methods for initial contact by those
seeking employment are to mail or e-mail a resume
with a covering letter. G.F.I. Control Systems Inc.
does hire students for summer and co-op work terms.
Contact: Marg Gallinger.

G.M. SERNAS & ASSOCIATES LTD.
110 Scotia Court, Unit 41
Whitby, ON L1N 8Y7

Tel. 905-686-6402
Fax 905-432-7877

G.M. Sernas & Associates Ltd. provides municipal,
environmental, water resources, power distribution
and land use planning services to both public and
private sector clients in Southern and Eastern Ontario from offices in Mississauga, Whitby and
Belleville. Graduates most likely to be hired come
from the following academic areas: Bachelor of Arts
(Urban Geography), Bachelor of Engineering (Civil,
Environmental, Electrical), Master of Business Administration, Master of Engineering (Civil, Environmental), and Community College Diploma (Engineering Technician). During the initial years of employment, graduates are placed on personally-tailored
development programs to expose them to all aspects

of the company's consulting work within their field of specialization. Depending upon the individuals capabilities and interests, careers may lead to specialized technical work, supervisory responsibilities or project management in the long term. Good planning, organization skills, strong written and oral communication skills, and able to work with minimal supervision are all listed as desirable non-academic qualifications. In addition, applicants should be interested in working with the demands, and interpersonal contacts experienced in consulting work. Company benefits are rated above average. The potential for advancement is listed as being good. The starting salary depends upon the position being considered, and the qualifications and experience of the applicant. The most suitable method for initial contact by those seeking employment is to mail a resume with a covering letter. G.M. Sernas & Associates Ltd. does hire summer and work term students. *Contact:* Mrs. Jone Webster, Human Resources Manager.

G.N. JOHNSTON EQUIPMENT CO. LTD.
1400 Courtney Park Drive
Mississauga, ON L5T 1H1

Tel. 416-675-6460
Fax 905-564-1698

G.N. Johnston Equipment Co. Ltd. sells and services material handling equipment. There are more than 100 employees at this location. Graduates most likely to be hired come from the following academic areas: Bachelor of Commerce/Business Administration (General, Marketing, Accounting), Certified Management Accountant, Certified General Accountant, and Community College Diploma (Accounting, Business, Mechanic, Engineering Technician, Electrical Technician). Graduates would occupy Field Service Technician, Shop Mechanic, Junior/Intermediate Accountant, and Salesperson positions. Company benefits are rated as industry standard. The potential for advancement is listed as being good. The average annual starting salary falls within the $25,000 to $30,000 range, and is commission based for Sales positions. The most suitable method for initial contact by those seeking employment is to mail a resume with a covering letter. *Contacts:* Beth McKenney, Director, Employee Relations or Ingrid Lambert, Employee Relations Assistant.

GARDENWORKS
6250 Lougheed Highway
Burnaby, BC V5B 2Z9

Tel. 604-299-9622
Fax 604-299-4403

Gardenworks operates six retail garden centre outlets which offer a full range of home and garden products. Open 12 months a year, Gardenworks is the leading independent retailer of garden supplies in British Columbia. There are more than 50 employees at this location and approximately 160 employees in the company. Graduates most likely to be hired come from the following academic areas: Bachelor of Arts (Horticulture), Bachelor of Science (Horti-

culture, Plant Sciences), Certified Management Accountant, Certified General Accountant, Community College Diploma (Business, Forestry, Horticulture), and High School Diploma. Graduates would occupy Sales Clerk and Management Trainee positions. Previous work experience in retail merchandising, team player, and a genuine interest/hobby in gardening are all listed as desirable non-academic qualifications. Company benefits are rated as excellent. The potential for advancement is listed as being good. The average annual starting salary depends on the position being considered. The most suitable method for initial contact by those seeking employment is to mail a resume with a covering letter. Gardenworks does hire summer students. *Contact:* Bruce Meyers, Vice President Finance and Administration.

GATEWAY FREIGHT SYSTEMS
243 North Service Road, Suite 302
Oakville, ON L6M 3E5

Tel. 905-842-3600
Fax 905-842-6210
Email .... gpo@gatewayfrt.com

Gateway Freight Systems is a truck transport and freight forwarding company. Graduates most likely to be hired are Business, Purchasing/Logistics, and Secretarial graduates with a Community College Diploma. Graduates would occupy Dispatcher, Logistics Coordinator, Clerk, Bookkeeper, and Customer Service Representative positions. Previous work experience in the truck transportation industry is listed as a desirable non-academic qualification. Company benefits are rated above average. The potential for advancement is listed as being good. The most suitable method for initial contact by those seeking employment is to fax a resume with a covering letter. Gateway Freight Systems does hire summer and co-op work term students. *Contact:* Bill Charney.

GE CANADA
2300 Meadowvale Boulevard
Mississauga, ON L5N 5P9

Tel. 905-858-5705
Fax 905-858-5641
Website .... www.ge.com

GE is a diversified and global technology, manufacturing, and services company. GE Canada is involved in diverse business activities that GE operates worldwide, including: Financial/Capital Services, Hydro, Electrical Distribution and Control, Nuclear Products, Motors and Industrial Systems, Industrial Automation, Aircraft Engines, Major Home Appliances, Lighting, Medical Systems, Plastics, Silicones, Transportation Systems, Meters, and Information Services. GE Canada operates facilities across

Canada employing a total of 9,200 people. GE employs over 250,000 people worldwide, and is one of the world's largest public companies. Graduates most likely to be hired come from the following academic areas: Bachelor of Science (Computer Science, Mathematics), Bachelor of Engineering (Chemical, Electrical, Mechanical, Automation/Robotics, Biomedical Electronics, Computer Systems, Engineering Physics, Industrial Production, Power/Hydro), Bachelor of Commerce/Business Administration (General, Accounting, Finance, Information Systems, Marketing), Master of Business Administration (General, Human Resources), and Master of Engineering. Graduates would occupy Design Engineer, Process/Manufacturing Engineer, Sales Engineer, Financial Analyst, Human Resources Specialist, and Sales/Marketing Specialist positions. Initiative, self-motivated, change oriented, team player, good communication skills, and an ability to inspire and influence others are all listed as desirable non-academic qualifications. Company benefits and the potential for advancement are both rated as excellent. The average annual starting salary falls within the $35,000 to $45,000 range. The most suitable method for initial contact by those seeking employment is to mail a resume with a covering letter. GE Canada does hire a limited number of summer students annually. *Contact:* Mr. Terry Peach, University Recruitment.

GE HARRIS
Energy Control Systems Canada, Inc.

GE HARRIS ENERGY CONTROL SYSTEMS, INC.
4525 Manilla Road SE
Calgary, AB T2G 4B6

Tel.	403-214-4400
Fax	403-287-9900
Email	HR@hdap.com
Website	www.geharris-ecs.com

GE HARRIS Energy Control Systems Inc. is part of a joint venture between General Electric Power Systems and Harris Corporation, Transcomm Division (Electronic Systems Sector). Based in Calgary, with sales support offices in Perth, Australia, Winnersh, England and Hong Kong. Pioneers of the supervisory control and data acquisitions business, GE HARRIS has more than 30 years experience in supplying the utility industry with the world's most technologically advanced monitoring and control systems. GE HARRIS is the major force in the development of the most innovative systems for substation automation, distribution automation and hydro generation plant automation. Electric, gas and water utilities around the world use the Company's systems to monitor, control and automate their operations effectively and efficiently. GE HARRIS records an installed base of over 12,000 systems in genera-

tion, transmission and distribution facilities in Canada coast to coast, throughout the United States, within Latin America, across Europe, in Africa, and widespread in Asia and the Pacific Rim. Customers range from national utilities to investor-owned corporations to rural and municipal utilities all employing GE HARRIS' systems to ensure the best and most reliable service to their industrial, commercial and residential customers. Graduates most likely to be hired come from the following academic areas: Bachelor of Engineering (Electrical, Mechanical, Computer Systems), Bachelor of Commerce/Business Administration (Accounting, Finance, Human Resources, Information Systems, Marketing), Certified Management Accountant, Certified General Accountant, Doctorate of Engineering, Community College Diploma (Accounting, Administration, Facility Management, Human Resources, Information Systems, Secretarial, CAD/CAM/Autocad, Computer Science, Electronics Technician, Engineering Technician), and High School Diploma. Graduates would occupy Software Developer, Analyst, Specialist, Coordinator, and Engineering positions. Previous work term experience, good interpersonal skills, team player, creativity, and excellent communication skills are all listed as desirable non-academic qualifications. Company benefits are rated above average. The potential for advancement is listed as excellent. The average annual starting salary falls within the $35,000 to $40,000 range. The most suitable method for initial contact by those seeking employment is to fax a resume with a covering letter. GE HARRIS does hire students for summer and co-op work terms. *Contact:* Judy Conrad, Manager, Human Resources.

GEC ALSTHOM AMF TRANSPORT INC.
1830, rue Le Ber
Montreal, QC H3K 2A4

Tel.	514-925-3693
Fax	514-925-3514

GEC Alsthom AMF Transport Inc. employs approximately 750 people in the remanufacturing of railroad cars and locomotives. Graduates most likely to be hired come from the following academic areas: Bachelor of Science (Chemistry, Computer Science, Environmental Science), Bachelor of Engineering (Chemical, Industrial Chemistry, Metallurgy, Pollution Treatment, Electrical, Mechanical), Bachelor of Commerce/Business Administration (General, Accounting, Finance, Human Resources, Information Systems, Marketing), Master of Business Administration, and Community College Diploma (Purchasing/Logistics, Secretarial, Architecture/Drafting, CAD/CAM/Autocad, Computer Science, Welding). Graduates would occupy Engineer, Technician, and junior positions in Marketing, Human Resources etc. Previous work experience in the railroad industry, hard working and team player are listed as desirable non-academic qualifications. Fluency in both French and English is a must. Company benefits and the potential for advancement are both rated as excellent. The average annual starting salary is dependent upon the type of position, experience and education of the applicant. The most suitable method for initial contact by those seeking employment is to mail a resume with a covering letter. *Contact:* Michel Martin, Manager, Human Resources.

GEMINI ENGINEERING LTD.
5940 Macleod Trail SW, Suite 700
Calgary, AB T2H 2G4

Tel.	403-255-2006
Fax	403-252-5338
Email	sgsmith@geminieng.com
Website	www.geminieng.com

Gemini Engineering provides high quality engineering, project management and procurement services globally. Headquartered in Calgary, Gemini focuses on providing service to the upstream oil and gas sector. As a full discipline engineering firm, Gemini can supply EPCM as well as EPC services. There are 120 employees at this location and a total of 240 employees in Canada. Graduates most likely to be hired come from the following academic areas: Bachelor of Engineering (Chemical, Civil, Electrical, Mechanical), Bachelor of Commerce/Business Administration (Accounting, Human Resources), and Community College Diploma (Accounting, Secretarial, CAD/CAM/Autocad, Electronics Technician, Engineering Technician, Welding), and High School Diploma. Graduates would occupy Project Engineer, Design Engineer, Designer, Technologist, Technician, Clerical, Accountant, and Secretarial positions. Team player and good communication skills are both listed as desirable non-academic qualifications. Company benefits are rated above average. The potential for advancement is listed as excellent. The average annual starting salary falls within the $25,000 to $30,000 range. The most suitable method for initial contact by those seeking employment is to e-mail a resume with a covering letter. Gemini Engineering Ltd. does hire summer and co-op work term students. *Contact:* Stacy Smith, Manager, Human Resources.

GENDIS INC./SAAN STORES LTD.
1370 Sony Place
Winnipeg, MB R3C 3C3

Tel.	204-474-5308
Fax	204-474-5471

Gendis Inc./Saan Stores Ltd. operates retail department stores. There are approximately 350 employees at this location and a total of 3,000 employees in Canada. Graduates most likely to be hired come from the following academic areas: Bachelor of Commerce/Business Administration (General, Accounting, Finance, Human Resources, Information Systems, Marketing, Public Administration), Certified Management Accountant, Certified General Accountant, Master of Business Administration (General, Accounting, Finance, Human Resources, Information Systems, Marketing, Public Administration), Community College Diploma (Accounting, Administration, Advertising, Business, Financial Planning, Human Resources, Marketing/Sales, Secretarial), and High School Diploma. Previous work experience, good references, team player, and a good attitude are

all listed as desirable non-academic qualifications. Company benefits are rated as excellent. The potential for advancement is listed as being good. The most suitable method for initial contact by those seeking employment is to mail a resume with a covering letter. Gendis Inc./Saan Stores Ltd. does hire summer students. *Contact:* Ms. B. Scardina, Human Resources & Training.

GENERAL ELECTRIC CAPITAL FLEET SERVICES
2300 Meadowvale Boulevard
Mississauga, ON L5N 5P9

Tel.	905-858-4947
Website	www.ge.com

General Electric Capital Fleet Services provides automobile leasing services for company car fleets. There are more than 100 employees at this location. Graduates most likely to be hired come from the following academic areas: Bachelor of Arts (General), Bachelor of Commerce/Business Administration, and Master of Business Administration. Graduates would occupy Client Service and Administrative positions. Experience in the automotive industry or in leasing is considered a definite asset. Company benefits and the potential for advancement are both rated as excellent. The average annual starting salary falls within the $25,000 to $30,000 range. The most suitable method for initial contact by those seeking employment is to mail a resume with a covering letter. *Contact:* Susan Chisholm, Human Resources.

GENESIS MICROCHIP INC.
200 Town Centre Blvd., Suite 400
Markham, ON L3R 8G5

Tel.	905-470-2742
Fax	905-470-2447
Email	hr@genesis-microchip.on.ca
Website	www.genesis-video.com

Established in 1987 and publicly traded on Nasdaq, Genesis Microchip Inc. is a leader in digital video graphics technology. With offices in Markham, Ontario and Mountain View, California, Genesis sets the standard for high quality, state-of-the-art digital video scaling and line doubling IC's. Employing over 100 people worldwide, and with design wins in the digital projection and growing LCD monitor markets, in video editing, video teleconferencing, medical imaging, broadcast and avionics, Genesis' goal is to become the leading developer and provider of high quality video, graphics and image manipulation IC solutions that address evolving standards of digital display systems. Genesis' responsiveness and relationships with market leaders, together with its understanding of market trends, allows the Company to develop products more quickly. Genesis is also able to provide manufacture-ready reference designs that allow its customers to ramp into production quickly while controlling development costs. Graduates most likely to be hired come from the following academic areas: Bachelor of Engineering (Electrical), Bachelor of Commerce/Business Administration (Finance, Information Systems), Master of Business Administration (Marketing), Master of Engineering (Electrical), and Community College Diploma (Business, Journalism, Electronics Technician, Engineering Technician). Graduates would occupy Engineer, Technician, Technologist, and IS Support positions. Co-op work term or previous work experience, team player, initiative, and good communication skills are all listed as desirable non-academic qualifications. Genesis offers a quality working environment with advanced up-to-date design tools, clean and modern work stations, healthy interactions, opportunities for continuous development and learning, flexible working hours, incentive initiatives, and share options and purchase plans. Accordingly, company benefits and the potential for advancement are both rated as excellent. The average annual starting salary falls within the $45,000 to $50,000 range, and the Company keeps track of pay levels in the industry to make sure that salaries remain competitive. The most suitable methods for initial contact by those seeking employment are to mail, fax or e-mail a resume with a covering letter, or by applying through the company's website at www.genesis-video.com. Genesis Microchip Inc. does hire summer and co-op work term students. *Contact:* Manager, Human Resources & Administration.

GENNUM CORPORATION
P.O. Box 489, Station A
Burlington, ON L7R 3Y3

Tel. 905-632-2996
Fax 905-632-2055
Email .... career@gennum.com
Website .... www.gennum.com

Gennum Corporation, formed in 1973 and ISO9001-94 registered, is a Canadian high technology company which designs, manufactures and markets electronic components, primarily silicon integrated circuits (IC's) and thick-film hybrid circuits, for specialized applications in the information world. The company's products include low voltage audio electronic amplifiers and analog signal processing circuitry supplied to the world hearing instrument industry, video signal distribution and processing components sold to the professional video and broadcast television markets, and user specific integrated circuits for a wide variety of specific applications where information is being conditioned, transmitted or interpreted. The company employs 400 people at this location and a total of 410 people worldwide. Graduates most likely to be hired come from the following academic areas: Bachelor of Engineering (Chemical, Electrical, Mechanical, Engineering Physics, Microelectronics, Telecommunications), Bachelor of Commerce/Business Administration (Accounting), Master of Business Administration (Marketing), Master of Engineering (Electrical, Engineering Physics), Doctorate of Engineering (Electrical), and Community College Diploma (Purchasing/Logistics, Secretarial, Graphic Arts, CAD/CAM/Autocad, Computer Science, Electronics Technician, Engineering Technician). Graduates would occupy Design Engineer, Technologist, Technician, Test Engineer, Proc-

ess Engineer, Production Engineer, Product Definition Specialist, Marketing Specialist/Manager, Account Representative, and Applications Engineer positions. Team skills, leadership abilities, creativity, business skills, innovation, and good interpersonal and communication skills are all listed as desirable non-academic qualifications. Company benefits and the potential for advancement are both rated as excellent. The average annual starting salary falls within the $40,000 to $50,000 range. The most suitable methods for initial contact by those seeking employment are to mail, fax or e-mail a resume with a covering letter, or by applying through the company's website at www.gennum.com. Gennum Corporation does hire students for summer and co-op work terms. *Contact:* Gary D. Gambacort, Director, Human Resources.

GEON CANADA INC.
P.O. Box 1026
Niagara Falls, ON L2E 6V9

Tel. 905-374-5651
Fax 905-374-5614

Geon Canada Inc. is a manufacturer of vinyl (VCM) resins and compounds. There are approximately 180 employees at this location, a total of 250 in Canada, and 2,000 Geon employees worldwide. Graduates most likely to be hired come from the following academic areas: Bachelor of Engineering (Chemical, Industrial Chemistry), Master of Business Administration, and Community College Diploma (Accounting, Computer Science, Engineering Technician). Graduates would occupy Process Engineer, Project Engineer, Chemical Technician, and Accounting positions. An entrepreneurial drive, accountability, and a positive attitude are all listed as desirable non-academic qualifications. Company benefits and the potential for advancement are both rated as excellent. The average annual starting falls within the $40,000 to $45,000 range. The most suitable method for initial contact by those seeking employment is to mail a resume with a covering letter. *Contact:* Manager, Human Resources.

GEORGE BROWN COLLEGE
P.O. Box 1015, Station B
Toronto, ON M5T 2T9

Tel. 416-415-2107

George Brown College is a community college with locations throughout Toronto, employing approximately 1,700 staff and faculty. Graduates are hired from the entire academic spectrum for a wide variety of positions, including Teaching and Faculty, Technical, Clerical and Administrative positions. Relevant work experience, and excellent oral and written communication skills are listed as desirable non-academic qualifications. Relevant work experience is emphasized as a critical qualification. Employee benefits and the potential for advancement are both rated as excellent. The average annual starting salary for support staff falls within the $20,000 to $25,000 range, and for faculty and administrative staff, the starting salary falls within the $30,000 to $35,000 range. The most suitable method for initial contact by those seeking employment is to mail a resume with a covering letter. George Brown College does hire summer students on a regular basis. *Contact:* Manager, Employment Services.

GEORGE KELK CORPORATION
48 Lesmill Road
Don Mills, ON M3B 2T5

Tel. 416-445-5850
Fax 416-445-5972
Email .... personnel@kelk.com
Website .... www.kelk.com

George Kelk Corporation employs 100 people in the design, manufacture and selling of sensors for the metals rolling industry. These sensors include load, force and tension measuring equipment, optoelectronics gauges for the dimensional measurement of steel strip and plate, and laser velocimeters. Graduates most likely to be hired come from the following academic areas: Bachelor of Engineering (Electrical, Software Development, Mechanical), and Doctorate (Photonics), and Community College Diploma (Electronics, Software Development, Mechanical). Graduates would occupy Technician, Technologist, Field Service Representative, and Design and Development Engineer positions. Reliability, creativity, interpersonal skills, team spirit and previous work experience are all listed as desirable non-academic qualifications. In addition to paying competitive salaries, company benefits are rated above average. The potential for advancement is listed as being good. The most suitable methods for initial contact by those seeking employment are to mail, fax or e-mail a resume with a covering letter, stating the position of interest. Additional information can be obtained from the company's website at www.kelk.com. *Contact:* Mrs. P. Worton - Personnel Manager.

GESCO INDUSTRIES INC.
1965 Lawrence Avenue West
Weston, ON M9N 1H5

Tel. 416-243-0040
Fax 416-243-1263

Gesco Industries Inc. is a floorcovering manufacturer and distributor. There are approximately 150 employees at this location, with over 250 employees in Canada. Graduates most likely to be hired come from the following academic areas: Bachelor of Arts (General, Economics, Fine Arts), Bachelor of Engineering (Industrial), Certified Management Accountant, Certified General Accountant, Master of Business Administration, and Community College Diploma (Accounting, Administration, Business). Graduates are hired to occupy Accounting Clerk, Financial Analyst, Accountant, Controller, and Marketing Assistant positions. Good communication skills, and previous work experience are both listed as desirable non-academic qualifications. Company benefits are rated above average. The potential for advance-

ment is listed as being good. The average annual starting salary is dependent upon the department and the position being considered. The most suitable method for initial contact by those seeking employment is to mail a resume with a covering letter. Gesco Industries Inc. does hire summer students, usually for specific projects in Accounting, Engineering and Administration. *Contact:* Elaine MacIsaac, Human Resources Manager.

GIENOW
3812 Edmonton Trail N.E.
Calgary, AB T2E 5T6

Tel. 403-276-1171
Fax 403-230-9309
Email .... oneill@gienow.com
Website .... www.gienow.com

Gienow is Canada's premier manufacturer of custom windows and doors. Manufacturing of Gienow's products takes place at its head office, located in Calgary, with distribution worldwide. In addition, the Company has several branches in Alberta and British Columbia. Gienow has been in business for over 50 years. Graduates most likely to be hired come from the following academic areas: Bachelor of Science (Computer Science), Bachelor of Engineering (General, Electrical, Mechanical, Computer Systems, Industrial Engineering, Industrial Production/Manufacturing), Bachelor of Commerce/Business Administration (General, Accounting, Finance, Human Resources, Information Systems, Marketing), Master of Business Administration (General), and Community College Diploma (Accounting, Administration, Business, Facility Management, Human Resources, Information Systems, Marketing/Sales, Purchasing/Logistics, Secretarial). Graduates would occupy Production Control, Engineering, Research and Development, System Analyst, Programmer, Junior Accountant, Cost Accounting, Buyer, Inside Sales, Customer Service, and Administrative Assistant positions. Initiative, a very positive attitude, time management skills, manufacturing background, and excellent communication skills are all listed as desirable non-academic qualifications. Company benefits are rated above average. The potential for advancement is listed as excellent. The average annual starting salary falls within the $25,000 to $35,000 range, depending on the position being considered. The most suitable methods for initial contact by those seeking employment are to mail, fax, or e-mail a resume with a covering letter, through the company's website at www.gienow.com, or via campus recruitment initiatives (visit your campus career centre). Gienow does hire summer and co-op work term students. *Contact:* Leslie O'Neill, Human Resources Manager.

GIFFELS ASSOCIATES LIMITED
30 International Boulevard
Toronto (Rexdale), ON M9W 5P3

Tel. 416-675-5950
Fax 416-675-4620

Email .... info@giffels.com
Website .... www.giffels.com

In business for nearly 50 years, Giffels Associates Limited is a full-service, employee owned, Canadian-based, consulting and contracting organization offering a broad range of architectural, engineering, management and construction services worldwide. The company's services incorporate all aspects of design, construction and operations, from architecture, and engineering design, to infrastructure development project/construction management, process engineering and operations consulting. There are 300 employees at this location, a total of 350 in Canada, and a total of 420 employees worldwide. Graduates most likely to be hired come from the following academic areas: Bachelor of Engineering (Civil, Architectural/Building, Surveying, Electrical, Automation/Robotics, Computer Systems, Instrumentation, Power, Mechanical, Industrial Design, Industrial Production, Mining), Bachelor of Architecture, Bachelor of Commerce/Business Administration (Information Systems), and Community College Diploma (Architecture/Drafting, CAD/CAM/Autocad, Computer Science, Engineering Technician, HVAC Systems). Graduates would occupy Engineer-in-Training and Junior Technician or Technologist positions. Results-driven, team player, superb communication and interpersonal skills, natural leadership abilities, a demonstrated track record of success and hands-on management, design, engineering or consulting experience all listed as desirable non-academic qualifications. Company benefits are rated as excellent. The potential for advancement is listed as being good. The average annual starting salary falls within the $35,000 to $40,000 range. The most suitable methods for initial contact by those seeking employment are to mail, fax or e-mail a resume with a covering letter, or by applying through the company's website at www.giffels.com. Giffels Associates Limited does hire students for summer and co-op work terms. *Contacts:* John S. MacDonald, Director of Human Resources or Linda Janeway, Human Resources Administrator.

GLOBAL TRAVEL COMPUTER SERVICES
7550 Birchmount Road
Markham, ON L3R 6C6

Tel. 905-479-4949
Fax 905-479-5420
Email .... lindah@global-travel.on.ca
Website .... www.global-travel.on.ca

Global Travel Computer Services provides transaction processing computer services. There are 59 employees at this location. Graduates most likely to be hired come from the following academic areas: Bachelor of Science (Computer Science), Bachelor of Commerce/Business Administration (Accounting), Master of Business Administration (Accounting), and Community College Diploma (Computer Science). Graduates would occupy positions that relate directly to their academic backgrounds. Team player, initiative, and good communication skills are all listed as desirable non-academic qualifications.

Company benefits are rated above average. The potential for advancement is listed as average. The average annual starting salary falls within the $30,000 to $35,000 range. The most suitable method for initial contact by those seeking employment is to mail a resume with a covering letter. Global Travel Computer Services occasionally hires summer students. *Contact:* Human Resources.

GLOBE & MAIL, THE
444 Front Street West
Toronto, ON M5V 2S9

Tel. 416-585-5000
Fax 416-585-5675

The Globe and Mail, Canada's national newspaper, is produced at six regional printing plants across Canada, and publishes seven magazines: Report on Business, Domino, Destinations, Broadcast Week, Toronto, Montreal Magazine and West. The Info Globe Division provides a variety of online news and financial database products and services and publishes specialized periodicals and books. There are more than 500 employees at this location. Graduates most likely to be hired come from the following academic areas: Bachelor of Arts (Journalism, General), Bachelor of Commerce/Business Administration, Master of Arts (Journalism, General), and Community College (General, Journalism). Applicants should possess appropriate experience and maintain a "good fit" with the corporate operating style. Company benefits and the potential for advancement are both rated as excellent. The average annual starting salary is dependent upon the position being considered. The most suitable method for initial contact by graduates seeking employment is to respond to positions advertised in The Globe and Mail. A small number of summer internships are available each year. Apply to the Deputy Managing Editor no later than October 31 of the prior year. *Contact:* Manager, Human Resources.

GMSI INC.
275 Michael Cowpland Drive
Kanata, ON K2M 2G2

Tel. 613-599-5161
Fax 613-599-6425
Email .... dthomson@gmsiworld.com
Website .... gmsiworld.com

GMSI Inc. develops fleet management and wireless communications systems for the transportation and service industries. GMSI's customers are organizations with fleets of 10 to 10,000 vehicles, in industries ranging from home services, couriers and taxis, to buses, distribution and long-haul trucking. Each uses GMSI's dispatch and tracking applications to optimize the usage and efficiency of their fleet by analyzing real-time work order and location information obtained over radio or satellite networks, from GMSI's in-vehicle radio modems and mobile terminals. Graduates most likely to be hired come from the following academic areas: Bachelor of Engineering (General, Computer Systems), Master of Engineering (Computer Systems), and Community College Diploma (Computer Science, Electronics Technician, Engineering Technician). Graduates would occupy Software Developer and Systems Installation positions. Team player and specialized knowledge of certain computer languages are listed as desirable non-academic qualifications. Company benefits are rated as industry standard. The potential for advancement is listed as being good. The average annual starting salary falls within the $45,000 to $50,000 range. The most suitable methods for initial contact by those seeking employment are to mail or fax a resume with a covering letter. *Contact:* Diahanne Thomson, Project Coordinator.

GOLDFARB CONSULTANTS
4950 Yonge Street
Suite 1700
Toronto, ON M2N 6K1

Tel. 416-221-9200
Fax 416-221-2214
Email .. wendy.beh@goldfarb.global.ibmmail.com

Goldfarb Consultants conducts custom research to gather, process and analyse data about a client's products or services and those segments of the population to which they are marketed. This includes research on attitudes, behaviours and opinions, as well as on advertising, media usage, customer satisfaction, brand equity and management, new product testing and package design. The company employs approximately 100 full-time and 350 part-time employees. Graduates most likely to be hired come from the following academic areas: Bachelor of Arts (Economics, Philosophy, Political Science, Psychology, Sociology), Bachelor of Commerce/Business Administration (Accounting, Finance, Human Resources, Marketing), Chartered Accountant, Certified Management Accountant, Certified General Accountant, Master of Business Administration (Marketing), and Community College Diploma (Business, Marketing/Sales, Secretarial, Computer Science). Graduates would occupy Market Research Analyst (qualitative/quantitative), Project Director, Accounting Clerk, Accounting Manager, Word Processor, Field Coordinator, Clinic Research Analyst, and Clinic Project Director positions. Self starter, bright, energetic, competitive, curious, superior writing skills (for analyst positions), knowledge of and excellent skills with computer software (eg. Word, Excel, PowerPoint), and quality oriented are all listed as desirable non-academic qualifications. The most suitable method for initial contact by those seeking employment is to mail a resume with a covering letter. Goldfarb Consultants does hire summer students, applications should be made in the preceding February or March. *Contact:* Wendy Behm, Human Resources.

GOODWILL TORONTO
234 Adelaide Street East
Toronto, ON M5A 1M9

Tel. 416-362-4711
Fax 416-362-0720

Email .... info@goodwill.on.ca
Website .... www.goodwill.on.ca

Goodwill Toronto is a not-for-profit, charitable organization that funds and provides work training and job-related services to people facing employment barriers. For more than 60 years, it has helped Toronto communities build better futures by helping people find gainful employment. With 187 Goodwills in North America and 52 international affiliates, Goodwill Toronto is part of a worldwide network of Goodwill agencies. All are not-for-profit, charitable agencies governed individually by local boards. Goodwills across Canada include Toronto, Hamilton, London, St. Catharines, Sarnia, Edmonton, and Montreal. Goodwill Toronto is 90% self-reliant through the sale of donated goods and other revenue-generating enterprises. Each year, over 25 million pounds of reusable clothing, housewares and furniture are sold in more than 30 Goodwill stores across southeastern Ontario. Beyond funds generated internally, Goodwill Toronto receives support through innovative partnerships with the government and corporate sector, allowing the agency to develop and offer a wide range of training programs that meet the changing employment needs of surrounding communities. With its three Employment Resource Centres, three Training Centres and 25 employment-related programs, Goodwill Toronto was able to help nearly 3,000 people reach their employment goals in 1997. Goodwill Toronto employs 1,100 people in the Greater Toronto Area. Graduates most likely to be hired come from the following academic areas: Bachelor of Arts (Sociology/Social Work - BSW), Bachelor of Education (Special Needs), and Community College Diploma (Information Systems, Social Work/DSW, Carpentry, Welding). Graduates would occupy IT, Career Assessment Facilitator, and Store Manager positions. Previous work experience in career/job counselling is listed as a definite asset. Company benefits are rated above average. The potential for advancement is listed as excellent. The most suitable method for initial contact by those seeking employment is to mail a resume with a covering letter. Goodwill Toronto does hire summer students. *Contact:* Human Resources Co-ordinator.

GOWLING, STRATHY AND HENDERSON
160 Elgin Street, Suite 2600
P.O. Box 466, Station D
Ottawa, ON K2P 2C4

Tel. 613-233-1781
Fax 613-563-9869
Email .... info@gowlings.com
Website .... www.gowlings.com

Gowling, Strathy and Henderson was founded in 1887 and has grown to become one of the largest law firms in Canada, with over 340 professionals, and offices in Ottawa, Toronto, Hamilton, Waterloo Region, Vancouver and Moscow. The firm provides a full range of legal services in virtually every field of law, including environmental service, municipal planning, real estate, corporate finance, administrative tribunals and government agencies, banking, civil litigation, international trade, foreign investment, securities and taxation. Clients include a broad spectrum of corporations, public bodies, interest groups, professionals and individuals. The firm employs approximately 340 people at this location, a total of 902 in Canada, and a total of 918 people worldwide. Graduates most likely to be hired come from the following academic areas: Bachelor of Laws, and Community College Diploma (Accounting, Administration, Business, Secretarial). Graduates would occupy Lawyer, Patent Agent, Trade-Mark Agent, Legal Clerk, Data Processor, Accounting Clerk, Secretary, Assistant, and Technical Support positions. Team player, and enthusiasm are both listed as desirable non-academic qualifications. The most suitable method for initial contact by those seeking employment is to mail a resume with a covering letter to the Human Resources Coordinator. *Contacts:* Sharon Mitchell, Chief Operating Officer or Holly Glenn, Human Resources Coordinator.

GRANT THORNTON
200 Bay Street, Box 55
10th Floor, North Tower, Royal Bank Plaza
Toronto, ON M5J 2P9

Tel. 416-366-0100
Fax 416-360-4944

Grant Thornton is one of Canada's major chartered accounting firms providing professional accounting, taxation, business advisory and consulting services to growing entrepreneurial enterprises. The company maintains 50 offices across the country, with international affiliates in over 75 countries. There are approximately 2,300 employees across Canada and a total of 17,000 worldwide. Graduates most likely to be hired come from the following academic areas: Bachelor of Commerce/Business Administration (Accounting), Chartered Accountant, and Master of Business Administration (Accounting). Graduates would be hired to occupy the position of Staff Accountant. Good interpersonal and problem solving skills, a high level of motivation, and a professional bearing and attitude are all listed as desirable non-academic qualifications. Company benefits are rated above average. The potential for advancement is listed as excellent. The average annual starting salary varies with location across Canada. The most suitable method for initial contact is to mail a resume, covering letter, and a copy of your academic transcript. Grant Thornton does hire a small number of summer students. *Contact:* John Gunn, FCA National Human Resources Partner.

GREAT ATLANTIC & PACIFIC CO. OF CANADA LTD., THE
P.O. Box 68, Station A
Toronto, ON M5W 1A6

Tel. 416-239-7171
Fax 416-234-6583

The Great Atlantic & Pacific Co. of Canada Ltd. is a food/grocery retailer operating approximately 260 stores, warehouses and bakery facilities across Canada. There are approximately 500 employees at the head office location. Graduates most likely to be hired come from the following academic areas: Bachelor of Arts (General, Criminology, Economics, Psychology), Bachelor of Science (Actuarial, Chemistry, Mathematics), Bachelor of Engineering (General), Chartered Accountant (Finance), Certified Management Accountant (Finance), Certified General Accountant (Finance), Master of Business Administration (Marketing), Community College Diploma (Accounting, Administration, Advertising, Business, Marketing/Sales, Secretarial, Human Resources, Security, Architecture/Drafting, Computer Science), and High School Diploma. Graduates are hired to occupy Financial Analyst, Accounting Clerk, Benefits Clerk, Computer Operator, Graphic/Layout Artist, and Security positions. In addition to setting goals, applicants should possess related work experience. Company benefits and the potential for advancement are both rated as excellent. The average annual starting salary falls within the $20,000 to $30,000 range, ultimately depending upon the type of position being considered. The most suitable methods for initial contact by graduates seeking employment are to mail or fax a resume with a covering letter. Summer students are hired, beginning in March and April. *Contacts:* Louisa Furtado, Personnel Manager or Mary Lajmanovski, Personnel Assistant.

GREAT PACIFIC COMPANY LTD.
1125 Howe Street
Vancouver, BC V6Z 2K8

Tel. 604-669-1143
Fax 604-669-0310

Great Pacific Company Ltd. is a brokerage firm specializing in mutual funds and tax shelter sales. The company employs 100 people at this location and a total of 210 people in Canada. Graduates most likely to be hired come from the following academic areas: Bachelor of Commerce/Business Administration (Accounting, Information Systems, Marketing), Certified Management Accountant, Certified General Accountant, Master of Business Administration (Marketing), and Community College Diploma (Accounting, Administration, Financial Planning, Insurance, Marketing/Sales, Secretarial). Graduates would occupy Sales and Sales Assistant positions, and Clerical positions in Accounting, Administration, and Data Entry. Team player and good communication skills are both listed as desirable non-academic qualifications. Company benefits are rated as industry standard. The potential for advancement is listed as average. The average annual starting salary for administrative positions ranges from $20,000 to $35,000, and is commission based for some sales positions. The most suitable method for initial contact by those seeking employment is to mail a resume with a covering letter. Great Pacific Company Ltd. does hire summer students. *Contacts:* Sandra Richard, Administration or Michael Peacock, Sales.

THE
Great-West Life
ASSURANCE G___ COMPANY

GREAT-WEST LIFE ASSURANCE COMPANY, THE
100 Osborne Street North
Winnipeg, MB R3C 3A5

Tel. 204-946-7156
Fax 204-946-4116
Website .... www.gwl.ca

The Great-West Life Assurance Company is an international corporation based in Winnipeg. Together with its subsidiary, London Life, the Company employs 5,000 individuals serving the financial needs of more than 8 million people through the network of Great-West and London Life field offices across Canada. The company offers individuals, businesses and organizations a growing range of life and disability insurance, and retirement savings, investment, and employee benefits plans. Great-West has also joined the Information Systems divisions of Great-West, London Life and its sister company, Investors Group, to provide I.S. support to all three companies. This move has made the Company's I.S. organization one of the largest in Canada. Graduates most likely to be hired come from the following academic areas: Bachelor of Arts (General, Economics, English, French), Bachelor of Science (General, Actuarial, Computer Science, Mathematics, Nursing, Occupational Therapy), Bachelor of Engineering (Computer Systems), Bachelor of Laws, Bachelor of Commerce/Business Administration (Accounting, Finance, Information Systems, Marketing), Chartered Accountant, Certified Management Accountant, Certified General Accountant, Master of Business Administration (Accounting, Finance, Information Systems), Master of Science (Actuarial), Community College Diploma (Accounting, Administration, Advertising, Business, Communications, Financial Planning, Insurance, Marketing, Purchasing/Logistics, Real Estate, Secretarial, Graphic Arts, Legal Assistant, Computer Science, HVAC, Nursing RN), and High School Diploma. Graduates would occupy Administrative, Clerical, Technical, and Management positions. Leadership abilities, bilingualism, and strong communication skills are all listed as desirable non-academic qualifications. Company benefits and the potential for advancement are both rated as excellent. The most suitable method for initial contact by those seeking employment is to mail a resume with a covering letter. The Great-West Life Assurance Company does hire students for summer and co-op work terms. Contact: Val Johnston, Manager, Human Resources.

GREATER EDMONTON FOUNDATION
10050 - 112 Street, Suite 810,
Edmonton, AB T5K 2J1

Tel. 403-482-6561
Fax 403-488-3561

The Greater Edmonton Foundation supplies subsidized housing for functionally independent senior citizens. There are 30 employees at this location, and a total of 340 employees in Edmonton. Graduates most likely to be hired come from the following academic areas: Bachelor of Arts (Recreation Studies, Sociology), Bachelor of Science (Computer Science), Bachelor of Education (Adult, Physical and Health), Bachelor of Commerce/Business Administration (Accounting, Human Resources, Public Administration), Certified Management Accountant, Master of Business Administration (Human Resources, Public Administration), Community College Diploma (Accounting, Administration, Business, Human Resources, Marketing/Sales, Cooking, Hospitality), and High School Diploma. Graduates would occupy Activity Coordinator, Accountant, Marketing Coordinator, Director, Human Resource Administrator, Assistant Manager, and Manager positions. Previous work experience, positive attitude, initiative, complete thought process, and confidence are all listed as desirable non-academic qualifications. The most suitable methods for initial contact by those seeking employment are to mail a resume with a covering letter, via telephone, or walk-in applications. The Greater Edmonton Foundation does hire summer students. Contact: Francine Leidl, Human Resources Administrator, Human Resources Department.

GREATER VICTORIA HOSPITAL SOCIETY
2101 Richmond Avenue
Victoria, BC V8R 4R7

Tel. 250-370-8523
Fax 250-370-8570

The Greater Victoria Hospital Society employs approximately 6,000 people in the provision of health care and health related services. Graduates most likely to be hired come from the following academic areas: Bachelor of Arts (Criminology, Recreation Studies, Social Work), Bachelor of Science (Biology, Chemistry, Microbiology, Nursing, Nutritional Sciences, Occupational Therapy, Pharmacy, Physical Therapy, Psychology, Speech Pathology), Chartered Accountant, Certified Management Accountant, Certified General Accountant, Master of Business Administration (Accounting, Finance, Human Resources, Information Systems, Public Administration), and Community College Diploma (Human Resources, Recreation Studies, Laboratory Technician, Nuclear Medicine Technician, Radiology Technician, Respiratory Therapy, Ultra-Sound Technician). Previous work experience (1 to 2 years) is listed as a definite asset. The most suitable method for initial contact by those seeking employment is to mail a resume with a covering letter. Contacts: Donna Scott, Manager, Employment Services, Human Resources or Marlane Worthington, Employment Services Representative, Human Resources.

GROUP 4 CPS LIMITED
2 Lansing Square, Suite 204
Toronto, ON M2J 4P8

Tel. 416-490-8329

Group 4 CPS Limited employs more than 500 people in the provision of protection and security services for various needs. Although post-secondary education is not required for employment consideration, Group 4 CPS Limited has historically employed students at various stages of their educational programs as Security Officers. Company benefits are rated as industry standard. The potential for advancement is listed as being good. The average annual starting salary falls in the $15,000 plus range. The most suitable methods for initial contact by those seeking employment are via telephone, or by applying in person. Group 4 CPS Limited does hire summer students on a regular basis. *Contact:* Personnel Manager.

GROUPE CONSEIL TS
325, de L'Espinay
Quebec, QC G1L 2J2

Tel.	418-647-1402
Fax	418-648-9288
Email	gctsqc@total.net
Website	www.groupets.com

Groupe Conseil TS is a subsidiary of Groupe TS, an association of eight companies working in fields of engineering, personnel training, and environment. The services offered by Groupe Conseil TS cover all aspects of the implementation of environmental characterization studies, of the development and implementation of decontamination and restoration programs, and the application of specific environmental techniques. Groupe Conseil TS employs 25 people at this location, and a total of 60 employees across Canada. Graduates most likely to be hired come from the following academic areas: Bachelor of Science (Geology), Bachelor of Engineering (Environmental/Resources, Geological, Industrial Chemistry, Pollution Treatment, Water Resources). Graduates would occupy Field Technician and Project Engineer positions. Company benefits are rated above average. The potential for advancement is listed as being good. The average annual starting salary for Technician positions falls within the $15,000 to $20,000 range. For Engineer positions, the average annual starting salary falls within the $30,000 to $35,000 range. The most suitable method for initial contact by those seeking employment is to mail a resume with a covering letter. Groupe Conseil TS does hire summer students. *Contacts:* Michel Drolet, Director or Richard Tardif, Assistant.

GROUPE HBA EXPERTS CONSEILS
150, Place Marchand
Drummondville, QC J2C 4N1

Tel.	819-478-8191
Fax	819-478-2994
Email	hbadrv@hba.qc.ca

Groupe HBA Experts Conseils is a engineering consulting company. Consulting activities include agriculture, environment, construction, urban infrastructure, transportation, geomatics, energy, telecommunications, and industry. There are 220 employees at this location, and a total of 250 employees worldwide. Graduates most likely to be hired come from the following academic areas: Bachelor of Science (Agriculture, Environmental, Forestry, Geography), and Bachelor of Engineering (Pollution Treatment, Electrical, Automation/Robotics, Biomedical Electronics, Computer Systems, Instrumentation, Microelectronics, Power, Telecommunications, Mechanical, Industrial Design, Industrial Production). Graduates would occupy Engineering positions. Applicants should be business minded. Company benefits are rated as industry standard. The potential for advancement is listed as average. The most suitable method for initial contact by those seeking employment is to mail a resume with a covering letter. Groupe HBA Experts Conseils does hire summer students, recruiting locally. *Contact:* Michel N. Houle, Vice President, Engineering.

GUARDIAN INSURANCE COMPANY OF CANADA
181 University Avenue
Toronto, ON M5H 3M7

Tel.	416-941-5201
Fax	416-941-5198

Guardian Insurance Company of Canada is a general insurance company, providing property and casualty insurance. Guardian operates as a decentralized company with offices across Canada, and branches in each region (East, Quebec, Central, West) serving the immediate community. Guardian's parent company is located in the United Kingdom. There are 100 employees at this location, and a total of 900 employees in Canada. Graduates most likely to be hired come from the following academic areas: Bachelor of Arts (Economics, Political Science), Bachelor of Science (Actuarial, Computer Science), Bachelor of Engineering (Computer Systems, Telecommunications), Bachelor of Commerce/Business Administration (Accounting, Finance, Human Resources, Information Systems), Chartered Accountant (Accounting, Audit), Certified Management Accountant, Certified General Accountant, Master of Business Administration (Accounting, Finance), and Community College Diploma (Accounting, Administration, Business, Human Resources, Insurance, Secretarial). Graduates would occupy Insurance Trainee, Programmer Trainee, Administrative Assistant/Clerk, and Accounting Clerk positions. Team player, ambitious, goal oriented, volunteer work, outside interests, and previous work experience are all listed as desirable non-academic qualifications. Company benefits are rated above average. The most suitable method for initial contact by those seeking employment is to mail a resume with a covering letter. Guardian Insurance Company of Canada does hire summer students. *Contact:* Human Resources Department.

GUSDORF CANADA LTD.
8620 Delmeade Road, T.M.R.
Montreal, QC H4T 1L6

Tel.	514-731-2242

Fax 514-731-9856
Website .... www.gusdorf.com

Gusdorf Canada Ltd. is a furniture manufacturer employing approximately 150 people. Graduates most likely to be hired come from the following academic areas: Bachelor of Engineering (Mechanical, Industrial Design), Bachelor of Commerce/Business Administration (Human Resources, Information Systems, Marketing), and Community College Diploma (Accounting, Business, Human Resources, Information Systems, Marketing/Sales, Architectural Technician, CAD/CAM Autocad). The most suitable methods for initial contact by those seeking employment are to mail or fax a resume with cover letter. *Contacts:* Nancy Leib, President; Shawn Leib, Vice President or Kathy Strasser, Human Resources Manager.

GUTHRIE PHILLIPS GROUP INC.
1200 West 73rd Avenue
Suite 340 Airport Square
Vancouver, BC V6P 6G5

Tel. 604-263-9347
Fax 604-261-2336
Email .... gpg@gpg.bc.ca
Website .... www.gpg.bc.ca

The Guthrie Phillips Group Inc. (GPG) is a privately owned company, incorporated in February 1990. GPG is a firm of computer systems specialists providing customized applications to extend and enhance business systems. GPG provides the following services: Information Systems Consulting (Strategic Plans, System Selection, etc.), Custom Systems Development, Project Management, Computer Application Systems and Support, General Computer Systems Services, and Documentation Services (Reports, Procedures, On-Line Help, Websites). GPG provides systems in a wide range of industries, specializing in areas where business systems typically do not support or adequately address. As one example, GPG has provided specialty banking systems for many large Banks, Trust Companies, and Credit Unions. GPG solutions include: reconciliation, chequing and EFT, mortgage-backed securities, collections, utility bill payments, suspense, foreign exchange, and fraud detection. The company employs a total of 15 people. Graduates most likely to be hired come from the following academic areas: Bachelor of Science (Computer Science, Mathematics, Physics), Bachelor of Commerce/Administration (General, Accounting, Finance, Information Systems, Marketing), Master of Business Administration (Finance), and Community College Diploma (Advertising, Business, Information Systems, Marketing/Sales, Computer Science). Graduates would occupy Programmer, Systems Analyst, Business Analyst, Documentor, Quality Assurance, and Marketing positions. Previous work experience in banking and financial services, and experience in visual/object oriented programming are listed as desirable non-academic qualifications. Company benefits are rated as industry standard. The potential for advancement is listed as excellent. The average annual starting salary falls within the $40,000 to $45,000 range. The most suitable methods for initial contact by those seeking employment are to mail, fax or e-mail a resume with a covering letter. The Guthrie Phillips Group Inc. does hire co-op work term students. *Contacts:* David Phillips, President or Human Resources.

HAEFELY TRENCH
71 Maybrook Drive
Toronto, ON M1V 4B6

Tel. 416-298-8108
Fax 416-298-6290

Haefely Trench designs, tests and manufactures high voltage electrical equipment. The company employs approximately 315 people at this location, and a total of 450 people in Canada. Graduates most likely to be hired come from the following academic areas: Bachelor of Arts (Economics, Geography, History, Languages, Music, Political Science), Bachelor of Science (Chemistry, Computer Science, Mathematics, Physics), Bachelor of Engineering (Industrial Chemistry, Materials Science, Electrical, Power), Bachelor of Commerce/Business Administration (General, Accounting, Finance, Human Resources, Information Systems, Marketing), Certified Management Accountant, Certified General Accountant, Master of Business Administration (General, Human Resources, Marketing), Master of Arts (Industrial Relations), Master or Engineering, Doctorate (Engineering), Community College Diploma (Accounting, Administration, Business, Human Resources, Marketing/Sales, Purchasing/Logistics, Secretarial, CAD/CAM/Autocad, Electronics Technician, Engineering Technician, Welding), and High School Diploma. Graduates would occupy Finance, Human Resources, Marketing, Sales, Engineering, Research and Development, Design, CAD Drafting, Industrial Engineering, High Voltage Testing, Quality Assurance, and Production positions. A willingness to learn throughout career, good oral and written communication skills, team player, positive attitude, previous work experience (depending upon position), and an ability to get along with co-workers and supervisors are all listed as desirable non-academic qualifications. Company benefits are rated above average. The potential for advancement is listed as being good. The average annual, entry level salary for non-managerial positions falls within the $25,000 to $35,000 range. The most suitable method for initial contact by those seeking employment is to mail a resume with a covering letter. Haefely Trench occasionally hires summer students, this varies from year to year. *Contact:* Katherine Jordan, Human Resources Manager.

HALIFAX INSURANCE
75 Eglinton Avenue East
Toronto, ON M4P 3A4

Tel. 416-440-1000
Fax 416-440-0191
Website .... www.halifaxinsurance.com

Halifax Insurance provides personal and commercial insurance products through the independent broker system. There are 323 employees at this location, and a total of 823 employees across Canada. Graduates most likely to be hired come from the following academic areas: Bachelor of Arts (General, Criminology, Economics), Bachelor of Science (General, Actuarial, Computer Science), Bachelor of Engineering (Computer Systems), Bachelor of Education (General, Adult), Bachelor of Commerce/Business Administration (Accounting, Finance, Human Resources, Information Systems, Marketing), Chartered Accountant, Certified General Accountant, Master of Business Administration (Accounting, Finance, Human Resources, Information Systems, Marketing), and Community College Diploma (Accounting, Advertising, Business, Communications, Human Resources, Insurance, Marketing/Sales, Secretarial, Computer Science). Graduates would occupy Underwriting, Claims, and Human Resources (Compensation and Training) positions. Relationship building skills, teamwork, cooperation, team leadership skills, innovation, initiative, a concern for order, and customer service skills are all listed as desirable non-academic qualifications. Company benefits are rated above average. The potential for advancement is listed as being good. The average annual starting salary falls within the $20,000 to $25,000 range. The most suitable methods for initial contact by those seeking employment are to mail or fax a resume with a covering letter. Halifax Insurance does hire summer students. *Contact:* Human Resources.

HALIFAX SHIPYARD LIMITED
P.O. Box 9110
Halifax, NS B3K 5M7

Tel. 902-423-9271
Fax 902-494-5554

Halifax Shipyard Limited employs approximately 750 people in new ship construction and ship repair. Graduates most likely to be hired come from the following academic areas: Bachelor of Engineering (Civil, Electrical, Computer Systems, Mechanical, Industrial Design, Industrial Production, Marine, Welding), Bachelor of Commerce/Business Administration (General, Accounting, Finance, Human Resources, Information Systems), Master of Business Administration (Accounting, Finance, Human Resources, Information Systems), Master of Engineering, and Community College Diploma (Accounting, Administration, Financial Planning, Human Resources, Purchasing/Logistics, Secretarial, Mechanic, Drafting, CAD/CAM/Autocad, Computer Science, Electronics Technician, Engineering Technician, HVAC Systems, Marine Engineering, Welding). An ability to work independently and with little supervision, previous work experience relating to position, team player, and a willingness to take on and learn new ideas and concepts are all listed as desirable non-academic qualifications. Company benefits are rated as industry standard. The potential for advancement is listed as average. The most suitable method for initial contact by those seeking

employment is to mail a resume with a covering letter. Halifax Shipyard Limited does hire summer students. *Contacts:* David Thompson, Manager of Human Resources or Rennée Woodworth, Labour Control Administrator.

HAMILTON CIVIC HOSPITALS
237 Barton Street East
Hamilton, ON L8L 2X2

Tel. 905-527-0271
Fax 905-546-0412

Hamilton Civic Hospitals employ 4,500 full and part time staff in the provision of health care and related services. Graduates most likely to be hired come from the following academic areas: Bachelor of Arts (General), Bachelor of Science (Chemistry, Computer Science, Microbiology, Nursing, Nutritional Sciences, Occupational Therapy, Pharmacy, Physical Therapy), Bachelor of Engineering (Biomedical Electronics, Computer Systems), Bachelor of Commerce/Business Administration (Accounting, Finance, Human Resources, Information Systems), Chartered Accountant, Certified Management Accountant, Certified General Accountant, Master of Business Administration (Accounting, Human Resources), Master of Science (Speech Pathology), Master of Health Sciences, and Community College Diploma (Accounting, Administration, Business, Human Resources, Purchasing/Logistics, Photography, Social Work, Computer Science, Electronics Technician, Engineering Technician, HVAC Systems, Dental Assistant, Dietician, Laboratory Technician, Nuclear Medicine Technician, Nursing RN/RNA, Radiology Technician, Respiratory Therapy, Ultra-Sound Technician). Possessing related work experience is listed as a desirable non-academic qualification. Company benefits are rated as excellent. The potential for advancement is rated as being good. The most suitable methods for initial contact by those seeking employment are to mail a resume with a covering letter, or in response to advertised positions. *Contact:* Shelley DaCosta, Compensation & Benefits Specialist.

HAMILTON-WENTWORTH CHILDREN'S AID SOCIETY
143 Wentworth Street South
P.O. Box 1170, Depot 1
Hamilton, ON L8N 4B9

Tel. 905-522-1121
Fax 905-572-9733
Email .... bsnider@hamiltoncas.com

Hamilton-Wentworth Children's Aid Society provides protection of children, family education, placement of children, visitation, and adoption services. The Society employs 150 people. Graduates most likely to be hired come from the following academic areas: Master of Arts (Social Work) and Community College Diploma (Social Work/DSW). Graduates would occupy Frontline Social Worker positions. Good assessment, counselling, communication and investigative skills are all listed as desirable non-academic qualifications. Company benefits are rated as excellent. The potential for advancement is listed as being good. The average annual starting salary falls within the $30,000 to $35,000 range. The most suitable methods for initial contact by those seeking employment are to mail or fax a resume with a covering letter. Hamilton-Wentworth Children's Aid Society does hire summer students. *Contact:* Brenda Snider, Director of Human Resources.

IMPROVING YOUR ODDS AGAINST CANADA'S #1 KILLER.

HEART AND STROKE FOUNDATION OF ONTARIO

477 Mount Pleasant Road, 4th Floor
Toronto, ON M4S 2L9

Tel. 416-489-7100
Fax 416-482-0948

Heart and Stroke Foundation of Ontario is a fund raising organization whose mandate is to reduce disability/death from heart disease and stroke. There are approximately 100 employees at this location. Graduates most likely to be hired come from the following academic areas: Bachelor of Arts (General, Recreation Studies), Bachelor of Science (General, Nutritional Sciences, Wellness), Bachelor of Education (General, Physical and Health), Bachelor of Commerce/Business Administration (Accounting, Finance, Human Resources, Information Systems, Marketing), Chartered Accountant, Certified Management Accountant, Certified General Accountant, Master of Business Administration (General, Marketing) Master of Science (Epidemiology), and Community College Diploma (Accounting, Administration, Advertising, Business, Human Resources, Secretarial, Recreation Studies, Dietician/Nutrition). Graduates would occupy Entry Level Clerk, Secretary/Assistant, and Coordinator positions. Volunteer exposure, team player, positive attitude, self-starter, innovative, self-directed, planning and organization skills, and good interpersonal and leadership skills are all listed as desirable non-academic qualifications. Company benefits are rated as excellent. The potential for advancement is listed as average. The average starting salaries are listed as follows: Clerk - $20,000 to $22,000, Secretary/Assistant - $22,000 to $26,000, Coordinator - $28,000 to $33,000. The most suitable methods for initial contact by those seeking employment are to mail or fax a resume with a covering letter, or via telephone. The Heart and Stroke Foundation does hire summer students, depending upon HRDC grants. *Contact:* Veronica Utton, Manager, Human Resources.

HEBDO MAG INC.

130, rue de Liege
Montreal, QC H2P 1J1

Tel. .... 514-384-7902 x 416
Fax 514-384-2056
Email .... johanneg@hebdomag.com

Hebdo Mag Inc. is a periodical publisher employing 160 people at this location, a total of 700 people in Canada, and a total of 3,000 people worldwide. Graduates most likely to be hired come from the following academic areas: Bachelor of Arts (Graphic Arts), Bachelor of Science (Computer Science), Bachelor of Commerce/Business Administration (General, Accounting, Finance, Human Resources, Information Systems, Marketing), Chartered Accountant, Certified Management Accountant, Certified General Accountant, Master of Business Administration (General, Accounting, Finance, Human Resources, Information Systems, Marketing), and Community College Diploma (Accounting, Administration, Business, Human Resources, Marketing/Sales, Purchasing/Logistics, Secretarial). Graduates would occupy Director, Manager, Clerk, Supervisor and Sales Representative positions. Company benefits are rated above average. The potential for advancement is listed as being good. The average annual starting salary falls within the $20,000 to $25,000 range. The most suitable method for initial contact by those seeking employment is to mail a resume with a covering letter. *Contact:* Johanne Gagnon, Human Resources Director - North America.

HERITAGE COLLEGE

325 Cité des Jeunes
Hull, QC J8Y 6T3

Tel. 819-778-2270
Fax 819-778-7364
Email .... mcharlebois@cegep-heritage.qc.ca
Website .... www.cegep-heritage.qc.ca

Heritage College is an English language, post-secondary institution employing approximately 150 people. As an educational institution, graduates from almost all academic disciplines are hired for positions as Professors, Managers, Professionals, Technicians, and for Clerical and Administrative positions. Bilingualism, team player, initiative, and previous work experience are all listed as desirable nonacademic qualifications. Company benefits are rated as excellent. The potential for advancement is listed as being good. The average annual starting salary falls within the $25,000 to $30,000 range. The most suitable methods for initial contact by those seeking employment are to mail or fax a resume with a covering letter. *Contact:* Michele Charlebois, Human Resouces.

HERMES ELECTRONICS INC.

40 Atlantic Street
Dartmouth, NS B2Y 4N2

Tel. 902-466-7491
Fax 902-463-6098

Hermes Electronics Inc. is an internationally recognized manufacturing firm active in industrial and defence electronics markets. Hermes' diversified products through partnering, include multi-resonant power supplies and mobile SATCOM transmitters. Other products include transmitters for Argos satellites, ice beacons, remote weather stations and HF receiver loop antennas. The Defence Division, Hermes Electronics, is a world leader in ASW Sonobuoy technology, with a history of success in acoustic monitoring within challenging ocean environments. The company employs approximately 280 people. Graduates most likely to be hired come from the following academic areas: Bachelor of Science (Occupational Therapy), Bachelor of Engineering (Electrical, Mechanical, Industrial Design, Industrial Production), Bachelor of Commerce/Business Administration (Accounting, Finance, Human Resources, Information Systems, Marketing), Chartered Accountant, Certified Management Accountant, Certified General Accountant, Master of Business Administration (Accounting, Finance, Human Resources, Information Systems, Marketing), Master of Engineering (Electrical, Mechanical), Doctorate (Engineering, Physics), and Community College Diploma (Accounting, Administration, Secretarial, Computer Science, Electronics, Engineering Technician, Quality Assurance, Tool & Die, Machinist). Graduates would occupy R&D Engineer, Design Engineer, Industrial Engineer, Quality Engineer, Technical Sales Representative, Customer Service Representative, Marketing Assistant, Purchasing Agent, Contracts Manager, Program Manager, Product Development Manager, Accountant, Electrician, Industrial Mechanic, Carpenter, Machinist, and Assembler positions. Results driven, value added doers, dynamic, team players, and problem solving skills are listed as desirable non-academic qualifications. Company benefits are rated above average. The potential for advancement is listed as being good. The average salary for new graduates falls within the $30,000 to $40,000 range. The most suitable method for initial contact by those seeking employment is to mail a resume and covering letter. Hermes does hire summer students. *Contacts:* Donna Somerville, Director, Human Resources or Glenda Hill, Human Resources Generalist.

HERSHEY CANADA INC.
2350 Matheson Boulevard East
Mississauga, ON L4W 5E9

Tel. 905-602-9200
Fax 905-602-8766

Hershey Canada Inc. is involved in the manufacture and marketing of grocery and confectionery products. There are approximately 130 employees at this location. Graduates most likely to be hired come from the following academic areas: Bachelor of Arts (Social Sciences), Bachelor of Commerce/Business Administration (Marketing), Chartered Accountant, Certified Management Accountant, Master of Business Administration (Finance, Marketing), and Community College Diploma (Administration, Secretarial, Human Resources, Information Services).

Graduates would occupy Marketing Coordinator, Sales Representative, Accountant, Accounting Clerk, Promotional Cost Analyst, Assistant Brands Manager, and Associate Brands Manager positions. Reliable, good problem solving skills, goal oriented, determined, and strong analytical skills are all listed as desirable non-academic qualifications. Company benefits are rated above average. The potential for advancement is listed as being good. The average annual starting salary for most of the positions listed falls within the $30,000 to $35,000 range. The most suitable method for initial contact by those seeking employment is to mail a resume with a covering letter. Hershey Canada Inc. does hire summer students as the need arises. *Contact:* Human Resources Department.

HEWITT ASSOCIATES
25 Sheppard Avenue West
Toronto, ON M2N 6T1

Tel. 416-225-5001
Fax 416-225-5121

Hewitt Associates is an international firm of consultants and actuaries specializing in the design, financing, administration and communication of benefits, compensation and human resources programs and strategies. The company employs more than 100 people at this location and more than 5,000 people worldwide. Graduates most likely to be hired come from the following academic areas: Bachelor of Science (Actuarial, Computer Science, Mathematics), Bachelor of Laws, Bachelor of Commerce/Business Administration (Finance, Information Systems), Master of Business Administration (General, Finance), and Community College Diploma (Human Resources, Secretarial). Within various practices there are available, from time to time, entry level administrative consultant positions for new graduates. New graduates should demonstrate strong quantitative, analytical and systems skills, as well as the ability to learn the business. In addition, strong communication and interpersonal skills, a willingness to work hard, team player, good project management skills and prior work experience in a financial consulting environment are all listed as desirable non-academic qualifications. The most suitable method for initial contact by those seeking employment is to mail a resume with a covering letter. Hewitt Associates occasionally hires summer students. *Contacts:* Anne Burrows, Human Resources or Laurie Arevalo, Human Resources.

HILL AND KNOWLTON CANADA/DECIMA RESEARCH
160 Bloor Street East, Suite 700
Toronto, ON M4W 3P7

Tel. 416-413-1218
Fax 416-413-1550
Email .... rclark@hillandknowlton.ca
Website .... www.hillandknowlton.com

Hill and Knowlton Canada/Decima Research is involved in public relations, public affairs consulting, and public opinion research and consulting activities. The company employs approximately 85 people at this location and a total of 140 people in Canada. Graduates most likely to be hired come from the following academic areas: Bachelor of Arts (English, Journalism, Political Science), Bachelor of Science (Psychology), Bachelor of Commerce/Business Administration (Marketing), Master of Business Administration (Marketing), Master of Arts (Communications/Public Relations, Political Science, Social Sciences, Sociology), Master of Science (Consumer Behaviour), and Community College Diploma (Communications/Public Relations). Graduates would occupy Assistant Consultant, and Research Analyst positions. Initiative, team work, problem solving, organization, time management, and presentation skills are all listed as desirable non-academic qualifications. Company benefits and the potential for advancement are both rated as excellent. The average annual starting salary falls within the $25,000 to $30,000 range. The most suitable methods for initial contact by those seeking employment are to mail, fax or e-mail a resume with a covering letter, or by applying through the company's website at www.hillandknowlton.com. Hill and Knowlton Canada/Decima Research does hire summer and co-op work term students. *Contact:* Ruth Clark, Vice President, Human Resources.

HINCKS-DELCREST CENTRE, THE
440 Jarvis Street
Toronto, ON M4Y 2H6

Tel. 416-924-1164
Fax 416-924-8208

The Hincks-Dellcrest Centre is a children's mental health centre providing a wide range of prevention, early intervention and treatment services to children, youth and their families. The centre focuses on helping clients deal with situations that are causing emotional and behavioural problems. Programs include outpatient counselling, day treatment and residential treatment services. The centre employs more than 300 people. Graduates most likely to be hired come from the following academic areas: Master of Arts (Psychology, Child Development Social Work), Doctorate (Psychology), and Community College Diploma (Child and Youth Worker, Social Service Worker, Correctional Worker). Graduates are hired as Social Workers, Child and Youth Workers, and Prevention Workers. Previous work experience in a social service setting, and knowledge and experience in different modes of individual, group and family therapy are all listed as desirable non-academic qualifications. Company benefits are rated above average. The potential for advancement is listed as average. The average annual starting salary falls within the $25,000 to $30,000 range. The most suitable method for initial contact by those seeking employment is to mail a resume with a covering letter. The Hincks-Dellcrest Centre does hire summer and co-op work term students when government funding is available. *Contact:* Human Resources.

HOFFMANN-LA ROCHE LIMITED
2455 Meadowpine Boulevard
Mississauga, ON L5N 6L7

Tel. 905-542-5555
Fax 905-542-7130

Hoffmann-La Roche Limited is a health care company with the following operational divisions: Pharmaceutical, Fine Chemicals (Cambridge, Ontario), and Diagnostics (Laval, Quebec). There are 250 employees at this location and a total of 450 employees in Canada, including field staff. Graduates most likely to be hired come from the following academic areas: Bachelor of Arts (Economics), Bachelor of Science (Biology, Chemistry, Pharmacology, Computer Science), Bachelor of Commerce/Business Administration, Chartered Accountant, Certified Management Accountant, Certified General Accountant, and Master of Science (Biology, Chemistry, Pharmacology). Graduates would occupy Medical Sales, Clinical Research, Quality Control, Regulatory Affairs and Medical Information positions. Possessing related work experience is listed as a desirable non-academic qualification. Compensation and other forms of remuneration such as group health benefits are highly competitive within the pharmaceutical industry. The opportunities for career and professional development are very good. To inquire about employment opportunities, send a resume with a covering letter describing career objectives or goals to the Human Resources Department. Hoffmann-La Roche Limited also operates a summer student hiring program. (Other Locations: Hoffman-La Roche Limited - Fine Chemicals Division, P.O. Box 877, Cambridge, ON, N1R 5X9, Phone 519-622-2200, Fax 519-623-4849; Hoffman-La Roche Limited - Diagnostics Division, 201, boul. Armand-Frappier, Laval, PQ, H9V 4A2, Phone 514-686-7050, Fax 514-686-7697). *Contact:* Catherine Meyer, Director, Human Resources.

HOLDERBANK ENGINEERING CANADA LTD.
2310 Lakeshore Road West
Mississauga, ON L5J 1K2

Tel. 905-822-1693
Fax 905-822-1698
Email .... general@holderbank.ca
Website .... www.holderbank.ca

Holderbank Engineering Canada Ltd. offers a complete range of engineering services to cement industry producers throughout the Americas. This includes assisting manufacturers of cement, lime and related products in all aspects of the design, construction and operation of their plant facilities. As the Canadian-based engineering office of Holderbank Financière Glaris Ltd., Switzerland, the company is associated with more than 70 cement plants of the Holderbank Group. This international network of producers provides an unparalleled source of information and experience in all aspects of cement manufacture and plant operation, and helps make Holderbank a leader among cement-industry consultants. There are approximately 110 employees at this location, and over 4,500 Holderbank employees worldwide. Graduates most likely to be hired come from the following academic areas: Bachelor of Science (Chemistry), Bachelor of Engineering (Chemical, Electrical, Mechanical), Master of Engineering (Civil), and Community College Diploma (CAD/CAM/Autocad, Electronics Technician). Graduates are hired for Technician and Trainee positions. Applicants should be team players. Company benefits are rated as industry standard. The potential for advancement is listed as being good. The average annual starting salary falls within the $35,000 to $40,000 range. The most suitable methods for initial contact by those seeking employment are to mail or fax a resume with a covering letter (no phone calls please). Holderbank Engineering Canada Ltd. does hire summer and co-op work term students. *Contact:* Wayne Gallant, Vice President, Finance & Administration.

HOLIDAY INN, EXPRESS
50 Estate Drive
Toronto, ON M1H 2Z1

Tel. 416-439-9666
Fax 416-439-4295

The Holiday Inn, Express Hotel provides full service accommodation and banquet services. Operational activities also include administrative functions. The hotel employs more than 25 people. Graduates most likely to be hired come from the following academic areas: Bachelor of Commerce/Business Administration (Marketing), and Community College Diploma (Hospitality, Travel/Tourism, Marketing). Graduates would occupy Night Auditor, Banquet Porter, Room Attendant, and Front Desk Clerk positions. Initiative, good interpersonal skills, friendly, outgoing, and confidence are all listed as desirable non-academic qualifications. Company benefits are rated above average. The potential for advancement is listed as excellent. Employees are paid on a hourly wage scale. The most suitable method for initial contact by those seeking employment is to mail a resume with a covering letter. The Holiday Inn, Express Hotel does employ summer students. *Contact:* General Manager.

HONDA CANADA INC.
715 Milner Avenue
Toronto, ON M1B 2K8

Tel. 416-284-8110

Honda Canada Inc. is involved in the sales, marketing, and distribution of auto, motorcycle, and power (eg. lawn mowers) products. There are 300 associates at this location, a total of 2,500 associates in Canada, and 80,000 Honda employees worldwide. Graduates most likely to be hired come from the following academic areas: Bachelor of Arts (Economics), Bachelor of Science (Computer Science, Mathematics), Bachelor of Engineering (Automation/Robotics, Industrial Design, Industrial Production), Bachelor of Commerce/Business Administration (Accounting, Finance, Human Resources, Information Systems, Marketing), Chartered Accountant,

Certified Management Accountant, Certified General Accountant, Master of Business Administration (Accounting, Finance, Information Systems, Marketing), and Community College Diploma (Accounting, Marketing/Sales, Auto Mechanic, Computer Science). Graduates would occupy Market Research Analyst, Product Planning, Field Sales Representative, Accounting Coordinator, Sales Operations Coordinator, Human Resources, and Employee Relations positions. Strong communication skills, industrious, team player, international focus, and an interest in the automotive industry are all listed as desirable non-academic qualifications. Company benefits are rated as excellent. The potential for advancement is listed as being good. The average annual starting salary falls within the $25,000 to $30,000 range. The most suitable method for initial contact by those seeking employment is to mail a resume with a covering letter. Summer students are hired for Honda's parts distribution centre, and manufacturing plant. *Contacts:* Mr. A. S. Thomas, Senior Manager, Administration or Mr. J. Descoteaux, Manager, Human Resources.

HONEYWELL LIMITED
740 Ellesmere Road
Toronto, ON M1P 2V9

Tel. 416-293-8111

Honeywell Limited employs more than 500 people at this location, in the manufacture and marketing of environmental controls. These include HVAC systems for commercial buildings, residential heat and air conditioning controls, and industrial process controls. Graduates most likely to be hired come from the following academic areas: Bachelor of Engineering (Mechanical, Electrical), Certified Management Accountant, and Master of Business Administration. Graduates would occupy Manufacturing Engineer, System Designer, Quality Control, Process and Sales positions. Company benefits are rated above average. The potential for advancement is listed as being good. The most suitable method for initial contact by those seeking employment is to mail a resume with a covering letter. Honeywell Limited occasionally hires summer students (summer job seekers should inquire before applying.). *Contact:* Human Resources.

HOSPITAL FOR SICK CHILDREN, THE
555 University Avenue
Toronto, ON M5G 1X8

Tel. 416-813-1500
Fax 416-813-5671

The Hospital For Sick Children is a major Canadian pediatric hospital employing approximately 4,500 people. Graduates most likely to be hired come from the following academic areas: Bachelor of Arts (Psychology), Bachelor of Science (Biology, Chemistry, Computer Science, Microbiology, Audiology, Dentistry, Nursing, Nutritional Sciences, Occupational Therapy, Pharmacy, Physical Therapy, Psychology, Speech Pathology), Bachelor of Education (Early

Childhood), Bachelor of Commerce/Business Administration (Accounting, Finance, Human Resources, Information Systems), Chartered Accountant, Certified Management Accountant, Certified General Accountant, Master of Business Administration (Accounting, Finance, Public Administration), Master of Science (General, Health Sciences), Medical Doctor, and Community College Diploma (Administration, Human Resources, Hospitality, Security, Computer Science, Nursing RN/RNA, Radiology Technician, Respiratory Therapy, Ultra-Sound Technician). Prior work experience is listed as a desirable non-academic qualification. The most suitable method for initial contact by those seeking employment is to mail a resume with a covering letter. The Hospital For Sick Children does hire summer students. *Contacts:* Anna Demasi, Human Resource Specialist or Keith Spiller, Human Resource Representative.

HOTEL PLAZA II
90 Bloor Street East
Toronto, ON M4W 1A7

Tel. 416-961-8000
Fax 416-961-9581

The Hotel Plaza II is a 256 room, "Four Diamond" hotel employing approximately 150 people. Graduates most likely to be hired come from the following academic areas: Bachelor of Arts (General), and Community College Diploma (Hospitality, Hotel Administration, Tourism, Culinary/Cooking). Graduates would occupy Waiter, Kitchen and Housekeeping staff positions, as well as front office Clerk positions. The ability to work shifts (including weekends), a strong command of the English language, good customer service and communication skills, and a strong interest in the hospitality and service industry are all listed as desirable non-academic qualifications. Company benefits are rated as industry standard. The potential for advancement is listed as average. The average annual starting salary falls within the $18,000 to $23,000 range. The most suitable methods for initial contact by those seeking employment are to mail a resume with a covering letter, or via telephone. The Hotel Plaza II does hire summer students depending upon the level of business. Summer students must also be available to work on weekends. *Contact:* Gail Loder, Human Resources Manager.

HOUSESITTERS CANADA
530 Queen Street East
Toronto, ON M5A 1V2

Tel. 416-947-1295
Fax 416-947-9869

Housesitters Canada provides house sitting, pet sitting, and general property management services. There are approximately 50 employees at this location and an additional 20 employees in Quebec. Graduates most likely to be hired come from the following academic areas: Bachelor of Arts (General), Bachelor of Engineering (Computer Systems), Bach-

elor of Commerce/Business Administration (General, Accounting, Finance), and Community College Diploma (Accounting, Administration, Advertising). Company benefits are rated as industry standard. The potential for advancement is listed as average. The average annual starting salary falls within the $30,000 to $35,000 range. The most suitable methods for initial contact by those seeking employment are to mail or fax a resume with a covering letter. Housesitters Canada does hire summer and co-op work term students. *Contact:* William H. Murphy.

HOWARD JOHNSON PLAZA - HOTEL TORONTO EAST
40 Progress Court
Toronto, ON M1G 3T5

Tel. 416-439-6200
Fax 416-439-5689

The Howard Johnson Plaza - Hotel Toronto East is a full service hotel with 186 guest rooms, one restaurant, one lobby lounge, and 16 meeting rooms. The hotel employs more than 75 people. Graduates most likely to be hired come from the following academic areas: Bachelor of Arts (French Language), Community College Diploma (Administration, Cooking, Hospitality, Travel/Tourism), and High School Diploma. Graduates would occupy Front Desk, Secretary, Night Auditor, Sales and Supervisory positions. Enthusiastic, team player, and an outgoing personality are listed as desirable non-academic qualifications. Company benefits and the potential for advancement are both rated as excellent. The average annual starting salary falls within the $15,000 to $20,000 range. The most suitable method for initial contact by those seeking employment is to mail a resume with a covering letter. The Howard Johnson Plaza - Hotel Toronto East does employ summer students. *Contact:* Eleanor Pope, Human Resources Manager.

HUANG & DANCZKAY LIMITED
370 Queen's Quay West, 3rd Floor
Toronto, ON M5V 3J3

Tel. 416-260-2333
Fax 416-260-2347

Huang & Danczkay Limited is an engineering, construction, and land development firm employing more than 10 people at this location. Graduates most likely to be hired come from the following areas: Bachelor of Engineering (Civil, Environmental), Bachelor of Architecture, Bachelor of Landscape Architecture, and Community College Diploma (Business, Marketing/Sales, Secretarial, Engineering, Industrial Design). Graduates are hired to occupy Clerk, Draughtsperson, Architect, and Accountant positions. Company benefits are rated above average. The potential for advancement is listed as being good. The most suitable method for initial contact by those seeking employment is to mail a resume with a covering letter. *Contact:* Controller.

HUDSON BAY MINING AND SMELTING CO., LIMITED

P.O. Box 1500
Flin Flon, MB R8A 1N9

Tel. 204-687-2050
Fax 204-687-3582

Hudson Bay Mining and Smelting Co., Limited employs approximately 2,140 people in mining and smelting activities. Graduates most likely to be hired come from the following academic areas: Bachelor of Science (Chemistry, Metallurgy), Bachelor of Engineering (Chemical, Industrial Chemistry, Metallurgy, Electrical, Instrumentation, Mechanical, Mining), Bachelor of Commerce/Business Administration (Accounting, Finance, Information Systems), Certified Management Accountant, Certified General Accountant, Master of Business Administration (Accounting, Finance, Information Systems), and Community College Diploma (CAD/CAM/ Autocad, Computer Science, Electronics Technician). Graduates would be hired to occupy Technician/ Technologist, Junior Engineer Engineer, Planner, Accountant, Programmer/Analyst, and Supervisor positions. Good communication skills, leadership abilities, team player, and industrial experience are all listed as desirable non-academic qualifications. Company benefits are rated above average. The potential for advancement is listed as being good. The average annual starting salary ranges between $30,000 and $45,000 and is dependent upon the vacancy being filled, as well as being commensurate with the education and experience of the applicant. The most suitable method for initial contact by those seeking employment is to mail a resume with a covering letter. Hudson Bay Mining and Smelting Co., Limited does hire summer and co-op work term students (check with your campus career centre). *Contact:* Personnel Department.

HUDSON GENERAL AVIATION SERVICES INC.

Pearson Airport, P.O. Box 31, Toronto AMF
Mississauga, ON L5P 1A2

Fax 905-676-4894

Hudson General Aviation Services Inc. is an air transportation ground handling company employing more than 500 people at Pearson Airport, and a total of 1,500 people in Canada. Graduates and non-graduates would occupy Aircraft Service Attendants, Check-In Agents, Equipment Maintenance Mechanics, and Cabin Service Attendants. Company benefits are rated above average. The potential for advancement is listed as average. The most suitable methods for initial contact by those seeking employment are to mail or fax a resume with a covering letter. *Contacts:* N. Maramieri, Manager, Ramp Services; Dianne McEwan, Manager, Administration or C. Scott, Manager, Customer Services.

HUMBER RIVER REGIONAL HOSPITAL

2111 Finch Avenue West
Downsview, ON M3N 1N1

Tel. 416-744-2500
Fax 416-747-3758

Humber River Regional Hospital is a newly merged acute care hospital serving the culturally diverse northwest metropolitan Toronto area. The hospital is comprised of the former hospitals, Humber Memorial, Northwestern, and York Finch General. The hospital employs a total of 2,200 people. Graduates most likely to be hired come from the following academic areas: Bachelor of Arts (General, English, Fine Arts, Journalism, Psychology, Recreation Studies, Sociology/Social Work), Bachelor of Science (General, Computer Science, Mathematics, Microbiology, Audiology, Nursing, Nutritional Sciences, Occupational Therapy, Pharmacy, Physio/Physical Therapy, Psychology, Speech Pathology), Bachelor of Engineering (General, Mechanical, Computer Systems, Environmental/Resources), Bachelor of Education (General, Adult), Master of Business Administration (General, Finance, Human Resources, Information Systems), Master of Science (Nursing), Community College Diploma (Accounting, Administration, Business, Communications/Public Relations, Facility Management, Financial Planning, Human Resources, Information Systems, Secretarial, Audio/Visual Technician, Graphic Arts, Recreation Studies, Security/ Enforcement, Social Work/DSW, Computer Science, Plumber, Health/Home Care Aide, Laboratory Technician, Nuclear Medicine Technician, Nursing RN/ RNA, Radiology, Respiratory Therapy, Ultra-Sound Technician), and High School Diploma. Graduates would occupy entry level positions relating to their academic backgrounds. Team work, collaborative, customer service skills, initiative, and a non-discriminatory attitude are all listed as desirable non-academic qualifications. The average annual starting salary falls within the $20,000 to $25,000 range. The most suitable method for initial contact by those seeking employment is to mail a resume with a covering letter. Humber River Regional Hospital does hire summer and co-op work term students. *Contact:* Recruitment Specialist, Human Resorces Planning (Phone Extension 2511).

HUMMINGBIRD COMMUNICATIONS LTD.

1 Sparks Avenue
Toronto, ON M2H 2W1

Tel. 416-496-2200
Fax 416-496-2207
Email .... frank.nemeth@hummingbird.com
Website .... www.hummingbird.com

Hummingbird Communications Ltd. is Canada's 4th largest software development company, and growing fast. Currently there are 330 employees at this location, 460 in Canada, and a total of 660 employees worldwide. Hummingbird has made its mark in Enterprise Network Connectivity with products like Exceed, NFS-Maestro, and HostExplorer. In addition Hummingbird is active in developing new products for the rapidly growing Data Warehousing market. The company is on the leading edge of the Network Connectivity and Business Intelligence software business. For further information, visit Hummingbird's website at www.hummingbird.com. Graduates most likely to be hired come from the following academic areas: Bachelor of Science (Computer Science, Mathematics), Bachelor of Engineering (Computer Science, Telecommunications), Master of Business Administration (Information Systems, Marketing), Community College Diploma (Communications/Public Relations, Information Systems, Marketing/Sales, Computer Science, Engineering Technician), and those with an MCSE accreditation. Graduates would occupy Technical Support Representative, Quality Assurance Analyst, Pretest Engineer, Programmer Analyst, and Junior Software Developer positions. Strong interpersonal and communication skills, entrepreneurial, relevant work experience, excellent problem solving skills, energetic and motivated are all listed as desirable non-academic qualifications. Hummingbird offers a very competitive benefits package, including tuition, health club dues, RRSP's, bonuses, options, etc. The potential for advancement is listed as being good. The most suitable methods for initial contact by those seeking employment are to mail, fax or e-mail a resume with a covering letter. Hummingbird Communications Ltd. does hire summer and co-op work term students. *Contact:* Frank Nemeth, Manager, Human Resources.

HUSKY

HUSKY INJECTION MOLDING SYSTEMS LTD.
560 Queen Street South
Bolton, ON L7E 5S5

Tel. 905-951-5000
Fax 905-951-5335
Website .... www.husky.on.ca

Husky Injection Molding Systems Ltd. is one of the leading suppliers of complete injection molding systems to the plastics industry. Bolton is Husky's Corporate Office, as well as one of its five manufacturing locations. This state-of-the-art facility comes complete with on-site fitness and wellness centres. Similar facilities are located in the United States and Europe. Graduates most likely to be hired come from the following academic areas: Bachelor of Science (Computer Science, Mathematics), Bachelor of Engineering (General, Electrical, Mechanical, Automation/Robotics, Computer Systems, Environmental/Resources, Industrial Design, Industrial Engineering, Industrial Production/Manufacturing, Instrumentation), and Community College Diploma (CAD/CAM/Autocad, Computer Science, Electronics Technician, Engineering Technician, Tool and Die, Machinist, Welding). Graduates are hired to occupy Machine Design, Mold Design, Robotic Design, Assembly Technician, and Test Technician positions in one of the following areas: Total Factory Solutions, Molds and Hot Runners, Injection Molding Machines, Information Services, and Components Manufacturing. Husky also has opportunities for professionals to work in Sales and Service and other corporate and support positions. Quality-focused, committed to excellence, enjoy working in a fast-paced and changing environment, ambitious, self-motivated, team player, able to take pride in the work accomplished, a genuine desire to contribute and learn, and a positive attitude are all listed as desirable non-academic qualifications. The most suitable method for initial contact by those seeking employment is to apply through the company's website at www.husky.on.ca. Husky Injection Molding Systems Ltd. does hire students for summer and co-op work terms. *Contacts:* Chris Cowan, Manager, Human Resources - Components or Paul Pierrozi, Manager, Human Resources - Machine Business.

HUSKY OIL LIMITED
Box 6525, Station D
Calgary, AB T2P 3G7

Tel. 403-298-6111
Fax 403-298-6799
Website .... www.husky-oil.com

Husky Oil Limited is a Canadian based, privately held integrated oil and gas company headquartered in Calgary, Alberta. The Company's operations include the exploration for and development of crude oil and natural gas, as well as the production, purchase, transportation, upgrading, refining and marketing of crude oil, natural gas, natural gas liquids, sulphur and petroleum coke, and the marketing of refined petroleum products, including gasoline, alternative fuels and asphalt. Husky ranks among Canada's top producers of crude oil, natural gas and sulphur. The company employs approximately 1,500 permanent employees located in Calgary, the Lloydminster and Prince George refineries, the Lloydminster Upgrader, and Production Districts and Marketing Offices throughout Western Canada and Ontario. Graduates most likely to be hired come from the following academic areas: Bachelor of Science (Computer Science, Geology), Bachelor of Engineering (Chemical, Civil, Electrical, Power, Mechanical, Resources/Environmental, Petroleum), Bachelor of Laws, Bachelor of Commerce/Business Administration (General, Accounting, Finance, Human Resources, Marketing), Chartered Accountant, Certified Management Accountant, Master of Business Administration, Master of Engineering, and Community College Diploma (Accounting, Administration, Communications). Good communication and interpersonal skills, flexibility, initiative, innovation, team work skills, and knowledge of Microsoft Office are all listed as desirable non-academic qualifications. The most suitable method for initial contact by those seeking employment is to mail a resume with a covering letter. Husky Oil Limited is a dynamic employer that values workplace diversity. *Contact:* Human Resources Department.

I.M.P. GROUP LIMITED
2651 Dutch Village Road, Suite 400
Halifax, NS B3L 4T1

Tel. 902-453-2400
Fax 902-453-6931
Email .... rob.burns@impgroup.com
Website .... www.impgroup.com

I.M.P. Group Limited is a diversified company involved in the Aerospace Industry (Components, Avionics, etc.), Precision Machining, Aviation (Corporate), Commercial Aviation (Air Atlantic), Industrial Marine, Hotel Properties (Holiday Inn Select, Aerostar Hotel - Moscow), and other Commercial Holdings (Retail/Wholesale). There are 2,600 employees in Canada, and a total of 3,000 employees worldwide. Graduates most likely to be hired come from the following academic areas: Bachelor of Engineering (Computer Systems, Instrumentation, Microelectronics, Mechanical, Aeronautical, Industrial Design, Industrial Production, Marine, Welding), Bachelor of Laws, Bachelor of Commerce/Business Administration (Accounting, Finance, Human Resources, Information Systems), Master of Business Administration (Accounting, Finance, Human Resources, Information Systems, Marketing), and Community College Diploma (Accounting, Facility Management, Human Resources, Marketing/Sales, Aircraft Maintenance, Architecture/Drafting, CAD/CAM/Autocad, Computer Science, Electronics Technician, Engineering Technician, Marine Engineering, Welding). Computer skills, work experience, corporate fit, and a multi-disciplined academic background are all listed as desirable attributes. Company benefits are rated as industry standard. The potential for advancement is listed as good. The average annual starting salary depends upon the position being considered. The most suitable method for initial contact by those seeking employment is to mail a resume with a covering letter. I.M.P. Group Limited rarely hires summer students. Contact: Rob Burns, Human Resources Administrator - Corporate.

IBM CANADA LTD.
3600 Steeles Avenue East
Markham, ON L3R 9Z7

Tel. 800-426-4968

IBM Canada Ltd. is the Canadian arm of IBM World Trade Corp. (New York). IBM Canada Ltd. is the largest Canadian company involved in the manufacture, design and marketing of computer hardware and software. There are over 5,000 employees at this location. Graduates most likely to be hired come from the following academic areas: Bachelor of Science (Computer Science), Bachelor of Engineering (Electrical), Bachelor of Laws, Chartered Accountant, and Master of Business Administration. Graduates would occupy entry-level Programmer, Systems Engineer and Marketing positions. Company benefits and the potential for advancement are both rated as excellent. The most suitable method for initial contact by those seeking employment is to mail a resume with a covering letter. IBM Canada Ltd. does hire summer students on a limited basis. Contact: Human Resource Department.

IBM - FOOTPRINT DEVELOPMENT
330 University Avenue, 4th Floor
Toronto, ON M5G 1R7

Tel. 416-340-1200
Fax 416-340-7772
Website .... www.footprint.com

The IBM - Footprint Development lab specializes in the creation of software solutions for visionary companies who want to increase the profitability and bottom-line efficiency of their customer interactions. Over the past decade, the team at Footprint have earned a reputation as successful innovators and market leaders in the creation and development of products that automate, streamline, and help manage the sales process. Footprint has pursued the belief that financial institutions benefit from employing fully-integrated systems, with the scalability to grow and flexibility to adapt. This vision has led to the creation of the Visual Banker enterprise solutions. Starting with the branch, the company develops solutions for the Teller and then the Call Centre, Internet, Mobile and Kiosk channels. From Software development and systems integration, to Footprint's engagement methodology, consulting and training, the Company continues to deliver a competitive advantage to its customers around the world. Visual Banker enterprise solutions are IBM strategic for the global financial services industry. Footprint has successfully set a new standard for enterprise-wide sales automation within the financial services industry, and is committed to developing software solutions that build and strengthen customer relationships. Graduates most likely to be hired come from the following academic areas: Bachelor of Science (Computer Science), and Bachelor of Engineering (Computer Systems). Company benefits and the potential for advancement are both rated as excellent. The most suitable method for initial contact by those seeking employment is to mail a resume with a covering letter. The IBM - Footprint Development lab does hire summer and co-op work term students. Contact: Human Resources.

ILCO UNICAN INC.
7301, boulevard Décarie
Montreal, QC H4P 2G7

Tel. 514-735-5411
Fax 514-735-5732
Email .... cv@ilcounican.com
Website .... www.ilcounican.com

ILCO UNICAN Inc. operates internationally and is a world leader in the design and manufacture of key blanks, key machines, mechanical pushbutton and electronic access controls. With locations worldwide, the company reaches original equipment manufacturers, locksmiths, businesses, hotels, and hardware stores in over fifty countries on all continents. ILCO

UNICAN maintains the Electronic Access Control Division and its head office in Montreal. There are 450 employees at this location, a total of 1,000 in Canada and 5,000 employees worldwide. Graduates most likely to be hired come from the following academic areas: Bachelor of Arts (Graphic Arts), Bachelor of Engineering (Electrical, Mechanical, Materials Science, Automation, Microelectronics, Telecommunications, Industrial Design/Production), Bachelor of Commerce/Business Administration (Accounting, Finance, Human Resources, Information Systems, Marketing), Chartered Accountant (Cost Accounting), Certified Management Accountant (Finance), Certified General Accountant (Finance), Master of Business Administration (Accounting, Finance, Human Resources, Information Systems, Marketing), Master of Engineering (Electrical, Electronics, Mechanical), and Community College Diploma (Accounting, Administration, Advertising, Business, Communications, Financial Planning, Human Resources, Marketing/Sales, Purchasing/Logistics, Secretarial, Security, CAD/CAM/Autocad, Computer Science, Electronics Technician, Engineering Technician). Graduates would occupy Mechanical Designer, Hardware Engineer, Programmer Analyst, Project Coordinator, Human Resources Coordinator, Assistant Divisional Controller, Administrative Assistant, Product Manager, Export Technician, Translator, and Graphic Artist positions. Bilingualism, flexibility, team player and good communication skills are all listed as desirable non-academic skills. Company benefits are rated above average. The potential for advancement is listed as being excellent. The average annual starting salary falls within the $30,000 to $35,000 range. The most suitable method for initial contact by those seeking employment is to mail a resume with a covering letter. ILCO UNICAN Inc. does hire summer and co-op work term students. *Contacts:* Lise Pilon, Executive Director, Human Resources or Gaétan Olivier, Human Resources Consultant.

IMPERIAL OIL LIMITED
111 St. Clair Avenue West
Toronto, ON M5W 1K3

Tel. 416-968-8312
Fax 416-968-8129

Imperial Oil Limited has been a leading member of Canada's petroleum industry for more than a century. In addition to being the country's largest producer of crude oil and a major producer of natural gas, Imperial Oil is also the largest refiner and marketer of petroleum products, with a coast-to-coast supply network, and a major manufacturer of petrochemicals. Imperial's 7,500 employees work in major cities and in communities across Canada. Graduates most likely to be hired from the following academic areas: Bachelor of Arts (Economics), Bachelor of Science (Chemistry, Computer Science, Geology, Mathematics, Metallurgy), Bachelor of Engineering (Chemical, Civil, Electrical, Mechanical, Resources/Environmental), Bachelor of Commerce/Business Administration (Accounting, Finance, Human Resources, Information Systems,

Marketing), Certified Management Accountant, Certified General Accountant, Master of Business Administration (Accounting, Finance, Human Resources, Information Systems, Marketing), Master of Engineering, and Community College Diploma (Engineering Technician). Previous work experience, mobility, team player, and initiative are all listed as desirable non-academic qualifications. Company benefits are rated above average. The potential for advancement is listed as being good. The most suitable method for initial contact by those seeking employment is to mail a resume, covering letter, and a recent transcript (the months of August and September are best). On-campus recruitment requires CACEE forms and transcripts (see your career centre for opportunities with Imperial Oil). Imperial Oil Limited does hire students for summer and co-op work terms. *Contact:* Recruitment Co-ordinator.

IMPERIAL TOBACCO LIMITED
3810, rue Saint-Antoine ouest
Montreal, QC H4C 1B5

Tel. 514-932-6161

Imperial Tobacco Limited is Canada's largest tobacco enterprise employing over 2,500 people in all phases of the industry, from the raw leaf to the final product. The company operates three manufacturing plants located in Montreal, Guelph Ontario, and Joliette Quebec, in addition to two tobacco processing plants located in Aylmer Ontario, and LaSalle Quebec. Imperial Tobacco Limited also maintains sales and distribution centres in six major Canadian cities, Moncton, Montreal, Toronto, Winnipeg, Calgary, and Vancouver. This location is the head office. The major corporate divisions are finance, marketing, manufacturing, materials management, human resources, and research and development. Graduates most likely to be hired come from the following academic areas: Bachelor of Arts (Psychology), Bachelor of Science (Chemistry, Computer Science, Health Sciences, Physics, Psychology), Bachelor of Engineering (Chemical, Civil, Environmental, Electrical, Industrial, Mechanical), Bachelor of Laws, Bachelor of Commerce/Business Administration (Accounting, Finance, Marketing), Chartered Accountant (Finance), Certified Management Accountant (Finance), Certified General Accountant (Finance), Master of Business Administration (Finance, Marketing), and Community College Diploma (Human Resources). Company benefits and the potential for advancement are both listed as excellent. The average annual starting salary falls within the $30,000 to $35,000 range. The most suitable method for initial contact by those seeking employment is to mail a resume with a covering letter. Imperial Tobacco Limited does hire summer students. *Contact:* Human Resources.

IMPRIMERIE INTERWEB INC.
1603 boulevard Montarville
Boucherville, QC J4B 5Y2

Tel. 450-655-2801
Fax 450-641-3650

Imprimerie Interweb Inc. is a commercial printing company that specializes in the production of magazines, newspapers, and inserts. Founded in 1981, the Company is a subsidiary of Groupe Transcontinentale. Interweb has about 300 permanent employees that work from their central office in Boucherville, Quebec, and a total of 370 employees in Canada. Graduates most likely to be hired come from the following academic areas: Bachelor of Commerce/Business Administration (Marketing), Community College Diploma (Administration, Marketing/Sales, Purchasing/Logistics, Mechanic, Electronics Technician), and High School Diploma. Graduates would occupy Production (eg. General Help and Stackerman), and Customer Service positions. Creative, communicative, responsible, diligent, organized, enthusiastic, and productive are all listed as desirable non-academic qualifications. Company benefits and the potential for advancement are both rated as excellent. The average annual starting salary falls within the $15,000 to $20,000 range. The most suitable method for initial contact by those seeking employment is to fax a resume with a covering letter. Imprimerie Interweb Inc. does hire summer and co-op work term students. *Contact:* Lucie Gérin, Human Resources.

INDUSTRIES LASSONDE INC.
170 5 E Avenue
Rougemont, QC J0L 1M0

Tel. 514-469-4926
Fax 514-469-2505

Industries Lassonde Inc. is involved in food processing, primarily juices and drinks. The company employs 300 people at this location and a total of 500 people in Canada. Graduates most likely to be hired come from the following academic areas: Bachelor of Science (Chemistry, Microbiology, Nutritional Sciences), Bachelor of Engineering (Food Processing, Automation/Robotics, Computer Systems, Industrial Design, Industrial Production), Bachelor of Commerce/Business Administration (Accounting, Finance, Human Resources, Information Systems, Marketing, Public Administration), Chartered Accountant, Certified Management Accountant, Certified General Accountant, and Community College Diploma (Accounting, Administration, Human Resources, Secretarial). Graduates would occupy Manager, Controller, Chief Accountant, Technician, Clerk, and Engineering positions. Good communication skills, leadership abilities, the ability to make decisions, and being a team player are all listed as desirable non-academic qualifications. Company benefits are rated as above average. The potential for advancement is listed as being good. The average annual starting salary falls within the $25,000 to $35,000 range. The most suitable method for initial contact by those seeking employment is to mail a resume with a covering letter. Industries Lassonde Inc. does hire summer students. *Contacts:* Michel Simard, Vice President, Human Resources or Jacques Tartif, Manager, Human Resources.

INFORMATION SYSTEMS MANAGEMENT CORPORATION

IBM Global Services

INFORMATION SYSTEMS MANAGEMENT CORPORATION (ISM)
245 Consumers Road, BK9
Toronto, ON M2J 1R3

Tel. 416-490-2568
Fax 416-490-4790
Website .... www.ism.ca

Information Systems Management Corporation (ISM) is one of Canada's premier providers of information system management services. ISM is a wholly owned subsidiary of IBM Canada Ltd., and a member of the IBM Global Services team. There are 1,500 employees at this location, and a total of 6,500 employees in Canada. Graduates most likely to be hired come from the following academic areas: Bachelor of Science (Computer Science), Bachelor of Engineering (Computer Systems), Bachelor of Commerce/Business Administration (Information Systems), Master of Business Administration (Information Systems), and Community College Diploma (Computer Science). Graduates would occupy IT Specialist, Network Operations Analyst, Help Desk Support, Customer Service Representative, Software/Hardware Administrator, Disaster Recovery Analyst, and Programmer/Analyst positions. Team player, good written and verbal communication skills, and a strong customer service orientation are all listed as desirable non-academic qualifications. Company benefits and the potential for advancement are both rated as excellent. The average annual starting salary falls within the $35,000 to $45,000 range. The most suitable methods for initial contact by those seeking employment are to apply online through www.ism.ca, or to fax or mail a resume with a covering letter. Information Systems Management Corporation does hire summer and co-op work term students. *Contact:* Recruitment Services - TCD.

INFORMATION & TECHNOLOGY SERVICES (ITS)
700 Lawrence Avenue West, Suite 370
Toronto, ON M6A 3B4

Tel. 416-256-6512
Fax 416-256-6513

Information & Technology Services (ITS) is the technology division of the Ontario Housing Corporation (OHC). ITS develops in-house application systems for the client group, which is the Local Housing Authorities (LHA) in Ontario. A Help Support Centre is also provided. Systems developed are in the areas of accounting, human resources, budgeting and asset management. ITS employs a total of 60 personnel. Graduates most likely to be hired come from the following academic areas: Bachelor of Science (Computer Science), Bachelor of Engineering (Computer Systems), Bachelor of Commerce/Business Administration (Information Systems), and Community College Diploma (Computer Science).

Graduates would occupy Programmer/Analyst, Application Developer, Business Analyst, Software Tester, Software Implementer/Trainer, and Help Centre Analyst positions. Good communication skills and flexibility are both listed as desirable non-academic qualifications. Company benefits are rated as industry standard. The potential for advancement is listed as being good. The average annual starting salary falls within the $40,000 to $45,000 range. The most suitable method for initial contact by those seeking employment is via telephone. ITS does hire summer and co-op work term students. *Contact:* Christopher Gomes, Human Resources Administrator.

INGENIUS ENGINEERING

30 Rosemount Avenue, Suite 200
Ottawa, ON K1Y 1P4

Tel.	613-729-6400
Fax	613-729-6770
Email	recruit@ingenius.on.ca
Website	www.ingenius.on.ca

InGenius Engineering is a software engineering and technical consulting firm specializing in telecom applications and systems integration. The company's core competencies include real-time software development, enterprise networking, and telecommunications systems. InGenius provides both technical contractors and custom software development services to clients in the telecom industry and in government. Special expertise includes technical recruiting and contracting (developers, system administrators, web and multimedia developers, project managers) and telecommunications product development (multimedia applications, internet applications, computer-telephony integration). InGenius employs 90 people at this location, and a total of 100 people in Canada. Graduates most likely to be hired come from the following academic areas: Bachelor of Science (Computer Science), Bachelor of Engineering (Electrical, Computer Systems), and Community College Diploma (Information Systems, Computer Science). Graduates would occupy System Administrator, Software Developer, Project Manager, Multimedia Developer, and Technical Writer positions. Good interpersonal and people skills, able to work well in a group or alone, customer service experience, good communication skills, and able to meet deadlines are all listed as desirable non-academic qualifications. Company benefits are rated as industry standard. The potential for advancement is listed as excellent. The average annual starting salary falls within the $40,000 to $45,000 range. The most suitable method for initial contact by those seeking employment is to e-mail a resume with a covering letter. InGenius Engineering does hire summer and co-op students. *Contact:* Recruitment.

INGERSOLL-RAND CANADA INC.

51 Worcester Road
Rexdale, ON M9W 4K2

Tel.	416-213-4500
Fax	416-213-4616

Ingersoll-Rand Canada Inc. manufactures and sells industrial machinery such as air compressors, air tools, construction and mining machinery, hoists, bearings, and architectural hardware. The company employs approximately 115 people at this location, a total of 750 across Canada, and 48,000 people worldwide. Graduates most likely to be hired come from the following academic areas: Bachelor of Engineering (Mechanical), Bachelor of Commerce/Business Administration (Accounting), and Community College Diploma (Accounting). Graduates would occupy Application Engineer and Financial/Accounting positions. Good communication skills, high integrity, team player, and an ability to make decisions and follow through are all listed as desirable non-academic qualifications. Company benefits are rated above average. The potential for advancement is listed as being good. The average annual starting salary falls within the $35,000 to $40,000 range. The most suitable method for initial contact by those seeking employment is to mail a resume with a covering letter. *Contact:* Agako Nouch, Vice President, Finance & Administration.

INGLIS LIMITED

1901 Minnesota Court
Mississauga, ON L5N 3A7

Tel.	905-821-6400
Fax	905-821-3462
Website	inglislimited.com

Inglis Limited employs approximately 225 people at this location in the sales, marketing and service of household appliances. Inglis employs over 450 people across Canada and is a wholly owned subsidiary of Whirlpool Corporation, USA, employing 40,000 people worldwide. Graduates most likely to be hired come from the following academic areas: Bachelor of Engineering, Chartered Accountant, Certified Management Accountant, Certified General Accountant, Master of Business Administration, Master (for different areas in organization), and Community College Diploma (Accounting, Administration, Advertising, Information Systems, Marketing/Sales, Purchasing/Logistics, Electronics Technician). Graduates are recruited for Sales and Marketing, Accounting, Clerical, and Customer Service positions in the company's call-centre. Inglis seeks high potential employees. Company benefits are rated as excellent. The potential for advancement is listed as being good. The average annual salary falls within the $30,000 to $35,000 range. The most suitable method for initial contact by those seeking employment is to mail a resume with a covering letter. Inglis Limited hires summer students depending upon their requirements. *Contact:* Human Resources.

INNOVEX, QUINTILES CANADA INC.

100 Alexis-Nihon, Suite 800
St-Laurent, QC H4M 2P4

Tel.	514-855-0888
Fax	514-855-1348
Website	www.innovexglobal.com

Innovex, a Division of Quintiles Canada Inc., offers custom designed solutions to healthcare companies that allows them to accelerate their commercial success. As a world leader in contract pharmaceutical services, Innovex provides contract sales and marketing services, late phase clinical (IIIB -IV) services, as well as health management services. Graduates most likely to be hired come from Bachelor of Science (Biology, Microbiology, Nursing, Pharmacy), and Bachelor of Commerce/Business Administration programs. Innovex hires full-time employees across Canada, for Sales and Sales Management positions on specific customer projects, that may range from 6 to 18 months in duration. Enthusiasm, good communication skills, team player, initiative, and a business acumen are all listed as desirable nonacademic qualifications. Company benefits are rated as industry standard. The potential for advancement is listed as being good. The average annual starting salary varies according to the applicants level of experience in pharmaceutical sales or clinical research. The most suitable method for initial contact by those seeking employment is through Innovex's website at www.innovexglobal.com (Fax Number 514-855-0800). *Contact:* Human Resources.

INTELCAN TECHNOSYSTEMS INC.
69 Auriga Drive
Nepean, ON K2E 7Z2

Tel. 613-228-1150
Fax 613-228-1149
Email .... hr@intelcan.com
Website .... www.intelcan.com

Intelcan Technosystems Inc. is a turnkey contractor and systems integrator for telecommunications and civil aviation projects, primarily in emerging markets. The company employs approximately 44 people at this location and an additional 13 people outside of Canada. Graduates most likely to be hired come from the following academic areas: Bachelor of Engineering (Civil, Electrical, Telecommunications), Bachelor of Architecture, Bachelor of Commerce/Business Administration (Accounting, Human Resources, Information Systems), Chartered Accountant, Certified Management Accountant, and Certified General Accountant. Graduates would occupy Electrical Engineer, Civil Engineer, Architect, Accountant, and Accounting Clerk positions. A minimum of two years work experience for junior engineering positions, team player, and the ability to travel are listed as desirable non-academic qualifications. Company benefits are rated above average. The potential for advancement is listed as being good. The average annual starting salary depends on the position being considered. The most suitable methods for initial contact by those seeking employment are to mail or e-mail a resume with a covering letter. Intelcan Technosystems Inc. does hire co-op work term students. *Contact:* Tracy Hearty, Human Resources.

INTERACTIVE CHANNEL TECHNOLOGIES
150 Dufferin Avenue, Suite 906
London, ON N6A 5N6

Tel. 519-663-4460
Fax 519-663-0339
Email .... hr@ichanneltech.com
Website .... www.sourcemedia.com

Interactive Channel Technologies Inc. is a dynamic hi-tech organization leading the industry in interactive television system development. The company's technology, VirtualModem, provides consumers with a variety of interactive television applications and on-demand services including: internet access, e-mail, electronic program guide, electronic home shopping, and video-on-demand. The VirtualModem television system utilizes industry standard digital MPEG set-top boxes. Trials and deployments are ongoing with cable television and telephone companies, as well as in other commercial and business areas around the world. Interactive Channel Technologies employs 48 people at this location, and a total of 200 people worldwide. Graduates most likely to be hired come from the following academic areas: Bachelor of Science (Computer Science), Bachelor of Engineering (Electrical, Computer Systems), Master of Science (Computer Science), and Master of Engineer (Computer Systems). Graduates would occupy Software and Hardware Programmer/Developer positions. Team player, good communication skills, and previous work experience are all listed as desirable non-academic qualifications. Company benefits are rated as excellent. The potential for advancement is listed as average. The average annual starting salary falls within the $30,000 to $40,000 range. The most suitable method for initial contact by those seeking employment is to e-mail a resume with a covering letter. Interactive Channel Technologies does hire students for summer and co-op work terms. *Contact:* Mary Donnelly, Human Resources Manager.

INTERNATIONAL FOREST PRODUCTS LIMITED (INTERFOR)
1055 Dunsmuir Street
P.O. Box 49114, Four Bentall Centre, Suite 3500
Vancouver, BC V7X 1H7

Tel. 604-689-6800
Fax 604-688-0313

International Forest Products Limited is one of western Canada's largest logging and sawmilling companies producing a diversified range of quality wood products for sale to world markets. It harvests timber and manufactures and markets lumber products, logs, and wood chips. The company has 46 logging operations and six sawmills in the southern coastal region of British Columbia and has one logging operation and one sawmill in the central interior region of the province. The company employs approximately 2,100 people directly and a further 700 people through logging contractors operating under its direction. Graduates most likely to be hired come from the following academic areas: Bachelor of Science (Forestry), Bachelor of Engineering (Mechanical), Bachelor of Commerce/Business Administration (Accounting, Marketing), Master of Business Administration (Accounting, Marketing), and Community College Diploma (Forestry). Graduates would occupy Timber Cruiser, Assistant Forestry Engineer, Assistant Silviculturist, Manufacturing Management Trainee, Production, and Sales positions. Applicants should be team players and self starters. Company benefits and the potential for advancement are both rated as excellent. The average annual starting salary falls within the $35,000 to $40,000 range. The most suitable methods for initial contact by those seeking employment are to mail or fax a resume and covering letter. International Forest Products Limited does hire summer students. *Contact:* Human Resources Department.

INTERNATIONAL LEISURE SYSTEMS INC.
511 King Street West, Suite 303
Toronto, ON M5V 2Z4

Tel. 416-598-9494
Fax 416-598-0040
Email .... 103177,1014@compuserve.com

International Leisure Systems Inc. is a rapidly growing entertainment company employing 150 people worldwide. The company seeks graduates for training in the urban entertainment industry with the potential to work internationally. Graduates most likely to be hired come from the following academic areas: Bachelor of Arts (General), Master of Business Administration, and Community College Diploma (Business, Facility Management, Financial Planning, Hospitality, Recreation Studies, Urban Planning). Graduates would be hired to occupy Assistant Manager positions. Enthusiasm, a willingness to travel, positive attitude, and a desire to gain experience in different areas of the urban entertainment industry are all listed as desirable non-academic qualifications. Company benefits are rated above average. The average annual starting salary is negotiable with the position and qualifications of the applicant. The most suitable method for initial contact by those seeking employment is to mail a resume with a covering letter. *Contact:* Laura Tweedy, Administration.

INTERTEC SECURITY & INVESTIGATION LIMITED
939 Eglinton Avenue East, Suite 119
Toronto, ON M4G 4E8

Tel. 416-424-2002

Intertec Security & Investigation Limited provides contract security services for condominium, industrial, commercial, and residential facilities, as well as providing investigation services. Graduates most likely to be hired come from the following academic areas: Bachelor of Arts, Bachelor of Commerce/Business Administration, and Community College Diploma (Law Enforcement, Business). Graduates would occupy supervisory positions in the Security Division and possible management positions within

the Personnel/Training or Operations Department. Good public relations, communication, and English language skills are all listed as desirable non-academic qualifications. Company benefits are rated as industry standard. The potential for advancement is listed as excellent. The average annual starting salary falls within the $15,000 to $20,000 range, and is commission based for some positions. The most suitable methods for initial contact by those seeking employment are to mail a resume with a covering letter, or by applying in person. Intertec Security & Investigation Limited does hire summer students. *Contact:* Human Resources Manager.

INVESTORS GROUP (CORPORATE HEADQUARTERS)
447 Portage Avenue, One Canada Centre
Winnipeg, MB R3C 3B6

Tel. 204-956-8359
Fax 204-942-0967
Email .... humanresources@investorsgroup.com
Website .... www.investorsgroup.com

Investors Group is one of the leading financial services companies in Canada. Canadian owned and operated, Investors Group is a dominant player in the mutual fund industry. In addition to mutual funds, the company offers other individual and group investment products (eg. life, health and disability insurance, mortgage financing, and tax preparation services). Distribution of all services is handled by more than 3,300 representatives working from more than 95 sales offices across Canada. One Canada Centre is the corporate headquarters for Investors Group. Corporate functions are divided into 10 corporate divisions: Client Services, Corporate Affairs, Corporate Services and Internal Audit, Finance, Information Technology, Investment, Marketing, Property, Sales, and Strategic Initiatives. Graduates most likely to be hired come from the following academic areas: Bachelor of Arts (Economics), Bachelor of Science (Computer Science), Bachelor of Commerce/Business Administration (Accounting, Finance, Marketing), Certified Management Accountant, Certified General Accountant, Master of Business Administration (Accounting, Finance, Marketing), and Community College Diploma (Administration). Company benefits and the potential for advancement are rated as excellent. Starting salaries are based on a combination of education, experience, the position and its responsibilities. The most suitable method for initial contact by those seeking employment is to forward a resume with a covering letter. Investors Group does hire summer students. *Contacts:* Kendra Noel, Human Resources Consultant or Colleen MacInnes, Human Resources Consultant.

INVESTORS GROUP (WESTMOUNT)

4 Westmount Square
Suite 250
Westmount, QC H3Z 2S6

Tel. 514-935-3520
Fax 514-935-2930
Website .... www.investorsgroup.com

Investors Group is one of the leading financial services companies in Canada. Investors Group is a dominant player in the mutual fund industry. In addition to mutual funds, the Company offers other individual and group investment products (eg. life, health and disability insurance, mortgage financing, and tax preparation services). Investors Group employs approximately 60 people at this office, and a total of 4,000 people in Canada (see previous listing). Graduates hired for this location come from the following academic areas: Bachelor of Arts (Economics), Bachelor of Commerce/Business Administration (General, Accounting, Finance, Marketing), Chartered Accountant, Certified Management Accountant, Certified General Accountant, Master of Business Administration (Finance), and Community College Diploma (Accounting, Business, Financial Planning, Marketing/Sales). Graduates are hired as Sales Representatives in the financial planning field. The starting salary is commission based. Excellent human relations skills, self starter, ambitious, competitive, and business oriented are all listed as desirable nonacademic qualifications. Company benefits and the potential for advancement are both rated as excellent. The most suitable methods for initial contact by those seeking employment are to mail or fax a resume with a covering letter. *Contact:* Babis Chronopoulos, Region Manager.

IRVING OIL LIMITED

10 Sydney Street
P.O. Box 1421
Saint John, NB E2L 3W4

Tel. 506-632-2000
Fax 506-632-7161

Irving Oil Limited is involved in oil refining, and the sale and marketing of oil products. Graduates most likely to be hired come from the following academic areas: Bachelor of Engineering (Chemical, Civil, Environmental, Mechanical, Bachelor of Commerce/Business Administration (Accounting, Finance, Marketing, Information Systems), Chartered Accountant (Finance), Certified Management Accountant (Finance), Certified General Accountant (Finance), Master of Business Administration (Accounting, Finance, Marketing, Information Systems), and Community College Diploma (Accounting, Administration, Advertising, Business). The most suitable methods for initial contact by those seeking employment are to mail a resume with a covering letter, or through on-campus recruitment programs (see your campus career centre for details). Irving Oil Limited does hire summer students. *Contact:* Human Resources.

IRWIN TOY LIMITED

43 Hanna Avenue
Toronto, ON M6K 1X6

Tel. 416-533-3521
Fax 416-533-3257

Irwin Toy Limited is involved in the manufacture and distribution of toy products. Activities also include importing and exporting, sales and marketing. There are more than 250 employees at this location. Graduates most likely to be hired come from the following academic areas: Bachelor of Arts, Bachelor of Science, Bachelor of Education, Bachelor of Commerce/Business Administration, Chartered Accountant, Certified Management Accountant, Master of Business Administration, and Community College Diploma (General/Related). Graduates would occupy Manager, Controller, Sales Representative, and Public Relations Assistant positions. Excellent communication and organizational skills are both listed as desirable non-academic qualifications. Company benefits are rated as excellent. The potential for advancement is listed as being good. The most suitable methods for initial contact by those seeking employment are to mail a resume with a covering letter, or via telephone. Irwin Toy Limited does hire summer students on a regular basis. *Contact:* Director Human Resources.

ISL INTERNATIONAL SURVEYS LTD.

151 Placer Court
Willowdale, ON M2H 3R5

Tel. 416-495-0909
Fax 416-495-1369

ISL International Surveys Ltd. provides a wide range of market research services from initial design, through data collection and collation, to tabulation and interpretation. There are more than 100 employees at this location. Graduates most likely to be hired come from the following academic areas: Bachelor of Arts (Statistics, General), Bachelor of Science, Bachelor of Commerce/Business Administration (Marketing), Certified Management Accountant, and Community College Diploma (Secretarial, Clerical). Graduates would occupy Report Preparations Processor/Programming, Intermediate Accounting Clerk, Data Entry Operator, Secretary, and Management Assistant positions. Company benefits are rated above average. The potential for advancement is listed as being good. The average annual starting salary falls within the $20,000 to $25,000 range. The most suitable methods for initial contact by those seeking employment are to mail a resume with a covering letter, or via telephone. ISL International Surveys Ltd. does hire summer students, occasionally. *Contacts:* Caren Healy, Human Resources Manager or Karrie Kong, Administrative Assistant, Human Resources.

ITS Electronics Inc.
Response, Innovation, Craftsmanship

ITS ELECTRONICS INC.
200 Edgeley Blvd., Units 24-26
Concord, ON L4K 3Y8

Tel. 905-660-0405
Fax 905-660-0406
Email .... itselectronics@sympatico.ca
Website .... itselectronics.com

ITS Electronics Inc., a private Canadian company, is an established global supplier of active and passive RF/microwave and millimetrewave components and subsystems. The company's business is diversified, catering to various industries such as wireless communications, satellite communications, telecommunications, and defence. Graduates most likely to be hired come from the following academic areas: Bachelor of Engineering (Electrical, Mechanical, Aerospace, Engineering Physics, Telecommunications), Bachelor of Commerce/Business Administration (General, Accounting), Master of Science, Master of Engineering (Mechanical, Electrical, Engineering Physics), Doctorate (Mechanical Engineering, Electrical Engineering, Engineering Physics). Graduates would occupy Analog/Digital Designer, RF/Microwave Assembler, Digital Engineer, Electrical Engineer, Mechanical Engineer, RF/Microwave Engineer, RF/Microwave Technicians/Technologist, Administrative Clerk, and Accounting Clerk positions. Team player, initiative, self-motivated, exceptional communication and interpersonal skills, quick learner, and at least two years of previous work experience are all listed as desirable non-academic qualifications. Company benefits are rated above average. The potential for advancement is listed as excellent. The average annual starting salary falls within the $30,000 to $35,000 range, and could fall into a higher range depending on the position being considered. The most suitable methods for initial contact by those seeking employment are to mail, fax or e-mail a resume with a covering letter. ITS Electronics Inc. does hire summer and co-op students. *Contacts:* Ana P. Fini, Human Resources Administrator or Michael A. Earle, Vice President.

IVANHOÉ INC.
413, rue St-Jacques, bureau 700
Montreal, QC H2Y 3Z4

Tel. 514-841-7600
Fax 514-841-7795

Ivanhoé Inc. is a real estate management, development and investment company, specializing in shopping centre properties. The company employs approximately 150 employees at this location and a total of 200 full-time and 50 temporary employees in Canada. Graduates most likely to be hired come from the following academic areas: Bachelor of Engineering (Civil, Architectural/Building), Bachelor of Laws, Bachelor of Commerce/Business Administration (Accounting, Marketing), Chartered Accountant, Certified Management Accountant, Certified General Accountant, and Community College Diploma (Accounting, Advertising, Secretarial, HVAC Systems). Graduates would occupy Secretary, Accounting Manager, Project Manager, Publicity and Promotions Administrator, Assistant Manager, and Technical positions in the shopping centres. Previous work experience, bilingualism, computer skills, and service oriented are all listed as desirable non-academic qualifications. Company benefits are rated as excellent. The potential for advancement is listed as being good. The average annual starting salary falls within the $30,000 to $35,000 range. The most suitable method for initial contact by those seeking employment is to mail a resume with a covering letter. *Contact:* Carmela Rubiano, Human Resources Department.

IVL TECHNOLOGIES LTD.
6710 Bertram Place
Victoria, BC V8M 1Z6

Tel. 250-544-4091
Fax 250-544-4100
Email .... info@ivl.com
Website .... www.ivl.com

IVL Technologies Ltd. is a world leader in innovative vocal and musical signal processing. IVL designs and manufactures award winning products for the professional music, audio, and multimedia markets. The company has 80 creative employees working in engineering, manufacturing, sales and support at IVL's modern facilities located in Victoria, British Columbia. Graduates most likely to be hired come from the following academic areas: Bachelor of Science (Computer Science), Bachelor of Engineering (Electrical, Computer Systems, Industrial Design), Master of Science (Computer Science), Master of Engineering (Electrical, Computer Systems). Graduates would occupy Junior-Senior DSP Engineer, Junior-Senior Embedded Software Engineer, and Junior-Senior Research Engineer positions. Excellent problem solving skills, strong team-players and a passion for music are all listed as desirable non-academic qualifications. Applicants with demonstrated related work experience, and real-time experience are preferred. Company benefits are rated as excellent. The potential for advancement is listed as average. The average annual starting salary falls within the $45,000 to $50,000 range. The most suitable method for initial contact by those seeking employment is to mail a resume with a covering letter. IVL Technologies Ltd. does hire co-op work term students. *Contact:* Human Resources.

J. D. SMITH AND SONS LIMITED
700 Flint Road
Downsview, ON M3J 2J5

Tel. 416-661-2500
Fax 416-661-7680
Email .... sblackwell@jdsmith.com
Website .... www.jdsmith.com

J. D. Smith and Sons Limited specializes in truck transportation, including general common carrier and dedication contract. Services include warehousing, distribution and dedicated services. The company employs more than 300 people across Canada. Graduates most likely to be hired come from the following academic areas: Bachelor of Arts (General), Bachelor of Commerce/Business Administration (General), Community College Diploma (Administration, Business, Facility Management, Purchasing/Logistics), and High School Diploma. Graduates would occupy Clerical, Supervisor Trainees for trucking and warehousing operations, Management Trainees, and Business Analyst/Logistics positions. Honesty, dedication, good interpersonal skills, and a good attitude towards work and business environments are all listed as desirable non-academic qualifications. Company benefits are rated as excellent. The potential for advancement is listed as being good. The average annual starting salary falls within the $25,000 to $30,000 range. The most suitable method for initial contact by those seeking employment is to mail a resume with a covering letter. J. D. Smith and Sons Limited does hire summer students, traditionally for Clerical, Warehouse, and Truck Driving positions. Summer students demonstrating appropriate skills may be considered for permanent positions upon graduation. *Contacts:* Susan Blackwell or Joseph Libralesso.

J. M. SCHNEIDER INC.
321 Courtland Avenue
Kitchener, ON N2G 3X8

Tel. 519-741-5000

J. M. Schneider Inc. is a food manufacturer primarily involved in the manufacture of consumer meat products. There are more than 1,000 employees at this location. Graduates most likely to be hired come from the following areas: Bachelor of Arts (General, English), Bachelor of Science (Chemistry, Computer Science, Mathematics), Bachelor of Commerce/Business Administration, Chartered Accountant, Master of Business Administration (Marketing), and High School Diploma. Graduates are hired to occupy positions relating to their specific specialty. Previous work experience, outside interests, and related specialized qualifications are all listed as desirable non-academic qualifications. Company benefits are rated above average. The potential for advancement is listed as being good. The average annual starting salary ranges between $20,000 and $25,000 and will ultimately depend upon the position being considered. The most suitable method for initial contact by those seeking employment is to mail a resume with a covering letter. J. M. Schneider Inc. does hire summer students. *Contact:* Alfred Lowrick, Human Resources, Management.

JACQUES, WHITFORD AND ASSOCIATES LTD.
3 Spectacle Lake Drive
Dartmouth, NS B3B 1W8

Tel. 902-468-7777
Fax 902-468-9009

Founded in 1972, Jacques, Whitford and Associates Limited provides consulting services in six disciplines in the engineering and environmental sciences. These disciplines are as follows: Environmental Engineering, Environmental Sciences, Geotechnical Engineering, Hydrogeology, Materials Engineering and Research, and Mining Services. There are approximately 100 employees at this location, and a total of 325 across Canada. Graduates most likely to be hired come from the following academic areas: Bachelor of Arts (Geography, Urban Geography, Archeology), Bachelor of Science (Biology, Geography), Bachelor of Engineering (General, Chemical, Industrial Chemistry, Materials Science, Pollution Treatment, Civil, Environmental, Forest Resources, Water Resources, Petroleum, Geological, Geotechnical), Bachelor of Commerce/Business Administration (Accounting, Human Resources, Marketing), Certified Management Accountant, Master of Business Administration (Accounting, Finance), Master of Science (Biology, Geography), Master of Engineering (General, Chemical, Industrial Chemistry, Materials Science, Pollution Treatment, Civil, Environmental, Forest Resources, Water Resources, Petroleum, Geological, Geotechnical), and Community College Diploma (Accounting, Administration, CAD/CAM/Autocad, Engineering Technician, Laboratory Technician, Environmental Engineering Technician). Graduates would occupy Junior Engineer, Junior Scientist, Secretarial, and Accounting positions. Good communication skills, community involvement, and related work experience or completion of co-op work terms are all listed as desirable non-academic qualifications. Company benefits are rated above average. The potential for advancement is listed as excellent. The average annual starting salary falls within the $25,000 to $30,000 range. The most suitable method for initial contact by those seeking employment is to mail a resume with a covering letter. Jacques, Whitford and Associates Limited does hire summer students, mainly through organized co-op programs. *Contact:* Kim Crowell, Human Resources Coordinator.

JAMES RIVER CANADA INC.
137 Bentworth Avenue
Toronto, ON M6A 1P6

Tel. 416-789-5151
Fax 416-789-3590

James River Canada Inc. employs approximately 450 people in the manufacture and distribution of paper and plastic cups, plates and cutlery. Graduates most likely to be hired come from the following academic areas: Bachelor of Engineering (Mechanical, Chemical, Electrical), Bachelor of Commerce/Business Administration, Chartered Accountant, and Community College Diploma (Purchasing/Logistics, Mechanic, Engineering Technician). Self-starter, upwardly mobile, and a strong team player are all listed as desirable non-academic qualifications. Graduates would occupy Purchasing, Scheduling, Finance, Maintenance, Traffic and Engineering positions. Company benefits are rated above average. The potential for advancement is listed as being good. The most suitable method for initial contact by graduates seeking employment is to mail a resume with a covering letter. *Contact:* Fay Lue Kim, Employee Relations Coordinator.

JANNA SYSTEMS INC.
3080 Yonge Street, Suite 6020
Toronto, ON M4N 3N1

Tel.	416-483-7711
Fax	416-483-3220
Email	hr@janna.com
Website	www.janna.com

Janna Systems Inc. is a quick-paced, independent software vendor, and award-winning Microsoft Solution Provider based in Toronto. The company designs, develops and markets relationship management solutions that provide industry leading organizations with integrated contact, document, time, and Web management. Corporate alliances and strategic partners include Microsoft, Oracle, Sybase, Intel, and Nokia. Employing approximately 80 people, Janna Systems offers an upstart attitude and an entrepreneurial environment where individuals are able to make a difference. The Company was ranked the third fastest growing hi-tech company in Canada in 1997, and clients are Fortune 500 financial and telecommunications industry leaders. Graduates most likely to be hired come from the following academic areas: Bachelor of Science (Computer Science, Mathematics), Bachelor of Engineering (General, Computer Systems), and Master of Business Administration (Information Systems). Graduates would occupy Software Developer, Professional Services Consultant, and Quality Assurance Analyst positions. An ability to work with minimal supervision in a team environment, good communication skills, motivated, willing to make a commitment to success, and the ability to learn the skills of the "Big Six" consulting firms are all listed as desirable non-academic qualifications. Janna Systems offers an extremely competitive compensation package and excellent opportunities for professional growth. The most suitable method for initial contact by those seeking employment is to e-mail a resume with a covering letter. Janna Systems Inc. does hire summer and co-op work term students. *Contact:* Human Resources.

JAS F. GILLANDERS CO. LIMITED
33 Atomic Avenue
Toronto, ON M8Z 5K8

Tel.	416-259-5446
Fax	416-259-5614

Jas F. Gillanders Co. Ltd. is a custom millwork manufacturer of all types of cabinets, furniture, panelling, etc. The company employs more than 50 people. Graduates most likely to be hired come from the following academic areas: Community College Diploma (Accounting, Secretarial, Architecture/Drafting, Industrial Design), and High School Diploma. Possessing relevant work experience and technical trades would be a definite asset. Company benefits are rated as excellent. The potential for advancement is listed as being good. The average annual starting salary falls within the $15,000 to $20,000 range. The most suitable methods for initial contact by those seeking employment are to mail a resume with a covering letter, or via telephone. Jas F. Gillanders Co. Ltd. does hire summer students. *Contact:* Mr. Bill Vincent, Vice President, Administration.

JEWELSTONE SYSTEMS INC.
1 Richmond Street West, Suite 400
Toronto, ON M5H 3W4

Tel.	416-364-5800
Fax	416-364-5448
Email	positions@unitrax.com
Website	www.unitrax.com

Jewelstone Systems Inc. is a thriving Canadian software company that provides shareholder management record keeping solutions for the Canadian Investment Fund industry. Presently, Jewelstone Systems Inc. employs 45 people. Graduates most likely to be hired come from the following academic areas: Bachelor of Science (Computer Science), Bachelor of Commerce/Business Administration (General, Accounting, Finance, Human Resources, Information Systems, Marketing), Chartered Accountant, Certified Management Accountant, Certified General Accountant, Master of Business Administration (General), and Community College Diploma (Accounting, Administration, Human Resources, Information Systems, Marketing/Sales, Secretarial, Computer Science). Graduates would occupy Technical Support, Computer Programmer, Office Administration, Accounts Payable, Accounts Receivable, and Human Resources positions. Previous work experience in the mutual fund industry, self-motivated, the ability to work well in a team environment, and good communication skills are listed as a desirable non-academic qualifications. Jewelstone offers competitive industry salaries and flexible working hours. Company benefits and the potential for advancement are both rated as excellent. The average annual starting salary falls within the $30,000 to $35,000 range. The most suitable method for initial contact by those seeking employment is to apply through the company's website at www.unitrax.com. Jewelstone Systems Inc. does hire summer and co-op work term students. *Contacts:* Human Resources Manager or Executive Assistant.

JIM PATTISON SIGN GROUP, THE
555 Ellesmere Road
Toronto, ON M1R 4E8

Tel.	416-759-6796
Fax	416-759-9560

The Jim Pattison Sign Group employs more than 100 people in Ontario involved in the manufacture and sale of signs. Graduates most likely to be hired come from the following academic areas: Bachelor of Arts (Economics), Bachelor of Science (Metallurgy), Bachelor of Commerce/Business Administration (Accounting, Marketing), Chartered Accountant, Certified Management Accountant, Certified General Accountant, Master of Business Administration (Marketing), Community College Diploma (Accounting, Advertising, Business, Marketing/Sales), and High School Diploma. Graduates would occupy Accounting, Artist, Sales Representative, Draftsman, and Estimator positions. Community involvement and possessing related work experience are both listed as desirable non-academic qualifications. Company benefits are rated above average. The potential for advancement is listed as average. The average annual starting salary for clerical positions falls within the $20,000 to $25,000 range, and for all others it is dependent upon the position being considered. The most suitable method for initial contact by graduates seeking employment is to mail a resume with a covering letter. The Jim Pattison Sign Company does hire summer students. *Contacts:* Controller or Sales Manager or Plant Manager.

JML SHIRT LTD.
12 Long Street
Edmunston, NB E3V 3H3

Tel. 506-735-1920
Fax 506-735-1923

JML Shirt Ltd. is a manufacturer of men's and women's dress and uniform shirts and men's boxer shorts. The company employs approximately 215 people. Graduates most likely to be hired come from the following academic areas: Bachelor of Science (Computer Science), Bachelor of Engineering (Computer Systems, Industrial Production), Bachelor of Commerce/Business Administration (Accounting, Finance, Human Resources, Information Systems, Marketing, Public Administration), Certified General Accountant (Accounting Comptroller), Community College Diploma (Accounting, Business, Secretarial, Computer Science, Engineering Technician), and High School Diploma. Graduates would occupy Accounting Clerk, Payroll Clerk and Receptionist positions. Good work ethic, team player, and conscientious are listed as desirable non-academic qualifications. Company benefits are rated as industry standard. The potential for advancement is listed as average. The most suitable method for initial contact by those seeking employment is to mail a resume with a covering letter. *Contacts:* Jacques Mongeau or Dale Soucy.

JOHN FORSYTH COMPANY INC., THE
36 Horner Avenue
Toronto, ON M8Z 5Y1

Tel. 416-252-6231
Fax 416-253-4147

The John Forsyth Company Inc. is one of Canada's leading suppliers of apparel and a growing presence in the United States. The company was started in 1903 by John Forsyth, a manufacturer of men's quality shirts and accessories. Today, Forsyth product lines include men's shirts, sweaters, overcoats, raincoats, jackets, activewear, casual pants and jeans, pajamas, and robes, ties and scarves and women's shirts and blouses, sweaters, pants, skirts and activewear. The company's Penmans subsidiary produces T-shirts and fleece products for men, women, youths and children. The company maintains 3 warehouses in Toronto for distribution and processing, employing sales persons, merchandisers, sourcers, and artists. The company also maintains a manufacturing facility in Cambridge, Ontario. There are approximately 180 employees at this location and a total 1,000 employees in Canada. Graduates most likely to be hired come from the following academic areas: Bachelor of Arts (Economics), Bachelor of Commerce/Business Administration (Accounting, Finance), and Community College Diploma (Accounting, Merchandising, Secretarial, Artist, Fashion Design). Graduates would occupy Accounts Payable Clerk, Accounts Receivable Clerk, Secretary, Receptionist, Merchandiser, Sourcer, and Artist positions. Team player, committed, and enthusiastic are listed as desirable non-academic qualifications. Company benefits are rated as industry standard. The potential for advancement is listed as being good. The most suitable method for initial contact by those seeking employment is to mail a resume with a covering letter. John Forsyth Company Inc. does hire summer students for warehouse positions. *Contact:* Maria Rice, Benefits Administrator.

JOHN WILEY & SONS CANADA LIMITED
22 Worcester Road
Rexdale, ON M9W 1L1

Tel. 416-236-4433
Fax 416-236-4447

John Wiley & Sons Canada Limited is an educational and trade publishing company employing more than 60 people at this location and a total of 75 people in Canada. Graduates most likely to be hired come from the following academic areas: Bachelor of Arts, Bachelor of Science, Bachelor of Education, Bachelor of Commerce/Business Administration, Chartered Accountant, and Community College Diploma (Business). Graduates would occupy Editorial Assistant, Marketing Assistant, Sales Representative, and Sales Assistant positions. Good communication and interpersonal skills, strong work ethic, positive attitude, computer literacy, and excellent organizational skills are all listed as desirable non-academic qualifications. Company benefits are rated above average. The potential for advancement is listed as being good. The average annual starting salary falls within the $22,000 to $25,000 range. The most suitable method for initial contact by those seeking employment is to mail a resume with a covering letter. John Wiley & Sons Canada Limited does hire summer students. *Contact:* Ms Berni Galway, Director of Human Resources.

JOHNSON & JOHNSON, MEDICAL PRODUCTS
1421 Lansdowne Street West
Peterborough, ON K9J 7B9

Tel. 705-741-6100
Fax 705-743-1545
Email .... csmith@medca.jnj.com

Johnson & Johnson, Medical Products is involved in the sales and distribution of medical devices. There are 95 employees at this location and a total of 350 employees in Canada. Graduates most likely to be hired come from the following academic areas: Bachelor of Arts (General), Bachelor of Science (General, Biology, Computer Science), Bachelor of Commerce/Business Administration (General, Accounting, Finance, Human Resources, Information Systems, Marketing), Certified Management Accountant, Certified General Accountant, and Community College Diploma (Accounting, Administration, Business, Human Resources, Information Systems, Secretarial, Computer Science). Graduates would occupy Product Specialist, Secretary, Product Manager, Accountant, Financial Controller, Associate Field Representative (non-grad), Sales Representative, and Human Resources Manager positions. Previous work experience, assertive, innovative, self-directed, collaborative, and good interpersonal skills are all listed as desirable non-academic qualifications. Company benefits are rated above average. The potential for advancement is listed as being good. The most suitable methods for initial contact by those seeking employment are to mail, fax or e-mail a resume with a covering letter. Johnson & Johnson, Medical Products does hire summer and co-op work term students. *Contact:* Carole Smith, Manager, Recruitment & Support Services.

JOHNSON MATTHEY LIMITED
130 Glidden Road
Brampton, ON L6W 3M8

Tel. 905-454-6848
Fax 905-454-6849

Johnson Matthey Limited is a precious metals refiner and manufacturer. The company employs approximately 180 people at this location, a total of 216 people in Canada, and 6,250 people worldwide. Graduates most likely to be hired come from the following academic areas: Bachelor of Science (Chemistry, Metallurgy), Bachelor of Engineering (Industrial Chemistry, Metallurgy, Industrial Production), Chartered Accountant, and Community College Diploma (Marketing/Sales). Graduates would occupy Junior Engineering and Special Project positions. Team player, resourceful, dependable, and an ability to work unsupervised are all listed as desirable non-academic qualifications. Company benefits are rated above average. The potential for advancement is listed as average. The average annual starting salary is dependent upon the position being considered. The most suitable method for initial contact by those seeking employment is to mail a resume with a covering letter. Johnson Matthey Limited does hire summer students when they are required. *Contacts:* Linda

Szeli, Human Resources Assistant or Andy McCullough, Human Resources Manager.

JUNE WARREN PUBLISHING LTD.
9915 - 56 Avenue N.W.
Edmonton, AB T6E 5L7

Tel. 403-944-9333
Fax 403-944-9500
Website .... www.junewarren.com

June Warren Publishing Ltd. is a privately owned, Alberta company specializing in the development and distribution of trade publications for the Canadian oil, gas and construction industries. Utilizing leading edge in-house database and production technology, the company publishes a family of six premier trade publications. The Canadian Oilfield Service & Supply Directory, Oil & Gas Inquirer, and Canadian Oilfield Gas Plant Atlas are all geared to the needs of the Canadian oil and gas industry. Alberta Construction Service & Supply Directory, Alberta Construction '97, and Alberta Construction Association Membership Roster & Buyers Guide are geared towards the Alberta construction industry. June Warren employs over 35 people in offices located in Calgary and Edmonton. Graduates most likely to be hired come from the following academic areas: Bachelor of Arts (English, Journalism), Bachelor of Science (Computer Science), Bachelor of Commerce/Business Administration (Information Systems, Marketing), Master of Business Administration (Information Systems, Marketing), and Community College Diploma (Advertising, Marketing/Sales, Graphic Arts, Journalism). Company benefits are rated as industry standard. The potential for advancement is listed as being good. The average annual starting salary depends on the position being considered. The most suitable method for initial contact by those seeking employment is to mail a resume with a covering letter. *Contact:* Human Resources.

KEANE CANADA INC.
439 University Avenue, Suite 500
Toronto, ON M5G 1Y8

Tel. 416-596-1532
Fax 416-596-1546

Keane Canada Inc. is a U.S. based information technology consulting firm employing almost 160 people in Canada. Areas of expertise include Application Development, Year 2000 Compliance, Application Outsourcing, and BaaN Implementation. Graduates most likely to be hired come from the following academic areas: Bachelor of Science (Computer Science), Bachelor of Engineering (Computer. System Design), Master of Business Administration (Information Systems), and Master of Science (Computer Science). Graduates would occupy a Consultant role and should possess 3 to 4 years' experience (minimum) in a structural problem-solving environment working with structured analysis methods and tools. Company benefits are rated above average. The potential for advancement is listed as excellent. The average annual starting salary fall in the $35,000 plus.

The most suitable method for initial contact by graduates seeking employment is to mail a resume with a covering letter. This location is also involved in hiring for positions located in Calgary, Halifax, and Kingston, and affiliates in the United States. *Contact:* Kathy Kadoch, Manager, Human Resources.

KELOWNA, CITY OF
1435 Water Street
Kelowna, BC V1Y 1J4

Tel. 604-862-3339
Fax 604-862-3318

The City of Kelowna employs 600 people in the provision of a full range of municipal government services. Graduates most likely to be hired come from the following academic areas: Bachelor of Arts (Recreation Studies, Urban Geography/Planning), Bachelor of Science (Computer Science), Bachelor of Engineering (Civil, Architectural/Building, Electrical, Instrumentation), Bachelor of Landscape Architecture, Bachelor of Commerce/Business Administration (Accounting, Human Resources, Information Systems, Public Administration), Certified Management Accountant, Certified General Accountant, Master of Business Administration, Master of Arts (Urban Planning), Community College Diploma (Accounting, Purchasing/Logistics, Secretarial, Urban Planning, Auto Mechanic, Architecture/Drafting, CAD/CAM/Autocad, Computer Science, Engineering Technician), and High School Diploma. Graduates would occupy Transportation Engineer, Engineering Technician, CAD/CAM/Autocad, Programmer/Analyst, Records Management Coordinator, Landscape and Parks Planner, and Planning and Development Officer positions. Good communication skills, team player, creative, innovative, customer service skills, and an ability to learn are all listed as desirable non-academic qualifications. Company benefits are rated above average. The potential for advancement is listed as average. The average annual starting salary for new graduates falls within the $30,000 to $35,000 range. The most suitable method for initial contact by those seeking employment is to mail a resume with a covering letter. The City of Kelowna does hire summer students. *Contact:* Marsha Keen, Human Resources Officer.

KELOWNA HOME SUPPORT
1340 Ellis Street
Kelowna, BC V1Y 1Z8

Tel. 250-712-3160

Kelowna Home Support provides in-home health care, personal care, light housekeeping, respite and meal program services. Graduates most likely to be hired come from the following academic areas: Bachelor of Science (Nursing), Community College Diploma (Health/Home Care Aide, Nursing RN), and High School Diploma. Company benefits are rated as excellent. The potential for advancement is listed as average. The average annual starting salary falls within the $25,000 to $30,000 range. The most suitable method for initial contact by those seeking employment is to apply in person at this location. Kelowna Home Support does hire summer students. *Contact:* Stuart Ballard, Human Resoruces.

KENNAMETAL LTD.
115 - B Matheson Boulevard West, Suite 211
Mississauga, ON L5R 3L1

Tel. 905-568-2288
Fax 905-568-4955

Kennametal Ltd. is the Canadian subsidiary of the United States based multinational corporation, specializing in the design, manufacture and marketing of tungsten carbide cutting tools, tooling systems, supplies and services to the metal working industry. There are six offices and plants in Canada, employing a total of 200 people. Graduates most likely to be hired come from the following academic areas: Bachelor of Arts (General), Bachelor of Science (Metallurgy), Bachelor of Engineering (Mechanical, Design), Bachelor of Commerce/Business Administration (Accounting), and Community College Diploma (Engineering, Accounting, Business). Personable, good telephone manner, and keyboard skills are listed as desirable non-academic qualifications. Company benefits are rated above average. The potential for advancement is listed as being good. The most suitable method for initial contact by graduates seeking employment is to mail a resume with a covering letter. *Contact:* Grant Adam, Manager of Human Resources.

KERNELS POPCORN LIMITED
40 Eglinton Avenue East, Suite 250
Toronto, ON M4P 3A2

Tel. 416-487-4194

Kernels Popcorn Ltd. is a retailer of flavoured gourmet popcorn. There are 68 stores in Canada, located in major regional shopping malls. Kernels currently has 4 stores operating in South Korea. Approximately 25% of the stores are corporately owned, and 75% are franchised. Graduates most likely to be hired come from the following academic areas: Bachelor of Arts (General), Bachelor of Commerce/Business Administration (Accounting, Marketing), Certified Management Accountant, Certified General Accountant, Master of Business Administration (Marketing), and Community College Diploma (Accounting, Marketing/Sales). Graduates would be hired to occupy Clerical, Accounting, Marketing, and Store Management positions. Hard working, a positive attitude, sharp, honest, and ethical are all listed as desirable non-academic qualifications. Company benefits are rated above average. The potential for advancement is listed as being good. The average annual starting salary is dependent upon the position and the qualifications of the applicant. The most suitable method for initial contact by graduates seeking employment is to mail a resume with a covering letter. Kernels Popcorn Ltd. does hire summer students. *Contacts:* Paula Hurley, Store Positions or Loreta Miskinis, Office Positions.

KIMBERLY-CLARK INC.
90 Burnhamthorpe Road West
Mississauga, ON L5B 3Y5

Tel.	905-277-6500
Fax	905-277-6894

Kimberly-Clark Inc. is involved in the manufacture of consumer packaged goods. The company employs approximately 100 people at this location and a total of 230 people in Canada. Graduates most likely to be hired come from the following academic areas: Bachelor of Arts (General), Bachelor of Science (General), Bachelor of Engineering (Chemical, Electrical, Mechanical), Bachelor of Commerce/Business Administration (General, Marketing), Master of Business Administration (General, Marketing), and Community College Diploma (Business, Marketing/Sales). Graduates would occupy Sales Representative and Marketing Assistant positions. Initiative, adaptability and flexibility are all listed as desirable non-academic qualifications. Company benefits are rated above average. The potential for advancement is listed as being good. The average annual starting salary falls within the $30,000 to $35,000 range. The most suitable method for initial contact by graduates seeking employment is to mail a resume with a covering letter. Kimberly-Clark Inc. does hire summer students for Sales Intern positions. *Contact:* Recruiting/Personnel Services.

KINARK CHILD AND FAMILY CARE SERVICES
240 Duncan Mill Road, Suite 402
Don Mills, ON M3B 3B2

Tel.	416-391-3884
Fax	416-444-8896
Email	Kinark@inforamp.net

Kinark Child and Family Care Services is one of the largest and most respected child and family mental health service providers in Ontario. A non-profit organization established in 1984, Kinark operates six Program Centres in the province through the Ministry of Community and Social Services. Services provided include: child, family and group counselling, professional assessments, residential treatment, family preservation, therapeutic foster care, and a special needs camp. Graduates most likely to be hired come from the following academic areas: Master of Social Work, and Community College Diploma (Child and Youth Worker, Early Childhood Educator). Graduates would occupy Social Worker, Child and Youth Worker, and Early Childhood Educator positions. Computer literacy, team player, leadership skills, and excellent communication skills are all listed as desirable non-academic qualifications. Company benefits are rated as excellent. The potential for advancement is listed as being good. The average annual starting salary falls within the $35,000 to $40,000 range. The most suitable method for those seeking employment is to mail a resume with a covering letter. Kinark does hire co-op work term students and summer students, usually for the Outdoor Camping Facility. *Contacts:* Lesley Ford, Manager Human Resources Services or Jane Dawes, Director Human Resources.

KIPLING ACRES HOME FOR THE AGED
2233 Kipling Avenue North
Toronto, ON M9W 4L3

Tel.	416-392-2300
Fax	416-392-3360

Kipling Acres Home for the Aged is a non-profit home for seniors run by the Municipality of Metropolitan Toronto. The home provides a wide range of services for 335 residents in the home, and for nearly 200 seniors in the surrounding community. Kipling Acres employs approximately 450 full and part-time staff in a variety of departments. These include: Administration, Social Work, Recreation, Dietary, Nursing, Housekeeping, Maintenance, Rehabilitation, and Staff Development. Graduates most likely to be hired come from the following academic areas: Bachelor of Arts (Fine Arts, Psychology, Recreation Studies, Sociology, Gerontology), Bachelor of Science (Health Sciences, Nursing, Psychology), Bachelor of Commerce/Business Administration, Master of Arts (Social Work), Master of Science (Health Care Administration, Nursing, Dietary), and Community College Diploma (Accounting, Facility Management, Cooking, Human Resources, Recreation, Social Work, Food/Nutrition, RN, RNA), and High School Diploma. Company benefits are rated as excellent. The potential for advancement is listed as being good. The average annual starting salary falls within the $25,000 to $30,000 range. The most suitable methods for initial contact by those seeking employment are to mail a resume with a covering letter, or by applying in person at this address. *Contact:* Personnel Department.

KLÖCKNER STADLER HURTER LTD.
1400, rue du Fort, bureau 900
Montreal, QC H3H 2T1

Tel.	514-932-4611
Fax	514-932-9700

Klöckner Stadler Hurter Ltd. employs 360 people in the design and supply of pulp and paper mills and other industrial plants in Canada and internationally. Graduates most likely to be hired come from the following academic areas: Bachelor of Engineering (Pollution Treatment, Pulp and Paper, Civil, Electrical, Instrumentation, Mechanical), and Community College Diploma (CAD/CAM/Autocad, Engineering Technician, HVAC Systems Technician). Bachelor of Engineering graduates would occupy Junior Engineer and Junior Specialist positions. Technical Diploma graduates would occupy Technician and Drafting positions. Company benefits are rated as excellent. The potential for advancement is listed as being good. The average annual starting salary for Technicians falls within the $20,000 to $25,000 range. The starting salary for Bachelor of Engineering graduates falls within the $30,000 to $35,000 range. The most suitable method for initial contact by those seeking employment is to mail a resume with a covering letter. *Contact:* Peter Almeida, Vice-President, Human Resources.

KMART CANADA CO.

8925 Torbram Road
Brampton, ON L6T 4G1

Tel. 905-792-4423
Fax 905-792-4576

Kmart Canada Co. is a national retail chain operating stores in all provinces. Kmart employs approximately 12,000 people across Canada. There are 330 employees at the home office. Graduates most likely to be hired come from the following academic areas: Bachelor of Commerce/Business Administration (General, Accounting, Finance, Human Resources, Information Systems), Certified Management Accountant, Certified General Accountant, Master of Business Administration, Community College Diploma (Administration, Business, Human Resources), and High School Diploma. Graduates are hired for Management Trainee positions, progressing to Store Management positions, and for professional positions in Finance, Accounting and Human Resources. The company emphasizes promotion from within where appropriate skills are available. Excellent communication skills, professionalism, team player, management experience, enthusiasm and energy, positive attitude, willingness to relocate, and strong interpersonal skills are all listed as desirable non-academic qualifications. Company benefits are rated above average. The potential for advancement is listed as excellent. The average annual starting salary falls within the $20,000 to $25,000 range, increasing after six month training program. The most suitable methods for initial contact by those seeking employment are to mail or fax a resume with a covering letter. Kmart Canada Co. hires co-op students and students for office assistance at the home office, and retail associates at individual store locations (contact store directly for more information - see your yellow/white pages for nearest location). Contacts: Jackie Chavarie, Director, Human Resource Development or Melissa Law, Human Resource Coordinator.

KNOLL NORTH AMERICA CORP.

1000 Arrow Road
Toronto, ON M9M 2Y7

Tel. 416-741-5453
Fax 416-741-7568
Website .... www.knoll.com

Knoll North America Corp. is a manufacturer of high end wood office furniture. Publicly traded on the New York Stock Exchange, Knoll's head office is located in East Greenville, Pennsylvania. The company operates three plants in Toronto with 75% of its production being exported to the United States. There are 750 employees at this location, a total of 1,000 employees in Canada and a total of 4,800 employees worldwide. Graduates most likely to be hired come from the following academic areas: Bachelor of Science (Chemistry), Bachelor of Engineering (General, Chemical, Electrical, Mechanical, Automation/Robotics, Industrial Design, Industrial Engineering, Industrial Production/Manufacturing), Bachelor of Commerce/Business Administration (Accounting, Human Resources, Marketing), Chartered Accountant, Certified Management Accountant, Certified General Accountant, Master of Business Administration (General, Marketing), Master of Engineering (Industrial Production/Manufacturing), Community College Diploma (Accounting, Communications/Public Relations, Purchasing/Logistics, Secretarial, CAD/CAM/Autocad, Carpentry, Electronics Technician, Engineering Technician, HVAC Systems, Marine Engineering, Welding), and High School Diploma. Graduates would occupy Accounting, Management, and Technical positions in Plant Operations and Plant Support. A high energy level, enthusiasm, common sense, drive, initiative, decision making abilities, and good communication skills are all listed as desirable non-academic qualifications. Company benefits are rated above average. The potential for advancement is listed as excellent. The average annual starting salary falls within the $40,000 to $45,000 range. The most suitable method for initial contact by those seeking employment is to fax a resume with a covering letter. Knoll North America Corp. does hire summer students. Contact: Human Resources.

KNOWLEDGE POWER INCORPORATED

50 Pippy Place, Suite 10B
St. John's, NF A1B 4H7

Tel. 709-726-8866
Fax 709-726-8868
Email .... gpower@knowledgepower.com
Website .... www.knowledgepower.com

Knowledge Power Incorporated (KPI) is an information management and technology consulting firm that provides information technology skills and services to organizations in the public and private sector. Services offered include Marketing Consulting for IT, Resource Contracting Services, IT Training, and IT Consulting. KPI offers the latest in technology skills to help its customers become more productive, efficient and effective. KPI employs a total of 12 professionals. Graduates most likely to be hired come from the following academic areas: Bachelor of Science (General, Computer Science, Mathematics), Bachelor of Engineering (Computer Systems, Instrumentation), Bachelor of Commerce/Business Administration (General, Information Systems, Marketing), Master of Business Administration (General, Information Systems), and Community College Diploma (Information Systems, CAD/CAM/Autocad, Computer Science). Graduates would occupy Junior Programmer, Programmer, and Technical Support positions. Good written and oral communication skills, team player, and self starter are all listed as desirable non-academic qualifications. Company benefits are rated as industry standard. The potential for advancement is listed as excellent. The average annual starting salary falls within the $30,000 to $35,000 range. The most suitable method for initial contact by those seeking employment is to e-mail a resume with a covering letter. Knowledge Power Incorporated does hire summer and co-op work term students. Contact: Human Resources.

KODAK CANADA INC.
3500 Eglinton Avenue West
Toronto, ON M6M 1V3

Tel.	416-766-8233
Fax	416-760-4462
Website	www.kodak.ca

Kodak Canada Inc. is Canada's only major manufacturer of photographic products and the leading supplier of business imaging products for commercial, industrial, government, and health care markets. Kodak employs more than 1,000 people at this location and a total of 1,500 people in Canada. Graduates most likely to be hired come from the following academic areas: Bachelor of Arts (General), Bachelor of Science (General, Chemistry, Computer Science, Health Sciences), Bachelor of Engineering (General, Chemical, Electrical, Industrial, Mechanical), Bachelor of Commerce/Business Administration (Finance, Marketing), Master of Business Administration (Finance, Marketing), Community College Diploma (Accounting, Administration, Business, Electronics Technician), and High School Diploma. Graduates would occupy Service Technician, Financial Analyst, Systems Analyst, Chemical Engineer, Electrical Engineer, Industrial Engineer, Mechanical Engineer, Sales and Marketing, Manufacturing, and Clerical positions. Possessing directly related work experience for the specific position is a definite asset. Company benefits and the potential for advancement are both rated as excellent. The average annual starting salary falls within the $25,000 to $35,000 range. The most suitable method for initial contact by graduates seeking employment is to mail a resume with a covering letter. Kodak Canada Inc. does hire summer students. *Contact:* F.R. Fries, Human Resource Services.

KPMG
P.O. Box 31
Station Commerce Court
Toronto, ON M5L 1B2

Tel.	416-777-8500
Fax	416-777-8818

KPMG provides accounting, bookkeeping and related services to individuals and organizations. Practice areas include: Audit, Tax, Computer Audit, Forensics, Solvency Services, Valuations/Mergers and Acquisitions, and Management Consulting. There are more than 500 people employed at this location. KPMG maintains office locations across Canada. Graduates most likely to be hired come from the following academic areas: Bachelor of Arts (Economics, Business Related), Bachelor of Laws, Bachelor of Commerce/Business Administration (Accounting, Finance), Chartered Accountant, Master of Business Administration (Accounting), Master of Arts (Economics), and Community College Diploma (Accounting). Business and people oriented work experience, good interpersonal and communication skills, and extra-curricular involvement are all listed as desirable non-academic qualifications. Company benefits and the potential for advancement are both rated as excellent. The average annual starting salary falls within the $25,000 to $30,000 range. The most suitable method for initial contact by those seeking employment is to mail a resume with a covering letter. KPMG does hire a limited number of summer students annually (traditionally summer is not the busiest season). *Contact:* Manager, Human Resources.

KUEHNE & NAGEL INTERNATIONAL LTD.
5935 Airport Road
Mississauga, ON L4V 1X3

Tel.	905-673-3981
Fax	905-673-0006

Kuehne & Nagel International Ltd. is a international transportation and logistics company active in freight forwarding, international logistics, customs brokerage, warehousing and distribution services. There are 200 employees at this location, a total of 1,000 employees in Canada, and 12,000 employees worldwide. Graduates most likely to be hired come from the following academic areas: Bachelor of Arts (General), Bachelor of Commerce/Business Administration (General, International Business), Community College Diploma (International Business, Purchasing/Logistics), and C.I.F.F.A., C.S.C.B., P.LOG. accreditations. Graduates would occupy Trainee/Apprentice, Clerk, Customer Service Representative, and Sales Support positions. Good communication and problem solving skills, fluency in foreign languages (Spanish in particular), and previous experience in international freight movement are all listed as desirable non-academic qualifications. Company benefits and the potential for advancement are both rated as excellent. The average annual starting salary falls within the $20,000 to $25,000 range. The most suitable method for initial contact by those seeking employment is to mail a resume with a covering letter. Kuehne & Nagel International Ltd. does hire summer students. *Contacts:* Cathy Bilotta, Manager, Human Resources - Head Office or Ray Getson, Manager, Human Resources - KN Logistics.

LAIDLAW INC.
3221 North Service Road
P.O. Box 5028
Burlington, ON L7R 3Y8

Tel.	905-336-1800
Fax	905-336-3900
Email	dblock@laidlaw.com

Laidlaw Inc. is recognized as the leading North American service company providing school busing and public transit, emergency and non-emergency healthcare transportation, and the management of physician's practices within hospital emergency departments. Laidlaw's 94,500 employees operate from more than 900 locations throughout the United States and Canada. There are 150 employees at this location and a total of 9,500 employees in Canada. Laidlaw is dedicated to delivering predictable and growing returns to its shareholders. The company has grown through acquisition, by improving its operations, and by gaining new customers. Graduates most likely to be hired come from the following academic areas: Bachelor of Science (Computer Science), Bachelor of Commerce/Business Administration (Accounting, Finance, Human Resources, Information Systems), Chartered Accountant, Certified Management Accountant, Certified General Accountant, Master of Business Administration (Accounting, Finance), Community College Diploma (Accounting, Business, Communications/Public Relations, Human Resources, Information Systems, Secretarial, Legal Assistant, Computer Science, Ambulance/Emergency Care), and High School Diploma. Graduates would occupy Clerk, Accountant, Secretary, Computer Programmer, Systems Analyst, Business Analyst, and Sales Representative positions. Previous related work experience, good oral and written communication skills, adaptable to change, team player, computer skills, and an ability to think strategically are all listed as desirable non-academic qualifications. Company benefits are rated as industry standard. The potential for advancement is listed as average. The most suitable method for initial contact by those seeking employment is to mail a resume with a covering letter. Laidlaw Inc. does hire summer and co-op work term students, generally in the finance and tax department. *Contact:* Debbie Block, Manager, Human Resources.

LAMBERT SOMEC INC.
1505 Des Tanneurs
Quebec, QC G1N 4S7

Tel. 418-687-1640
Fax 418-688-7577

Lambert Somec Inc. is a specialized construction contractor providing electrical, plumbing, piping, HVAC and industrial mechanical services. The company employs approximately 400 people. Graduates most likely to be hired come from the following academic areas: Bachelor of Science (Metallurgy, Physics), Bachelor of Engineering (General, Metallurgy, Pulp and Paper, Electrical, Instrumentation, Hydro-Power, Mechanical, Welding, Petroleum), Bachelor of Commerce/Business Administration, Chartered Accountant, Certified Management Accountant, and Community College Diploma (Engineering Technician, HVAC Systems Technician, Welding). Work experience in the construction field, good team work habits, and a willingness to learn are all listed as desirable non-academic qualifications. Company benefits are rated above average. The potential for advancement is listed as average. The average annual starting salary falls within the $25,000 to $30,000 range. The most suitable methods for initial contact by those seeking employment are to mail a resume with a covering letter, or through personal contacts. Lambert Somec Inc. does hire summer students. *Contact:* Ann Martell, Human Resource Director.

LAMSON & SESSIONS OF CANADA LIMITED
5190 Bradco Boulevard
Mississauga, ON L4W 1G7

Tel. 905-624-4490
Fax 905-624-6195

Lamson & Sessions of Canada Limited employs more than 50 people in the manufacture and sale of industrial fasteners to the automotive industry. Graduates most likely to be hired are Community College graduates from Engineering Technology programs. Graduates would occupy Technician, Engineer, and Manager positions. Able to translate theory into practical applications, be independently motivated requiring no strong supervision, and good problem solving and supervisory skills are all listed as desirable non-academic qualifications. Company benefits are rated above average. The potential for advancement is listed as average. The most suitable method for initial contact by those seeking employment is to mail a resume with a covering letter. Lamson & Sessions of Canada Limited does hire summer students as needs require. *Contact:* Mr. C.L. Dahl, General Manager.

LANZAROTTA WHOLESALE GROCERS LTD.
10 Ronrose Drive
Concord, ON L4K 4R3

Tel. 905-669-9814
Fax 905-669-9570

Lanzarotta Wholesale Grocers Ltd. is a privately owned, wholesale grocery distributor of dry goods and frozen foods, including dairy products. Operating within Ontario are six cash and carry locations (Metro Toronto), and five retail grocery stores (Northern Communities only). Lanzarotta's main customers are independent grocers and grocery chains. There are approximately 150 employees at this location and a total of 365 employees in the company. Graduates most likely to be hired come from the following academic areas: Bachelor of Commerce/Business Administration (General, Accounting, Finance, Human Resources, Information Systems, Marketing), Community College Diploma (Accounting, Administration, Business, Human Resources, Marketing/Sales, Purchasing/Logistics), and High School Diploma. Graduates would occupy Accounts Payable Clerk, Accounts Receivable Clerk, Human Resources Assistant, Payroll Clerk, Data Entry Clerk, Accounting Clerk, Secretary/Receptionist, Customer Service Representative, Junior Buyer, Buyer, Administrative Assistant, Order Selector, Stock Clerk, Store Manager, Assistant Manager, and Grocery Manager positions. A positive attitude towards work, good interpersonal and communication skills, team player, organized, good problem solver and decision maker, related work experience, and a willingness to learn and adapt to change are all listed as desirable non-academic qualifications. Company benefits are rated above average. The potential for advancement is listed as average. The most suitable method for initial contact by those seeking employment is to mail a resume with a covering letter. *Contact:* Robert Santobuono, Human Resources Supervisor.

LAURA SECORD
1500 Birchmount Road
Toronto, ON M1P 2G5

Tel. 416-285-2505

Fax 416-751-8976
Email .... hr.birchmount@ca.nestle.com

Laura Secord is involved in the manufacturing and retailing of confectionery products. The company employs 300 people across Canada. Graduates most likely to be hired come from the following academic areas: Bachelor of Arts (General), Bachelor of Science (General), Bachelor of Commerce/Business Administration (Accounting, Finance, Human Resources, Information Systems, Marketing), Certified General Accountant, and Community College Diploma (Accounting, Administration, Advertising, Business, Communications, Facility Management, Human Resources, Marketing/Sales, Purchasing/Logistics, Secretarial, Computer Science, Dietician/Nutrition, Laboratory Technician, Nursing RN). Good communication skills, leadership abilities, and problem solving skills are all listed as desirable non-academic qualifications. Company benefits and the potential for advancement are both rated as excellent. The most suitable method for initial contact by those seeking employment is to mail a resume with a covering letter. Laura Secord does hire a limited number of summer and co-op work term students. Contacts: Ms Jo-Ann Latham, Human Resources Manager (Factory) or Mr. Rob Takimoto, Human Resources Manager (Office).

LAURENTIAN BANK OF CANADA
130 Adelaide Street West
Ground Floor
Toronto, ON M5H 3P5

Tel. 416-947-5100

Laurentian Bank of Canada is a full service financial institution offering consumer banking products to their client base, including deposit accounts, GIC's, RRSP's, mutual funds, personal loans, mortgages, and lines of credit. There are more than 25 employees at this location. Graduates most likely to be hired come from the following academic areas: Bachelor of Arts (Economics), Bachelor of Science (Computer Science, Mathematics), Bachelor of Commerce/Business Administration (Accounting, Marketing), Master of Business Administration, and Community College Diploma (Accounting, Administration, Business, Communications, Marketing/Sales, Secretarial). A professional attitude and appearance, sales and marketing orientation, and a quality customer service orientation are all listed as desirable non-academic qualifications. Graduates would occupy entry level Customer Service Representative positions, with the Management Training Program available after one year of service. Company benefits are rated above average. The potential for advancement is listed as being good. The average annual starting salary falls within the $20,000 to $30,000 range. The most suitable method for initial contact by those seeking employment is to mail a resume with a covering letter (no telephone calls please). Laurentian Bank of Canada does hire summer students. Contact: Cindy Gunderson, Human Resources.

LE CHÂTEAU
5695 Ferrier
Montreal, QC H4P 1N1

Tel. 514-738-7000
Fax 514-738-8288

Le Château is a leading retailer of apparel, accessories and footwear aimed at young spirited, fashion conscious men, women and kids. It is the company's vertically integrated approach, combined with its design strength, the gives Le Château a competitive edge and allows it to maintain its brand appeal in a rapidly changing market. Le Château's brand name clothing is sold mainly through its 145 retail stores. Stores average 3,000 square feet in size, and all are located in Canada with the exception of three which are located in the United States. The company is committed to research, design and product development, and manufactures approximately 65% of its goods in its own Canadian production facilities, located at the head office in Montreal. Le Château employs 300 people at this location and a total of 2,000 people. Graduates most likely to be hired come from the following academic areas: Bachelor of Commerce/Business Administration (Accounting), Community College Diploma (Fashion Arts, Graphic Arts, Computer Science), and High School Diploma. Enthusiastic, a high energy level, and hard working are listed as desirable non-academic qualifications. Company benefits are rated as industry standard. The potential for advancement is listed as being good. The most suitable method for initial contact by those seeking employment is to fax a resume with a covering letter. Le Château does hire summer students. Contacts: Coleen Mann, Human Resources Director or Nicole Fortier, Human Resources Manager.

LEADER-POST, THE
1964 Park Street
Regina, SK S4P 3G4

Tel. 306-565-8211
Fax 306-565-7484

The Leader-Post publishes Regina's daily newspaper and a wide range of commercial print products. The Leader-Post employs approximately 400 people. Graduates most likely to be hired come from the following academic areas: Bachelor of Arts (English, Journalism, Political Science), Bachelor of Science (Computer Science), Bachelor of Engineering (Computer Systems), Bachelor of Commerce/Business Administration (Accounting), Certified Management Accountant, and Community College Diploma (Accounting, Advertising, Marketing/Sales, Secretarial, Graphic Arts, Journalism, Computer Science, Electronics Technician, Engineering Technician). Good oral and written communications skills, flexibility, leadership potential, experience, attitude, and focused personal objectives are all listed as desirable non academic qualifications. Company benefits are rated as excellent. The potential for advancement is listed as being good. The average entry level starting salary falls within the $15,000 to $20,000 range, and is commission based for some positions.

The most suitable method for initial contact by those seeking employment is to mail a resume with a covering letter. The Leader-Post hires 4 month journalism interns twice a year. Also, the Paper has contract positions that may become available during the summer months. *Contact:* Ms. J. Dockham, Human Resources Manager.

LEGO CANADA INC.
380 Markland Street
Markham, ON L6C 1T6

Tel.	905-887-5346
Fax	905-887-1171

LEGO Canada Inc. is involved in the distribution of construction toys. There are 70 employees at this location, a total of 115 in Canada, and a total of 10,000 employees worldwide. Graduates most likely to be hired come from the following academic areas: Bachelor of Arts (General), Bachelor of Science (General, Computer Science), Bachelor of Commerce/Business Administration (Accounting, Finance, Human Resources, Information Systems, Marketing), Chartered Accountant, Certified General Accountant, and Community College Diploma (Accounting, Administration, Business, Human Resources, Marketing/Sales, Computer Science). Graduates would occupy Sales Planning Analyst, Credit Representative, Accountant, Programmer/ Analyst, Consumer Services Representative, and Assistant Brand Manager positions. Team player, able to work in fast paced environment, self-motivated, energetic, and detail oriented are all listed as desirable non-academic qualifications. Company benefits are rated as excellent. The most suitable method for initial contact by those seeking employment is to mail a resume with a covering letter. LEGO Canada Inc. hires summer students for the LEGO Creative Play Centre at Ontario Place in Toronto. *Contact:* Wendy LaValle, Human Resources Manager.

LEHNDORFF MANAGEMENT LIMITED
390 Bay Street
Toronto, ON M5H 2Y2

Tel.	416-869-7800
Fax	416-869-7851

Lehndorff Management Limited is a real estate development company. Activities include, Property Management, Real Estate Investment, Risk Management, Asset Management, Development, Re-Development, Syndication and Mutual Fund Management. The company employs approximately 80 staff at this location and a total of 280 employees across Canada. Graduates most likely to be hired come from the following academic areas: Bachelor of Engineering (Computer Systems, Mechanical), Bachelor of Laws (Corporate), Bachelor of Commerce/Business Administration (Accounting, Finance, Human Resources, Information Systems), Chartered Accountant, Certified Management Accountant, Certified General Accountant, Community College Diploma (Accounting, Administration, Business, Human Resources, Insurance, Secretarial, Computer Science, HVAC Systems), and High School Diploma. Graduates would be hired to occupy Managerial, Clerical, Technical, Secretarial and Administrative positions. Related work experience, team player, positive work attitude, professionalism, and good problem solving skills are all listed as desirable non-academic qualifications. Company benefits are rated above average. The potential for advancement is listed as average. The average annual starting salary falls within the $30,000 to $35,000 range. The most suitable method for initial contact by those seeking employment is to mail a resume with a covering letter. Lehndorff Management Limited does employ summer students. *Contact:* Michelle Ziegler, Manager, Human Resources.

LENNOX INDUSTRIES (CANADA) LTD.
400 Norris Glen Road
Toronto, ON M9C 1H5

Tel.	416-621-9302
Fax	416-621-6303

Lennox Industries (Canada) Ltd. is a leading manufacturer of heating, ventilation and air conditioning products. The corporate head office is located in Dallas, Texas. Sales and distribution districts are located throughout Canada in most major cities. There are more than 100 employees at the Canadian head office located in Toronto. Graduates most likely to be hired come from the following academic areas: Bachelor of Arts (General, Psychology), Bachelor of Science (Computer Science, Psychology), Bachelor of Engineering (Mechanical, Industrial), Bachelor of Commerce/Business Administration (General, Accounting, Finance), Chartered Accountant, Certified Management Accountant, Certified General Accountant (Finance), Master of Engineering, and Community College Diploma (Administration, Marketing/Sales, HVAC Systems, Industrial Design). An exciting blend of Technical and Administrative opportunities are available for graduates. Leadership potential, computer literacy, and good communication, interpersonal and organizational skills are all listed as desirable non-academic qualifications. Company benefits are rated above average. The potential for advancement is listed as being good. The average annual starting salary falls within the $30,000 to $35,000 range. The most suitable method for initial contact by those seeking employment is to mail a resume with a covering letter. *Contacts:* Wendy Purvis, Manager, Safety, Health & Labour Relations; Brian Hughes, Manager, Human Resources or Doug Ross, Director, Organization Development.

LENWORTH METAL PRODUCTS LIMITED
275 Carrier Drive
Rexdale, ON M9W 5Y8

Tel.	416-675-9390
Fax	416-675-6874

Lenworth Metal Products Limited employs more than 25 people in the manufacture and metal fabrication of steel containers. Graduates most likely to be hired come from the following academic areas: Bachelor of Engineering, Bachelor of Commerce/Bachelor Business Administration, Chartered Accountant, and Certified Management Accountant. Graduates would occupy Office Manager, Controller, Quality Assurance, and Drafting/Estimator positions. Aggressiveness, reliability, initiative, dedication and promptness are all listed as desirable non-academic qualifications. Company benefits are rated as industry standard. The potential for advancement is listed as being good. The average annual starting salary falls within the $20,000 to $25,000 range. The most suitable method for initial contact by graduates seeking employment is to mail a resume with a covering letter. *Contact:* Payroll Department.

LEVI STRAUSS & CO. (CANADA) INC.
1725 16th Avenue
Richmond Hill, ON L4B 4C6

Tel. 905-763-2777
Fax 905-763-4401

Levi Strauss & Co. (Canada) Inc. is a major manufacturer of jeans and jean related products. The company employs approximately 250 people at this location, a total of 2,200 people in Canada, and 35,000 people worldwide. Graduates most likely to be hired come from the following academic areas: Bachelor of Arts (General), Bachelor of Science (Textiles), Bachelor of Commerce/Business Administration, Chartered Accountant, Certified Management Accountant, Certified General Accountant, Master of Business Administration, Community College Diploma (Accounting, Administration, Business, Human Resources, Marketing/Sales, Purchasing/Logistics, Secretarial, CAD/CAM/Autocad, HVAC Systems), and High School Diploma. Graduates would occupy various positions relating to their academic backgrounds. Team player and initiative are both listed as desirable non-academic qualifications. Company benefits are rated above average. The potential for advancement is listed as being good. The most suitable method for initial contact by those seeking employment is to mail a resume with a covering letter. Levi Strauss & Co. (Canada) Inc. hires a few summer students annually. *Contact:* Human Resources Specialist.

LEVY PILOTTE, CHARTERED ACCOUNTANTS
5250 Decarie Blvd.
7th Floor
Montreal, QC H3X 3Z6

Tel. 514-487-1566
Fax 514-488-5145
Email .... levypilotte@levypilotte.com
Website .... www.levypilotte.com

Levy Pilotte, Chartered Accountants is a chartered accountancy firm employing approximately 45 people in Montreal. Graduates most likely to be hired come from the following academic areas: Bachelor of Commerce/Business Administration (Accounting, Information Systems), Chartered Accountant, Certi-

fied General Accountant, Master of Business Administration (Accounting), and Community College Diploma (Accounting). Graduates would occupy Audit Trainee and Junior Accountant positions. Team player, leadership qualities, and previous accounting work experience are all listed as desirable non-academic qualifications. Company benefits are rated above average. The potential for advancement is listed as excellent. The average annual starting salary falls within the $25,000 to $30,000 range. The most suitable method for initial contact by those seeking employment is to fax a resume with a covering letter. Levy Pilotte, Chartered Accountants does hire students for summer and co-op work terms. *Contacts:* Raouf Guirguis, Partner or Nick Vannelli, Partner.

LGS GROUP INC.
1155 Metcalfe Street
12th Floor
Montreal, QC H3B 2V6

Tel. 514-861-2673
Fax 514-861-3832
Email .... rrichter@lgs.ca
Website .... www.lgs.ca

LGS Group Inc. is one of Canada's leading systems integration firms, providing consulting in all aspects of information technology and management. The company's aim is to establish state-of-the-art solutions, adapted and suited to the business environments of its clients. LGS Group Inc. employs approximately 300 people at this location, a total of 1,100 people in Canada, and a total of 1,200 people worldwide. Graduates most likely to be hired come from the following academic areas: Bachelor of Science (Computer Science, Mathematics), Bachelor of Engineering (Computer Systems), Master of Business Administration (Finance, Information Systems), Master of Science (Computer Science), Master of Engineering (Electrical, Computer Systems), and Doctorate (Information/Computer Systems). Graduates would occupy Programmer/Analyst, Technical Support Technician, Analyst, and Technical Analyst. Excellent written and spoken and communication skills, and the practical application of academic courses are listed as desirable non-academic qualifications. Company benefits and the potential for advancement are both rated as excellent. The average annual starting salary falls within the $30,000 to $35,000 range. The most suitable method for initial contact by those seeking employment is to mail a resume with a covering letter. LGS Group Inc. does hire summer students. *Contacts:* Lisa Gabrielle or Rick Richter.

LICHTMAN'S NEWS AND BOOKS
24 Ryerson Avenue, Suite 400
Toronto, ON M5T 2P3

Tel. 416-703-7773
Fax 416-703-1078
Email .... lichtman@ican.net
Website .... www.lichtman.com

Lichtman's News and Books operates a chain of retail stores, specializing in newspapers, magazines and books. Lichtman's features over 240 newspapers from around the world, 4,400 magazine titles, and over 60,000 book titles. There are 13 employees at the head office, and a total of 165 employees in the company. Graduates most likely to be hired are Bachelor of Arts and Bachelor of Science graduates. Graduates would occupy Management Trainee, Book Buyer, Operations Co-ordinator, and Store Manager positions. An entrepreneurial spirit coupled with unparalleled customer service skills are listed as desirable non-academic qualifications. Company benefits are rated above average. The potential for advancement is listed as being good. The average annual starting salary falls within the $15,000 to $20,000 range. The most suitable method for initial contact by those seeking employment is to mail a resume with a covering letter. Lichtman's News and Books hires summer students for store positions. *Contact:* General Manager.

LILY CUPS INC.
2121 Markham Road
Toronto, ON M1B 2W3

Tel. 416-691-2181
Fax 416-691-3665

Lily Cups Inc. is involved in the manufacture of paper and polystyrene cups and food containers for the food service industry. Lily Cups Inc. is a leader within the industry on environmental issues. The company is committed to the concepts of waste reduction, reuse, recycling and recovery in the context of environmental stewardship. The company employs a total of 450 people. Graduates most likely to be hired come from the following academic areas: Bachelor of Science (Chemistry, Computer Science), Bachelor of Engineering (General), Bachelor of Commerce/Business Administration (Accounting, Finance, Information Systems, Marketing), and Community College Diploma (Accounting, Administration, Human Resources, Marketing/Sales, Secretarial). Graduates would occupy Laboratory Technician, Engineer, Junior and Intermediate Accountant, Human Resources Administration, Secretarial, and Junior Sales and Marketing positions. Applicants must be team players, organized, possess appropriate work experience, knowledge of Total Quality Management, and be able to work independently and manage pressure/deadline situations. Company benefits are rated above average. The potential for advancement is listed as being good. The average annual starting salary falls within the $25,000 to $30,000 range. The most suitable method for initial contact by those seeking employment is to mail a resume with a covering letter (no telephone calls please). Lily Cups does hire summer students for plant positions and occasionally for office positions, as well as occasionally hiring co-op work term students. *Contacts:* Diane Budd, Human Resources Coordinator (Salaried Personnel) or Suzanne Ruffo, Benefits Administrator (Hourly Personnel).

LINCOLN PLACE NURSING HOME
429 Walmer Road
Toronto, ON M5P 2X9

Tel. 416-967-6949
Fax 416-928-1965

Lincoln Place Nursing Home employs approximately 260 people in the operation of a nursing home for the aged. Graduates most likely to be hired come from the following academic areas: Bachelor of Arts (Music, Recreation Studies, Sociology), Bachelor of Science (Nursing, Nutritional Sciences, Occupational Therapy, Physical Therapy, Speech Pathology), Bachelor of Education (Adult), Bachelor of Commerce/Business Administration (Human Resources, Information Systems, Marketing, Public Administration), Master of Business Administration (Human Resources, Information Systems, Marketing), and Community College Diploma (Recreation Studies, Health Promotion, Massage Therapy, Nursing RN/RNA, Social Work). Graduates would occupy Nurse, Nurses Aide, Music Therapist, Art Therapist, Recreational Therapist, Nurse Educator, Information Management Specialist, Nurse Manager, and Health Promotion Therapist positions. Team player (very important), group skills, innovative problem solving skills, and creativity are all listed as desirable non-academic qualifications. Company benefits are rated as industry standard. The potential for advancement is listed as average. The average annual starting salary falls within the $15,000 to $50,000 range, depending on the position being considered. The most suitable method for initial contact by those seeking employment is to mail a resume with a covering letter. *Contacts:* Marie Colliss, Nurse Manager (NSG) or Tulia Ferreira, Administrator (Administration).

LINK COMPUTER CONSULTING LTD.
1275 West 6th Avenue, Suite 332
Vancouver, BC V6H 1A6

Tel. 604-732-5012
Fax 604-738-7134
Email .... sunnyk@linkconsulting.com
Website .... www.linkconsulting.com

Link Computer Consulting Ltd. is a consulting firm which specializes in placing information technology professionals into contract opportunities with clients in British Columbia. Presently, the company has over 20 contract professionals located in the province. Graduates most likely to be recruited come from the following academic areas: Bachelor of Science (Computer Science), Bachelor of Commerce/Business Administration (Information Systems), Master of Science (Computer Science), and Community College Diploma (Computer Science). Graduates are recruited for Programmer Analyst, Systems Analyst, Project Manager, Business Analyst, Technical Writer, and Telecommunication Specialist positions. Applicants should have a minimum of three years experience. The most suitable methods for initial contact by those seeking employment are to mail, fax or e-mail a resume with a covering letter. *Contacts:* Sunny L. Kae or Andy J. Fitzpatrick.

LOCKHEED MARTIN CANADA

6111 avenue Royalmount
Montreal, QC H4P 1K6

Tel. 514-340-8317
Fax 514-340-8314
Email .... imcda.hr@lmco.ca
Website .... www.lmco.com/canada

Lockheed Martin Canada is a highly diversified global enterprise, principally engaged in the research, design, manufacture and integration of advanced-technology products. The company is a leader in systems integration, software development and large scale program management, and Canada's premier supplier of electronic defence and surveillance systems. Primary capabilities encompass the integration and management of complex computer-based electronic systems; the design, manufacture and supply of military-standard computers; electronic warfare; sonar and security systems; and the provision of life cycle support for major platforms. Lockheed Martin employs 175 people at this location, a total of 700 people in Canada, and 190,000 people worldwide. Graduates most likely to be hired come from the following academic areas: Bachelor of Science (Computer Science, Mathematics, Physics), Bachelor of Engineering (Electrical, Mechanical, Aerospace, Computer Systems), Master of Science (Computer Science), Master of Engineering (Electrical Engineering, Computer Systems), and Community College Diploma (Computer Science). Graduates would occupy Software Engineering Specialist, Hardware Engineering Specialist, and Systems Engineering Specialist positions. Team player, initiative, and creativity are listed as desirable non-academic qualifications. Company benefits are rated above average. The potential for advancement is listed as being good. The average annual starting salary falls within the $35,000 to $40,000 range. The most suitable methods for initial contact by those seeking employment are to mail, fax or e-mail a resume with a covering letter. Lockheed Martin Canada does hire summer and co-op work term students. *Contact:* Lucie-Marie Gauthier, Human Resources, Montreal.

LOMBARD CANADA LTD.

105 Adelaide Street West
Toronto, ON M5H 1P9

Tel. 416-350-4400
Fax 416-350-4106

Lombard Canada Ltd. is one of Canada's top ten general/property and casualty insurance companies. The company is 100% Canadian owned, employs 500 people at this location, and a total of 700 people across the country. Graduates most likely to be hired come from the following academic areas: Bachelor of Arts (General, Economics, Psychology, Sociology), Bachelor of Science (General, Actuarial, Computer Science, Mathematics), Bachelor of Engineering (Computer Systems, Mechanical), Bachelor of Commerce/Business Administration (General, Accounting, Finance, Human Resources, Information Systems, Marketing), Chartered Accountant (General, Insurance), Certified Management Accountant (General, Insurance), Certified General Accountant (General, Insurance), Master of Business Administration (Finance, Marketing), and Community College Diploma (Accounting, Administration, Business, Facility Management, Financial Planning, Human Resources, Insurance, Computer Science). Graduates would occupy Underwriting Trainee (commercial and personal lines), Claims Trainee, Computer Technician, Financial Analyst, Business Analyst, Human Resources Consultant, Customer Service Representative, and Accounting positions. Previous related work experience, good communication skills, customer focus, commitment, positive attitude, accountable, team player, leadership skills, motivated, creative, and innovative are all listed as desirable non-academic qualifications. Company benefits are rated as excellent. The potential for advancement is listed as being good. The average annual starting salary falls within the $28,000 to $35,000 range. The most suitable method for initial contact by those seeking employment is to mail a resume with a covering letter. Lombard Canada Ltd. does hire summer students on a limited basis. *Contact:* Diana Iddon, Human Resources Administrator.

LONG & MCQUADE LIMITED

1744 Midland Avenue
Toronto, ON M1P 3C2

Tel. 416-751-9785

Long & McQuade Limited operates music instrument sales and rental stores. In addition to this head office location there are three store locations in Metropolitan Toronto. Graduates most likely to be hired at this location are Bachelor of Commerce/Business Administration, and Chartered Accountant graduates. Graduates would occupy various Accounting and Administration positions. Graduates should possess a strong business background. The most suitable method for initial contact by graduates seeking employment is to mail a resume with a covering letter. *Contact:* Controller.

LOTEK ENGINEERING INC.

115 Pony Drive
Newmarket, ON L3Y 7B5

Tel. 905-836-6680
Fax 905-836-6455
Email .... positions@lotek.com
Website .... www.lotek.com/lotek

Lotek Engineering Inc. designs and manufactures wildlife telemetry products for use in biological research. Lotek's sister company, Lotek Marine Technologies, is located in St. John's, Newfoundland and specializes in marine applications. The company's technology is considered leading edge and its customer base is worldwide. Lotek employs 60 people at this location and a total of 100 people in Canada. Graduates most likely to be hired come from the following academic areas: Bachelor of Science (Biology), Bachelor of Engineering (Electrical, Microelectronics), Bachelor of Commerce/Business Administration (Marketing), Community College Diploma (Accounting, Marketing/Sales, Electronics Technician), and High School Diploma. Graduates would occupy Marketing and Sales Specialist, Sales Person, Accounting Clerk, Software Engineer, Hardware Engineer, Assembler, and Electronics Technician positions. Organized, good communication skills, confidence, energetic, team player, initiative, and adaptability are all listed as desirable non-academic qualifications. Company benefits are rated above average. The potential for advancement is listed as being good. The average annual starting salary falls within the $25,000 to $30,000 range. The most suitable method for initial contact by those seeking employment is to mail a resume with a covering letter. Lotek Engineering Inc. does hire summer and co-op work term students. *Contact:* Human Resources Manager.

LOVAT INC.
441 Carlingview Drive
Toronto, ON M9W 5G7

Tel. 416-675-3293
Fax 416-675-6702
Email .... tbm@lovat.com
Website .... www.lovat.com

Lovat Inc. is the Canadian based world leader in the manufacture of customized Tunnel Boring Machines (TBMs) utilized for the construction of tunnels for the transportation, sewer, water main, mining and telecommunications industries. The company was founded in 1972 to improve safety and efficiency of tunnelling operations. Since then, Lovat has built over 180 TBM's which have completed more than 350 tunnelling projects on six continents. From Seattle to Cairo to Bangkok, Lovat machines have excavated more than 825,000m of tunnel in over twenty countries. Lovat specializes in shield rock, mixed face, soft ground, EPB and Slurry TBMs, and open face tunnel shields ranging from 1.5 metres to 14 metres in diameter. Continually expanding with market demands, the company presently employs 276 specialized engineering, production, sales, service support, and marketing personnel at its head office and manufacturing facilities in Toronto. Even with more than 98 percent of sales being exports, 90 percent of all Lovat products are built at the Toronto plant. Throughout Europe and Asia, first-line support of all TBMs operation on the continents is provided by Lovat's Europe office (based near Birmingham, United Kingdom), and Lovat's Asia office (based in Alexandria, Australia). Elsewhere, an international network of Representatives assist to monitor global tunnelling activity, open new markets and support operating TBMs within their territories. Graduates most likely to be hired come from the following academic areas: Bachelor of Arts (General), Bachelor of Engineering (Electrical, Mechanical), Certified Management Accountant, Certified General Accountant, and Community College Diploma (CAD/CAM/Autocad, Fluid Power Technologist, Mechanical Technologist, Electrical Technologist). Graduates would occupy Junior Draftsperson, Junior Designer, Intern Accountant, Receptionist, Administrative Assistant, and Plant Helper positions. Creativity, innovation, team player, and flexibility are all listed as desirable non-academic qualifications. Company benefits are rated above average. The potential for advancement is listed as being good. The average annual starting salary falls within the $30,000 to $35,000 range. The most suitable methods for initial contact by those seeking employment are to mail or fax a resume with a covering letter. Lovat Inc. does hire summer and co-op work term students. *Contact:* Human Resources.

LOYALTY MANAGEMENT GROUP CANADA INC.
4110 Yonge Street, 2nd Floor
Toronto, ON M2P 2B7

Tel. 416-228-6500
Fax 416-733-9712
Website .... www.airmiles.ca

Loyalty Management Group Canada Inc. is the owner of the highly successful Air Miles Rewards Program in Canada. Loyalty's data driven organization is recognized for its leading edge database capabilities, as well as its insight on the motivations and actions of its Air Miles Collectors. Founded in 1991 as a data management company, the Company's business has grown to include expertise in loyalty programs (Air Miles), direct marketing, marketing research and analysis, retail systems technical development, retail database warehouse development consulting services and the company's very own full service travel agency (Extra Miles Agency). Presently, the company employs 425 people. Graduates most likely to be hired come from the following academic areas: Bachelor of Arts (General, Economics, Psychology), Bachelor of Science (Computer Science, Mathematics), Bachelor of Engineering (Computer Systems), Bachelor of Commerce/Business Administration (General, Accounting, Finance, Human Resources, Information Systems, Marketing), Certified Management Accountant, Certified General Accountant, Master of Business Administration (General, Information Systems, Marketing), and Community College Diploma (Advertising, Marketing/Sales, Travel/Tourism). Graduates would occupy Business Analyst, Account Executive, Account Manager, Programmer/Analyst, Marketing/Sales Representative, Travel Service Representative, Travel Specialist, Analytics, Accounting, and Finance positions. Team oriented, professional, articulate, results oriented, driven, ambitious, entrepreneurial, able to balance work with outside interests, and possessing previous work experience relevant to the field are all listed as desirable non-academic qualifications. Company benefits and the potential for advancement are both rated as excellent. The average annual starting salary falls within the $35,000 to $40,000 range. The most suitable methods for initial contact by those seeking employment are to mail or fax a resume with a covering letter. Loyalty Management Group Canada Inc. does hire college and university students for summer and co-op work terms. *Contact:* Corporate Recruiter, Human Resources.

LUMONICS

105 Schneider Road
Kanata, ON K2K 1Y3

Tel.	613-592-4375
Fax	613-599-2550
Email	hr@lumonics.com
Website	www.lumonics.com

Founded in 1970, Lumonics is a public company and a world leader in the development, design, manufacture and marketing of laser-based advanced manufacturing systems for the semiconductor, electronics, aerospace, automotive and packaging markets. These systems are used in highly automated environments for applications such as cutting, drilling, welding and coding a wide range of products and materials. Global demand for Lumonics' products has opened up new job opportunities in the company's Kanata facility. Presently, Lumonics employs 135 people at this location, a total of 200 people in Canada, and 1,000 employees worldwide. Graduates most likely to be hired come from the following academic areas: Bachelor of Science (Computer Science, Physics) and Bachelor of Engineering (Electrical, Mechanical, Engineering Physics). Team oriented, enthusiastic, and flexible are listed as desirable non-academic qualifications. Company benefits are rated above average. The potential for advancement is listed as excellent. The average annual starting salary falls within the $35,000 to $40,000 range. The most suitable method for initial contact by those seeking employment is to e-mail a resume with a covering letter. Lumonics does hire summer and co-op work term students. *Contacts:* Shelley Browne, Manager, Human Resources or Beth Typhair, Human Resources Administrator.

M3I SYSTEMS INC.

1111, St-Charles ouest, 11th Floor
Longueuil, QC J4K 5G4

Tel.	514-928-4600
Fax	514-442-5076

M3i Systems Inc. is a world leader in the development, implementation and support of integrated software systems for distribution operations and dispatch management. Specializing in command centre support systems, M3i provides innovative operational solutions for electric, gas and water utilities, for emergency response organizations, and for the transportation and telecommunications industries. Initially created within the operations of Hydro-Québec, M3i Systems Inc. was incorporated in 1990 and has since grown from seven to over 400 employees, and today has offices in Ottawa, Los Angeles, Chicago, Pittsburgh, Seattle, Birmingham (United Kingdom), Paris, and Singapore. Graduates most likely to be hired come from the following academic areas: Bachelor of Arts (English), Bachelor of Science (Computer Science), Bachelor of Engineering (Computer Systems, Microelectronics), and Community College Diploma (Computer Science, Electronics Technician). Graduates would occupy Programmer (all levels, in all categories), Technical Writer, Hardware Specialist, Network Specialist, Applications Specialist, Systems Architect, and Project Manager positions. Creativity, flexibility, initiative, autonomy, team player, dedication, working knowledge of latest programming tools and methods, and previous relevant work or co-op experience are all listed as desirable non-academic qualifications. Company benefits and the potential for advancement are both rated as excellent. The average annual starting salary for those with previous work experience, falls within the $30,000 to $35,000 range. The most suitable method for initial contact by those seeking employment is to mail a resume with a covering letter. M3i Systems Inc. does hire summer students. *Contact:* Human Resources Director.

MACDONALD DETTWILER & ASSOCIATES

13800 Commerce Parkway
Richmond, BC V6V 2J3

Tel.	604-278-3411
Fax	604-278-2117
Email	jobs@mda.ca
Website	www.mda.ca

MacDonald Dettwiler & Associates is truly a global business with customers and employees from all over the world. The company collects and processes information about the world, including the development of computer based systems and solutions that address basic societal needs in the area of monitoring the Earth's resources, and information about the Earth, air navigation, defence applications, and data communications markets worldwide. MacDonald Dettwiler is one of Canada's largest diversified systems engineering companies, leading technology development in a growing number of disciplines. There are 600 employees at this location, a total of 725 employees in Canada, and 900 employees worldwide. Graduates most likely to be hired come from the following academic areas: Bachelor of Science (Computer Science, Mathematics, Physics), Bachelor of Engineering (Electrical, Computer Systems), Bachelor of Commerce/Business Administration (General, Accounting), and Community College Diploma (Business, Computer Science). Graduates would occupy Software Engineer, Systems Engineer, and Systems Architect positions. Team player, leadership skills, and possessing an awareness of budget and schedule restraints are all listed as desirable non-academic qualifications. Company benefits and the potential for advancement are both rated as excellent. The average annual starting salary falls within the $40,000 to $45,000 range. The most suitable methods for initial contact by those seeking employment are to mail or e-mail a resume with a covering letter, or by applying through the company's website at www.mda.ca. MacDonald Dettwiler & Associates does hire summer and co-op work term students. *Contact:* Recruiting Office.

MACKENZIE FINANCIAL CORPORATION

150 Bloor Street West
Toronto, ON M5S 3B5

Tel.	416-922-5322
Fax	416-922-1278

Email .... hr@mackenziefinancial.com
Website .... www.mackenziefinancial.com

Mackenzie Financial Corporation is one of Canada's leading mutual fund companies, managing over $20 billion in assets on behalf of more than 800,000 investors across Canada. There are 800 employees at this location, and a total of 1,200 employees in Canada. Graduates most likely to be hired come from the following academic areas: Bachelor of Arts (Economics, English, French, Psychology), Bachelor of Science (Computer Science), Bachelor of Commerce/ Business Administration (General, Finance, Information Systems, Marketing), Chartered Accountant, Certified Management Accountant, Certified General Accountant, Master of Business Administration (General, Accounting, Finance, Information Systems, Marketing), and Community College Diploma (Accounting, Administration, Business, Information Systems, Secretarial). Graduates would occupy Data Processing Clerk, Customer Service Representative, Training and Documentation Coordinator, Trust Accountant, Accounting Clerk, Computer Operator, Junior Programmer, Desktop Publisher, Graphic Designer, Receptionist, and Secretary positions. Good organizational skills, team player, a willingness to do any kind of work, and strong problem solving skills are all listed as desirable non-academic qualifications. Company benefits and the potential for advancement are both rated as excellent. The average annual starting salary falls within the $25,000 to $30,000 range. The most suitable methods for initial contact by those seeking employment are to mail, fax or e-mail a resume with a covering letter, or by applying through Mackenzie's website at www.mackenziefinancial.com. Mackenzie Financial Corporation does hire co-op work term students during the winter season, January through May. *Contact:* Human Resources Consultant.

MACLEAN HUNTER PUBLISHING LTD.
777 Bay Street, 9th Floor
Toronto, ON M5W 1A7

Tel. 416-596-5270
Fax 416-596-5967

Maclean Hunter Publishing Ltd. publishes Canadian business and consumer magazines, including Maclean's, Canada's Weekly Newsmagazine. There are approximately 800 employees at this location, and a total of 1,000 employees in Canada. Graduates most likely to be hired come from the following academic areas: Bachelor of Arts (General, English, Journalism, Political Science), Bachelor of Science (Computer Science), Bachelor of Commerce/Business Administration (General, Information Systems, Marketing), and Community College Diploma (Accounting, Administration, Advertising, Graphic Arts, Journalism). Graduates would occupy Editorial Assistant, Assistant Editor, Sales Coordinator, Inside Sales Representative, Administrative Assistant, Marketing Coordinator, PC Specialist, and Assistant Art Director positions. Good communication and organizational skills, detail oriented, able to work well in a team environment, high energy level, computer software knowledge (word processing and spreadsheets), and previous work experience are all listed as desirable non-academic qualifications. The most suitable methods for initial contact by those seeking employment are to mail or fax a resume with a covering letter. Maclean Hunter Publishing Ltd. hires a limited number of summer students each year, the type and number of summer positions is generally known by May (sometimes late April). Maclean Hunter also hires co-op work term students. *Contact:* Receptionist, Human Resources.

MACMILLAN BATHURST - WHITBY PLANT
220 Water Street, P.O. Box 150
Whitby, ON L1N 5R7

Tel. 905-686-2600
Fax 905-427-0892

MacMillan Bathurst is a corrugated box manufacturer. There are approximately 185 employees at the Whitby Plant, and a total of 1,800 employees in Canada. Graduates most likely to be hired come from the following academic areas: Bachelor of Science (Biology, Chemistry, Computer Science, Environmental, Forestry), Bachelor of Engineering (Chemical, Materials Science, Pulp and Paper, Electrical, Instrumentation, Mechanical, Industrial Design, Industrial Production), Bachelor of Commerce/Business Administration (General, Accounting, Human Resources), and Community College Diploma (Accounting, Human Resources, Secretarial, Electronics Engineering, Engineering Technician, Production Engineering). Graduates would occupy Quality Facilitator, Production Leadhand, and Accounting positions. Previous work experience in the paper and corrugated box industry would be a definite asset. Company benefits and the potential for advancement are both rated as excellent. The average annual starting salary falls within the $25,000 to $30,000 range. The most suitable method for initial contact by those seeking employment is to mail a resume with a covering letter. MacMillan Bathurst does hire summer students, applications must be received before April 30th. *Contacts:* Steve Ashby, Employee Relations or Ken Gills, Production Manager.

MACMILLAN BLOEDEL LIMITED
925 West Gorgia Street
Vancouver, BC V6C 3L2

Tel. 604-661-8324
Fax 604-688-8256

MacMillan Bloedel is a forestry company employing approximately 450 people. Graduates most likely to be hired come from the following academic areas: Bachelor of Science (Environmental, Forestry), Bachelor of Engineering (Pulp and Paper, Forest Resources), Bachelor of Commerce/Business Administration (Accounting, Finance, Human Resources, Information Systems, Marketing), Master of Business Administration (Accounting, Finance, Human Resources), and Community College Diploma (Accounting, Financial Planning, Human Resources,

Marketing/Sales, Secretarial). Graduates would be hired to occupy a broad range of positions, from Forester to Accountant, depending upon their academic backgrounds. The most suitable method for initial contact by those seeking employment is to mail a resume with a covering letter. MacMillan Bloedel does hire engineering students for summer positions. *Contact:* Darlene Donaldson, Employee Relations Coordinator, Human Resources Department.

MAGNA PROJECTS INC.
4393 - 14th Street N.E.
Suite 200
Calgary, AB T2E 7A9

Tel. 403-250-4676
Fax 403-219-3149
Email .... projcal@magnaiv.com

Magna Projects Inc. is an international engineering firm that can provide complete single or multi-discipline engineering, procurement and construction management services to the oil and gas, utility and industrial sectors. Magna Projects Inc. is a leader in technologies related to infrastructure, power, process industries and systems. Services range from feasibility studies to complete detailed design, construction management and start-up. After start-up Magna can provide training, troubleshooting, and plant optimization services. Magna is comprised of learned individuals who collectively deliver a wealth of experience and information to every project. The company's history of quality and commitment to service depicts a foundation from which Magna continually strives to build and excel upon. Graduates most likely to be hired come from the following academic areas: Bachelor of Engineering (Civil, Electrical, Mechanical, Computer Systems, Instrumentation, Petroleum/Fuels, Power/Hydro, Pulp and Paper, Telecommunications), and Community College Diploma (Administration, Human Resources, Information Systems, Secretarial). Team player, computer literate, and previous engineering experience are all listed as desirable non-academic qualifications. Company benefits and the potential for advancement are both rated as excellent. The most suitable methods for initial contact by those seeking employment are to mail, fax or e-mail a resume with a covering letter. Magna Projects Inc. does hire summer and co-op work term students. *Contact:* Christine Cole.

MANAC, A DIVISION OF THE CANAM MANAC GROUP INC.
51 Centennial Road
Orangeville, ON L9W 3R1

Tel. 519-941-2018
Fax 519-941-5321
Email .... lefebvre_patrick@canammanac.com
Website .... www.canammanac.com

Manac, A division of The Canam Manac Group Inc. is the largest manufacturer of quality, custom built semitrailers in North America. Manac specializes in the design, manufacture and marketing of custom products tailored to the specific needs of its custom-

ers. The company's head office is located in Saint-Georges de Beauce, Quebec. Manac employs over 1,000 people, and The Canam Manac Group Inc. employs over 4,400 throughout Canada, the United States, Mexico, and France. Graduates most likely to be hired come from the following academic areas: Bachelor of Arts (General), Bachelor of Engineering (General, Industrial Design, Industrial Production), Bachelor of Commerce/Business Administration, Chartered Accountant, Certified Management Accountant, Certified General Accountant, Community College Diploma (Technicians, Technologists Accounting, Administration), and High School Diploma. Graduates would occupy a variety of unskilled, semi-skilled and entry level professional positions in the following functional areas: Production, Engineering, Human Resources, Finance, and Administration. Customer orientation, team players, capacity to adapt to change, results oriented achievers, innovators, analytical thinkers, and problem solving skills are all listed as desirable traits. The average starting salary reaches up to $30,000 plus range. The most suitable methods for initial contact by those seeking employment are to mail, fax or e-mail a resume with a covering letter, stating geographic and positions preferences. Manac does hire summer students. *Contact:* Human Resources Team.

MANITOBA AGRICULTURE
401 York Avenue
Suite 803
Winnipeg, MB R3C 0P8

Tel. 204-945-3308
Fax 204-945-5024
Email .... humanresoruces@agr.gov.mb.ca
Website .... www.agr.gov.mb.ca

Manitoba Agriculture's mission is to sustain and enhance the economic and personal well-being of participants within the agriculture and food chain. In support of this mission the department's role is to provide leadership and a range of services to assist agriculture and food participants in creating a sustainable economic climate to improve their net income and general well-being. Manitoba Agriculture is composed of four divisions which are called the Management and Operations Division, Regional Agricultural Services Division, Agricultural Development and Marketing Division, and the Policy and Economics Division. The department employs 575 people throughout the province of Manitoba. Graduates most likely to be hired come from the following academic areas: Bachelor of Arts (General), Bachelor of Science (General, Agriculture, Computer Science, Microbiology, Human Ecology), Bachelor of Commerce/Business Administrator (General, Accounting, Finance, Human Resources, Marketing), Chartered Accountant, Certified Management Accountant, Certified General Accountant, Master of Business Administration (Finance, Human Resources, Marketing), Master of Science (Agriculture), Doctor of Veterinary Medicine, and Community College Diploma (Administration, Agriculture/Horticulture). Graduates would occupy Administrative

Clerk, Financial Clerk, Agrologist (Agricultural Representative, Specialist, etc.), Information Technologist, Medical Technologist, Agricultural Engineer, Financial Manager, Financial Analyst, Manager, Director, Home Economist, Veterinary Medical Officer, Livestock Technician, and Laboratory Technician positions. Excellent oral and written communication skills, and the ability to work cooperatively in a team environment and provide leadership are listed as desirable non-academic qualifications. Company benefits are rated above average. The potential for advancement is listed as being good. The most suitable method for initial contact by those seeking employment is to mail a resume with a covering letter. Manitoba Agriculture does hire summer and co-op work term students. *Contact:* Mrs. Angie Kudlak, Personnel Administrator, HR Management Services.

MANITOBA HYDRO
P.O. Box 815
Winnipeg, MB R3C 2P4

Tel. 204-474-4294
Fax 204-474-4868

Manitoba Hydro is responsible for providing electrical power for the people and industry of the province. This involves all activities from forecasting the province's future energy requirements, to designing, constructing, maintaining, and operating the numerous facilities needed to meet those requirements. Graduates most likely to be hired are: Bachelor of Science (Chemistry, Computer, Forestry), Bachelor of Engineering (Civil, Electrical, Mechanical), Bachelor of Laws, Bachelor of Commerce/Business Administration (Accounting, Finance, Marketing, Personnel), Chartered Accountant, Certified Management Accountant, Certified General Accountant, Master of Business Administration (Accounting, Finance, Marketing), Master of Engineering (Electrical, Mechanical, Civil), Community College Diploma (Accounting, Administration, Business, Communications, Marketing, Graphic Arts, Human Resources, Drafting, Computer Science, Electronics Technician, Engineering Technician, CAD/CAM/Autocad, Industrial Design), and High School Diploma. Graduates would occupy Clerk, Technician, Engineering Aid, Application Programmer Analyst, Accountant, Marketing Officer, Personnel Officer, Engineer-in-Training, Junior Engineer, Chemist, Forester, Auditor, Lawyer, and Apprenticeship Trainees (Power Line, Electrical, Mechanical, and Station Operator) positions. Strong interpersonal and communication skills are both listed as desirable non-academic qualifications. Company benefits are rated above average. The potential for advancement is listed as good. The most suitable methods for initial contact by those seeking employment are to mail a resume with a covering letter, or by applying in person at this location. Summer students are hired through Step Services (a Manitoba Government service). Manitoba Hydro is an employment equity employer. *Contact:* Rachelle Woodard, Employment Officer, Employment Department.

MAPLE LEAF MEATS, A MEMBER OF MAPLE LEAF FOODS INC.
150 Bartor Road
Weston, ON M9M 1H1

Tel. 416-741-7181
Fax 416-741-7693

Maple Leaf Meats is a meat processing company, employing approximately 400 people at this location. Graduates most likely to be hired come from the following academic areas: Bachelor of Science (Biology, Chemistry, Microbiology), Bachelor of Engineering (Industrial), Bachelor of Commerce/Business Administration, and Community College Diploma (Laboratory Technician). Graduates would occupy Laboratory Technician, Microbiologist, and Industrial Engineer positions. Possessing related food industry experience is listed as a definite asset. Company benefits and the potential for advancement are both rated as excellent. The average starting salary falls between the $25,000 to $40,000 plus range, and ultimately depends upon the position being considered. The most suitable method for initial contact by individuals seeking employment is to mail a resume with a covering letter. Maple Leaf Meats does hire a limited number of summer students annually. *Contact:* Marilyn Broderick, Manager, Human Resources.

MAPLE LODGE FARMS LTD.
RR #2
Norval, ON L0P 1K0

Tel. 905-455-8340
Fax 905-455-8370

Maple Lodge Farms Ltd. is a food (poultry) processing company, employing approximately 1,600 people. Graduates most likely to be hired come from the following academic areas: Bachelor of Science (Biology, Chemistry, Computer Science, Environmental, Nursing, Nutritional Sciences), Bachelor of Engineering (General, Chemical, Food Processing, Industrial Chemistry, Pollution Treatment, Electrical, Computer Systems, Mechanical, Industrial Design, Industrial Production, Welding, Resources/Environmental, Water Resources), Bachelor of Commerce/Business Administration (General, Accounting, Finance, Human Resources, Marketing), Chartered Accountant, Certified Management Accountant, Certified General Accountant, Master of Business Administration (Accounting, Finance, Human Resources, Information Systems, Marketing, Public Administration), Master of Science, Master of Engineering, Community College Diploma (Accounting, Administration, Business, Financial Planning, Human Resources, Insurance, Marketing/Sales, Purchasing/Logistics, Secretarial, Cooking, Graphic Arts, Security, CAD/CAM/Autocad, Computer Science, Electronics Technician, Engineering Technician, Welding, Dietician, Nursing RN/RNA), and High School Diploma. Graduates would occupy Food Technologist, Water/Waste Treatment, Microbiologist, Plant Nurse, Electrician, Maintenance, Welder, Refrigeration, Engineering Manager, Maintenance Manager, Computer Programmer, Accountant, Controller, Accounts Payable/Receivable Clerk, Human Resource Professional, Marketing, Sales Representative, Secretary, Purchasing Agent, Security Personnel, and Cafeteria Worker positions. Previous work experience, good references, team player, attitude and enthusiasm are all listed as desirable non-academic qualifications. Company benefits are rated above average. The average annual starting falls within the $25,000 to $30,000 range. The most suitable method for initial contact by those seeking employment is to mail a resume with a covering letter. Maple Lodge Farms Ltd. does hire summer students. *Contact:* John Botelho, Personnel Officer.

MARK'S WORK WAREHOUSE LTD.
1035 - 64th Avenue SE, Suite 30
Calgary, AB T2H 2J7

Tel. 403-255-9220
Fax 403-258-7575

Mark's Work Warehouse Ltd. is a Canadian retailer of clothing and footwear. The company employs approximately 100 people at this location, and a total of 1,800 people across Canada. Graduates most likely to be hired come from the following academic areas: Bachelor of Arts (Graphic Arts), Bachelor of Engineering (Computer Systems, Telecommunications, Industrial Design), Chartered Accountant, Certified Management Accountant, Certified General Accountant, Master of Business Administration (Accounting, Finance), Community College Diploma (Accounting, Administration, Facility Management, Financial Planning, Marketing/Sales, Purchasing/Logistics), and High School Diploma. Graduates would occupy Store Manager, Department Manager, Trainee and Clerical positions. Team player, dedicated, and dependable are all listed as desirable non-academic qualifications. Company benefits and the potential for advancement are both rated as excellent. The average annual starting salary falls within the $30,000 to $35,000 range and is commission based for some positions. The most suitable method for initial contact by those seeking employment is to mail a resume with a covering letter. Mark's Work Warehouse Ltd. does hire summer students. *Contact:* Human Resources.

MARKEL INSURANCE COMPANY OF CANADA
105 Adelaide Street West, 7th Floor
Toronto, ON M5H 1P9

Tel. 416-364-7800
Fax 416-364-1625

Markel Insurance Company of Canada is the largest commercial insurance company specializing in Long Haul Trucking Insurance. The company maintains branches in Montreal, Edmonton, Calgary, and subsidiary Tractor Trailer Driver Schools in Guelph, Ontario and Exeter, Ontario. There are more than 70 employees at this location, and a total of 110 employees in Canada. Graduates most likely to be hired come from the following academic areas: Bachelor of Science (Actuarial, Mathematics), Bachelor

of Commerce/Business Administration (Accounting, Finance), Master of Business Administration (Accounting, Finance), and Community College Diploma (Accounting, Business, Insurance). Graduates would occupy Underwriting Technical Assistant, Junior Underwriter, Junior Claims Examiner, Administrative Services Clerk, Secretary, Technician, and Computer Operator positions. Company benefits are rated above average. The potential for advancement is listed as being good. The average annual starting salary falls within the $30,000 to $35,000 range. The most suitable method for initial contact by those seeking employment is to mail a resume with a covering letter. Markel Insurance Company of Canada does occasionally hires summer and co-op work term students. *Contact:* Delores Johnson, Personnel Manager.

MARKHAM STREET SERVICES DEPARTMENT
101 Town Centre Boulevard
Markham, ON L3R 9W3

Tel. 905-475-4700
Fax 905-479-7774

The Town of Markham's Street Services Department is responsible for infrastructure, long-term planning and daily operations. This includes municipal roads, bridges, sidewalk, all drainage features, fresh water and waste water management traffic, and transportation systems. The Street Services Department employs approximately 80 people. Graduates most likely to be hired come from the following academic areas: Bachelor of Arts (Urban Geography/Planning), Bachelor of Engineering (Civil, Surveying, Water Resources), Bachelor of Commerce/Business Administration (Accounting, Public Administration), Certified Management Accountant, Community College Diploma (Accounting, Administration, Secretarial, CAD/CAM/Autocad, Computer Science, Engineering Technician), and High School Diploma. Employee benefits are rated as excellent. The potential for advancement is listed as average. The average annual starting salary falls within the $30,000 plus range. The most suitable methods for initial contact by those seeking employment are to mail or fax a resume with a covering letter. The Town of Markham's Street Services Department does hire summer students on a regular basis. *Contact:* Human Resources Department.

MARKHAM TRANSIT
101 Town Centre Boulevard
Markham, ON L3R 9W3

Tel. 905-475-4888
Fax 905-475-4709

The Town of Markham Transit Department is involved in the planning for and operation of municipal public transit in Markham. Transit services include conventional bus operation and services for physically disabled persons. There are approximately 25 employees at this location. Graduates most likely to be hired come from the following academic areas: Bachelor of Arts (Urban Geography/Planning),

Bachelor of Engineering (Transportation), and Community College Diploma (Transportation Technology). The types of positions these graduates would occupy are as follows: Transit Planner, Transit Technician, and Operations Supervisor. Good interpersonal skills, previous work experience, and a geographic knowledge of the area are listed as desirable non-academic qualifications. Employee benefits are rated as excellent. The potential for advancement is listed as average. The average annual starting salary falls within the $25,000 to $30,000 range. The most suitable method for initial contact by graduates seeking employment is to mail a resume with a covering letter. *Contact:* Manager, Human Resources.

MARSHALL MACKLIN MONAGHAN LIMITED
80 Commerce Valley Drive East
Thornhill, ON L3T 7N4

Tel. 905-882-1100
Fax 905-882-0055

Marshall Macklin Monaghan Limited (est. 1952) is a privately held Canadian company, owned and managed by its practitioners, offering comprehensive consulting services to government and private sector clients across Canada and overseas. The practice currently employs more than 300 personnel, of whom one third are registered professionals. The company provides a multidisciplinary consulting service. The traditional discipline skills include Engineering, Surveying, and Planning. Offices are located in Toronto and Edmonton, with additional offices established as required for local or project needs. Graduates most likely to be hired come from the following academic areas: Bachelor of Arts (Urban Geography/Planning, General), Bachelor of Science (Geography, Chemistry), Bachelor of Engineering (Civil, Electrical, Mechanical, Environmental), Bachelor of Architecture, Bachelor of Landscape Architecture, Bachelor of Commerce/Business Administration (Accounting), Chartered Accountant, Certified Management Accountant, Masters (Environmental Studies, Chemistry), and Community College Diploma (Civil Engineering Technology). Excellent written and oral communication skills are listed as desirable non-academic qualifications. Company benefits are rated as excellent. The potential for advancement is listed as being good. The most suitable method for initial contact by graduates seeking employment is to mail a resume with a covering letter. Marshall Macklin Monaghan Limited does hire summer students. *Contact:* Rhonda Lawson, Manager, Human Resources.

MATROX ELECTRONIC SYSTEMS LTD.
1025, boul St-Regis
Dorval, QC H9P 2T4

Tel. 514-822-6000
Fax 514-822-6274
Email .... personnel@matrox.com
Website .... www.matrox.com/hrweb

Matrox designs and manufactures ASICs, hardware and software for computer graphics, desktop video, PC-based image processing and computer networking applications. The company produces state-of-the-art products, known worldwide for their quality and price-performance ratio. In addition to the 1,200 employees based in Montreal, Matrox has design centres in Markham, Ontario and in Boca-Raton, Florida. Graduates most likely to be hired come from the following academic areas: Bachelor of Engineering (Robotics, Computer Systems, Microelectronics, Telecommunications), Bachelor of Science (Computer Science, Mathematics, Physics), Bachelor of Commerce/Business Administration/MBA (Accounting, Finance, Human Resources, Information Systems, Marketing), Chartered Accountant, Bachelor of Arts (Graphic Art, Journalism), Master of Science (Physics), Master of Engineering (Electrical), Doctorate (Electrical Engineering), and Community College Diploma (Computer Science, Electronics Technician, Engineering Technician). Graduates would occupy Hardware Designer, Software Designer, New Product Introduction Specialist, ASIC Designer, ASIC Architect, Validation Specialist, Engineering Sales Representative, Applications/OEM Support Representatives, Quality Assurance Specialist, Production Support Specialist, Product Manager, Technical Support Representative, Software Quality Assurance Technician, Project Coordinator, Junior Buyer, Sales and Marketing Coordinator, Customer Service Representative, Technical Writer, and Inside Sales Representative positions. Team player, a high level of initiative and motivation, computer literacy, and strong interpersonal and communication skills are all listed as desirable non-academic qualifications. Company benefits are rated as excellent and include group insurance, profit sharing, on-site daycare, free parking, a fully equipped gym, a heated outdoor pool and volleyball and basketball courts. The potential for advancement is also rated as excellent. The average annual starting salary for engineering positions falls within the $35,000 to $40,000 range, and the average starting salary for non-engineering positions falls within the $25,000 to $30,000 range. The most suitable methods for initial contact by those seeking employment are to mail a resume with a covering letter, or by applying through the company's website at www.matrox.com/hrweb. Matrox also offers summer positions, internships, cooperative education terms, and part-time positions. *Contacts:* Anita Salvador, Human Resources Manager; Andrea Di Domenico, Recruiting Specialist or Catherine Masson, Recruiting Specialist.

MAVES INTERNATIONAL SOFTWARE, INC.
90 Allstate Parkway, Suite 400
Markham, ON L3R 6H3

Tel. 905-475-1300
Fax 905-475-9878
Email .... ackcha@tor.maves.ca
Website .... www.maves.com

Maves International Software, Inc. has been a leading provider of software solutions for the logistics industry for more than 25 years. Maves has over 100 employees at offices in Toronto and Vancouver, serving more than 250 clients in Canada, the United States, and the United Kingdom, with installations in over 1,100 warehouse locations. Graduates most likely to be hired come from the following academic areas: Bachelor of Science (Computer Science), Bachelor of Commerce/Business Administration (Computer Systems), and Community College Diploma (Information Systems, Purchasing/Logistics, Computer Science). Graduates would occupy Consulting/Project Management, Quality Assurance Testing, Technical/Programming, and Trainee positions. Bright, self-motivated, hard working, multitasked, good verbal and written communication skills, able to work independently as well as within a team, and excellent problem solving skills are all listed as desirable non-academic qualifications. Company benefits are rated above average. The potential for advancement is listed as being good. The average annual starting salary falls within the $35,000 to $40,000 range. Employment opportunities at Maves are ongoing, in the Toronto and Vancouver offices, and on a contract basis. The most suitable method for initial contact by those seeking employment is to e-mail a resume with a covering letter. (Vancouver Office: Maves International Software, Inc., 4940 Canada Way, Suite 203, Burnaby, BC, V5G 4K6, Phone 604-294-4722, Fax 604-294-4159). *Contact:* Charmaine Ackerman, Manager, Human Resources.

MAXAM M & S INC.
1 Holiday Street, East Tower, 5th Floor
Pointe-Claire, QC H9R 5N3

Tel. 514-694-3326
Fax 514-694-3126
Email .... maxam@total.net

MAXAM M & S Inc. employs a total of four people in the development of computer based data management systems. Graduates most likely to be hired come from the following academic areas: Bachelor of Science (Computer Science), Bachelor of Engineering (Computer Systems), and Community College Diploma (Computer Science). Graduates would be hired to occupy S/W Application Specialist, and Database Administrator positions. Applicants should be familiar with Unix, Oracle and SQL programming languages. Company benefits are rated as industry standard. The potential for advancement is listed as being excellent. The average annual starting salary falls within the $30,000 to $35,000 range. The most suitable method for initial contact by those seeking employment is to mail a resume with a covering letter. MAXAM M & S Inc. does hire summer students. *Contact:* Magdy Boghdady, Director of Operations.

MCCARNEY GREENWOOD
1300 Central Parkway West, Suite 300
Mississauga, ON L5C 4G8

Tel. 905-276-3891
Fax 905-896-8959

McCarney Greenwood is a chartered accounting firm providing a full range of public accounting services, including audits, reviews, compilations, and tax returns, as well as providing tax consulting and man-

agement consulting services. McCarney Greenwood employs 25 people at this location, and an additional 15 people in Canada. Graduates most likely to be hired come from the following academic areas: Bachelor of Arts (General), Bachelor of Commerce/Business Administration (General, Accounting), Chartered Accountant, Master of Business Administration (General, Accounting), and Community College Diploma (Accounting). Graduates would occupy the position of Student in Accounts. Strong analytical skills, organized, good verbal and written communication skills, personable, and professional are all listed as desirable non-academic qualifications. Company benefits are rated as industry standard. The potential for advancement is listed as being good. The average annual starting salary falls within the $25,000 to $30,000 range. The most suitable methods for initial contact by those seeking employment are to mail or fax a resume with a covering letter. McCarney Greenwood does hire co-op work term students. *Contact:* Ms. R. Dinshaw, Human Resources.

MCCORMICK CANADA INC.
316 Rectory Street
London, ON N6A 4Z2

Tel. 519-432-1166
Fax 519-673-0089

McCormick Canada Inc. is the industry leader in the area of processing, packaging and selling of spices, seasonings and flavourings. There are approximately 225 employees at this location, a total of 450 across Canada, and a total of 8,500 employees worldwide. Graduates most likely to be hired come from the following academic areas: Bachelor of Arts (General, Economics), Bachelor of Science (Microbiology, Nutritional Sciences), Bachelor of Engineering (Chemical, Food Processing, Electrical, Industrial Production), Bachelor of Commerce/Business Administration (Accounting, Finance, Human Resources, Information Systems, Marketing), Chartered Accountant, Certified Management Accountant, Certified General Accountant, Master of Business Administration (Accounting, Finance, Human Resources), Professional Designations CHRP and PMAC, Community College Diploma (Accounting, Communications, Human Resources, Marketing/Sales, Purchasing/Logistics, CAD/CAM/Autocad, Electronics Technician, Engineering Technician, HVAC Systems, Dietician), and High School Diploma. New graduates would occupy entry level Finance, Administration, Information Resources, Manufacturing, Technical, and Laboratory positions. Graduates with relevant work experience would occupy positions throughout the organization at every level. The ability to adapt and work in a team oriented environment, commitment to continuous improvement of both self and company, successful work experience, and stability of previous employment are all listed as desirable non-academic qualifications. Company benefits and the potential for advancement are both rated as excellent. The most suitable method for initial contact by those seeking employment is in response to advertised positions. McCormick Canada

Inc. hires summer students, primarily recruited from within the company. *Contacts:* George Ward, Human Resources Manager or Barb Stotts, Human Resources Co-ordinator.

MCDONALD'S RESTAURANTS OF CANADA LIMITED
McDonald's Place
Toronto, ON M3C 3L4

Tel. 416-446-3381
Fax 416-446-3376

McDonald's Restaurants of Canada Limited operates quick-service restaurant outlets throughout Canada. The primary activities at each restaurant are food preparation and customer service. Each restaurant location employs between 50 and 100 people, with over 60,000 employees in total across Canada. University and Community College graduates are hired from a wide variety of academic areas for the McDonald's Management Trainee program. Leadership abilities, good communication and people skills, a high energy level, and enthusiasm are all listed as desirable non-academic qualifications. Company benefits and the potential for advancement are both rated as excellent. The average annual starting salary falls within the $23,000 to $25,000 range. The most suitable method for initial contact by graduates seeking employment is to mail a resume with a covering letter. McDonald's Restaurants of Canada Limited does hire summer and part-time students for restaurant employee positions. Contact should be made at the individual restaurant regarding summer and part-time employment. *Contact:* Human Resources Department.

MCDONNELL DOUGLAS CANADA LTD., A BOEING COMPANY
P.O. Box 6013, Toronto AMF, Airport Road
Mississauga, ON L5P 1B7

Tel. 905-677-4341
Fax 905-673-4303

McDonnell Douglas Canada Ltd., a Boeing Company manufactures and assembles airplane wings. There are 1,800 employees at this location, while Boeing employs a total of 220,000 employees worldwide. Graduates most likely to be hired come from the following academic areas: Bachelor of Arts (English), Bachelor of Science (Metallurgy), Bachelor of Engineering (Aerospace, Industrial Design, Industrial Production, Metallurgy), Bachelor of Commerce/Business Administration (Accounting, Finance, Human Resources, Information Systems), Chartered Accountant, Master of Business Administration (Accounting), and Community College Diploma (Accounting, Human Resources, Aircraft Maintenance, CAD/CAM/Autocad, Computer Science, Electronics Technician, HVAC Systems). Graduates would occupy Clerk, Technician, Engineering Design, Computer Programming, Industrial Engineering, and Trouble Shooting positions. Good problem solving skills, process focus, team player, and an ability to make decisions are all listed as de-

sirable non-academic qualifications. Company benefits are rated above average. The potential for advancement is listed as average. The average annual starting salary is dependent upon the position being considered. The most suitable methods for initial contact by those seeking employment are to mail or fax a resume with a covering letter. McDonnell Douglas does hire students for summer and co-op work terms. *Contacts:* Judy Bis or Anna-Maria Andreucci.

MCELHANNEY CONSULTING SERVICES LTD.
780 Beatty Street, Suite L100
Vancouver, BC V6B 2M1

Tel. 604-683-8521
Fax 604-683-4350

McElhanney Consulting Services Ltd. is an employee owned, Canadian consulting company specializing in engineering, surveying, mapping/GIS, and technical services. The company employs 70 people at this location and a total of 200 people in Canada. Graduates most likely to be hired come from the following academic areas: Bachelor of Arts (General), Bachelor of Science (General, Computer Science, Forestry), Bachelor of Engineering (Computer Systems, Surveying), Bachelor of Accounting/Business Administration (Accounting), and Community College Diploma (CAD/CAM/Autocad). Company benefits are rated above average. The potential for advancement is listed as being good. The most suitable method for initial contact by those seeking employment is to mail a resume with a covering letter. McElhanney Consulting Services Ltd. does hire summer students. *Contact:* Human Resources.

MCGRAW-HILL RYERSON LTD.
300 Water Street
Whitby, ON L1N 9B6

Tel. 905-430-5000
Fax 905-430-5020

McGraw-Hill Ryerson Ltd. is involved in book publishing, marketing and selling of educational textbooks, teaching materials, reference books, and general interest books. There are more than 100 people employed at this location. Graduates most likely to be hired come from the following academic areas: Bachelor of Arts, Bachelor of Science, Bachelor of Laws, Bachelor of Education, Bachelor of Commerce/Business Administration, Certified Management Accountant, and Community College Diploma (General). Graduates would occupy Sales Representatives, Editorial Assistant, Production Assistant, Marketing Assistant, Marketing Coordinator, and Accounting Clerk positions. Applicants should possess good analytical and communication skills. Knowledge of Lotus 123 and Wordperfect (for Windows), Pagemaker and other computer software is also desirable. Company benefits are rated above average. The average annual starting salary falls within the $25,000 range, and is base or bonus structured for sales positions. The most suitable method for initial contact by graduates seeking employment is to mail a resume with a covering letter. McGraw-Hill Ryerson Ltd. does hire summer students with the total number varying from year to year. *Contact:* Manager, Human Resources.

MCMILLAN BINCH
Royal Bank Plaza
South Tower, Suite 3800
Toronto, ON M5J 2J7

Tel. 416-865-7947
Fax 416-865-7048
Website .... www.mcbinch.com

McMillan Binch is one of Canada's leading business law firms, committed to understanding its clients' needs and objectives and working with them to achieve effective and creative solutions. Since 1903, McMillan Binch has provided definitive legal advice to Canadian and international businesses, financial institutions, governments and private individuals. Today, McMillan Binch comprises approximately 160 lawyers with a total staff of 474 in Toronto. Graduates most likely to be hired come from the following academic areas: Bachelor of Laws, and Community College Diploma (Accounting, Information Systems, Secretarial, Legal Assistant, Computer Science). Graduates would occupy Associate Lawyer, Legal Secretary, Law Clerk, and a limited number of Accounting and Systems Technology positions. Team player, strong communication skills, and good organizational skills are all listed as desirable non-academic qualifications. Company benefits and the potential for advancement are both rated as excellent. The average annual starting salary depends on the position being considered. The most suitable method for initial contact by those seeking employment is to mail a resume with a covering letter. McMillan Binch does hire summer and co-op work term students. *Contacts:* Stephanie Wilson, Director, Student & Associate Programs or Nisha Mullick, Supervisor, Human Resources.

MCW CONSULTANTS LTD.
156 Front Street West
Suite 600
Toronto, ON M5J 2L6

Tel. 416-598-2920
Fax 416-598-5394

MCW Consultants Ltd. provides engineering consulting services. The company employs approximately 40 people at this location and a total of 100 people in Canada. Graduates most likely to be hired are Bachelor of Engineering (Electrical, Mechanical) graduates. Company benefits are rated as industry standard. The potential for advancement is listed as average. The average annual starting salary falls within the $25,000 to $30,000 range. The most suitable method for initial contact by those seeking employment is to mail a resume with a covering letter. MCW Consultants Ltd. does hire summer students. *Contact:* Virgilio De Melo.

MDS AUTOMED
13151 Vanier Place, Suite 170
Richmond, BC V6V 2J1

Fax 604-279-9295
Email .... kitot@ihermes.com

MDS Automed offers a wide range of engineering and design services. The company has a proven record of electro-mechanical experience in a variety of biomedical areas and, for the past five years, has been developing automated laboratory equipment. MDS Automed works with clients to move the technology from a vision to a market ready product. In addition, the company develops customer specific automation devices and systems, and provides custom integration of off-the-shelf automation equipment. There are 15 employees at this location, and a total of 9,000 employees worldwide. Graduates most likely to be hired come from the following academic areas: Bachelor of Engineering (Electrical, Mechanical, Automation/Robotics, Biomedical Electronics, Computer Systems), and Community College Diploma (Electronics Technician, Tool and Die, Machinist). Graduates would occupy Technician positions, and work in a design capacity as Junior Engineers, Senior Engineers, and Trainees. Company benefits are rated above average. The potential for advancement is listed as being good. The average annual starting salary falls within the $50,000 to $55,000 range. The most suitable method for initial contact by those seeking employment is to mail a resume with a covering letter. MDS Automed does hire summer and co-op students. *Contact:* Kito Tosetti, Engineering.

MEDIA SYNERGY
260 King Street East, Building C
Toronto, ON M5A 1K3

Tel. 416-369-1100
Fax 416-369-9482
Email .... hresources@mediasynergy.com
Website .... www.mediasynergy.com

Media Synergy is a fast-growing internet software company providing innovative online marketing solutions to corporations internationally. Some of Media Synergy's clients include Hallmark Cards, National Geographic, CBS Sportsline, Travelocity, and Teletoon. The company currently employs 35 people. Graduates most likely to be hired come from the following academic areas: Bachelor of Science (Computer Science, Mathematics), Bachelor of Engineering (Computer Systems), and Community College Diploma (Advertising). Graduates would occupy Software Developer, Software Engineer, Project Manager, Program Manager, and Account Executive positions. Team player, work experience, good problem solving and communication skills, self-motivated, energetic and creative are all listed as desirable non-academic qualifications. Company benefits and the potential for advancement are both rated as excellent. The average annual starting salary falls within the $40,000 to $45,000 range. The most suitable methods for initial contact by those seeking employment are to fax or e-mail a resume with a covering letter. *Contact:* Jessica Gelberg, Human Resources Manager.

MEDIASOFT TELECOM INC.
8600, boul Décarie, bureau 215
Montreal, QC H4P 2N2

Tel. 514-731-3838
Fax 514-731-3833
Email .... lindav@mediasoft.com
Website .... www.mediasoft.com

MediaSoft Telecom Inc. is a leading computer telephony and internet partner to CT application developers, OEMs and system integrators. MediaSoft builds sophisticated CT platforms that can use any combination of voice, fax, data, web and multimedia technologies. The company employs approximately 50 people. Graduates most likely to be hired come from the following academic areas: Bachelor of Science (Computer Science), Bachelor of Engineering (Computer Systems, Telecommunications), Bachelor of Commerce/Business Administration (Marketing), and Community College Diploma (Advertising, Marketing/Sales, Secretarial). Graduates would occupy Programmer/Developer, Secretary/Receptionist, Marketing Secretary, Sales Representative, Technical Support, Advertising, and Technical Writer positions. Team player, communicative, flexible, experienced, imaginative, and creative are all listed as desirable non-academic qualifications. Company benefits are rated as industry standard. The most suitable methods for initial contact by those seeking employment are to mail, fax or e-mail a resume with a covering letter. *Contacts:* Linda Villeneuve or Ahmed Aina.

MEMOTEC COMMUNICATIONS INC.
600 McCaffrey Street
Montreal, QC H4T 1N1

Tel. 514-738-4781
Fax 514-738-4436
Email .... aguzzis@memotec.com
Website .... www.memotec.com

Memotec Communications Inc. is a frame-relay networking vendor, offering carriers, ISPs and corporations a family of frame relay access devices and edge switches that are at the forefront of reliable and manageable networking solutions. The company employs 200 people at this location, and a total of 250 people worldwide. Graduates most likely to be hired come from the following academic areas: Bachelor of Arts (Economics, English, Graphic Arts), Bachelor of Science (Computer Science, Mathematics, Physics), Bachelor of Engineering (Electrical, Computer Systems, Microelectronics, Telecommunications, Mechanical, Industrial Design), Bachelor of Commerce/Business Administration, Chartered Accountant, Certified Management Accountant, Certified General Accountant, Master of Business Administration (General, Accounting), Master/Doctorate of Science, Master/Doctorate of Engineering, Community College Diploma (CAD/CAM/Autocad, Computer Science, Electronics Technician, Engineering Techni-

cian), and High School Diploma. Graduates would occupy Technician, Test Technician, CAD Technician, Electrical Designer, Software Designer, Mechanical Designer, Clerk, Secretary, and Receptionist positions. Team player, organized, leadership qualities, innovative, client dedicated, and good interpersonal skills are all listed as desirable non-academic qualifications. Company benefits are rated as excellent. The potential for advancement is listed as average. The most suitable methods for initial contact by those seeking employment are to mail, fax or e-mail a resume with a covering letter. Memotec Communications Inc. occasionally hires summer students. *Contact:* Sandra Aguzzi, Human Resources Coordinator.

METAFORE
154 Sheldon Drive
Cambridge, ON N1R 7K9

Tel. 519-623-9800
Fax 519-623-7400
Email .... recruiter@metaforegroup.com
Website .... www.metaforegroup.com

Metafore is an enterprise technology services provider and application developer. With over 100 associates, headquartered in Cambridge, Ontario, Metafore has professional education centres, and a global network of business partners. The company delivers comprehensive information technology (IT) services, education services, skill sourcing and application development offerings. Metafore works to develop skills and solutions that work. Graduates most likely to be hired come from the following academic areas: Bachelor of Science (Computer Science), Bachelor of Engineering (Computer Systems), Bachelor of Commerce/Business Administration (Information Systems), Community College Diploma (Computer Science), as well as other Information Technology accreditations. Graduates would occupy Senior Technical Analyst, Application Developer, Programmer and Systems Analyst, Project Leader, Technical Support Specialist, and Help Desk positions. Superior written and oral communication skills, team work, bilingual, and multi-tasking abilities are all listed as desirable non-academic qualifications. Company benefits are rated as excellent. The potential for advancement is listed as being good. The most suitable methods for initial contact by those seeking employment are to fax or e-mail a resume with a covering letter. Metafore does hire students for summer and co-op work term positions. *Contacts:* Brent Davidson, Director; Christina Laughren, IT Resource Specialist or Lars Pastrik, IT Resource Specialist.

METMART-GREENBERG STORES
3075 Trans Canada Highway
Pointe-Claire, QC H9R 1B4

Tel. 514-428-6700
Fax 514-697-1699

Metmart-Greenberg Stores is a junior department store and clothing retailer with 200 stores across

Canada. Retail locations are located coast to coast with the head office and distribution centre located in Pointe-Claire. There are approximately 330 employees at this location, and a total of 3,630 across Canada. Graduates most likely to be hired come from the following academic areas: Bachelor of Arts (General, Graphic Arts, Journalism), Bachelor of Commerce/Business Administration (Human Resources, Information Systems, Marketing), Certified General Accountant, and Community College Diploma (Accounting, Administration, Advertising, Marketing/Sales). Graduates would occupy Buyer, Assistant Buyer, Buyer-in-Training, Accounting positions from Clerk to Accountant level, and Marketing positions including Advertising and Graphic Design positions. Previous retail or store management experience, excellent speech delivery, aggressive, self-starter, motivated, extroverted, and personable are all listed as desirable non-academic qualifications. Company benefits are rated above average. The potential for advancement is listed as excellent. The average annual starting salary falls within the $15,000 to $20,000 range, and may be commission based for sales positions. The most suitable method for initial contact by those seeking employment is to mail a resume with a covering letter. *Contacts:* Gilles J. Ferland, Director of Human Resources or Odette Grenier, Human Resources Supervisor.

METRO ORTHOPAEDIC REHAB CLINICS
909 Jane Street, Suite 202
Toronto, ON M6N 4C6

Tel. 416-604-4404
Fax 416-604-4406

Metro Orthopaedic Rehab Clinics (M.O.R.C.) take a proactive approach to the rehabilitation of muscular-skeletal injuries, offering an individualized assessment, ongoing patient education, and using a complete multi-disciplinary approach to rehabilitation and pain management. This multi-disciplinary treatment approach optimizes input from each branch of expertise in order to provide an individualized rehabilitative package for each patient. M.O.R.C operates six clinics in Metro Toronto, employing a total of 25 people. Graduates most likely to be hired come from the following academic areas: Bachelor of Arts (General, Economics), Bachelor of Science (General, Physio/Physical Therapy, Psychology), and Community College Diploma (Accounting, Business, Health/Home Care Aide, Massage Therapy). Punctuality, team player, innovative, culturally sensitive, good people skills, and excellent customer service skills are all listed as desirable non-academic qualifications. Company benefits are rated as excellent. The potential for advancement is listed as average. The average annual starting salary falls within the $15,000 to $45,000 plus range, depending on the position being considered. The most suitable method for initial contact by those seeking employment is to mail a resume with a covering letter. Metro Orthopaedic Rehab Clinics occasionally hires summer and co-op work term students. *Contact:* Kash Handy, Manager.

MÉTRO-RICHELIEU INC.
11011, boul Maurice Duplessis
Montreal, QC H1C 1V6

Tel. 514-643-1000

Métro-Richelieu Inc. is involved in the merchandising of food and other consumer products. Graduates most likely to be hired come from the following academic areas: Bachelor of Arts (Industrial Relations), Bachelor of Engineering (Industrial), Bachelor of Commerce/Business Administration (Accounting, Finance, Marketing), Certified Management Accountant (Finance), Certified General Accountant (Finance), Master of Business Administration, and Community College Diploma (Human Resources, Security/Enforcement, Computer Science). Previous work experience is listed as a desirable non-academic qualification. The most suitable method for initial contact by those seeking employment is to mail a resume with a covering letter (no telephone calls please). Métro-Richelieu Inc. does hire summer students. *Contacts:* Renee Dupont, conseillere ressources humaines or Michel Turner, directeur renumeration developpement organisationnel.

METROPOLE LITHO INC.
1201, Marie-Victoria
St-Bruno, QC J3V 6C3

Tel. 514-441-1201
Fax 514-441-4242

Metropole Litho Inc. is active in commercial printing and binding. The company employs approximately 200 people. Graduates most likely to be hired come from the following academic areas: Bachelor of Engineering (Electrical, Automation/Robotics), Bachelor of Commerce/Business Administration, Community College Diploma (Accounting, Administration, Advertising, Financial Planning, Human Resources, Marketing/Sales, Purchasing/Logistics, Secretarial, Graphic Arts, Computer Science, Electronics Technician, Engineering Technician), and High School Diploma. Graduates would occupy related junior trainee positions. Previous work experience, leadership skills, and industry knowledge are listed as desirable non-academic qualifications. Company benefits are rated above average. The potential for advancement is listed as average. The average annual starting salary falls within the $20,000 to $25,000 range. The most suitable method for initial contact by those seeking employment is to mail a resume with a covering letter. Metropole Litho Inc. does hire summer students for production level positions. *Contact:* Sylvie Marceaux, Human Resources Director.

MEYERS NORRIS PENNY & CO.
508 - 1661 Portage Avenue
Winnipeg, MB R3J 3T7

Tel. 204-775-4531
Fax 204-772-5917

Meyers Norris Penny & Co. is an accounting firm employing 30 people at this location and a total of

250 people across Canada. Graduates most likely to be hired come from the following academic areas: Bachelor of Commerce/Business Administration (Accounting, Human Resources, Information Systems, Marketing), Chartered Accountant, Certified Management Accountant, Certified General Accountant, Master of Business Administration (Accounting, Human Resources, Information Systems, Marketing), and Community College Diploma (Accounting, Human Resources, Marketing, Secretarial, Computer Science). The most suitable method for initial contact by those seeking employment is to mail a resume with a covering letter. Meyers Norris Penny & Co. does hire summer students. *Contact:* Human Resources Department.

MICROSOFT CANADA CO.
320 Matheson Boulevard West
Mississauga, ON L5R 3R1

Tel. 905-568-0434
Fax 905-568-1527

Microsoft Canada Co. employs approximately 350 people in the sales, support, marketing and distribution of Microsoft software products in Canada. Graduates most likely to be hired come from the following academic areas: Bachelor of Science (Computer Science, Mathematics), and Bachelor of Engineering (Computer Systems, Electrical). Graduates would be hired to occupy Product Support and Systems Engineering positions. Applicants should be enthusiastic, self-starters, love PC's, and possess excellent written and verbal communication skills. Company benefits and the potential for advancement are both rated as excellent. The average annual starting salary is dependent upon the position being considered. The most suitable method for initial contact by graduates seeking employment is to mail a resume with a covering letter. Microsoft Canada Co. hires students for co-op work terms. *Contact:* Nancy Easton.

MILGRAM GROUP OF COMPANIES
407 McGill Street, Suite 500
Montreal, QC H2Y 2G7

Tel. 514-288-2161
Fax 514-288-2519
Website .... www.milgram.com

Milgram Group of Companies are involved in freight forwarding and customs brokering. There are approximately 160 employees at this location and a total of 209 employees in Canada. Graduates most likely to be hired come from the following academic areas: Bachelor of Science (General, Computer Science), Bachelor of Engineering (Computer Systems), Bachelor of Commerce/Business Administration (General, Accounting, Finance, Human Resources, Information Systems, Marketing, Public Administration), Master of Business Administration, Community College Diploma (Accounting, Administration, Business, Marketing/Sales, Secretarial), and High School Diploma. Graduates would occupy Secretarial, Clerk, and Technician, positions. Previous

work experience, team player, and a good attitude are listed as desirable non-academic qualifications. Company benefits are rated above average. The potential for advancement is listed as being good. The average annual starting salary falls within the $15,000 to $20,000 range. The most suitable methods for initial contact by those seeking employment are to mail or fax a resume with a covering letter, or by applying through the company's website at www.milgram.com. Milgram Group of Companies occasionally hires summer students. *Contact:* Linda Miller, Human Resources.

MINISTRY OF EDUCATION AND TRAINING, ONTARIO
900 Bay Street, 19th Floor, Mowat Block
Toronto, ON M7A 1L2

Tel. 416-327-9045
Fax 416-327-9043

The Ministry of Education and Training employs approximately 2,500 people. Graduates most likely to be hired come from the following academic areas: Bachelor of Arts, Bachelor of Science, Bachelor of Engineering, Bachelor of Education, Bachelor of Commerce/Business Administration, Master of Business Administration, Community College Diploma, and High School Diploma. Graduates are hired to occupy a wide variety of administrative, clerical, secretarial, and policy, etc. positions. Excellent written and verbal communication skills, team player, good interpersonal skills, and good organizational skills are all listed as desirable non-academic qualifications. Company benefits are rated above average. The potential for advancement is listed as being good. The average annual starting salary falls within the $30,000 to $35,000 range. The most suitable method for initial contact by those seeking employment is to mail a resume with a covering letter. The Ministry of Education and Training does hire summer students. *Contact:* Organization Development Team.

MINISTRY OF NATURAL RESOURCES, ONTARIO
900 Bay Street, Macdonald Block, Rm M173
Toronto, ON M7A 2C1

Tel. 416-314-2000

The Ministry of Natural Resources is responsible for the management of the renewable and non-renewable natural resources for the province of Ontario. This involves a wide variety of resource activities, including forest, wildlife and fisheries management, cartography, public education, provincial park operation, forest fire prevention, water resource management, as well as a multitude of administrative functions. In addition to this main office there are eight regional and forty-seven district offices spread across the province. Graduates most likely to be hired come from the following academic areas: Bachelor of Arts (Sociology, Recreation/Planning), Bachelor of Science (Forestry, Biology, Geography), Bachelor of Landscape Architecture, Bachelor of Commerce/Business Administration, Chartered Accountant,

Certified Management Accountant, Certified General Accountant, Master of Business Administration, Master of Arts (Related), Master of Science (Related), and Community College Diploma (Forestry Technology). Graduates would occupy a wide variety of related positions such as: Forester, Biologist, Resource Technician, Conservation Officer, Planner, and Administrative positions. Employee benefits and the potential for advancement are both rated as excellent. The most suitable method for initial contact by those seeking employment is to mail a resume with a covering letter. The Ministry of Natural Resources does hire summer students. *Contact:* Human Resources Branch.

MINISTRY OF THE SOLICITOR GENERAL & CORRECTIONAL SERVICES, ONTARIO

171 Judson Street
Southern Regional Office, Suite C
Toronto, ON M8Z 1A4

Tel. 416-314-0520
Fax 416-314-0527

Ministry of the Solicitor General and Correctional Services, Correctional Services Division is responsible for the supervision of adults awaiting trial, sentence, deportation or transfer to a correctional institution, as well as offenders sentenced to terms of probation or institutional custody of less than two years. Under the Young Offenders Act, the Ministry is also responsible for young offenders. The Correctional Services Division employs more than 1,000 people in the province. Graduates most likely to be hired come from the following academic areas: Bachelor of Arts (Criminology, Psychology, Recreation, Sociology, Social Work), Bachelor of Science (Nursing, Psychology), Bachelor of Education (Adult), Master of Arts (Social Work, Psychology), and Community College Diploma (Nursing RN, Correctional Worker, Recreation, Security/Enforcement). Graduates would occupy Probation/Parole Officer, Nurse, Social Worker, Psychologist, Teacher, Correctional Officer, Recreation Officer and Chaplain positions. Good interpersonal skills, an ability to use tact and judgement, and able to recognize and react to abnormal situations are all listed as desirable non-academic qualifications. Employee benefits are rated as excellent. The potential for advancement is listed as being good. The average annual starting salary falls within the $30,000 to $35,000 range. The most suitable method for initial contact by those seeking employment is to mail a resume with a covering letter. The Correctional Services Division does hire summer students through the Summer Experience Program (see your campus career centre for details). *Contact:* Personnel.

MINOLTA BUSINESS EQUIPMENT (CANADA), LTD.

369 Britannia Road East
Mississauga, ON L4Z 2H5

Tel. 905-890-6600
Fax 905-890-8997

Minolta Business Equipment (Canada), Ltd. is involved in the sales and service of business equipment, including photocopiers, facsimiles, and printers. There are 31 employees at this location, and a total of 600 employees in Canada. Graduates most likely to be hired come from the following academic areas: Bachelor of Arts (Economics, English, History, Political Science, Sociology), Bachelor of Commerce/Business Administration (Accounting, Finance, Marketing), and Community College Diploma (Electronics Technician, Engineering Technician). Graduates would occupy Sales Representative, Technician, Clerical, and Accounting positions. Previous work experience and a positive attitude are listed as desirable non-academic qualifications. Company benefits are rated above average. The potential for advancement is listed as average. The most suitable methods for initial contact by those seeking employment are to mail or fax a resume with a covering letter. Minolta Business Equipment (Canada), Ltd. rarely hires summer students. *Contact:* Tracie Bradshaw, Corporate Human Resources Manager.

MINTZ & PARTNERS

1446 Don Mills Road, Suite 100
Don Mills, ON M3B 3N6

Tel. 416-391-2900
Fax 416-391-2748

Mintz & Partners is a chartered accounting firm employing more than 100 people in the provision of a full range of financial and consulting services for the entrepreneurial, owner-managed client. Mintz & Partners are small enough to provide a personal touch to their service, yet are able to provide a full range of services on a national and international scale since they are affiliated with Nexia International. Graduates most likely to be hired come from the following academic areas: Bachelor of Commerce/Business Administration (Accounting), Chartered Accountant, Certified Management Accountant, Certified General Accountant, and Master of Business Administration (Accounting). Graduates would occupy positions as Staff Accountants/Students-in- Accounts, and Accounting Technicians. C.A. training is provided. Possessing strong interpersonal and communication skills, and small business work experience are listed as desirable non-academic qualifications. Company benefits are rated above average. The potential for advancement is listed as being good. The average annual starting salary falls within the $25,000 to $30,000 range. The most suitable method for initial contact by job hunters is to mail a resume with a covering letter. Mintz & Partners does hire summer students, primarily 3rd year Bachelor of Commerce, Bachelor of Business Administration and Management students. *Contacts:* Elliott Jacobson, C.A., Partner or Alex Gallacher, MBA, Manager, Human Resources.

MISSISSAUGA, CITY OF

300 City Centre Drive, 5th Floor
Mississauga, ON L5B 3C1

Tel. 905-896-5023

Fax 905-615-4185
Email .... hr.info@city.mississauga.on.ca
Website .... www.city.mississauga.on.ca

The City of Mississauga employs 2,500 full time and 1,900 temporary employees in the provision of a full range of municipal government services through various departments and affiliates. Departments include the City Manager's Office, Corporate Services, Transportation and Works, Community Services, and Planning and Building. Affiliates include Art Gallery of Mississauga, Mayor's Youth Advisory Committee, Mississauga Arts Council, Mississauga Heritage Foundation, and the Mississauga Sports Council. Graduates most likely to be hired come from the following academic areas: Bachelor of Arts (Geography, Urban Geography/Planning), Bachelor of Science (Computer Science, Geography), Bachelor of Engineering (Civil, Electrical, Mechanical, Architectural/Building, Computer Systems, Environmental/Resources, Surveying, Water Resources), Bachelor of Architecture, Bachelor Landscape Architecture, Bachelor of Commerce/Business Administration (Accounting, Finance, Human Resources, Information Systems, Marketing, Public Administration), and Community College Diploma (Accounting, Administration, Communications/Public Relations, Facility Management, Financial Planning, Human Resources, Information Systems, Recreation Studies, Security/Enforcement, Urban Planning, Agriculture/Horticulture, CAD/CAM/Autocad, Computer Science, Electronics Technician, Engineering Technician, Forestry, HVAC Systems). Good communication skills, team player, enthusiasm, and work experience are all listed as desirable non-academic qualifications. Company benefits are rated as industry standard. The potential for advancement is listed as average. The most suitable method for initial contact by those interested in working for the City of Mississauga is to mail, fax or drop off a resume, cover letter and an application form to the Corporate Services Department, Human Resources Division at this address. The Human Resources Division receives all applications submitted to the City and is responsible for reviewing them and maintaining the Applications Inventory File. All applications are kept on file for six months to be reviewed continuously for suitable vacancies that come open to external applicants. The City of Mississauga does hire students for summer and co-op work terms. Contact: Corporate Services Department, Human Resources Division.

MISSISSAUGA HOSPITAL, THE
100 Queensway West
Mississauga, ON L5B 1B8

Tel. 905-848-7580
Fax 905-848-5598

The Mississauga Hospital is a diversified community hospital with over 400 beds, servicing primarily the residents of the southern, central and eastern sections of Mississauga. Providing a variety of services, the hospital employs over 2,000 full and part-time staff and more than 300 medical staff. Graduates most likely to be hired come from the following academic areas: Bachelor of Arts (General, Economics, English, Languages, Philosophy, Political Science, Sociology, Psychology, Recreation), Bachelor of Science (General, Biology, Chemistry, Computer, Health Sciences, Mathematics, Microbiology, Nursing, Pharmacy, Physics, Psychology), Bachelor of Engineering (Systems, Electrical, Environmental, Industrial, Materials Science, Mechanical), Bachelor of Education (General, Adult, Childhood, Physical, Special Needs) Bachelor of Commerce/Business Administration (Accounting, Finance, Marketing, Information Systems, Public Administration), Chartered Accountant (Finance), Certified Management Accountant (Finance), Certified General Accountant (Finance), Master of Business Administration (Accounting, Finance, Marketing, Information Systems, Public Administration), Master of Science (Nursing), Master of Engineering (Biomedical Engineering), Master of Education (Adult Education), Doctorate (Psychology, Pathology, Gerontology), and Community College (Accounting, Administration, Business, Communications, Facility Management, Secretarial, Cooking, Hospitality, Human Resources, Recreation, Photography, Social Work, Computer, Electronics, Engineering, Mechanic, Ambulance/Emergency Care). Maturity, reliable, motivated, good work ethic, excellent communication skills, and leadership potential are all listed as desirable non-academic qualifications. The most suitable method for initial contact by those seeking employment is to mail a resume with a covering letter. The Mississauga Hospital does hire summer students. Contact: O. Rita DoCanto, Human Resources Advisor.

MISTAHIA HEALTH REGION
10320 - 99 Street, 2nd Floor, Provincial Building
Grande Prairie, AB T8V 6J4

Tel. 403-538-5387
Fax 403-538-5455
Website .... www.mhr.ab.ca

Mistahia Health Region was established as a part of regionalization to coordinate health services within an area which includes Grande Prairie, Fairview, Grimshaw, Worsley, Grande Cache, Hythe, Beaverlodge, Spirit River, and Valleyview. Mistahia Health Region directly serves 85,000 residents and employs a total of 2,200 people. Mistahia Health Region provides excellent opportunities for new graduates to gain experience in general and specialized areas of health care. Graduates most likely to be hired come from the following academic areas: Bachelor of Arts (Social Work), Bachelor of Science (Computer Science, Audiology, Nursing, Nutritional Sciences, Occupational Therapy, Pharmacy, Physical Therapy, Recreation Therapy), Bachelor of Commerce/Business Administration (Finance, Human Resources, Information Systems), Certified Management Accountant, Certified General Accountant, Master of Business Administration (Finance, Human Resources), Master of Science (Speech Pathology, Psychology), Medical Doctor (Psychiatry, General Medicine), and Community College Diploma (Accounting, Human Resources, Purchasing/Logistics, Secretarial, Recreation, Computer Science, Dental

Assistant/Hygienist, Nutrition, Laboratory Technician, Nuclear Medicine Technician, Nursing RN/RNA, Radiology Technician, Respiratory Therapy, Ultra-Sound Technician). Graduates from the Health Sciences would occupy positions related directly to their academic backgrounds. Other graduates would occupy Financial Analyst, Human Resources Officer, Labour Relations Consultant, Technical Support Analyst, and Programmer/Analyst positions. Team player, adaptable to change, and good communication skills are all listed as desirable non-academic qualifications. Company benefits are rated as industry standard. The potential for advancement is listed as being good. The most suitable method for initial contact by those seeking employment is to mail a resume with a covering letter. The Mistahia Health Region does hire a small number of summer students depending on programs available. In addition, Mistahia does hire co-op work term students. For more information visit the Mistahia Health Region's website at www.mhr.ab.ca. When telephoning long distance Mistahia can be reached toll free at 1-800-732-8981. *Contacts:* Human Resources (all Other Health Care Occupations) or Regional Medical Director (for Physicians).

MITEC ELECTRONICS LTD.
104 Gun Avenue
Pointe Claire, QC H9R 3X3

Tel. 514-694-6666
Fax 514-694-3731

Mitec Electronics Ltd. is active in the design and development of the following product lines: microwave communications components and subsystems; satellite communications equipment for earth stations; monitoring, alarm and control products, in both generic and dedicated forms; PCS and cellular base station subsystems and components. There are approximately 145 employees at this location and a total of 215 employees worldwide. Graduates most likely to be hired come from the following academic areas: Bachelor of Engineering (Chemical, Metallurgy, Electrical, Computer Systems, Telecommunications), Bachelor of Commerce/Business Administration (Accounting), Certified General Accountant, Master of Engineering, Community College Diploma (Secretarial, CAD/CAM/Autocad, Electronics Technician, Mechanical Technology), and High School Diploma. Graduates would occupy Development Engineer, Process Engineer, Controller, Process Planner, Electrical Test Technician, Typist, and CAD Operator positions. Previous related work experience is listed as a desirable non-academic qualification. The most suitable method for initial contact by those seeking employment is to mail a resume with a covering letter. Mitec Electronics Ltd. does hire summer students. *Contact:* Human Resources.

MITRA IMAGING INC.
455 Phillip Street
Waterloo, ON N2L 3X2

Tel. 519-746-2900
Fax 519-746-3745

Email .... hr@mitra.com
Website .... www.mitra.com

Mitra Imaging Inc. designs and implements integrated medical imaging and information systems. In association with world-renowned medical specialists and multinational partners such as Agfa, General Electric, Philips, and others, Mitra develops products that are used to manage medical images and other clinical information in hospitals worldwide. With just 90 employees, Mitra is the acknowledged leader in its chosen niches in information technology, with offices in three countries and a growing international reputation for excellence. Graduates most likely to be hired come from the following academic areas: Bachelor of Science (Computer Science, Mathematics, Physics), Bachelor of Engineering (Biomedical Electronics, Computer Systems, Engineering Physics), Master of Science (Computer Science), and Community College Diploma (Information Systems, Computer Science). Graduates would occupy Software Developer, Technical Support Specialist, Integration Specialist, Software Product Manager, and Software Verification Specialist positions. Team player, innovative, responsible, dedicated, quick learner, and good problem solving skills are all listed as desirable non-academic qualifications. Company benefits and the potential for advancement are both rated as excellent. The average annual starting salary falls within the $40,000 to $45,000 range. The most suitable methods for initial contact by those seeking employment are to fax or e-mail a resume with a covering letter. Mitra does hire co-op work term students. *Contact:* Julie Symons, Human Resources Administrator.

MOHAWK OIL CO. LTD.
6400 Roberts Street
Burnaby, BC V5G 4G2

Tel. 604-293-4114
Fax 604-293-7126

Mohawk Oil Co. Ltd. is involved in the retail of gasoline, convenience store marketing, and the manufacturing of lubricants and ethanol. The company employs 96 people at this location and a total of 282 people across Western Canada. Graduates most likely to be hired come from the following academic areas: Bachelor of Commerce/Business Administration (Accounting, Finance, Human Resources, Information Systems, Marketing), Certified Management Accountant, Community College Diploma (Accounting, Administration, Advertising, Business, Human Resources, Marketing/Sales, Legal Assistant), and High School Diploma. Graduates would occupy Entry Level Marketing and District Manager Trainee positions. Retail experience, industry experience, a willingness to move within Western Canada, a positive outlook, team player and strong leadership qualities are all listed as desirable non-academic qualifications. Company benefits are rated as excellent. The potential for advancement is listed as being good. The most suitable method for initial contact by those seeking employment is to mail a resume with a covering letter. Mohawk Oil Co. Ltd. does hire a limited number of summer students. *Contacts:* Neil B. Zambik, Director, People Development and Communications or Lucille Wright, Leader, People Support Services.

MONARCH COMMUNICATIONS INC.
361 First Street SE
Medicine Hat, AB T1A 0A5

Tel. 403-526-4529
Fax 403-526-4000

Monarch Communications Inc. employs 300 people in the operation of radio, television and cable television systems. Graduates most likely to be hired come from the following academic areas: Bachelor of Arts (Journalism), Bachelor of Engineering (Microelectronics, Telecommunications), Bachelor of Commerce/Business Administration (Marketing), and Community College Diploma (Accounting, Communications, Journalism, Television/Radio Arts, Electronics Technician). Graduates would occupy On-Air Announcer, News Reporter, Creative Writer, Production Editor, VTR Operator, Salesperson, Administrative Assistant, Master Control Operator, Electronic Technician, Data Processing, and Computer Technician positions. Creative, self-motivated, team player, and able to communicate in a professional manner are all listed as desirable non-academic qualifications. Company benefits and the potential for advancement are both rated as excellent. The average annual starting salary varies depending upon the position being considered. The most suitable method for initial contact by those seeking employment is to mail a resume with a covering letter. *Contact:* Heather Lemeshuk, Supervisor, Human Resources.

MONTREAL CHILDREN'S HOSPITAL
2300 Tupper Street
Montreal, QC H3H 1P3

Tel. 514-934-4403
Fax 514-934-4387

The Montreal Children's Hospital is a major pediatric, research and teaching hospital employing approximately 2,000 people. Graduates most likely to be hired come from the following academic areas: Bachelor of Arts (Psychology, Social Work), Bachelor of Science (Biology, Chemistry, Computer Science, Microbiology, Audiology, Nursing, Nutritional Sciences, Occupational Therapy, Pharmacy, Physical Therapy, Psychology, Speech Pathology), Bachelor of Engineering (Civil, Architectural/Building, Electrical, Biomedical Electronics, Computer Systems, Mechanical, Welding), Bachelor of Architecture, Bachelor of Education (General, Special Needs), Bachelor of Commerce/Business Administration (Accounting, Finance, Human Resources, Information Systems, Public Administration), Certified Management Accountant, Certified General Accountant, Master of Business Administration, Master of Arts (Psychology), Master of Science (Health Sciences), Medical Doctor, Community College Diploma (Accounting, Human Resources, Purchasing, Secretarial, Social Work, Architecture/Drafting, Dental Assistant, Dental Hygienist, Nutrition, Laboratory Technician, Massage Therapy, Nuclear Medicine, Nursing RN/RNA, Radiology, Respiratory Therapy, Ultra-Sound Technician), and High School Diploma. Previous work experience, good communication skills, motivated, flexible, team player, good interpersonal skills, initiative, autonomous, organized and good judgement are all listed as desirable non-academic qualifications. Company benefits are rated above average. The potential for advancement is listed as being good. The average starting salary is dependent upon the position being considered, with government scales applying in many cases. The most suitable methods for initial contact by those seeking employment are to mail a resume with a covering letter, or via telephone. The Montreal Children's Hospital does hire summer students. *Contact:* Human Resources Services.

MONTREAL GENERAL HOSPITAL
1650 Cedar Avenue
Montreal, QC H3G 1A4

Tel. 514-937-6011

Montreal General Hospital is an acute care hospital and trauma centre employing approximately 3,400 people. Graduates most likely to be hired come from the following academic areas: Bachelor of Arts (Psychology, Sociology/Social Work), Bachelor of Science (Biology, Chemistry, Computer Science, Microbiology, Audiology, Nursing, Nutritional Science, Occupational Therapy, Pharmacy, Physical Therapy, Psychology, Speech Pathology), Bachelor of Engineering (Biomedical Electronics, Instrumentation, Telecommunications, Welding), Bachelor of Commerce/Business Administration (Human Resources), Chartered Accountant, Master of Business Administration (Accounting, Finance, Human Resources, Information Systems), Master of Social Work, Master of Nursing Science, and Community College Diploma (Accounting, Administration, Facility Management, Human Resources, Purchasing/Logistics, Secretarial, Security/Enforcement, Social Work, Electronics Technician, Engineering Technician, Welding, Dietician, Laboratory Technician, Nuclear Medicine Technician, Nursing RN/RNA, Radiology Technician, Respiratory Therapy, Ultra-Sound Technician). Graduates would occupy positions related directly to their academic field of study. Good communication skills, team player, bilingual, and a customer service orientation are all listed as desirable non-academic qualifications. Employee benefits are rated above average. The potential for advancement is listed as average. The average annual starting salary falls within the $20,000 to $25,000 range, depending upon the position being considered. The most suitable method for initial contact by those seeking employment is to mail a resume with a covering letter. Montreal General Hospital does hire summer students. *Contact:* Recruiter's, Staffing Department, Division of Human Resources.

MOORE CANADA
5500 Explorer Drive
Mississauga, ON L4W 5C3

Tel.	905-602-1726
Fax	905-602-1731

Moore Canada is a leading manufacturer of business forms and is also involved in a variety of business activities, such as business information handling and processing support services, telesales, direct-mail marketing, data processing, and a variety of specialized services. There are approximately 138 employees at this location with a total of over 1,300 employees across Canada in over 50 sales offices and six manufacturing facilities. Graduates most likely to be hired come from the following academic areas: Bachelor of Arts (General), Bachelor of Commerce/Business Administration, Chartered Accountant, Certified Management Accountant, Master of Business Administration, and Community College Diploma (Administration, Business, Marketing/ Sales). Graduates would occupy Sales Assistant, Accounting Clerk, Customer Service Representative, Programmer, and Sales Representative positions. Adaptable, team-oriented, self-motivated, quality-conscious, and possessing initiative are all listed as desirable non-academic qualifications. Company benefits are rated above average. The potential for advancement is listed as being good. The average annual starting salary falls within the $25,000 to $30,000 range, and is commission based for sales positions. The most suitable method for initial contact by those seeking employment is to mail a resume with a covering letter. Moore Canada does hire summer students, the number hired varies annually with requirements. *Contact:* Manager, Recruitment, Human Resources.

MOORE STEPHENS HYDE HOUGHTON, CHARTERED ACCOUNTANTS
P.O. Box 122
Woodstock, ON N4S 7W8

Tel.	519-539-5623
Fax	519-537-5386
Email	dbullen@wdk.mshh.ca

Moore Stephens Hyde Houghton, Chartered Accountants is a public accounting, regional firm providing all related financial reporting and support to medium sized businesses. Office locations are found in Ontario and Quebec, and internationally through an affiliation with Moore Stephens. Specialties include tax, forensics, valuations, and litigation for a wide range of clients. Graduates most likely to be hired come from the following academic areas: Bachelor of Arts (Economics), Bachelor of Science (Mathematics), Bachelor of Commerce/Business Administration (General, Accounting, Finance), Chartered Accountant, Master of Business Administration (Accounting, Finance), and Community College Diploma (Accounting, Administration, Business, Secretarial). Graduates would occupy Audit, Accounting, Tax Specialist, and Forensic Accounting positions. Possessing 2 to 3 years of public accounting

experience is listed as desirable non-academic qualifications. Company benefits are rated above average. The potential for advancement is listed as excellent. The most suitable methods for initial contact by those seeking employment are to mail, fax, or e-mail a resume with a covering letter. Moore Stephens Hyde Houghton, Chartered Accountants does hire co-op work term students. *Contact:* Dixie Bullen, Director of Human Resources.

MORELAND RESOURCES INC.
717 - 7th Avenue SW, Suite 1480
Calgary, AB T2P 0Z3

Tel.	403-263-2330
Fax	403-278-1000

Moreland Resources Inc. is a junior oil and gas company. Graduates most likely to be hired come from the following academic areas: Bachelor of Science (Geology), and Bachelor of Engineering (Chemical, Electrical, Mechanical, Geological, Petroleum/Fuels). More that eight years related work experience, and good human relations skills are listed as desirable nonacademic qualifications. Company benefits are rated as excellent. The potential for advancement is listed as average. The average annual starting salary falls in the $60,000 plus range. The most suitable method for initial contact by those seeking employment is to mail a resume with a covering letter. (See listing for Veba Oil). *Contacts:* Kam Fard, P.Eng. or Human Resources.

MORRISON HERSHFIELD LIMITED
4 Lansing Square
Toronto, ON M2J 1T1

Tel.	416-499-3110
Fax	416-499-9658
Website	www.mhgroup.ca

Morrison Hershfield Limited is a prominent multi-disciplinary consulting engineering and management firm. The company's focus is in providing clients with expertise in communications infrastructure, civil and structural engineering, building science, facility management, fire and safety, transportation infrastructure, project and construction management, and specialized services in management and marketing consulting. There are approximately 140 employees at this location with a total of 230 employees in five office locations across Canada. Graduates most likely to be hired come from the following academic areas: Bachelor of Engineering (Civil, Architectural/ Building, Electrical, Telecommunications, Mechanical), and Community College Diploma (CAD/CAM/ Autocad, Engineering Technician). Graduates would occupy Engineers in Training, Junior Technician and Technologist, and CAD Operator positions. Previous work experience in the consulting field or in engineering are both listed as desirable non-academic qualifications. Company benefits are rated above average. The potential for advancement is listed as excellent. The average annual starting salary falls within the $30,000 to $35,000 range. The most suitable method for initial contact by those seeking employment is to mail a resume with a covering letter. Morrison Hershfield Limited does hire summer and co-op work term students, the number varies annually with requirements. *Contact:* Dennis Comand, Human Resources Officer.

MOTOROLA CANADA LIMITED
3900 Victoria Park Avenue
Toronto, ON M2H 3H7

Tel. 416-499-1441
Fax 416-499-6994
Website .... www.mot.com

Motorola Canada Limited is a leading provider of wireless communications, semiconductors and advanced electronic systems and services. Major equipment businesses include cellular telephone, two-way radio paging and data communications, personal communications, automotive, defence and space electronics and computers. Communication devices, computers and millions of other products are powered by Motorola semiconductors. Motorola Canada Limited's parent company, Motorola Inc., maintains sales, service and manufacturing facilities throughout the world, conducts business on six continents and employs more than 140,000 people worldwide. Graduates most likely to be hired come from the following academic areas: Bachelor of Engineering (Electrical, Computer Systems, Telecommunications), and Community College Diploma (Electronics Technician, Engineering Technician). Graduates would occupy Electrical Engineering, and Computer Science positions. Previous work experience that is relevant to position, telecommunications knowledge, and a willingness to learn new skills through constant training are all listed as desirable non-academic qualifications. Company benefits are rated above average. The potential for advancement is listed as excellent. The most suitable method for initial contact by those seeking employment is to mail a resume. Motorola Canada Limited does recruit Bachelor of Engineering students for co-op work terms (contact your campus career centre). *Contacts:* Staffing Department or Human Resources.

MOUNT SINAI HOSPITAL
600 University Avenue
Toronto, ON M5G 1X5

Tel. 416-586-5040
Fax 416-586-5045
Website .... www.mtsinai.on.ca

Mount Sinai Hospital is at the very forefront of the Canadian health care arena in the areas of patient care, teaching and research. Presently the hospital employs approximately 3,000 people. Graduates most likely to be hired come from the following academic areas: Bachelor of Science (Biology, Chemistry, Dentistry, Nursing, Nutritional Sciences, Occupational Therapy, Pharmacy, Physiotherapy, Speech Pathology), Bachelor of Engineering (General, Electrical, Mechanical, Biomedical Electronics, Computer Systems), Chartered Accountant, Certified Management Accountant, Certified General Account-

ant, Master of Business Administration (General, Health Care Administration), and Community College Diploma (Administration, Communications/Public Relations, Human Resources, Information Systems, Secretarial, Cook/Chef, Electronics Technician, Engineering Technician, HVAC Systems, Plumber, Animal Health, Dental Assistant, Dental Hygiene, Dietitian/Nutrition, Health/Home Care Aide, Nuclear Medicine, Radiology, Respiratory Therapy, Ultrasound Technician). Graduates would occupy Pharmacist, Physiotherapist, Occupational Therapist, Registered Nurse, Medical Secretary, Administrative Secretary, Research Technician, Biomedical Engineer, Computer Analyst, Electrician, etc. positions. Company benefits are rated as industry standard. The potential for advancement is listed as being good. The average annual starting salary falls within the $25,000 to $30,000 range. The most suitable methods for initial contact by those seeking employment are to mail or fax a resume with a covering letter. Mount Sinai Hospital does hire summer and co-op work term students. *Contacts:* Marilyn Gaul, Employment Relations Manager or Kerri McKenzie, Employment Relations Officer.

MTD PRODUCTS LIMITED
97 Kent Avenue, P.O. Box 1386
Kitchener, ON N2G 4J1

Tel. 519-579-5500
Fax 519-579-5730

MTD Products Limited is involved in the manufacture and assembly of outdoor power equipment, including all types of power mowers, yard tractors, and snow throwers. MTD Products Limited also has significant exposure as an OEM supplier of automotive stampings, primarily to the Ford Motor Company. The company employs approximately 750 people at this location, a total of 800 people in Canada, and 8,000 people worldwide. Graduates most likely to be hired come from the following academic areas: Bachelor of Science (Mathematics), Bachelor of Engineering (Robotics, Computer Systems, Instrumentation, Microelectronics, Mechanical, Industrial Design/Production), Bachelor of Commerce/Business Administration (Accounting, Finance, Information Systems, Human Resources, Marketing), Chartered Accountant, Certified Management Accountant, Certified General Accountant, Master of Business Administration (Accounting, Finance, Human Resources, Information Systems, Marketing), Community College Diploma (Accounting, Administration, Business, Advertising, Facility Management, Financial Planning, Human Resources, Marketing, Purchasing, CAD/CAM/Autocad, Computer Science, Electronics Technician, Engineering Technician, HVAC Technician, Welding), and High School Diploma. Positions would range from hourly rated unionized production positions, through junior and senior supervisors, all the way to senior management positions. Relevant work experience and good communication skills are listed as desirable non-academic qualifications. Preference in hiring would likely be shown to graduates of cooperative education programs. Company benefits are rated as industry standard. The potential for advancement is listed as average. The average annual starting salary falls within the $30,000 to $35,000 range. The most suitable method for initial contact by those seeking employment is mail a resume with a covering letter. MTD Products Limited does hire co-op students. *Contact:* Mark Schneider, Human Resources Manager.

MTS COMMUNICATIONS INC.
489 Empress Street, Box 6666
Winnipeg, MB R3C 3V6

Tel.	204-941-5096
Fax	204-772-0617
Website	www.mts.mb.ca

MTS Communications Inc. is the major supplier of telecommunications products and services in the province of Manitoba. MTS employs 3,500 people throughout the province. Graduates most likely to be hired come from the following academic areas: Bachelor of Science (Computer Science), Bachelor of Engineering (Electrical, Telecommunications), Bachelor of Commerce/Business Administration (Finance, Information Systems, Marketing), Chartered Accountant, Certified Management Accountant, Certified General Accountant, Master of Business Administration (Marketing), and Community College Diploma (Information Systems, Marketing/Sales, Computer Science). Graduates would occupy Engineer, Product Manager, Business Sales Representative, Account Manager, Programmer/Analyst, and System Analyst positions. Leadership, teamwork, innovation, and good communication skills are all listed as desirable non-academic qualifications. Company benefits are rated above average. The potential for advancement is listed as being good. The average annual starting salary falls within the $30,000 to $35,000 range. The most suitable method for initial contact by those seeking employment is to mail a resume with a covering letter. MTS Communications Inc. does hire summer and co-op work term students. *Contact:* Olga Ford, Human Resources.

MULTIVIEW INC.
1 Antares Drive, Suite 550
Nepean, ON K2E 8C4

Tel.	613-225-5050
Fax	613-225-0505

Multiview is a premier independent supplier of full-featured financial applications for the HP 3000, HP 9000, and Windows NT operating environments. With 1,800 applications installed, Multiview supports more that 500 clients worldwide representing more that 42 industries. Customers employ Multiview's integrated applications to improve the analysis of their financial information, better understand the details of their operations and improve the performance of their companies. Graduates most likely to be hired come from the following academic areas: Bachelor of Science (Computer Science), Bachelor of Engineering (Computer Systems), and Community College Diploma (Accounting). Graduates would occupy Software Engineer and Software Con-

sultant positions. Company benefits are rated above average. The potential for advancement is listed as excellent. The most suitable methods for initial contact by those seeking employment are to mail or fax a resume with a covering letter. Multiview Inc. does hire summer and co-op work term students. *Contact:* John Leslie.

MUSTANG SURVIVAL CORP.
3810 Jacombs Road
Richmond, BC V6V 1Y6

Tel.	604-270-8631
Fax	604-270-0489
Email	mustang@mustangsurvival.com
Website	www.mustangsurvival.com

Mustang Survival Corp. is a leader in the design, development, manufacturing and marketing of personal safety and survival equipment. Mustang Survival has created an extensive range of products to meet the specific needs of recreational, industrial and military uses. Based on a tradition of excellence built over 31 years, Mustang is driven by its commitment to continuous improvement and innovation through ongoing research and testing, total quality management and world class manufacturing practices, as well as developing strong partnerships with its employees and customers. The company employs 275 people in five locations in Canada, the United States, and the United Kingdom. Graduates most likely to be hired come from the following academic areas: Bachelor of Arts (General), Bachelor of Science (Computer Science), Bachelor of Engineering (Chemical, Mechanical, Engineering Physics, Industrial Engineering, Industrial Production), Bachelor of Commerce/Business Administration (Accounting, Human Resources, Information Systems, Marketing), Certified Management Accountant, Certified General Accountant, Community College Diploma (Accounting, Administration, Business, Communications/Public Relations, Human Resources, Information Systems, Marketing/Sales, Purchasing/Logistics, Secretarial, Graphic Arts, CAD/CAM/Autocad, Computer Science, Engineering Technician), and High School Diploma. Graduates would occupy Customer Service Representative, Credit Associate, Engineering Technologist, Quality Assurance Technician, Junior Engineer, Junior Scientist, Industrial Engineer, Operations, and Production positions. Adaptable, confident, productive, analytical, creative, efficient, innovative, dependable, communicative, team player, and leadership skills are all listed as desirable non-academic qualifications. Company benefits are rated above average. The potential for advancement is listed as being good. The average annual starting salary falls within the $25,000 to $35,000 range, depending on the education level of the applicant and the position being considered. The most suitable methods for initial contact by those seeking employment are to mail, fax or e-mail a resume with a covering letter. Mustang Survival Corp. does hire students for summer and co-op work terms. *Contacts:* Janice Robinson, Director, Human Resources or Caroline Mitchell, Assistant, Human Resources.

MUTUAL GROUP, THE - IT PROFILE
227 King Street South
Waterloo, ON N2J 4C5

Tel.	888-882-4268
Fax	519-888-3183
Email	itjobs@themutualgroup.com
Website	www.themutualgroup.com

Mutual Life of Canada, the core company of The Mutual Group, has for more than 125 years, provided dependable financial services, including life insurance and mutual funds. Along with the other companies of The Mutual Group, the company is one of the fastest growing and most diverse financial organizations in Canada. At Mutual, the innovative use of technology is key to maintaining a competitive advantage in the dynamic financial services industry. The company is a recognized leader in the development and use of state-of-the-art technology with an infrastructure designed to meet the rapidly changing needs of a world-class organization. Mutual's Information Technology (IT) is fundamental to the company's accelerated growth and ongoing success. Exciting challenges in IT exist within the Information Systems department in Waterloo, Ottawa, and the Application Delivery Centre in Mississauga. Mutual is looking for innovative people with an aptitude for technology and a desire for lifelong learning. These include graduates from Computer Science, Mathematics, Engineering, or Business programs, as well as those from other programs who have experience and a passion for IT. Candidates must have a strong aptitude for information technology, be self-starters, client and results focused, adaptable, must have excellent communication and interpersonal skills and a vision and ability to create quality solutions to a variety of information technology needs. The company has a variety of positions available ranging from application development roles to hands on technical roles. Starting salary is $35,000 to $45,000 depending on position and prior experience. Benefits include flexible group life and health benefits and a pension package, on-site fitness facilities and cafeteria (Waterloo location), and ongoing training and education. The most suitable methods for initial contact by those seeking employment are to mail, fax or e-mail a resume with a covering letter. *Contact:* Wanda Taylor, IT Resourcing Consultant.

MUTUAL GROUP, THE - SALES PROFILE
227 King Street South
Waterloo, ON N2J 4C5

Tel.	888-882-4268
Fax	519-888-2107
Email	Cindy.Schutt@TheMutualGroup.com
Website	www.themutualgroup.com

For more than 125 years, The Mutual Group has provided dependable financial services, including life insurance and mutual funds. Along with the other companies of The Mutual Group, the company is one of the fastest growing and most diverse financial organizations in Canada. The Mutual Group hires individuals from all kinds of academic backgrounds, but a university degree or college diploma is required. Candidates must be ambitious, energetic and service oriented and must also exhibit strong leadership and independence. A business background is considered an asset. The Mutual Group offers full time Sales positions, where each candidate is responsible for building their own financial services practice through the growth of their own client base. This involves assisting clients in creating a financial plan by offering a full range of financial products and services, including life insurance and mutual funds. The company offers a five month internship program to help each candidate learn the business, and a 17 month formal mentorship program that links the candidate to a successful agent. This opportunity provides an excellent track for personal growth and management opportunities, while providing unique benefits of running an independent business. A development allowance is paid during the initial internship period. Upon full agent contract, commissions and bonuses are paid, where the earning potential equals the effort invested. A complete benefits package is available upon successful completion of internship. The most suitalbe methods for initial contact by those seeking employment are to mail or fax a resume, cover letter, and a copy of most recent transcript. *Contact:* Cindy Schutt, University Recruiting.

NABISCO BRANDS LIMITED
2150 Lakeshore Boulevard West
Toronto, ON M8V 1A3

Tel.	416-503-6000
Fax	416-503-6022

Nabisco Brands Limited is involved in the manufacture of consumer packaged goods (primarily food products). There are 1,200 employees at this location and approximately 3,500 employees across Canada. Graduates most likely to be hired come from the following academic areas: Bachelor of Arts (General), Bachelor of Science (Microbiology, Nutritional Sciences), Bachelor of Engineering (General, Chemical, Food Processing, Industrial Chemistry, Materials Science, Electrical, Mechanical), Bachelor of Commerce/Business Administration (Accounting, Finance, Information Systems, Marketing), Chartered Accountant, Certified Management Accountant, Certified General Accountant, Master of Business Administration (Accounting, Finance, Information Systems), and High School graduates for bakery positions. Post-secondary graduates would occupy Financial Analyst, Production Supervisor, Assistant Product Manager, P.C. Coordinator, and Sales Representative positions. Outgoing, flexible, adaptable, results oriented, team player, excellent analytical skills, previous work experience, and good written and verbal communication skills are all listed as desirable non-academic qualifications. Company benefits are rated above average. The potential for advancement is listed as being good. The average annual starting salary falls within the $30,000 to $35,000 range. The most suitable method for initial contact by graduates seeking employment is to mail a resume with a covering letter. *Contacts:* Kelly Sheehan, Human Resources Representative or Susie Baggio, Human Resources Representative.

NACAN PRODUCTS LIMITED
60 West Drive
Brampton, ON L6T 4W7

Tel. 905-454-4466
Fax 905-796-1450
Email .... monica.wanner@nstarch.com
Website .... www.nationalstarch.com

Nacan Products Limited is a manufacturer and supplier to industry of adhesives, resins, specialty chemicals, specialty industrial food starches, seasonings and flavourings. The company maintains plant locations in Toronto, Collingwood, Surrey, and Boucherville. The Brampton location is Nacan's Corporate Office and R & D Centre employing over 100 people. There are total of 300 employees across Canada. Nacan Products Limited is part of the US based National Starch and Chemical Corporation which in turn is part of the ICI Group, one of the world's largest specialty products, coatings and material companies with an impressive record in innovation. Graduates most likely to be hired come from the following academic areas: Bachelor of Science (Chemistry), Bachelor of Engineering (Chemical), Bachelor of Commerce/Business Administration, and

Community College Diploma (Accounting, Business, Secretarial, Human Resources, Engineering Technician). Maturity, stability, a positive attitude, motivation, aptitude, and good communication, leadership and listening skills are all listed as desirable non-academic qualifications. Company benefits are rated above average. The potential for advancement is listed as excellent. The average starting salary falls within the $30,000 to $40,000 range, depending upon the position being considered. The most suitable methods for initial contact by those seeking employment are to mail, fax or e-mail a resume with a covering letter. Nacan Products Limited does hire summer students and NSERC eligible students for 4 and 8 month work term placements. Nacan is an equal opportunity employer. *Contact:* Monica A. Wanner, Manager, Employee Relations.

NATIONAL GROCERS CO. LTD./LOBLAWS SUPERMARKETS LIMITED
6 Monogram Place
Toronto, ON M9R 4C4

Tel. 416-240-3969
Fax 416-240-3953

National Grocers is at the heart of Canada's most successful grocery retail and wholesale organization. National Grocers is recognized by many as the leader in bringing unique and innovative products, such as G.R.E.E.N., President's Choice and No Name products, to the marketplace. There are more than 1,000 employees between this and the 22 St. Clair Avenue East (Toronto) locations, and approximately 60,000 employees across Canada. Graduates most likely to be hired come from the following academic areas: Bachelor of Arts (Economics, Psychology, Urban Planning), Bachelor of Science (Computer Science, Nutritional Sciences, Pharmacy, Psychology), Bachelor of Engineering (Computer Systems, Industrial), Bachelor of Laws (Labour Law), Bachelor of Commerce/Business Administration (Finance, Human Resources, Information Systems), Master of Business Administration (Accounting, Finance, Human Resources, Information Systems), Community College Diploma (Accounting, Business, Human Resources, Purchasing/Logistics, Secretarial, Computer Science), and High School Diploma. Graduates would occupy Human Resources Manager/Specialist, Project Engineer, Analyst, Secretary, Warehouse Assistant, Consultant, Legal Advisor, I.R. Consultant, Food Product Development Specialist, Store Management Trainee, Departmental Manager, and Continuous Process Improvement positions. Results oriented, innovative, leadership skills, proven track record of success, team player, and previous grocery store experience are all listed as desirable non-academic qualifications. Company benefits are rated as excellent. The potential for advancement is listed as being good. The most suitable method for initial contact by those seeking employment is to mail a resume with a covering letter. National Grocers hires summer students, applications should be made prior to the summer season. *Contact:* Human Resources.

NATIONAL LIFE ASSURANCE COMPANY OF CANADA

522 University Avenue
Toronto, ON M5G 1Y7

Tel.	416-598-2122
Fax	416-598-4574
Website	www.national-life.ca

National Life Assurance Company of Canada designs, markets and sells individual and group life and health insurance products, and retirement income plans. In business since 1899, National Life has office locations across Canada and in the Caribbean. There are approximately 360 employees at the Toronto head office. Candidates with a background in the following academic areas may be interested in career opportunities with the company: Bachelor of Arts (General), Bachelor of Science (General, Actuarial, Computer Science, Mathematics), Bachelor of Commerce/Business Administration, an Accounting Designation, and Community College Diploma (Accounting, Administration, Business, Communications, Insurance, Secretarial, Human Resources). Career opportunities would include Sales Representative, Claims Examiner, Trainee Underwriter, Administrator, Accountant, Actuarial Student, and Trainee Programmer/Analyst positions. Starting salaries are competitive and vary depending on the position being considered. National Life offers a comprehensive benefits package. Accordingly, company benefits are listed as excellent. Commitment to quality is an important part of the company's philosophy. The most suitable methods for initial contact by those seeking employment are to mail a resume with a covering letter, or by calling the Employment Information Line at (416) 585-8090. *Contacts:* Ana Cimolai, Administrator, Human Resources or Kellee Wells, Administrator, Human Resources.

NATIONAL SILICATES LIMITED

429 Kipling Avenue
Toronto, ON M8Z 5C7

Tel.	416-255-7771
Fax	416-255-0170

National Silicates Limited employs more than 50 people in the manufacture of inorganic chemicals - sodium silicates. Graduates most likely to be hired come from the following academic areas: Bachelor of Science (Chemistry), Bachelor of Engineering (Mechanical, Chemical), and Bachelor of Commerce/Business Administration. Engineering and Science graduates would occupy Laboratory Technician positions. Company benefits are rated as excellent. The potential for advancement is listed as being good. The average annual starting salary falls within the $25,000 to $30,000 range. The most suitable method for initial contact by graduates seeking employment is to mail a resume with a covering letter. National Silicates Limited does hire summer students on a regular basis. *Contact:* Lynda S. Ryder, Employee Relations Manager.

NATIONAL TRUST, A MEMBER OF THE SCOTIABANK GROUP

1 Adelaide Street East
One Financial Place, 9th Floor
Toronto, ON M5C 2W8

Tel.	416-361-3611
Fax	416-361-3906
Email	marteln@nationaltrust.com

National Trust, A Member of the Scotiabank Group provides Financial Services (Banking, Retail Lending, Mortgage Lending), Personal Trust Services, and Corporate Trust Services (Pensions and Mutual Funds). National Trust employs more than 500 employees at this location. Graduates most likely to be hired come from the following academic areas: Bachelor of Arts (Business, Economics), Bachelor of Commerce/Business Administration, Chartered Accountant, Certified Management Accountant, Certified General Accountant, and Community College Diploma (Business, Marketing, Accounting). Graduates would occupy positions in Finance, Accounting, Client Services and Administration. Company benefits are rated above average. The potential for advancement is listed as being good. The average annual starting salary falls within the $20,000 to $30,000 range. The most suitable methods for initial contact by those seeking employment are to mail a resume with a covering letter, or via telephone. National Trust does hire summer students. *Contact:* Nancy Martel, Human Resources Advisor.

NATURAL SCIENCES & ENGINEERING RESEARCH COUNCIL

350 Albert Street
Ottawa, ON K1A 1H5

Tel.	613-995-6061
Fax	613-943-8675

The Natural Sciences and Engineering Research Council's (NSERC) role is to secure a healthy research base in universities and, as a corollary, to secure a sound balance between the diversified research base and more targeted programs of research. Also, the NSERC works to secure an adequate supply of highly qualified personnel who have been well educated in basic science as well as trained with state-of-the-art facilities, and to facilitate collaboration between R&D performing sectors in Canada. This role is exercised through the delivery of the Program of Scholarships and Grants in Aid of Research. The Council employs 190 people. Graduates most likely to be hired come from the following academic areas: Bachelor of Science (Biology, Chemistry, Computer Science, Forestry, Geology, Geography, Mathematics, Metallurgy, Microbiology, Oceanography, Physics, Zoology), Bachelor of Engineering (Chemical, Civil, Electrical, Mechanical, Resources/Environmental), Master of Science, Master of Engineering, and Community College Diploma (Computer Science). A knowledge of the scientific community, administrative experience, strong interpersonal skills, and a team-player orientation are all listed as desirable non-academic qualifications. Company benefits are rated above average. The potential for advancement is listed as being good. The average annual starting salary falls within the $30,000 to $35,000 range. The most suitable method for initial contact by those seeking employment is to mail a resume with a covering letter. The NSERC does hire summer students. *Contact:* Human Resources.

NCR CANADA LTD.
320 Front Street West
Toronto, ON M5V 3C4

Tel. 416-599-4627
Fax 416-351-2159

NCR Canada Ltd. develops, manufactures, markets, and supports a full line of computer information systems and related products and services. NCR Canada Ltd. employs approximately 2,400 people across Canada. Graduates most likely to be hired come from the following academic areas: Bachelor of Arts (Business), Bachelor of Science (Computer Science), Bachelor of Engineering (Electrical, Computer Systems), Bachelor of Commerce/Business Administration (Marketing, Finance), Certified Management Accountant, Master of Business Administration (Marketing, Finance, Information Systems), and Community College Diploma (Secretarial, Administration, Electronics Technician). Graduates would occupy Accounts Manager, Systems Engineer, Finance and Administration Trainee, Administration Clerk, Financial Analyst, Information Systems, Programmer/Analyst, Field Engineer, Secretary, and Word-Processing Operator positions. Company benefits and the potential for advancement are both rated as excellent. The most suitable methods for initial contact by those seeking employment are to mail a resume with a covering letter, through campus placement centres (preferably using ACCIS forms and Transcript, 3), or through on-campus recruitment initiatives (see your campus career centre for details). NCR Canada Ltd. does hire summer students, occasionally. *Contacts:* Human Resources Manager (Toronto) or Ann Marie Quish (580 Weber St., Waterloo, N2J 4G5, Phone # 519-883-3710).

NELVANA LIMITED
32 Atlantic Avenue
Toronto, ON M6K 1X8

Tel. 416-588-5571
Fax 416-588-5252
Email .... laurak@nelvana.com
Website .... www.nelvana.com

Nelvana Limited is an animation studio, specializing in the production of children's animated television series. There are approximately 250 employees at this location, a total of 450 in Canada, and a total of 480 employees worldwide. Graduates most likely to be hired come from the following academic areas: Bachelor of Arts (General, Graphic Arts), Bachelor of Commerce/Business Administration (Accounting, Finance, Marketing), and Community College Diploma (Accounting, Marketing/Sales,

Secretarial, Graphic Arts, Legal Assistant, Television/Radio Arts, Classical Animation, Computer Animation). Graduates would occupy Storyboard Artist, Timing Director, Production Manager, Location Designer, Prop Designer, Animator, Producer, Digital Painter, Digital Compositor, Background Artist, Character Designer, Layout Artist, Poser, and Assistant Animator positions. Team player, strong interpersonal skills, previous work experience (not necessarily within the industry), and good computer skills are all listed as desirable non-academic qualifications. Company benefits are rated above average. The potential for advancement is listed as excellent. The average annual starting salary falls within the $25,000 to $30,000 range. The most suitable method for initial contact by those seeking employment is to mail a resume with a covering letter. For certain positions, applicants should include portfolio when mailing resume with covering letter. *Contact:* Human Resources.

NESTE RESINS CANADA
5865 McLaughlin Road, Suite 3
Mississauga, ON L5R 1B8

Tel. 905-712-0900
Fax 905-712-0901
Email .... deborah.journeaux@neste.com
Website .... www.neste.com

Neste Resins Canada, is a member of the Neste Group based in Finland. Neste is an oil, energy, and chemicals company employing 9,000 people worldwide. Neste Resins Canada is involved in the manufacturing of chemicals and adhesives (eg. formaldehyde resins etc.) for the pulp and paper industry. Neste employs 40 people at this location, and a total of 250 people in Canada. Graduates most likely to be hired come from the following academic areas: Bachelor of Science (Chemistry, Forestry), Bachelor of Engineering (Chemical, Environmental/Resources, Industrial Chemistry), Bachelor of Commerce/Business Administration (Accounting, Finance, Human Resources, Information Systems, Marketing), Master of Business Administration (Finance, Human Resources, Information Systems, Marketing), Master of Science, Master of Engineering, Community College Diploma (Accounting, Financial Planning, Human Resources, Information Systems, Marketing/Sales), and High School Diploma. Graduates would occupy Chemist, Laboratory Technician, Technical Sales, Technical Service, Accountant, EHS, Human Resources, Information Technology and Systems, Marketing Manager, Sales Manager, Laboratory Technician, and Research Chemist positions. Dedicated, challenges the status quo, professional, and honest are all listed as desirable non-academic qualifications. Company benefits are rated above average. The potential for advancement is listed as being good. The average annual starting salary falls within the $30,000 to $35,000 range. The most suitable method for initial contact by those seeking employment is to e-mail a resume with a covering letter. Neste Resins Canada does hire student for summer and co-op work terms. *Contact:* Human Resources.

NESTLE ENTERPRISES LTD.
25 Sheppard Avenue West
Toronto, ON M2N 6S8

Tel. 416-512-9000
Fax 416-218-2828

Nestle Enterprises Ltd. is involved in the manufacture and selling of a wide variety of food products. Activities encompass manufacturing, distribution, logistics, purchasing, marketing, sales, financial planning, accounting, information services, human resources, and other related activities. There are more than 250 employees at this location. Graduates most likely to be hired come from the following academic areas: Bachelor of Arts (General, Economics, Psychology, Sociology, English), Bachelor of Science (Biology, Biochemistry, Chemistry, Computer, Nutrition), Bachelor of Engineering (Mechanical, Electrical, Industrial), Bachelor of Commerce/Business Administration (Marketing, Accounting, Finance), Certified Management Accountant, Master of Business Administration (Marketing, Finance), Master of Arts (Economics, English), and Community College (Laboratory Technician, Administration). Hardworking, well rounded, and excellent interpersonal skills are all listed as desirable non-academic qualifications. Company benefits are rated above average. The potential for advancement is listed as being good. The average annual starting salary falls within the $25,000 to $30,000 range. The most suitable methods for initial contact by those seeking employment are to mail a resume with a covering letter, or via telephone. Nestle Enterprises Ltd. does hire summer students. Contact: Human Resources Manager.

NETWORK DESIGN AND ANALYSIS (NDA)
60 Gough Road, 2nd Floor
Markham, ON L3R 8X7

Tel. 905-477-9534
Fax 905-477-9572
Email .... nda@ndacorp.com
Website .... www.ndacorp.com

Network Design and Analysis Corporation (NDA) is a software company specialized in developing telecommunications network optimization, performance analysis and cost control tools. NDA has been servicing large scale international corporations since its foundation in 1983. NDA employs a total of 21 people in Canada. Graduates most likely to be hired come from the following academic areas: Bachelor of Science (Computer Systems, Telecommunications), Master of Business Administration (Information Systems), Master of Science (Computer Science, Operations), and Doctorate (Operations Research). Graduates would occupy Project Engineer, Scientist, and Product Manager positions. Good communication skills, able to use own initiative, and 2 years previous work experience are all listed as desirable non-academic qualifications. Company benefits and the potential for advancement are both rated as excellent. The average annual starting salary falls within the $40,000 to $45,000 range. The most suitable method for initial contact by those seeking em-

ployment is to fax a resume with a covering letter. Contact: Mrs. Maureen Tracey, Administrator.

NEW BRUNSWICK POWER CORPORATION
P.O. Box 2000
Fredericton, NB E3B 4X1

Tel. 506-458-4004
Fax 506-458-4000
Email .... jdoucett@nbpower.com

New Brunswick Power Corporation is a provincial crown corporation responsible for the generation, transmission and distribution of electricity. Electricity is generated using a variety of fuels and technologies, including hydro, nuclear, coal, orimulsion, oil and combustion turbines. The corporation participates in a program that shares training and technology with developing countries, and is a leader in technology throughout North America. There are approximately 2,500 employees throughout the province. Graduates most likely to be hired come from the following academic areas: Bachelor of Science (Computer Science), Bachelor of Engineering (Electrical, Computer Systems, Nuclear Power, Mechanical), Bachelor of Commerce/Business Administration (Accounting, Finance, Human Resources, Information Systems), Master of Business Administration (Accounting, Finance, Human Resources, Information Systems), and Community College Diploma (Administration, Human Resources, Computer Science, Electronics Technician). Graduates would occupy Accounting, Business, Administration, Programming, Technical and Engineering positions. Customer service orientation, positive attitude towards new experiences, good verbal and written communication skills, and related work experience are all listed as desirable non-academic qualifications. The potential for advancement is listed as being good. The most suitable methods for initial contact by those seeking employment are to mail or e-mail a resume with a covering letter. New Brunswick Power Corporation actively recruits individuals for summer and co-op work term positions. Contacts: Jill Doucett, Manager, Employment or Karen Stafford, Director, Personnel Services.

NEW BRUNSWICK TELEPHONE CO., THE
One Brunswick Square, P.O. Box 1430
Saint John, NB E2L 4K2

Tel. 506-658-7439
Fax 506-694-2392

The New Brunswick Telephone Co. employs approximately 2,300 people, and is the prime provider of telephone service, and data-information systems in the province of New Brunswick. Graduates most likely to be hired come from the following academic areas: Bachelor of Science (Computer Science) and Bachelor of Engineering (General, Electrical, Industrial Engineering). Leadership skills, entrepreneurial, team player, risk taker, and analytical are all listed as desirable non-academic qualifications. In addition, the ability to communicate in New Brunswick's two official languages would be an asset. Company benefits and the potential for advancement are both listed as excellent. The most suitable method for initial contact by those seeking employment is to mail a resume with a covering letter. The New Brunswick Telephone Co. does hire summer and co-op work term students. *Contact:* John Hebert, Human Resources Consultant.

NEWFOUNDLAND & LABRADOR HYDRO
P.O. Box 12400
St. Johns, NF A1B 4K7

Tel.	709-737-1400
Fax	709-737-1231

Newfoundland & Labrador Hydro is responsible for the generation and transmission of electricity throughout the province. The company employs a total of 1,250 people. Graduates most likely to be hired come from the following academic areas: Bachelor of Engineering (Civil, Electrical, Power, Telecommunications, Mechanical, Industrial Design), Bachelor of Commerce/Business Administration (Accounting, Human Resources, Information Systems), Chartered Accountant, Certified Management Accountant, Certified General Accountant, Master of Business Administration (Human Resources), and Community College Diploma (Accounting, Human Resources, CAD/CAM/Autocad, Computer Science, Electronics Technician, Engineering Technician). Graduates would occupy Technician, Clerk, Human Resources, Accounting, and Engineering positions. Team player and good communication skills are both listed as desirable non-academic qualifications. Company benefits are rated as excellent. The potential for advancement is listed as average. The average annual starting salary falls within the $25,000 to $30,000 range. The most suitable method for initial contact by those seeking employment is to mail a resume with a covering letter. Newfoundland & Labrador Hydro does hire summer students (students must be enrolled in a post secondary institute for year prior and must be returning the following autumn). *Contact:* Mr. Alan Evans, Human Resources Specialist.

NEWFOUNDLAND POWER
55 Kenmount Road, P.O. Box 8910
St. John's, NF A1B 3P6

Tel.	709-737-5776
Fax	709-737-2967

Newfoundland Power is an electrical distribution company providing service to almost 250,000 customers on the island portion of the province of Newfoundland. There are more than 800 employees at this location. Graduates most likely to be hired come from the following academic areas: Bachelor of Engineering (Civil, Environmental, Electrical, Industrial, Mechanical), Bachelor of Laws, Bachelor of Commerce/Business Administration (Accounting, Information Systems), Chartered Accountant (Finance), Certified Management Accountant (Finance), Certified General Accountant (Finance), Master of Business Administration (Finance), and Community

College Diploma (Human Resources, Computer Science, Electronic Technician, Engineering Technician, Mechanic Technician). Graduates would occupy Analyst, Engineer, Technician, and Programmer, etc. positions. Strong interpersonal and communications skills are both listed as desirable non-academic qualifications. Company benefits are rated as excellent. The potential for advancement is listed as being good. The average annual starting salary falls within the $25,000 to $30,000 range. The most suitable method for initial contact by those seeking employment is to mail a resume with a covering letter. Newfoundland Power does hire summer students. *Contact:* Douglas Chafe, Director, Employee Services.

NIKON CANADA INC.
1366 Aerowood Drive
Mississauga, ON L4W 1C1

Tel.	905-625-9910
Fax	905-625-0103

Nikon Canada Inc. is the Canadian distributor of photographic goods and accessories, ophthalmic measuring instruments, microscopes, electronic image engineering products. There are more than 25 employees at this location. Graduates most likely to be hired come from the following academic areas: Bachelor of Arts, and Bachelor of Commerce/Business Administration. Graduates are hired as Clerks, Repair Technicians or Trainees. A basic knowledge of office routines, computer oriented background, and accounting experience at various levels are all listed as desirable non-academic qualifications. Also, for Repair Technician positions, possessing a basic knowledge of cameras is desirable. Company benefits are rated above average. The potential for advancement is listed as being good. The average annual starting salary falls within the $15,000 to $20,000 range. The most suitable method for initial contact by graduates seeking employment is to mail a resume with a covering letter. Nikon Canada Inc. does hire summer students, occasionally. *Contact:* Mr. H.K.S. Surty, Treasurer & Controller.

NLK CONSULTANTS INC.
855 Homer Street
Vancouver, BC V6B 5S2

Tel.	604-689-0344
Fax	604-443-1000
Email	info@nlkvcr.nlkeng.com
Website	www.nlkeng.com

NLK Consultants Inc. is a consulting engineering firm active in the pulp and paper industry. There are 200 employees at this location, a total of 300 in Canada, and a total of 325 employees worldwide. Graduates most likely to be hired come from the following academic areas: Bachelor of Engineering (Chemical, Pulp and Paper, Civil, Architectural/Building, Electrical, Instrumentation, Power, Mechanical, Industrial Production), and Community College Diploma (Architecture/Drafting, CAD/CAM/Autocad, Engineering Technician). Graduates would occupy Engineer (in all disciplines), CAD

Designer, and Drafting positions. Previous work experience in the pulp and paper industry, team player and a strong work ethic are all listed as desirable non-academic qualifications. Company benefits are rated as excellent. The potential for advancement is listed as being good. The average annual starting salary depends on the position being considered. The most suitable methods for initial contact by those seeking employment are to mail, fax or e-mail a resume with a covering letter. NLK Consultants Inc. does hire summer and co-op work term students. (Montreal Office: NLK Consultants Inc., 1425 boul. Réné Lévesque ouest, 8e étage, Montreal, QC, H3G 1T7, Phone 514-875-7950, Fax 514-397-1535). *Contacts:* Patricia Marion, Manager, Administration - Montreal or Barbara MacDonald, Office Manager - Vancouver.

NORANDA MINING AND EXPLORATION INC., BRUNSWICK DIVISION

P.O. Box 3000
Bathurst, NB E2A 3Z8

Tel. 506-547-3442
Fax 506-547-6162

Noranda Mining and Exploration Inc., Brunswick Division employs 990 people in mining activities. Graduates most likely to be hired come from the following academic areas: Bachelor of Arts (Economics), Bachelor of Science (Chemistry, Computer Science, Environmental, Geology, Metallurgy), Bachelor of Engineering (Chemical, Industrial Chemistry, Metallurgy, Surveying, Automation/Robotics, Computer Systems, Instrumentation, Microelectronics, Power, Industrial Design, Industrial Production, Welding, Mining), Bachelor of Commerce/Business Administration (Accounting, Finance, Human Resources, Information Systems), Chartered Accountant, Certified Management Accountant, Master of Business Administration (Accounting, Finance), Master of Science, Master of Engineering, and Community College Diploma (Human Resources, Purchasing/Logistics, Architecture/Drafting, CAD/CAM/Autocad, Computer Science, Electronics Technician, Engineering Technician, HVAC Systems, Welding). Graduates would occupy Professional, Engineer, and Technician positions. Team player, flexibility, and bilingualism (French/English) are all listed as desirable non-academic qualifications. Company benefits and the potential for advancement are both rated as excellent. The average annual starting salary falls within the $40,000 to $45,000 range. The most suitable method for initial contact by those seeking employment is to mail a resume with a covering letter. Brunswick Mining Division does hire summer and co-op work term students. *Contact:* Bruno Couteille, Human Resources Supervisor.

NORBORD INDUSTRIES INC.

1 Toronto Street, Suite 500
Toronto, ON M5C 2W4

Tel. 416-365-0710
Fax 416-360-2243

Fully owned by Noranda Forest Inc., Norbord Industries Inc. is an international manufacturer and marketer of wood and wood fibre products for construction and industrial purposes. Norbord employs 1,400 people in the manufacture of lumber and panel board products (eg. oriented structural board, medium density fibreboard, and hardwood plywood), and 1,300 people through its 50% interest in CSC Forest Products of Cowie, Scotland. The company is also an award-winning marketer of softwood lumber, and plywood on behalf of major Canadian producers. Graduates most likely to be hired come from the following academic areas: Bachelor of Science (Forestry), Bachelor of Engineering (Environmental, Mechanical), Bachelor of Commerce/Business Administration (Human Resources, Marketing), Chartered Accountant (Finance), Certified Management Accountant (Finance), Master of Business Administration (Accounting, Human Resources, Marketing), and Community College Diploma (Secretarial, Human Resources, Forestry). Team player, flexibility, adaptability, excellent interpersonal and communication skills, enthusiasm, drive to continually improve self and quality of work, and fluency in French (Other Languages: Dutch, Japanese, German, Italian) are all listed as desirable non-academic qualifications. Company benefits and the potential for advancement are both rated as excellent. The most suitable method for initial contact by those seeking employment is to mail a resume with a covering letter. Norbord Industries Inc. does hire summer students. *Contacts:* Lisa Irwin, Co-ordinator, Recruitment, Training and Development, or Human Resources Department.

NORCEN ENERGY RESOURCES LIMITED

425 - 1st Street SW, P.O. Box 2595, Station M
Calgary, AB T2P 4V4

Tel. 403-231-0111
Fax 403-231-0187

Norcen is a major Canadian-owned natural resource enterprise with three business segments: oil and gas, propane marketing, and mineral resources. In its core business of oil and gas, Norcen explores for, develops and produces hydrocarbons in Canada, the United States, Australia and Argentina. In propane marketing, Superior distributes propane across Canada and in the midwestern United States. In mineral resources, Norcen's principal assets are an equity interest in Iron Ore Company of Canada. The company employs approximately 3,000 people. Graduates most likely to be hired come from the following academic areas: Bachelor of Science (Computer Science, Geology), Bachelor of Engineering (Chemical, Electrical, Mechanical, Petroleum), Bachelor of Commerce/Business Administration (Accounting, Marketing, Land Management), Masters (Geology, Geophysics), and Community College Diploma (Engineering Technician). Graduates would occupy Engineer-in-Training, Junior Geologist, Junior Geophysicist, Accountant-in-Training, and positions in the Business Training Program (Accounting, Marketing, Land Management). Initiative, enthusiasm, adaptability, flexibility, and a demonstrated ability to work in a team environment are all listed as desirable non-academic qualifications. Company benefits and the potential for advancement are both rated as excellent. The average annual starting salary falls within the $30,000 to $35,000 range. The most suitable method for initial contact by those seeking employment is to mail a resume with a covering letter. Norcen Energy Resources Ltd. does hire summer students. *Contact:* Human Resources.

NORPAC CONTROLS LTD.
30 Gostick Place
North Vancouver, BC V7M 3G3

Tel.	604-980-5701
Fax	604-986-0483
Website	www.norpaccontrols.com

Norpac Controls designs and sells industrial control solutions. Norpac employs a total of 50 people. Graduates most likely to be hired come from the following academic areas: Bachelor of Science (Computer Science), Bachelor of Engineering (Chemical, Pulp and Paper, Electrical, Computer Systems, Instrumentation, Microelectronics, Telecommunications, Mechanical, Industrial Design, Industrial Production, Welding, Petroleum), Bachelor of Commerce/Business Administration (Accounting, Human Resources, Information Systems, Public Administration), Master of Business Administration (General, Accounting), Master of Engineering (Mechanical), and Community College Diploma (Administration, Electronics Technician). Graduates would occupy Technician, Applications Engineer, Accountant, and Trainee positions. Team player, hard worker, eager to learn, and practical experience are all listed as desirable non-academic qualifications. Company benefits and the potential for advancement are both rated as excellent. The average annual starting salary falls within the $30,000 to $35,000 range. The most suitable method for initial contact by those seeking employment is to mail a resume with a covering letter. Norpac Controls hires university students for summer positions, primarily engineering students. *Contacts:* Dave Wall, Vice President or Cynde Downs, Administration Manager.

NORTEL (NORTHERN TELECOM)
P.O. Box 3511, Station C
Ottawa, ON K1Y 4H7

Tel.	613-763-8232
Fax	613-765-3900
Website	www.nortel.com

Nortel is the world's most diversified provider of digital network solutions and is active in shaping the standards for internet access and high-speed data transmission. Nortel has earned a reputation for its expertise in networks, designing, building and integrating information, entertainment and communications networks globally. Nortel's environment is innovative, challenging, dynamic, culturally diverse, flexible and fun. The atmosphere inspires teamwork, breakthrough thinking and a passion for work. Nortel recruits recent graduates who thrive on creativity and individuality, and hold a degree in Engineering, Computer Science, Business or Marketing. Nortel employs some 73,000 people worldwide, 25% of which work in R&D. Key lines of business include Enterprise Networks, Enterprise Data Networks, Wireless Networks, Broadband Networks and Public Carrier Networks. Nortel owns and operates R&D, sales and manufacturing facilities across Canada. The corporate headquarters is located in Brampton, Ontario. Unique opportunities exist in Ottawa, Montreal, Belleville, Toronto, Calgary, and Vancouver. Exciting opportunities also exist in the United States, where the Company has a presence in North Carolina, Texas, Georgia, California and Tennessee. Graduates would occupy positions in Software Design and Development, Test and Verification, Hardware Design and Development, Network Engineer, Radio Systems Development, Technical Support Engineer, Installation Engineer, Information Technology, Systems Engineer and Architecture, Component Engineer, Marketing/Product Marketing, Finance, and Business/Information Systems. Company benefits and the potential for advancement are rated as excellent. Co-op and non co-op students are hired during the fall, winter and summer terms. Other programs that support students include the High School Co-op Program and the Career Edge Program. For detailed information about available positions please access Nortel's website at www.nortel.com, or mail or e-mail a resume with a cover letter and a copy of the most recent transcripts to the address listed above. *Contact:* North American Resourcing Centre.

NORTH SHORE NEWS
1139 Lonsdale Avenue
North Vancouver, BC V7M 2H4

Tel.	604-985-2131
Fax	604-985-1157

North Shore News employs 95 people in the publishing of a community newspaper in one of Canada's richest markets. Graduates most likely to be hired come from the following academic areas: Bachelor of Arts (Graphic Arts, Journalism), Bachelor of Engineering (General), and Community College Diploma (Advertising, Business, Communications, Marketing/Sales, Journalism). Graduates would occupy Trainee Sales Representative, Freelance Journalist, and Sales Representative positions. Energy, enthusiasm, drive, determination, and good communication skills are all listed as desirable non-academic qualifications. Company benefits and the potential for advancement are both rated as excellent. The average annual starting salary falls within the $20,000 to $25,000 range. The most suitable method for initial contact by those seeking employment is to mail a resume with a covering letter. *Contact:* Dee Dhaliwal.

NORTH YORK COMMUNITY CARE ACCESS CENTRE
45 Sheppard Avenue East, 7th Floor
Toronto, ON M2N 5W9

Tel.	416-222-2241
Fax	416-224-1470

North York Community Care Access Centre is a non-profit corporation employing approximately 200 people. The centre plans, co-ordinates and delivers a full range of services required to support clients and their caregivers in their homes. Services are also provided in schools throughout North York. Services provided include, nursing, nutritional counselling, occupational therapy, physiotherapy, social work, speech-language pathology, personal support, drug, hospital equipment, laboratory services, medical supplies, and transportation for medical appointments. Graduates most likely to be hired come from the following academic areas: Bachelor of Arts (Social Work), Bachelor of Science (Nursing, Occupational Therapy, Physiotherapy), Bachelor of Commerce/Business Administration (Accounting, Finance, Human Resources, Information Systems), Masters (Speech/Language Pathology, Social Work), Community College Diploma (Accounting, Communications, Human Resources, Secretarial), and High School Diploma. Graduates would occupy Secretary, Human Resources Associate, Supervisor, Case Manager Co-ordinator, Physiotherapist, Speech-Language Pathologist, Social Worker, Clerk, and Network Administrator positions. Customer service skills, team player, knowledge of commercial software applications, keyboard skills, analytical, good organizational skills, problem solving ability, ability to handle concurrent tasks without close supervision, communication skills, knowledge of medical terminology, and fluency in other languages are all listed as desirable non-academic qualifications. Company benefits are rated above average. The potential for advancement is listed as average. Starting salary falls within the $24,000 to $29,000 range for Clerical positions, and is $43,000 plus for professional positions. The most suitable method for initial contact by those seeking employment is to mail a resume with a covering letter. North York Community Care Access Centre hires summer students on a regular basis. *Contact:* Suzanne Jones, Human Resources.

NORTH YORK GENERAL HOSPITAL, BRANSON

555 Finch Avenue West
Willowdale, ON M2R 1N5

Tel. 416-633-9420
Fax 416-635-2537

North York General Hospital, Branson is a general hospital employing approximately 1,100 people. Graduates most likely to be hired come from the following academic areas: Bachelor of Arts (General, Social Work/Sociology), Bachelor of Science (Nursing, Nutritional Sciences, Occupational Therapy, Pharmacy, Physical Therapy), Bachelor of Commerce/Business Administration (Accounting, Finance), Master of Business Administration (Accounting), Master of Arts (Social Work/Sociology), and Community College Diploma (Accounting, Administration). Graduates would occupy Secretary, Clerk, Nurse, Paramedic, Technologist, and Technician positions. Employee benefits are rated as industry standard. The potential for advancement is listed as average. The average annual starting salary falls within the $25,000 to $30,000 range. The most suit-able method for initial contact by those seeking employment is to mail a resume with a covering letter. North York General Hospital, Branson does hire summer students. *Contact:* Ashton White, Human Resources Manager.

NORTHERN ALBERTA INSTITUTE OF TECHNOLOGY (NAIT)

11762 - 106 Street
Edmonton, AB T5G 2R1

Tel. 403-471-7018
Fax 403-471-7533

NAIT is one of Canada's foremost institutes of technical training dedicated to offering quality career education that fulfills the goals and expectations of students while serving the needs of the economy. NAIT employs approximately 700 instructional and 700 support staff. Graduates most likely to be hired come from the following academic areas: Bachelor of Arts (General, English, Graphic Arts), Bachelor of Science (General, Biology, Chemistry, Computer Science, Forestry, Geology, Mathematics, Metallurgy, Microbiology, Physics, Dentistry, Nutrition), Bachelor of Engineering (General, Industrial Chemistry, Materials Science, Metallurgy, Building, Surveying, Electrical, Biomedical Electronics, Computer Systems, Instrumentation, Microelectronics, Power, Telecommunications, Mechanical, Aeronautical, Industrial Design, Welding, Fish/Wildlife, Forest Resources, Mining, Petroleum, Water Resources), Bachelor of Architecture, Bachelor of Landscape Architecture, Bachelor of Education (General, Adult), Bachelor of Commerce/Business Administration (General, Accounting, Finance, Human Resources, Information Systems Marketing, Public Administration), Certified Management Accountant, Certified General Accountant, Master of Business Administration (General, Accounting, Finance, Human Resources, Information Systems, Marketing), and Community College Diploma (Accounting, Business, Financial Planning, Television/Radio Arts, Mechanic, Drafting, Animal Health, Dental Assistant/Hygienist). Graduates would be hired to occupy support and instructional (no teaching qualifications required) positions. Five to ten years previous work experience, empathy with students, team player, and quality/customer orientation are all listed as desirable non-academic qualifications. Company benefits are rated above average. The potential for advancement is listed as being good. The average annual starting salary for instructional positions falls within the $30,000 to $35,000 range. The most suitable methods for initial contact by those seeking employment are to mail a resume with a covering letter, or via telephone. *Contacts:* Mike Maitre; Donna Foerster or Marian Pangburn.

NORTHERN COMPUTER SYSTEMS, INC.

93 James Street
Parry Sound, ON P2A 1T7

Tel. 705-746-5873
Fax 705-746-5178
Email .... ncs@northerncomputer.com

Northern Computer Systems, Inc. (NCS) was established in 1983, and developed the world's first finite capacity scheduling solution for manufacturing and fabrication companies. Some of NCS' clients include INCO, the world's largest nickel supplier, who achieved a 25% increase in throughput in divisional shops through the implementation of NCS' scheduling technology. Vision 4000 is easily tailored through user features that allow a diverse range of industries to utilize and benefit from the company's technology. Some of these industries include the General Motors Proving Ground, The Timken Company, American Cast Iron Pipe Company, and both divisions of the second largest supplier to the Boeing Company, Menasco Aerospace. Northern Computer Systems, Inc. employs a total of 17 people. Graduates most likely to be hired come from the following academic areas: Bachelor of Science (Computer Science, Mathematics), Bachelor of Engineering (General, Chemical, Mechanical), Master of Engineering (Industrial Engineering), and Community College Diploma (Information Systems, Computer Science). Graduates would occupy Industrial Engineer, Applications Engineer, and Software Systems Engineer. Able to work well on individual projects as well as in a team environment, manufacturing knowledge and experience, results oriented, able to meet deadlines, and excellent communication skills are all listed as desirable non-academic qualifications. Company benefits are rated as industry standard. The potential for advancement is listed as excellent. The average annual starting salary falls within the $30,000 to $35,000 range. The most suitable method for initial contact by those seeking employment is to e-mail a resume with a covering letter. Northern Computer Systems, Inc. does hire summer and co-op work term students. *Contacts:* Geoff Osborne, Senior Applications Engineer or David Cox, President and Manager of Development.

NORTHERN TELECOM, TORONTO LAB
522 University Avenue, 14th Floor
Toronto, ON M5G 1W7

Tel. 416-597-7000

Northern Telecom's Toronto Lab, is involved in the development of advanced voice processing and call management applications for the evolving business communications market. The Toronto Lab location works closely with Northern Telecom's manufacturing sites in Canada, the United States and overseas. There are more than 100 employees at the Toronto Lab location. Graduates most likely to be hired come from the following academic areas: Bachelor of Science (Computer Science), Bachelor of Engineering (Electrical), Master of Science (Computer Science), Master of Engineering (Electrical), and Master of Business Administration. Graduates would occupy Digital Signal Processing Software Engineer, Applications Designer, Operating Systems Designer, and Hardware Design Engineer positions. Highly motivated, team player, and good interpersonal skills are all listed as desirable non-academic qualifications. Company benefits and the potential for advancement are both rated as excellent. The average annual start-

ing salary is dependent upon each applicant's degree program and level of experience. The most suitable methods for initial contact by those seeking employment are to mail a resume with a covering letter, or through campus career centres using ACCIS forms (visit your campus career centre). Northern Telecom - Toronto Lab does hire students for co-op work term assignments. *Contacts:* Cathy Tsujimoto, Human Resources Manager or (No Phone Calls Please).

NORTHWESTEL INC.
P.O. Bag 790
Yellowknife, NT X1A 2R3

Tel. 867-920-3645
Fax 867-873-3053
Email .... recruitment@nwtel.ca
Website .... www.nwtel.ca

Northwestel Inc. is a telecommunications company, providing voice, data, cellular, satellite, mobile, cable television and internet services in the Yukon, Northwest Territories and Northern British Columbia. The company employs approximately 600 people. Graduates most likely to be hired come from the following academic areas: Bachelor of Arts (Economics), Bachelor of Science (Computer Science), Bachelor of Engineering (Civil, Electrical, Computer Systems, Telecommunications), Bachelor of Commerce/Business Administration (General, Accounting, Finance, Human Resources, Information Systems, Marketing, Chartered Accountant, Certified Management Accountant, Certified General Accountant, Master of Business Administration (General, Accounting, Finance, Human Resources, Information Systems, Marketing), Master of Engineering (Electrical), and Community College Diploma (Accounting, Administration, Business, Communications/Public Relations, Human Resources, Information Systems, Marketing/Sales, Legal Assistant, Computer Science, Electronics Technician, Engineering Technician), and High School Diploma. Team player, highly motivated, adaptable, focused on quality customer service, and strong interpersonal and communication skills are all listed as desirable non-academic qualifications. Company benefits and the potential for advancement are both rated as excellent. The average annual starting salary falls in the $45,000 plus range. The most suitable method for initial contact by those seeking employment is to mail a resume with a covering letter. Northwestel Inc. does hire summer students. *Contact:* Laura Chapman, Manager, Recruitment and Benefits.

NOVA CHEMICALS LTD.
P.O. Box 5006
Red Deer, AB T4N 6A1

Tel. 403-342-8611
Fax 403-342-8787
Website .... www.novachem.com

NOVA Chemicals Ltd., headquartered in Calgary, Alberta (see next listing), is an aggressively expanding and dynamic petrochemicals company which operates two commodity chemicals businesses, olefins/

polyolefins and styrenics. NOVA Chemicals has more than a dozen petrochemical and plastics plants in Canada and the United States. There are 600 employees at this location, a total of 2,680 in Canada, and 3,600 employees worldwide. Graduates most likely to be hired come from the following academic areas: Bachelor of Science (Computer Science, Nursing), Bachelor of Engineering (Chemical, Civil, Electrical, Mechanical, Computer Systems, Instrumentation), Bachelor of Commerce/Business Administration (Finance, Human Resources, Information Systems, Marketing), Certified Management Accountant, Certified General Accountant, Master/Doctorate of Engineering (Process Control), and Community College Diploma (Accounting, Administration, Information Systems, Secretarial, Computer Science, Ambulance/Emergency Care, Laboratory Technician, Power Engineering - Minimum 4th Class, Chemical Technology). Graduates would occupy Programmer, Desktop Support, Occupational Health Nurse, Graduate Engineer, Secretarial, Accountant, Human Resources Consultant, Systems Analyst, Buyer, Loss Prevention Technician, Laboratory Technician, and Operating Technician positions. Good communication skills, a customer service orientation, leadership skills, problem solving and decision making abilities, self management skills, team player, change management skills, and good interpersonal skills are all listed as desirable non-academic qualifications. Company benefits and the potential for advancement are both rated as excellent. Accordingly, NOVA Chemicals supports diversity initiatives, offers alternative work arrangements, leadership programs, and a flexible benefits program. The average annual starting salary depends on the applicant and the position being considered. Career opportunities at NOVA Chemicals appear on the FWJ job board at www.fwj.com, or can by listened to by calling 1-888-371-0161 (toll free). The most suitable methods for initial contact by interested and qualified job seekers are to mail or fax a resume with a covering letter, or by applying through campus career centres. NOVA Chemicals Ltd. does hire summer and co-op work term students. *Contacts:* Connie Maundrell, Human Resources Consultant or Melody Jones, Human Resources Consultant.

NOVA CORPORATION - NOVA GAS TRANSMISSION LTD. / NOVA CHEMICALS LTD.
801 - 7th Avenue SW, P.O. Box 2535, Station M
Calgary, AB T2P 2N6

Tel. 403-290-6732
Fax 403-290-8989
Email .... lisa.morgan@pipe.nova.ca

NOVA Corporation is the parent company of both NOVA Gas Transmission Ltd. (NGT), based in Calgary, and NOVA Chemicals Ltd., based in Red Deer/Joffre, Alberta. NGT is the largest volume carrier of natural gas in North America, transporting natural gas through NGT's 13,500 mile system for use within Alberta and to provincial boundary points for connection with pipelines serving markets elsewhere in Canada and the United States. NOVA Chemicals Ltd. (see previous listing) is one of North America's largest petrochemical producing companies, producing ethylene and polyethylene, a vital building block for the plastic and petrochemical industries. There are 3,500 employees at this location, a total of 5,200 employees in Canada, and a total of 6,000 employees worldwide. Graduates most likely to be hired come from the following academic areas: Bachelor of Arts (Economics, English, Political Science), Bachelor of Science (Chemistry, Computer Science, Environmental, Nursing, Occupational Therapy), Bachelor of Engineering (Chemical, Industrial Chemistry, Surveying, Power, Instrumentation), Bachelor of Laws, Bachelor of Commerce/Business Administration (Accounting, Finance, Human Resources, Information Systems, Marketing, Public Administration), Certified General Accountant, Master of Business Administration (Accounting), Master of Science, Master of Engineering (Chemical, Instrumentation), Community College Diploma (Accounting, Administration, Business, Communication, Human Resources, Secretarial, CAD/CAM/ Autocad, Computer Science, Electronics Technician, Engineering Technician, Paramedic, Laboratory Technician), and High School Diploma. Team player, integrity, resourceful, intuition, pragmatic, proactive, good time management and interpersonal skills, self motivated, results oriented, and good written and verbal communication skills are all listed as desirable non-academic qualifications. Company benefits are rated above average. The potential for advancement is listed as excellent. The average annual starting salary falls within the $30,000 to $35,000 range. The most suitable method for initial contact by those seeking employment is to mail a resume with a covering letter. Nova Corporation does hire summer students. *Contact:* People Resource Centre at (403) 290-6262.

NOVA SCOTIA REHABILITATION CENTRE
1341 Summer Street
Halifax, NS B3H 4K4

Tel. 902-422-1787
Fax 902-425-6466

The Nova Scotia Rehabilitation Centre is an active treatment centre employing more than 250 people. The centre employs the broad concept of total rehabilitation for the physically disabled through a "multidisciplinary" approach. Although possessing certain characteristics of a hospital, its approach and method are more functional than clinical and in many cases concerned with adjustment rather than cure. Graduates most likely to be hired come from the following academic areas: Bachelor of Arts (Recreation), Bachelor of Science (Nursing), Bachelor of Education (Adult), Bachelor of Commerce/Business Administration, Master of Business Administration (Finance), Master of Science (Physiotherapy, Occupational Therapy), Master of Engineering (Biomedical), Doctorate (Psychology), and Community College Diploma (Accounting, Secretarial, Human Resources, Recreation, Social Work, Food/Nutrition, Nursing RN/RNA, Orthotic/Prosthetic Technician, Orthotic Footwear Technician). Graduates would occupy entry level positions relating to their specific area of study. Excellent communication skills, team player, adaptable, and a commitment to patient care are all listed as desirable non-academic qualifications. Company benefits are rated as industry standard. The potential for advancement is listed as average. The average annual starting salary falls within the $20,000 to $35,000 range and ultimately depends upon the position being considered. The most suitable method for initial contact by those seeking employment is to mail a resume with a covering letter. The Nova Scotia Rehabilitation Centre does hire summer students. *Contact:* Joy Stevens, Human Resources Services Manager.

NOWSCO WELL SERVICE LTD.
801 - 6th Avenue SW, Suite 1300
Calgary, AB T2P 4E1

Tel.	403-531-5151
Fax	403-265-7810

Nowsco Well Service Ltd. is involved in oil well servicing (nitrogen, fracturing, coiled tubing, cement), and pipeline services. The company employs approximately 300 people at this location, a total of 800 people in Canada, and 1,831 people worldwide. Graduates most likely to be hired come from the following academic areas: Bachelor of Science (Chemistry, Computer Science, Geology), Bachelor of Engineering (Chemical, Metallurgy, Computer Systems, Welding, Petroleum), Bachelor of Commerce/Business Administration (Accounting, Finance, Human Resources, Information Systems, Marketing), and Community College Diploma (Accounting, Administration, Business, Communications, Financial Planning, Human Resources, Insurance, Marketing/Sales, Secretarial, CAD/CAM/Autocad, Computer Science, Engineering Technician, Laboratory Technician). Graduates would occupy Accounting Clerk, Petroleum Engineer, Sales and Marketing, and Human Resource positions. Team player, creativity, and enthusiasm are listed as desirable non-academic qualifications. Company benefits and the potential for advancement are both rated as excellent. The average annual starting salary falls within the $25,000 to $35,000 range. The most suitable method for initial contact by those seeking employment is to mail a resume with a covering letter. Nowsco Well Service Ltd. does hire summer students. *Contacts:* Shirleen Becker, Manager, Human Resources or Debbie Charlton, Human Resources.

NRI INDUSTRIES INC.
394 Symington Avenue
Toronto, ON M6N 2W3

Tel.	416-652-4236
Fax	416-652-4213

NRI Industries Inc. was founded in 1927 and currently operates five plants in Canada and the United States. Through its expertise in rubber compounding and product design the company has become North America's leading manufacturer of automotive and industrial rubber parts based on recycled materials. Annual sales exceed $60 million with more than 80% from export sales. The company's objective is to remain the lowest total cost producer of value-added products using recycled materials and meet the highest specifications for quality. NRI achieved QS9000 certification in 1997. There are 350 employees at this location, a total of 450 in Canada, and a total of 600 employees in Canada and the United States. Graduates most likely to be hired come from the following academic areas: Bachelor of Science (Chemistry), Bachelor of Engineering (Chemical, Industrial Chemistry, Materials Science, Instrumentation, Industrial Design, Industrial Production), and Master of Business Administration (Marketing). Graduates would occupy Marketing, Production Management, Chemical Engineering, Mechanical Engineering, and Electrical Engineering positions. Applicants should be enthusiastic and active participants. Company benefits are rated as industry standard. The potential for advancement is listed as being good. The average annual starting salary falls within the $30,000 to $35,000 range. The most suitable method for initial contact by those seeking employment is to mail a resume with a covering letter. NRI Industries Inc. does hire summer students. *Contacts:* Sheila Kendall, Manager, Human Resources or Randy Garrett, Vice President, Human Resources.

NSI COMMUNICATIONS
4610 Chemin Bois Franc
St-Laurent, QC H4S 1A7

Tel.	514-956-8880
Fax	514-956-8251
Email	nsi@nsicomm.com

NSI Communications manufactures, designs and markets state of the art satellite based telecommunications equipment and services worldwide. There are approximately 40 employees at this location, 50 across Canada, and a total of 60 employees worldwide. Graduates most likely to be hired come from the following academic areas: Bachelor of Science (Computer Science, Mathematics, Physics), Bachelor of Engineering (General, Electrical, Computer Systems, Telecommunications, Mechanical, Industrial Design), Bachelor of Commerce/Business Administration (Accounting, Finance, Human Resources, Information Systems, Marketing), Chartered Accountant, Master of Business Administration (Marketing), Master of Science (Computer Science), Master of Engineering (Electronic Circuits, Computer Science), Doctorate (Engineering), and Community College Diploma (Accounting, Business, Human Resources, Marketing, Purchasing/Logistics, Secretarial, Graphic Arts, CAD/CAM/Autocad, Computer Science, Electronics Technician, Engineering Technician). Graduates would occupy Technical positions in Research and Development, Production, and Systems, as well as positions in Marketing and Accounting. Depending upon the level of experience and academic background of the applicant, positions would range from the Junior to Director levels. An ability to speak and write properly in both official languages where applicable, good work ethic, self-starter, proactive, reliable, punctual, non-smoker, and good presentation skills are all listed as desirable non-academic qualifications. Company benefits are rated as industry standard. The potential for advancement is listed as being good. The average annual starting salary depends upon the level and function of the position being considered. The most suitable method for initial contact by those seeking employment is to mail a resume with a covering letter. NSI Communications does hire summer students. *Contact:* Ms. Diane Malboeuf.

NUMAC ENERGY INC.
321 - 6 Avenue SW
Calgary, AB T2P 3H3

Tel. 403-260-9484
Fax 403-294-3402
Email .... patti-lou.barron@numac.com

Numac Energy Inc. is involved in oil and gas exploration and production. There are 160 employees at this location, and a total of 240 employees in Canada. Graduates most likely to be hired come from the following academic areas: Bachelor of Arts (Economics), Bachelor of Science (Computer Science, Geology, Geography), Bachelor of Engineering (Industrial Production, Petroleum), Bachelor of Laws, Bachelor of Commerce/Business Administration (Accounting, Finance, Human Resources, Information Systems, Marketing), Chartered Accountant, Certified Management Accountant, Certified General Accountant, Master of Business Administration (Accounting, Finance, Human Resources, Information Systems, Marketing), Master of Science, Master of Engineering, Community College Diploma (Accounting, Administration, Business, Human Resources, Computer Science, Engineering Technician), and High School Diploma. Graduates would occupy Facilities Engineer, Production Engineer, Reservoir Engineer, Operations Engineer, Drilling Engineer, Geologist, Geophysicist, Marketing, Computer/IS Department, Human Resources, Land Acquisitions/Divestitures, Finance, Tax, and General Accounting positions. Team player, self motivated, independent thinker, and previous industry experience are all listed as desirable non-academic qualifications. Company benefits are rated as excellent. The potential for advancement is listed as being good. The average annual starting salary for new graduates falls within the $25,000 to $30,000 range. The most suitable methods for initial contact by those seeking employment are to mail a resume with a covering letter, or through networking contacts. Numac Energy Inc. hires 15 to 20 students per year for summer and co-op work terms. *Contact:* Patti Lou Barron.

NYGÅRD INTERNATIONAL INC.
1771 Inkster Boulevard
Winnipeg, MB R2X 1R3

Tel. 204-982-5000
Fax 204-697-1254

Nygård International Inc. manufactures and retails ladies apparel. There are 1,300 employees at this location, and a total of 2,000 employees worldwide. Graduates most likely to be hired come from the following academic areas: Bachelor of Engineering (Industrial), Bachelor of Commerce/Business Administration (Finance, Human Resources, Information Systems), Chartered Accountant, Certified Management Accountant, Certified General Accountant, Master of Engineering (Industrial), and Community College Diploma (Administration, Business, Human Resources, Legal Assistant, Security/Enforcement, Travel/Tourism, CAD/CAM/Autocad, Computer Science, Electronics Technician). Garment manufacturing, design and construction experience, computer literate, team oriented, able to work with a minimum of supervision, and deadline oriented are all listed as desirable non-academic qualifications. Company benefits and the potential for advancement are both rated as excellent. The average annual starting salary falls within the $20,000 to $25,000 range. The most suitable method for initial contact by those seeking employment is to mail a resume with a covering letter. Nygård International Inc. does hire a limited number of summer students annually. *Contact:* Manager, Human Resources.

A Division of Canon Canada Inc.

OE, A DIVISION OF CANON CANADA INC.
1490 Denison Street
Markham, ON L3R 9T7

Tel. 905-683-9857
Fax 905-305-3913
Email .... hrmarkham@canada.canon.com
Website .... www.usa.canon.com

OE was founded in 1906 and its relationship with Canon Canada Inc. (see Canon's listing) first began in 1964, becoming a wholly owned subsidiary in 1990, and then a division of the company in 1995. OE is responsible for the sale and servicing of Canon Office Equipment throughout the Greater Toronto Area, Hamilton, Montreal, Ottawa and Quebec City. OE's dedication to service and responsiveness to customer needs, has earned it a reputation of being an innovative and trusted provider of global solutions for business and consumer products. The company's quality Canon products and superb customer service contribute to Canon's attainment of the largest share of the imaging solutions market. This reputation has been built and maintained by the concerted efforts of individuals who work in a variety of challenging and rewarding careers in Sales, Sales Support, Service and Technology, Marketing, and Administration. OE offers graduates a team environment that recognizes individual effort and achievement. In addition, OE provides excellent career growth opportunities and comprehensive benefits and rewards. The most suitable methods to inquire about current job opportunities are to e-mail (hrmarkham@canada.canon.com) or fax (905-305-3913) a resume with a covering letter. *Contact:* Human Resources.

OERLIKON AEROSPACE INC.
225, boul du Séminaire sud
St-Jean-sur-Richelieu, QC J3B 8E9

Tel. 514-358-2000
Fax 514-358-1744

Oerlikon Aerospace Inc. is a high tech company, supplying the Canadian Armed Forces with its ADATS low-level air defense missile system. The company employs approximately 300 people. Graduates most likely to be hired come from the following academic areas: Bachelor of Science (Computer Science, Physics), Bachelor of Engineering (Electrical, Telecommunications, Mechanical, Aeronautical), Bachelor of Commerce/Business Administration (Accounting, Finance, Information Systems), Master of Business Administration (Marketing), and Community College Diploma (Accounting, CAD/CAM/Autocad, Electronics Technician). Applicants should possess related work experience. Company benefits and the potential for advancement are both rated as being excellent. The most suitable method for initial contact by those seeking employment is to mail a resume with a covering letter. *Contact:* Human Resources Department.

OFFICE OF THE AUDITOR GENERAL, CANADA
240 Sparks Street
Ottawa, ON K1A 0G6

Tel. 613-995-3708
Fax 613-954-0441
Email .... emploi@oag-bvg.gc.ca
Website .... www.oag-bvg.gc.ca

The Office of the Auditor General of Canada maintains a vision of making a difference for the Canadian people by promoting, in all its work for Parliament, answerable, honest, and productive government. The Auditor General's mission is to conduct independent audits and examinations that provide objective information, advice and assurance to Parliament. The Office promotes accountability and best practices in government operations. The Auditor General offers a variety of work in government departments, Crown corporations and agencies touching all aspects of national life. Transportation, finance, culture, the environment, foreign aid, broadcasting and scientific research are just a few of the areas covered by auditors. The Office is recognized internationally as a leader in developing innovative approaches, software packages and applications to assist in auditing government activities. The Office of the Auditor General employs a total of 550 people across Canada in offices located in Halifax, Montreal, Ottawa, Winnipeg, Edmonton and Vancouver (450 in Ottawa). Graduates with a Bachelor level degree would enter the Financial Audit Trainee program. These graduates would be required to obtain an accounting designation, with preference given to candidates who have successfully completed or enrolled in advanced courses in financial accounting, management accounting or auditing. Undergraduate degree specialization must be in accounting, commerce, administration, finance, or other related disciplines. Graduates with a Master degree or Professional qualification in public/business administration, social science, applied science, applied science (including environmental science), mathematics, computer science, law, engineering or other disciplines related to the work of the Office, would enter the Value-for-Money Audit Trainee program. The Office maintains a commitment to Audit Trainees by offering high quality and lively training, both on the job and in the classroom, and has designed an extensive professional development curriculum for all its staff, ranging from technical knowledge courses to training in management skills. Audit Trainees also have the opportunity to enter into the mentoring program. Bilingualism is listed as a definite asset. The average annual starting salary falls within the $25,000 to $30,000 range. The most suitable methods for initial contact by those seeking employment are to mail, fax or e-mail a resume, cover letter and most recent transcript. The Office of the Auditor General does hire summer and co-op work term students. *Contacts:* Dominique Martel (x 4229) or Lucie Smith.

OFFICE SPECIALTY
67 Toll Road
Holland Landing, ON L9N 1H2

Tel. 905-836-7676
Fax 905-836-6000

Office Specialty employs 425 people in the manufacturing of office furniture. Graduates most likely to be hired come from the following academic areas: Bachelor of Arts (Economics, Psychology), Bachelor of Science (Environmental, Metallurgy), Bachelor of Engineering (General, Metallurgy, Architectural/Building, Industrial Design, Industrial Production, Welding), Bachelor of Commerce/Business Administration (Accounting, Finance, Human Resources, Information Systems, Marketing, Public Administration), Chartered Accountant, Certified Management Accountant, Certified General Accountant, Master of Business Administration (Accounting, Finance, Human Resources, Information Systems, Marketing, Public Administration), Community College Diploma (Accounting, Administration, Human Resources, Welding), and High School Diploma. Graduates would occupy Human Resources Administrator/Coordinator, Industrial Engineer, Mechanical Engineer, Product Engineer, Marketing Coordinator, Accountant, Controller, Cell Operator/Assembler, Fabrication Supervisor, Plant Supervisor, and Production Manager positions. Strong interpersonal skills, team player, previous work experience, an ability to meet deadlines, detail oriented, and strong organizational skills are all listed as desirable non-academic qualifications. The potential for advancement is listed as excellent. The most suitable method for initial contact by those seeking employment is to mail a resume with a covering letter. *Contacts:*

Raihana Ansari, Human Resources Coordinator or Karen Copeland, Human Resources Coordinator.

OLAND BREWERIES LIMITED
3055 Agricola Street
Halifax, NS B3K 4G2

Tel. 902-453-3811
Fax 902-453-5664

Oland Breweries Limited is involved in the brewing and marketing of beer. The company employs 196 people at this location and a total of approximately 3,000 people in Canada. Graduates most likely to be hired come from the following academic areas: Bachelor of Arts (General), Bachelor of Science (Chemistry), Bachelor of Engineering (Food Processing, Industrial Production), Bachelor of Commerce/ Business Administration (Accounting, Finance, Human Resources, Information Systems, Marketing), Master of Business Administration (Accounting, Finance, Human Resources, Information Systems, Marketing), and Community College Diploma (Accounting, Business, Human Resources, Marketing/ Sales, Laboratory Technician). The positions graduates would occupy depend upon the specific openings, but usually they are entry level Clerical, Technical or Sales positions. Results oriented, analytical, team work, and possessing good communication, people, leadership, problem solving, and decision making skills are all listed as desirable non-academic qualifications. Company benefits are rated as excellent. The potential for advancement is listed as being good. The average annual starting salary falls within the $25,000 to $30,000 range. The most suitable method for initial contact by those seeking employment is to mail a resume with a covering letter. Oland Breweries Limited occasionally hires summer students. *Contacts:* John Stacey, Director of Human Resources or Eleanor Grodett, Human Resources Coordinator.

OLYMEL
2200 Leon Pratte
Saint-Hyacinthe, QC J2S 4B6

Tel. 514-771-0400
Fax 514-771-0519

Olymel is involved in meat processing and packaging. There are approximately 2,200 employees at separate locations in Canada. Graduates most likely to be hired come from the following academic areas: Bachelor of Science (Biology, Computer Science), Bachelor of Engineering (Civil), Bachelor of Commerce/Business Administration (Accounting, Marketing), Chartered Accountant (Finance), Certified General Accountant, and Community College Diploma (Computer Science). Company benefits are rated above average. The potential for advancement is listed as average. The average annual starting salary falls within the $30,000 to $35,000 range. The most suitable method for initial contact by those seeking employment is to mail a resume with a covering letter. *Contact:* M. Louis Banville.

OMNIMARK TECHNOLOGIES CORPORATION
1400 Blair Place, 4th Floor
Ottawa, ON K1J 9B8

Tel. 613-745-4242
Fax 613-745-5560
Email .... hr@omnimark.com
Website .... www.omnimark.com

Founded in 1986, OmniMark Technologies Corporation makes the industry's most advanced server-side programming language for managing and delivering personalized content on the Web. This language enables organizations to build robust content management and delivery applications that provide dynamic content to meet the needs of the individual user. It provides high-quality interaction, integration of large volumes of text, data, graphics, hyperlinks and other objects, unlimited scalability and an open-ended growth strategy. OmniMark powers some the world's most innovative websites, including The Wall Street Journal Interactive Edition, Hewlett-Packard, and Airbus Industries. OmniMark has installed at over 1,000 companies in more than 35 countries worldwide. Privately owned by its management, OmniMark Technologies Corporation is a profitable, financially sound and growing company, with over 80 full-time employees at its corporate headquarters in Ottawa, as well as direct sales and technical support offices in France, Belgium, Sweden, and the United Kingdom. Graduates most likely to be hired come from the following academic areas: Bachelor of Arts (General, English, Journalism, Languages, Philosophy, Psychology), Bachelor of Science (Computer Science), Bachelor of Engineering (General, Computer Systems), Master of Science (Computer Science), Master of Engineering (Computer Systems), Master of Arts, and Community College Diploma (Computer Science). Graduates would occupy Software Developer, Customer Solutions Developer, and Technical Coordinator positions. Team player, interest in technology, and strong communication skills are all listed as desirable non-academic qualifications. Company benefits and the potential for advancement are both rated as excellent. The average annual starting salary ranges widely, depending on the position and the applicant's experience and skill set. The most suitable method for initial contact by those seeking employment is to apply through the company's website. OmniMark Technologies Corporation does hire students for co-op work terms. *Contact:* Doris Kiffner, Human Resources Generalist.

ONTARIO COLLEGE OF ART & DESIGN
100 McCaul Street
Toronto, ON M5T 1W1

Tel. 416-977-6000
Fax 416-977-3034
Email .... ocad.on.ca
Website .... www.ocad.on.ca

The Ontario College of Art & Design is the oldest and largest college of art and design in Canada. There are 350 employees. The College provides post-secondary students with a 4 Year Diploma Program in such areas as Fine Art, Industrial and Environmental Design, Ceramics, Wood and Metal Work, Film, Photography, etc. Graduates most likely to be hired come from the following academic areas: Bachelor of Arts (Fine Art/Design, Journalism), Bachelor of Education (Arts/Design), Bachelor of Commerce (Accounting, Finance, Human Resources, Information Systems, Marketing), Masters (Fine Art/Design), Community College Diploma (Accounting, Administration, Advertising, Communications, Financial Planning, Human Resources, Marketing/Sales, Purchasing/Logistics, Secretarial, Fine Art/Graphics/Design, Journalism, Photography, Security/Enforcement), and High School Diploma. Good oral and written communication skills, able to work as a member of a team, detail oriented, able to prioritize and meet deadlines, computer skills (word processing, spreadsheet and database), and good interpersonal skills are all listed as desirable non-academic qualifications. Employee benefits are rated as excellent. The potential for advancement is listed as being good. The most suitable method for initial contact by those seeking employment is to mail a resume with a covering letter. The Ontario College of Art & Design hires summer students depending on need. *Contacts:* Nicky Davis, Director, Human Resources or Suzanne Smith, Assistant, Human Resources.

ONTARIO FOOD TERMINAL BOARD
165 The Queensway
Toronto, ON M8Y 1H8

Tel. 416-259-5479

The Ontario Food Terminal Board operates the Ontario Food Terminal (located at same address), which is a Schedule II Ontario Government agency. The Board rents space to tenants who in turn sell their produce to retailers. There are more than 25 employees with the Board. Graduates most likely to be hired come from the following academic areas: Master of Business Administration (Accounting), Community College Diploma (Business, Mechanic). Graduates would occupy office, maintenance, security and sanitation positions. Company benefits are rated as excellent. The average annual starting salary falls within the $25,000 to $30,000 range. The most suitable method for initial contact by those seeking employment is to mail a resume with a covering letter. The Ontario Food Terminal Board does hire summer students. *Contact:* Mr. C.E. Carsley, General Manager.

ONTARIO HOSPITAL ASSOCIATION (OHA)
200 Front Street West
Suite 2800
Toronto, ON M5V 3L1

Tel. 416-205-1300
Fax 416-205-1392
Website .... www.oha.com/

The Ontario Hospital Association (OHA) is a voluntary non-profit organization of hospitals and health care institutions in Ontario. The OHA's mission is to promote excellence of delivery of health care through effective utilization of available resources. The OHA employs approximately 100 people. Graduates most likely to be hired come from the following academic areas: Bachelor of Arts (Journalism, Political Science), Bachelor of Laws (Health), Bachelor of Commerce/Business Administration (Accounting, Finance, Human Resources, Public Administration), Chartered Accountant, Certified Management Accountant, Certified General Accountant, Master of Business Administration (Human Resources, Public Administration, Health Administration), Masters (Health Administration, Industrial Relations), and Community College Diploma (Administration, Secretarial). The most suitable method for initial contact by those seeking employment is to mail a resume with a covering letter. *Contact:* Human Resources.

ONTARIO HYDRO
20 Dundas Street West, 14th Floor
Toronto, ON M5G 2C2

Tel. 416-592-5111

Ontario Hydro provides electricity to industrial, residential, and commercial customers throughout Ontario, either directly or through local municipal services. Activities include design, construction, maintenance of hydro electric, thermal and nuclear power plants, research and development into alternative power sources, energy management, nuclear safety, etc. Graduates most likely to be hired come from the following academic areas, Bachelor of Science (Biology, Chemistry, Computer Science), Bachelor of Engineering (Mechanical, Electrical, Civil, Industrial, Computer Systems), Bachelor of Laws, Bachelor of Architecture, Bachelor of Commerce/Business Administration, Chartered Accountant, Master of Business Administration (Finance, Marketing), Master of Science/Engineering (Environmental Studies), Community College Diploma (Engineering Technician, Secretarial, Computer Science). Good management skills, oral and written communication skills, and an ability to work in a team environment are all listed as desirable non-academic qualifications. Positions are advertised in The Globe & Mail, The Toronto Star, and at campus career centres. Otherwise, the most suitable method for initial contact by those seeking employment is to mail a resume with a covering letter. Ontario Hydro does hire summer students. *Contact:* Staffing Department.

ONTARIO HYDRO TECHNOLOGIES
800 Kipling Avenue
Toronto, ON M8Z 5S4

Tel. 416-207-6550
Fax 416-207-5875

Ontario Hydro Technologies (OHT) is one of the largest single source technology centres in the world. As a subsidiary of Ontario Hydro, OHT's mandate is to support the technology development needs of Ontario Hydro and its business units and, in addition, to commercialize promising technologies and to market its technical services more broadly throughout the energy and process industries. Graduates most likely to be hired come from the following academic areas: Bachelor of Science (Chemistry, Biology, Computer Science, Mathematics, Metallurgy, Materials Science), Bachelor of Engineering (Mechanical, Civil, Electrical, Computer Systems, Materials Science), Bachelor of Commerce/Business Administration (Marketing), Master/Doctorate of Science (Chemistry, Biology, Computer Science, Mathematics, Metallurgy, Materials Science), and Master/Doctorate of Engineering (Mechanical, Civil, Electrical, Computer Systems, Materials Science). Graduates are hired as Technicians, Scientists, Engineers, and Researchers. Creativity, commitment, flexibility and strong communication skills are all listed as desirable non-academic qualifications. Company benefits are rated as excellent. The potential for advancement is listed as being good. The average starting salary falls within the $35,000 plus range. The most suitable method for initial contact by those seeking employment is to mail a resume with a covering letter. Ontario Hydro Technologies does hire summer students. *Contact:* Human Resources Officer.

ONTARIO JOCKEY CLUB, THE
P.O. Box 156
Rexdale, ON M9W 5L2

Tel. 416-675-3993
Fax 416-213-2130

The Ontario Jockey Club is involved in the sports and entertainment industry, particularly horse racing. The Ontario Jockey Club employs a total of 2,100 people worldwide. Graduates most likely to be hired come from the following academic areas: Bachelor of Arts (General), Bachelor of Science (General, Computer Science), Bachelor of Commerce/Business Administration (Accounting, Finance, Human Resources, Information Systems, Marketing), Chartered Accountant, Certified Management Accountant, Certified General Accountant, Master of Business Administration (Accounting, Finance), Community College Diploma (Accounting, Advertising, Business, Communications, Facility Management, Human Resources, Marketing/Sales, Purchasing/Logistics, Secretarial, Cooking, Hospitality, Security/Enforcement, Television/Radio Arts, Computer Science), and High School Diploma. Team player, adaptable to change, good communication skills, initiative, attention to detail, customer service focus, good organizational skills, and previous work experience are all listed as desirable non-academic qualifications. Company benefits are rated as industry standard. The potential for advancement is listed as being good. The most suitable method for initial contact by those seeking employment is to mail a resume with a covering letter. The Ontario Jockey Club hires summer students for maintenance and customer service positions. *Contact:* Human Resources Services.

ONTARIO MARCH OF DIMES
10 Overlea Boulevard
Toronto, ON M4H 1A4

Tel. 416-425-3463
Fax 416-425-1920

Ontario March of Dimes provides support services to individuals with disabilities. There are a total of 1,100 employees, of which approximately 750 are engaged directly in the provision of support services. Graduates most likely to be hired come from the following academic areas: Bachelor of Arts (General, Psychology, Sociology/Social Work), Chartered Accountant, Certified General Accountant, and Master of Business Administration (Accounting). Graduates would occupy Secretarial, Clerical, Finance, Accounting, and Attendant and Support Service positions. Team player, flexible, and empathetic to customer needs are all listed as desirable non-academic qualifications. Company benefits are rated as industry standard. The potential for advancement is listed as average. The average annual starting salary for full-time positions falls within the $25,000 to $30,000 range. The most suitable method for initial contact by those seeking employment is to mail a resume with a covering letter. Ontario March of Dimes does hire a few summer students annually. *Contacts:* Birgit Matthaes, Human Resources Assistant (x 385) or Jim Davidson, Director of Human Resources & Quality (x 334).

OPAL MANUFACTURING LTD.
105 Brisbane Road
Suite 12
Downsview, ON M3J 2K6

Tel. 416-665-6605

Opal Manufacturing Ltd. employs approximately 40 people in the design and manufacture of vending machines and liquid dispensing devices. Opal Manufacturing is a small but aggressive and fast growing company with international distribution. Graduates most likely to be hired come from the following academic areas: Bachelor of Engineering (Electrical, Mechanical), Bachelor of Commerce/Business Administration, and Community College Diploma (Electronics, Mechanic Technician). Graduates would occupy Service Manager, Technician, Designer, Production Manager, and Casual Labour positions. Company benefits are rated above average. The potential for advancement is listed as excellent. The most suitable method for initial contact by those seeking employment is to mail a resume with a covering letter. Opal Manufacturing Ltd. does hire summer students, depending upon production demand. *Contact:* Garnet Rich.

OPEN LEARNING CANADA
4355 Mathissi Place
Burnaby, BC V5G 4S8

Tel. 604-431-3000
Fax 604-431-3384
Website .... www.olcanada.edu

Open Learning Canada (OLC) is a non-profit, fully accredited educational institution providing flexible and innovative education and training to British Columbians through a variety of technologies (that are among the most advanced used anywhere in the world) and a variety of services, including the Knowledge Network, Open University of Canada, Open College of Canada, Open School of Canada, and Workplace Training Systems. To ensure that OLC's offerings reach the broadest possible audience, it works with a wide variety of partners from industry, government, and other educational institutions. OLC is funded by the British Columbia government and by grants, tuition fees, sales, donations, sponsorships, and partnerships. Employing approximately 600 people, OLC is headquartered in Burnaby, British Columbia. Graduates most likely to be hired come from the following academic areas: Bachelor of Arts, Bachelor of Science, Bachelor of Education, Bachelor of Commerce/Business Administration, Chartered Accountant, Certified Management Accountant, Certified General Accountant, Master of Business Administration, Master of Arts, Master of Science, Master of Engineering, Community College Diploma (Accounting, Communications/Public Relations, Facility Management, Human Resources, Information Systems, Purchasing/Logistics, Audio/Visual Technician, Graphic Arts, Television/Radio Arts, Computer Science, Dental Assistant, Dental Hygiene, Nursing RN/RNA), and High School Diploma. Good communication, interpersonal and organizational skills, ability to work in a team environment, high energy level, positive attitude, creative, motivated, computer skills, and related work experience are all listed as desirable non-academic qualifications. Company benefits are rated above average. The potential for advancement is listed as being good. The average annual starting salary depends upon the level and function of the position being considered. The most suitable methods for initial contact by those seeking employment are to mail or fax a resume with a covering letter, quoting the relevant competition number (OLC does not accept unsolicited resumes). *Contact:* Human Resources.

OPTIMAL ROBOTICS CORP.
4700 De La Savane, Suite 101
Montreal, QC H4P 1T7

Tel. 514-738-8885
Fax 514-738-2284
Email .... jobs@optimal-robotics.com
Website .... www.optimal-robotics.com

Optimal Robotics Corp. is the leader in the development and implementation of automated self-checkout systems for retail applications. The U-Scan Express system is designed to reduce the cost of checkout transactions to retailers and increase shopper's convenience by providing a level of service and convenience similar to that provided in the banking industry by ATMs. Optimal Robotics employs a total of 85 people. Graduates most likely to be hired come from the following academic areas: Bachelor of Science (Computer Science), Bachelor of Engineering (Electrical), and Community College Diploma (Computer Science). Graduates would occupy Programmer, Technician, Help Desk, and Quality Assurance positions. Previous work experience, flexible and a willingness to travel are listed as desirable non-academic qualifications. Company benefits are rated as industry standard. The potential for advancement is listed as excellent. The average annual starting salary falls within the $35,000 to $40,000 range. The most suitable methods for initial contact by those seeking employment are to fax or e-mail a resume with a covering letter. Optimal Robotics Corp. does hire a limited number of summer students. *Contacts:* Charles Morris, Programmers or Brett Johnson, Technicians.

ORTHOPAEDIC & ARTHRITIC HOSPITAL
43 Wellesley Street East
Toronto, ON M4Y 1H1

Tel. 416-967-8655
Fax 416-967-8593

The Orthopaedic & Arthritic Hospital is an acute care hospital specializing in orthopaedics and arthritic type disorders. The hospital employs more than 250 people. Graduates most likely to be hired come from the following academic areas: Bachelor of Science (Chemistry, Health Sciences, Nursing, Pharmacy), Bachelor of Engineering (Computer Systems), Chartered Accountant (Finance), and Community College Diploma (Accounting, Secretarial, Human Resources, Laboratory Technician, Nursing RN/RNA, Radiology Technician). Graduates would be hired to occupy Service positions (Housekeeping, Dietary), Technical positions (Lab, X-Ray), and Professional positions (RN, Physiotherapy). Friendly, good with people, polite, good communication skills, and related customer service work experience are all listed as desirable non-academic qualifications. Employee benefits are rated as excellent. The potential for advancement is listed as being good. The average annual starting salary falls within the $25,000 to $35,000 range, and ultimately depends upon the position being considered. The most suitable method for initial contact by those seeking employment is to mail a resume with a covering letter. The Orthopaedic & Arthritic Hospital does hire summer students. *Contacts:* Laurette Sauer, Supervisor, Human Resources or Marilyn Reddick, Director, Human Resources.

OSHAWA GENERAL HOSPITAL
24 Alma Street
Oshawa, ON L1G 2B9

Tel. 905-433-4393
Fax 905-433-2859

The Oshawa General Hospital is a 650 bed hospital employing 2,300 people. Graduates most likely to be hired come from the following academic areas: Bachelor of Arts (Social Work), Bachelor of Science (Nursing, Nutritional Sciences, Occupational Therapy, Pharmacy, Physical Therapy, Psychology,

Speech Pathology), Bachelor of Engineering (Architectural/Building, Biomedical Electronics, Computer Systems), Chartered Accountant, Certified General Accountant, Master of Arts (Social Work), Master of Science (Nursing, Nutritional Sciences, Occupational Therapy, Pharmacy, Physical Therapy, Psychology, Speech Pathology), and Community College Diploma (Accounting, Human Resources, Purchasing/Logistics, Secretarial, Recreation Studies, Computer Science, Electronics Technician, HVAC Systems, Laboratory Technician, Nuclear Medicine Technician, Nursing RN/RNA, Radiology Technician, Respiratory Therapy, Ultra-Sound Technician). Computer literacy, and excellent communication, interpersonal, organizational and written skills are all listed as desirable non-academic qualifications. Employee benefits are rated above average. The potential for advancement is listed as being good. The most suitable method for initial contact by those seeking employment is to mail a resume with a covering letter. *Contact:* Janet Walker, Human Resources Consultant, Human Resources Department.

OSHAWA GROUP LIMITED, THE
302 The East Mall
Toronto, ON M9B 6B8

Tel. 416-236-1971
Fax 416-236-3255
Email .... jobs@oshawagroup.ca

The Oshawa Group's two business segments are Agora Food Merchants and SERCA Foodservice Inc. Agora is Canada's largest food retail franchisor, known for its many banners such as IGA, Price Chopper, Knechtel, and Food Town. SERCA is the country's only national foodservice wholesaler, distributing to restaurants, hospitals, hotels and institutional accounts. There are approximately 350 employees at this location, and a total of 17,000 employees across Canada. Graduates most likely to be hired come from the following academic areas: Bachelor of Arts (General), Bachelor of Science (Computer Science), Bachelor of Engineering (Industrial Engineering), Bachelor of Commerce/Business Administration (General, Accounting, Finance, Human Resources, Information Systems, Marketing), Chartered Accountant, Master of Business Administration (General), Community College Diploma (Accounting, Business, Human Resources, Information Systems, Marketing/Sales, Purchasing/Logistics, Computer Science), and High School Diploma. Graduates would occupy Technical Specialist, Administrative Staff, and Management Level positions. Action and results driven, innovative, excellent problem solving skills, customer driven, and the ability to build positive relationships are all listed as desirable non-academic qualifications. Company benefits are rated above average. The potential for advance-

ment is listed as being good. The average annual starting salary depends on the position being considered. The most suitable methods for initial contact by those seeking employment are to fax or e-mail a resume with a covering letter. The Oshawa Group Limited does hire summer and co-op work term students. *Contacts:* Joan Andersen, Senior Director, Human Resources (Agora & The Oshawa Group) or Grace Palombo, Director, Human Resources (Serca).

OSRAM SYLVANIA LTD.
2001 Drew Road
Mississauga, ON L5S 1S4

Tel. 905-673-6171
Fax 905-673-6290

Osram Sylvania Ltd., is the Canadian subsidiary of Osram Sylvania Inc. based in Danvers, Massachusetts, which is the North American operation of Osram GmbH, a wholly owned subsidiary of Munich based Siemens AG. The Mississauga office provides general lighting sales, marketing, distribution and related services to the Canadian market. With regional offices across the country, Osram's sales staff work as partners with a significant distributor base in Canada to service customers. Osram Sylvania Ltd. manufactures lighting products in a facility in Drummondville, Quebec. There are approximately 140 employees at this location, a total of 500 in Canada, and 27,000 Osram employees worldwide. Graduates most likely to be hired come from the following academic areas: Bachelor of Arts (French, Languages), Bachelor of Science (Computer Science, Psychology), Bachelor of Engineering (Electrical, Computer Systems, Industrial Production), Bachelor of Commerce/Business Administration (Accounting, Finance, Human Resources, Information Systems, Marketing), Chartered Accountant, Certified Management Accountant, Certified General Accountant, Master of Engineering (Lighting Systems), Community College Diploma (Accounting, Administration, Advertising, Business, Communications/Public Relations, Facility Management, Human Resources, Marketing, Purchasing, Secretarial, Computer Science, Electrical Engineering Technician), and High School Diploma. Graduates would occupy Finance, Human Resources, Logistics/Distribution, Sales/Marketing, Information Systems, Operations, Lighting Applications, Customer Service, and Administration positions. Team player, a customer service orientation, flexible, adaptable, and a commitment to continuous improvement are all listed as desirable non-academic qualifications. Company benefits are rated above average. The potential for advancement is listed as excellent. The average annual starting salary falls within the $25,000 to $45,000 plus range, depending upon the position being considered. The most suitable method for initial contact by those seeking employment is to mail a resume with a covering letter. *Contacts:* David Ribardy, Human Resources Manager or Wanda Menge, Human Resources Administrative Assistant.

OTTAWA HOSPITAL, CIVIC CAMPUS
1053 Carling Avenue
Ottawa, ON K1Y 4E9

Tel. .... 613-798-5555 x 6995
Fax 613-761-5374

The Ottawa Hospital is a major academic health sciences centre affiliated with the University of Ottawa. The hospital is dedicated to the provision of quality patient care in an atmosphere of academic and research excellence. The hospital employs approximately 7,000 people. Graduates most likely to be hired come from the following academic areas: Bachelor of Arts (French, Graphic Arts, Psychology, Recreation, Social Work/Sociology), Bachelor of Science (Biology, Chemistry, Computer Science, Audiology, Nursing, Nutritional Sciences, Occupational Therapy, Pharmacy, Physical Therapy, Psychology, Speech Pathology), Bachelor of Commerce/Business Administration (Accounting, Finance, Human Resources, Information Systems, Marketing, Public Administration), Certified Management Accountant, Certified General Accountant, Master of Business Administration, Master of Science, Master of Health Sciences, Community College Diploma (Accounting, Administration, Advertising), and High School Diploma. Excellent communication and interpersonal skills are both listed as desirable non-academic qualifications. Company benefits and the potential for advancement are both rated as excellent. The most suitable method for initial contact by those seeking employment is to mail a resume with a covering letter. The Ottawa Hospital occasionally hires summer students. Contacts: Sandii Paquette, Employment Services Officer or Adele Savoie, Employment Services Officer.

OWENS-CORNING CANADA
3450 McNicoll Avenue
Toronto, ON M1V 1Z5

Tel. 416-292-4000
Fax 416-292-5837

Owens-Corning Canada is the largest manufacturer of glass fibre insulation products for the Canadian market. The Toronto plant employs more than 100 people, and is located in the Steeles/Markham Road area. Graduates most likely to be hired come from the following academic areas: Bachelor of Science (Chemistry), Bachelor of Engineering (Mechanical), Chartered Accountant, Certified Management Accountant (Finance, Accounting), and Community College Diploma (Architectural Technician, Sciences). Graduates are hired to occupy Accounting, Engineering and Technical positions. Good communication skills, an interest in team work, and previous job experience in a manufacturing environment are all listed as desirable non-academic qualifications. Company benefits are rated as excellent. The potential for advancement is listed as being good. The most suitable method for initial contact by those seeking employment is to mail a resume with a covering letter. Owens-Corning Canada does hire a limited number of summer students. Contact: Employee Relations Manager.

OXFORD PROPERTIES GROUP INC.
120 Adelaide Street West
Suite 1700
Toronto, ON M5H 1T1

Tel. 416-865-8300
Fax 416-868-0701

Oxford Properties Group Inc. is one of North America's leading real estate corporations. The company was formed in 1960, and manages approximately 45 million square feet of prime real estate assets throughout North America. There are approximately 400 employees at this location. Graduates most likely to be hired come from the following academic areas: Bachelor of Commerce/Business Administration (Accounting, Finance, Information Systems), Chartered Accountant (Finance), Certified Management Accountant (Finance), Certified General Accountant (Finance), and Master of Business Administration (Finance). Possessing work experience specifically related to real estate or building management is listed as a desirable non-academic qualification. Company benefits are rated as excellent. The potential for advancement is listed as being good. The average annual starting salary depends upon the specific position being considered and the qualifications of each individual applicant. The most suitable method for initial contact by those seeking employment is to mail a resume with a covering letter. Contact: Human Resources Department.

PAFCO INSURANCE COMPANY LIMITED
1243 Islington Avenue
Suite 300
Toronto, ON M8X 2Y3

Tel. 416-231-2835
Fax 416-231-2806

Pafco Insurance Company Limited underwrites and settles claims for a variety of specialty insurance lines and comprehensive packages. The company employs more than 150 people across Canada. Graduates most likely to be hired come from the following academic areas: Chartered Accountant, Certified General Accountant (Accounting, Finance), Community College Diploma (Clerical, Underwriting, Claims, Marketing, Secretarial), A.I.I.C Designation and F.I.I.C. designation preferred. Graduates are hired to occupy the following General positions: Telephone Adjuster, Claims Examiner, Underwriter, Marketing Representative, Secretary, Accountant, Reinsurance Clerk, Clerical Support; and Managerial positions in the following areas: Underwriting, Marketing, Claims, Administration/Personnel, and Accounting. Insurance knowledge, computer skills, mathematical aptitude, initiative, ability to work independently or as part of a team, good communication skills, ability to meet deadlines, a mature attitude, and reliability are all listed as desirable non-academic qualifications. Company benefits are rated above average. The potential for advancement is listed as being good. The average annual starting salary is dependent upon the position being considered. The most suitable method for initial contact by those seeking employment is to mail or fax a resume with a covering letter. Pafco Insurance Company Limited does hire summer students. *Contact:* Karyn E. O'Neill, Manager, Human Resources.

PAGE + STEELE INCORPORATED - ARCHITECTS PLANNERS
95 St. Clair Avenue West
Suite 200
Toronto, ON M4V 1N6

Tel. 416-924-9966
Fax 416-924-9067

Page + Steele Incorporated is a full service architectural firm involved in urban planning, design of the architectural built environment in commercial, residential and institutional spheres. Both new construction and renovations are executed. Page + Steele employs a total of 75 people. Graduates most likely to be hired come from the following areas: Bachelor of Architecture, Bachelor of Arts (Urban Planning), and Community College Diploma (Architecture/ Drafting, Urban Planning). Graduates would occupy Junior Designer and Junior Technician positions. Previous stable work experience, length of employment at previous locations, team player, organization skills, solid work ethic, previous employment records and references are all considered upon application. Company benefits are rated as industry standard. The potential for advancement is listed as being good. The average annual starting salary falls within the $25,000 to $30,000 range, and is dependent upon skills and previous work experience. The most suitable method for initial contact by those seeking employment is to mail a resume with a covering letter. Page + Steele Incorporated does hire summer students, primarily University students. *Contact:* Denis G. Rioux.

PALLISER FURNITURE LTD. (AIRDRIE)
Box 3520
Airdrie, AB T4B 2B7

Tel. 403-948-5931
Fax 403-948-4532
Website .... www.palliser.com

This location of Palliser Furniture Ltd. is involved in the manufacturing of upholstered motion furniture. The company employs approximately 140 people at this location, a total of 1,700 people across Canada, and 2,100 people worldwide. Graduates most likely to be hired at this location come from the following academic areas: Community College Diploma (Upholstery), and High School Diploma. These graduates would occupy Upholsterer, Sewer, and Woodshop Worker positions. Company benefits are rated above average. The potential for advancement is listed as being good. The most suitable methods for initial contact by those seeking employment are to mail a resume with a covering letter, or via telephone. *Contact:* Harley Winborn, Human Resources Manager.

PALLISER FURNITURE LTD. (WINNIPEG)
80 Furniture Park
Winnipeg, MB R2G 1B9

Tel. 204-988-0827
Fax 204-988-5657
Website .... www.palliser.com

Palliser Furniture Ltd. is Canada's largest furniture manufacturer, specializing in leather upholstery and wood products. The corporate head office is located in Winnipeg. The company employs approximately 3,000 people in Manitoba, 3,300 throughout Canada, and at total of 3,600 people worldwide. Palliser is a team based, multicultural company dedicated to leadership in design, service and customer value. Graduates most likely to be hired come from the following academic areas: Bachelor of Arts (Criminology), Bachelor of Science (Computer Science), Bachelor of Engineering (Electrical, Mechanical, Computer Systems, Industrial Engineering, Industrial Production), Bachelor of Commerce/Business Administration (Accounting, Finance, Human Resources, Marketing), Chartered Accountant, Certified Management Accountant, Certified General Accountant, and Community College Diploma (Accounting, Administration, Human Resources, Information Systems, Marketing/Sales, Secretarial, Graphic Arts, Journalism, CAD/CAM/Autocad, Carpentry, Computer Science, Tool and Die, Machinist, Welding). Palliser has many opportunities for those seeking career changes and for new graduates. Team player, honesty, integrity, and solid work ethic are all listed as desirable non-academic qualifications. Company benefits and the potential for advancement are both rated as excellent. The average annual starting salary falls within the $20,000 to $30,000 range. The most suitable methods for initial contact by those seeking employment are to mail or fax a resume with a covering letter, or by applying in person. Palliser Furniture Ltd. does hire summer and co-op work term students. *Contact:* Corporate Human Resources, Employment Services.

PAPINEAU GROUP
CP 100
St-Jerome, QC J7Z 5T7

Tel. 514-432-7555
Fax 514-538-7304

Papineau Group provides general merchandise transportation services in Quebec, Ontario, and the United States. There are approximately 384 employees at this location and a total of 512 employees in Canada. Graduates most likely to be hired come from the following academic areas: Bachelor of Science (Computer Science), Bachelor of Commerce/Business Administration (General, Accounting, Finance, Human Resources, Information Systems, Marketing), Chartered Accountant, Community College Diploma (Accounting, Administration, Business, Human Resources, Secretarial, Computer Science), and High School Diploma. Bilingualism, good judgement, dedication, good work skills and two years previous work experience are all listed as desirable non-academic qualifications. Company benefits are rated as industry standard. The potential for advancement is listed as being good. The average annual starting salary falls within the $20,000 to $25,000 range. The most suitable method for initial contact by those seeking employment is to mail a resume with a covering letter. Papineau Group does hire summer students. *Contact:* Christine Arcad, Human Resource Services.

PARAGON PROTECTION LTD.
1210 Sheppard Avenue East
Toronto, ON M2K 1E3

Tel.	416-498-4000
Fax	416-498-1648

Paragon Protection Ltd. provides protection of people, property and information for select clientele. There are 550 employees at this location, and a total of 650 employees in Canada. Graduates most likely to be hired come from the following academic areas: Bachelor of Arts (General, Criminology, Psychology, Sociology), Bachelor of Science (General), Bachelor of Engineering (General), Bachelor of Education (General), Bachelor of Laws, Bachelor of Commerce/Business Administration (General), and Community College Diploma (Administration, Security/Enforcement, Nursing RN/RNA). Graduates are hired to occupy the position of Security Officer. Good decision making abilities, physically fit, team and individual worker, able to work under stress and with or without supervision, attention to detail, calm during emergency situations, computer literate, goal oriented, and excellent communication, interpersonal, time management, conflict resolution, problem solving, report writing, public relations and customer service skills are all listed as desirable nonacademic qualifications. Company benefits are rated above average. The potential for advancement is listed as being good. The average annual starting salary falls within the $15,000 to $20,000 range. The most suitable methods for initial contact by those seeking employment are to mail a resume with a covering letter, or by applying in person at this location. Paragon Protection Ltd. does hire summer students. *Contact:* Mr. Terry Jackman, Human Resources.

PARK PROPERTY MANAGEMENT INC.
16 Esna Park Drive
Suite 200
Markham, ON L3R 5X1

Tel.	905-940-1718
Fax	905-940-2898

Park Property Management Inc. employs more than 25 people in residential and industrial property management activities. Positions requiring post-secondary academic qualifications are very few. Park Property generally hires semi-qualified people who can be trained accordingly. When graduates are hired, those most likely to be hired come from the following academic areas: Chartered Accountant (Finance, Real Estate), Certified Management Accountant (In-training), Certified General Accountant (In-training), Community College Diploma (HVAC Systems,

Mechanic Technician), and High School Diploma. Graduates are hired to occupy Accountant, Accounts Receivable Clerk, Accounts Payable Clerk, Secretary, Property Manager, and Maintenance Department positions. Company benefits are rated above average. The potential for advancement is listed as average. The average annual starting salary falls within the $20,000 to $25,000 range. The most suitable method for initial contact by those seeking employment is to mail a resume with a covering letter. *Contact:* Human Resources.

PARKLAND SAVINGS AND CREDIT UNION LTD.
4901 - 48th Street
Suite 601
Red Deer, AB T4N 6M4

Tel.	403-343-0144
Fax	403-347-6686
Email	pquesnel@parklandsavings.com
Website	www.parklandsavings.com

Parkland Savings and Credit Union Ltd. provides a variety of financial services and employs approximately 206 people throughout central Alberta. Graduates most likely to be hired come from the following academic areas: Bachelor of Commerce/Business Administration (General, Accounting, Finance, Information Systems, Marketing), Chartered Accountant, Certified Management Accountant, Master of Business Administration (Accounting, Finance, Information Systems), Community College Diploma (Accounting, Administration, Business, Communications/Public Relations, Financial Planning, Human Resources, Information Systems, Insurance, Marketing/Sales, Computer Science), and High School Diploma. Graduates would occupy Accountant, Human Resources Consultant, Marketing Specialist, Financial Planner, Lending Specialist, and Investment Specialist positions. Good communication skills, entrepreneurial, and strong interpersonal skills are listed as desirable non-academic qualifications. Company benefits and the potential for advancement are both listed as excellent. The average annual starting salary falls within the $15,000 to $20,000 range for entry level positions, $25,000 to $30,000 range for permanent staff positions, and $40,000 to $45,000 for management positions. The most suitable method for initial contact by those seeking employment is to mail a resume with a covering letter. Parkland Savings and Credit Union Ltd. does hire summer students. *Contacts:* Herb Der, General Manager or Mr. Pat Quesnel, Vice President, Human Resources.

PC WORLD DIVISION OF CIRCUIT WORLD CORP.
250 Finchdene Square
Toronto, ON M1X 1A5

Tel.	416-299-4000 x 253
Fax	416-292-4308
Email	pwenzel@circtwrld.com

PC World Division of Circuit World Corp. employs approximately 150 people in the manufacture of printed circuit boards. Graduates most likely to be hired come from the following academic areas: Bachelor of Arts (General), Bachelor of Science (Chemistry, Computer Science), Bachelor of Engineering (Chemical, Civil, Electrical, Mechanical, Environmental/Resources, Industrial Chemistry, Industrial Engineering, Metallurgy), Bachelor of Commerce/Business Administration (Accounting, Finance, Information Systems, Marketing), Certified Management Accountant, Certified General Accountant, and Community College Diploma (Accounting, Administration, Business, Facility Management, Marketing/Sales, CAD/CAM/Autocad, Computer Science, Electronics Technician, Engineering Technician). Graduates would occupy Product Engineer, Process Engineer, Operations Analyst, Systems Engineer, Environmental Coordinator, Accountant, and CAM Operator positions. Computer literacy, team player, strong people skills, multitasking abilities, and good organizational skills are all listed as desirable nonacademic qualifications. Company benefits are rated above average. The potential for advancement is listed as being good. The average annual starting salary falls within the $30,000 to $35,000 range. The most suitable method for initial contact by those seeking employment is to fax a resume with a covering letter. PC World Division of Circuit World Corp. does hire co-op work term students on occasion. *Contact:* Ms. Pat Wenzel, Human Resources Administrator.

PEACOCK INC.
8600, rue St. Patrick
Montreal, QC H8N 1V1

Tel. 514-366-5900
Fax 514-366-9804

Peacock Inc. is involved in the distribution and repair of industrial products. These products include pumps, filtration equipment, instrumentation and material handling equipment. Peacock's activities serve the mining, pulp and paper, oil and gas, and power generation industries. The company employs approximately 280 people at this location, a total of 680 across Canada, and more than 5,000 employees worldwide. Graduates most likely to be hired come from the following academic areas: Bachelor of Science (Metallurgy), Bachelor of Engineering (Materials Science, Metallurgy, Pollution Treatment, Pulp and Paper, Instrumentation, Mechanical, Industrial Production, Welding), Bachelor of Commerce/Business Administration (General, Accounting, Finance, Human Resources, Information Systems, Marketing), Chartered Accountant, Certified Management Accountant, Certified General Accountant, Master of Business Administration (Accounting, Information Systems), Master of Engineering, Community College Diploma (Accounting, Administration, Business, Human Resources, Secretarial, Engineering, Forestry, Machinist, Millwright, Welding), and High School Diploma. Bilingualism is a definite asset. Company benefits are rated as excellent. The potential for advancement is listed as being good. The average annual starting salary is dependent upon the position being considered. The most suitable method for initial contact by those seeking employment is to

mail a resume with a covering letter. Peacock Inc. hires summer students. *Contacts:* Carole Proulx, Human Resources Administrator or Louis Tassé, Director of Human Resources.

PEEL MEMORIAL HOSPITAL
20 Lynch Street
Brampton, ON L6W 2Z8

Tel. 905-796-4477
Fax 905-451-9888

Peel Memorial Hospital is a 422 bed, active treatment, community hospital employing approximately 1,900 people. Graduates most likely to be hired come from the following academic areas: Bachelor of Science (Nursing, Pharmacy, Health Sciences, Physiotherapy, Speech Audiology), Chartered Accountant, Certified Management Accountant, and Community College Diploma (Nursing RN/RNA, Laboratory Technician, X-Ray/Radiology Technician, Respiratory Technician, Recreation Studies, Secretarial). Graduates would occupy Registered Nurse, Accountant, Physiotherapist, Occupational Therapist, Speech Therapist, Technicians, and Secretarial positions. Employee benefits are rated as excellent. The potential for advancement is listed as being good. The most suitable method for initial contact by those seeking employment is to mail a resume with a covering letter, or via telephone. Peel Memorial Hospital does hire summer students on a regular basis. *Contact:* Employee Services Department.

PEOPLES JEWELLERS LIMITED
1440 Don Mills Road
Don Mills, ON M3B 3M1

Tel. 416-441-1515
Fax 416-391-7756
Website .... www.peoplesjewellers.com

Peoples Jewellers Limited is Canada's leading jewellery retailer. There are more than 130 employees at this location. Graduates most likely to be hired come from the following academic areas: Bachelor of Commerce/Business Administration (General, Accounting, Finance, Marketing), and Community College Diploma (Accounting, Administration, Business, Architectural Technician). Graduates would occupy Sales Representative, Store Manager, Clerk, Financial Analyst, and Information Systems positions. Company benefits and the potential for advancement are both rated as excellent. The average annual starting salary depends upon the position being considered. The most suitable methods for initial contact by graduates seeking employment are to mail or fax a resume with a covering letter. Peoples Jewellers Limited does hire summer and co-op work term students. *Contact:* Human Resources.

PEPSI-COLA CANADA LTD.
5205 Satellite Drive
Mississauga, ON L4W 5J7

Tel. 905-212-7377
Website .... www.pepsico.com/

Pepsi-Cola Canada Ltd. is the Canadian division of PepsiCo Inc., based in Purchase, New York. PepsiCo is among the most successful consumer products companies in the world. Pepsi-Cola Canada Ltd. employs more than 100 people at this location, and is primarily involved in administration and marketing activities. Recent graduates most likely to be hired are Community College graduates from Secretarial and Administrative programs. These graduates are hired for Clerical and Secretarial positions. A minimum of 3 to 5 years experience in the packaged-goods industry is required for management positions in Marketing, Sales, and Trade Development. Company benefits and the potential for advancement are both rated as excellent. The most suitable method for initial contact by graduates seeking employment is to mail a resume with a covering letter. Pepsi-Cola Canada Ltd. does hire summer students at this location. *Contact:* Human Resources Representative.

PETER KIEWIT SONS CO. LTD.
2600 Skymark Avenue, Building #2, Suite 201
Mississauga, ON L4W 5B2

Tel. 905-206-1490
Fax 905-206-1513

Peter Kiewit Sons Co. Ltd. is engaged in heavy civil engineering construction, mining and related businesses throughout Canada. There are 42 people employed at this location, approximately 200 employees across Canada, and approximately 2,900 employees worldwide. Graduates most likely to be hired are Bachelor of Engineering graduates from Civil and Mechanical Engineering programs. Graduates would occupy Field Engineer, Field Supervisor, Maintenance Engineer, Project Engineer, Project Manager, Engineer/Estimator, Job Superintendent, and Office Engineer positions. Initiative, mobility, strong leadership and interpersonal skills, and extra-curricular involvement while at school are all listed as desirable non-academic qualifications. Company benefits are rated as industry standard. The potential for advancement is listed as being good. The average annual starting salary falls within the $30,000 to $35,000 range. The most suitable method for initial contact by those seeking employment is to mail a resume with a covering letter. Peter Kiewit Sons Co. Ltd. does hire summer students. *Contact:* Ted Chant, Area Manager.

PETO MACCALLUM LTD.
165 Cartwright Avenue
Toronto, ON M6A 1V5

Tel. 416-785-5110
Fax 416-785-5120

Peto MacCallum Ltd. is an independent, Canadian consulting engineering company. The company provides a broad range of specialized engineering and technical services related to the following fields of activity: Geotechnical Engineering, Geo-Environmental and Hydrogeological Services, Construction Materials Engineering, Quality Control - Testing and Inspection, and Building Science Services. Peto MacCallum maintains seven Ontario locations, with approximately 200 employees in total. In addition to the Toronto head office, locations can be found in Aurora, Barrie, Brampton, Hamilton, Kitchener, and Oshawa. Graduates most likely to be hired come from the following academic areas: Bachelor of Science (Chemistry, Geology), Bachelor of Engineering (Chemical, Civil, Environmental, Materials Science, Geotechnical), Master of Engineering (Geotechnical, Hydrogeology, Environmental), and Community College Diploma (Engineering Technician). Graduates would be most to occupy related positions as Engineers, Technologists, and Technicians. Company benefits and the potential for advancement are both rated as excellent. The most suitable method for initial contact by graduates seeking employment is to mail a resume with a covering letter. Peto MacCallum Ltd. does hire summer students. *Contact:* Manager, Human Resources.

PETRO-CANADA PRODUCTS
5140 Yonge Street
Suite 200
Toronto, ON M2N 6L6

Tel. 416-730-2000
Fax 416-730-2151

Petro-Canada Products is the division of Petro-Canada involved in the refining, marketing and distribution of "downstream" petroleum products. Graduates most likely to be hired come from the following academic areas: Bachelor of Science (Computer Science), Bachelor of Engineering (Mechanical, Chemical), Bachelor of Commerce/Business Administration (Accounting), Certified Management Accountant, Certified General Accountant, and Master of Business Administration. Graduates would occupy Accountant, Credit Representative, Marketing Representative Trainee, Marketing Analyst Trainee, Engineer, and Computer Programmer positions. Leadership and good communication skills, team player, continuous improvement and service mindset, ability to adapt to an ever changing environment, and the ability to manage a number of priorities within tight time frames are all listed as desirable attributes. Company benefits are rated as excellent. The potential for advancement is listed as average. The average annual starting salary falls within the $30,000 to $36,000 range. The most suitable method for initial contact by those seeking employment is to mail a resume with a covering letter. Petro-Canada Products does hire summer students who are returning to full-time post secondary studies in the fall. *Contact:* Human Resources, Central.

PHILIP ENVIRONMENTAL INC.
P.O. Box 423, Depot 1
Hamilton, ON L8L 7W2

Tel. 905-544-6687

Philip Environmental Inc. is active in waste management and recycling. There are approximately 200 employees at this location and a total of 1,500 employees in Canada. Graduates most likely to be hired come from the following academic areas: Bachelor of Science (Chemistry), Bachelor of Engineering (Architectural/Building, Industrial Production, Welding), Bachelor of Commerce/Business Administration (Accounting, Marketing), Chartered Accountant, Certified Management Accountant, Master of Business Administration (Accounting), Master of Engineering (Construction), Community College Diploma (Accounting, Administration, Business, Purchasing/Logistics, Secretarial, Truck Mechanic, Architecture/Drafting, CAD/CAM/Autocad, Welding), and High School Diploma. Graduates would occupy Welder, Mechanic, Millwright, Electrician, Accountant (with/without designation), and Secretarial positions. A positive attitude, flexibility, an ability to work well with others, and three to five years related work experience (depending upon the position) are all listed as desirable non-academic qualifications. Company benefits are rated as excellent. The potential for advancement is listed as being good. The average annual starting salary for Clerical positions falls within the $20,000 to $25,000 range. The starting salary for Technical positions falls within $35,000 to $40,000 range. The most suitable methods for initial contact by those seeking employment are to mail a resume with a covering letter, or by responding to advertised positions in the paper. Philip Environmental Inc. hires a few summer students each year. *Contact:* Mr. Rennie Mohammed, Human Resources Supervisor.

PICARD TECHNOLOGIES INC.
9916 Cote de Liesse
Lachine, QC H8T 1A1

Tel. 514-422-8404
Fax 514-422-8406
Email .... bferris@picardtech.com

Picard Technologies Inc. (PTI) is a systems integration and project management company servicing the pharmaceutical industry. Employing approximately 10 people, PTI provides resources that are well-versed in industrial communications, controls and automation for the manufacturing and process industries. PTI focuses on the pharmaceutical industry extending these services to where experience with GMP approaches to automation and equipment is critical. Graduates most likely to be hired are Bachelor of Engineering graduates from Chemical, Electrical, and Mechanical Engineering programs. Graduates would occupy the position of Project Specialist. Team player, versatile, and committed are listed as desirable non-academic qualifications. Company benefits are rated above average. The potential for advancement is listed as being good. The average annual starting salary falls within the $45,000 to $50,000 range. The most suitable method for initial contact by those seeking employment is to e-mail a resume with a covering letter. Picard Technologies Inc. does hire co-op work term students. *Contact:* Brenda Ferris.

PICKERING PLANNING DEPARTMENT
1 The Esplanade, Pickering Civic Complex
Pickering, ON L1V 6K7

Tel. 905-420-4617

The Town of Pickering Planning Department is primarily concerned with planning, development and redevelopment of land in the town of Pickering. Activities include processing development applications, setting of official plan and development guidelines for the municipality, providing information (written and oral) on public inquiries concerning land use and other planning related concerns. The department employs fewer than 25 people. Graduates most likely to be hired come from the following academic areas: Bachelor of Arts (Urban Planning/Geography), and Master of Arts (Urban Planning/Geography). Recent graduates would occupy entry-level positions as a Planning Technician or Draftsperson. Good oral and written communication skills, independent work habits, and able to handle a wide variety of tasks are all listed as desirable non-academic qualifications. Company benefits are rated above average. The potential for advancement is listed as average. The average annual starting salary falls within the $20,000 to $25,000 range. The most suitable method for initial contact by those seeking employment is to mail a resume with a covering letter. The Planning Department hires three students annually, each for four month work terms. *Contact:* Director of Human Resources.

PINE FALLS PAPER COMPANY LIMITED
P.O. Box 10
Pine Falls, MB R0E 1M0

Tel. 204-367-5206
Fax 204-367-2442

Pine Falls Paper Company Limited is a newsprint manufacturer employing approximately 475 people. Graduates most likely to be hired come from the following academic areas: Bachelor of Arts (General), Bachelor of Science (Biology, Chemistry), Bachelor of Engineering (Chemical, Pulp and Paper, Electrical, Mechanical, Forest Resources), Bachelor of Commerce/Business Administration (Accounting, Finance, Human Resources), Certified Management Accountant, and Master of Business Administration (Accounting). Graduates are hired to occupy non-union supervisory positions. Team player and previous work experience are both listed as desirable non-academic qualifications. Company benefits are rated above average. The potential for advancement is listed as being good. The average annual starting salary falls within the $25,000 to $30,000 range. The most suitable method for initial contact by those seeking employment is to mail a resume with a covering letter. Pine Falls Paper Company Limited does hire local students for summer positions. *Contact:* Human Resource Department (Human Resources direct line: 204-367-5205).

PIONEER GRAIN COMPANY, LIMITED
2800 One Lombard Place
Winnipeg, MB R3B 0X8

Tel. 204-934-5961
Pioneer Grain Company, Limited employs more than 500 people involved in grain wholesaling. Graduates most likely to be hired come from the following academic areas: Bachelor of Science (Computer Science), Bachelor of Engineering (General), Bachelor of Commerce/Business Administration (Accounting, Finance, Marketing, Information Systems), Chartered Accountant (Finance), Certified Management Accountant (Finance), Certified General Accountant (Finance), Master of Business Administration (Accounting, Finance, Marketing, Information Systems), and Community College Diploma (Accounting, Administration, Business, Marketing/Sales, Purchasing/Logistics, Secretarial, Human Resources, Architecture/Drafting, Computer Science, Engineering, Industrial Design). Company benefits are rated as excellent. The potential for advancement is listed as being good. The most suitable method for initial contact by those seeking employment is to mail a resume with a covering letter. Pioneer Grain Company, Limited does hire summer students. *Contacts:* Sherrie Rauth, Human Resource Administrator (Staffing & Recruiting) or Colleen Johnston, Manager, Human Resources.

PIONEER STANDARD CANADA INC.
3415 American Drive
Mississauga, ON L4V 1T4

Tel. 905-405-8300
Pioneer Standard Canada Inc. maintains locations across Canada and is involved in the distribution of electronic components. There are two divisions within the company. The first deals with electronic semi-conductors, passive and non passive products while the second serves the computer marketplace. The company employs approximately 75 people at this location. Graduates most likely to be hired come from the following academic areas: Bachelor of Arts (General), Bachelor of Science (Computer Science), Bachelor of Engineering (Electrical) and Bachelor of Commerce/Business Administration. Graduates would occupy Technician, Sales Representative, Buyer and various head office positions. Applicants should possess drive, motivation and sales skills, accordingly. Company benefits and the potential for advancement are both rated as excellent. The average annual starting salary varies according to the position being considered. The most suitable method for initial contact by those seeking employment is to mail a resume with a covering letter. *Contact:* John Turner.

PIZZA PIZZA LIMITED
580 Jarvis Street
Toronto, ON M4Y 2H9

Tel. 416-967-1010
Fax 416-967-0891

Pizza Pizza Limited is one of Canada's leading pizza chains, a franchised operation consisting mainly of takeout and delivery stores. The head office provides services and administration for a network of franchised and company-operated stores throughout Ontario. After more than 30 years in business, the company continues to be a fast-paced, entrepreneurial corporation - a market leader. Part of this success can be attributed to its famous leading-edge marketing programs and technology systems. Activities at the Head Office include Accounting, Marketing, Architecture and Real Estate, Customer Service, Commissary, Operations, Franchising, Warehousing, and a Training Centre. Graduates most likely to be hired come from the following academic areas: Bachelor of Commerce/Business Administration, Certified Management Accountant, and Community College Diploma (Administration, Advertising, Business, Marketing/Sales, Secretarial, Hospitality). Graduates would occupy Store Manager, Area Representative, Secretarial, Accounting, and Marketing positions. Flexibility, enthusiasm, initiative, a high energy level, leadership skills and good communication skills are all listed as desirable non-academic qualifications. Company benefits are rated above average. The potential for advancement is listed as excellent. The average annual starting salary falls within the $20,000 to $28,000 range. The most suitable methods for initial contact by those seeking employment are to mail a resume with a covering letter, or via telephone. *Contact:* Human Resources.

PLACER DOME NORTH AMERICA LTD.
1055 Dunsmuir Street
Suite 600
Vancouver, BC V7X 1L3

Tel. 604-661-1991
Fax 604-661-3722

Placer Dome North America Ltd. is a wholly owned subsidiary of international mining corporation Placer Dome Inc. Headquartered in Vancouver, Placer Dome operates six mines across the country. With five gold mines in Ontario and Quebec and a molybdenum mine in British Columbia, Placer Dome is one of the largest gold producers in Canada. Graduates most likely to be hired come from the following academic areas: Bachelor of Arts (Economics), Bachelor of Science (Computer Science, Geology, Metallurgy), Bachelor of Engineering (Mining, Environmental, Electrical, Mechanical), Bachelor of Laws, Bachelor of Commerce/Business Administration (Accounting, Finance, Marketing, Information Systems), Chartered Accountant (Finance), Certified Management Accountant (Finance), Certified General Accountant (Finance), Master of Business Administration (Accounting, Finance, Marketing), Master of Engineering (Mining, Geology, Metallurgy), Doctorate (Geostatistics, Geology), and Community College Diploma (Accounting, Administration, Secretarial, Human Resources, Computer Science, Electronic Technician, Engineering Technician, Mechanic, Industrial Design). Graduates would develop careers in Geology, Mining, Engineering, Metallurgy, Mechanical and Electrical Maintenance and related fields, as well as corporate functions in Finance and Administration. Company benefits and the potential for advancement are both listed as excellent. The average annual starting salary is dependent upon position and performance. The most suitable method for initial contact by those seeking employment is to mail a resume with a covering letter. Placer Dome North America Ltd. does hire summer and co-op work term students. *Contacts:* Karen Walsh, Manager, Human Resources Department or Human Resources Department.

PMC-SIERRA, INC.
8555 Baxter Place
Suite 105
Burnaby, BC V5A 4V7

Tel. 604-415-6000
Fax 604-415-6209
Email .... careers@pmc-sierra.com
Website .... www.pmc-sierra.com

PMC-Sierra Inc. is a leading provider of high speed internetworking component solutions emphasizing ATM, SONET/SDH, TI/EI and ethernet applications. The company's quality system is registered with Quality Management Institute to the ISO 9001 standard. As co-founder of the SATURN Development Group, PMC-Sierra works with over 40 other member companies to define and develop interoperable, standard-compliant solutions for high speed networking applications. Headquartered near Vancouver, British Columbia, PMC-Sierra offers technical and sales support in California, Texas, Illinois, Massachusetts, Europe and Asia. In addition, continuing growth has added to development capabilities that now include a Beaverton, Oregon facility that is developing ethernet switching solutions and new Design Centres in Montreal, Quebec; Saskatoon, Saskatchewan; San Jose, California; and Gaithersburg, Maryland. There are 350 employees in Burnaby, a total of 375 in Canada, and a total of 475 employees worldwide. Graduates most likely to be hired come from the following academic areas: Bachelor of Engineering (Electrical, Microelectronics, Telecommunications), and Master of Engineering (Microelectronics, Telecommunications). Graduates would occupy Digital Designer, Analog Designer, CAD Engineer, Physical Design Engineer, I/O Library Engineer, Validation Engineer, Application Engineer, Product Marketing Engineer, DSP H/W Designer, Product Engineer, and Test Engineer positions. Team building skills and good interpersonal skills are both listed as desirable non-academic qualifications. Company benefits and the potential for advancement are both rated as excellent. The average annual starting salary falls within the $40,000 to $45,000 range. The most suitable methods for initial contact by those seeking employment are to mail, fax or e-mail a resume with a covering letter. PMC-Sierra Inc. does hire summer students. *Contact:* Teri McNaughton, Manager, Employment Services.

PNG GLOBE ENVELOPES
400 Humberline Drive
Toronto, ON M9W 5T3

Tel. 416-675-9370
Fax 416-675-3724

PNG Globe Envelopes employs more than 100 people in the manufacture, printing, and distribution of envelopes. Post-secondary education is not a prerequisite for employment application. Intelligent, motivated, committed, adaptable, able to work well with colleagues, and related work experience are all listed as a desirable non-academic qualification. Applicants would occupy Accounting, Sales, Marketing, Operations Management and Traffic positions. Company benefits are rated above average. The potential for advancement is listed as being good. The average annual starting salary falls within the $20,000 to $30,000 range. The most suitable method for initial contact by those seeking employment is to mail or fax a resume with a covering letter. PNG Globe Envelopes does hire summer students. *Contact:* Mary Neto, Human Resources Manager.

POLYGRAM CANADA INC.
1345 Denison Street
Markham, ON L3R 5V2

Tel. 905-415-9900
Fax 905-415-7369

PolyGram Canada Inc. is a music and film entertainment company employing approximately 150 people at this location and a total of 254 people across Canada. Graduates most likely to be hired come from the following academic areas: Bachelor of Arts (General, Graphic Arts, Journalism, Music), Bachelor of Laws (Entertainment/Contract), Bachelor of Commerce/Business Administration (Accounting, Finance, Human Resources, Information Systems, Marketing), Chartered Accountant, Certified Management Accountant, Certified General Accountant, Master of Business Administration (Accounting, Finance), Community College Diploma (Accounting, Administration, Business, Communications, Human Resources, Marketing/Sales, Secretarial, Graphic Arts, Television/Radio Arts), and High School Diploma. Graduates would occupy Clerk and Assistant positions. Previous music or film industry experience, team player, enthusiastic, motivated, and good interpersonal and communications skills are all listed as desirable non-academic qualifications. Company benefits and the potential for advancement are both rated as excellent. The average annual starting salary for entry level positions falls within the $20,000 to $30,000 range. The most suitable method for initial contact by those seeking employment is to mail a resume with a covering letter. PolyGram Canada Inc. does hire one or two summer students for office services and mailroom positions. In addition, PolyGram also hires co-op students for unpaid work terms. *Contacts:* Lorie McMackin, Vice President of Human Resources or Voula Vagdatis, Human Resources Administrator.

POSITRON FIBER SYSTEMS INC.
5101 Buchan Street
Montreal, QC H4P 2R9

Tel. 514-345-2200
Fax 514-345-2252
Email .... pbarry@positronfiber.com
Website .... www.positronfiber.com

Positron Fiber Systems Inc. (PFS) designs, develops, markets and supports advanced broadband access network systems for local telecommunications carriers. The company's products enable local telecommunication carriers to provide a range of high capacity voice, video and data communication services to their business and residential customers rapidly and cost effectively using advanced fiber optic technology. PFS employs more than 135 professionals in sales, marketing, product research and development, engineering, product management, customer service, technical support and administration. The Company's products include fiber optic add/drop multiplexers based on the synchronous optical network ("SONET") and synchronous digital hierarchy ("SDH") transmission standards. Graduates most likely to be hired come from the following academic areas: Bachelor of Science (Computer Science), and Bachelor of Engineering (Electrical). Graduates would occupy Electrical Engineer, Software Engineer, Hardware Engineer, Software Designer, and Hardware Engineer positions. PFS seeks professionals who are motivated by the challenge of shaping the future through fiber-optic technologies. Graduates should enjoy working in a highly dynamic, forward-looking organization, where each individual is able to evolve within a positive, multidisciplinary team environment that encourages the exchange of creative ideas and professional development. Company benefits are rated above average. The potential for advancement is listed as excellent. The average annual starting salary falls within the $45,000 to $50,000 range. The most suitable methods for initial contact by those seeking employment are to mail, fax or e-mail a resume with a covering letter. Positron Fiber Systems Inc. does hire co-op work term students. Contact: Patricia Barry, Director, Human Resources.

POSTAL PROMOTIONS LIMITED
1100 Birchmount Road
Toronto, ON M1K 5H9

Tel. 416-752-8100
Fax 416-752-8239

Postal Promotions Limited is a direct mail advertising service employing more than 100 people. Activities include, data processing, data base management, printing, and direct mail advertising. Graduates most likely to be hired come from the following academic areas: Chartered Accountant, Master of Business Administration, and Community College Diploma (Graphic Arts, Data Processing). Graduates would occupy Accounting, Client Service, and Sales and Marketing positions. Adaptability to specific training, a willingness to accept a challenge, and possessing good communication skills are all listed as desirable non-academic qualifications. Company benefits are rated above average. The potential for advancement is listed as being good. The average annual starting salary falls within the $20,000 to $25,000 range, and is based upon commission for sales positions. The most suitable method for initial contact by graduates seeking employment is to mail a resume with a covering letter. Postal Promotions Limited does employ summer students on a regular basis. Contact: Operations Manager.

POTACAN MINING CO.
P.O. Box 5005
Sussex, NB E0E 1P0

Tel. 506-839-2146
Fax 506-839-6415

Potacan Mining Co. employs approximately 500 people in the mining of potash. Graduates most likely to be hired come from the following academic areas: Bachelor of Arts (Economics), Bachelor of Engineering (Electrical, Computer Systems, Instrumentation, Mechanical, Industrial Design, Welding, Mining), Master of Business Administration (Accounting, Finance, Human Resources, Information Systems), and Community College Diploma (Accounting, Administration, Business, Human Resources, Auto Mechanic, CAD/CAM/Autocad, Computer Science, Electronics Technician, Engineering Technician, Welding, Nursing RNA). Company benefits are rated above average. The potential for advancement is listed as being good. The average annual starting salary falls within the $35,000 to $40,000 range. The most suitable method for initial contact by those seeking employment is to mail a resume with a covering letter. Contact: Employee Relations, Personnel & Benefits Administrator.

PPG CANADA INC., WORKS 81, OSHAWA
155 First Avenue, P.O. Box 340
Oshawa, ON L1H 7L3

Tel. 905-725-1144
Fax 905-725-3422
Website .... www.ppg.com

PPG Canada Inc., Works 81 in Oshawa employs 400 people in the manufacture of automotive safety glass. PPG employs a total of 3,200 people in Canada and a total of 30,000 people worldwide. Graduates most likely to be hired at this location come from Bachelor of Engineering programs in Electrical, Mechanical, Automation/Robotics, and Environmental/Resources disciplines. Graduates would occupy Engineering Trainee positions. Team player and good communication skills are both listed as desirable non-academic qualifications. Company benefits are rated above average. The potential for advancement is listed as being good. The average annual starting salary falls within the $30,000 to $35,000 range. The most suitable method for initial contact by those seeking employment is to mail a resume with a covering letter. Summer students are hired occasionally, subject to requirements. Contact: Director, Human Resources.

PRATT & WHITNEY CANADA INC.
1801 Courtney Drive
Mississauga, ON L5T 1J3

Tel. 905-564-7500
Fax 905-564-4114
Website .... www.pwc.com

Pratt & Whitney Canada (P&WC) is the world's leading manufacturer of small and medium sized gas turbine engines. As a member of The Pratt & Whitney Group and a subsidiary of United Technologies Corporation (UTC) of Hartford, Connecticut, P&WC operates with a world mandate to design, develop, manufacture, market and support small and medium sized gas turbine engines. The company employs 1,000 people at this location, a total of 7,760 people in Canada, and 9,047 people worldwide. Graduates most likely to be hired come from the following academic areas: Bachelor of Science (Computer Science), Bachelor of Engineering (Electrical, Mechanical, Aerospace, Industrial Engineering), Master of Engineering (Mechanical, Aerospace), and Community College Diploma (Aircraft Maintenance, CAD/CAM/Autocad, Electronics Technician). Graduates would occupy Trainee positions. Company benefits and the potential for advancement are both rated as excellent. The most suitable method for initial contact by those seeking employment is to mail a resume with a covering letter. Pratt & Whitney Canada does hire co-op work term students. *Contact:* Ed Wyzykowski, Manager, Human Resources.

PRECISION DRILLING CORPORATION
112 - 4 Avenue SW, Suite 700
Calgary, AB T2P 0H3

Tel. 403-264-4882
Fax 403-266-1480

Precision Drilling Corporation is involved in oil and gas well drilling. There are approximately 100 employees at this location, and an approximate total of 2,000 employees across Canada. Graduates most likely to be hired come from the following academic areas: Bachelor of Arts (English), Bachelor of Science (Computer Science), Bachelor of Engineering (Industrial Design, Petroleum), Bachelor of Commerce/Business Administration (Accounting, Finance, Human Resources, Information Systems, Marketing), Chartered Accountant, Certified Management Accountant, Certified General Accountant, Master of Business Administration (Accounting, Human Resources, Information Systems, Marketing), and Community College Diploma (Accounting, Administration, Business, Communications, Human Resources, Marketing, Secretarial, Computer Science). Graduates would occupy Accounts Payable Clerk, Accounts Receivable Clerk, Accountant, Payroll and Benefits Clerk, Personnel Administrator, Purchaser, and Engineer positions. Computer literacy, team player, inquisitive, adaptable and versatile are all listed as desirable non-academic qualifications. Company benefits and the potential for advancement are both rated as excellent. The average annual starting salary varies widely between the $20,000 to $45,000 range, depending upon the position being considered. The most suitable method for initial contact by those seeking employment is to mail a resume with a covering letter. Precision Drilling Corporation does hire summer students. *Contact:* Jackie Swartout, Manager, Human Resources.

PREMIS SYSTEMS CANADA
3500 Steeles Avenue East, Suite 1300
Markham, ON L3R 0X1

Tel. 905-477-4155
Fax 905-477-9949
Email .... jalbers@premis.com
Website .... www.premis.com

Premis Systems Canada develops retail software, including POS, Back Office, Head Office, and communications. There are 40 employees at this location, and a total of 75 employees worldwide. Graduates most likely to be hired come from the following academic areas: Bachelor of Science (Computer Science), Bachelor of Engineering (Computer Systems), and Community College Diploma (Computer Science, Information Systems). Graduates would occupy Programmer, Business Analyst and Customer Support Analyst positions. Team player, independent worker, high caliber, POS experience, professional, and co-op work experience are all listed as desirable non-academic qualifications. Company benefits are rated above average. The potential for advancement is listed as excellent. The average annual starting salary falls within the $50,000 to $55,000 range, depending upon experience. The most suitable method for initial contact by those seeking employment is to mail a resume with a covering letter. *Contact:* Human Resources.

PRICEWATERHOUSECOOPERS
Box 82, Royal Trust Tower, TD Centre, Suite 3000
Toronto, ON M5K 1G8

Tel. 416-863-1133
Fax 416-947-8993
Website .... www.pw.com/ca

PricewaterhouseCoopers is a major chartered accountancy and management consulting firm employing approximately 1,300 people in the Metropolitan Toronto area. Activities range from accounting services to management consulting services. PricewaterhouseCoopers maintains office locations across Canada. Graduates most likely to be hired come from the following academic areas: Bachelor of Arts (General, Economics), Bachelor of Science (General, Computer Science), Bachelor of Engineering (General), Bachelor of Commerce/Business Administration (General, Accounting), Chartered Accountant, Master of Business Administration (General, Accounting, Finance, Human Resources, Information Systems, Marketing, Public Administration), and Community College Diploma (Accounting, Administration, Business, Communications, Facility Management, Financial Planning). Recent graduates are primarily hired for Staff Accounting positions and occasionally for more senior positions. Strong interpersonal and communication skills are both listed as desirable non-academic qualifications. Company benefits are rated above average. The potential for advancement is listed as excellent. The average annual starting salary falls in the $30,000 plus range. The most suitable method for initial contact by those seeking employment is to mail a resume, covering letter, and a transcript of academic marks. PricewaterhouseCoopers does hire a limited number of summer students. *Contact:* Manager, Human Resources.

PRINCE ALBERT, CITY OF
1084 Central Avenue
Prince Albert, SK S6V 7P3

Tel.	306-953-4330
Fax	306-953-4353
Email	cityp@sk.sympatico.ca
Website	www.CityLightsNews.com

The City of Prince Albert employs 520 people in the provision of municipal government, fire, and police services. Graduates most likely to be hired come from the following academic areas: Bachelor of Arts (General, Criminology, Geography, Recreation Studies, Urban Geography), Bachelor of Science (Computer Science), Bachelor of Engineering (General, Civil), Bachelor of Commerce/Business Administration (Accounting, Finance, Human Resources, Information Systems, Public Administration), Certified Management Accountant, Master of Business Administration (Human Resources, Public Administration), and Community College Diploma (Accounting, Human Resources, Information Systems, Secretarial, Urban Planning, CAD/CAM/Autocad, Engineering Technician). Company benefits are rated above average. The potential for advancement is listed as being good. The average annual starting salary falls within the $30,000 to $35,000 range. The most suitable method for initial contact by those seeking employment is to mail a resume with a covering letter. The City of Prince Albert does hire summer and co-op work term students. *Contact:* Laurent Mougeot, Director, Human Resources.

PRINCE ALBERT HEALTH DISTRICT
1220 - 25th Street West
Human Resources Department, Box 3000
Prince Albert, SK S6V 5T4

Tel.	306-953-0207
Fax	306-764-2818

Prince Albert Health District employs approximately 1,700 people in the provision of health care services. Graduates most likely to be hired come from the following academic areas: Bachelor of Arts (Psychology, Recreation Studies), Bachelor of Science (Nursing, Occupational Therapy, Pharmacy, Physio/Physical Therapy, Psychology, Speech Pathology), Bachelor of Engineering (Computer Science, Power/Hydro), Bachelor of Commerce/Business Administration (Accounting, Finance, Human Resources Information Systems), Master of Business Administration (Accounting, Finance, Human Resources,

Information Systems), and Community College Diploma (Human Resources, Information Systems, Secretarial, Cook/Chef, Dental Hygiene, Dietitian/Nutrition, Nursing RN/Special Care Aide, Respiratory Therapy, Ultra-Sound Technician). Graduates would occupy positions relating to their academic backgrounds, from labour positions (housekeeping, maintenance), semi-professional positions (finance, human resources, health records), to professional positions (doctor, nurse, social worker, psychologist). A positive mental attitude, a willingness and desire to work, and the ability to get along with other people are all listed as desirable non-academic qualifications. Company benefits are rated above average. The potential for advancement is listed as being good. The average annual starting salary falls within the $25,000 to $35,000 range, depending on the position being considered. The most suitable methods for initial contact by those seeking employment are to mail a resume with a covering letter, or complete an application with the Human Resources Department. The Prince Albert Health District does hire summer students. *Contact:* Bette Hartsfield, Employment Officer, Human Resources.

PROCTER & GAMBLE INC.
P.O. Box 355, Station A
Toronto, ON M5W 1C5

Tel.	416-730-4711
Fax	416-730-4684
Website	www.pg.com/careers

Procter & Gamble Inc. is a recognized leader in the development, manufacture, and marketing of a broad range of quality consumer products. Procter & Gamble markets more than 300 brands to nearly five billion consumers in over 140 countries. These brands include: Tide, Ivory, Cover Girl, Pantene Pro-V, Crest, Always, Whisper, Folgers, Pringles, Pampers, and Oil of Olay. The company employs 650 people at this location, a total of 2,600 in Canada, and more than 100,000 people worldwide. Graduates most likely to be hired come from the following academic areas: Bachelor of Arts (General), Bachelor of Science (General), Bachelor of Engineering (General, Chemical, Civil, Electrical, Mechanical), Bachelor of Commerce/Business Administration (Accounting, Finance, Information Systems, Marketing), and Master of Business Administration (Accounting, Finance, Information Systems, Marketing). Graduates would occupy entry level management positions in Marketing (Assistant Brand Manager), Customer Business Development (Sales), Product Supply (Manufacturing), Finance (Financial Analyst), and Management Systems. Leadership ability, good communication skills, an ability to work effectively with others, initiative, follow through, and good thinking and problem solving skills are all listed as desirable non-academic qualifications. Company benefits and the potential for advancement are both rated as excellent. The most suitable methods for initial contact by those seeking employment are to mail a resume with a covering letter, or through on-campus recruitment initiatives (see your campus career centre for details). Procter & Gamble Inc. does hire summer students. *Contact:* Corporate Recruiting, Human Resources Department.

PUBLIC OPTICAL
1140 Sheppard Avenue West, Unit 12B
Downsview, ON M3K 2A2

Tel. 416-638-2075

Public Optical dispenses eyewear directly to the public, providing services and products for all eyecare needs. Graduates most likely to be hired are Bachelor of Science graduates from Opthalmic programs. Graduates would occupy Optometrist positions. Working in a retail environment, graduates would be responsible for contact lens and spectacle fitting. Team player, enthusiasm, self-motivated, energetic, sales skills, and a willingness to learn are all listed as desirable non-academic qualifications. Company benefits and the potential for advancement are both rated as excellent. The average annual starting salary is dependent upon applicant's experience. The most suitable method for initial contact by those seeking employment is to mail a resume with a covering letter. *Contact:* Human Resources Department.

PURDUE FREDERICK
575 Granite Court
Pickering, ON L1W 3W8

Tel. 905-420-6400
Fax 905-420-0385

Purdue Frederick is a pharmaceutical manufacturer employing 100 people at this location, and a total of 140 people in Canada. Graduates most likely to be hired come from the following academic areas: Bachelor of Arts (Economics, English), Bachelor of Science (Chemistry, Computer Science, Nursing, Pharmacy, Psychology), Bachelor of Engineering (Chemical, Industrial Chemistry, Computer Systems), Bachelor of Education (Adult), Bachelor of Commerce/Business Administration (General, Finance, Human Resources, Information Systems, Marketing), Chartered Accountant, Certified Management Accountant, Master of Business Administration (Finance, Human Resources, Information Systems, Marketing), Master of Science, Master of Health Sciences, Community College Diploma (Accounting, Business, Human Resources, Purchasing/Logistics, Secretarial, CAD/CAM/Autocad, Computer Science, Laboratory Technician, Nursing RN), C.H.R.P., and High School Diploma. Graduates would occupy entry level and more advanced positions, including Chemist, Technician, Product Manager, Human Resources Manager, Assistant Controller, Controller, Accounting Clerk, Secretarial, and Clerical positions. Previous work experience, team player, good work ethic, initiative, organized, and leadership skills are all listed as desirable non-academic qualifications. Company benefits are rated as excellent. The potential for advancement is listed as being good. The average annual starting salary is dependent upon the position being considered. The most suitable method for initial contact by those seeking employment is to mail

a resume with a covering letter. Summer students are hired. These are usually University level students recruited from within the company. *Contact:* Manager, Human Resources.

PUROLATOR COURIER LTD.
11 Morse Street
Training & Recruitment, 2nd Floor
Toronto, ON M4M 2P7

Tel. .... 416-461-9031 x 301
Fax 416-461-3994
Website .... www.purolator.com

Purolator Courier Ltd. is the largest overnight courier in Canada. Purolator is a fully Canadian owned corporation, and today employs approximately 10,000 people across Canada. Over 375,000 envelopes and parcels are funnelled through the company's system each night, and Purolator now serves over 175 countries worldwide. Graduates most likely to be hired come from the following academic areas: Bachelor of Arts (General, English, French, Psychology), Bachelor of Engineering (Mechanical, Industrial Design, Transportation), Bachelor of Education (General, Adult), Bachelor of Commerce/Business Administration (General, Accounting, Finance, Human Resources, Information Systems, Marketing), Chartered Accountant, Certified Management Accountant, Certified General Accountant, Master of Business Administration (General, Accounting, Finance, Human Resources, Information Systems, Marketing), Master of Engineering (Industrial), Community College Diploma (Accounting, Administration, Advertising, Business, Communications, Facility Management, Human Resources, Marketing/Sales, Purchasing/Logistics, Secretarial, Legal Assistant, Aircraft Maintenance, Auto Mechanic, Computer Science), and High School Diploma. Graduates would occupy Operations/Sorter, Administrative, Coordinator, Customer Service, and Support Representative positions. Team player and previous work experience (depending upon the job) are both listed as desirable non-academic qualifications. Purolator offers employees competitive compensation and benefits packages. The most suitable methods for initial contact by those seeking employment are to mail or fax a resume with a covering letter, or by applying in person at this location. Purolator Courier Ltd. does hire summer and co-op work term students. *Contacts:* Debbie Kamino, Human Resources, Metro Recruiter or Erin Howden, Human Resources, Corporate.

QLT PHOTOTHERAPEUTICS INC.
520 West 6th Avenue, Suite 200
Vancouver, BC V5Z 4H5

Tel. 604-872-7881
Fax 604-871-1308
Email .... allisonalberts@qlt.ca
Website .... www.qlt-pdt.com

QLT PhotoTherapeutics Inc. is a world leader in the development and commercialization of proprietary pharmaceutical products for photodynamic therapy, a field of medicine that uses light activated drugs for the treatment of cancer diseases of the eye and other medical conditions. The company employs a total of 122 people. Graduates most likely to be hired come from the following academic areas: Bachelor of Science (Biology, Chemistry), Bachelor of Engineering (Biomedical Electronics, Mechanical), Bachelor of Commerce/Business Administration (Accounting, Finance, Human Resources, Information Systems, Marketing), Chartered Accountant, Certified General Accountant, Master of Business Administration (Marketing), Master of Science (Biology, Biochemistry, Chemistry), Doctorate (Biology, Biochemistry, Chemistry), Community College Diploma (Accounting, Human Resources, Computer Science), and High School Diploma. Graduates would occupy Clerk, Technician, Associate, Scientist, Manager, Engineer, and Analyst positions. Team player, good interpersonal skills, work experience, supervisory skills, adaptability and good written and verbal communication skills are all listed as desirable non-academic qualifications. Company benefits are rated above average. The potential for advancement is listed as being good. The most suitable method for initial contact by those seeking employment is to mail a resume with a covering letter. QLT Photo Therapeutics Inc. does hire summer students. *Contact:* Employment Jobsline.

QSR LIMITED
166 Pearl Street
Toronto, ON M5H 1L3

Tel. 416-597-0969
Fax 416-597-1776

QSR Limited is involved in gold mining and milling. There are approximately 100 people employed at this location and locations in Timmins, Ontario and Bachelor Lake, Quebec. Graduates most likely to be hired come from the following academic areas: Bachelor of Science (Geology), Bachelor of Engineering (Mining), Bachelor of Commerce/Business Administration (Accounting), and Chartered Accountant. Graduates would be hired for positions located at on-site operations and for administrative positions at this location in Toronto. Applicants should be willing and able to work in remote areas. Company benefits are rated as industry standard. The potential for advancement is listed as average. The average annual starting salary falls within the $20,000 to $25,000 range. The most suitable method for initial contact by those seeking employment is to mail a resume with a covering letter. *Contact:* Human Resources.

QUAKER OATS COMPANY OF CANADA LIMITED, THE
Quaker Park
Peterborough, ON K9J 7B2

Tel. 705-743-6330
Fax 705-876-4141

The Quaker Oats Company of Canada Limited is active in the manufacture and marketing of Oat-based food products, and Gatorade beverages for retail stores and the food service industry. There are approximately 200 employees at this location and a total of 1,000 employees in Canada. Graduates most likely to be hired come from the following academic areas: Bachelor of Arts (Economics), Bachelor of Science (Computer Science, Mathematics), Bachelor of Engineering (Food Processing, Electrical, Mechanical), Bachelor of Commerce/Business Administration (General, Accounting, Finance, Human Resources, Information Systems, Marketing, Public Administration), Chartered Accountant, Certified Management Accountant, Master of Business Administration (General, Accounting, Finance, Human Resources, Information Systems, Marketing), and Community College Diploma (Accounting, Human Resources, Marketing/Sales, Purchasing/Logistics, Secretarial, CAD/CAM/Autocad, Engineering Technician). Graduates would occupy Financial Manager (CA's), Financial Analyst, Programmer Analyst, Computer Operator, Buyer, Customer Service Representative, Sales Representative, Project Engineer, Cost Accountant, Marketing Assistant, Quality Assurance Technician, and Production Line Supervisor positions. Company benefits are rated as excellent. The potential for advancement is listed as being good. The average annual starting salary is dependent upon position and previous experience. The most suitable method for initial contact by those seeking employment is to mail a resume with a covering letter. *Contacts:* Denise Kouri, Human Resources or Fred Stanbury, Human Resources.

R. V. ANDERSON ASSOCIATES LIMITED
2001 Sheppard Avenue East, Suite 400
Willowdale, ON M2J 4Z8

Tel. 416-497-8600
Fax 416-497-0342

R. V. Anderson Associates Limited is an engineering consulting firm employing more than 100 people. Consultation activities include water pollution control, water supply, water resources, environmental planning, transportation, tunnels and shafts, municipal services, land development, structural and architectural consulting services. Graduates most likely to be hired come from the following academic areas: Bachelor of Engineering (Environmental, Transportation, Structural, Water Resources), Master of Engineering (Environmental, Transportation, Structural, Water Resources), and Community College Diploma (Engineering Technician). Graduates are hired as Junior Engineers (In-Training). The ability to work well with others, solid work ethic, and independent work habits are listed as desirable non-academic qualifications. Company benefits and the potential for advancement are both rated as excellent. The most suitable method for initial contact by those seeking employment is to mail a resume with a covering letter. R. V. Anderson Associates Limited does hire summer students on a regular basis, primarily for field work. *Contact:* Human Resources.

RADISSON PLAZA HOTEL ADMIRAL
249 Queens Quay West
Toronto, ON M5J 2N5

Tel. 416-203-3333
Fax 416-203-3100

Radisson Plaza Hotel Admiral is a hotel and restaurant, located on Toronto's waterfront. The hotel employs 110 people. Graduates most likely to be hired are Community College graduates from Hospitality and Travel/Tourism programs. Graduates would occupy Front Office, Food and Beverage Waitstaff, and Supervisory positions. Applicants should be outgoing and service oriented. The most suitable method for initial contact by those seeking employment is to mail a resume with a covering letter. Radisson Plaza Hotel Admiral does hire summer students, however there are very few summer positions available. *Contact:* Michèle L. Poisson, Human Resources Manager.

RAMADA HOTEL 400/401, CONFERENCE CENTRE
1677 Wilson Avenue
Toronto, ON M3L 1A5

Tel. 416-249-8171
Fax 416-243-7342

The Ramada Hotel 400/401, Conference Centre is a 200 bedroom, full service hotel with conference facilities to accommodate 1,500 guests. The hotel employs more than 100 people catering to corporate business conventions, small and large banquet functions, sports groups, tour groups, and individual travellers. Graduates most likely to be hired are Community College graduates from Hospitality/Hotel Administration, and Food and Beverage programs. Able to interact well with the public, enjoy working in a service oriented industry, and the ability to speak French, German, or Spanish are all listed as desirable non-academic qualifications. Company benefits are rated above average. The potential for advancement is listed as being good. The average annual starting salary falls within the $20,000 to $25,000 range, and varies a great deal depending upon the positions being considered. The most suitable method for initial contact by those seeking employment is to mail a resume with a covering letter. The Ramada Hotel 400/401 does hire summer students on a regular basis. *Contact:* Wenli Ho, General Manager.

RBC DOMINION SECURITIES INC.
P.O. Box 50, Royal Bank Plaza
Toronto, ON M5J 2W7

Tel. 416-842-8004
Fax 416-842-8033

RBC Dominion Securities Inc. is a security brokerage firm servicing individual and institutional clients. Activities and services include individual investor services, institutional sales and trading, research, treasury, and operational activities. There are more than 500 employees at this location. Graduates most likely to be hired come from the following academic areas: Bachelor of Arts, Bachelor of Science (Computer Science) Bachelor of Commerce/Business Administration, Chartered Accountant, Master of Business Administration, Masters (General/Related), and Community College (General/Related). Graduates would occupy a wide variety of entry-level positions in Corporate Finance, Clerical, and Computer Programming. Company benefits are rated above average. The potential for advancement is listed as being good. The average annual starting salary is dependent upon the level of position. The most suitable method for initial contact by those seeking employment is to mail a resume with a covering letter. RBC Dominion Securities Inc. does hire summer students. *Contact:* Recruitment Officer, Human Resources Department.

READER'S DIGEST ASSOCIATION (CANADA) LTD.
215 avenue Redfern
Montreal, QC H3Z 2V9

Tel. 514-934-0751
Fax 514-932-3637

Reader's Digest Association (Canada) Ltd. is a major publisher and direct marketer of published materials. There are approximately 365 people employed at this location with an additional 20 people employed at the Toronto office. In addition, Reader's Digest employs 6,700 people in 50 locations around the world. Graduates most likely to be hired come from the following academic areas: Bachelor of Arts (General, English, French, Graphic Arts, Journalism), Bachelor of Science (Computer Science, Mathematics), Bachelor of Commerce/Business Administration (General, Accounting, Finance, Human Resources, Information Systems, Marketing), Chartered Accountant, Certified Management Accountant, Certified General Accountant, Community College Diploma (Accounting, Administration, Advertising, Business, Communications, Marketing/Sales, Purchasing/Logistics, Secretarial, Graphic Arts, Journalism, Computer Science), and High School Diploma. Graduates would occupy Secretary, Clerk, Programmer Trainee, Programmer Analyst, Marketing Coordinator, Marketing Assistant, Marketing Analyst, Accounting Clerk, Cost Accountant, and Graphic Designer positions. Initiative, adaptability, flexibility, versatility, energy, motivation, good communication skills, team player, and a curious mind are all listed as desirable non-academic qualifications. Company benefits are rated as excellent. The potential for advancement is listed as very good. The average annual starting salary falls within the $25,000 to $30,000 range. The most suitable methods for initial contact by those seeking employment are to mail a resume with a covering letter, or through industry contacts and employee referrals. The Reader's Digest Association (Canada) Ltd. does hire summer students. *Contact:* Marc St-Pierre, Employee Relations Administrator, Human Resources Department.

RECKITT & COLMAN CANADA INC.
2 Wickman Road
Toronto, ON M8Z 5M5

Tel.	416-255-2300
Fax	416-255-5150

Reckitt & Colman Canada Inc. is a manufacturer and distributor of a variety of household and food products. Popular brand categories include Airwick, Wizard, Black Flag, Easy-Off, Sani-Flush, Sanifoam, Neet, Chore-Boy, Dettol, Down-to-Earth (environmental products), Mr. Bubble, Carpet Fresh, French's Mustard, Keen's Mustard, French's Assorted Sauces & Gravies, etc. The company's head office is located in the United Kingdom. Graduates most likely to be hired come from the following academic areas: Bachelor of Science (Chemistry), Bachelor of Engineering (Chemical), Bachelor of Commerce/Business Administration (Accounting, Finance, Marketing, Information Systems), Master of Business Administration (Finance, Marketing), and Community College Diploma (Accounting, Business, Marketing/Sales, Purchasing/Logistics, Secretarial, Human Resources). Graduates would occupy Laboratory Technician, Plant Engineer, Accounting Manager, Product Manager, Systems Analyst, Human Resources Associate, Credit Clerk, Accounts Payable Clerk, Buyer, Vendor Scheduler, and Secretarial positions. Team player, dedicated, self motivated, good communication skills, a professional image, initiative, and an interest in continual improvement and challenging the status quo are all listed as desirable non-academic qualifications. Company benefits and the potential for advancement are both rated as excellent. The most suitable method for initial contact by those seeking employment is to telephone directly. Reckitt & Colman Canada Inc. does hire summer students. *Contact:* Donna Gautreau, Human Resources Department.

RECOCHEM INC.
850 montée de Liesse
Montreal, QC H4T 1P4

Tel.	514-341-3550
Fax	514-341-1292
Website	www.recochem.com

Recochem Inc. is involved in the manufacturing, packaging, and distribution of automotive specialty chemicals for industries and consumers. There are 150 employees at this location, at total of 400 in Canada, and a total of 500 employees worldwide. Graduates most likely to be hired come from the following academic areas: Bachelor of Science (Chemistry, Computer Science), Bachelor of Engineering (Chemical, Industrial Chemistry, Computer Systems, Mechanical), Bachelor of Commerce/Business Administration (Accounting, Finance, Human Resources, Information Systems), Certified Management Accountant, Master of Business Administration (Accounting, Finance, Human Resources, Information Systems, Marketing), and Community College Diploma (Accounting, Computer Science, Electronics Technician, Engineering Technician). Graduates would occupy Network Integrator, Accounting

Clerk, Human Resource Manager, Payroll Supervisor, Plant Manager, Warehouse Manager and Chemist positions. Company benefits are rated above average. The potential for advancement is listed as average. The average annual starting salary depends upon the position being considered. The most suitable method for initial contact by those seeking employment is to mail a resume with a covering letter, specifying salary and range. *Contact:* Eva Kuchar, Vice President, Administration.

RED COAT TRAIL SCHOOL DIVISION #69
P.O. Box 1330
Assiniboia, SK S0H 0B0

Tel.	306-642-3341
Fax	306-642-3455

Red Coat Trail School Division #69 is a school board operating nine schools in rural Saskatchewan. The School Division employs approximately 130 people. Graduates most likely to be hired come from the following academic areas: Bachelor of Arts (General, Psychology), Bachelor of Science (General, Audiology, Psychology, Speech Pathology), Bachelor of Education (General, Early Childhood, Primary Junior, Junior Intermediate, Intermediate Senior, Physical and Health, Special Needs), Bachelor of Commerce/Business Administration, Community College Diploma (Accounting, Administration, Secretarial, Auto Mechanic, Computer Science, Electronics Technician), and High School Diploma. Depending upon academic background, graduates would occupy Teacher, Principal, Teacher's Aide, Secretarial, Administration, School Bus Driver, and Mechanic positions. Related work experience, enthusiasm, an ability to get along with children and adults, and knowledge and training in area of employment are all listed as desirable non-academic qualifications. Company benefits are rated as industry standard. The potential for advancement is listed as average. The average annual starting salary falls within the $15,000 to $20,000 range for non-academic positions, and within the $25,000 to $30,000 range for academic positions. The most suitable method for initial contact by those seeking employment is to mail a resume with a covering letter. Red Coat Trail School Division #69 does hire summer students, although rarely. *Contacts:* Edward H. Maksymiw, Director of Education or Arthur J. Warnecke, Secretary Treasurer.

RED DEER COLLEGE
P.O. Box 5005
Red Deer, AB T4N 5H5

Tel.	403-342-3273
Fax	403-342-3161
Email	hro@admin.rdc.ab.ca
Website	www.rdc.ab.ca

Established in 1963, Red Deer College is a learning-centered college committed to excellence and educational leadership. The goal of Red Deer College is to provide a wide range of quality educational opportunities which promote success of learners and the enrichment of life in the communities served. Red

Deer College is located in the City of Red Deer, Alberta, but also offers off-campus programming through distance delivery in many areas of the province. Programs include adult development, career oriented studies, apprenticeship training, and university undergraduate studies. Red Deer College also offers the citizens of Central Alberta the opportunity to complete degrees while remaining in Red Deer. Baccalaureate programs in Nursing and Elementary Education (middle years major) are offered in collaboration with the University of Alberta. A Bachelor of Arts degree is offered in collaboration with the University of Calgary. The College's comprehensive mandate together with its reputation as an excellent teaching institution with quality instruction attracts students. Graduates most likely to be hired come from the following academic areas: Bachelor of Arts (General, Economics, English, French, Geography, Fine Arts, History, Philosophy, Political Science, Psychology, Recreation Studies, Sociology/Social Work), Bachelor of Science (General, Biology, Chemistry, Computer Science, Mathematics, Microbiology, Physics, Nursing, Pharmacy, Psychology), Bachelor of Engineering (General, Electrical, Mechanical, Computer Systems, Water Resources, Welding), Bachelor of Education (General, Early Childhood, Adult, Special Needs), Bachelor of Commerce/Business Administration (General, Accounting, Finance, Human Resources, Information Systems, Marketing), Chartered Accountant, Certified Management Accountant, Certified General Accountant, and Master of Business Administration (General, Accounting, Finance, Human Resources, Information Systems, Marketing). Company benefits and the potential for advancement are both rated as excellent. The average annual starting salary falls within the $30,000 to $35,000 range. The most suitable method for initial contact by those seeking employment is to mail a resume with a covering letter. Red Deer College does hire summer students. *Contact:* Employee Support & Development.

REENA
927 Clark Avenue West
Thornhill, ON L4J 8G6

Tel. 905-889-6484

Reena is a non-profit, social service agency providing support to people who are developmentally handicapped. This primarily involves assisting in community integration. Reena has over 300 employees. Graduates most likely to be hired come from the following academic areas: Bachelor of Arts (Psychology, Sociology), Bachelor of Education (Special - Physically Challenged and Developmentally Handicapped), Certified Management Accountant, Master of Social Work, and Community College Diploma (Developmental Service Worker). Graduates would occupy Support Worker, Social Worker, Supervisor, and Accountant positions. Depending upon position, experience with people who have special needs in a supporting and teaching environment is listed as a desirable non-academic qualification. Company benefits are rated above average. The potential for advancement is listed as average. The average annual starting salary falls within the $20,000 to $30,000 range. The most suitable methods for initial contact by graduates seeking employment are to mail a resume with a covering letter, or by phoning the Human Resources Department directly. Reena does hire summer students to occupy positions with their summer cottage program. *Contact:* Roxanne Bird, Human Resources Manager.

REGAL CONSTELLATION HOTEL
900 Dixon Road
Toronto, ON M9W 1J7

Tel. 416-675-1500
Fax 416-675-1737

The Regal Constellation Hotel boasts the largest hotel convention and tradeshow facilities in Canada enabling service to over 3,000 people. The Hotel offers extensive recreation facilities, 708 guestrooms, and a variety of lounges and restaurants. The Hotel employs approximately 575 people. Graduates most likely to be hired come from the following academic areas: Bachelor of Science (Computer Science), Chartered Accountant, Certified Management Accountant, Master of Business Administration (Accounting, Human Resources), Community College Diploma (Business, Human Resources, Marketing/Sales, Cooking, Hospitality, Travel/Tourism), and High School Diploma. Graduates would occupy Room Attendant, Front Desk Clerk, Reservations Agent, Accounting Clerk, Sales/Catering Coordinator, and Restaurant Staff Management positions. Previous hotel experience, team player, and a customer service orientation are listed as desirable non-academic qualifications. Company benefits are rated above average. The potential for advancement is listed as excellent. The average annual starting salary falls within the $15,000 to $25,000 range. The most suitable method for initial contact by those seeking employment is to visit the Human Resource Department at the hotel from 2:00pm to 4:00pm, weekdays. The Regal Constellation Hotel hires 3 to 6 summer students annually. *Contact:* Human Resources Department.

REGENT HOLIDAYS LIMITED
6205 Airport Road, Building A, Suite 200
Mississauga, ON L4V 1E1

Tel. 905-673-0777
Fax 905-673-1717

Regent Holidays Limited is primarily involved in placing travel reservations and taking bookings from travel agents. Operational areas include, Customer Service, Product Development, Documentation, Sales, and Accounting. There are 116 employees at this location, and a total of 125 worldwide. Graduates most likely to be hired come from the following academic areas: Bachelor of Arts (Languages), Bachelor of Commerce/Business Administration (Accounting, Finance, Human Resources, Information Systems, Marketing), Master of Business Administration (Accounting, Finance, Human Resources, Information Systems), and Community College Diploma (Accounting, Administration, Advertising, Business, Hospitality, Travel/Tourism). Graduates would occupy positions ranging from entry-level Reservation, Sales and Clerical positions to Supervisory positions. Applicants should possess good communication skills. Company benefits are rated as industry standard. The potential for advancement is listed as being good. The average annual starting salary falls within the $15,000 to $20,000 range. The most suitable method for initial contact by graduates seeking employment is to mail a resume with a covering letter. *Contact:* Linda Johnston, Manager, Human Resources.

REGION 3 HOSPITAL CORPORATION
P.O. Box 9000
Fredericton, NB E3B 5N5

Tel.	506-452-5311
Fax	506-452-5680

Region 3 Hospital Corporation is a major health care corporation, including 15 facilities and employing 3,200 people throughout the region. Graduates most likely to be hired come from the following academic areas: Bachelor of Science (Audiology, Nursing, Nutritional Sciences, Occupational Therapy, Pharmacy, Physical Therapy, Speech Pathology), Bachelor of Engineering (Biomedical Electronics), Bachelor of Education (Adult), Master of Arts (Social Work), Master of Science (Clinical Psychology, Speech Pathology), and Community College Diploma (Dietician/Nutrition, Ambulance/Emergency Care Technician, Laboratory Technician, Nuclear Medicine Technician, Nursing RN/RNA, Radiology Technician, Respiratory Therapy). Graduates are hired to occupy Registered Nurse, Occupational Therapist, Physiotherapist, Speech Language Pathologist, Dietician, Clinical Psychologist, and related positions. Demonstrated communication, interpersonal and team building skills are all listed as desirable non-academic qualifications. Company benefits are rated above average. The potential for advancement is listed as being good. The average annual starting salary depends upon the position being considered. The most suitable method for initial contact by those seeking employment is to mail a resume with a covering letter. The Region 3 Hospital Corporation does hire summer students. *Contact:* Human Resources Officer.

REHABILITATION INSTITUTE OF TORONTO, THE
550 University Avenue
Toronto, ON M5G 2A2

Tel.	416-597-3093
Fax	416-597-6626

The Rehabilitation Institute of Toronto (formerly The Queen Elizabeth Hospital) is a rehabilitation and continuing care hospital which is affiliated with The University of Toronto. Graduates most likely to be hired come from the following academic areas: Bachelor of Arts (Recreation Studies), Bachelor of Science (Computer Science, Nursing, Pharmacy), Bachelor of Education (Adult), Bachelor of Commerce/Business Administration (Accounting, Finance, Information Systems), Chartered Accountant (Finance), Certified Management Accountant (Finance), Certified General Accountant (Finance), Master of Business Administration (Information Systems), Master of Science (Speech Pathology), Master of Education (Adult Education), and Community College Diploma (Accounting, Human Resources, Recreation, HVAC Systems, Mechanic, Dental Assistant, Laboratory Technician, Nursing RN/RPN, Radiology Technician). Graduates would occupy Staff Nursing, Nursing Management, and related positions. Organized, punctual, and excellent interpersonal and communication skills are listed as desirable non-academic qualifications. The most suitable method for initial contact by graduates seeking employment is to mail a resume with a covering letter. Applications are encouraged from qualified women and men, members of visible minorities, aboriginal peoples and persons with disabilities. Summer positions are available for Nursing students only. *Contact:* Marianne Chandler, Recruitment and Employee Relations.

REHABILITATION INSTITUTE OF TORONTO, THE
47 Austin Terrace
Toronto, ON M5R 1Y8

Tel.	416-537-3421
Fax	416-537-8628

The Rehabilitation Institute of Toronto (formerly Hillcrest Hospital) is a general rehabilitation hospital for orthopaedic and arthritic patients. Graduates most likely to be hired come from the following academic areas: Bachelor of Arts (General), Bachelor of Science (Health Sciences, Nursing, Pharmacy, Physiotherapy, Occupational Therapy), Bachelor of Commerce/Business Administration, Master of Science (Nursing), Community College Diploma (Accounting, Business, Secretarial, Human Resources, Food/Nutrition, Nursing RN/RNA, Pharmacy Technician, Central Supply Technician, Materials Management), and High School Diploma. Graduates would occupy Budget Officer, Accounts Receivable Clerk, Accounts Payable Clerk, Secretary, Health Records Technician, Health Records Manager, Director of Nursing Practice, Nursing Unit Manager, Nurse RN, Nurse RNA, Grad Nurse, Physiotherapist, Occupational Therapist, Central Supply Technician, Food Services Supervisor, Dietician, Pharmacy Technician, Pharmacist, Human Resources and Payroll Coordinator, and Store Supervisor positions. Related work experience is listed as a desirable non-academic qualification. Employee benefits are rated above average. The potential for advancement is listed as average. The average annual starting salary falls within the $25,000 to $30,000 range. The most suitable method for initial contact by those seeking employment is to mail a resume with a covering letter, or via telephone. The Rehabilitation Institute of Toronto does hire summer students. *Contact:* Recruitment and Employee Relations.

REICHHOLD LTD.
1919 Wilson Avenue
Weston, ON M9M 1B1

Tel. 416-742-0262

Reichhold Ltd. is involved in the research, development, manufacture and bulk sale of liquid and powder chemicals to industrial companies. Products include forest product adhesives for plywood, waferboard, etc., and products such as base paints, plastic resins, etc. Reichhold Ltd. employs more than 100 people at this location, and a total of 500 across Canada. Graduates most likely to be hired come from the following academic areas: Bachelor of Science (Chemistry, Forestry), Bachelor of Engineering (Chemistry, Forestry), Bachelor of Commerce/Business Administration, and Master of Business Administration (Marketing), Master of Science (Chemistry), Doctorate of Science (Chemistry), and Community College Diploma (Laboratory Technician). Good writing skills, entrepreneurial abilities, a strong work ethic, integrity and being "down to earth" are all listed as desirable non-academic qualifications. Company benefits are rated above average. The potential for advancement is listed as excellent. The average annual starting salary falls between the $25,000 to $35,000 plus range. The most suitable method for initial contact by those seeking employment is to mail a resume with a covering letter. Reichhold Ltd. hires a small number students for summer and co-op work terms, primarily co-op students. *Contact:* Manager, Human Resources.

RENAISSANCE VANCOUVER HOTEL HARBOURSIDE
1133 West Hastings
Vancouver, BC V6E 3T3

Tel. 604-689-9211
Fax 604-689-4358

Renaissance Vancouver Hotel Harbourside is a major Vancouver hotel and restaurant employing approximately 300 people. Graduates most likely to be hired come from the following academic areas: Bachelor of Arts (Languages), Bachelor of Engineering (Food Processing, Electrical, Mechanical, Welding), Bachelor of Commerce/Business Administration (General, Accounting, Finance, Human Resources, Marketing), Chartered Accountant, Certified Management Accountant, Certified General Accountant, Master of Business Administration (Accounting, Finance, Human Resources, Marketing), Community College Diploma (Accounting, Administration, Business, Facility Management, Financial Planning, Human Resources, Marketing/Sales, Purchasing/Logistics, Secretarial, Cooking, Hospitality, Travel/Tourism, HVAC Systems, Welding, Nutrition), and High School Diploma. Graduates would occupy Line Staff positions such as Cook, Front Desk Clerk, Reservations, General Maintenance, Server, Bartender, and Cleaner, and Management positions in Accounting, Sales, Human Resources, Secretarial, Food and Beverage, and Purchasing. Excellent customer service skills, prior work experience, an ability to balance many work tasks simultaneously, outgoing, professional, and computer literate are all listed as desirable non-academic qualifications. Company benefits are rated above average. The potential for advancement is listed as being good. The average annual starting salary falls within the $20,000 to $25,000 range. The most suitable method for initial contact by those seeking employment is to mail a resume with a covering letter. Renaissance Vancouver Hotel Harbourside hires summer students from March to September. *Contact:* Georgia Sanderson, Director of Human Resources.

RESEARCH IN MOTION LIMITED
295 Phillip Street
Waterloo, ON N2L 3W8

Tel. 519-888-7465
Fax 519-888-6906
Email .... careers@rim.net
Website .... www.rim.net

Founded in 1984, Research In Motion Limited (RIM) is a leading international developer, manufacturer, and worldwide marketer of battery efficient radio modem technology for a variety of innovative devices for the narrowband-PCS wireless data industry. RIM supplies two-way interactive pagers, wireless PC MCIA network adapters, and OEM radio modems for wireless data networks operating throughout the world, including Mobitex and Data TAC. RIM employs a total of 200 people. Graduates most likely to be hired come from the following academic areas: Bachelor of Science (Computer Science), Bachelor of Engineering (Electrical, Computer Systems, Telecommunications, Mechanical), Bachelor of Commerce/Business Administration (Information Systems), and Community College Diploma (CAD/CAM/Autocad, Electronics Technician). Graduates would occupy RF Technician/Technologist, Software Developer, Hardware Engineer, Mechanical Designer, ASIC Designer, Test Engineer, Process Engineer, Marketing Product Manager, and Business Development Manager positions. Previous, related work experience, flexibility, creativity, initiative, enthusiasm, team player, independence, good organizational skills, able to juggle multiple priorities, and good time management skills are all listed as desirable non-academic qualifications. Company benefits and the potential for advancement are both rated as excellent. The average annual starting salary depends upon the position being considered and the applicants background. The most suitable methods for initial contact by those seeking employment are to mail or e-mail a resume with a covering letter. Research In Motion Limited hires co-op students from local universities, on four month rotating terms all year round. *Contact:* Laura Druar, Recruiting Officer.

RESTAURANTS NORMANDIN INC., LES
2335, boul Bastien
Quebec, QC G2B 1B3

Tel. 418-842-9160
Fax 418-842-8916

Les Restaurants Normandin Inc. is a restaurant company with 27 locations, including corporate and franchise locations. There are approximately 45 employees at the head office and 1,300 throughout the Province of Quebec. Head office, located in Quebec will recruit and select Restaurant Managers and Assistant Managers for each facility as well as support staff and management. Graduates most likely to be hired come from the following academic areas: Bachelor of Arts (Sociology), Bachelor of Science (Computer Science, Nutritional Sciences), Bachelor of Engineering (Food Processing, Automation/Robotics, Instrumentation), Bachelor of Commerce/Business Administration (General, Accounting, Finance, Human Resources, Marketing), Chartered Accountant, Certified Management Accountant, Certified General Accountant, and Community College Diploma (Accounting, Administration, Advertising, Business, Communications, Facility Management, Human Resources, Marketing/Sales, Purchasing/Logistics, Secretarial, CAD/CAM/Autocad, Computer Science). Graduates are hired to occupy Manager, Associate Manager, Assistant Manager, Marketing Assistant, Human Resources Assistant, and Computer Programmer positions. Restaurant or food market experience is listed as a desirable non-academic qualification. The most suitable method for initial contact by those seeking employment is to mail a resume with a covering letter to the Human Resource Department. *Contacts:* Jean Dénommé, Director, Human Resources or Maude Gallichand, Assistant Director, Human Resources.

REUTERS INFORMATION SERVICES (CANADA) LIMITED, REUTERS CANADA DIVISION
121 King Street West, Suite 2000
Toronto, ON M5H 3T9

Tel.	416-941-8000
Fax	416-941-9064
Email	canada.employment@reuters.com

Reuters Canada Division is the Canadian arm of Reuters Holdings PLC and employs approximately 125 people across Canada. Reuters is the world's leading news and information organization. For the financial community, Reuters provides real-time and delayed price information on every financial market in the world, and global coverage of business and market news. Reuters obtains information from exchanges and over-the-counter markets and from a vast network of journalists, photographers and camera persons. Reuters distributes this information through video terminals and teleprinters, using the latest technology to inform the world. Graduates most likely to be hired come from the following academic areas: Master of Business Administration (General, Finance), Bachelor of Arts (Journalism, Business), Bachelor of Science (Computer Science), Bachelor of Commerce/Business Administration, Chartered Accountant, Certified Management Accountant, and graduates with the Canadian Securities Institute (CSI) designation. Graduates would occupy Account Executive, Account Support Representative, Sales Specialist, Client Administrator, and Technician positions. Strategic thinking, energetic, entrepreneurial,

innovative, and creativity are all listed as desirable non-academic qualifications. Company benefits are rated above average. The potential for advancement is listed as average. The average annual starting salary falls within the $45,000 to $50,000 range, dependant on position sought. The most suitable methods for initial contact by those seeking employment are to mail, fax or e-mail a resume with a covering letter. *Contact:* Sharon E. Greenholt, Human Resources Manager.

REVENUE CANADA, INFORMATION TECHNOLOGY BRANCH
875 Heron Road, Suite 5082
Ottawa, ON K1A 0L8

Tel.	613-954-9105
Fax	613-941-3799
Website	www.rc.gc.ca

Revenue Canada is responsible for Canadian tax, trade, and border administration. The department draws its mandate from a federal statute, the Department of National Revenue Act, which gives the Minister of National Revenue federal responsibility for controlling, regulating, managing and supervising income and consumption taxes, as well as customs and excise duties. The Minister is also responsible for controlling the movement of people and goods into Canada. Revenue Canada carries out its mandate through four business lines: revenue generation, trade policy administration, customs border services, and income redistribution. Graduates most likely to be hired for the Information Technology Branch of Revenue Canada must have an University Degree from a recognized institution in Information Systems, Computer Science or Software Engineering. Graduates would occupy Programmers/Analyst, Technology Specialist, Database Administrator, Systems Programmer/Analyst, and LAN Support Specialist positions. Team player, strong interpersonal skills, good judgment, reliability, and motivation are all listed as desirable non-academic qualifications. Company benefits are rated as industry standard. The potential for advancement is listed as being good. The average annual starting salary falls within the $30,000 to $35,000 range. The most suitable method for initial contact by those seeking employment is to apply through Revenue Canada's website at www.rc.gc.ca. Revenue Canada - Information Technology Branch does hire students for summer and co-op work terms. *Contact:* Through Web Site Address.

REYNOLDS AND REYNOLDS (CANADA) LTD.
2100 Steeles Avenue East
Brampton, ON L6T 3X1

Tel.	905-791-4400
Fax	905-790-1381
Website	reyrey.com

Reynolds and Reynolds (Canada) Ltd. is involved in the manufacturing of business forms, and the programming and software/hardware support of computer systems for automotive dealerships. Reynolds and Reynolds employs approximately 311 people in

Canada and 4,500 people worldwide. Graduates most likely to be hired come from the following academic areas: Bachelor of Arts (General, Economics), Bachelor of Science (Computer Science), Bachelor of Engineering (Computer Systems), Bachelor of Commerce/Business Administration (Human Resources, Information Systems, Marketing), Master of Business Administration (Human Resources, Information Systems, Marketing), and Community College Diploma (Administration, Business, Human Resources, Marketing/Sales, Secretarial, Computer Science), and High School Diploma. Graduates would occupy various positions in manufacturing and computer systems/operations. Related work experience, initiative, drive, self starter, positive attitude, attendance and punctuality, and involvement in community and career related associations are all listed as desirable non-academic qualifications. Company benefits are rated as industry standard. The potential for advancement is listed as average. The average annual starting salary falls within the $25,000 to $30,000 range. The most suitable method for initial contact by those seeking employment is to mail a resume with a covering letter. *Contacts:* Christine Pascoe, Manager, Human Resources/Payroll or Christine Smith, Human Resources Specialist.

RICHARD & B. A. RYAN LIMITED

78 Logan Avenue
Toronto, ON M4M 2M8

Tel. 416-461-0791
Fax 416-461-7606

Richard & B. A. Ryan Limited is a general contractor and construction manager employing more than 50 people. Activities include industrial, commercial and institutional construction. Graduates most likely to be hired come from the following academic areas: Bachelor of Engineering (Civil, Architectural/Building), Bachelor of Commerce/Business Administration (Accounting), Chartered Accountant, Certified General Accountant, Community College Diploma (Accounting, Engineering Technician), and High School Diploma. Graduates would occupy Project Manager, Estimator, and Superintendent positions. Company benefits are rated as excellent. The potential for advancement is listed as being good. The average annual starting salary falls within the $20,000 to $30,000 range. The most suitable method for initial contact by those seeking employment is to mail a resume with a covering letter. Richard & B. A. Ryan Limited does hire summer students on a regular basis. *Contacts:* Y. Loisel, President & C.E.O. or B. Bridle, Purchasing Manager.

RICHMOND SAVINGS

5611 Cooney Road, Suite 300
Richmond, BC V6X 3J5

Tel. 604-273-8138
Fax 604-273-7612

Richmond Savings provides financial services to its more than 53,000 members through 9 branches in the lower mainland. Richmond Savings offers a full range of banking, investment, and insurance products. There are more than 250 employees at this location. Graduates most likely to be hired come from the following academic areas: Bachelor of Arts (General, Economics, English, History, Journalism, Languages, Political Science, Psychology, Sociology), Bachelor of Science (General, Computer Science, Mathematics, Psychology), Bachelor of Education, Bachelor of Commerce/Business Administration (Accounting, Finance, Marketing, Information Systems), Chartered Accountant (Finance), Certified Management Accountant (Finance), Certified General Accountant (Finance), Master of Business Administration (Accounting, Finance, Marketing, Information Systems), Community College Diploma (Accounting, Administration, Advertising, Communications, Insurance, Marketing/Sales, Human Resources, Journalism, Computer Science, Electronics Technician, Engineering Technician), and High School Diploma. Graduates would occupy Banking, Systems, Marketing, Investment, and Insurance positions. Team player, self motivated, strong organizational skills, a willingness to learn and grow with the company, and previous work experience in the financial industry are all listed as desirable non-academic qualifications. Company benefits and the potential for advancement are both rated as excellent. The average starting salary falls within the $20,000 to $25,000 range. The most suitable method for initial contact by those seeking employment is to mail a resume with a covering letter. Richmond Savings does hire summer students. *Contact:* Personnel Department.

RICHTER, USHER & VINEBERG/RICHTER & ASSOCIATES

2 Place Alexis Nihon, Suite 1950
Montreal, QC H3Z 3C2

Tel. 514-934-3400
Fax 514-934-3539

Richter, Usher & Vineberg was founded in 1926 and today has grown to offer a wide range of business services including: accounting, auditing, management consulting, taxation, insolvency consulting, business counselling, financial litigation and business valuation. Graduates most likely to be hired come from the following academic areas: Bachelor of Engineering (Computer Systems), Bachelor of Commerce/Business Administration (General, Accounting, Finance, Information Systems), Chartered Accountant, Certified Management Accountant, Certified General Accountant, Master of Business Administration (General, Information Systems), and Community College Diploma (Accounting, Administration, Secretarial). Graduates would occupy Audit Trainee, Audit Technician, Tax Technician, Chartered Accountant, Secretary, Typist, Clerk, Systems Analyst, Programmer, Project Leader, Systems Trainer, and Customer Service Technician positions. Good communication skills, team player, dynamic, self-starter, and strong interpersonal skills are all listed as desirable non-academic qualifications. The most suitable method for initial contact by those seeking employment is to mail a resume with a covering letter. Richter, Usher & Vineberg does hire summer students. *Contact:* Human Resources Department.

RIO ALTO EXPLORATION LTD.
205 - 5 Avenue SW
Suite 2500
Calgary, AB T2P 2V7

Tel. 403-264-8780
Fax 403-261-7626

Rio Alto Exploration Ltd. is an oil and gas production company based in Calgary, Alberta. The company's focus is on exploration, development and production, with an emphasis on meeting production and financial targets. This emphasis makes Rio Alto one of the lowest cost operators in the industry. There are 97 employees at this location and a total of 236 employees in Canada. Graduates most likely to be hired come from the following academic areas: Bachelor of Science (Geology), Bachelor of Engineering (General, Mechanical, Environmental/Resources, Geological Engineering, Petroleum/Fuels), Bachelor of Commerce/Business Administration (Accounting, Human Resources, Marketing), Chartered Accountant, Certified Management Accountant, Master of Business Administration (Accounting, Marketing), Master of Engineering, and Community College Diploma (Accounting, Administration, Financial Planning, Human Resources). Graduates would occupy Accountant, Accounting Clerk, Human Resources Assistant, Engineer, and Geologist positions. Competent, team player, and good verbal and written communication skills are all listed as desirable non-academic qualifications. Company benefits are rated above average. The potential for advancement is listed as excellent. The average annual starting salary is dependent upon the position being considered. The most suitable method for initial contact by those seeking employment is to fax a resume with a covering letter. Rio Alto Exploration Ltd. does hire summer and co-op work term students. *Contact:* Liz Ganton.

RISDON COSMETIC CONTAINERS INC.
137 John Street
Barrie, ON L4N 2L1

Tel. 705-726-6571
Fax 705-726-7934

Risdon Cosmetic Containers Inc. manufactures plastic lipstick containers using the injection molding, hot die stamping and auto assembly processes. The company operates three shifts on a five, six or seven day basis. There are 270 employees at this location, while Risdon's parent company (CMB) employs 34,000 people worldwide. Graduates most likely to be hired come from the following academic areas: Bachelor of Engineering (Automation/Robotics, Mechanical, Industrial Design, Industrial Production, Quality Engineer - ASQC), Master of Business Administration (Finance, Human Resources), Community College Diploma (Accounting, Administration, Business, Human Resources, Marketing/Sales, Pur-

chasing/Logistics, Engineering Technician, Mold Maker), and High School Diploma. Graduates would occupy Moldmaker, Injection Molding Technician, Automation/Robotics Technician, Engineer, and various Administrative positions. Previous injection molding experience, high energy level, self starter, and team player are all listed as desirable non-academic qualifications. Company benefits are rated above average. The potential for advancement is listed as average. The most suitable method for initial contact by those seeking employment is to mail a resume with a covering letter. Risdon Cosmetic Containers Inc. does hire summer students. *Contact:* JoAnne Ayres, Human Resources Manager.

ROBCO INC.
7200 St. Patrick
La Salle, QC H8N 2W7

Tel. 514-368-2723
Fax 514-367-4884

Robco Inc. manufactures and distributes industrial sealing and maintenance repair products for all sorts of industry. Robco Inc. employs 160 people at this location, and a total of 225 people across Canada. Graduates most likely to be hired come from the following academic areas: Bachelor of Arts (General), Bachelor of Science (General, Chemistry, Computer Science, Forestry), Bachelor of Engineering (General, Chemical, Industrial Chemistry, Materials Science, Metallurgy, Pollution Treatment, Pulp and Paper, Computer Systems, Mechanical, Industrial Design, Industrial Production, Marine, Forest Resources, Mining, Petroleum, Water Resources), Bachelor of Commerce/Business Administration (Accounting, Finance, Information Systems, Marketing), Chartered Accountant, Certified Management Accountant, Certified General Accountant, Master of Business Administration (Accounting, Finance, Marketing), and Community College Diploma (Accounting, CAD/CAM/Autocad, Forestry). Self-starter and entrepreneurial are both listed as desirable non-academic qualifications. Company benefits are rated as industry standard. The potential for advancement is listed as excellent. The average annual starting salary falls within the $20,000 to $25,000 range. The most suitable method for initial contact by those seeking employment is to mail a resume with a covering letter. Robco Inc. does hire summer students. *Contacts:* Mr. R. Duguay or Mr. J. T. White.

ROBERTS COMPANY CANADA LIMITED
2070 Steeles Avenue
Bramalea, ON L6T 1A7

Tel. 905-791-4444
Fax 905-791-1998

Roberts Company Canada Limited employs more than 25 people in the manufacture of floor covering installation products and accessories, including adhesives, smoothedge, tape, etc. Graduates most likely to be hired come from the following academic areas: Bachelor of Science (Chemistry), Bachelor of

Engineering (Industrial), Bachelor of Commerce/ Business Administration (Marketing), Chartered Accountant (Finance), Certified General Accountant, Community College Diploma (Administration, Business), and High School Diploma. Graduates would occupy Laboratory Technician, Marketing Assistant, and Accounting positions. Applicants should be a suitable match with the company. Company benefits are rated above average. The potential for advancement is limited due to the company's size, and is therefore listed as average. Although job vacancies in the areas listed are rare, the most suitable method for initial contact by graduates seeking employment is to mail a resume with a covering letter. Roberts Company Canada Limited does hire 2 to 3 summer students annually for general labour positions. *Contact:* Personnel Manager.

ROCTEST LTÉE
665 avenue Pine
St-Lambert, QC J4P 2P4

Tel. 450-465-1113
Fax 450-465-1938
Email .... info@roctest.com
Website .... www.roctest.com

Founded in 1967, Roctest Ltée specializes in the manufacture and marketing of high-technology instruments designed for monitoring major civil engineering and environmental projects. By measuring parameters such as pressure, bearing capacity, permeability, displacement, deformation and inclination, its instruments can assess the stability and potential risks of failure of large-scale construction works. Roctest instruments and monitoring systems are incorporated into hundreds of dams, mines, tunnels, nuclear power stations, buildings and bridges in over 75 countries. The company employs 55 people at this location, a total of 75 people in Canada, and 120 people worldwide. Graduates most likely to be hired come from the following academic areas: Bachelor of Science (Geology), Bachelor of Engineering (Civil, Electrical, Mechanical, Computer Systems, Environmental/Resources, Geological Engineering, Instrumentation, Mining, Water Resources), Bachelor of Commerce/Business Administration (Accounting), Certified Management Accountant, Certified General Accountant, and Community College Diploma (Accounting, Administration, Marketing/Sales, CAD/CAM/Autocad, Electronics Technician, Engineering Technician, Tool and Die, Machinist). Graduates would occupy Production Technician, R&D Technician, Production Engineer, R&D Engineer, Junior Accountant, Sales Representative, and Project Director positions. Company benefits are rated above average. The potential for advancement is listed as being good. The average annual starting salary falls within the $20,000 to $30,000 range. The most suitable methods for initial contact by those seeking employment are to mail, fax or e-mail a resume with a covering letter. Roctest Ltée does hire summer students. *Contact:* Human Resources.

ROGERS BROADCASTING LIMITED
36 Victoria Street
Toronto, ON M5C 1H3

Tel. 416-864-2000
Fax 416-864-2133
Email .... s.foreste@rci.rogers.com
Website .... www.rogers.com

Rogers Broadcasting Limited is involved in radio broadcasting, both AM and FM stations across Canada, and television broadcasting, including CFMT, a multicultural station in Toronto, and The Shopping Channel (see Directory listings). There are 120 employees at this location, and a total of 1,200 employees across Canada. Graduates most likely to be hired come from the following academic areas: Bachelor of Engineering (Computer Systems), and Community College Diploma (Accounting, Administration, Marketing/Sales, Secretarial, Graphic Arts, Television/Radio Arts). Graduates would occupy Accountant, Accounting Clerk, Administrator, Administrative Assistant, Sales Representative, Copy Writer, Radio Talent, and Television/Radio Technical Crew positions. Natural talent (for on-air work), industry related work experience (eg. radio/television station experience), flexibility, commitment and aptitude are all listed as desirable non-academic qualifications. Company benefits are rated as excellent. The potential for advancement is listed as being good. The average annual starting salary falls within the $20,000 to $25,000 range, depending on the position being considered, geographic location, and the experience of the applicant. For certain positions the salary is commission based. The most suitable method for initial contact by those seeking employment is to mail a resume with a covering letter. *Contact:* Human Resources Administrator.

ROGERS CABLE TV LTD.
855 York Mills Road
Don Mills, ON M3B 2S7

Tel. 416-446-6500
Fax 416-446-0250
Email .... cablehr@rci.rogers.com
Website .... www.rogers.com/RNS/

Rogers Cable TV Ltd. has 14 cable systems that serve 1.8 million subscribers in British Columbia, Alberta and Ontario and also owns and operates services for pay television, pay-per-view, hotel pay television, converter rentals, local telecommunications, cable classified advertising, a chain of 70 video rental stores, and 93.2% of the Canadian Home Shopping Network (CHSN) Ltd. Graduates most likely to be hired come from the following academic areas: Bachelor of Arts (Journalism, Urban Geography), Bachelor of Science (Computer Science, Environmental, Mathematics), Bachelor of Engineering (General, Computer Systems, Microelectronics, Power, Telecommunications), Bachelor of Commerce/Business Administration (Accounting, Finance, Human Resources, Information Systems, Marketing, Public Administration), Certified Management Accountant,

Certified General Accountant, Master of Business Administration (Marketing), Community College Diploma (Accounting, Administration, Human Resources, Marketing/Sales, Journalism, Television/Radio Arts), and High School Diploma. Good communication and customer service skills, an ability to be trained, and a desire to work in a dynamic industry are all listed as desirable non-academic qualifications. Company benefits are rated above average. The potential for advancement is listed as excellent. The average annual starting salary falls within the $25,000 to $30,000 range for Junior/Clerical positions, $25,000 to $30,000 range for Administrative positions, $40,000 to $45,000 range for Professional positions, and commission based for Sales positions. The most suitable method for initial contact by those seeking employment is to mail a resume with a covering letter. Rogers Cable TV Ltd. does hire summer students. *Contact:* Human Resources.

ROSEMOUNT INSTRUMENTS LIMITED
808 - 55th Avenue NE
Calgary, AB T2E 6Y4

Tel. 403-730-3135
Fax 403-275-2856

Rosemount Instruments Ltd. is the Canadian division of Fisher-Rosemount, the world's leading manufacturer of industrial process instrumentation. Rosemount Instruments has sales offices across Canada, with headquarters and a manufacturing plant in Calgary. Through Fisher-Rosemount, and its parent corporation, Emerson Electric Co., Rosemount employees have the opportunity to take on assignments around the world. There are approximately 70 employees here at the Calgary location, a total of 150 employees across Canada, and through Emerson Electric Co., there are 60,000 employees worldwide. Graduates most likely to be hired come from the following academic areas: Bachelor of Science (Chemistry, Environmental), Bachelor of Engineering (Chemical, Instrumentation, Resources/Environmental), Chartered Accountant, Certified Management Accountant, Certified General Accountant, and Community College Diploma (Accounting, Secretarial, Industrial Instrumentation). Graduates would occupy Inside/Outside Instrument Sales, Product Marketing Specialist, Accountant, Secretary, Service and Technical positions. Relevant work experience, personal initiative, positive outlook, and a customer focus are all listed as desirable non-academic qualifications. The most suitable method for initial contact by those seeking employment is to mail a resume with a covering letter. *Contact:* Human Resources Manager.

ROSS ROY COMMUNICATIONS CANADA LIMITED
1737 Walker Road, P.O. Box 2235
Windsor, ON N8Y 4R8

Tel. 519-258-7584
Fax 519-258-4242

Ross Roy Communications Canada Limited is involved in "below the line" advertising or merchandising for large automobile clients. Activities include training, direct marketing, telemarketing, print production and new car announcement shows for sales personnel. The company employs approximately 130 people. Graduates most likely to be hired come from the following academic areas: Bachelor of Arts (General, English, French, Journalism), Bachelor of Science (Computer Science), Bachelor of Commerce/Business Administration (Accounting, Finance, Human Resources, Information Systems, Marketing), Chartered Accountant, Certified Management Accountant, Certified General Accountant, Master of Business Administration (Finance, Marketing), and Community College Diploma (Accounting, Administration, Advertising, Business, Communications, Human Resources, Marketing/Sales, Secretarial, Graphic Arts/Design, Computer Science). Graduates would occupy Accounting, Human Resources, Administration, Operations, Marketing, Computer Operations, Creative Writing, and Creative Art/Design positions. Work experience, a good attitude, personable, and an ability to work under pressure are all listed as desirable non-academic qualifications. Company benefits are rated above average. The potential for advancement is listed as being good. The average annual starting salary for entry level positions falls within the $20,000 to $25,000 range. The most suitable methods for initial contact by those seeking employment are to mail a resume with a covering letter, or through personnel agencies. Ross Roy Communications Canada Limited does hire summer students. *Contacts:* Claudette Parent, Vice President, Human Resources or Jean Dawson, Manager, Human Resources.

ROYAL BANK
970 Lawrence Avenue West
Suite 110
Toronto, ON M6A 3B6

Tel. 416-256-0088
Fax 416-256-0282
Email .... emp@rb-erc.com
Website .... www.royalbank.com

Royal Bank is Canada's premier global financial services group. As one of North America's largest financial institutions, Royal Bank and its key subsidiaries, Royal Trust, RBC Dominion Securities, RBC Insurance, and Royal Bank Action Direct have 58,134 employees who serve 10 million clients through 1,500 branches and offices in 36 countries. Graduates most likely to be hired come from the following academic areas: Bachelor of Arts (General, Economics), Bachelor of Science (Actuarial, Computer Science, Mathematics), Bachelor of Commerce/Business Administration (General, Accounting, Finance, Human Resources, Information Systems, Marketing), Chartered Accountant, Certified Management Accountant, Certified General Accountant, Master of Business Administration (General, Accounting, Finance, Human Resources, Information Systems, Marketing, Public Administration), Master of Arts (Economics), Master of Science (Computer Science), and Community College Diploma (Accounting, Administration, Advertising,

Business, Human Resources, Information Systems, Marketing/Sales, Computer Science). Graduates would enter Career Management Programs. In 1997, Royal Bank invested more than $100 million in employee training. Achievement, motivation, impact and influence, customer service skills, initiative, leadership skills, teamwork, and adaptability are all listed as desirable non-academic qualifications. Company benefits and the potential for advancement are both rated as excellent. The average annual starting salary varies with the position being considered, and the education and experience of the applicant. The most suitable methods for initial contact by those seeking employment are to mail, fax or e-mail a resume with a covering letter, or by applying through the Royal Bank's website at www.royalbank.com. Interested applicants should visit Royal Bank's website to learn more about products, services, and career opportunities. Royal Bank does hire summer and co-op work term students. Royal Bank values diversity in the workplace and is committed to employment equity. *Contact:* Employment Resources Centre.

ROYAL LEPAGE REAL ESTATE SERVICES LTD.
39 Wynford Drive
Don Mills, ON M3C 3K5

Tel. 416-510-5678

Royal LePage Real Estate Services Ltd. is the largest full service real estate company in Canada. Activities include residential, commercial and investment real estate, property management, consulting, mortgage administration and real estate appraisal. Royal LePage maintains numerous locations throughout Canada (see your local telephone white pages). Graduates most likely to be hired come from the following academic areas: Bachelor of Arts, Bachelor of Commerce/Business Administration, Chartered Accountant, Certified Management Accountant, Master of Business Administration, Community College Diploma (General/Related), and Real Estate courses (contact your local Real Estate Board). Graduates would occupy Finance, Computer Operations, Systems, Human Resources, Appraisal, Marketing, Mortgage Administration, Consulting, and commission based Sales positions. Company benefits are rated above average. The potential for advancement is listed as being good. The average annual starting salary falls within the $15,000 and $35,000 range, depending greatly upon the position being considered. The most suitable method for initial contact by those seeking employment is to mail a resume with a covering letter. Royal LePage Real Estate Services Ltd. does hire summer students. *Contacts:* Employment Services Co-ordinator or Human Resources.

ROYAL MERIDIEN KING EDWARD HOTEL, LE
37 King Street East
Toronto, ON M5C 1E9

Tel. 416-863-3215
Fax 416-863-5232

Le Royal Meridien King Edward Hotel is a downtown, luxury hotel employing more than 300 people. Graduates most likely to be hired come from the following academic areas: Bachelor of Arts (General, Languages), Community College Diploma (Business, Cook/Chef Training, Hospitality, Travel/Tourism), and Cles D'Or (Concierge). Graduates would occupy Front Office Agent, Food and Beverage Server, Chef, Kitchen Help, and Professional positions in the Business Office. Team player, proactive, quick learner, flexible, and able to manage change well are all listed as desirable non-academic qualifications. Company benefits are rated above average. The potential for advancement is listed as being good. The average annual starting salary falls within the $20,000 to $25,000 range. The most suitable method for initial contact by graduates seeking employment is to mail a resume with a covering letter. Le Royal Meridien King Edward Hotel does hire summer students, depending upon the position and the area of employment. *Contacts:* Laurie Hewson, Human Resources Director or Anne Hardacre, Human Resources Consultant.

ROYCO HOTELS & RESORTS LTD./ TRAVELODGE CANADA
5940 Macleod Trail South, Suite 500
Calgary, AB T2H 2G4

Tel. 403-259-9800
Fax 403-255-6981
Email .... bannon@royco.com
Website .... www.travelodge.com

Royco Hotels & Resorts Ltd. is a hotel/resort management company concerned with developing standards and an improved bottom line for owners/investors of hotel and resort properties. Royco is also the parent company of Travelodge Canada, the Master Franchisor of Travelodge and Thriftlodge. There are over 80 employees at the corporate office in Calgary with responsibilities for managing hotels in Canada and the United States. Graduates most likely to be hired come from the following academic areas: Bachelor of Commerce/Business Administration (Hotel and Food Administration), Community College Diploma (Travel and Tourism, Hotel and Catering), and High School Diploma. Graduates are hired to occupy Trainee Manager positions at the Hotel locations. Successful applicants would participate in a 12 to 18 month training program. Good interpersonal skills, leadership potential, organization skills, deadline orientation, initiative, practical hands-on ability and an enthusiasm for the hotel and catering industry are all listed as desirable non-academic skills. Company benefits are rated as industry standard. The potential for advancement is listed as excellent. The average annual starting salary falls within the $20,000 to $25,000 range. The most suitable method for initial contact by those seeking employment is to mail a resume with a covering letter. Summer students are hired, subject to the business demands of individual property locations. *Contact:* Sue Wadland, Vice President, Human Resources.

RUBBERMAID CANADA INC.
2562 Stanfield Road
Mississauga, ON L4Y 1S5

Tel. 905-279-1010
Fax 905-279-2993

Rubbermaid Canada Inc. is a leading manufacturer of plastic household products. The company employs approximately 310 people. Graduates most likely to be hired come from the following academic areas: Bachelor of Arts (General, Economics), Bachelor of Science (Chemistry), Bachelor of Engineering (Electrical, Industrial Production), Bachelor of Commerce/Business Administration (Finance, Human Resources, Marketing), Certified Management Accountant, Community College Diploma (Accounting, Business, Secretarial, Computer Science, Engineering Technician), and High School Diploma. Graduates would occupy Marketing Manager, Production Supervisor, Industrial Engineer, Customer Service Representative, Administrative Assistant, and Production Worker positions. Community involvement and previous related work experience are listed as desirable non-academic qualifications. Company benefits are rated above average. The potential for advancement is listed as being good. The average annual starting salary falls within the $35,000 to $40,000 range. The most suitable method for initial contact by those seeking employment is to mail a resume with a covering letter. Rubbermaid Canada Inc. does hire students for summer and co-op work terms. Contact: Human Resources Department.

RUSSEL METALS INC.
1900 Minnesota Court, Suite 210
Mississauga, ON L5N 3C9

Tel. 905-567-8500
Email .... hrdept@russelmetals.com
Website .... www.russelmetals.com

Russel Metals Inc. is involved in the processing, warehousing and distribution of steel. The company employs approximately 2,000 people worldwide. Graduates most likely to be hired come from the following academic areas: Bachelor of Science (General, Metallurgy), Bachelor of Engineering (General, Mechanical), Bachelor of Commerce/Business Administration (Accounting, Finance, Marketing, Information Systems), Chartered Accountant (Finance), Certified Management Accountant (Finance), Certified General Accountant (Finance), and Community College Diploma (Accounting, Administration, Business). Graduates would occupy Sales, Accounting, and Administration positions. Team player, and strong people skills are listed as desirable non-academic qualifications. The potential for advancement is listed as average. The average annual starting salary falls within the $30,000 to $35,000 range, and is ultimately dependent upon position, qualifications, and experience. The most suitable method for initial contact by graduates seeking employment is to mail a resume with a covering letter. Russel Metals Inc. does hire summer students. Contact: Lori Hawley, Human Resources.

S & C ELECTRIC CANADA LTD.
90 Belfield Road
Toronto, ON M9W 1G4

Tel. 416-249-9171
Fax 416-249-1893

S & C Electric Canada Ltd. is involved in the manufacturing of high voltage switching and protection equipment. S & C Electric Canada Ltd. is a wholly owned subsidiary of S & C Electric Company, Chicago, Illinois. There are approximately 260 employees at the Toronto location, and a total of 1,800 employees worldwide. Graduates most likely to be hired come from the following academic areas: Bachelor of Science (Computer Science), Bachelor of Engineering (Chemical, Industrial Chemistry, Pollution Treatment, Electrical, Power, Mechanical, Industrial Design, Industrial Production), Bachelor of Commerce/Business Administration (Accounting, Finance, Information Systems), and Community College Diploma (Accounting, CAD/CAM/Autocad, Computer Science, Engineering Technician, Manufacturing Engineer, CNC Machinist). Graduates would occupy Engineer, Technician, Technologist, and Specialist positions. Self motivated, team player, positive attitude, and an ability to focus on the job and the company are all listed as desirable non-academic qualifications. Company benefits are rated above average. The potential for advancement is listed as being good. The average annual starting salary for college graduates falls within the $25,000 to $30,000 range, and for university graduates it falls within the $30,000 to $35,000 range. The most suitable method for initial contact by those seeking employment is to mail a resume with a covering letter. S & C Electric Canada Ltd. does hire summer and co-op work term students. Contacts: Douglas J. Patten, Director Human Resources or Carmel Foster, Personnel Administrator.

SAJO INC.
1212 Louvain Street West
Montreal, QC H4N 1G5

Tel. 514-385-0333
Fax 514-389-8622

Since 1977, SAJO Inc. has established itself as one of the most trusted specialized contractors in the construction industry and has developed into one of the largest interior finishing companies. SAJO provides, throughout Canada, the United States and Europe, a full range of services in the construction, renovation and project management sectors. The company's Montreal office is supported by millwork operations, architectural metal manufacturing facilities and warehouse distribution facilities. SAJO's principal services are general contracting, project management, sourcing and distribution of store fixtures. The general contracting of the firm is concentrated in the high-end fashion retail chains (interior finishing). The company also manages its customers' capital expenditure budgets. The sourcing and distribution of store fixtures involves coordinating and installing store fixtures for multiple sites. Yearly, SAJO executes more than 250 projects and 750 soft shops. The company employs a total of 100 people. Graduates most likely to be hired come from the following academic areas: Bachelor of Engineering (Civil, Architectural/Building, Industrial Design), Bachelor of Architecture, Bachelor of Landscape Architecture, Master of Engineering, and Community College Diploma (Architectural Technician, Carpentry). Graduates would occupy Account Manager, Project Manager, and Assistant Project Manager positions. Good communication skills, strong interpersonal skills, multi-task oriented, eagerness to learn and improve, and excellent time management skills are all listed as desirable non-academic qualifications. Company benefits are rated as industry standard. The potential for advancement is listed as excellent. The average annual starting salary falls within the $25,000 to $30,000 range. The most suitable methods for initial contact by those seeking employment are to mail or fax a resume with a covering letter, or via telephone. SAJO Inc. does hire summer and co-op work term students. *Contact:* Director of Human Resources.

SALOMON BROTHERS CANADA INC.
161 Bay Street
BCE Place, Suite 4600
Toronto, ON M5J 2S1

Tel. 416-866-2300
Fax 416-866-7484

Salomon Brothers Canada Inc. is a full service global investment banking firm located in Toronto. Salomon Brothers Canada Inc. is an indirect, wholly owned subsidiary of Salomon Inc. located at 7 World Trade Center, New York, New York. There are approximately 30 employees in Toronto, while Salomon Inc. employs approximately 6,600 people worldwide. Graduates most likely to be hired come from the following academic areas: Bachelor of Arts (Economics, Political Science), Bachelor of Science (Mathematics), Bachelor of Engineering (General), Bachelor of Commerce/Business Administration (General, Finance, Marketing), Master of Business Administration (General, Finance), and Community College Diploma (Business, Marketing/Sales). In Corporate Finance graduates could occupy the following professional positions: Analyst, Associate, and Vice President. In Sales and Trading, graduates would occupy Fixed Income Sales, Fixed Income Trading, and Training positions. Applicants must possess a high degree of intelligence, excellent analytical skills, aggressiveness, excellent sales skills, knowledge of the industry, and very high ethical standards. Company benefits and the potential for advancement are both rated as excellent. The most suitable method for initial contact by those seeking employment is to mail a resume with a covering letter. Salomon Brothers Canada Inc. does hire summer students. *Contacts:* Robert J. Gemmell, Managing Director, Corporate Finance or Jerry E. Brown, Director, Fixed Income Sales and Trading.

SALVATION ARMY GRACE GENERAL HOSPITAL
241 LeMarchant Road
St. John's, NF A1E 1P9

Tel. 709-778-6222
Fax 709-778-6640

The Salvation Army Grace General Hospital is an acute care hospital employing approximately 1,000 people. Graduates most likely to be hired come from the following areas: Bachelor of Arts (Sociology/ Social Work), Bachelor of Science (Biology, Chemistry, Computer Science, Microbiology, Audiology, Occupational Therapy, Pharmacy, Speech Pathology), Bachelor of Engineering (Architectural/Building, Biomedical Electronics, Computer Systems, Industrial Design, Welding), Bachelor of Education (General, Physical and Health), Bachelor of Commerce/Business Administration (Accounting, Human Resources, Information Systems, Public Administration), Master of Business Administration (Accounting, Human Resources, Information Systems, Public Administration), and Community College Diploma (Accounting, Administration, Business, Facility Management, Financial Planning, Human Resources, Purchasing/Logistics, Cooking, Social Work, Electronics Technician, Welding, Dental Assistant, Dietician, Laboratory Technician, Nuclear Medicine Technician, Nursing RN/RNA, Radiology Technician, Respiratory Therapy, Ultra-Sound Technician). Good communication skills, an ability to adapt to change, team player, enthusiasm, and common sense are all listed as desirable non-academic qualifications. Company benefits are rated as industry standard. The potential for advancement is listed as average. The most suitable methods for initial contact by those seeking employment are to mail a resume with a covering letter, or via telephone to arrange an appointment with a Recruiting Officer. The Salvation Army Grace General Hospital does hire summer students. *Contact:* Mr. John Gillis, Human Resources Manager, Human Resources Department.

SANDOZ CANADA INC.
Case Postale 385
Dorval, QC H9R 4P5

Tel. 514-631-6775
Fax 514-631-8525

Sandoz Canada Inc., a world leader in the research and development of pharmaceutical and chemicals, maintains one of Canada's broadest programs of clinical research in immunology, neurology, endocrinology, asthma and cardiovascular diseases. Graduates most likely to be hired come from the following academic areas: Bachelor of Arts (Journalism, Languages, Psychology), Bachelor of Science (Biology, Chemistry, Computer Science, Health Sciences, Microbiology, Nursing, Pharmacy, Physics, Psychology), Bachelor of Engineering (Chemical), Bachelor of Commerce/Business Administration (Accounting, Finance, Information Systems, Marketing), Chartered Accountant (Finance), Certified Management Accountant (Finance), Certified General Accountant (Finance), Master of Business Administration (Accounting, Finance, Information Systems, Marketing), Masters/Doctorate of Science (Immunology, Oncology, Central Nervous System, Cardiovascular, Neurology), and Community College Diploma (Marketing, Purchasing/Logistics, Secretarial, Human Resources, Journalism, Computer, Nursing RN/RNA). Graduates would occupy Sales Representative, Regional/National Sales Manager, Marketing Research Analyst, Product Manager, Associate Product Manager, Training Manager, Analyst, Technical Support, Medical Liaison Associate, New Product Manager, and Clinical Research positions. Bilingual, an ability to work in a team environment, and excellent interpersonal and communication skills are listed as desirable non-academic qualifications. Company benefits and the potential for advancement are both rated as excellent. The most suitable methods for initial contact by those seeking employment are to mail or fax a resume with a covering letter. Sandoz Canada Inc. does hire summer students. *Contacts:* Ginette Dubuc, Manager of Recruitment or Patsy Palmen, Recruiter.

SANFORD CANADA
2670 Plymouth Drive
Oakville, ON L6H 5R6

Tel.	905-829-5051
Fax	905-829-3074

Sanford Canada (Formerly Faber Castell Canada Inc.) employs approximately 40 people in Canada in the wholesale of writing instruments and related products. Graduates most likely to be hired come from the following academic areas: Bachelor of Arts (General), Bachelor of Commerce/Business Administration, Chartered Accountant, Certified Management Accountant, Certified General Accountant, Master of Business Administration (General, Marketing), and Community College Diploma (Accounting, Administration, Business, Human Resources, Marketing/Sales, Secretarial). Graduates would occupy Clerical, Customer Service, Marketing, and Administration positions. Self motivated, independent worker, team player, and excellent communication skills are all listed as desirable non-academic qualifications. Company benefits are rated above average. The potential for advancement is listed as being good. The most suitable method for initial contact by those seeking employment is to mail a resume with a covering letter. Sandford Canada does hire summer students. *Contact:* Fiona Morrison, Human Resources and Payroll.

SAPUTO GROUP INC.
6869, boulevard Metropolitan est
St-Leonard, QC H1P 1X8

Tel.	514-328-3325
Fax	514-328-3322
Email	saprh@cam.org
Website	www.saputo.com

Saputo Group Inc. is a Canadian leader in cheese manufacturing and food distribution. There are approximately 75 employees at this location, and a total of 700 employees across Canada. Graduates most likely to be hired come from the following academic areas: Bachelor of Science (Biology, Chemistry, Computer Science, Nutritional Science), Bachelor of Engineering (General, Chemical, Food Processing, Industrial Chemistry, Electrical, Robotics, Instrumentation, Mechanical, Industrial Design, Industrial Production), Bachelor of Commerce/Business Administration (General, Accounting, Finance, Human Resources, Information Systems, Marketing), Chartered Accountant, Certified Management Accountant, Certified General Accountant, Community College Diploma (Accounting, Administration, Marketing/Sales, Computer Science, Engineering Technician, Laboratory Technician), and High School Diploma. Graduates would occupy Clerk, Technician, Engineer, Accountant and Assistant Manager positions. Previous work experience, entrepreneurial skills, team player and creativity are all listed as desirable non-academic qualifications. Company benefits are rated as excellent. The potential for advancement is listed as being good. The average annual starting salary falls within the $20,000 to $25,000 range. The most suitable method for initial contact by those seeking employment is to mail a resume with a covering letter. Saputo Group Inc. does hire summer students. *Contacts:* Pierre Leroux, Vice President, Quality and Human Resources or Christine Morris, Human Resources Manager.

SASKATCHEWAN CROP INSURANCE CORPORATION
P.O. Box 3000
Melville, SK S0A 2P0

Tel.	306-728-7200
Fax	306-728-7260

Saskatchewan Crop Insurance Corporation (SCIC) provides crop insurance to growers in Saskatchewan. The main purpose of crop insurance is to provide customers peace of mind while they farm. SCIC employs approximately 550 people. In addition to the head office in Melville there are 21 Customer Service Offices located across the province. Within the head office there are several divisions, these include: Audits, Communications, Field Operations, Finance and Administration, Systems, Processing, Planning and Development, and Human Resources. Graduates most likely to be hired come from the following academic areas: Bachelor of Science (Actuarial, Agriculture, Computer Science), Bachelor of Engineering (Computer Systems), Bachelor of Commerce/Business Administration (Accounting, Finance, Human Resources, Information Systems, Public Administration), Master of Business Administration (Accounting, Finance, Human Resources, Information Systems, Marketing, Public Administration), Master of Science (Agriculture, Actuarial Studies), Master of Engineering (Computer Systems), Community College Diploma (Accounting, Administration, Business, Communications, Human Resources,

Secretarial, Journalism, Computer Science, Engineering Technician), and High School graduates with sufficient related work experience. Excellent interpersonal and communication skills, ambition, team player, confidence, and an ability to deal with customers and fellow employees in a business setting are all listed as desirable non-academic qualifications. The most suitable method for initial contact by those seeking employment is to mail a resume with a covering letter. SCIC does hire summer students, though the number varies with program and workload changes. *Contacts:* Louise Sawyer, Manager, Employee Relations, Human Resources or Sharon Granquist, Personnel Officer, Human Resources.

SASKATCHEWAN RESEARCH COUNCIL (SRC)
15 Innovation Boulevard
Saskatoon, SK S7N 2X8

Tel. 306-933-5400
Fax 306-933-7446

The Saskatchewan Research Council is a member of the Association of Provincial Research Organizations. It exists to help the people of Saskatchewan develop a viable economy with quality jobs and a secure environment. The SRC employs 200 people, and is a leader in the province's science and technology infrastructure, through technology development, implementation and innovation. Graduates most likely to be hired come from the following academic areas: Bachelor of Arts (Journalism, Psychology), Bachelor of Science (Biology, Chemistry, Computer, Forestry, Geography, Geology, Meteorology, Microbiology), Bachelor of Engineering (Chemical, Electrical, Mechanical), Bachelor of Commerce/Business Administration, Chartered Accountant, Certified Management Accountant, Certified General Accountant, Master of Business Administration, Master of Arts (Journalism, Psychology), Master of Science (Geology, Biology, Chemistry, Forestry, Meteorology, Microbiology), Master of Engineering (Industrial, Mechanical), Doctorate of Science (Geology, Biology, Chemistry, Forestry, Meteorology, Microbiology, Psychology), Doctorate of Engineering (Chemical, Electrical, Industrial, Mechanical), and Community College Diploma (Facility Management, CAD/CAM/Autocad, Computer Science, Electronics Technician, Engineering Technician, Forestry, Laboratory Technician). Graduates would occupy Research Scientist I-IV, Research Engineer I-IV, Research Technician I-IV, Controller, Administrative Support I-III, Human Resources, Marketing, and Facilities Manager positions. Team player, work and supervisory experience, and good interpersonal and communication skills are all listed as desirable non-academic qualifications. Company benefits are rated as industry standard. The potential for advancement is listed as excellent. The most suitable method for initial contact by those seeking employment is to mail a resume with a cover letter. The Saskatchewan Research Council does hire summer students. *Contact:* Jonathan France, Human Resources.

SASKPOWER
2025 Victoria Avenue
Regina, SK S4P 0S1

Tel. 306-566-2157
Fax 306-566-2087

SaskPower is a crown-owned electrical utility which operates a number of generating stations to meet the province of Saskatchewan's demands for energy. This includes coal-fired and multi-fuel steam powered stations, as well as hydro and gas facilities. SaskPower employs a total of 2,200 people in the province. Graduates most likely to be hired come from the following academic areas: Bachelor of Arts (Journalism), Bachelor of Science (Chemistry, Computer Science, Environmental, Metallurgy), Bachelor of Engineering (Chemical, Industrial Chemistry, Metallurgy, Civil, Electrical, Instrumentation, Power, Mechanical, Welding, Environmental, Water Resources), Bachelor of Education (Adult), Bachelor of Commerce/Business Administration (Accounting, Finance, Human Resources, Information Systems, Marketing), Chartered Accountant, Certified Management Accountant, Certified General Accountant, Master of Business Administration (Accounting, Finance, Human Resources, Information Systems, Marketing, Public Administration), Master of Engineering, and Community College Diploma (Accounting, Administration, Business, Financial Planning, Human Resources, Marketing/Sales, Secretarial, Graphic Arts, Journalism, Industrial Mechanic, Instrument Mechanic, CAD/CAM/Autocad, Computer Science, Electrician, Engineering, Power Engineer, Welding, Chemical Laboratory Technician, Millwright). Graduates would occupy Engineer, Analyst, Coordinator, Consultant, Technologist, Clerk, Stenographer, Secretary, Electrician, Industrial Mechanic, Welder, Machinist, Instrument Mechanic, Chemical Technician, Lineman, Power Engineer, Drafting Technician, and Apprentice positions. Knowledge of business, leadership, problem solving skills, innovative, good interpersonal skills, entrepreneurial, and computer literacy are all listed as desirable non-academic qualifications. Company benefits are rated as excellent. The potential for advancement is listed as being good. The average annual starting salary falls within the $25,000 to $30,000 range. The most suitable method for initial contact by those seeking employment is to mail a resume with a covering letter. SaskPower does hire summer students. *Contact:* Jackie Bonsal, Human Resources Analyst, Strategic Skills.

SASKTEL
2121 Saskatchewan Drive, 13th Floor
Regina, SK S4P 3Y2

Tel. 306-777-2029
Fax 306-359-0653

SaskTel is a highly competitive technology leader committed to delivering outstanding customer service and cost-effective communications solutions for customers in the province of Saskatchewan. SaskTel employs 4,000 people throughout the Province. Graduates most likely to be hired come from the following academic areas: Bachelor of Arts (English), Bachelor of Engineering (Electrical, Microelectronics, Telecommunications), Bachelor of Commerce/Business Administration (Accounting, Human Resources, Information Systems, Marketing), Chartered Accountant, Certified Management Accountant, Certified General Accountant, Master of Business Administration (Finance, Marketing), and Community College Diploma (Accounting, Business, Marketing/Sales, Electronics Technician). Graduates would occupy Trainee, Engineering Assistant, etc. positions. Team player, positive attitude, creative, flexible, highly skilled, and focused on excellence are all listed as desirable non-academic qualifications. Company benefits are rated as excellent. The potential for advancement is listed as being good. The average annual starting salary falls within the $30,000 to $35,000 range. The most suitable methods for initial contact by those seeking employment are to mail a resume with a covering letter, or by applying through campus recruitment initiatives (see your campus career centre for details). SaskTel does hire summer and co-op work term students. *Contacts:* Stacy Schiefner, Selection & Staffing Manager or Sherry Moe, Recruiter.

SCARBOROUGH DEPARTMENT OF PLANNING

150 Borough Drive
Toronto, ON M1P 4N7

Tel. 416-396-7526

The Scarborough Department of Planning is involved in land use planning and development. The department is the focus point for land developers dealing within Scarborough, and is the liaison with council members. Activities include processing of legal documents, facilitating the completion of land development applications, and the preparation of technical, graphic, and mapping material. The department employs more than 100 people. Graduates most likely to be hired come from the following academic areas: Bachelor of Arts (Urban Geography, Economic Geography, Cartography, Graphic Arts), Bachelor of Architecture/Landscape Architecture, and Master of Arts (Urban Geography). Graduates would occupy positions in the following areas: Planning, Graphic Design, Architecture/Landscape Architecture, Cartography and Community Planning. Good communication and presentation skills, and membership in the relevant professional body are listed as desirable non-academic qualifications. The most suitable method for initial contact by those seeking employment is to mail a resume with a covering letter to the City of Toronto Human Resources Division. The Department of Planning does hire summer students. The Scarborough Department of Planning is part of the new City of Toronto Urban Planning and Development Services. *Contact:* Personnel Department.

SCARBOROUGH GENERAL HOSPITAL

3050 Lawrence Avenue East
Toronto, ON M1P 2V5

Tel. 416-431-8126
Fax 416-431-8186

Scarborough General Hospital is a full service, general hospital employing approximately 2,200 professional and non-professional staff. Graduates most likely to be hired come from the following academic areas: Bachelor of Arts (Psychology, Recreation Studies), Bachelor of Science (Audiology, Nursing, Occupational Therapy, Pharmacy, Physio/Physical Therapy, Psychology), Bachelor of Engineering (Computer Science), Bachelor of Education (Adult), Bachelor of Commerce/Business Administration (Accounting, Finance, Human Resources, Information Systems), Master of Business Administration (General), Master of Science (Health Sciences), Master of Education, and Community College Diploma (Human Resources, Recreation Studies, Laboratory Technician, Nuclear Medicine, Nursing RN/RPN, Radiology, Respiratory Therapy, Ultra-Sound Technician). Graduates would occupy Nursing RN/RPN, Service Technical Aide, Engineer, Unit Clerk, Dietician, Food Services Supervisor, Occupational Therapist, Physiotherapist, Clerk, and Technician positions. Team work, customer service skills, accountability, professionalism, and a dedication to continuous improvement. Employee benefits are rated above average. The potential for advancement is listed as average. The average annual starting salary ranges widely over professional and non-professional positions. The most suitable methods for initial contact by individuals seeking employment are to mail or fax a resume with a covering letter. The Scarborough General Hospital does hire co-op work term students. *Contact:* Human Resources Department.

SCHERING-PLOUGH HEALTH CARE PRODUCTS

6400 Northam Drive
Mississauga, ON L4V 1J1

Tel. 905-673-6242

Schering-Plough Health Care Products is a leading manufacturer and marketer of brand name products (eg. Coppertone, Dr. Scholl's, Correctol, Waterbabies). There are more than 100 employees at this location. Graduates most likely to be hired come from the following academic areas: Bachelor of Arts (General), Bachelor of Science (General), Bachelor of Engineering (General), Bachelor of Commerce/Business Administration (Finance, Marketing), Certified Management Accountant, and Master of Business Administration. Graduates are hired to occupy Marketing Assistant, Sales Representative Trainee, Accounting Clerk, Customer Service Representative, Production Assistant, and Maintenance Trainee positions. Teamwork, a positive attitude, competitiveness, and assertiveness are listed as desirable non-academic qualifications. Company benefits are rated as excellent. The potential for advancement is listed as being good. The average annual starting salary falls within the $30,000 to $35,000 range. The most suitable method for initial contact by those seeking employment is to mail a resume with a covering letter. Schering-Plough Health Care Products does hire summer students. *Contact:* Manager, Human Resources.

SCHOLARSHIP CONSULTANTS OF NORTH AMERICA INC.
P.O. Box 3084, South
Halifax, NS B3J 3G6

Tel. 902-425-1100
Fax 902-425-1915
Website .... www.resp-usc.com

Scholarship Consultants of North America Inc. (USC) provides group and individual presentations, explaining a special savings plan for children's future post-secondary education (RESP) and assistance in applying for additional Canada Education Savings Grant. The company's business is focused on marketing and financial planning. Scholarship Consultants of North America Inc. employs approximately 30 people at this location. Graduates most likely to be hired come from the following academic areas: Bachelor of Commerce/Business Administration (Finance, Marketing), and Master of Business Administration (Finance, Human Resources, Marketing). Graduates would occupy Enrollment Representative, Sales Manager, and Agency Director positions. Working in partnership with USC, which has agencies and sales professionals across Canada, Enrollment Representatives will receive support and training to ensure that their business succeeds. USC provides sales support materials, state-of-the-art computer based training, local agency support, conferences and seminars, and ongoing recognition and award programs. Entrepreneurial attitude, extremely self-motivated, previous sales and marketing work experience, computer literacy, honest, mature, and professional are all listed as desirable non-academic qualifications. All representatives are licensed by their Provincial Securities Commissions, while the company provides a comprehensive training program designed to ensure that all representatives are well prepared to represent USC's leading edge education savings plans. Company benefits are rated as industry standard. The potential for advancement is listed as excellent, with the level of success ultimately determined by the individual's effort. The average annual starting is commission based following a industry leading, and very generous compensation structure. The most suitable method for initial contact by those seeking employment is to fax a resume with a covering letter. *Contacts:* Laura Coulombe, Executive Agnecy Director or Mark Corkum, Director of Marketing.

SCIENTIFIC-ATLANTA INC.
120 Middlefield Road
Toronto, ON M1S 4M6

Tel. 416-299-6888
Fax 416-754-4266
Email .... hr.stnd@sciatl.com
Website .... www.sciatl.com

Scientific-Atlanta Inc. is a leading supplier of broadband communications systems, satellite-based video, voice and data communications networks and worldwide customer service and support. The Satellite Television Networks Division leads in the design and manufacture of video processing equipment for the encryption and transmission of satellite signals. Scientific-Atlanta employs 5,000 people worldwide. Graduates most likely to be hired come from the following academic areas: Bachelor of Engineering (Electrical, Computer Systems, Engineering Physics), and Community College Diploma (Computer Science). Graduates would occupy Design Engineer positions. Company benefits are rated as industry standard. The most suitable method for initial contact by those seeking employment is to e-mail a resume with a covering letter. Scientific-Atlanta Inc. does hire co-op work term students. *Contact:* Human Resources.

SDL OPTICS INC.
6703 Rajpur Place
Saanichton, BC V8M 1Z5

Tel. 250-544-2244
Fax 250-544-2225
Email .... HROptics@sdli.com
Website .... www.sdli.com

SDL Optics Inc. designs and markets fibre-coupled laser diodes for a wide range of fibre optic applications used in telecommunications, CATV, data communications, sensing and various industrial and scientific applications. The company's primary area of focus is the communications industry. SDL is recognized for innovation in product design and manufacturing yielding high quality, reliable devices at competitive prices. The company combines stringent quality standards with extensive experience in order to meet the quality, reliability and performance requirements of its customers. SDL Optics Inc. employs 150 people at this location, and is a wholly owned subsidiary of SDL, Inc., based in San Jose, California, and traded on the Nasdaq Exchange under the symbol SDLI. Graduates most likely to be hired come from the following academic areas: Bachelor of Science (Physics), Bachelor of Engineering (Electrical, Mechanical, Engineering Physics, Telecommunications), Master of Science (Physics), and Master of Engineering (Electrical, Mechanical, Engineering Physics, Telecommunications). Graduates would occupy Process Engineer, Product Engineer, and Project Engineer positions. Excellent team skills, SPC, DOE, ISO and ESD experience, and five years experience in fibre optics and telecommunications are all listed as desirable non-academic qualifications. Company benefits and the potential for advancement are both rated as excellent. The most suitable methods for initial contact by those seeking employment are to mail, fax or e-mail a resume with a covering letter, apply through the company's website at www.sdli.com, or via telephone. SDL Optics Inc. does hire co-op work term students. *Contact:* Kathy Neeves, Human Resources Manager.

SECOND CUP LTD., THE
175 Bloor Street East
South Tower, Suite 801
Toronto, ON M4W 3R8

Tel. 416-975-5541
Fax 416-975-5207
Website .... www.secondcup.com

The Second Cup Ltd. is a North American leader in the specialty coffee market. The company is the market leader with more than 300 stores in Canada. There are 45 employees at this location and a total of 160 employees across Canada. Graduates most likely to be hired come from the following academic areas: Bachelor of Arts (General, Economics, French, Geography, Urban Geography/Planning), Bachelor of Commerce/Business Administration (General, Accounting, Finance, Marketing), and Community College Diploma (Accounting, Administration, Business, Marketing/Sales). Graduates would occupy Clerk and Administrative Assistant positions in various departments. Team player, fast learner, and computer literate are listed as desirable non-academic qualifications. Company benefits are rated as industry standard. The potential for advancement is listed as being good. The average annual starting salary falls within the $30,000 to $35,000 range. The most suitable methods for initial contact by those seeking employment are to mail or fax a resume with a covering letter (no phone calls please). *Contact:* Human Resources Department.

SEDGWICK LIMITED
P.O. Box 439
Toronto Dominion Centre
Toronto, ON M5K 1M3

Tel. 416-361-6700
Fax 416-361-6777

Sedgwick Limited is an Insurance Broker for both general insurance and group benefits. Sedgwick employs more than 250 people. Graduates most likely to be hired come from the following academic areas: Bachelor of Science (Mathematics, Actuarial Science, Computer Science), Bachelor of Engineering (Civil), Bachelor of Laws, Chartered Accountant, Masters (Library Science), and Community College Diploma (Business, Human Resources, Computer, Accounting, Secretarial). Technical Positions exist in Computer Programming, Benefits Administration, Pension Administration, Accounting, Customer Service, Marketing and Sales. Consulting positions exist in Risk Management, Actuary, Research, Legal Counsel, and Administration. Company benefits are rated above average. The potential for advancement is listed as being good. The average starting salary falls within the $25,000 to $30,000 range. The most suitable methods for initial contact by those seeking employment are to mail a resume with a covering letter, or through on-campus recruitment initiatives (see your campus career centre for details). Sedgwick Limited does hire summer students. *Contact:* Nazaneen Parson, Human Resources.

SENECA COLLEGE OF APPLIED ARTS AND TECHNOLOGY
1750 Finch Avenue East
Toronto, ON M2J 2X5

Tel. 416-491-5050
Fax 905-479-4162

Seneca College of Applied Arts and Technology is a major educational institution offering post-secondary courses, certificates, diplomas, post-diplomas, and contract training. Seneca employs approximately 1,200 staff (all campuses), and offers more than 120 diploma programs. Employment opportunities exist for graduates from all levels and disciplines. Graduates are hired to occupy positions in three main staff groups: Administrative, Faculty, and Support Staff. Sample positions include Clerk, Secretary, Support Services Officer, Technician, Technologist, Programmer, Technical Support Specialist, Professor, Manager, Chair, Supervisor, Director, etc. Good communication skills, relevant work experience, team player, good interpersonal skills, an ability to relate effectively with a multicultural, multiracial and multiable student population, good problem solving skills, strong analytical skills, and competency with a variety of computer software applications, are all listed as desirable non-academic qualifications. Company benefits are rated above average. The potential for advancement is listed as average. The average annual starting salary, depending upon the staff group, falls within the $25,000 to $60,000 range. The most suitable methods for initial contact by those seeking employment are to mail or fax a resume with a covering letter, or via telephone. Seneca College does hire summer and co-op work term students through their own and through government sponsored programs. *Contact:* Jane Wilson, Personnel Officer, Employee Relations.

SHARP ELECTRONICS OF CANADA LTD.
335 Britannia Road East
Mississauga, ON L4Z 1W9

Tel. 905-890-2100

Sharp Electronics of Canada Ltd. is the Canadian head office and distributor for electronic products in Canada. There are approximately 200 employees at this location. Graduates most likely to be hired come from the following academic areas: Bachelor of Arts (General, Economics), Bachelor of Science (Mathematics), Bachelor of Engineering (General), Bachelor of Commerce/Business Administration (Accounting, Finance, Marketing, Information Systems), Chartered Accountant (Finance), Certified Management Accountant (Finance), Certified General Accountant (Finance), Master of Business Administration (Accounting, Finance, Marketing), and Community College Diploma (Accounting, Advertising, Administration, Business, Communications, Facility Management, Marketing/Sales, Purchasing/Logistics, Secretarial, Human Resources, Computer Science, Electronics, Engineering). Graduates would occupy a variety of Head Office positions. Excellent presentation skills, outgoing, and strong communication skills are listed as desirable non-academic qualifications. Company benefits are rated above average. The potential for advancement is listed as being good. The average annual starting salary falls within the $30,000 to $35,000 range, and is commission based for certain positions. The most suitable method for initial contact by graduates seeking employment is to mail a resume with a covering letter. Sharp Electronics of Canada Ltd. does hire a small number of summer students annually. *Contact:* Tracy Savage, Recruitment, Employment Practices & Training Specialist.

SHAW INDUSTRIES LTD.
25 Bethridge Road
Toronto, ON M9W 1M7

Tel. 416-743-7111
Fax 416-743-8194

Shaw Industries Ltd. is a global energy services company specializing in products and services for the exploration and production, pipeline and downstream sectors of the oil and gas industry. Through its 50/50 joint venture with Dresser Industries, Inc., the company is the world leader in the design and manufacture of corrosion insulation and weight coating products utilized in the pipeline industry for oil and gas gathering and long distance transmission applications. The joint venture operates 29 plants located in all major energy producing markets, and in addition to these permanent facilities, employs its engineering expertise to install temporary project-specific plants anywhere in the world. The company's wholly owned divisions and subsidiaries also provide proprietary ultrasonic weld inspection services and heat shrinkable sleeves utilized for corrosion protection applications by the global pipeline industry. In the exploration and production sector, the company provides seismic equipment for gathering geophysical data, drill string components for drilling oil and gas wells, and inspection and refurbishment services for drill pipe production tubing and casing. For petrochemical, utility and industrial markets, the company manufactures wire and cable for use in process instrumentation and control systems and heat shrinkable tubing used for electrical, electronic and telecommunications applications. There are 280 employees at this location, a total of 702 in Canada, and a total of 1,592 employees worldwide. Graduates most likely to be hired come from the following academic areas: Bachelor of Science (Metallurgy), Bachelor of Engineering (Chemical, Electrical, Mechanical, Environmental/Resources, Industrial Engineering, Industrial Production/Manufacturing, Instrumentation, Power/Hydro), Bachelor of Commerce/Business Administration (Accounting, Human Resources, Marketing), Chartered Accountant, Certified Management Accountant, Certified General Accountant, Master of Business Administration (Accounting, Finance, Human Resources, Marketing), Master of Science, Master of Engineering, and Community College Diploma (Accounting, Administration, Business, Marketing/Sales, Secretarial, Computer Science, Electronics Technician, Engineering Technician). Computer literacy, nego-

tiation skills, previous work experience, and good written and verbal communication skills are all listed as desirable non-academic qualifications. The average annual starting salary falls within the $40,000 to $45,000 range. The most suitable method for initial contact by those seeking employment is to fax a resume with a covering letter. Shaw Industries Ltd. does hire summer and co-op work term students. *Contacts:* Mr. J.M. Lamb, Corporate Human Resources Manager or Ms A.M. Campoli, Recruiter.

SHELL CANADA PRODUCTS LIMITED
P.O. Box 2000
Corunna, ON N0N 1G0

Tel. 519-481-1100
Fax 519-481-1288

Shell Canada Products Limited is involved in the refining of petrochemicals. There are more than 300 employees at this location. Graduates most likely to be hired come from the following academic areas: Bachelor of Science (Chemistry), Bachelor of Engineering (Chemical, Mechanical), Bachelor of Commerce/Business Administration (Accounting), and Community College Diploma (Electronics Technician, Engineering Technician, Mechanic, Instrumentation, Process Operations). Graduates would occupy positions as Process Operators, Chemists, and positions in Engineering. Previous work experience, motivated, innovative, excellent problem solving skills, an ability to work in a team environment, and strong communication and interpersonal skills are all listed as desirable non-academic qualifications. Company benefits and the potential for advancement are both rated as excellent. The average annual starting salary falls within the $30,000 to $35,000 range, and ultimately depends upon the position being considered. The most suitable methods for initial contact by those seeking employment are to mail or fax a resume with a covering letter, by responding to campus recruitment listings and programs (see your campus career centre for details), or by responding to advertised positions in newspapers. Shell Canada Products Limited does hire summer and co-op work term students. *Contact:* Human Resources Analyst.

SHERATON CENTRE TORONTO HOTEL
123 Queen Street West
Toronto, ON M5H 2M9

Tel. 416-947-4900
Fax 416-361-6223

Sheraton Centre Toronto Hotel provides lodging, food and beverage services, and large convention service facilities. The Hotel employs a total of 960 people. Graduates most likely to be hired come from the following academic areas: Bachelor of Arts (General, Hospitality and Tourism), Bachelor of Science (Computer Science), Bachelor of Commerce/Business Administration (General, Human Resources, Marketing), Chartered Accountant, Certified Management Accountant, Certified General Accountant, Master of Business Administration, Community College Diploma (Accounting, Business, Facility

Management, Human Resources, Cooking, Hospitality, Computer Science), and High School Diploma. Graduates would occupy Guest Service Agent in Reception, Sales Coordinator, Food and Beverage Supervisor, Trainee positions, and Entry Level Management and Non-Management positions. Friendly, enthusiastic, problem solving skills, outgoing, initiative, quality awareness, business savvy, entrepreneurship, and customer service oriented are all listed as desirable non-academic qualifications. Company benefits are rated above average. The potential for advancement is listed as being good. The starting salary and benefit level varies with the position. The most suitable method for initial contact by those seeking employment is by calling the Job Hotline at (416) 947-4900. Sheraton Centre Toronto Hotel hires a limited number of students, these are mostly part-time term contract positions. *Contacts:* Anthony Hopkins, Director, Human Resources; Tracey Kraus, Human Resources Consultant or Anna Salvati, Human Resources Consultant.

SHERATON PARKWAY HOTEL, TORONTO NORTH
600 Highway #7 East
Richmond Hill, ON L4B 1B2

Tel. 905-881-2121
Fax 905-881-7841

The Sheraton Parkway Hotel employs more than 250 people in the provision of accommodation, food and beverage, and convention services to tourists, corporations and associations. Graduates most likely to be hired come from the following academic areas: Bachelor of Arts, Bachelor of Science, Bachelor of Commerce/Business Administration, Chartered Accountant, Certified Management Accountant, and Community College Diploma (Travel/Tourism, Hotel/Hospitality, Culinary/Cooking). Graduates are hired to occupy Managerial positions for the following departments: Front Office, Lounge and Restaurants, Kitchen, Banquets, Housekeeping, Maintenance, Security, Accounting, Human Resources, Catering, and Sales and Marketing. Computer literacy, outgoing, friendly, a helpful attitude, and excellent communication and public relations skills are all listed as desirable non-academic qualifications. Company benefits and the potential for advancement are both rated as excellent. The average annual starting salary falls within the $15,000 to $20,000 range. The most suitable method for initial contact by those seeking employment is to mail a resume with a covering letter. The Sheraton Parkway Hotel does hire summer students, depending upon the level of business. *Contact:* Human Resources Manager.

SHERATON TORONTO EAST HOTEL
2035 Kennedy Road
Toronto, ON M1T 3G2

Tel. 416-299-1500
Fax 416-299-8959
Email .... sheraton@interhop.net

The Sheraton Toronto East Hotel is a full service hotel providing accommodation, food and beverage, and convention services. The Hotel employs approximately 400 people. Graduates most likely to be hired come from the following academic areas: Bachelor of Commerce/Business Administration, and Community College Diploma (Administration, Hospitality). Graduates are hired to occupy Guest Service Agent, Sales Coordinator, Restaurant Supervisor, Security Officer/Supervisor, and Accounting Clerk positions. Team player, enthusiastic, self-driven, and a pleasant personality are all listed as desirable non-academic qualifications. Company benefits and the potential for advancement are both rated as excellent. The average annual starting salary falls within the $20,000 to $25,000 range. The most suitable methods for initial contact by those seeking employment are to mail a resume with a covering letter, or by applying in person at the office, Monday through Friday, 1:30 pm to 4:30 pm. The Sheraton Toronto East Hotel does hire a few summer students annually. *Contacts:* Colleen Welter-Gavey, Human Resources Manager or Carminha Caneira, Assistant Human Resources Manager.

SHERWOOD CREDIT UNION
P.O. Box 1960, Station Main
Regina, SK S4P 4M1

Tel. 306-780-1649
Fax 306-780-1521
Email .... lynn.hunter@sherwoodcu.com

Sherwood Credit Union is a financial institution offering a variety of financial services and products. The company employs 145 people at this location and a total of 325 people within Saskatchewan. Graduates most likely to be hired come from the following areas: Bachelor of Arts (General, Economics, English), Bachelor of Science (Computer Science), Bachelor of Education (Adult), Bachelor of Commerce/Business Administration (Accounting, Finance, Human Resources, Information Systems, Marketing, Public Administration), Chartered Accountant, Certified Management Accountant, Certified General Accountant, and Community College Diploma (Accounting, Administration, Business, Communications, Financial Planning, Human Resources, Insurance, Marketing/Sales). Graduates would occupy Financial Services Representative, Lending Representative, Service Centre Manager, Sales and Service Leader, and Information Technology Specialist positions. An ability to work with the public, friendliness, team player, and sales experience are all listed as desirable non-academic qualifications. Company benefits and the potential for advancement are both rated as excellent. The average annual starting salary falls within the $20,000 to $25,000 range. The most suitable method for initial contact by those seeking employment is to mail a resume with a covering letter. Sherwood Credit Union does hire summer and co-op students. *Contact:* Human Resource Coordinator, Human Resources Department.

SHIRMAX FASHIONS LTD.
3901 Jarry Street East
Montreal, QC H1Z 2G1

Tel. 514-729-8980
Fax 514-729-3018

Shirmax Fashions Ltd. is a retailer of women's fashions. There are 150 employees at this location and a total of 1,000 employees across Canada. Graduates most likely to be hired come from the following academic areas: Bachelor of Science (Computer Science), Bachelor of Engineering (Computer Systems), Bachelor of Architecture, Bachelor of Commerce/Business Administration (Accounting, Finance, Human Resources, Information Systems, Marketing), Chartered Accountant, Master of Business Administration (Accounting, Finance, Marketing), Community College Diploma (Accounting, Administration, Advertising, Business, Human Resources, Marketing/Sales, Secretarial, Graphic Arts, Architecture/Drafting, Computer Science), and High School Diploma. Company benefits are rated as excellent. The potential for advancement is listed as being good. The average annual starting salary falls within the $20,000 to $25,000 range. The most suitable method for initial contact by those seeking employment is to mail a resume with a covering letter. Shirmax Fashions Ltd. does hire summer students. *Contact:* Josée Trudel, Human Resources.

SHL SYSTEMHOUSE (OTTAWA)
50 O'Connor Street, Suite 501
Ottawa, ON K1P 6L2

Tel. 613-236-9734
Fax 613-236-2043
Email .... 471hire@shl.com
Website .... www.systemhouse.mci.com

SHL Systemhouse, The Network Enterprise Company, is MCI's global information technology services company. The industry's only single source provider of convergence products and services that address businesses' total networking, communications and consulting needs, SHL Systemhouse has 120 offices and approximately 9,400 professionals worldwide. There are a total of 3,600 employees in Canada. With a comprehensive offering of Network Enterprise solutions and services for the new millennium, MCI-Systemhouse serves major corporate, mid-sized and public sector clients throughout North and South America, Europe and Asia. Graduates most likely to be hired come from the following academic areas: Bachelor of Science (Computer Science, Mathematics), Bachelor of Engineering (Electrical, Computer Systems, Telecommunications), Bachelor of Commerce/Business Administration (Information Systems), Master of Business Administration (Information Systems), and Community College Diploma (Information Systems, CAD/CAM/Autocad, Computer Science). Graduates would occupy Programmer, Computer Technician, Systems Engineer, Analyst, and Business Analyst positions. Innovative, professional, creative, logical, analytical, team player, proactive, strong leadership skills, and good verbal and written communication skills are all listed as desirable non-academic qualifications. Company benefits are rated as excellent. The potential for advancement is listed as being good. The average annual starting salary falls within the $30,000 to $35,000 range. The most suitable methods for initial contact by those seeking employment are to mail, fax (1-800-471-HIRE) or e-mail (471hire@shl.com) a resume with covering letter, or by by applying through SHL's website at www.systemhouse.mci.com. SHL Systemhouse does hire summer and co-op work term students, with postings made at campus career centres. *Contact:* Contact Local Human Resource Departments for Specific Opportunities.

SHL SYSTEMHOUSE (REGINA)
1881 Scarth Street, Suite 1800
Regina, SK S4P 4K9

Tel. 306-525-7100
Fax 306-352-8001
Email .... lchalupiak@shl.com
Website .... www.shl.com

SHL Systemhouse, The Network Enterprise Company, is MCI's global information technology services company. The industry's only single source provider of convergence products and services that address businesses' total networking, communications and consulting needs, SHL Systemhouse employs 180 people at this location. Graduates most likely to be hired at the Regina location come from the following academic areas: Bachelor of Science (Computer Science), and Bachelor of Engineering (Computer Systems). Graduates would occupy Programmer and Associate Technical Services Representative. Team player, professional self presentation, and excellent interpersonal skills all listed as desirable non-academic qualifications. Company benefits are rated above average. The potential for advancement is listed as being excellent. The average annual starting salary falls within the $35,000 to $40,000 range. The most suitable methods for initial contact by those seeking employment are to mail, fax or e-mail a resume with a covering letter. SHL Systemhouse does hire summer and co-op work term students. *Contact:* Manager, Human Resources.

SHOPPING CHANNEL, THE - TELEMARKETING/WAREHOUSE
1400 Castlefield Avenue
Toronto, ON M6B 4H8

Tel. 416-785-3500
Fax 416-785-0493

The Shopping Channel produces a Canadian televised home shopping service. The service is video taped live from the broadcast centre in Mississauga. The Shopping Channel sells jewellery, fashions, fitness equipment, home decorating items, cosmetics, etc. There are a total of 500 employees at the Toronto and Mississauga locations. Graduates most likely to be hired come from the following academic areas: Bachelor of Engineering (Electrical), Bachelor of Commerce/Business Administration (General,

Accounting, Finance, Human Resources, Information Systems, Marketing), Certified Management Accountant, Certified General Accountant, and Community College Diploma (Accounting, Administration, Communications/Public Relations, Audio Visual Technician, Graphic Arts, Television/Radio Arts, Broadcasting, Electronics Technician, Engineering Technician). Graduates would occupy Merchandising Assistant, AIP Clerk, Controller, General Accounting, and Camera Operator positions. Previous work experience, and an ability to work flexible hours are listed as desirable non-academic qualifications. Company benefits are rated above average. The potential for advancement is listed as being good. The most suitable methods for initial contact by those seeking employment are to mail or fax a resume with a covering letter, or by applying in person. The Shopping Channel does hire summer students. (Head Office Location: The Shopping Channel, 59 Ambassador Drive, Mississauga, Ontario, L5T 2P9). *Contact:* Recruitment Specialist.

SIDUS SYSTEMS INC.
66 Leek Crescent
Richmond Hill, ON L4B 1H1

Tel. 905-882-1600
Fax 905-882-2430
Website .... www.sidus.ca

Sidus Systems Inc. is involved in computer manufacturing, sales and customer support. Graduates most likely to be hired come from the following academic areas: Bachelor of Engineering (Computer Systems, Industrial Production/Manufacturing), Bachelor of Commerce/Business Administration (Accounting, Finance), Chartered Accountant, Certified Management Accountant, Certified General Accountant, Community College Diploma (Computer Science, Electronics Technician, Engineering Technician), and graduates with Microsoft Certified Systems Engineer (MCSE), Certified Novell Administrator (CNA 3, 4), and Certified Novell Engineer (CNE 3) accreditations. Graduates would occupy Systems Engineer, Computer Technician, Technical Service Representative, Manufacturing Engineer, Credit and Collections, Accounting, Computer Assembly, and Sales positions. Previous experience, team player, team builder, initiative, motivation, and the ability to work independently are all listed as desirable non-academic qualifications. Company benefits are rated as industry standard. The potential for advancement is listed as being good. The average annual starting salary falls within the $20,000 to $25,000 range. The most suitable method for initial contact by those seeking employment is to fax a resume with a covering letter. Sidus Systems Inc. does hire summer and co-op work term students. *Contact:* Carolyn Jaswal, Human Resources.

SIEMENS CANADA LIMITED
2185 Derry Road West
Mississauga, ON L5N 7A6

Tel. 905-819-8000
Fax 905-819-5777
Email .... jobs@siemens.ca
Website .... www.siemens.ca

Siemens is one of the largest and most diversified companies in the world, working in areas such as healthcare, energy and power, industry, communications, transportation, components, information and lighting. In Canada, Siemens is headquartered in Mississauga, Ontario and has 40 offices and 11 manufacturing facilities across Canada. Locations span from coast to coast staffed by 3,900 employees. Siemens employs approximately 400,000 people worldwide. Graduates most likely to be hired come from the following academic areas: Bachelor of Engineering (Microelectronics, Computer Systems, Mechanical, Industrial Production), Bachelor of Commerce/Business Administration (Accounting, Human Resources, Marketing), Master of Business Administration (Accounting, Finance, Information Systems), and Community College Diploma (CAD/CAM/Autocad, Electronics Technician, Engineering Technician, HVAC Systems). Graduates would be hired to occupy a variety of Technical, Administrative (eg. human resources, accounting, warehouse, purchasing, maintenance), and Marketing (eg. sales, customer service) positions. Strong communication and interpersonal skills, self-starter, related work experience, computer literacy (company standards - MS Word, Excel, and Power Point), and a working knowledge of the German language are all listed as desirable non-academic qualifications. Company benefits are rated above average. The potential for advancement is listed as being good. The most suitable method for initial contact by those seeking employment is to mail a resume with a covering letter. Siemens Canada Limited does hire summer and co-op work term students. These may be referrals from present employees or through job placement programs (contact your campus career centre). *Contact:* Human Resources.

SIERRA SYSTEMS CONSULTANTS INC.
880 Douglas Street, Suite 500
Victoria, BC V8W 2B7

Tel. 250-385-1535
Fax 250-385-4761
Email .... erutherf@sierrasys.com
Website .... www.sierrasys.com

Sierra Systems Consultants Inc. (Sierra) is a British Columbia based company with branches in both the United States and Canada that offers high quality, cost effective information technology based business solutions. The extensive range of services Sierra provides includes Business and Technical Consulting, Systems Integration and Delivery, Technology Management, and Internet Development and Delivery. While working in large variety of industries and business functional areas, Sierra's main areas of focus are Human Resources and Payroll, Finance, Government, Health Care, Education, and Justice. Since its establishment in 1966, Sierra has offered practical advice and technical expertise to clients in a myriad of industries including government, health care, banking, hospitality, insurance, utilities, airlines and unions. Company growth has been substantial, yet managed in a controlled fashion to ensure financial stability and long-term viability. Today, Sierra is a $66 million company with over 620 employees and 11 branches across North America. Graduates most likely to be hired come from the following academic areas: Bachelor of Science (Computer Science), Bachelor of Commerce/Business Administration (Information Systems), Master of Business Administration (Information Systems), and Community College Diploma (Information Systems, Computer Science). Graduates would occupy Applications Developer, Business Analyst, Technical Architect, and Technical Analyst positions. Excellent oral and written communication skills, able to think in business terms, a willingness to travel, and enjoy the challenge of solving business problems are all listed as desirable non-academic qualifications. Sierra provides an innovative remuneration plan, including profit sharing and a comprehensive benefits package. The company is committed to ongoing education and career development for its employees. The average annual starting salary falls within the $35,000 to $40,000 range for Junior positions and for those with two to three years experience. The most suitable method for initial contact by those seeking employment is to e-mail a resume with a covering letter. Sierra Systems Consultants Inc. does hire co-op work term students. *Contact:* Evelyn Rutherford, Human Resources Director.

SILCORP LIMITED
10 Commander Boulevard
Toronto, ON M1S 3T2

Tel. 416-291-4441
Fax 416-291-4947

Silcorp Limited is active in Canada in the retailing of groceries, fast food, gasoline, confectionery items, and specialty ice cream and yogurt items through Mac's, Mac's Plus, Mike's Mart, La Maissonee, Baskin Robbins, Yogurty's, and Yogurt Discovery stores. The company employs approximately 110 employees at this location and a total of 280 employees in Canada. Graduates most likely to be hired come from the following academic areas: Bachelor of Arts (General, Economics), Bachelor of Science (Computer Science, Mathematics), Bachelor of Engineering (Computer Systems), Bachelor of Commerce/Business Administration (General, Accounting, Finance, Human Resources, Information Systems), Chartered Accountant, Certified Management Accountant, Certified General Accountant, Master of Business Administration (General, Accounting, Finance), Community College Diploma (Accounting, Business, Financial Planning), and High School Diploma. Company benefits are rated above average. The potential for advancement is listed as being good. The average annual starting salary falls within the $15,000 to $45,000 range. The most suitable method for initial contact by those seeking employment is to mail a resume with a covering letter. Silcorp Limited does hire summer students, primarily through employee referrals. *Contact:* Human Resources.

SIMON FRASER HEALTH REGION
260 Sherbrooke Street
New Westminster, BC V3L 3M2

Tel. 604-524-2845
Fax 604-520-4204

Simon Fraser Health Region is a major teaching and referral facility consisting of six hospitals including the Royal Columbian Hospital and Queen's Park Care Centre in New Westminster, Eagle Ridge Hospital in Port Moody, Ridge Meadows Hospital in Maple Ridge, Burnaby Hospital and Fellburn Care Centre in Burnaby, as well as providing community programs and services within these communities. In total, the Simon Fraser Health Region employs more than 8,000 people. Graduates most likely to be hired come from the following areas: Bachelor of Arts (Psychology, Recreation Studies, Sociology), Bachelor of Science (Computer Science, Nursing, Nutritional Science, Occupational Therapy, Pharmacy, Physio/Physical Therapy, Psychology, Speech Pathology), Bachelor of Engineering (Biomedical Electronics), Bachelor of Education (Adult), Bachelor of Commerce/Business Administration (Accounting, Finance, Human Resources, Information Systems), Chartered Accountant, Certified Management Accountant, Certified General Accountant, Master of Business Administration (Accounting, Finance, Human Resources, Information Systems), and Community College Diploma (Cooking, Recreation Studies, CAD/CAM/Autocad, Computer Science, HVAC Systems, Laboratory Technician, Nuclear Medicine Technician, Nursing RN/RNA, Radiology Technician, Respiratory Therapy, Social Work, Ultrasound Technician). Graduates would occupy a variety of positions relating directly to their field of study. The average annual starting salary ranges widely, depending upon the position and experience of the applicant. Good communication skills, demonstrated team player, previous work experience, and good interpersonal and organizational skills are all listed as desirable non-academic qualifications. Company benefits are rated above average. The potential for advancement is listed as being good. The most suitable methods for initial contact by those seeking employment are to mail or fax a resume with a covering letter. The Simon Fraser Health Region does hire summer and co-op work term students. *Contact:* Employment Services.

SIMPLEX
6300 Viscount Road
Mississauga, ON L4V 1H3

Tel. 905-677-7000
Fax 905-677-7812
Website .... www.simplex.net.com

Simplex is involved in the manufacturing, distribution, sales and service of fire detection, security and time data systems. There are 100 employees at this location, and a total of 250 employees in Canada. Graduates most likely to be hired come from the following academic areas: Bachelor of Arts (Economics, Journalism, Psychology), Bachelor of Science (Computer Science, Mathematics, Psychology), Bachelor of Engineering (Computer Systems, Instrumentation, Microelectronics), Bachelor of Commerce/Business Administration (Accounting, Finance, Human Resources, Information Systems, Marketing), Certified Management Accountant, Certified General Accountant, Master of Business Administration (Accounting, Finance, Human Resources, Information Systems, Marketing), Master of Engineering (Electronics), Community College Diploma (Accounting, Administration, Business, Financial Planning, Human Resources, Marketing/Sales, Purchasing/Logistics, Secretarial, CAD/CAM/Autocad, Computer Science, Electronics Technician), and High School Diploma. Graduates would occupy Electronic Technician, Electronic Project Engineer, Network Administrator, Sales Representative, Human Resources Administrator, Purchasing, Accounting, Secretarial/Administration, Payroll, and Accounts Payable positions. Excellent communication and leadership skills, team player, driven, determined, and good people skills are all listed as desirable nonacademic qualifications. Company benefits are rated as excellent. The potential for advancement is listed as being good. The average annual starting salary falls within the $30,000 to $35,000 range. The most suitable method for initial contact by those seeking employment is to mail a resume with a covering letter. *Contact:* Sophie Cabaj, Human Resources Consultant.

SIMWARE INC.
2 Gurdwara Road
Ottawa, ON K2E 1A2

Tel.	613-228-5109
Fax	613-224-3804
Email	hr@simware.com
Website	www.simware.com

Simware Inc. helps companies create corporate extranets that bring business applications closer to company stakeholders. For more than 16 years, the company has provided software solutions that have enabled their global 2000 customers to leverage their enterprise systems to dramatically improve service delivery, reduce costs, increase revenues and gain strategic advantages. Simware Inc. is a publicly traded company (NASDAQ:SIMWF), headquartered in Ottawa, with offices in the United Kingdom and Belgium, and alliances with leading customer solution providers globally. There are 110 employees at the Ottawa location, and a total of 125 employees worldwide. Graduates most likely to be hired come from the following academic areas: Bachelor of Science (Computer Science), Bachelor of Engineering (Computer Systems), Bachelor of Commerce/Business Administration (Accounting, Finance, Human Resources, Marketing), Certified Management Ac-

countant, Master of Business Administration (Marketing), and Community College Diploma (Accounting, Communications/Public Relations, Human Resources, Marketing/Sales, Secretarial, Computer Science). Graduates would occupy Accountant, Clerical, Finance, Marketing Specialist, Sales Manager, Software Developer, Technical Support Technician, Technical Consultant, Programmer, and Network Analyst positions. Team player, good oral and written communication skills, innovative, and a high energy level are all listed as desirable nonacademic qualifications. Company benefits are rated above average. The potential for advancement is listed as excellent. The average annual starting salary falls within the $ 30,000 to $35,000 range. The most suitable methods for initial contact by those seeking employment are to mail, fax or e-mail a resume with a covering letter, or by applying through the company's website at www.simware.com. *Contact:* Human Resources.

SITEL CANADA
350 Bloor Street East, 5th Floor
Toronto, ON M4W 3J6

Tel.	416-932-2000
Fax	416-964-8966
Email	pamelat@sitelcan.sit.com
Website	www.sitelcorp@aol.com

SITEL Canada is Canada's leading provider of dedicated, outsourced telephone based sales and customer service solutions to large and fast growing corporations worldwide. SITEL Canada has coast to coast coverage of the Canadian and U.S. marketplaces, with offices and call centre operations in Montreal, Toronto and Calgary. SITEL Canada employs 450 people at this location, and a total of 1,200 people in Canada. SITEL Canada's parent company, SITEL Corporation, employs 22,000 people worldwide and is a global leader in providing outsourced teleservices to Fortune 500 companies worldwide. The company has 70 call centres in more than 17 countries. Graduates most likely to be hired come from the following academic areas: Bachelor of Commerce/Business Administration (Human Resources, Information Systems), and Community College Diploma (Business, Financial Planning, Human Resources, Information Systems). Graduates would occupy Systems Analyst, Client Services Manager/Analyst, Operations Supervisor, Quality Assurance Representative, Human Resources Recruiter, Trainer, and Sales/Customer Services Representative positions. Great communication skills, experience, a willingness to learn, and a can-do attitude are all listed as desirable nonacademic qualifications. Company benefits are rated above average. The potential for advancement is listed as being excellent. The average annual starting salary falls within the $25,000 to $30,000 range. The most suitable methods for initial contact by those seeking employment are to mail, fax or e-mail a resume with a covering letter, or via telephone. SITEL Canada does hire summer and co-op work term students. (Other Canadian Locations: Montreal 514-482-6188, Toronto 416-932-2000, and Calgary 403-269-3333). *Contacts:* Vice President, Human

Resources (for Client Services, Human Resources, Training, and Finance positions) or Manager, Human Resources (for Operations positions).

SKYJACK INC.
55 Campbell Road
Guelph, ON N1H 1B9

Tel. 519-837-0888
Fax 519-837-3102

Skyjack Inc. manufactures scissor lift platforms. These are self propelled lifts, powered by battery, diesel or gas engines, and range from 15 feet to 50 feet high. In addition, the Company offers various related options such as rollout platforms. Skyjack Inc. exports to the U.S.A., Europe and Asia. There are 470 employees at this location and a total of 1,000 worldwide. Graduates most likely to be hired come from the following academic areas: Bachelor of Science (Metallurgy), Bachelor of Engineering (Metallurgy, Industrial Design, Industrial Production, Welding), Bachelor of Commerce/Business Administration (Accounting, Finance, Human Resources, Information Systems, Marketing), Certified Management Accountant, Certified General Accountant, and Community College Diploma (Accounting, Administration, Human Resources, Marketing/Sales, Purchasing/Logistics, Auto Mechanic). Graduates would occupy Welder Fitter, NC Saw Operator, Assembler with Hydraulics and Pneumatics, CNC Lathe Operator, Painter - Electrostatic, Grinder, General Machinist, Engineering Technician, Accounts Payable/ Receivable Clerk, Purchasing/Buyer, and Sales/Marketing positions. Manufacturing experience, excellent work history, team player, good communication skills, able to work with minimal supervision, common sense, and motivation are all listed as desirable non-academic qualifications. Company benefits are rated as excellent. The potential for advancement is listed as being good. The average annual starting salary falls within the $25,000 to $30,000 range. The most suitable method for initial contact by those seeking employment is to mail a resume with a covering letter. Skyjack Inc. does hire students for summer and co-op work terms. Co-op students are recruited through various co-op programs while summer students are recruited internally. *Contact:* Dale McKay, Human Resources Manager.

SMED INTERNATIONAL INC.
10 SMED Lane SE
Calgary, AB T2C 4P8

Tel. 403-279-1400
Fax 403-720-6460
Email .... resumes@smednet.com
Website .... www.SMEDnet.com

SMED International Inc. designs, markets and manufactures complete office solutions. Products include cellular flooring, work surfaces, and moveable walls. SMED employs 1,800 people at this location, a total of 1,950 people in Canada, and an additional 175 people outside of the country. Graduates most likely to be hired come from the following academic areas: Bachelor of Engineering (Mechanical, Industrial Design), Bachelor of Commerce/Business Administration (Finance, Human Resources, Information Systems), Community College Diploma (Human Resources, Information Systems), and High School Diploma. Team player, self motivation, and a solid work history are all listed as desirable non-academic qualifications. Company benefits are rated above average. The potential for advancement is listed as excellent. The average annual starting salary falls within the $20,000 to $30,000 range, depending on the position and area of employment (Production: $9.00/hour, Administration: +$30,000). The most suitable methods for initial contact by those seeking employment are to e-mail or fax a resume with a covering letter. SMED International does hire summer and co-op work term students. *Contact:* Human Resources.

SMITH INTERNATIONAL CANADA LTD.
335 - 8th Avenue SW, Suite 1600
Calgary, AB T2P 1C9

Tel. 403-264-6077
Fax 403-269-3269

Smith International Canada Ltd. is involved in the manufacturing and sales of drill bits. The company employs 35 people at this location, and a total of 85 people in Canada. Graduates most likely to be hired come from the following academic areas: Bachelor of Science (Geology), Bachelor of Engineering (General, Industrial Design, Industrial Production, Welding, Petroleum), Certified Management Accountant, Certified General Accountant, Master of Business Administration (Information Systems), and Community College Diploma (Financial Planning, Purchasing/Logistics, Engineering Technician, Welding). Graduates would occupy entry level Clerk, Technician, Sales, Information Systems, and Assistant positions. Outgoing, self-motivated, diverse, easy-going, and a positive attitude are all listed as desirable non-academic qualifications. Company benefits are rated as excellent. The potential for advancement is listed as average. The average annual starting salary falls within the $25,000 to $30,000 range. The most suitable method for initial contact by those seeking employment is by telephone. Smith International Canada Ltd. does hire summer students. *Contact:* Lisa Kinzell, Office Administrator.

SMITHKLINE BEECHAM
2030 Bristol Circle
Oakville, ON L6H 5V2

Tel. 905-829-2030
Fax 905-829-6063
Email .... stephen.picyk@sb.com
Website .... www.sb.com

Smithkline Beecham (SB) is one of the world's leading healthcare companies, employing a total of 53,000 employees worldwide. SB discovers, develops, manufactures and markets pharmaceuticals, vaccines, over-the-counter medicines and health-related consumer products. Smithkline Beecham also provides healthcare services, including disease management, clinical laboratory testing, and pharmacy benefit management. Graduates most likely to be hired come from the following academic areas: Bachelor of Science (General, Biology, Chemistry, Nursing, Pharmacy, Psychology), Bachelor of Commerce/Business Administration, and Master of Business Administration. Graduates would occupy Medical Sales Representative, Specialist Sales Representative, Oncology Sales Representative, and Biological Sales Representative positions. Previous experience in sales (especially pharmaceutical sales), detail oriented, and able to work with little supervision are all listed as desirable non-academic qualifications. Company benefits are rated above average. The potential for advancement is listed as excellent. The average annual starting salary falls within the $40,000 to $45,000 range. The most suitable method for initial contact by those seeking employment is to mail a resume with a covering letter. Smithkline Beecham does hire summer students. *Contacts:* Stephen Picyk or Shelley Brown.

SNC-LAVALIN INC. (CHEMICALS & PETROLEUM BUSINESS UNIT)
909 - 5 Avenue SW
Calgary, AB T2P 3G5

Tel. 403-294-2100
Fax 403-294-2193
Email .... cval@snc-lavalin.com
Website .... www.snc-lavalin.com

Founded 80 years ago, SNC-Lavalin Inc., is one of the largest engineering and construction management firms in the world. It has successfully implemented major projects in over 120 countries. In addition to offices across Canada (see the following listings), SNC-Lavalin operates from strategically located bases in Africa, Asia, Europe, Latin America, and the Middle East. SNC-Lavalin's Chemicals and Petroleum Business Unit is headquartered in Alberta with offices in Calgary and Edmonton. The Chemicals and Petroleum Business Unit's demonstrated commitment to quality project excellence, has earned it a world-class reputation for process design, engineering procurement and construction of facilities for the chemicals and petroleum industries. Graduates most likely to be hired for the Chemical's and Petroleum Business Unit come from the following academic areas: Bachelor of Engineering (Chemical, Civil, Electrical, Mechanical, Instrumentation, Metallurgy, Mining, Telecommunications), and Community College Diploma (CAD/CAM/Autocad, Engineering Technician). Graduates would occupy Technician and Engineer positions. Generic competency is listed as desirable non-academic qualifications. Company benefits are rated above average. The potential for advancement is listed as average. The average annual starting salary falls within the $40,000 to $45,000 range. The most suitable method for initial contact by those seeking employment is to e-mail a resume with a covering letter. The Chemicals and Petroleum Business Unit does hire summer and co-op work term students. (Head Office: SNC-Lavalin Groupe, 455 Rene-Levesque Boulevard West, Montreal, Quebec, H2Z 1Z3). *Contact:* Human Resources.

SNC-LAVALIN INC. (ONTARIO DIVISION)
2235 Sheppard Avenue East
Willowdale, ON M2J 5A6

Tel. 416-756-2300
Fax 416-756-2266
Website .... www.snc-lavalin.com

SNC-Lavalin Inc., Ontario Division provides engineering consulting services in the following areas: environmental, municipal (eg. water, waste water, sewage), transportation, bridges and structures, and highway lighting. There are 175 employees at the Ontario Division, while SNC-Lavalin Inc. employs 4,000 people across Canada, and a total of 6,500 people worldwide. Graduates most likely to be hired at the Ontario Division come from the following academic areas: Bachelor of Arts (Urban Geography), Bachelor of Science (Biology, Chemistry, Environmental, Geology), Bachelor of Engineering (Architectural/Building, Instrumentation, Industrial Design), Bachelor of Commerce/Business Administration (Human Resources), Certified Management Accountant, Certified General Accountant, and Community College Diploma (Accounting, Human Resources, Architectural Technician, CAD/CAM/Autocad, HVAC Systems Technician). Graduates would occupy Engineer-in-Training, Technician, Drafting/Designing, Engineer, Librarian, and Human Resource positions. Entrepreneurial, self-starter, time oriented, team player, creative and dedication are all listed as desirable non-academic qualifications. Company benefits are rated above average. The potential for advancement is listed as being good. The average annual starting salary falls within the $20,000 to $40,000 range, depending on the position being considered. The most suitable methods for initial contact by those seeking employment are to mail or e-mail a resume with a covering letter. SNC-Lavalin Inc., Ontario Division does hire summer and co-op work term students. (Head Office Location: SNC-Lavalin Groupe, 455 Rene-Levesque Boulevard West, Montreal, Quebec, H2Z 1Z3). *Contacts:* Keri Christensen, Human Resources or Marcy Principio, Human Resources.

SNC-LAVALIN INC. (POWER DIVISION)
1100, boul René Lévesque ouest
Montreal, QC H3B 4P3

Tel. 514-393-1000
Fax 514-871-4913
Website .... www.snc-lavalin.com

SNC-Lavalin Inc., Power Division is an operating division of SNC Lavalin Group Inc., which provides engineering consulting, procurement, construction and management services in Canada and abroad. There are approximately 300 employees at this location. Graduates most likely to be hired come from the following academic areas: Bachelor of Science (Geology), Bachelor of Engineering (Civil, Electrical, Automation/Robotics, Instrumentation, Power,

Telecommunications, Mechanical, Industrial Design, Hydraulics, Geotechnical), and Community College Diploma (CAD/CAM/Autocad. The most suitable method for initial contact by those seeking employment is to mail a resume with a covering letter. (Head Office: SNC-Lavalin Groupe, 455 Rene-Levesque Boulevard West, Montreal, Quebec, H2Z 1Z3.) *Contact:* Nicole Giroux, Human Resources and Personnel Planning Coordinator.

SNS/ASSURE CORP.
5090 Orbitor Drive
Mississauga, ON L4W 5B5

Tel. 905-602-8374
Fax 905-602-7831
Email .... jill_ellis@sns.ca
Website .... www.sns.ca

SNS/Assure Corp. is a leading Canadian-based provider of electronic commerce products and value-added services primarily to the financial services, health care, transportation, logistics, retail and manufacturing industries. The company offers a broad range of customized and proprietary solutions in the areas of point-of-sale ("POS") transaction processing, health benefits processing, electronic data interchange ("EDI") and workflow and document management. These solutions are designed to automate and accelerate the creation, use, communication and transmission, electronically, of traditionally paper-based information, both within an organization and in its relationships with customers and suppliers. To provide a complete customer solution, SNS/Assure also offers specialized consulting, implementation, training and technical or business support services across its four business segments. SNS/Assure has 436 employees at this location, a total of 445 in Canada, and a total of 509 employees worldwide. Graduates most likely to be hired come from the following academic areas: Bachelor of Science (Computer Science, Mathematics, Nursing), Bachelor of Engineering (General, Computer Science, Telecommunications), Bachelor of Commerce/Business Administration (General, Accounting, Finance, Human Resources, Information Systems, Marketing), Master of Science (Computer Science), Master of Engineering (Computer Systems), and Community College Diploma (Accounting, Administration, Business, Financial Planning, Human Resources, Information Systems, Marketing/Sales, Secretarial, Computer Science, Electronics Technician). Graduates would occupy Programmer/Analyst, System Architect, Occupational Health Nurse, Sales, Accounts Payable/Receivable, and Administration positions. Previous work experience is listed as a desirable non-academic qualifications. Company benefits are rated as excellent. The potential for advancement is listed as being good. The average annual starting salary falls within the $35,000 to $40,000 range. The most suitable method for initial contact by those seeking employment is to e-mail a resume with a covering letter. SNS/Assure Corp. does hire summer and co-op work term students. *Contacts:* Jill Ellis, Human Resources Coordinator or Darlene LeGree, Human Resources Manager.

SOCIÉTÉ LAURENTIDE INC.
4660 - 12e Avenue
Shawinigan-Sud, QC G9N 6T5

Tel. 819-537-6636
Fax 819-537-5293

Société Laurentide Inc. is active in the manufacturing of chemicals, such as wood finishes, paints, antifreeze, solvents, and plastics. The company employs approximately 125 people at this location and a total of 300 employees in Canada. Graduates most likely to be hired come from the following academic areas: Bachelor of Science (Chemistry), Bachelor of Engineering (Industrial Chemistry, Industrial Production), Bachelor of Commerce/Business Administration (General, Accounting, Finance, Human Resources, Marketing), Certified Management Accountant, Certified General Accountant, and Community College Diploma (Business, Secretarial). Graduates would occupy Clerk, Technician, and Director positions. Bilingual, positive attitude, and determination are all listed as desirable non-academic qualifications. Company benefits and the potential for advancement are both rated as excellent. The most suitable method for initial contact by those seeking employment is to mail a resume with a covering letter. Société Laurentide Inc. does hire summer students. *Contact:* Denis Hogue.

SODEXHO MARRIOTT CANADA LTD./SODEXHO MARRIOTT QUÉBEC LTÉE
774, St-Paul ouest
Montreal, QC H3C 1M5

Tel. 514-866-7070
Fax 514-866-2212

Sodexho Marriott is a leading food and facilities management services provider to corporations, healthcare institutions, higher education institutions, school systems, and remote sites in Canada and the United States. The company employs 1,500 people in Quebec and a total of 5,000 people in Canada. Graduates most likely to be hired come from the following academic areas: Bachelor of Arts (General), Bachelor of Science (Nutritional Sciences), Bachelor of Commerce/Business Administration (General, Accounting, Marketing), Community College Diploma (Accounting, Administration, Business, Facility Management, Marketing/Sales, Secretarial, Cook/Chef Training, Hospitality, Nutrition), and High School Diploma. Graduates would occupy Account Manager, Secretary, Accounting Clerk, Chef, Dietician, and Sales Representative positions. Organized, a good attitude, creative, and service oriented are all listed as desirable non-academic qualifications.

Company benefits are rated above average. The potential for advancement is listed as being good. The average annual starting salary falls within the $25,000 to $30,000 range. The most suitable methods for initial contact by those seeking employment are to mail or fax a resume with a covering letter. Sodexho Marriott does hire summer students. *Contacts:* Stéphane Rivet, Directeur, Ressources Humaines - Québec or John Law, Director of Human Resources - Canada.

SOLCORP

5925 Airport Road, 9th Floor
Mississauga, ON L4V 1W1

Tel. 905-676-6568
Fax 905-672-1322
Email .... recruiting@solcorp.com
Website .... www.solcorp.com

SOLCORP is a global organization with customers ranging across five continents. In close to 20 years as a leading provider of software and solutions to life insurance companies, SOLCORP has established an unique partnership with many of the world's major players in the industry. Well over 150 project implementations for more than 75 companies, including a long list of industry leaders, have been successfully completed. SOLCORP is dedicated to serving the life insurance industry by providing customer-driven solutions that give companies the flexibility to launch innovative policies, bring new products quickly to market and to increase revenue by distributing customer and policy information directly to the point-of-sale. SOLCORP is a wholly-owned subsidiary of EDS, and employs 500 people worldwide, in offices in Mississauga, Montreal, Downers Grove, Illinois, West Sussex, England, and North Sydney, Australia. Graduates most likely to be hired come from the following academic areas: Bachelor of Science (General, Actuarial, Computer Science, Forestry, Mathematics), Bachelor of Engineering (General, Computer Systems), Bachelor of Commerce/Business Administration (Information Systems, Marketing), Master of Business Administration (Information Systems, Marketing), Master of Engineering (General, Information Systems), and Community College Diploma (Information Systems, Insurance, Marketing/Sales, Computer Science, Electronics Technician, Engineering Technician). SOLCORP seeks talented Programmer Analysts and Business Analysts with extensive COBOL, CICS, VisualC++, and individual life insurance administration systems experience (eg. CAPSIL, Life 70, Paxus) to work on research and development of their products and implementation at client sites throughout the world. In addition to Analyst positions, graduates would occupy Database Administrator, Project Manager, Team Leader, and Technical Support Analyst positions. Team player, life insurance knowl-

edge, customer service skills, a willingness to travel for extended periods of time, and strong communication skills are all listed as desirable non-academic qualifications. Company benefits and the potential for advancement are both rated as excellent. The average annual starting salary falls within the $50,000 to $55,000 range. The most suitable methods for initial contact by those seeking employment are to apply online at www.solcorp.com, e-mail to recruiting@solcorp.com, or fax to (905) 672-1322. SOLCORP does hire students for summer, intern and co-op work terms. *Contact:* Christina Paoletta, Recruiter.

SONY MUSIC CANADA

1121 Leslie Street
Toronto, ON M3C 2J9

Tel. 416-391-7995
Fax 416-391-7969
Website .... www.sony.ca

Sony Music Canada is involved in the production and distribution of recorded music, music publishing, as well as sales and marketing of their products and related support services. The company maintains regional branches across Canada in Toronto, Vancouver, Calgary and Montreal with representatives in Edmonton, Moncton, and Halifax. Sony Music Canada employs approximately 300 people at this location, and an additional 100 people across Canada. Graduates most likely to be hired come from the following areas: Bachelor of Arts (General, English, Graphic Arts, Journalism, Music), Bachelor of Engineering (Chemical, Civil, Electrical, Automation/Robotics, Computer Systems, Telecommunications, Mechanical, Welding), Bachelor of Architecture, Bachelor of Commerce/Business Administration (Accounting, Finance, Human Resources, Information Systems, Marketing, Public Administration), Chartered Accountant, Certified Management Accountant, Certified General Accountant, and Community College Diploma (Accounting, Administration, Advertising, Business, Communications, Facility Management, Financial Planning, Human Resources, Marketing, Purchasing/Logistics, Secretarial, Graphic Arts, Journalism, Photography, Television/Radio Arts, CAD/CAM/Autocad, Computer Science, Electronics Technician, Engineering Technician, HVAC Systems, Welding). Graduates would occupy Mechanical Technician, Electrical Technician, General Operator, Chemical Engineer, Administrative Assistant, Account Service Representative, Accountant, Financial Analyst, Computer Operator, Accounts Payable Clerk, and Warehouse Clerk positions. Company benefits and the potential for advancement are both rated as excellent. The most suitable method for initial contact by those seeking employment is to mail a resume with a covering letter. Sony Music Canada does hire summer students. *Contact:* Human Resources.

SOUTH-EAST HEALTH CARE CORPORATION

135 MacBeath Avenue
Moncton, NB E1C 6Z8

Tel. 506-857-5585
Fax 506-857-5590

South-East Health Care Corporation encompasses three hospitals, and two community based health centres. The Moncton Hospital is a tertiary care regional hospital, and the Sackville Memorial Hospital, and the Albert County Hospital are smaller hospitals. The corporation employs 2,000 people in total. Graduates most likely to be hired come from the following academic areas: Bachelor of Arts (Graphic Arts, Psychology, Recreation Studies), Bachelor of Science (Computer Science, Microbiology, Audiology, Dentistry, Nursing, Nutritional Sciences, Occupational Therapy, Pharmacy, Physical Therapy, Psychology, Speech Pathology), Bachelor of Engineering (Biomedical Electronics, Industrial Design), Bachelor of Education (General, Adult, Physical and Health), Bachelor of Commerce/Business Administration (Accounting, Finance, Human Resources, Information Systems), Chartered Accountant, Certified Management Accountant, Certified General Accountant, Master of Business Administration (Accounting, Finance, Human Resources, Information Systems), Master Science (Health Sciences), Medical Doctor, Community College Diploma (Accounting, Administration, Business, Human Resources, Secretarial, Cooking, Computer Science, Electronics Technician, Dietician, Ambulance/Emergency Care, Laboratory Technician, Nuclear Medicine Technician, Nursing RN/RNA, Radiology Technician, Respiratory Therapy, Social Work, Ultra-Sound Technician), and High School Diploma. Graduates from health related disciplines would occupy positions related to the staffing of health care facilities (eg. Nurses, Pharmacists, Social Workers, Laboratory Technicians, etc.), while graduates from other disciplines are hired for positions related to the functioning of the health care facilities (eg. Food Services, Administrative Staff, Maintenance Staff, etc.). Relevant work experience, team player, and good previous work references and attendance record are listed as desirable non-academic qualifications. Company benefits are rated above average. The potential for advancement is listed as average. The average annual starting salary varies widely depending on the position being considered. The most suitable methods for initial contact by those seeking employment are to mail a resume with a covering letter, or via telephone. The South-East Health Care Corporation does hire summer students. *Contacts:* Phyllis Hope, Director, Human Resources or Simone Jobin, Recruitment Manager.

SOUTHAM INC.
1450 Don Mills Road
Don Mills, ON M3B 2X7

Tel. 416-445-6641
Fax 416-442-2208

Southam Inc. is a diversified, Canadian owned Corporation in the information industry. The company is active in newspaper publishing, business communications and electronic media. There are more than 500 employees at this location. Graduates most likely to be hired come from the following academic areas: Bachelor of Arts (General, English, Fine Arts, Journalism), Bachelor of Science (General), Bachelor of Commerce/Business Administration (Accounting, Finance), Certified Management Accountant (Finance), Certified General Accountant (Finance), and Community College Diploma (Accounting, Administration, Advertising, Business, Marketing/Sales, Secretarial, Graphic Arts, Human Resources, Journalism). Graduates would occupy Editorial Assistant, Inside Sales Representative, Junior Sales Representative, Accounting Clerk, Administrative Assistant, and Clerical Support Staff positions. Team player, initiative, flexibility, and creativity are all listed as desirable non-academic qualifications. Company benefits are rated above average. The potential for advancement is listed as being good. The average annual starting salary falls within the $20,000 to $25,000 range. The most suitable method for initial contact by those seeking employment is to mail a resume with a covering letter. Southam Inc. does hire a few summer students annually. *Contacts:* Stacey Shepherd, Human Resources Representative or Hayley Parkinson, Human Resources Specialist.

SPECTRA COMPUTER SERVICES LTD.
383 Dovercourt Drive, Suite 200
Winnipeg, MB R3Y 1G4

Tel. 204-489-9790
Fax 204-489-1667
Email .... info@spectra.ca
Website .... www.spectra.ca

Spectra Computer Services Ltd. is a North American leader in developing real estate management software. Spectra's professional team of software developers continues to expand due to corporate growth and expansion. Currently, the Company employs 20 people. Graduates most likely to be hired are Bachelor of Science graduates in Computer Science. Graduates are hired as Software Developers using Microsoft development tools. Initiative, self-motivated, team player, and good communication skills are all listed as desirable non-academic qualifications. Company benefits are rated as industry standard. The potential for advancement is listed as average. The average annual starting salary falls within the $35,000 to $40,000 range. The most suitable method for initial contact by those seeking employment is to mail a resume with a covering letter. Spectra Computer Services Ltd. does hire co-op work term students. *Contact:* Vice President of Development.

SPECTRUM SIGNAL PROCESSING INC.
8525 Baxter Place, Suite 100
Burnaby, BC V5A 4V7

Tel. 604-421-5422
Fax 604-421-1764
Email .... jobs@spectrumsignal.com
Website .... www.SpectrumSignal.com

Spectrum Signal Processing, Inc., a technology company founded in 1987, leads the worldwide market in the development and integration of superior quality Digital Signal Processing (DSP) products. Spectrum designs, develops and markets programmable DSP Solutions which are incorporated into high-performance applications. All of the product solutions possess a very unique quality: they are all based on software programmable DSPs, rather than fixed function DSPs. This allows maximum system flexibility and provides a better more flexible system for customers. By incorporating these high-end programmable processors into all of their hardware products, Spectrum offers their customers the option to simply upgrade their old system, rather than completely replacing it. The company's proven engineering capabilities and expertise in programmable DSP software, hardware and ASIC designs, position it as the leading provider of programmable DSP System Solutions worldwide. Spectrum employs 150 people at this location and a total of 175 people worldwide. Graduates most likely to be hired come from the following academic areas: Bachelor of Science (Computer Science), and Bachelor of Engineering (Electrical, Computer Systems, Engineering Physics). Graduates would occupy Development Engineer and Field Application Engineers. Team player, related DSP experience, innovative, and good problem solving skills are all listed as desirable non-academic qualifications. Company benefits and the potential for advancement are both listed as excellent. The average annual starting salary falls within the $40,000 to $45,000 range. The most suitable method for initial contact by those seeking employment is to mail a resume with a covering letter. Spectrum Signal Processing Inc. does hire co-op work term students. *Contact:* Carol Schulz, Human Resources Committee Chairperson.

SPEEDWARE CORPORATION
9999 Cavendish Boulevard, Suite 100
St-Laurent, QC H4M 2X5

Tel. 514-747-7007
Fax 514-747-3380
Email .... HR@speedware.com
Website .... www.speedware.com

Speedware Corporation develops and markets rapid application development tools that enable their customers to create specialized computer applications for their businesses. The company also sells client server applications for accounting, database reporting and executive information systems. Speedware products run on stand alone and networked computers under most popular operating systems. There are 130 employees at this location, a total of 150 in Canada, and 230 worldwide. Graduates most likely to be hired come from the following academic areas: Bachelor of Science (Computer Science, Mathematics), Bachelor of Engineering (Computer Systems, Telecommunications), Bachelor of Commerce/Business Administration (Information Systems), Master of Business Administration (Information Systems), Master of Science (Computer Science), Master of Engineering (Computer Systems), and Community College Diploma (Accounting, Administration, Computer Science). Graduates would occupy Programmer, Software Developer, Systems Analyst, Software Systems Tester, Quality Assurance Specialist, Software Systems Support, Customer Support Specialist, Technical Product Manager, Marketing Specialist, Technical Writer, Training Course Developer, and Administrative Clerk positions. Flexible, organized, detail oriented, fast learner, work with minimal supervision and to tight deadlines, willing to accept a variety of assignments, interested in maintaining up-to-date technical knowledge, and experience with business systems, internet and networked computers are all listed as desirable non-academic skills. Company benefits are rated above average. The potential for advancement is listed as being good. The average annual starting salary falls within the $30,000 to $35,000 range, depending upon qualifications. The most suitable methods for initial contact by those seeking employment are to mail or e-mail a resume with a covering letter. Speedware Corporation occasionally hires summer and co-op work term students for programming, technical writing and graphic design positions. (Other Canadian Locations: Speedware, Quebec City: 2600 boul. Laurier, Suite 2350, Sainte Foy, QC, G1V 4M6, Phone 418-650-6567, Fax 418-650-5887; Speedware, Toronto: 150 John Street, 10th Floor, Toronto, ON, M5V 3E3, Phone 416-408-2880, Fax 416-408-2872.) *Contact:* Rose Church, Manager, Human Resources.

SPORT MART DISCOUNT SUPERSTORES
945 Columbia Street, Suite 214
Kamloops, BC V2C 1L5

Tel. 250-372-3128
Fax 250-828-2558
Email .... sportmart@wkpowerlink.com
Website .... www.sportmart.ca

Sport Mart Discount Superstores operates sporting goods retail superstores in Western Canada. There are approximately 18 employees at this location and a total of 450 employees in the company. Graduates with a High School Diploma are hired, post secondary education is not listed a prerequisite for employment application. Company benefits are rated above average. The potential for advancement is listed as being excellent. The average annual starting salary falls within the $15,000 to $20,000 range. The most suitable method for initial contact by those seeking employment is to mail a resume with a covering letter. Sport Mart Discount Superstores does hire summer students. *Contacts:* Shawn Fiddick, Vancouver; James Marchand, Edmonton or Bob Hrynchuk, Calgary.

SPRINT CANADA INC.
2550 Victoria Park Avenue, Suite 400
Toronto, ON M2J 5E6

Tel. 416-496-1644
Fax 416-496-0975
Website .... www.sprintcanada.ca

Sprint Canada Inc. provides long-distance voice and data transmissions throughout the world for Canadian businesses and consumers. Sprint Canada is committed to being the number one long distance alternative to the local telephone companies, and the number one in customer service. The company employs approximately 500 staff at this location and a total of 1,300 people across Canada. Graduates most likely to be hired come from the following academic areas: Bachelor of Arts (General, French, Languages), Bachelor of Science (Computer Science, Mathematics), Bachelor of Engineering (General, Telecommunications), Bachelor of Laws, Bachelor of Commerce/Business Administration (General, Accounting, Finance, Human Resources, Information Systems), Chartered Accountant, Master of Business Administration (Human Resources, Information Systems, Marketing), and Community College Diploma (Human Resources). Graduates would occupy Financial Analyst, Programmer/Analyst, Human Resources Assistant, Recruiter, Computer Operator, and Customer Services Representative positions. Adaptable, flexible, positive, team player, and able to work well independently are all listed as desirable non-academic qualifications. Company benefits are rated above average. The potential for advancement is listed as excellent. The average annual starting salary falls within the $30,000 to $35,000 range. The most suitable method for initial contact is to mail a resume with a covering letter. Sprint Canada Inc. does hire summer students. *Contact:* Kellye MacAdam, Manager, Human Resources.

SQL TECHNOLOGIES INC. (SQL TECH)
2323 Yonge Street, Suite 605
Toronto, ON M4P 2C9

Tel. 416-483-7383
Fax 416-483-8102

SQL Technologies Inc. is an organization specializing in the planning and delivery of client server solutions. Employing more than 25 people, SQL is a sales organization and the master distributor for Gupta Technologies, the leader in client server software in the computing industry. Graduates most likely to be hired come from the following academic areas: Bachelor of Science (Computer Science), Master of Business Administration (Marketing), and High School Diploma. Graduates would occupy Computer Programmer/Consultant, Marketing Assistant, and positions in Administration. Integrity, a forthright manner, self-motivated, excellent communication skills, a high energy level, and customer relations skills are all listed as desirable non-academic qualifications. Company benefits are rated as industry standard. The potential for advancement is listed as being good. The average annual starting salary falls within the $20,000 to $30,000 range, and is commission based for certain positions. The most suitable method for initial contact by those seeking employment is to mail a resume with a covering letter. SQL Technologies Inc. does hire summer students. *Contact:* Frank McCrea, President/Owner.

ST. ELIZABETH VISITING NURSES' ASSOC.
698 King Street West, Cathedral Square
Hamilton, ON L8P 1C7

Tel. 905-522-6887
Fax 905-522-5579

St. Elizabeth Visiting Nurses' Association (SEN) provides health care to clients in their home environment. SEN employs approximately 300 people. Graduates most likely to be hired come from the following academic areas: Bachelor of Arts (Psychology, Sociology/Social Work), Bachelor of Science (Nursing), Bachelor of Education (Adult), Bachelor of Commerce/Business Administration (Human Resources, Information Systems), Master of Business Administration (Accounting), Master of Health Sciences, Community College Diploma (Accounting, Administration, Business, Secretarial, Social Work, Computer Science, Nursing RN/RNA, HCA, HSW2, HSW3), and High School Diploma. Graduates would occupy Home Support Worker in the community, Nursing in the community, and Clerk positions. Previous work experience, excellent verbal and communication skills, conscientious, team player, and strong organizational skills are all listed as desirable non-academic qualifications. Company benefits are rated as industry standard. The potential for advancement is listed as average. The most suitable method for initial contact by those seeking employment is to mail a resume with a covering letter. The St. Elizabeth Visiting Nurses' Association does hire summer students. *Contact:* Pat Ordowich, Acting CEO & President.

ST. JOHN'S REHABILITATION HOSPITAL
285 Cummer Avenue
Toronto, ON M2M 2G1

Tel. 416-226-6780
Fax 416-226-6265

The St. John's Rehabilitation Hospital provides quality short term rehabilitation services to adolescent and adult populations. Patients are referred to St. John's from active treatment hospitals where they have undergone surgery/treatment in orthopaedics, amputation, and general surgery. St. John's focuses on interdisciplinary patient care including nursing, social work, patient education, physical and occupational therapy. The hospital employs 300 people. Graduates most likely to be hired come from the following academic areas: Bachelor of Arts (Social Work), Bachelor of Science (Computer Science, Nursing, Occupational Therapy, Pharmacy, Physical Therapy, Speech Pathology), Bachelor of Engineering, Bachelor of Commerce/Business Administration (Finance, Human Resources, Information Systems), Chartered Accountant, Master of Business Administration, Masters (Health Sciences Administration, All Health Science Disciplines), Community College Diploma (Accounting, Administration, Communications, Human Resources, Secretarial, Journalism, Computer Science, Engineering Technician, Nursing RN/RNA, Social Work/DSW), and High School Diploma. Graduates would occupy related clerical, administrative and professional service positions. Positive, good interpersonal skills, and previous work experience in a health care or social service setting are listed as desirable non-academic qualifications.

Company benefits are rated above average. The potential for advancement is listed as being good. The average annual starting salary falls within the $30,000 to $35,000 range. The most suitable method for initial contact by graduates seeking employment is to mail a resume with a covering letter. St. John's Rehabilitation Hospital does hire summer students. *Contacts:* Terry McMahon, Director of Human Resources or Mita Suri, Human Resources Assistant.

ST. JOSEPH PRINTING LTD.
50 MacIntosh Boulevard
Concord, ON L4K 4P3

Tel. 905-660-3111
Fax 905-660-6820

St. Joseph Printing Ltd. is a high quality commercial printer on the cutting edge in the application of new technologies. It is the largest privately owned printing corporation in Canada employing approximately 425 people. Network Studios, a division of St. Joseph Printing provides state of the art photography and pre-press activities. Together, St. Joseph Printing and Network Studios offer services from concept to doorstep. Graduates most likely to be hired come from the following academic areas: Bachelor of Arts, Bachelor of Science (Computer Science), Bachelor of Commerce/Business Administration, Certified Management Accountant, Community College Diploma (Business, Graphic Arts, Commercial Photography), and High School Diploma. Career opportunities for graduates exist in Creative and Art Direction, Customer Service, Accounting, Administration and Operations. Possessing previous work experience in the printing or fashion photography industries would be desirable. St. Joseph Printing Limited is a growing company committed to employee and business excellence. Graduates interested in a career with St. Joseph Printing Limited should mail a resume with covering letter to the above address. The company does hire summer students. *Contact:* Helen Ploumis, Director of Human Resources.

ST. JOSEPH'S HEALTH CENTRE
30 The Queensway
Toronto, ON M6R 1B5

Tel. 416-530-6460
Fax 416-530-6034

St. Joseph's Health Centre is one of the largest hospitals in Metropolitan Toronto, employing approximately 2,000 people. General and acute patient care are the Health Centre's main focus. Graduates most likely to be hired come from the following academic areas: Bachelor of Arts (General), Bachelor of Science (Nursing, Pharmacy), Bachelor of Education (Adult/Nursing), Masters (Nursing/Health Administration, Human Resources), and Community College Diploma (General, Nursing, Food/Nutrition, Health Technicians, Secretarial). Graduates would occupy a wide variety of positions in Administration, Nursing, Technical Services, Nutrition Services, and Human Resources. High School graduates are also hired for clerical and service related positions. Reliable, and excellent written and verbal communication skills are listed as desirable non-academic qualifications. Company benefits are rated above average. The most suitable method for initial contact by those seeking employment is to mail a well prepared resume with a covering letter. St. Joseph's Health Centre does hire a few summer students each year. *Contact:* Alison Walton, Recruitment Specialist.

ST. MICHAEL'S HOSPITAL
30 Bond Street
Toronto, ON M5B 1W8

Tel. 416-867-7415
Fax 416-867-7488

Established in 1892 by the Sisters of St. Joseph to care for the sick and the poor, St. Michael's Hospital is a Catholic teaching hospital affiliated with the University of Toronto. Presently the hospital employs more than 3,000 people. Graduates most likely to be hired come from the following academic areas: Bachelor of Science (Audiology, Nursing, Nutritional Sciences, Occupational Therapy, Pharmacy, Physical Therapy, Speech Pathology), Bachelor of Engineering (Biomedical Electronics, Telecommunications), Bachelor of Commerce/Business Administration (Information Systems), and Community College Diploma (Laboratory Technician, Nuclear Medicine Technician, Nursing RN/RNA, Radiology Technician, Respiratory Technician). Graduates would occupy positions which are directly related to their academic field of study. The most suitable method for initial contact by those seeking employment is to mail a resume with a covering letter. *Contact:* Heather Fong, Employment Coordinator.

STAGE WEST ALL SUITE HOTEL & THEATRE RESTAURANT
5400 Dixie Road
Mississauga, ON L4W 4T4

Tel. 905-238-0159
Fax 905-238-9820

Stage West is a hotel and theatre restaurant employing approximately 250 people. Graduates most likely to be hired come from the following academic areas: Bachelor of Arts (General), Bachelor of Commerce/Business Administration (Marketing, Finance), Certified Management Accountant, and Community College Diploma (Hotel/Restaurant, Culinary/Cooking). Graduates with relevant experience would be hired for Chef/Cook, Controller, and Middle Management positions in the Front Office, Restaurant, Administration, Food and Beverages, and Sales and Marketing. Punctual, reliable, excellent communication and public relations skills, and a willingness to work shifts and extra hours are all listed as desirable non-academic qualifications. Company benefits are rated as industry standard. The potential for advancement is listed as being good. The most suitable method for initial contact by those seeking employment is to mail a resume with a covering letter. Stage West does hire summer students. *Contact:* Sylvia Gimenez, Human Resources Coordinator.

STANDARD AERO LIMITED
33 Allen Dyne Road
Winnipeg, MB R3H 1A1

Tel. 204-775-9711
Fax 204-788-2333
Email .... human_resources@standardaero.ca
Website .... www.standardaero.com

Standard Aero is one of the world's largest gas turbine engine and accessory repair and overhaul companies. With facilities located around the globe, Standard Aero serves the ever-changing needs of aircraft, marine and industrial engine operators in over eighty countries. The company's customers include corporate and charter aircraft organizations, governments/militaries, power generation and gas line pumping companies, and some of the largest regional airlines in the world. Standard Aero is headquartered in Winnipeg and employs over 1,550 people in facilities worldwide. Graduates most likely to be hired come from the following academic areas: Bachelor of Science (Computer Science), Bachelor of Engineering (Chemical, Mechanical, Aerospace, Metallurgy), Bachelor of Education (Adult), Bachelor of Commerce/Business Administration (General, Accounting, Human Resources, Information Systems, Marketing), Chartered Accountant, Certified Management Accountant, Certified General Accountant, Master of Engineering, Doctorate of Engineering, and Community College Diploma (Accounting, Business, Human Resources, Purchasing/Logistics, Aircraft Maintenance, Computer Science, Engineering Technician, Tool and Die, Machinist). Team player, proficient with Microsoft Office, and excellent communication skills are all listed as desirable non-academic qualifications. Company benefits and the potential for advancement are both rated as excellent. The average annual starting salary falls within the $20,000 to $25,000 range. The most suitable method for initial contact by those seeking employment is to e-mail a resume with a covering letter. Standard Aero Limited does hire students for summer and co-op work term positions. *Contacts:* Alex Yoong, Director of Human Resources or Sandra Hawryluk, Human Resources Assistant.

STANDARD AUTO GLASS
334 Rowntree Dairy Road
Woodbridge, ON L4L 8H2

Tel. 905-856-9100
Fax 905-850-4242

Standard Auto Glass installs and repairs automotive glass and accessories, ensuring the highest quality of work and customer service, through its network of Standard Auto Glass stores. There are approximately 30 people employed at the head office location, and a total of 400 employees across Canada.

Graduates with a High School Diploma are hired as Glass Installers. Good communication skills, an ability to work well with others in a cooperative manner, driver's license, physically able to able to lift 50lbs, mechanical aptitude, and service oriented are all listed as desirable non-academic qualifications. Company benefits are rated above average. The potential for advancement is listed as average. The most suitable method for initial contact by those seeking employment is to complete an application at the individual store location (check your yellow/white pages for nearest location). Standard Auto Glass does hire summer students. *Contacts:* Barbara Rick, Personnel Manager (Head Office) or Store Manager (for local Standard Auto Glass Stores).

STANDARD LIFE ASSURANCE COMPANY
1245, rue Sherbrooke ouest
Montreal, QC H3G 1G3

Tel. 514-284-6711
Fax 514-499-4908
Website .... www.standardlife.ca/

Standard Life Assurance Company is a financial services company providing group life and health insurance, individual life and health insurance, group pension, individual pension, mutual funds and other investment vehicles. The company employs approximately 900 people at this location and a total of 2,000 people in Canada. Graduates most likely to be hired come from the following academic areas: Bachelor of Arts (General), Bachelor of Science (Actuarial, Nursing), Chartered Accountant, Certified Management Accountant, Certified General Accountant, Master of Business Administration (General, Finance, Information Systems, Marketing), Master of Science (Computer Science), Community College Diploma (Accounting, Administration, Financial Planning, Human Resources, Information Systems, Insurance, Marketing/Sales, Purchasing/Logistics, Secretarial, Graphic Arts, Computer Science). Leadership skills, teamwork, action oriented, business acumen, and a customer focus are all listed as desirable non-academic qualifications. Company benefits and the potential for advancement are both rated as excellent. The average annual starting salary is dependent upon the position being considered. The most suitable method for initial contact by graduates seeking employment is to mail a resume with a covering letter. Standard Life Assurance Company does hire summer students. *Contact:* Pierrette Roussel, Staffing Officer.

STANDEN'S LIMITED
P.O. Box 67, Station T
Calgary, AB T2H 2G7

Tel. 403-258-7000
Fax 403-258-7808

Standen's Limited manufactures leaf springs, and other industrial, automotive, and agricultural machinery parts. The company employs a total of 450 people. Graduates most likely to be hired come from the following academic areas: Community College

Diploma (Administration, Purchasing/Logistics, Mechanic, Engineering Technician, Welding, Tool and Die Maker, Millwright), and High School Diploma. Graduates would occupy Administrative, Clerical, and Skilled Trade positions. Previous work experience, good communication skills, self-starter, and focused career objectives are all listed as desirable non-academic qualifications. The most suitable method for initial contact by those seeking employment is to mail a resume with a covering letter. Standen's Limited does hire summer students for manufacturing positions. *Contact:* Roland Osske, Manager, Human Resources.

STANLEY TECHNOLOGY GROUP INC.
10160 - 112 Street
Edmonton, AB T5K 2L6

Tel. 403-917-7000
Fax 403-917-7330

Stanley Technology Group Inc. through its member companies, provides a broad range of engineering and professional consulting services to private and public sector clients in Canada, the United States, and internationally. The principle services offered include environmental consulting, infrastructure design and development, industrial engineering, and land development services and project management. Founded in 1954, the group employs 300 people at this location, a total of 1,000 people in Canada, and a total of 1,200 people worldwide. Graduates most likely to be hired come from the following academic areas: Bachelor of Arts (Economics, Journalism, Urban Geography), Bachelor/Master of Science (Biology, Chemistry, Computer Science, Environmental, Forestry, Geology, Metallurgy), Bachelor/Master of Engineering (Chemical, Civil, Industrial Chemistry, Metallurgy, Pollution Treatment, Pulp and Paper, Building, Structural, Land Development, Surveying, Transportation, Computer Systems, Instrumentation, Microelectronics, Power, Telecommunications, Mechanical, Industrial Design/Production, Environmental, Forest Resources, Mining, Petroleum, Water Resources), Bachelor of Landscape Architecture, Bachelor of Laws (Corporate, Environmental), Bachelor of Commerce/Business Administration (Accounting, Finance, Human Resources, Information Systems, Marketing), Chartered Accountant, Master of Business Administration (Accounting, Finance, Information Systems), Community College Diploma (Accounting, Administration, Communications, Financial Planning, Human Resources, Insurance, Marketing/Sales, Purchasing/Logistics, Secretarial, Journalism, Legal Assistant, Recreation Studies, Urban Planning, Architectural Technician, CAD/CAM/Autocad, Computer Science, Electronics, Engineering, Forestry, HVAC Systems) and High School Diploma. Graduates would occupy Clerk, Administrator, Technician, and Trainee (with professional component) positions. Those with a Masters degree may be hired at the Project Management level if they possess a number of years experience. A positive attitude, team player, flexibility, and initiative are all listed as desirable non-academic qualifications. Company benefits are rated above

average. The average starting salary falls within the $25,000 to $30,000 range. The most suitable method for initial contact by those seeking employment is to mail a resume with a covering letter. Stanley Technology Group Inc. hires summer students for engineering fieldwork positions. *Contact:* Corporate Human Resources Manager.

STAR DATA SYSTEMS INC.
7030 Woodbine Avenue, 8th Floor
Markham, ON L3R 1A2

Tel. 416-479-7827
Email .... hr@stardata.ca
Website .... www.stardata.com

Star Data Systems Inc. provides high tech delivery of online, real-time financial information systems, solutions and data to over 16,000 wealth managers in Canada. The Applications Service Division provides a comprehensive range of administrative, investment and asset management services to the financial services industry. Star Data's head office is in Markham, with additional office locations in Vancouver, Calgary, Winnipeg, Toronto, Montreal, Halifax, and London, United Kingdom. There are 300 employees at this location, a total of 500 employees in Canada, and a total of 505 employees in the United Kingdom and Canada. Graduates most likely to be hired come from the following academic areas: Bachelor of Arts (General, Economics, English, French, Psychology, Sociology), Bachelor of Science (General, Computer Science, Mathematics), Bachelor of Engineering (General, Computer Systems, Telecommunications), Bachelor of Laws, Bachelor of Commerce/Business Administration (Accounting, Finance, Human Resources, Information Systems, Marketing), Chartered Accountant, Certified General Accountant, Master of Business Administration (Accounting, Finance, Information Systems), and Community College Diploma (Accounting, Administration, Human Resources, Computer Science, Electronics Technician). Graduates would occupy Finance and Administration, Programming, High Technology/Telecommunications, Sales and Marketing, Human Resource, Training, and Technology Assisted Learning positions. Strong interpersonal skills and PC literacy (Word/Spreadsheet/PowerPoint) are listed as desirable non-academic qualifications. Company benefits and the potential for advancement are both rated as excellent. The average annual starting salary is based upon the position being considered. The most suitable method for initial contact by those seeking employment is via referrals through employees. Star Data Systems Inc. does hire summer students. *Contacts:* Vaugnn McIntyre, SVP Organization and Professional Development or Brenda Arcangeli, Human Resources Manager.

STATE FARM INSURANCE COMPANIES
100 Consilium Place, Suite 102
Toronto, ON M1H 3G9

Tel. 416-290-4100

State Farm Insurance Companies are involved in the

sale and service of automobile, life, and homeowners insurance policies. There are more than 500 employees at this location. Graduates most likely to be hired come from the following academic areas: Bachelor of Arts, Bachelor of Science, Bachelor of Engineering, Bachelor of Education, Bachelor of Laws, Bachelor of Commerce/Business Administration, and Community College Diploma (Business). Graduates would occupy Claims Service Representative, Underwriter, Computer Operator, Accounting Trainee, and Accounting Clerk positions. Good communication skills and a customer service background are both listed as desirable non-academic qualifications. Company benefits and the potential for advancement are both rated as excellent. The average annual starting salary falls within the $25,000 to $30,000 range. The most suitable method for initial contact by those seeking employment is to mail a resume with a covering letter. State Farm Insurance Companies does hire summer students on a limited basis. *Contact:* Carolyn Maugeri, Sr. Personnel Specialist.

STEELCASE CANADA LTD.
1 Steelcase Road West
Markham, ON L3R 0T3

Tel. 905-475-6333
Fax 905-475-6073
Website .... www.steelcase.com

Steelcase Canada Ltd. is the country's leading provider of office furnishings and knowledge about workplace performance. The company is a subsidiary of Steelcase Inc., headquartered in Grand Rapids, Michigan, the world's leader in the industry. There are approximately 650 employees at this location, while Steelcase Inc. employs 19,000 people worldwide. Graduates most likely to be hired come from the following academic areas: Bachelor of Engineering (Mechanical, Industrial Production, Manufacturing Engineer, Product Engineer), Bachelor of Commerce/Business Administration (General, Accounting), Community College Diploma (Human Resources, Marketing/Market Managers), and High School Diploma. Applicants should be able to work in a team based environment. Company benefits and the potential for advancement are both rated as excellent. The average annual starting salary falls within the $35,000 to $40,000 range. The most suitable methods for initial contact by those seeking employment are to mail or fax a resume with a covering letter. Steelcase Canada Ltd. does hire summer and co-op work term students. For more information about Steelcase, visit their website at www.steelcase.com. *Contact:* Human Resources.

STERLING PULP CHEMICALS, LTD.
2 Gibbs Road
Toronto, ON M9B 1R1

Tel. 416-239-7111
Fax 416-237-0431
Website www.clo2.com

Sterling Pulp Chemicals is one of the world's largest producers of sodium chlorate, an industrial salt used primarily for the manufacture of chlorine dioxide, the cornerstone of an important bleaching process that reduces pollution. This process, known as Elemental Chlorine-Free bleaching, has a superior environmental track record and yields high quality, environmentally friendly white paper products. The company also licenses and constructs large-scale chlorine dioxide generators, used in the bleaching process by the pulp and paper industry. In addition, Sterling Pulp Chemicals produces sodium chlorite, caustic, chlorine, hydrochloric acid, and calcium hypochlorite. There are 150 employees in Toronto, 465 across Canada, and a total of 500 worldwide. The company operates facilities in Buckingham, Quebec, Thunder Bay, Ontario, Saskatoon, Saskatchewan, Grande Prairie, Alberta, Vancouver, British Columbia, and Valdosta, Georgia. The company's business headquarters, its research and development facilities and the ERCO Systems Group are located at this address in Toronto. Sterling Pulp Chemicals, Ltd. is owned by Sterling Chemicals Holdings, Inc. based in Houston, Texas. Graduates most likely to be hired come from the following academic areas: Bachelor of Science (Chemistry), Bachelor of Engineering (Chemical, Environmental, Electrical, Mechanical), Bachelor of Commerce/Business Administration (Accounting, Finance, Marketing), Chartered Accountant (Finance), Certified Management Accountant (Finance), Certified General Accountant (Finance), and Community College Diploma (Secretarial, Human Resources, Computer Science). Graduates would occupy R & D Laboratory, Instrumentation, Technical Service, Process Engineering, Project Engineering, Finance, Accounting, Sales and Marketing, Purchasing, Clerical, Secretarial, and Human Resource positions. Company benefits and the potential for advancement are both rated as excellent. The most suitable methods for initial contact by those seeking employment are to mail a resume with a covering letter, or by applying through the company's website at www.clo2.com. Sterling Pulp Chemicals, Ltd. does hire summer and co-op students for R & D Laboratory positions. *Contact:* Human Resources Department.

STONE & WEBSTER CANADA LIMITED
2300 Yonge Street
Toronto, ON M4P 2W6

Tel. 416-932-4400
Fax 416-482-2865
Email .... swcl.hr@stoneweb.com
Website .... www.stoneweb.com

Stone & Webster Canada Limited is a full service engineering, procurement and construction management firm, operating in the petrochemical, refining, power generation, and heavy industrial sectors. There are approximately 450 employees at this location and a total of 550 employees in Canada. The parent company of Stone & Webster Canada Limited employs approximately 8,000 people worldwide. Graduates most likely to be hired come from the following academic areas: Bachelor of Engineering (Chemical, Civil, Electrical, Instrumentation, Mechanical),

Bachelor of Commerce/Business Administration (Accounting, Human Resources, Information Systems), Master of Engineering (Mechanical, Electrical, Civil), and Community College Diploma (Architecture/Drafting, CAD/CAM/Autocad, Computer Science). Graduates would occupy Engineer in Training, Drafter, and Designer positions. A willingness to travel, team oriented, and effective communication skills are all listed as desirable non-academic qualifications. The most suitable methods for initial contact by those seeking employment are to mail or e-mail a resume with a covering letter. Stone & Webster Canada Limited does hire summer and co-op work term students. *Contacts:* Lisa Dantas, Human Resources Representative or Paul Farkas, Human Resources Manager.

STRAIT CROSSING INFRASTRUCTURE INC.
1177 - 11th Avenue SW, Suite 700
Calgary, AB T2R 1K9

Tel. 403-244-9090
Fax 403-228-8643
Email .... johnf@groupsci.com

Strait Crossing Infrastructure Inc. is a construction management group dedicated to infrastructure design, build and operation of construction projects. Strait Crossing is the builder of the Confederation Bridge, and is involved in construction management projects in Canada, the United States and Europe. There are 25 employees at this location and a total of 35 employees in Canada. Graduates most likely to be hired come from the following academic areas: Bachelor of Engineering (Civil, Electrical, Mechanical, Environmental/Resources), Bachelor of Commerce/Business Administration (Finance), Master of Business Administration (Finance), and Community College Diploma (CAD/CAM/Autocad, Engineering Technician). Graduates would occupy Field Engineer, Office Engineer, Surveyor, and Draftsmen positions. Team player, analytical, and hard working are all listed as desirable non-academic qualifications. Company benefits are rated as industry standard. The potential for advancement is listed as being good. The average annual starting salary falls within the $45,000 to $50,000 range. The most suitable methods for initial contact by those seeking employment are to mail or fax a resume with a covering letter. Strait Crossing Infrastructure Inc. does hire summer and co-op work term students, depending on the projects available. *Contact:* John Forgeron, Manager, Human Resources.

STRONGCO MATERIAL HANDLING, DIVISION OF STRONGCO INC.
29 Regan Road
Brampton, ON L7A 1B2

Tel. 905-846-5910
Fax 905-846-3368

Strongco Material Handling, Division of Strongco Inc. employs more than 50 people in the sales and service of material handling equipment. Post-secondary education is not listed as a prerequisite for employment application. Strongco Material Handling hires people to occupy Service Technician positions. Relevant work experience and applied education would be a definite asset. Company benefits are rated as excellent. The potential for advancement is listed as being good. The most suitable method for initial contact regarding employment opportunities is to mail a resume with a covering letter. *Contacts:* Grant McCarole, General Manager or Patty McArthur, Human Resources.

STURGEON LAKE BOARD OF EDUCATION
Bag #5
Valleyview, AB T0H 3N0

Tel. 403-524-4590
Fax 403-524-3696
Email .... sturglke@telusplanet.net

Sturgeon Lake Board of Education is the primary controlling body of Sturgeon Lake School. The School is located 365 km north of Edmonton, Alberta. Sturgeon Lake School has 24 employees, both teachers and paraprofessionals. The School has an enrollment of 250 students in ECS to grade 12. Graduates most likely to be hired are Bachelor of Education (General, Early Childhood, Primary Junior - Grades 0-6, Junior Intermediate - Grades 4-10, Intermediate Senior - Grades 7 - 12, Physical and Health, Special Needs) graduates. Graduates are hired to occupy Teacher positions. Team player, experience teaching Native students, and a willingness to get involved in the community are all listed as desirable non-academic qualifications. Company benefits are rated above average. The School is located near two Provincial Parks, Williamson's and Young's Point, for those who enjoy various outdoor pursuits. The potential for advancement is listed as average. The average annual starting salary falls within the $30,000 to $35,000 range. The most suitable method for initial contact by those seeking employment is to mail a resume with a covering letter. *Contacts:* Tim Martens, Principal or Carol Goodswimmer, Education Administrator.

SUN LIFE OF CANADA
225 King Street West, 8th Floor
Toronto, ON M5V 3C5

Tel. 416-408-7585
Fax 416-595-1587

Sun Life of Canada is active in selling life insurance products, pensions and savings, and group benefits. The company employs approximately 4,200 people in Canada, and a total of 10,000 employees worldwide. Graduates most likely to be hired come from the following academic areas: Bachelor of Arts (Economics), Bachelor of Science (Actuarial, Computer Science, Mathematics), Bachelor of Commerce/Business Administration (Accounting, Finance, Human Resources, Information Systems), Master of Business Administration (Accounting, Finance, Human Resources, Information Systems, Marketing), and Community College Diploma (Legal Assistant). Excellent organizational skills, creative, innovative, good verbal and written communication skills, flexibility, adaptability, team player, and good interpersonal, consultative and negotiating skills are all listed as desirable non-academic qualifications. Company benefits are rated above average. The potential for advancement is listed as being good. The most suitable method for initial contact by those seeking employment is to mail a resume with a covering letter. Sun Life of Canada does hire summer students. *Contact:* Human Resources.

SUNBURY TRANSPORT LIMITED
P.O. Box 905, Station A
Fredericton, NB E3B 5B4

Tel. 506-453-1133
Fax 506-453-7658

Sunbury Transport Limited is a transportation company providing full truck load carrier services. Safety conscious and aiming to be the best possible carrier, Sunbury Transport uses the most advanced satellite technology in the industry to communicate with their vehicles on the road. There are 90 employees at this location, and a total of 110 employees in Canada. Graduates most likely to be hired come from the following academic areas: Bachelor of Engineering (General), Bachelor of Education (Adult), Bachelor of Commerce/Business Administration (Accounting, Human Resources, Information Systems, Marketing), Certified Management Accountant, and Community College Diploma (Administration, Marketing/Sales). Graduates would occupy Management Trainee, Operations Trainee, and Sales Associate positions. Team player, positive attitude, good communication skills, initiative, and relevant work experience are all listed as desirable non-academic qualifications. Company benefits and the potential for advancement are both rated as excellent. The average annual starting salary falls within the $20,000 to $25,000 range, depending upon the position being considered. The most suitable method for initial contact by those seeking employment is to mail a resume with a covering letter. Sunbury Transport Limited occasionally hires summer students. *Contacts:* Cathy Colpitts or Todd Stewart.

SUNOCO INC.
36 York Mills Road
Toronto, ON M2P 2C5

Tel. 416-733-7056
Fax 416-733-1233

Sunoco Inc. is a fully owned subsidiary of Suncor Energy Inc., a 100% publicly owned Canadian integrated oil and gas company. Headquartered in Toronto, Sunoco manufactures, distributes and markets transportation fuels, petrochemicals, and heating oils primarily in Ontario and Quebec. Sunoco also markets natural gas to Ontario households. Sunoco's main refinery is located in Sarnia, Ontario. There are 250 employees at this location, and a total of 700 employees in Canada. Graduates most likely to be hired come from the following academic areas: Bachelor of Science (Computer Science), Bachelor of

Engineering (Chemical, Electrical, Environmental/Resources), Bachelor of Commerce/Business Administration (Accounting), and Community College Diploma (Accounting, Business, Information Systems). Graduates would occupy Business Analyst, Business Development Specialist, and Distribution Analyst positions. Analytical skills, customer focus, and good problem solving skills are listed as desirable non-academic qualifications. Company benefits are rated above average. The potential for advancement is listed as excellent. The average annual starting salary falls within the $40,000 to $45,000 range. The most suitable method for initial contact by those seeking employment is to mail a resume with a covering letter. Sunoco Inc. does hire summer and co-op work term students. *Contacts:* Julia Bucciarelli or Suzanne Jordan.

SUPER FITNESS CENTRES INC.
P.O. Box 84539
Toronto, ON M6S 1T0

Tel. 416-762-6070

Super Fitness Centres Inc. employs more than 250 people in the operation of commercial health clubs. Graduates most likely to be hired come from the following academic areas: Bachelor of Arts, Bachelor of Science, Bachelor of Education (Physical Education), and Chartered Accountant. Graduates would occupy positions in Membership Enrollment, Fitness Instruction, Reception/Clerical, and Managerial functions. An athletic background, good personality, a "people-person", and an athletic appearance are all listed as desirable non-academic qualifications. Company benefits are rated as industry standard. The potential for advancement is listed as excellent. Most employee positions are salary based plus commission. The average starting salary falls within the $15,000 to $20,000 range, and may be supplemented through commission earnings (potential earnings can be high). The most suitable methods for initial contact by those seeking employment are to mail a resume with a covering letter, or via telephone. Super Fitness Centres Inc. does hire summer students on a regular basis. *Contact:* Christine Steiger, Vice President.

SUPERIOR ACCEPTANCE CORPORATION LTD.
22 St. Clair Avenue East, Suite 1201
Toronto, ON M4T 2S3

Tel. 416-924-7494
Fax 416-924-1117

Superior Acceptance Corp. Ltd. is a consumer loan company operating 89 branches across Canada, five in the Metropolitan Toronto area. This location is the head office branch with 25 employees. Graduates most likely to be hired are Community College graduates from business related programs. High School graduates are also hired. Graduates and non-post secondary graduates would occupy Credit, Collections, Accounting and Clerical positions. An ability to deal with the public, proper telephone manner, basic math and bookkeeping skills, and familiarity with credit evaluation, collection and small claims court procedures are all listed as desirable non-academic qualifications. Company benefits are rated as industry standard. The potential for advancement is listed as being good. The average annual starting salary falls within the $15,000 to $20,000 range. The most suitable method for initial contact by those seeking employment is to mail a resume with a covering letter. *Contacts:* John Cavanagh or R.W. 'Bud' Eckhard.

SWIFT CURRENT HEALTH DISTRICT
429 - 4th Avenue NE
Swift Current, SK S9H 2J9

Tel.	306-778-5105
Fax	306-773-9513
Email	smonti@scdhb.sk.ca

The Swift Current Health District is a multifaceted health care delivery organization dedicated to excellence in community health, long term care, acute care and home based services for a population of about 20,000. The Swift Current Health District is the host district for southwest Saskatchewan and supplies outreach services to the two neighbouring health districts. The Swift Current Health District employs a total of 1,000 people. Graduates most likely to be hired come from the following academic areas: Bachelor of Science (Nursing, Nutritional Sciences, Occupational Therapy, Pharmacy, Physio/Physical Therapy, Psychology, Speech Pathology), Bachelor of Education (Early Childhood), Bachelor of Commerce/Business Administration (General, Accounting, Finance, Human Resources), Chartered Accountant, Community College Diploma (Accounting, Administration, Human Resources, Secretarial, Social Work/DSW, Dietitian/Nutrition, Health/Home Care Aide, Laboratory Technician, Nursing RN, Radiology Technician, Ultra-Sound Technician). Graduates would occupy Social Worker, Psychologist, RN, RPN, Physiotherapist, Medical Radiation Technician, Laboratory Technician, and Accounting positions. Good written and verbal communication skills, computer literacy, team player, strong interpersonal and leadership skills, and previous work experience are all listed as desirable non-academic qualifications. Company benefits are rated as excellent. The potential for advancement is listed as being good. The average annual starting salary falls within the $20,000 to $25,000 range. The most suitable method for initial contact by those seeking employment is to mail a resume with a covering letter. The Swift Current Health District does hire summer students. *Contacts:* Cheryl James, Manager of Human Resources or Katy Wasiak, Communications.

SYNERVISION DIGITAL PRODUCTIONS
47 Clarence Street, Suite 200
Ottawa, ON K1N 9K1

Tel.	613-562-0464
Fax	613-562-0116
Email	hr@synervisiondpi.com
Website	www.synervisiondpi.com/main.html

Synervision Digital Productions is a leading developer of learning and performance improvement and measurement technology. Synervision products are delivered across server based intranet and internet environments. Traditional CD-ROM and satellite technology is also available. The company's work is entirely focused on training and corporate performance improvement. Synervision is an innovator in their field, working to exceed customer expectations in the areas of human resources development, strategic planning, learning systems design, instructional design, programming integrity, graphic design, and learning measurement. The company directly serves three main vertical markets: financial services, telecommunications, and transportation, as well as using indirect channels to serve other vertical markets. Synervision employs a total of 52 people worldwide. Graduates most likely to be hired come from the following academic areas: Bachelor of Science (Computer Science), Bachelor of Engineering (Computer Systems), Bachelor of Education (Adult), Bachelor of Commerce/Business Administration (Accounting, Finance, Human Resources, Information Systems, Marketing, Public Administration), Chartered Accountant, Certified Management Accountant, Master of Business Administration (General, Accounting, Finance, Human Resources, Marketing), Masters (Educational Technology), and Community College Diploma (Accounting, Administration, Advertising, Business, Communications/Public Relations, Human Resources, Information Systems, Marketing/Sales, Graphics Arts/Design, Computer Science). Graduates would occupy Instructional Designer, Programmer, Learning Consultant (Sales), Senior Software Engineer, Software Applications Engineer, Product Manager, Marketing, Graphic Designer, Accounting Clerk, Client Services, and Office Administrator positions. Team player, motivated, previous experience in the educational technology area, and experience in Synervision's vertical markets are all listed as desirable non-academic qualifications. The most suitable methods for initial contact by those seeking employment are to mail or e-mail a resume with a covering letter, or by applying through the company's website at www.synervisiondpi.com/main.html. Synervision does hire co-op work term students. *Contacts:* Peter McKercher, Vice President, Operations or Human Resources Department.

SYSTEMATIX (EDMONTON)
10405 Jasper Avenue, Suite 120
Edmonton, AB T5J 3N4

Tel.	403-421-7767
Fax	403-428-1775
Email	sciedm@systematix.com
Website	www.systematix.com

Systematix is a leading information technology consulting firm, currently working with over 500 IT consultants across Canada. There are 50 employees and consultants at this location. Systematix enjoys a good reputation with both consultants and clients. Graduates most likely to be hired at the Edmonton location come from the following academic areas: Bachelor of Science (Computer Science), Bachelor of Commerce/Business Administration (Information Systems), Master of Business Administration (Information Systems), and Community College Diploma (Computer Science). In addition, Systematix typically requires consultants who have solid technical skills, and experience in mainframe, mini or PC environments. These graduates would occupy Programmer, Analyst, Project Leader, Network Analyst, and Network Support positions. The most suitable methods for initial contact by those seeking employment are to mail, fax or e-mail a resume with a covering letter, or by applying through the company's website at www.systematix.com. *Contact:* Janice Fernie, Manager, Consultant Resourcing.

SYSTEMATIX (TORONTO)
320 Front Street West, Suite 830
Toronto, ON M5V 3B6

Tel.	416-595-5331
Fax	416-595-1525
Email	scitor@systematix.com
Website	www.systematix.com

Systematix is a leading information technology consulting firm, currently working with over 500 IT consultants across Canada. There are 30 employees and consultants at this location. Systematix enjoys a good reputation with both consultants and clients. Graduates most likely to be hired at the Toronto location come from the following academic areas: Bachelor of Science (Computer Science), Bachelor of Commerce/Business Administration (Information Systems), Master of Business Administration (Information Systems), and Community College Diploma (Computer Science). In addition, Systematix typically requires consultants who have solid technical skills, and experience in mainframe, mini, or PC environments. These graduates would occupy Programmer, Analyst, Project Leader, Network Analyst, and Network Support positions. The most suitable method for initial contact by those seeking employment is to mail a resume with a covering letter. *Contacts:* Norbert Rozko, Lisette Silva or Jeannette Kalkounis.

TALISMAN ENERGY INC.
855 - 2nd Street SW, Suite 2400
Calgary, AB T2P 4J9

Tel.	403-237-1234
Fax	403-237-1601
Email	tlm@Talisman-energy.com
Website	www.Talisman-energy.com

Talisman Energy Inc. is a senior oil and gas company active both domestically and internationally. The company's head office is located in Calgary, Alberta. Talisman employs 650 people in Canada and a total of 950 people worldwide. Graduates most likely to be hired come from the following academic areas: Bachelor of Arts (Economics), Bachelor of Science (Geology), Bachelor of Engineering (Chemical, Civil, Mechanical, Environmental/Resources, Geological Engineering), Bachelor of Laws, Bachelor of Commerce/Business Administration (General,

Accounting, Finance, Human Resources), Chartered Accountant, Certified Management Accountant, Certified General Accountant, Master of Business Administration (Finance), Master of Science (Geology), and Community College Diploma (Accounting, Secretarial, Automotive Mechanic, Engineering Technician). Effective communication skills, team player, good organization skills, and independence are all listed as desirable non-academic qualifications. Company benefits are rated above average. The potential for advancement is listed as excellent. The most suitable methods for initial contact by those seeking employment are to mail or fax a resume with a covering letter. Talisman Energy Inc. does hire summer and co-op work term students. *Contact:* Mary Meenagh, Human Resources Advisor.

TANDEM INTERNATIONAL INC.
3625 Dufferin Street, Suite 300
Downsview, ON M3K 1Z2

Tel.	416-630-8971
Fax	416-630-9211
Email	wrightre@tandemconsult.com

Tandem International Inc. is a management consulting firm, active in sales and marketing consulting. The company employs a total of 35 people. Graduates most likely to be hired come from the following academic areas: Bachelor of Commerce/Business Administration (General, Accounting, Information Systems), and Master of Business Administration (General, Marketing). Graduates would occupy Project Analyst positions. Computer skills (Microsoft Word and Excel), self-starter, smart, and relevant summer work experience are all listed as desirable non-academic qualifications. Company benefits and the potential for advancement are both rated as excellent. The average annual starting salary falls within the $30,000 to $40,000 range. The most suitable method for initial contact by those seeking employment is to mail a resume with a covering letter. *Contact:* Robert E. Wright, Vice-President, Finance and Administration.

TAXPREP INFORMATION SYSTEMS
2700 Matheson Boulevard East
8th Floor, West Tower
Mississauga, ON L4W 4V9

Tel.	905-624-2060
Fax	905-602-0239

Taxprep Information Systems is involved in the development and sales of tax software and related products for the accounting and bookkeeping profession. Taxprep is the largest distributor of such software. As part of the Softkey Group of Companies, Taxprep has the most complete variety of tax software and services in Canada. There are approximately 75 employees at this location, a total of 130 across Canada, and 500 worldwide. Graduates most likely to be hired come from the following academic areas: Bachelor of Science (Computer Science), Bachelor of Commerce/Business Administration (Marketing), Master of Business Administration (Marketing),

Community College Diploma (Administration, Marketing/Sales, Secretarial, Computer Science), and High School Diploma. Graduates would occupy Sales and Marketing, Sales and Service, Customer Support, and Administration positions. A willingness to contribute, positive attitude, good written and oral communication skills, and a neat and professional appearance are all listed as desirable non-academic qualifications. Company benefits are rated above average. The potential for advancement is listed as being good. The average annual starting salary falls within the $20,000 to $45,000 plus range, depending upon the position being considered. The most suitable method for initial contact by those seeking employment is to mail a resume with a covering letter. Taxprep Information Systems does hire co-op work term students for quality assurance and support positions throughout the year. *Contact:* Domenic Sicilia, President.

TECHNILAB INC.
17800 Lapointe
Mirabel, QC J7J 1P3

Tel. 514-433-7673
Fax 514-433-7434

Technilab Inc. is involved in the fabrication and distribution of pharmaceutical products, specializing in generic drugs. There are approximately 155 employees at this location and a total of 187 employees across Canada. Graduates most likely to be hired come from the following academic areas: Bachelor of Science (General, Chemistry, Computer Science, Pharmacy), Bachelor of Engineering (Chemical, Industrial Chemistry), Bachelor of Commerce/Business Administration (Accounting, Finance, Human Resources, Information Systems, Marketing), Chartered Accountant, Certified Management Accountant, Master of Science (Chemistry), and Community College Diploma (Accounting, Secretarial, Laboratory Technician). Graduates would occupy Laboratory Technician, Programmer Analyst, Medical Representative, Analytical Development Technician, Accounting Clerk, Secretary, Regulatory Affairs Director, Quality Assurance Director/Supervisor, and Quality Assurance Technician/Inspector positions. Pharmaceutical experience is listed as a desirable non-academic qualification. Company benefits are rated as industry standard. The potential for advancement is listed as being good. The average annual starting salary falls within the $25,000 to $30,000 range. The most suitable method for initial contact by those seeking employment is to mail a resume with a covering letter. *Contact:* Human Resources Department.

TECHNOLOGY CONNECTIONS LTD.
425 - 1 Street S.W., Suite 3400
Calgary, AB T2P 3L8

Tel. 403-245-9522
Fax 403-244-0644
Email .... inquire@technologyconnections.com
Website .... www.technologyconnections.com

Technology Connections Ltd. is a Calgary based provider of information technology (IT) services. The company provides people on a contract or permanent basis, develops custom applications, project management and planning, and develops and delivers customized training to the non-technical user. Technology Connections Ltd. works in mainframe, client/server desktop, and networked environments. The company's clients range from major multinational corporations, through to small and medium sized companies. Graduates most likely to be hired come from the following academic areas: Bachelor of Science (Computer Science, Mathematics), Bachelor of Engineering (Computer Systems), Bachelor of Commerce/Business Administration (Human Resources, Information Systems, Marketing), and Community College Diploma (Information Systems). Graduates would occupy positions that would vary from entry level and include Technical Support, Application Development, Network Support, and Analyst/Programmer positions. Strong communication skills, self-motivated, positive attitude, and the ability to work well independently as well as in a team environment are all listed as desirable non-academic qualifications. Company benefits are rated as industry standard. The potential for advancement is listed as being good. The average annual starting salary falls within the $30,000 to $35,000 range. The most suitable method for initial contact by those seeking employment is to fax a resume with a covering letter. *Contacts:* Leslie P. Purkis or Human Resources.

TECK EXPLORATION LTD.
1 First Canadian Place, P.O. Box 170
Toronto, ON M5X 1G9

Tel. 416-862-7102
Fax 416-365-7747

Teck Exploration Ltd. employs many people in mining exploration activities throughout the world. Graduates most likely to be hired come from the following academic areas: Bachelor of Science (Geology), and Bachelor of Engineering (Mining). Applicants would be hired as Geologists or Mining Engineers. An interest in the outdoors, and previous work experience are both listed as desirable non-academic qualifications. Company benefits are rated as excellent. The potential for advancement is listed as being good. The most suitable method for initial contact by those seeking employment is to mail a resume with a covering letter (applicants should be able to furnish references upon request). Teck Exploration Ltd. does hire summer students on a regular basis. *Contact:* Mr. B. D. Simmons.

TEKLOGIX INC.
2100 Meadowvale Boulevard
Mississauga, ON L5N 7J9

Tel. 905-813-9900
Website .... www.teklogix.com

Teklogix Inc. employs more than 50 people in the manufacturing of Radio Frequency Data Communications Systems for warehousing and distribution facilities. Graduates most likely to be hired come from the following academic areas: Bachelor of Science (Computer Science), Bachelor of Engineering (Electrical), and Community College Diploma (Electronic Technician). Graduates would occupy Technician, Technologist, and Engineer positions. Company benefits are rated as industry standard. The potential for advancement is listed as average. The average annual starting salary falls within the $20,000 and $30,000 range. The most suitable method for initial contact by those seeking employment is to mail a resume with a covering letter. Teklogix Inc. does hire summer students as the need arises. *Contact:* Human Resources.

TEKNION FURNITURE SYSTEMS
1150 Flint Road
Downsview, ON M3J 2J5

Tel.	416-661-3370
Fax	416-661-2647
Email	jacquie.little@teknion.com
Website	www.teknion.com

Established in 1983, Teknion Furniture Systems is an award-winning Canadian designer, manufacturer and marketer of leading edge furniture systems, serving an international client base. The company helps customers create workspaces that advance their strategic intent. As a customer-centered organization, Teknion works with architects, interior designers, and facilities managers to develop valuable customer driven solutions. The company's superior products have won recognition around the world for innovation and excellence. Teknion's international capabilities include a worldwide network of dealers and service providers that can help its customers define their needs, specify the products and create a work setting that will advance their business goals. Teknion products unite simplicity with layered performance. They are designed to provide solutions for a business environment transformed by technology and new work styles. Teknion products easily accommodate the changing needs of the user, the team, or the organization. The company has three manufacturing facilities in the Toronto area, and sales offices in the United States and overseas. There are 1,134 employees at this location and a total of 1,160 in Canada. Teknion is ISO 9001 registered and was named one of the 50 Best Managed Private Companies in Canada for three years. Teknion recently went public (July 1998) and is part of the Global Group of Companies. Graduates most likely to be hired come from the following academic areas: Bachelor of Engineering (General, Mechanical, Automation/Robotics, Industrial Design, Industrial Engineering, Indus-

trial Production/Manufacturing), Bachelor of Commerce/Business Administration (Accounting, Finance, Human Resources, Information Systems, Marketing), Certified General Accountant, and Community College Diploma (Accounting, Human Resources, Information Systems, Marketing/Sales, Graphic Arts, CAD/CAM/Autocad). Graduates would occupy Manufacturing Engineer, Production Supervisor, MRP Purchaser, CSR, Design Engineer, Industrial Engineer, Technical Support Specialist, Financial Analyst, Administrative Assistant, Accounts Receivable/Payable Clerk, Marketing Coordinator, and Industrial Designer positions. Team player, good interpersonal and organizational skills, ability to multitask, and computer literacy are all listed as desirable non-academic qualifications. Company benefits are rated as industry standard. The potential for advancement is listed as excellent. The average annual starting salary varies with the position being considered. The most suitable method for initial contact by those seeking employment is to fax a resume with a covering letter. Teknion Furniture Systems does hire summer and co-op work term students. *Contacts:* Jacquie Little, Manager, Employee Relations or Jayne Canning, Recruitment Specialist.

TELÉBEC LTÉE
7151, rue Jean Talon est
Montreal, QC H1M 3N8

Tel.	514-493-5394
Fax	514-493-5352
Email	spotente@telebec.qc.ca
Website	www.telebec.qc.ca

Telébec Ltée is a telecommunications company operating wholly in the province of Quebec. Telébec Ltée is a subsidiary of BCE Inc. There are approximately 250 employees at this location, and a total of 960 employees in the province of Quebec. Graduates most likely to be hired come from the following academic areas: Bachelor of Arts (Journalism), Bachelor of Science (Computer Science, Mathematics), Bachelor of Engineering (Telecommunications, Electrical, Computer Systems), Bachelor of Commerce/Business Administration (Finance, Information Systems, Marketing), Chartered Accountant, and Master of Business Administration (Marketing). Graduates would occupy Programmer, Analyst, Marketing Analyst, Marketing Manager, and a variety of positions in the Engineering Department. Team work, entrepreneurship, action-oriented, fast learner, excellent communication and interpersonal skills, innovative, and experience in pertinent field are all listed as desirable non-academic qualifications. Fluency in French is required. Company benefits are rated above average. The potential for advancement is listed as being good. The average annual starting salary falls within the $30,000 to $40,000 range for recent graduates. Those with related work experience can expect a higher starting salary. The most suitable methods for initial contact by those seeking employment are to mail, fax or e-mail a resume with a covering letter. Telébec Ltée does hire summer and co-op work term students. *Contact:* Sandra Potente, Manager, Human Resources.

TELEGLOBE CANADA INC.
1000, rue de la Gauchetière ouest
Montreal, QC H3B 4X5

Tel.	514-868-7272
Fax	514-868-8179
Website	www.teleglobe.ca

Teleglobe is a global North American-based overseas carrier whose capabilities can be accessed in virtually all countries. Teleglobe develops and provides overseas telecommunications services. It meets the global connectivity needs of established and emerging carriers around the world, as well as those of cable network operators, broadcasters and other large telecommunications services users, and is expanding to service select consumer markets. In key markets, the corporation establishes its presence through its own gateways. There are 700 employees at this location, a total of 850 in Canada, and 1,100 employees worldwide. Graduates most likely to be hired come from the following academic areas: Bachelor of Arts (Economics), Bachelor/Master of Science (Computer Science), Bachelor of Engineering (Electrical, Computer Systems, Telecommunications), Bachelor of Laws, Bachelor of Commerce/Business Administration (Accounting, Finance, Human Resources, Information Systems, Marketing), Chartered Accountant, Certified Management Accountant, Certified General Accountant, Master of Business Administration (Accounting, Finance, Information Systems, Marketing), Master of Engineering (Electrical, Telecommunications), and Community College Diploma (Accounting, Administration, Business, Secretarial, Computer Science, Electronics Technician, Engineering Technician). Graduates would occupy professional positions such as Engineer, Accountant, Account Manager, Product Manager, IT Specialist, management positions such as Associate Director, Director, and Technician and specialized Clerk positions. Team player, innovative, an ability to work in a changing environment, dynamic, and bilingual are all listed as desirable non-academic qualifications. Company benefits are rated as excellent. The potential for advancement is listed as being good. The average annual starting salary falls within the $30,000 to $35,000 range. The most suitable methods for initial contact by those seeking employment are to mail or fax a resume with a covering letter, or via telephone. Teleglobe does hire summer and co-op work term students. *Contacts:* Carole Rhéaume, Senior Advisor, Human Resources or Danielle Monette, Senior Advisor, Human Resources.

TELEPHONE COMMUNICATORS CANADA LIMITED
60 Bloor Street West
Suite 209
Toronto, ON M4W 3B8

Tel.	416-961-1155
Fax	416-961-7147

Telephone Communicators Canada Limited is a marketing service bureau employing more than 100 people. The company plays the role of liaison between the client and the client's customers. Post-secondary education is not a prerequisite for employment application. A strong command of the English and/or French languages, sales aptitude, sense of humour, good telephone manner, and a customer service orientation are all listed as desirable non-academic qualifications. Applicants would occupy Telemarketer, Customer Service Representative, Account Manager, Supervisor, and Assistant Supervisor positions. Company benefits are rated as industry standard. The potential for advancement is listed as excellent. The average annual starting salary falls within the $20,000 to $28,000 range, and may be commission based depending upon the specific client. The most suitable methods for initial contact by those seeking employment are to mail a resume with a covering letter, or via telephone. Telephone Communicators Canada Limited does hire summer students. *Contact:* Human Resources.

TELESAT CANADA
1601 Telesat Court
Gloucester, ON K1B 5P4

Tel.	613-748-0123
Fax	613-748-8865
Email	info@telesat.ca
Website	www.telesat.ca

Telesat is a world leader in satellite communications and systems management. Created in 1969, the Company made history with the launch of Anik A1 in 1972 - the world's first commercial domestic communications satellite placed in geostationary orbit. Currently regulated by the Canadian Radio-television Telecommunications Commission, the Company's satellites carry television and radio broadcasting, voice and data communication networks. Poised to start offering its telecommunications and broadcast services internationally, Telesat is now finalizing plans for its next generation of fixed Service Satellites, and is investigating how best to provide interactive multimedia services to customers in Canada and beyond. This location is Telesat's headquarters, where the majority of its 500 employees are located. The remainder are located in sales offices and satellite communications centres across Canada, with several teams of employees on international assignment around the world. Graduates most likely to be hired come from the following academic areas: Bachelor of Science (Computer Science, Mathematics), Bachelor of Engineering (Electrical, Telecommunications, Aerospace), Master of Engineering (Electrical), and Community College Diploma (Electronics Technician, Engineering Technician). Graduates would occupy Engineer, Systems Engineer, Scientific Programmer, Programmer Analyst, and Technologist positions. Good communication skills, flexible and team player are listed as desirable non-academic qualifications. Company benefits are rated above average. The potential for advancement is listed as average. The average annual starting salary falls within the $35,001 to $40,000 range, depending upon the position being considered. The most suitable method for initial contact by those seeking employment is to mail a resume with a covering letter.

Telesat Canada does hire summer and co-op work term students. *Contact:* Staffing and Relocation Officer.

TELLABS CANADA
2433 Meadowvale Boulevard
Mississauga, ON L5N 5S2

Tel. 905-858-2058
Fax 905-858-0418

Tellabs Canada is involved in the research and development, marketing, sales and service of telecommunication products. There are 50 employees at this location, a total of 70 employees across Canada, and approximately 2,800 employees worldwide. Graduates most likely to be hired come from the following academic areas: Bachelor of Arts (General), Bachelor of Science (Computer Science), Bachelor of Engineering (General, Electrical), Bachelor of Commerce/Business Administration (Accounting, Finance, Marketing), Chartered Accountant (Finance), Certified Management Accountant (Finance), Certified General Accountant (Finance), Master of Business Administration (Accounting, Finance, Marketing, Management), Master of Science (Computer Science), Master of Engineering (Electrical, Technical), and Community College Diploma (Accounting, Administration, Marketing/Sales, Purchasing/Logistics, Secretarial, Human Resources, Computer Science, Electronics Technician, Engineering Technician). Graduates would occupy Intermediate Software Designer, Technical, Engineering and Business/Sales related positions. Applicants should be motivated and maintain a positive attitude. Company benefits are rated as excellent. The potential for advancement is listed as being good. The average annual starting salary falls within the $35,000 to $40,000 range. The most suitable method for initial contact by those seeking employment is to mail a resume with a covering letter. Tellabs Canada occasionally requires temporary assistance that is clerical or warehouse related. *Contact:* Human Resources Supervisor.

TEMBEC INC.
Case Postale 3000
Témiscaming, QC J0Z 3R0

Tel. 819-627-4323
Fax 819-627-3946

Tembec Inc. is a Canadian forest products company operating primarily in wood products and market pulp. Tembec has grown from its original mill in Témiscaming, Quebec to an integrated forest products company with over 2,000 employees. The company's operations remain centered in Témiscaming with additional facilities in the Northwestern and Gaspé regions of Quebec, Northeastern Ontario and in Boston, Massachusetts. Tembec's products are sold worldwide and include softwood and hardwood lumber, market sulfite pulp, high-yield chlorine-free Temcell pulp and lignin-derived co-products. Graduates most likely to be hired come from the following academic areas: Bachelor of Science (Chemistry, Microbiology), Bachelor of Engineering (Chemical, Environmental, Industrial, Mechanical), Chartered Accountant, Certified General Accountant, Master of Science (Pulp and Paper), Master of Engineering (Pulp and Paper), Community College Diploma (Electronics Technician, Pulp and Paper), and High School Diploma. Graduates would occupy Junior Engineer, Accountant, and Labourer positions. Company benefits are rated above average. The potential for advancement is listed as excellent. The average annual starting salary falls within the $25,000 to $30,000 range. The most suitable method for initial contact by those seeking employment is to mail a resume with a covering letter. Tembec Inc. does hire summer students. *Contacts:* Yves Ouellet, Personnel Manager or Denis Lacourse, Personnel Supervisor.

TENNECO AUTOMOTIVE
1400 - 17th Street East, P.O. Box 800
Owen Sound, ON N4K 5Z9

Tel. 519-376-9650
Fax 519-376-9656

Tenneco Automotive employs 300 people in manufacturing automobile parts. Graduates most likely to be hired come from the following academic areas: Bachelor of Science (Computer Science, Environmental, Metallurgy), Bachelor of Engineering (Automation/Robotics, Mechanical, Industrial Design, Industrial Production), Bachelor of Commerce/Business Administration (General, Accounting, Finance, Human Resources, Information Systems, Marketing, Public Administration), Certified Management Accountant, Community College Diploma (Accounting, Administration, Business, Communications, Human Resources, Marketing/Sales, Secretarial, Journalism, CAD/CAM/Autocad), and High School Diploma. Company benefits and the potential for advancement are both rated as excellent. The average annual starting salary falls within the $20,000 to $25,000 range, and is subject strictly to each applicant's qualifications. The most suitable method for initial contact by those seeking employment is to mail a resume with a covering letter (no phone calls please). Tenneco Automotive does hire summer students. *Contact:* Evan Ewasko, Manager, Human Resources.

TETRA PAK
10 Allstate Parkway, 2nd Floor
Markham, ON L3R 5P8

Tel. 905-305-9777

Tetra Pak manufactures and supplies packaging systems and materials to the food and dairy industry. The company employs 220 people at this location, 300 people across Canada, and a total of 33,000 people worldwide. Graduates most likely to be hired come from the following academic areas: Bachelor of Arts (Economics), Bachelor of Science (Biology, Chemistry), Bachelor of Engineering (Pulp and Paper, Electrical, Automation/Robotics, Mechanical, Industrial Production), Bachelor of Commerce/Business Administration (Accounting, Finance, Human Resources, Marketing), Chartered Accountant, Certified Management Accountant, Certified General Accountant, Master of Business Administration (Accountant, Finance, Marketing), and Community College Diploma (Accounting, Business, Communications, Human Resources, Marketing/Sales, Electronics Technician, Millwright). Graduates would occupy Technician, Supervisor, Management, Development, Sales Representative, Sales Manager, Accountant, and Controller positions. Flexible, comfortable in a fast paced environment, adaptable to change, team player, and good decision making abilities are all listed as desirable non-academic qualifications. The most suitable method for initial contact by those seeking employment is to mail a resume with a covering letter. Tetra Pak does hire summer students. *Contact:* Human Resources Department.

THE PAS HEALTH COMPLEX INC.
P.O. Box 240
The Pas, MB R9A 1K4

Tel.	204-623-9240
Fax	204-623-5372

The Pas Health Complex Inc. is a regional health complex consisting of an acute care hospital, personal care home, and addiction rehabilitation centre. There are approximately 350 employees. Graduates most likely to be hired come from the following academic areas: Bachelor of Science (Nursing, Physical Therapy), Medical Doctor, and Community College Diploma (Dietician/Nutrition, Laboratory Technician, Nursing RN/RNA, Radiology Technician, Ultra-Sound Technician). Graduates would occupy Nurse, Health Care Aide, Dietary Aide, Laboratory Technician, Radiology Technician, etc. positions. Employee benefits are rated above average. The potential for advancement is listed as being good. The average annual starting salary falls within the $30,000 to $35,000 range. The most suitable method for initial contact by those seeking employment is to mail a resume with a covering letter. *Contact:* Personnel Department.

THG WORLDWIDE
20 Toronto Street, 10th Floor
Toronto, ON M5C 2B8

Tel.	416-955-0375
Fax	416-955-0380
Website	www.thgworldwide.com

THG Worldwide is a global provider of business services including corporate hospitality at major sporting events, conferences and training courses, world congresses and management forums, business reports and contract publishing. THG Worldwide employs 1,000 people in offices located in 16 countries around the world. Graduates most likely to be hired come from the following academic areas: Bachelor of Arts (General), Bachelor of Commerce/Business Administration (General, Marketing), and Community College Diploma (Administration, advertising, Business, Marketing/Sales, Hospitality). These graduates

should have an understanding of business and a strong desire to establish a successful sales career. In addition, good listening, presentation and selling skills, self-motivated, positive, organized, proactive, and ambitious are all listed as desirable non-academic qualifications. A business degree is advantageous. Graduates hired would learn selling methods, and upon establishing a track record of sales would be appointed to Sales Management positions domestically or internationally. Company benefits are rated as industry standard. The potential for advancement is listed as excellent. The average annual starting salary falls within the $35,000 to $40,000 range, and is salary and commission based. The most suitable method for initial contact by those seeking employment is to fax a resume with a covering letter. For further information, visit THG's website at www.thgworldwide.com. *Contact:* Melinda Mackey.

THINK SOFTWARE LTD.
180 Elgin Street, Suite 801
Ottawa, ON K2P 2K3

Tel.	613-237-3336
Fax	613-237-9693
Email	nshaw@think.ca
Website	www.think.ca

THINK Software Ltd. is a recognized leader and innovator in computer consulting practices in the Ottawa-area. As a Microsoft Solution Provider, THINK Software specializes in Access, Visual Basic and SQL Server. THINK Software designs and creates custom database software solutions which help its customers use information to gain competitive advantage. Established in 1994 by Nigel Shaw, THINK Software (formerly ICON Information Consultants) has established a reputation for being a leader in client-server consulting and development. The company's head office is in Ottawa, with a branch office in Vancouver. THINK presently has 17 full-time employees. The company's leading-edge application development creates a tremendous career opportunity for resourceful individuals with strong business and technical backgrounds. Graduates most likely to be hired come from the following academic areas: Bachelor of Science (Computer Science), Bachelor of Engineering (Computer Systems), and Community College Diploma (Information Systems). Graduates would occupy Systems Analyst, Programmers (Software), and Project Manager positions. Applicants should enjoy working in a fast-paced environment emphasizing achievement, creativity, resourcefulness, customer satisfaction, professionalism and personal respect for business partners. In addition, past work experience, dedication, vision, and initiative are all listed as desirable non-academic qualifications. Company benefits are rated above average, with a full benefit plan provided to employees, and a share option plan provided after one year's employment. The potential for advancement is listed as excellent. The average annual starting salary falls within the $45,000 to $50,000 range. The most suitable method for initial contact by those seeking employment is to e-mail a resume with a covering letter. THINK Software Ltd. does hire co-op work term students, and is an equal opportunity employer that values diversity. *Contact:* Leah Murray, Director, Business Development.

THOMAS COOK GROUP (CANADA) LIMITED
100 Yonge Street, Scotia Plaza, 14th Floor
Toronto, ON M5C 2W1

Tel. 416-359-3700

Thomas Cook Group (Canada) Limited employs more than 500 people in the provision of retail travel services, retail travellers cheques, and retail/wholesale of foreign currency and precious metals. Graduates most likely to be hired come from the following academic areas, Bachelor of Arts, Bachelor of Commerce/Business Administration, Chartered Accountant, Certified Management Accountant, Master of Business Administration, and Community College Diploma (General/Related). Graduates would occupy Clerical, Supervisory, Junior Management and some Professional positions. Company benefits are rated above average. The potential for advancement is listed as being good. The average annual starting salary falls within the $15,000 to $20,000 range. The most suitable method for initial contact by graduates seeking employment is to mail a resume with a covering letter. Thomas Cook Group (Canada) Limited does hire summer students. *Contact:* Human Resources.

THOMPSON'S TRANSFER COMPANY LIMITED
P.O. Box 670
Middleton, NS B0S 1P0

Tel. 902-825-3929

Thompson's Transfer Company Limited is a freight haulage trucking company and moving company. Graduates most likely to be hired come from the following academic areas: Bachelor of Arts (English), Bachelor of Science (Computer Science, Mathematics), Bachelor of Engineering (Computer Systems, Mechanical), Bachelor of Commerce/Business Administration (Accounting, Finance), Master of Business Administration (General, Accounting, Finance, Human Resources, Information Systems, Marketing, Public Administration), Community College Diploma (Accounting, Administration, Advertising, Business, Auto Mechanic, Computer Science), and High School Diploma. Graduates would occupy Accounting, Clerical, Mechanic, and Truck Driver positions. Previous work experience (two years), computer skills, friendly, an ability to get along with others, motivated, and an ability to work without guidance are all listed as desirable non-academic qualifications. Company benefits are rated as industry standard. The potential for advancement is listed as being good. The average annual starting salary falls in the $15,000 plus range. The most suitable method for initial contact by those seeking employment is to mail a resume with a covering letter. Thompson's Transfer Company Limited hires summer students for moving company activities. *Contacts:* David Boran, Director of Safety and Personnel or Darlene Marshall, Receptionist.

THUNDER CREEK SCHOOL DIVISION
P.O. Box 730
Moose Jaw, SK S6H 4P4

Tel. 306-694-2121
Fax 306-694-4955

Thunder Creek School Division operates elementary and secondary schools in the Moose Jaw area. Graduates most likely to be hired come from the following academic areas: Bachelor of Education (General, Early Childhood ECE, Primary Junior, Junior Intermediate, Intermediate Senior, Special Needs), Bachelor of Commerce/Business Administration (General, Accounting, Finance), and Community College Diploma (Accounting, Administration, Business, Communications, Secretarial, Auto Mechanic). The most suitable method for initial contact by those seeking employment is to mail a resume with a covering letter. *Contact:* Human Resources.

TIP TOP TAILORS
637 Lakeshore Boulevard West
Toronto, ON M5V 1A8

Tel. 416-586-7173

Tip Top Tailors operates menswear clothing retail specialty stores across Canada, with the head office located in Toronto. The company employs approximately 2,500 people in Canada. Graduates most likely to be hired come from the following academic areas: Bachelor of Arts (English, History, Journalism, Sociology/Social Work), Bachelor of Science (Computer Science, Mathematics), Bachelor of Education (Adult), Bachelor of Commerce/Business Administration (Accounting, Finance, Human Resources, Information Systems, Marketing, Public Administration), Master of Business Administration (Accounting, Finance, Human Resources, Marketing), and Community College Diploma (Business, Communications, Facility Management, Financial Planning, Human Resources, Marketing/Sales). Graduates would occupy Clerk, Supervisory, Store Management, Department Management, and Analyst positions. Team player, service driven, results oriented, and a high energy level are all listed as desirable non-academic qualifications. Company benefits are rated above average. The potential for advancement is listed as being good. The average annual starting salary falls within the $15,000 to $20,000 range. The most suitable method for initial contact by those seeking employment is to mail a resume with a covering letter. Tip Top Tailors occasionally hires summer students. *Contacts:* Pat Hopkins, Personnel Administrator or Barb McDowell, Human Resources Area Partner.

TNL CONSTRUCTION LTD., INDUSTRIAL CONTRACTORS
7580 River Road
Suite 110
Richmond, BC V6X 1X6

Tel. 604-278-7424
Fax 604-278-7107

TNL Construction Ltd. is a heavy industrial construction firm. There are 15 employees at this location and a total of 600 employees across Canada. Graduates most likely to be hired come from the following academic areas: Bachelor of Engineering (Civil, Mechanical, Welding, Mining), Community College Diploma (Accounting, Purchasing/Logistics, Auto Mechanic, CAD/CAM/Autocad, Welding, Trades - Rigging, Millwright etc.), and High School Diploma. Graduates would occupy Project Engineer, Quality Control Field Engineer, and Site Administrator positions. Mechanical aptitude, self-starter, independent thinking, and previous work experience are all listed as desirable non-academic qualifications. Company benefits are rated as excellent. The potential for advancement is listed as being good. The average annual starting salary falls within the $35,000 to $40,000 range. The most suitable method for initial contact by those seeking employment is to mail a resume with a covering letter. TNL Construction Ltd. does hire summer students. *Contact:* Human Resources.

TNT CANADA
P.O. Box 3030, Station A
Mississauga, ON L5A 3S3

Tel. 905-625-7500
Fax 905-625-8567

TNT Canada Inc. is a large transportation company employing more than 2,500 people in the provision of provincial and inter-provincial trucking services. Terminals and Maintenance Centres are located throughout Canada and the United States. Graduates most likely to be hired come from the following academic areas: Bachelor of Arts, Bachelor of Science, Bachelor of Commerce/Business Administration, Chartered Accountant, Certified Management Accountant, and Community College Diploma (Transportation, Computer Science, Auto Mechanic, Secretarial). Graduates would occupy Clerk/Biller, Secretary, Dockworker, Driver, Dispatcher, and Management positions. A sincere and intelligent interest in their work, responsible, mature, and a willingness to learn are all listed as desirable non-academic qualifications. Company benefits are rated above average. The potential for advancement is listed as being good. The average annual starting salary falls within the $15,000 to $20,000 range. The most suitable method for initial contact by those seeking employment is to mail a resume with a covering letter. TNT Canada Inc. does hire summer students, usually for clerical or dockwork positions. *Contact:* Ms. Jancic, Human Resource Manager.

TOON BOOM TECHNOLOGIES
7 Laurier Street East
Montreal, QC H2T 1E4

Tel. 514-278-8666
Fax 514-278-2666

Toon Boom Technologies develops 2D animation software for the animation industry. There are 35 employees at this location and a total of 38 employees in the Company. Graduates most likely to be hired come from the following academic areas: Bachelor of Science (Computer Science), and Bachelor of Commerce/Business Administration (General, Marketing). Graduates would occupy Software Developer and Sales positions. Team player, good communication skills, hardworking, and initiative are all listed as desirable non-academic qualifications. Company benefits are rated above average. The potential for advancement is listed as being good. The most suitable method for initial contact by those seeking employment is to mail a resume with a covering letter. *Contact:* Natacha Renard, Administrative Assistant.

TOROMONT LIMITED
3131 Highway #7 West, P.O. Box 20011
Concord, ON L4K 4T1

Tel. 416-667-5511
Fax 416-667-5725

Toromont Limited is a heavy equipment dealership employing approximately 650 people. Activities at this location involve sales, service, and parts supply. Graduates most likely to be hired come from the following academic areas: Bachelor of Engineering (Electrical, Mechanical, Metallurgy, Mining), Chartered Accountant (Finance), Certified Management Accountant (Finance), Certified General Accountant, Master of Business Administration (Accounting, Marketing). Graduates are hired to occupy specific salaried positions. A high energy level, outgoing personality, and good interpersonal and communication skills are all listed as desirable non-academic qualifications. Company benefits are rated above average. The potential for advancement is listed as being good. The average annual starting salary falls within the $25,000 to $40,000 plus range, depending upon the position being considered, and is commission based for sales positions. The most suitable method for initial contact by those seeking employment is to mail a resume with a covering letter. Toromont Limited does hire summer students. *Contact:* Bob Sleva, Director, Human Resources.

TORONTO AMBULANCE
4330 Dufferin Street
Toronto, ON M3H 5R9

Tel. 416-392-2000
Fax 416-392-2039

Toronto Ambulance is a government run Municipal Ambulance Service employing more than 500 people. The Service serves in excess of 2.4 million people in the Toronto area, and is the largest municipal Emergency Medical Service (EMS) in Canada. Toronto Ambulance is the sole licensee providing ambulance services within the new city of Toronto, and provides 24-hour pre-hospital emergency and non-emergency care and transportation to and between hospitals for individuals experiencing injury or illness. Graduates most likely to be hired come from Community College Diploma programs in Ambulance and Emergency Care. Graduates are hired to occupy Ambulance Officer, and Ambulance Dispatcher positions. Opportunities are also available for Clerical support, and Maintenance staff. Employee benefits are rated above average. The potential for advancement is listed as being good. The average annual starting salary falls within the $35,000 to $40,000 range. The most suitable methods for initial contact by those seeking employment are to mail or fax a resume with a covering letter to City of Toronto, Corporate and Human Resources at 55 St John Street, Toronto, Ontario, M5V 3C6 (Fax 416-397-9818). Toronto Ambulance is part of the new City of Toronto Works and Emergency Services Department. *Contact:* Corporate and Human Resources.

TORONTO ASSOCIATION FOR COMMUNITY LIVING

20 Spadina Road
Toronto, ON M5R 2S7

Tel. 416-968-0650
Fax 416-968-6463

The Toronto Association for Community Living provides residential, vocational and other support services for persons with a developmental disability and their families. The Association employs approximately 1,000 people. Graduates most likely to be hired come from the following academic areas: Bachelor of Arts (Social Work, Sociology, Social Services, Psychology), Bachelor of Education (Early Childhood Education, Special Needs), Master of Arts (Social Work, Psychology) and Community College Diploma (Social Work). Graduates would occupy Residential Counsellor, Instructor, Vocational Counsellor, Resource Teacher, and Consultant positions. Previous work experience, and a positive, caring attitude towards persons with developmental disabilities are listed as desirable non-academic qualifications. Company benefits are rated above average. The potential for advancement is listed as being good. The average annual starting salary falls within the $25,000 to $30,000 range. The most suitable method for initial contact by those seeking employment is to mail a resume with a covering letter. The Toronto Association for Community Living does hire summer students for the Shadow Lake Camp. *Contact:* Human Resources.

TORONTO COLONY HOTEL, THE

89 Chestnut Street
Toronto, ON M5G 1R1

Tel. 416-977-0707
Fax 416-585-3164

The Toronto Colony Hotel is a superior quality hotel located in the heart of downtown Toronto, with a total of 717 guest bedrooms. The Hotel employs a total of 364 people, and is part of a wider group that employs a total of 900 people in Canada, and 5,000 people worldwide. The Colony Hotel is located just blocks away from the City's main attractions such as The Eaton Centre, The Art Gallery of Ontario, City Hall, Skydome, and the CN Tower. The Hotel hosts a variety of services including two restaurants, indoor and outdoor pools, 25 meeting rooms, a revolving Lakeview Room that offers spectacular city views, weight room, sauna, whirlpool, as well as other services. Graduates most likely to be hired come from the following academic areas: Bachelor of Arts (General, Criminology, Psychology), Bachelor of Engineering (General, Electrical), Bachelor of Commerce/Business Administration (General, Accounting, Human Resources, Information Systems, Marketing, Public Administration), and Community College Diploma (Accounting, Administration, Advertising, Business, Communications/Public Relations, Human Resources, Information Systems, Marketing/Sales, Secretarial, Electronics Technician, Engineering Technician). Graduates would occupy the entry level positions of Lobby Attendant and Waitstaff, as well as Clerk, Sales Person, Accountant, Receiver/Purchaser, Engineer, Human Resources Manager, Reservationist, Secretarial, Door/Bell Person, Front Desk Manager, Food and Beverage Manager, Security Officer, Payroll Clerk, and Fitness Attendant positions. Outgoing, excellent people skills, professional demeanor, organized, and conscientious are all listed as desirable non-academic qualifications. Company benefits are rated as industry standard. The potential for advancement is listed as being good. The average annual starting salary falls within the $25,000 to $30,000 range. The most suitable methods for initial contact by those seeking employment are to mail or fax a resume with a covering letter. The Toronto Colony Hotel does hire summer and co-op work term students. *Contact:* Shelley Edwards, Human Resources Assistant.

TORONTO COMMUNITY AND NEIGHBOURHOOD SERVICES

55 John Street
Metro Hall, 9th Floor
Toronto, ON M5V 3C6

Tel. 416-392-8700

Toronto Community and Neighbourhood Services Department provides a variety of social and educational services for the residents in the new City of Toronto. Graduates most likely to be hired come from the following academic areas: Bachelor of Arts (Family Studies, History, Economics), Bachelor of Education (Adult/Gerontology, Early Childhood Education), Masters (Social Work), and Community College Diploma (Social Work). The majority of entry-level positions require some relevant work experience, attained through summer work, field placements or volunteer work. Also, some clerical and computer experience (eg. database, word processing) is desirable. Employee benefits are rated as excellent. The potential for advancement is listed as being good. The average annual starting salary falls within the $15,000 to $20,000 range. The most suitable method for initial contact by those seeking employment is to mail a resume with a covering letter. Toronto Community and Neighbourhood Services does hire summer students from designated programs of study. *Contact:* Staffing Coordinator.

TORONTO EAST GENERAL HOSPITAL
825 Coxwell Avenue
Toronto, ON M4C 3E7

Tel. 416-469-6300
Fax 416-469-7982

The Toronto East General Hospital is an acute care hospital with approximately 2,000 employees. Graduates most likely to be hired come from the following academic areas: Bachelor of Science (General, Nursing, Physical Therapy), Bachelor of Education, Bachelor of Commerce/Business Administration, Master of Business Administration, Masters (Health Care/Nursing Administration), and Community College Diploma (Business, Laboratory Technician, Nursing RN/RNA). Applicants should have some familiarity with or working exposure to hospital operations. Company benefits are rated above average. The potential for advancement is listed as being good. The average annual starting salary falls within the $25,000 to $30,000 range, and is dependent upon the position being considered. The most suitable method for initial contact by those seeking employment is to mail a resume with a covering letter. Contact: Alice Drody, Recruitment & Benefits Coordinator.

TORONTO FIRE SERVICES
4330 Dufferin Street
Toronto, ON M3H 5R9

Tel. 416-392-0162
Fax 416-392-0599
Email .... rbarrow@city.toronto.on.ca
Website .... old.city.toronto.on.ca/

On January 1st 1998, Toronto Fire Services was created when the six municipal fire departments of Metropolitan Toronto amalgamated, creating the largest fire service in Canada, and the fifth largest in the world. The Service employs 3,100 people. Applicants must be legally entitled to work in Canada, possess a secondary school diploma or have the equivalent combination of education and experience, understand and be able to communicate clearly in English under stressful conditions, and possess a pardon if previously convicted of a criminal offence. When applying, applicants must submit the following documents: an original and valid (conducted within 6 months of the application deadline) Occupation Specific Vision, Hearing and Fitness Assessment Certificate from York University, a copy of the current certification in Cardiopulmonary Resuscitation, Basic Rescuer Level 'C' (or approved equivalent), a copy of the current St. John Ambulance Standard First Aid (or approved equivalent), an original and valid Ontario driver's abstract (current within 30 days, showing not more than five demerit points and no unpaid fines). This standard must be maintained throughout the hiring process. At the time of the job offer, applicants must also present a valid Ontario Class 'D' licence (minimum), with a 'Z' air brake endorsement. Applicants are hired to occupy Probationary Fire Fighter positions. In addition to excellent physical fitness and strength abilities, a mechanical aptitude, ability to work shifts, and team player are listed as desirable non-academic qualifications. In the Fire Service teamwork is everything, since Fire Fighters depend on each other to successfully perform their duties. Company benefits are rated as excellent and include paid vacation, 11 designated holidays annually, sick pay, a comprehensive dental, prescription, and, supplemental hospital plan, life insurance, long-term disability insurance, uniform issue and cleaning allowance, and financial rewards for long service. The potential for advancement is also rated as excellent. The average annual starting salary falls within $40,000 to $45,000 range. Applicants are encouraged to attend one of the job orientation information sessions at the Toronto Fire Academy, 895 Eastern Avenue. Information about the sessions will be available on the recruitment hotline (416) 392-FIRE (416) 392-3473, and in community newspapers. Initial contact may also be made by mailing or faxing a resume with a covering letter. Contacts: Fire Hotline at 416-392-3473 or Ron Barrow, Recruitment Officer (895 Eastern Avenue, Toronto, ON, M4L 1A2, Phone 416-392-0163).

TORONTO HILTON
145 Richmond Street West
Toronto, ON M5H 2L2

Tel. 416-869-3456
Fax 416-860-6820

The Toronto Hilton is a major full-service hotel, located in the heart of Toronto's downtown. The Toronto Hilton employs a total of 350 people, and offers accommodation, recreation, restaurant and bar, and meeting facilities. Graduates most likely to be hired come from the following academic areas: Bachelor of Commerce/Business Administration (General, Human Resources), and Community College Diploma (Business, Human Resources, Hospitality). Graduates would occupy entry level Front Office, Guest Services Agent, Food and Beverage, and Restaurant Supervisor positions. Previous work experience and a hospitality attitude are listed as desirable non-academic qualifications. The most suitable method for initial contact by those seeking employment is to mail a resume with a covering letter. Contacts: Director, Human Resources or Assistant Director, Human Resources.

TORONTO HOSPITAL, THE
101 College Street
CW2-335
Toronto, ON M5G 2C4

Tel. 416-340-4141
Fax 416-595-5441
Email .... lkaukula@torhosp.toronto.on.ca
Website .... www.thehosp.org/index.html

The Toronto Hospital employs over 6,000 people in the provision of tertiary patient care. The hospital is also a major teaching, and medical research centre. Graduates most likely to be hired come from the following academic areas: Bachelor of Arts (General, Economics, English, Psychology, Sociology), Bachelor of Science (General, Biology, Chemistry, Computer Science, Mathematics, Dentistry, Immunology, Nursing, Nutritional Sciences, Occupational Therapy, Pharmacy, Physical Therapy, Psychology, Speech Pathology), Bachelor of Engineering (Computer Systems, Telecommunications), Bachelor of Education (General, Physical and Health), Bachelor of Commerce/Business Administration (Accounting, Finance, Human Resources, Information Systems, Marketing, Public Administration), Chartered Accountant, Certified Management Accountant, Certified General Accountant, Master of Business Administration (Human Resources), Master of Science (General, Health Sciences), Medical Doctor, Community College Diploma (Accounting, Administration, Facility Management, Human Resources, Purchasing/Logistics, Secretarial, Cooking, Journalism, Recreation Studies, Security, Television/Radio Arts, Computer Science, Health Sciences), and High School Diploma. Graduates would occupy positions relating to their specific area of study. Competent, compassionate, team player, honesty, integrity, confidentiality, and good decision making and communication skills are all listed as desirable non-academic qualifications. Employee benefits are rated above average. The potential for advancement is listed as being good. The average annual starting salary falls within the $25,000 to $30,000 range. The most suitable method for initial contact by those seeking employment is to mail a resume with a covering letter. The Toronto Hospital does hire summer students. *Contacts:* Darlene M. Tye, Manager, Employment Services and Records or Linda Kaukula, Employment Specialist.

TORONTO HUMANE SOCIETY, THE
11 River Street
Toronto, ON M5A 4C2

Tel. 416-392-2273
Fax 416-392-9978

The Toronto Humane Society employs 85 full time staff in providing animal protection services. Activities include lost and found, adoption, vaccination clinic, spay and neuter clinic, emergency rescue for injured stray animals, and education/awareness programs on issues of animal exploitation and abuse. Graduates most likely to be hired come from the following academic areas: Bachelor of Arts (General, but prefer English, Sociology, Philosophy), Bachelor of Laws (Animal Rights), Bachelor of Education, Bachelor of Commerce/Business Administration, Community College Diploma (Animal Health), and Doctor of Veterinary Medicine. Bright, hardworking, reliable and a commitment to animal protection are all listed as desirable non-academic qualifications. Employee benefits are rated as excellent. The potential for advancement is listed as being good. The average annual starting salary depends on the position being considered. The most suitable method for initial contact by graduates seeking employment is to mail a resume with a covering letter. The Toronto Humane Society does hire summer students. *Contact:* Human Resources.

TORONTO HYDRO
14 Carlton Street, 9th Floor
Toronto, ON M5B 1K5

Tel. 416-599-0400
Fax 416-591-4721

Toronto Hydro employs approximately 1,400 people in the provision of electrical services to the city of Toronto. Graduates most likely to be hired come from the following academic areas: Bachelor of Arts (Journalism), Bachelor of Science (Computer Science), Bachelor of Engineering (Architectural/Building, Electrical, Computer Systems, Telecommunications, Industrial Design), Bachelor of Architecture, Bachelor of Commerce/Business Administration (Accounting, Finance, Human Resources, Information Systems, Marketing), Certified Management Accountant, Certified General Accountant, Master of Business Administration (Accounting, Finance, Human Resources, Information Systems, Marketing), Master of Engineering, and Community College Diploma (Accounting, Administration, Business, Communications, Facility Management, Financial Planning, Human Resources, Marketing/Sales, Purchasing/Logistics, Secretarial, Journalism, Architecture, Drafting, CAD/CAM/Autocad, Computer Science, Electronics Technician, Engineering Technician/Technologist, Welding). Graduates would occupy Clerical, Administrative, Technical, and Field positions. Initiative, creativity, analytical skills, previous work experience, customer service orientation, strong verbal and written communication skills, team player, and good interpersonal skills are listed as desirable non-academic qualifications. Company benefits and the potential for advancement are both rated as excellent. Toronto Hydro does hire students for summer and co-op work terms. *Contact:* Personnel Services.

TORONTO LIFE MAGAZINE
59 Front Street East, 3rd Floor
Toronto, ON M5E 1B3

Tel. 416-364-3333
Fax 416-861-1169

Toronto Life Magazine is a monthly city magazine concerned with business stories, citizen profiles, calendar events, and other articles which directly relate to Toronto. The Magazine attempts to celebrate the city while featuring important articles that Torontonians would find relevant to their everyday lives, or may simply better inform them of the city in which they live. Toronto Life employs 50 people. Graduates most likely to be hired come from the following academic areas: Bachelor of Arts (Economics, English, History, Journalism, Political Science), Bachelor of Commerce/Business Administration (Marketing), Master of Business Administration (Marketing), Master of Arts (English, Journalism), and Community College Diploma (Graphic Arts, Journalism). Related work experience is a must. The amount of work experience required depends upon the department being considered. Graduates with the appropriate amount of work experience would occupy Copy Editor, Circulation Assistant, Sales Representative, Production Coordinator, Administrative Assistant, and Sales and Marketing Assistant positions. Other qualifications sought include the ability to work in a team environment, the desire to advance the magazine as well as oneself, a good sense of humour, and a strong belief and love for magazines and the industry. Toronto Life Magazine offers a relaxed and informal work environment and employees must feel comfortable with this style. Company benefits are rated above average. The potential for advancement is listed as average. The average annual starting salary falls within the $20,000 to $25,000 range. The most suitable method for initial contact by those seeking employment is through the Key Publishers JOBLINE. With this voice-mail service, callers will receive information on all available positions within Key Publishers, who in addition to Toronto Life publish, TL Fashion, Canadian Geographic, Where Magazines, Wedding Bells, Owl & Chickadee, among others. Toronto Life has Editorial Internships available year-round, including summer (these are not paid positions). *Contact:* For information on job openings call the JOBLINE at 416-360-0044 x330.

TORONTO MUTUAL LIFE INSURANCE CO.
112 St. Clair Avenue West
Toronto, ON M4V 2Y3

Tel. 416-960-3463
Fax 416-960-9927

Toronto Mutual Life Insurance Co. offers life, accident, and short term disability insurance products and services in most provinces within Canada. There are approximately 25 employees at this location. Graduates most likely to be hired come from the following academic areas: Bachelor of Arts (Social Sciences), and Community College Diploma (Business, Marketing). Graduates are hired for entry-level Clerk positions. Good customer service skills, successful completion of business related courses, excellent interpersonal skills, and business related work experience are all listed as desirable non-academic qualifications. Company benefits are rated as industry standard. The potential for advancement is listed as average. The average annual starting salary falls within the $15,000 to $20,000 range. The most suitable method for initial contact by those seeking employment is to mail a resume with a covering letter. Toronto Mutual Life Insurance Co. does hire summer students on a regular basis. *Contact:* Geoffrey Harrison, Vice President & Secretary.

TORONTO PRINCE HOTEL
900 York Mills Road
Toronto, ON M3B 3H2

Tel. 416-444-2511
Fax 416-444-9597

The Toronto Prince Hotel is a full-service hotel employing approximately 315 people. Graduates most likely to be hired come from the following academic areas: Master of Business Administration, Commu-

nity College Diploma (Accounting, Human Resources, Secretarial, Travel/Tourism), and High School Diploma. Graduates would occupy Accounting, Front Desk, Reservations, Human Resources and Secretarial positions. Work experience, positive attitude, personality and appearance are all listed as desirable non-academic qualifications. Company benefits are rated above average. The potential for advancement is listed as being good. The average annual starting salary ranges from $15,000 to $22,000. The most suitable method for initial contact by those seeking employment is to mail a resume with a covering letter. The Toronto Prince Hotel does hire summer students as required. *Contact:* Isobel Millar, Director of Personnel.

TORONTO PUBLIC WORKS AND THE ENVIRONMENT
100 Queen Street West, 23rd Floor, East Tower
Toronto, ON M5H 2N2

Tel. 416-392-7729
Fax 416-392-0816

The Toronto Public Works and the Environment Department employs more than 1,000 people in the following operational areas: Engineering, Planning/ Scheduling, Inspection, By-Law Enforcement, Surveying, Administration, Clerical, Technical Support, Drafting (Manual and CAD), Computer Services, and Operational activities (eg. Manual Labour, Vehicle, Equipment Operation, Plant and Shop). Graduates most likely to be hired come from the following academic areas: Bachelor of Science (Surveying), Bachelor of Engineering, Bachelor of Commerce/Business Administration (Accounting), and Community College Diploma (Related Technical Programs). Graduates would occupy Administrative, Clerical, and Technical positions. Initiative, creativity, a positive work attitude, and good interpersonal skills are all listed as desirable non-academic qualifications. Company benefits and the potential for advancement are both rated as excellent. The average annual starting salary falls within the $15,000 to $35,000 range, depending on the position being considered. In order to be considered for employment graduates must complete an employment application form at City Hall. The department does hire summer students for positions related to their academic studies. The Toronto Public Works and the Environment Department is part of the new City of Toronto Works and Emergency Services Department. *Contact:* Personnel Services Supervisor.

TORONTO STOCK EXCHANGE, THE
2 First Canadian Place
Toronto, ON M5X 1J2

Tel. 416-947-4700
Fax 416-947-4792

The Toronto Stock Exchange (TSE) is Canada's number one marketplace for the trading of equities and related investments. The second largest exchange in North America, the TSE develops innovative derivatives, indices, and information products to suit the needs of investors at home and abroad. The TSE also develops policies ranging from trading, corporate governance to telecommunications. The Exchange employs 550 people. Graduates most likely to be hired come from the following academic areas: Bachelor of Arts (Economics), Bachelor of Science (Computer Science), Bachelor of Engineering (Computer Systems), Bachelor of Laws, Bachelor of Commerce/Business Administration (General, Accounting, Finance), Chartered Accountant, Certified Management Accountant, Certified General Accountant, Master of Business Administration (General, Accounting, Finance, Human Resources, Marketing), and Community College Diploma (Accounting, Administration, Business). The most suitable method for initial contact by those seeking employment is to mail a resume with a covering letter. The Toronto Stock Exchange does hire summer students. *Contact:* Human Resources.

TORONTO TRANSIT COMMISSION (TTC)
1138 Bathurst Street
Toronto, ON M5R 3H2

Tel. 416-393-4564
Fax 416-532-6319

The Toronto Transit Commission (TTC) provides public transit services for residents of the amalgamated city of Toronto. This involves the maintenance and operation of transit equipment as well as associated services. The TTC is an equal opportunity employer, with approximately 10,700 employees in a variety of operational areas. Graduates most likely to be hired come from the following academic areas: Bachelor of Arts, Bachelor of Science (Computer Science), Bachelor of Engineering (Mechanical, Electrical, Structural, Architectural, Civil), and Community College Diploma (Business, Computer, Engineering Technician, Mechanic, Electrical Technician). Graduates would occupy Clerk, Technician, Tradesperson, Administrative Staff, Labourer, Professional, and Driver positions. Applicants should be service oriented individuals. Company benefits and the potential for advancement are both rated as excellent (90% of promotions are internal). The average annual starting salary varies widely with the position being considered. The most suitable method for initial contact by graduates seeking employment is to visit the TTC Employment Office at this address. Summer job applications should be made between September and December for the following summer. The Employment Office is open Monday through Friday, from 7:45am to 3:00pm. *Contact:* Outreach Recruiter.

TORONTO ZOO
361A Old Finch Avenue
Toronto, ON M1B 5K7

Tel. 416-392-5900
Fax 416-392-5934

The Toronto Zoo employs 250 full-time staff and over 130 seasonal staff (summer students) in zoo operations. The Toronto Zoo maintains four operational goals; recreation, education, conservation and research. Graduates most likely to be hired come from the following academic areas: Bachelor of Science (Biology, Computer Science, Zoology, Nursing, Nutritional Sciences), Bachelor of Engineering (Civil), Bachelor of Commerce/Business Administration (Accounting, Human Resources), Chartered Accountant, Master of Business Administration (Public Administration), and Community College Diploma (Accounting, Advertising, Human Resources, Information Systems, Marketing/Sales, Secretarial, Graphic Arts, Hospitality, Journalism, Security/Enforcement, Travel/Tourism, Agriculture/Horticulture, Automotive Mechanic, Carpentry, Computer Science, Electronics Technician, HVAC Systems, Plumber, Welding, Animal Health, Dietitian/Nutrition, Laboratory Technician, Nursing RN). Graduates would occupy positions in the three main operational areas: Administrative & Site Services, Biology and Conservation, and Marketing and Communications. Positions include, Computer Services, Registered Nurse, Animal Keeper, Commissary Assistant, Project Management, Financial Services, Purchasing Agent, Personnel Clerk, Human Resource Officer, Building Trades, Public Relations, and Animal Health Unit positions. Outgoing, customer service oriented, initiative, and the ability to work with minimum supervision are all listed as desirable nonacademic qualifications. Company benefits are rated as excellent. The potential for advancement is listed as being good. The most suitable method for initial contact by those seeking employment is to mail a resume with a covering letter. The Toronto Zoo does hire summer students. *Contact:* Human Resources.

TORONTO-DOMINION BANK, THE
55 King Street West, 14th Floor, TD Tower
Toronto, ON M5K 1A2

Tel. 416-307-8123
Website .... www.tdbank.ca

The Toronto-Dominion Bank (TD) is a recognized leader in the financial services industry with approximately 30,000 employees worldwide. The TD offers customers a full line of retail, commercial, corporate, investment banking and treasury products and services. The TD actively seeks college and university graduates for their Management Development Programmes across Canada. Graduates most likely to be hired come from the following academic areas: Bachelor of Arts (General, Economics), Bachelor of Science (Actuarial, Computer Science, Mathematics, Physics), Bachelor of Engineering (General, Computer Systems, Telecommunications), Bachelor of Commerce/Business Administration (Accounting, Finance, Human Resources, Information Systems, Marketing), Chartered Accountant, Certified Management Accountant, Certified General Accountant, Master of Business Administration (Accounting, Finance, Information Systems, Marketing), and Community College Diploma (Financial Planning, Marketing/Sales, Computer Science). Customer service skills, team player, motivation, and a commitment to ongoing learning are all listed as desirable nonacademic qualifications. Company benefits and the potential for advancement are both rated as excellent. The average annual starting salary varies significantly, based upon the experience and educational background of the applicant. The most suitable method for initial contact by those seeking employment is to mail a resume with a covering letter. The Toronto-Dominion Bank does hire summer students. *Contact:* Manager, Recruitment.

TOTAL CARE TECHNOLOGIES INC.
1708 Dolphin Avenue, Suite 500
Kelowna, BC V1Y 9S4

Tel.	250-763-0034
Fax	250-763-0039
Email	tctcareers@total-care.com
Website	www.total-care.com

Total Care Technologies Inc. is a dynamic software development, marketing and services organization focusing on staff scheduling solutions for health care organizations. The company has become Canada's leading provider of innovative staff scheduling systems in the Canadian health care industry. Total Care has developed marketing initiatives with national and international business partners in Quebec, the United States and Holland, and has produced ESP (Environment for Scheduling Personnel), a world-class product installed in three languages, in three countries. Total Care has grown continuously to meet the needs of its expanding client base resulting in very high client satisfaction, and has twice won Science Council of British Columbia competitions for research and development. Graduates most likely to be hired come from the following academic areas: Bachelor of Science (Computer Science, Mathematics), and Bachelor of Engineering (Computer Systems). Graduates would occupy Project Manager, Human Resources Manager, Product Managers, Product Design Personnel, Software Quality Manager, Software Quality Analyst, Software Support Analyst, Applications Consultant, Applications Instructor, and Software Development Staff positions. A positive attitude, team player, high standards, and strong technical and interpersonal skills are all listed as desirable non-academic qualifications. The most suitable methods for initial contact by those seeking employment are to mail or e-mail a resume with a covering letter, or browse available opportunities listed on the company's website at www.total-care.com, or telephone (250) 763-0034 to obtain detailed descriptions of available positions. Total Care Technologies Inc. does hire students for summer and co-op work terms. *Contact:* Human Resources.

TOURISM YUKON, YUKON
P.O. Box 2703
Whitehorse, YT Y1A 2C6

Tel.	403-667-3009
Fax	403-667-8844

Tourism Yukon is responsible for the development and marketing of tourism in Yukon. In addition, Tourism Yukon is responsible for historic site management, implementation of heritage specific land claim agreements, and scientific research, including archaeology and paleontology. There 45 full time employees, and 35 seasonal employees. Graduates most likely to be hired come from the following academic areas: Bachelor of Commerce/Business Administration (Human Resources, Information Systems, Marketing, Public Administration), and Community College Diploma (Marketing/Sales, Travel/Tourism). Graduates would occupy Marketing Manager, Marketing Officer, Finance and Systems Manager, and Personnel Technician positions. Company benefits are rated as excellent. The potential for advancement is listed as average. The average annual starting salary falls within the $40,000 to $45,000 range. The most suitable method for initial contact by those seeking employment is to mail a resume with a covering letter. Tourism Yukon does hire summer students, generally students returning home to Yukon from outside universities. *Contact:* Ms. C. Jenkins, Director, Corporate Services.

town❀shoes
THE SHOE COMPANY
A DIVISION OF TOWN SHOES

TOWN SHOES
44 Kodiak Crescent
Downsview, ON M3J 3G5

Tel.	416-638-5342
Fax	416-638-0639

Town Shoes is involved in the ladies, high fashion footwear and accessories business. Town Shoes consists of 14 retail stores and the head office location (this address). Stores are located in Kitchener, Ottawa, Toronto and vicinity. Town Shoes has been in business for over 45 years and today has approximately 700 employees in Canada. Town Shoes also operates The Shoe Company. This is a value oriented, assisted service operation which is being rapidly expanded across Canada, and presently consists of 31 stores. Graduates most likely to be hired come from the following academic areas: Bachelor of Arts (General, Economics, Fine Arts), Bachelor of Commerce/Business Administration (General), Master of Business Administration (General), and Community College Diploma (Advertising, Fashion Merchandising, Marketing). Graduates would occupy Executive Trainee, Management Trainee, and Retail Sales Associate positions. Previous retail experience, a passionate interest in fashion, and excellent people skills are listed as desirable non-academic qualifications. Company benefits and the potential for advancement are both rated as excellent. The average annual starting salary falls within the $20,000 to $25,000 range for sales representatives, and within the $25,000 to $30,000 range for trainee positions. The most suitable methods for initial contact by those seeking employment are to fax a resume with a covering letter, or via telephone. *Contact:* Ms. Terry Tracey, Director of Recruiting.

TOYOTA CANADA INC.
One Toyota Place
Toronto, ON M1H 1H9

Tel. 416-438-6320
Fax 416-431-1871

Toyota Canada Inc. is involved in the purchase of vehicles and auto parts from Japan and North America, the sale of passenger vehicles, parts, fork-lift vehicles and trucks, and subsequently the distribution of those vehicles and parts to locations throughout Canada. This location is also involved in the marketing of Toyota's products throughout Canada. There are approximately 300 employees at this location. Graduates most likely to be hired come from the following academic areas: Bachelor of Commerce (Marketing), and Community College Diploma (Marketing, Human Resources, Auto Technician/Mechanic, Materials Management, Purchasing/Logistics). Graduates would occupy Automotive Technician, Marketing Coordinator, and Analyst positions. Flexible, promotable, and excellent communication skills are all listed as desirable non-academic qualifications. Company benefits are rated above average. The potential for advancement is listed as being good. The average annual starting salary falls within the $30,000 plus range. The most suitable method for initial contact by graduates seeking employment is to mail a resume with a covering letter. Toyota Canada Inc. does hire summer students. *Contact:* Jeff Zarb, Human Resources Manager.

TOYS R US (CANADA) LTD.
2777 Langstaff Road
Concord, ON L4K 4M5

Tel. 905-660-2000
Fax 905-660-2022
Email .... HELANDER2@ToysRUs.COM

Toys "R" Us (Canada) Ltd. operates retail toy stores across Canada following the warehouse store concept. There are 200 employees at this location, and a total of 3,000 employees across Canada. Graduates most likely to be hired come from the following academic areas: Bachelor of Arts (Economics), Bachelor of Science (Computer Science), Bachelor of Education (Adult), Bachelor of Commerce/Business Administration (Accounting, Finance, Human Resources, Information Systems, Marketing), Certified Management Accountant, Certified General Accountant, and Community College Diploma (Accounting, Facility Management, Human Resources, Marketing/Sales, Graphic Arts). At the head office, graduates are hired to occupy Accounting Clerk, Marketing, and Advertising positions, and at store locations, graduates would occupy Management Trainee positions. Previous retail work experience, teamwork, and strong written and oral communication skills are all listed as desirable non-academic qualifications. Company benefits and the potential for advancement are both rated as excellent. The average annual starting salary falls within the $25,000 to $30,000 range. The most suitable methods for initial contact by those seeking employment are to mail, fax or e-mail a resume with a covering letter. Toys "R" Us (Canada)

Ltd. does hire summer students. *Contact:* Randall K. Helander, Director of Human Resources.

TRANS MOUNTAIN PIPE LINE COMPANY LTD.
1333 West Broadway, Suite 900
Vancouver, BC V6H 4C2

Tel. 604-739-5000
Fax 604-739-5335

Trans Mountain Pipe Line Company Ltd. owns and operates a pipeline system, originating in Edmonton, for the transportation of refined products, crude petroleum, and other refinery feedstocks to Kamloops and Burnaby. At the U.S. border, the Company's pipeline connects with a pipeline owned and operated by a wholly-owned subsidiary, Trans Mountain Oil Pipe Line Corporation, which delivers Canadian petroleum to refineries in northwestern Washington State. Another subsidiary, Trans Mountain Enterprises of British Columbia Limited, owns and operates a pipeline for the transportation of jet fuel to Vancouver International Airport. Graduates most likely to be hired come from the following areas: Bachelor of Arts (Economics), Bachelor of Science (Chemistry, Computer Science), Bachelor of Engineering (General, Environmental, Electrical, Mechanical, Metallurgy), Bachelor of Laws (Environmental), Bachelor of Commerce/Business Administration (Accounting, Finance), Chartered Accountant, Certified General Accountant, and Community College Diploma (Purchasing/Logistics, Secretarial, Computer Science). Graduates would occupy Pipeline Engineer, Draftsperson, Environmental Technician, Journeyman Electrician, H.D. Mechanic, Millwright, Instrumentation, Financial Analyst, Clerical and Accounting positions. Company benefits are rated as excellent. The potential for advancement is listed as being good. The most suitable method for initial contact by those seeking employment is to mail a resume with a covering letter. Trans Mountain Pipe Line Company Ltd. does hire summer and co-op work term students. *Contact:* Human Resources.

TRANSAMERICA LIFE INSURANCE COMPANY OF CANADA
300 Consilium Place
Toronto, ON M1H 3G2

Tel. 416-290-6221
Fax 416-290-2911

Transamerica Life Insurance Company of Canada provides financial security services, innovative and affordable life insurance, and annuity products. Transamerica has operated in Canada since 1927 and is the sixth largest life insurance company in Canada. There are approximately 250 employees at this location. Graduates most likely to be hired come from the following academic areas: Bachelor of Arts (Economics, Psychology, General), Bachelor of Science (Actuarial, Mathematics), Bachelor of Commerce/Business Administration, and Community College Diploma (Business, Communications, Graphic Arts). Graduates are hired to occupy a variety of positions including Customer Service Representative and Policy Accounting Clerk. Good communication skills, flexibility, customer service skills, and computer literacy (eg. word processing and spreadsheet applications) are all listed as desirable non-academic qualifications. Company benefits are rated above average. The potential for advancement is listed as average. The average annual starting salary falls within the $20,000 to $30,000 range. The most suitable methods for initial contact by those seeking employment are to mail or fax a resume with a covering letter. Transamerica Life Insurance Company of Canada does hire summer students on a limited basis. *Contact:* Leslie Quarrington-Turnbull, Human Resources.

TRANSCANADA PIPELINES
P.O. Box 1000, Station M
Calgary, AB T2P 4K5

Tel. 403-267-6100
Fax 403-267-6444
Email .... careers@transcanada.com
Website .... www.transcanada.com

TransCanada Pipelines is a leading North American energy services company with businesses in transmission, marketing, and processing. The company, through its $21 Billion (CDN) asset base, provides high value-added energy service solutions to the North American and international marketplace. TransCanada Pipelines employs 6,500 people in total. Graduates most likely to be hired come from the following academic areas: Bachelor of Science (Chemistry, Computer Science), Bachelor of Engineering (General, Chemical, Civil, Electrical, Mechanical, Computer Systems, Industrial Design, Telecommunications), Bachelor of Commerce/Business Administration (General, Accounting, Finance, Human Resources, Information Systems), Chartered Accountant, Certified Management Accountant, Certified General Accountant, Master of Business Administration (General, Accounting, Finance, Human Resources, Information Systems), Master of Science, and Master of Engineering. Graduates would occupy Analyst, Engineer, and Specialist positions. In order to succeed in the competitive energy services world, TransCanada employs creative and innovative people who are encouraged to realize their full potential. The company fosters a working environment that emphasizes teamwork, initiative, involvement, communication and continuous improvement. Accordingly, leadership, business acumen, customer focus, project management, team player, problem solving and good communication skills are all listed as desirable non-academic qualifications. TransCanada helps employees improve their performance by providing a wide range of internal and external training opportunities. The company sponsors memberships in professional associations and provides financial support to employees who wish to further their education in areas of benefit to the company. The most suitable methods for initial contact by those seeking employment are to mail, fax or e-mail a resume with a covering letter, or by applying through the company's website. TransCanada

Pipelines does hire summer students (on a limited basis), and co-op work term students. *Contact:* Human Resources.

TRANSCO PLASTIC INDUSTRIES
150 Merizzi
Ville St. Laurent, QC H4T 1S4

Tel. 514-733-9951
Fax 514-733-5481

Transco Plastic Industries is a vertically integrated (extrusion/printing/converting) plastic bag manufacturer. The company employs approximately 140 people at this location and a total of 190 across Canada. Graduates most likely to be hired come from the following academic areas: Bachelor of Engineering (General, Electrical, Automation/Robotics, Industrial Production, Process), Community College Diploma (Electronics Technician, Engineering Technician), and High School Diploma. Graduates would occupy Trainee, Process Engineering, Clerical, and General Production positions. Initiative, team player, and a minimum of 2 to 3 years work experience are all listed as desirable non-academic qualifications. Company benefits are rated above average. The potential for advancement is listed as being good. The average annual starting salary is dependent upon the position being considered. The most suitable method for initial contact by those seeking employment is to mail a resume with a covering letter. Transco Plastic Industries does hire summer students. *Contacts:* Irwin Rapkin, Director of Human Resources or Michel Boulanger, Operations Manager.

TREBAS INSTITUTE
451, rue St-Jean
Montreal, QC H2Y 2R5

Tel. 514-845-4141
Website .... www.trebas.com

Trebas Institute is a private career college with campuses in Montreal, Toronto and Vancouver. Since 1979, Trebas has offered training programs in the digital media, including: Interactive Multimedia, Film and Television Production, Music Business Administration, Audio Engineering, and Recorded Music Productions. There are 30 employees at the Montreal campus (head office), 40 in Toronto, and 30 employees at the Vancouver campus. Graduates most likely to be hired for instructor positions come from backgrounds in Multimedia Development, 3D Animation, Digital Audio, Music Business, and Film/TV Production. Excellent communication skills, problem solving and analytical abilities are listed as desirable non-academic qualifications. The most suitable method for initial contact by those seeking employment is to mail a resume with a covering letter. Trebas Institute does hire summer students. (Toronto Location: 410 Dundas Street East, Toronto, ON, M5A 2A8, Phone 416-966-3066; Vancouver Location: 112 East 3rd Avenue, Suite 305, Vancouver, BC, V5T 1C8, Phone 604-872-2666). *Contact:* The Director.

TRIPLE-A MANUFACTURING COMPANY LIMITED, THE
44 Milner Avenue
Toronto, ON M1S 3P8

Tel. 416-291-4451
Fax 416-291-1292

The Triple-A Manufacturing Co. Ltd. employs more than 50 people in the manufacturing of a wide variety of storage systems. Graduates most likely to be hired come from the following academic areas: Bachelor of Arts (General), Bachelor of Science (Computer Science), Bachelor of Engineering (Mechanical), Bachelor of Commerce/Business Administration (Accounting), Certified Management Accountant, Certified General Accountant, Community College Diploma (Accounting, Marketing/Sales, Purchasing/Logistics, Secretarial, Architecture/Drafting, Industrial Design CAD/CAM/Autocad), and High School Diploma. In addition to unskilled labour positions in the manufacturing plant, graduates would occupy Receptionist, Order Desk Clerk, Engineer, Estimator, Secretary, Clerical, and Computer Operator positions. Company benefits are rated as excellent. The potential for advancement is listed as average. The average annual starting salary falls within the $20,000 to $25,000 range. The most suitable method for initial contact by those seeking employment is to mail a resume with a covering letter. The Triple-A Manufacturing Co. Ltd. does hire summer students. *Contacts:* Ms. D. Partridge or Mr. A. Lerman.

TRISTAN & ISEUT/AMERICA
20 Des Seigneurs
Montreal, QC H3K 3K3

Tel. 514-937-4601
Fax 514-935-1233

Tristan & Iseut/America operates retail chain stores with boutiques in Quebec, Ontario and the United States. The head office is located in Montreal, complete with Buying, Design, and Production departments. There are 200 employees at this location, a total of 1,200 employees across Canada, and an additional 200 employees in the United States. Graduates most likely to be hired come from the following academic areas: Bachelor of Arts (Languages), Bachelor of Science (Computer Science), Bachelor of Engineering (Computer Systems), Bachelor of Commerce/Business Administration (Accounting, Finance, Human Resources, Information Systems, Marketing), Chartered Accountant, Master of Business Administration (Accounting, Finance, Information Systems, Marketing), Community College Diploma (Computer Science), and High School Diploma. Graduates are hired to occupy Accounting Clerk, Accounts Payable Clerk, Data Entry Clerk, Import Clerk, Distribution Clerk, and Receptionist positions. Previous work experience, alertness, good attention span, character, quickness, and good references are listed as desirable non-academic qualifications. Company benefits are rated as industry standard. The potential for advancement is listed as average. The average annual starting salary depends upon the po-

sition being considered and the applicant's experience. The most suitable methods for initial contact by those seeking employment are to mail a resume with a covering letter, or through an employment agency. Tristan & Iseut/America does hire summer students at their boutique locations for Sales Staff positions. *Contact:* Connie Fuoco, Human Resources Director.

TUFF CONTROL SYSTEMS LTD.
5 Director Court, Unit 104
Vaughan, ON L4L 4S5

Tel. 905-850-8560
Fax 905-850-8577

Tuff Control Systems Ltd. provides security services, assisting retailers in controlling losses. The company employs approximately 50 people. Graduates most likely to be hired come from Community College programs in Law and Security. Graduates would occupy the position of Retail Investigator. Applicants must be responsible, possess good judgment, a mature attitude, and "keen powers of observation". Applicants must have no criminal record. Positions are available for graduates throughout Ontario in various cities. Company benefits are rated as industry standard. The potential for advancement is listed as average. The average annual starting salary falls within the $15,000 to $20,000 range. The most suitable methods for initial contact by graduates seeking employment are to fax a resume with a covering letter, or via telephone. Tuff Control Systems Ltd. does employ students for summer, part-time and co-op work terms. *Contact:* Debi Bellis.

TURNBULL AND TURNBULL LTD.
1850 Main Street
Winnipeg, MB R2V 3J4

Tel. 204-982-7843
Fax 204-334-2048

Turnbull and Turnbull Ltd. provides business consulting services. These services include the design and creation of employee benefit programs, special employment agreements and other similar arrangements, the administration of health, welfare and pension plans, the development of automated data processing systems and procedures, the selection of a suitable organization to provide investment or insurance services to benefit programs, assessment of investment performance, assistance to trustees in making investment decisions, selection and training of personnel, and actuarial services. These services may be provided alone or in conjunction with other organizations. There are 73 employees at this location and a total of 82 across Canada. Graduates most likely to be hired come from the following academic areas: Bachelor of Science (Actuarial, Computer Science, Mathematics), Bachelor of Commerce/Business Administration (Information Systems), Certified Management Accountant, and Community College Diploma (Accounting, Secretarial, Computer Science). Graduates would occupy Clerk, Assistant, Accounting Technician, Accounting Assistant,

Actuarial Technician, and Actuarial Student positions. Team player, a solid work history, and relevant work experience are all listed as desirable non-academic qualifications. Company benefits and the potential for advancement are both rated as excellent. The most suitable method for initial contact by those seeking employment is to mail a resume with a covering letter. Turnbull and Turnbull Ltd. does hire summer students as required. *Contact:* Karen Luff, Manager, Personnel & Building Operations.

TVONTARIO
P.O. Box 200, Station Q
Toronto, ON M4T 2T1

Tel. 416-484-2658
Fax 416-484-2633

TVOntario is an Educational Telecommunications Provincial Agency whose primary objectives are the acquisition, production and distribution of programs and materials (teacher's guides) in French and English within the educational broadcasting field. TVOntario employs between 350 and 500 people. Graduates most likely to be hired come from the following academic areas: Bachelor of Arts (Fine Arts, Languages, Communications), Community College Diploma (Secretarial, Radio and Television Arts), Bachelor of Education (Adult, Childhood), Bachelor of Commerce/Business Administration, and Master of Business Administration (Finance). Graduates are hired to occupy Technician, Production, Equipment Maintenance, Programming, Accounting, Clerical, Marketing, and Public Relation positions. Bilingualism is a definite asset. Company benefits are rated as excellent. The potential for advancement is listed as average. The average annual starting salary falls within the $25,000 to $30,000 range. The most suitable method for initial contact by graduates seeking employment is to mail a resume with a covering letter. *Contact:* Human Resources Department.

TWINPAK INC.
1255 route Transcanadienne
Bureau 210
Dorval, QC H9P 2V4

Tel. 514-684-7070
Fax 514-684-3128
Website .... www.twinpak.com

Twinpak Inc. is a Canadian leader in plastic, paper and composite material packaging. Headquartered in Dorval, Quebec, Twinpak operates through a network of more than a dozen manufacturing facilities and sales offices across North America. There are 20 employees at this location, 1,270 employees in Canada, and a total of 1,462 employees in the Company. Twinpak serves customers in the food, beverage, pharmaceutical, cosmetic and construction industries. Graduates most likely to be hired come from the following academic areas: Bachelor of Engineering (General, Chemical, Mechanical, Environmental/Resources, Industrial Chemistry), Bachelor of Commerce/Business Administration (General, Accounting, Finance, Human Resources, Informa-

tion Systems, Marketing), Chartered Accountant, Certified Management Accountant, Certified General Accountant, Master of Business Administration (General, Marketing), Community College Diploma (Accounting, Administration, Human Resources, Information Systems, Secretarial, CAD/CAM/Autocad, Computer Science, Tool and Die, Machinist), and High School Diploma. Graduates would occupy Plant Engineer, Secretary, Accounting Clerk, Laboratory Technologist, Customer Service Representative, Sales Representative, and Operator positions. Initiative, great communication skills, computer skills, team player, positive attitude, flexibility, and an ability to learn are all listed as desirable non-academic qualifications. Company benefits are rated as excellent. The potential for advancement is listed as being good. The average annual starting salary falls within the $25,000 to $30,000 range. The most suitable methods for initial contact by those seeking employment are to mail or fax a resume with a covering letter. Twinpak Inc. does hire summer students. *Contact:* Katherine Axiuk, Director of Human Resources.

TYCO INTERNATIONAL OF CANADA LTD.
8069 Lawson Road
P.O. Box 1001
Milton, ON L9T 4B6

Tel. 905-878-0541
Fax 905-878-3888

TYCO International of Canada Ltd. manufactures gas and water flow equipment (eg. valves and hydrants), pipe fittings (eg. nipples, plugs, bushings), and provides installation and servicing of fire protection equipment (eg. sprinklers, alarms, extinguishers). The company employs a total of 900 people across Canada. Graduates most likely to be hired come from the following academic areas: Bachelor of Engineering (Industrial Design, Industrial Production), Bachelor of Commerce/Business Administration (Marketing), Certified General Accountant (Manufacturing), and Community College Diploma (Accounting, Marketing/Sales). Graduates would occupy Cost Accountant, Sales Representative, Design Engineer, and Manufacturing Engineer positions. Company benefits are rated as excellent. The potential for advancement is listed as being good. The average annual starting salary depends upon the position being considered. The most suitable methods for initial contact by those seeking employment are to mail or fax a resume with a covering letter. TYCO International of Canada Ltd. does hire summer students. *Contact:* Wendall F. Gillis, Manager, Human Resources.

UBI SOFT ENTERTAINMENT INC.
5505 Saint-Laurent, Suite 5000
Montreal, QC H2T 1S6

Tel. 514-490-2000
Fax 514-490-0882
Email .... recruitment@ubisoft.qc.ca
Website .... www.ubisoft.qc.ca

As a leader in the multimedia field, Ubi Soft Entertainment Inc. handles every stage of the creation of new interactive software games, from their design and production to their distribution. These activities offer a wide variety of career opportunities to creative and innovative young graduates who are high-tech enthusiasts. Established in 1986, Ubi Soft is an international company employing over 1,100 people in five production studios and 13 subsidiaries located in Europe, North America and Asia. Presently, Ubi Soft distributes its catalogue of over 1,200 products in 50 countries in 22 different languages. Established in Montreal in July of 1997, Ubi Soft has over 300 employees at this location and is always seeking talented young graduates eager to take on new creative challenges in the video games industry. Graduates most likely to be hired come from the following academic areas: Bachelor of Arts (Fine Arts, Music), Bachelor of Science (General), Bachelor of Engineering (General, Computer Systems), Bachelor of Commerce/Business Administration (General, Accounting, Marketing), Chartered Accountant, Certified Management Accountant, Certified General Accountant, Master of Business Administration (Marketing, Management, International Business), and Community College Diploma (Animation, Audio/Visual Technician, Graphic Arts, Music, Computer Science, Engineering Technician). Graduates would occupy Marketing Manager and Project Coordinator positions. A bona fide video game enthusiast is listed as desirable non-academic skill. Company benefits and the potential for advancement are both rated as excellent. The most suitable method for initial contact by those seeking employment is to apply through Ubi Soft's website at www.ubisoft.qc.ca. Ubi Soft Entertainment Inc. does hire summer and co-op work term students. *Contact:* Human Resources.

UNDERWRITERS ADJUSTMENT BUREAU LTD.
4300, rue Jean-Talon ouest
Montreal, QC H4P 1W3

Tel. 514-735-3561
Fax 514-735-8439
Email .... uabØ98@attmail.com

The Underwriters Adjustment Bureau Ltd. is an independent adjusting firm. There are approximately 75 employees at this location and a total of 550 employees across Canada. Graduates most likely to be hired come from the following academic areas: Bachelor of Commerce, Bachelor of Business Administration, and Community College Diploma (Insurance). Graduates are hired to occupy the position of Insurance Claims Adjuster. Autonomous, and self-starting are both listed as desirable non-academic qualifications. Company benefits are rated above average. The average annual starting salary falls within the $23,000 to $25,000 range. The most suitable method for initial contact by those seeking employment is to mail a resume with a covering letter. The Underwriters Adjustment Bureau Ltd. does hire summer and co-op work term students. *Contact:* Personnel Department.

UNI-SELECT INC.
170, boul Industriel
Boucherville, QC J4B 2X3

Tel. 514-641-2440
Fax 514-641-6566
Website .... www.uni-select.com

Uni-Select Inc. distributes automobile parts and supplies. There are 215 employees at this location, and a total of 818 employees in Canada. Graduates most likely to be hired come from the following areas: Bachelor of Science (Computer Science), Bachelor of Commerce/Business Administration (Accounting, Finance, Human Resources, Information Systems, Marketing), Certified Management Accountant, Certified General Accountant, Master of Business Administration (Accounting, Finance, Human Resources, Information Systems, Marketing), and Community College Diploma (Accounting, Administration, Business, Human Resources, Information Systems, Marketing/Sales, Purchasing/Logistics, Secretarial, Computer Science). Graduates are hired to occupy Clerk, Technician, Coordinator, and Accountant positions. Team work, flexible, leadership skills, communicative, efficient, dynamic, and previous work experience are all listed as desirable non-academic qualifications. The most suitable methods for initial contact by those seeking employment are to mail or fax a resume with a covering letter. Uni-Select Inc. does hire summer students. *Contact:* Marie-Josée Ladouceur, Human Resources Coordinator.

UNION GAS LIMITED
200 Yorkland Boulevard
Toronto, ON M2J 5C6

Tel. 416-491-1880
Fax 416-496-5309

Union Gas Limited is a natural gas utility company, distributing gas to northern, north-western, and eastern Ontario. Approximately 100 Ontario communities are serviced through 35 separate locations. There are more than 100 employees at this location. Graduates most likely to be hired come from the following academic areas: Bachelor of Arts (Economics), Bachelor of Engineering (Civil, Mechanical), Bachelor of Commerce/Business Administration (Marketing, Accounting), Certified Management Accountant, Master of Business Administration (Marketing, Accounting), Master of Arts (Economics), and Community College Diploma (Engineering Technician, Electronics Technician, Instrumentation, Secretarial, Human Resources). Co-Op work experience is listed as a desirable non-academic qualification. Company benefits and the potential for advancement are both rated as excellent. The average annual starting salary falls within the $25,000 to $30,000 range. The most suitable method for initial contact by those seeking employment is to mail a resume with a covering letter. Union Gas Limited does hire summer students on a limited basis. *Contact:* Coordinator, Staffing and Training.

UNISYS CANADA INC. (TORONTO)
2001 Sheppard Avenue East
Toronto, ON M2J 4Z7

Tel.	416-495-0515
Fax	416-495-4652
Website	www.unisys.com

Unisys Canada Inc. is involved in the design, manufacture, and marketing of computer hardware and software. There are more than 250 employees at this location. Graduates most likely to be hired come from the following academic areas: Bachelor of Arts (General), Bachelor of Science (Computer Science), Bachelor of Engineering (Electrical), Bachelor of Laws, Bachelor of Commerce/Business Administration, Chartered Accountant, Certified Management Accountant, and Master of Business Administration. Graduates would occupy Systems, Marketing, Sales, Finance, and Administration positions. Company benefits are rated as industry standard. The potential for advancement is listed as excellent. The average annual starting salary falls within the $30,000 to $35,000 range. The most suitable method for initial contact by those seeking employment is to mail a resume with a covering letter. Unisys Canada Inc. does hire summer students on a limited basis. *Contact:* Human Resources Department.

UNISYS CANADA INC. (WINNIPEG)
51 Burmac Road
Winnipeg, MB R2J 4C9

Tel.	204-253-3000
Fax	204-257-9224
Email	hr.winnipeg@unisys.com
Website	www.unisys.com

The Winnipeg location of Unisys Canada Inc. manufactures high capacity computer disk systems. Graduates most likely to be hired come from the following academic areas: Bachelor of Engineering (Electrical, Mechanical, Computer Systems, Industrial Engineering, Microelectronics), Bachelor of Commerce/Business Administration (General, Accounting, Finance, Operations), Master of Business Administration (Accounting, Finance), and Community College Diploma (Information Systems, Computer Science, Electronics Technician). Graduates would occupy Engineer and Analyst positions. Able to work well in a team environment, quick, and innovative are listed as desirable non-academic qualifications. Company benefits are rated above average. The potential for advancement is listed as being good. The average annual starting salary falls within the $30,000 to $35,000 range. The most suitable methods for initial contact by those seeking employment are to mail or e-mail a resume with a covering letter. Unisys Canada Inc. does hire summer and co-op work term students. *Contact:* Human Resources.

UNIVERSAL FLAVORS (CANADA) LTD.
110 Vulcan Street
Rexdale, ON M9W 1L2

Tel.	416-245-6610
Fax	416-245-6379

Universal Flavors (Canada) Ltd. employs more than 50 people in the manufacture of food flavours and fruit preparations for all areas of the food industry. Graduates most likely to be hired come from the following academic areas: Bachelor of Science (Chemistry, Microbiology, Food Sciences), and Community College Diploma (Science, Laboratory Technician). Graduates would occupy Product Development Technologist, and QC Laboratory Technician positions. A good work ethic, flexibility, and excellent communication skills are all listed as desirable non-academic qualifications. Company benefits are rated above average. The potential for advancement is listed as being good. The average annual starting salary is dependent upon the position being considered. The most suitable method for initial contact by those seeking employment is to mail a resume with a covering letter. Universal Flavors (Canada) Ltd. does hire summer students. *Contact:* Personnel Manager.

UNLEASH CORPORATION
5397 Eglinton Avenue West, Suite 210
Toronto, ON M9C 5K6

Tel.	416-622-7658
Fax	416-622-7631
Email	lkistner@unleashcorp.com

Unleash Corporation provides solutions integration of business computer systems, specializing in sales force automation, accounting and distribution systems. The company employs a total of 20 people. Graduates most likely to be hired come from the following academic areas: Bachelor of Science (Mathematics - UofW), Bachelor of Engineering (Computer Systems), Bachelor of Commerce/Business Administration (General, Accounting, Finance, Information Systems), Certified Management Accountant, Master of Business Administration (General, Accounting, Finance, Information Systems, Marketing), Community College Diploma (Accounting, Information Systems, Marketing/Sales, Computer Science), and graduates with a Microsoft Certified Systems Engineer (MCSE) accreditation. Graduates would occupy Junior Developer, Business Analyst, and System Engineer position. Team player and professional appearance are both listed as desirable non-academic qualifications. Company benefits are rated above average. The potential for advancement is listed as excellent. The average annual starting salary falls within the $30,000 to $35,000 range. The most suitable method for initial contact by those seeking employment is to mail a resume with a covering letter. *Contact:* Larry Kistner, President.

URBAN SYSTEMS LTD.
286 St. Paul Street, Suite 200
Kamloops, BC V2C 1G4

Tel.	250-374-8311
Fax	250-374-5334
Email	kamloops@urban-systems.com
Website	www.urban-systems.com

Urban Systems Ltd. is a multidisciplinary firm of engineers, planners and landscape architects located in four offices throughout British Columbia and Alberta. The company's clients include small municipalities, land developers, and First Nations. Urban Systems is a client focused organization rather than a project focused one. Graduates most likely to be hired come from the following academic areas: Bachelor of Arts (Geography, Urban Geography/Planning), Bachelor of Science (Geography), Bachelor of Engineering (Civil), Bachelor of Landscape Architecture, Bachelor of Laws (Local Government Consulting), Master of Engineering (Civil, Environmental, Hydrology, Transportation), Community College Diploma (Business, CAD/CAM/Autocad, Engineering Technician), and High School Diploma. Graduates would occupy Consulting Engineer, Planner, Landscape Architect, Local Government Consultant, Civil Engineering Technologist/Technician, Landscape Architect Technician, Administrative and Accounting positions. The company places a tremendous emphasis on the development of its staff, ensuring that they are challenged, stimulated and have the necessary tools to better serve clients. Urban Systems' work environment is informal and friendly, but intense. As a demanding business, the company stays competitive by seeking people that want to do challenging work as opposed to "doing a job". Urban Systems creates an environment of freedom and responsibility to provide every employee with the ability to manage their own career. Accordingly, enthusiasm, team mindset, responsible, hardworking and eager to learn are all listed as desirable non-academic qualifications. Company benefits are rated above average. The potential for advancement is listed as excellent. The average annual starting salary falls within the $35,000 to $40,000 range. The most suitable methods for initial contact by those seeking employment are to mail or fax a resume with a covering letter. Urban Systems Ltd. does hire summer and co-op work term students. *Contacts:* Shannon McQuillan, Staffing Resources Advisor or Tizina Wamboldt, Office Administrator.

UWI UNISOFT WARES INC. (UWI.COM)
1095 McKenzie Avenue, Suite 400
Victoria, BC V8P 2L5

Tel.	250-479-8334
Fax	250-479-3772
Email	info@uwi.com
Website	www.uwi.com

UWI Unisoft Wares Inc. (UWI.Com), developer of the first internet forms software, is the leader in the internet forms market segment. The company's InternetForms System helps businesses develop cost-effective, internet based business forms that save both time and money over traditional paper forms. All products in the InternetForms System support the Universal Forms Description Language (UFDL), which describes InternetForms much like HTML describes web pages. UWI.Com offers UFDL to the public as a common, open standard for forms design. The company also offers organizations complete solutions in areas such as workflow, legacy and ODBC data access, and Palm Top integration with the enterprise. UWI.Com employs 30 people at this location and a total of 40 people worldwide. Graduates most likely to be hired come from the following academic areas: Bachelor of Arts (English, Fine Arts, History, Journalism), Bachelor of Science (Computer Science, Mathematics), Bachelor of Engineering (Electrical, Computer Systems, Microelectronics), Bachelor of Commerce/Business Administration (Accounting, Finance, Information Systems, Marketing), Master of Arts (English, Visual Arts), Master of Science (Computer Science), Master of Engineering (Computer Systems), Community College Diploma (Accounting, Administration, Advertising, Business, Communications/Public Relations, Financial Planning, Information Systems, Marketing/Sales, Secretarial, Animation, Audio/Visual Technician, Fashion Arts, Graphic Arts, Journalism, Computer Science), and High School Diploma. Graduates would occupy Technical Writer, Programmer, Marketing, Sales, and Web Development positions. Hardworking, driven, creative, and HTML experience are all listed as desirable non-academic qualifications. Company benefits and the potential for advancement are both listed as excellent. The average annual starting salary falls within the $30,000 to $35,000 range. The most suitable method for initial contact by those seeking employment is to e-mail a resume with a covering letter. UWI.Com does hire summer and co-op work term students. *Contact:* info@uwi.com.

VAN HORNE CONSTRUCTION LIMITED
3279 Caroga Drive
Mississauga, ON L4V 1A3

Tel.	905-677-5150
Fax	905-677-7291

Van Horne Construction Limited is a general contracting firm employing fewer than 10 people. Graduates most likely to be hired come from the following academic areas: Bachelor of Engineering (General, Industrial), Master of Engineering (Structural), and Community College Diploma (Engineering Technician). Graduates would occupy the positions of Estimator and Project Manager (Trainee). Company benefits are rated above average. The potential for advancement is listed as being good. The average annual starting salary depends upon the applicant's level of experience. The most suitable method for initial contact by those seeking employment is to mail a resume with a covering letter. *Contact:* Doug Lock.

VanCity

It's right here.™

VANCOUVER CITY SAVINGS CREDIT UNION

183 Terminal Avenue
Vancouver, BC V6A 4G2

Tel. 604-877-8298
Fax 604-877-8299
Email .... pesonnel_resumes@vancity.com
Website .... www/vancity.com

The Vancouver City Savings Credit Union (VanCity) is a financial institution providing a full range of financial services. As Canada's largest credit union, VanCity employs approximately 1,500 people in the province of British Columbia. Graduates most likely to be hired come from the following academic areas: Bachelor of Arts (Economics), Bachelor of Science (Computer Science), Bachelor of Commerce/ Business Administration (Accounting, Finance, Information Systems, Marketing), Chartered Accountant, Certified Management Accountant, Certified General Accountant, Community College Diploma (Accounting, Business, Financial Planning, Information Systems, Insurance, Marketing/Sales, Purchasing/Logistics, Computer Science), and High School Diploma. Applicants should possess exceptional communication, relationship building, sales and service skills to apply towards VanCity's goal of building and maintaining financial relationships. Company benefits and the potential for advancement are both rated as excellent. The average annual starting falls within the $25,000 to $35,000 range, depending on the position being considered. The most suitable method for initial contact by those seeking employment is to mail, fax or e-mail a resume with a covering letter. VanCity does hire summer and co-op work term students. *Contact:* Personnel Department.

VANCOUVER HOSPITAL AND HEALTH SCIENCES CENTRE

855 - West 12th Avenue
Vancouver, BC V7A 2Z5

Tel. 604-875-4202
Fax 604-875-4761

Vancouver Hospital and Health Sciences Centre is an adult tertiary care, teaching and research facility. The Hospital's area of emphasis are: Neuro Sciences, Oncology, Orthopedics, and Trauma. Located on two separate sites, the hospital employs approximately 9,000 people. Graduates most likely to be hired come from the following academic areas: Bachelor of Science (Audiology, Nursing, Nutritional Sciences, Occupational Therapy, Pharmacy, Physical Therapy, Psychology, Speech Pathology), Bachelor of Engineering (Electrical, Automation/Robotics, Biomedical Electronics), Bachelor of Commerce/Business Administration (Human Resources, Information Systems), Certified General Accountant, Master of Business Administration, Master of Health Sciences, Community College Diploma (Accounting, Human Resources, Purchasing/Logistics, Computer Science, Nursing RN, Radiology Technician, Respiratory Technician, Ultra-Sound Technician), and High School Diploma. Graduates would occupy positions relating directly to their particular academic background. A commitment to patient-centred delivery of care, and strong interpersonal and communication skills are listed as desirable non-academic qualifications. Company benefits and the potential for advancement are both rated as excellent. The average annual starting salary falls within the $30,000 to $35,000 range. The most suitable methods for initial contact by those seeking employment are to mail or fax a resume with a covering letter. *Contact:* Human Resources Office.

VAPOR CANADA INC.

10655, Henri Bourassa ouest
St-Laurent, QC H4S 1A1

Tel. 514-335-4200
Fax 514-335-4231

Vapor Canada Inc. designs and builds systems and sub-systems for the mass transit industry. The company employs approximately 160 people. Graduates most likely to be hired come from the following academic areas: Bachelor of Engineering (Electrical, Computer Systems, Telecommunications, Mechanical, Industrial Design), Bachelor of Commerce/ Business Administration (Accounting, Finance), Master of Business Administration (Finance), Master of Engineering (Electrical, Mechanical), Community College Diploma (Accounting, Administration, Business, Marketing/Sales, Secretarial, Drafting, CAD/CAM/Autocad, Computer Science, Electronics Technician, Engineering Technician, Technical Trades, Welding), and High School Diploma. Graduates would occupy Engineering Technician, Mechanical Engineering Technician, Electronics Technician, Electronics Technologist, Manufacturing Engineering Technician, Mechanical Engineer (Design), Electrical Engineer (Design), Software/ Hardware Engineer, Reliability/Maintainability Engineer, and Manufacturing Engineer positions. Creativity, initiative, team player, and good verbal and written communication skills are all listed as desirable non-academic qualifications. Company benefits are rated above average. The potential for advancement is listed as being good. The average annual starting salary falls within the $25,000 to $30,000 range. The most suitable method for initial contact by those seeking employment is to mail a resume with a covering letter. Vapor Canada Inc. occasionally hires summer students. *Contacts:* Manager, Human Resources or Manager, Engineering Department.

VAUGHAN ECONOMIC AND TECHNOLOGY DEVELOPMENT
2141 Major Mackenzie Drive
Vaughan, ON L6A 1T1

Tel. 905-832-8521
Fax 905-832-6248
Email .... ecdev@city.vaughan.on.ca
Website .... www.city.vaughan.on.ca

The City of Vaughan Economic and Technology Development Department is primarily involved in attracting and retaining commercial and industrial development, expediting the development process for developers, economic research activities, publishing city information, public relations and marketing the city to prospective firms and employers. The department employs approximately 15 people. Graduates most likely to be hired come from the following academic areas: Bachelor of Arts (Urban Geography/Planning, Journalism, Economics), and Bachelor of Commerce/Business Administration (Marketing). Graduates would occupy Economic Developer, Marketing and Communications Specialist, and Economic Researcher positions. Employee benefits are rated as excellent. The potential for advancement is listed as being good. The average annual starting salary is $35,000 plus. The most suitable method for initial contact by those seeking employment is to mail a resume with a covering letter. The Economic and Technology Development Department does hire summer students for the collection of data. *Contact:* Manager.

VAUGHAN ENGINEERING
P.O. Box 2045, Station M
Halifax, NS B3J 2Z1

Tel. 902-425-3980
Fax 902-423-7593
Email .... vaughan@mgnet.ca
Website .... www.mgnet.ca

Vaughan Engineering provides multi-disciplinary consulting engineering services to regional and international clients, through five divisions: Environmental, Municipal, Building Science, Structural, and Heavy Civil/Industrial. Vaughan specializes in project solutions which require integrating advanced engineering techniques with information technology and advanced materials. Vaughan is a member of the MacDonnell Group (MG) Limited, an alliance of companies and partnerships committed to world class technology and consulting solutions in the engineering, geomatics, environmental, computer graphics, and management consulting fields. Vaughan employs 45 people at this location, and a total of 110 employees in Canada. Graduates most likely to be hired come from the following academic areas: Bachelor of Science (Computer Science, Environmental), Bachelor of Engineering (General, Materials Science, Pollution Treatment, Civil, Architectural/Building, Surveying, Municipal, Ports and Marine Structures, Electrical, Instrumentation, Power, Mechanical, Industrial Design, Marine, Environmental), Master of Engineering (Advanced Composite Materials, Environmental), Doctorate (Advanced Composite Materials, Intelligent Structures), and Community College Diploma (Computer Science). Graduates are hired for a variety of positions relating directly to their educational background and experience level. Previous consulting experience, computer literacy (essential), and the ability to work independently are all listed as desirable non-academic qualifications. Company benefits and the potential for advancement are both rated as excellent. Average annual starting salaries are above the industry average, and are dependent upon the qualifications and experience of the applicant. The most suitable methods for initial contact by those seeking employment are to mail, fax or e-mail a resume with a covering letter. Vaughan Engineering does hire summer students. *Contact:* Human Resources.

VAUGHAN HYDRO ELECTRIC COMMISSION
2800 Rutherford Road
Vaughan, ON L4K 2N9

Tel. 905-832-8371
Fax 905-303-2000
Website .... www.city.vaughan.on.ca

The Vaughan Hydro Electric Commission provides hydro electric services to the city of Vaughan. The commission employs approximately 150 people. Graduates most likely to be hired come from the following academic areas: Bachelor of Engineering (Electrical), Bachelor of Commerce/Business Administration, Chartered Accountant, and Community College Diploma (Accounting, Business, Computer Science, Electrical, Drafting, CAD/CAM/Autocad). Graduates would occupy Engineer (in training), Technician, Draftsperson, Accounting Clerk, Billing Clerk, Revenue Clerk, Payroll Clerk, and Financial Analyst positions. Employee benefits are rated as excellent. The average annual starting salary falls within the $30,000 to $35,000 range. The most suitable method for initial contact by those seeking employment is to mail a resume with a covering letter. The Vaughan Hydro Electric Commission does hire summer students. *Contact:* Recruitment Officer, Human Resources.

VAUGHAN RECREATION AND CULTURE DEPARTMENT
2141 Major Mackenzie Drive
Maple, ON L6A 1T1

Tel. 905-832-8500
Fax 905-832-5630
Website .... www.city.vaughan.on.ca

The City of Vaughan Recreation and Culture Department employs more than 100 people and is responsible for the delivery of parks and recreation services, facility operations, administration, and the design and development of parks and heritage resources. Graduates most likely to be hired come from the following academic areas: Bachelor of Arts (General, Fine Arts, History, Journalism, Psychology, Recreation, Sociology, Urban Geography), Bachelor of Science (Forestry, Geography), Bachelor of Education (Adult, Child, Physical, Special Needs), Bachelor of Landscape Architecture, Bachelor of Commerce/Business Administration (Marketing), Master of Business Administration (Marketing, Information Systems), and Community College Diploma (Facility Management, Graphic Arts, Recreation, Architecture/Drafting, Industrial Design). Graduates would occupy Programmer, Landscape Architect, Landscape Technician, Facility Operator, Food Services Technician, and Administrative Assistant positions. Previous work experience or volunteer experience are listed as desirable non-academic qualifications. Employee benefits are rated as excellent. The average annual starting salary falls within the $30,000 to $35,000 range. The most suitable method for initial contact by those seeking employment is to mail a resume with a covering letter (no phone calls please). The Recreation and Culture Department does hire summer students. *Contact:* Human Resources Department.

VEBA OIL
717 - 7th Avenue S.W., Suite 1480
Calgary, AB T2P 0Z3

Tel. 403-263-2330
Fax 403-278-1000

Veba Oil is a major oil company in Libya, with an average production of 120,000 barrels of oil per day. Veba Oil Operations B.V. is active in the exploration development and production of oil and gas. Graduates most likely to be hired come from the following academic areas: Bachelor of Science (Geology), and Bachelor of Engineering (Chemical, Electrical, Mechanical, Geological, Petroleum/Fuels). Company benefits are rated as excellent. The potential for advancement is listed as average. The average annual starting salary falls in the $60,000 plus range. The most suitable method for initial contact by those seeking employment is to mail a resume with a covering letter. (See Listing for Moreland Resources Inc.). *Contact:* Kam Fard, P.Eng..

VELA INFORMATION MANAGEMENT CONSULTANTS
665 - 8th Street SW, Suite 300
Calgary, AB T2P 3K7

Tel. 403-263-2553
Fax 403-234-9033
Website .... www.vela.ca

VELA Information Management Consultants provides business consulting services, employing 13 people at this location, and a total of 25 people in Canada. Graduates most likely to be hired come from the following academic areas: Bachelor of Science (Computer Science), Bachelor of Engineering (General), Bachelor of Commerce/Business Administration (Information Systems), Master of Business Administration (Information Systems), and Community College Diploma (Computer Science). Graduates would occupy Programmer, Programmer Analyst, Business Analyst, and Project Manager positions. Entrepreneurial, creative, and able to work well in a

team environment are all listed as desirable non-academic qualifications. Company benefits are rated as excellent. The potential for advancement is listed as being good. The average annual starting salary falls within the $35,000 to $40,000 range. The most suitable method for initial contact by those seeking employment is to mail a resume with a covering letter. *Contact:* Human Resources.

VELTRI GLENCOE LTD.
73 Main Street, Box 460
Glencoe, ON N0L 1M0

Tel. 519-287-2283
Fax 519-287-2285

Veltri Glencoe Ltd. produces metal stamping, automotive parts for both Tier 1 and Tier 2 suppliers. The company supplies to both North American and Japanese companies. The company employs approximately 215 people at this location, and a total of 600 people worldwide. Veltri Glencoe Ltd. is a registered QS 9000 company. Graduates most likely to be hired come from the following academic areas: Bachelor of Engineering (Automation/Robotics, Computer Systems, Industrial Design, Industrial Production), Bachelor of Commerce/Business Administration (Accounting, Finance, Human Resources), Chartered Accountant, Certified Management Accountant, Certified General Accountant, and Community College Diploma (Accounting, Human Resources, Purchasing/Logistics, Secretarial, Engineering Technician). Graduates would occupy Tooling Engineer, Controller, General Accountant, Human Resources Generalist, Purchasing/Logistics, and Office Administration positions. Team player, enjoy working in a fast paced environment, and previous experience in the automotive industry are all listed as desirable non-academic qualifications. Company benefits are rated above average. The potential for advancement is listed as being good. The most suitable method for initial contact by those seeking employment is to mail a resume with a covering letter. *Contact:* Human Resources.

VERSA SERVICES LTD.
P.O. Box 950, Station U
Toronto, ON M8Z 5Y7

Tel. 416-255-1331
Fax 416-255-4706

Versa Services Ltd. is the largest contract service management company in Canada, providing food and housekeeping services across the country. There are more than 100 employees at this location, and over 15,000 employees nationwide. Graduates most likely to be hired come from the following academic areas: Bachelor of Arts (General), Bachelor of Science (Computer Science, Health Sciences), Bachelor of Commerce/Business Administration (Accounting, Finance), Certified Management Accountant (Finance), Certified General Accountant (Finance), Community College Diploma (Business, Cooking, Hospitality, Human Resources, Food/Nutrition), and High School Diploma. Related work experience, and good interpersonal and communication skills are listed as desirable non-academic qualifications. Company benefits are rated above average. The potential for advancement is listed as excellent. The average annual starting salary falls within the $20,000 to $25,000 range. The most suitable method for initial contact by those seeking employment is to mail a resume with a covering letter. Versa Services Ltd. does hire summer students. *Contact:* Manager, Human Resource Programs.

VERSATILE FARM EQUIPMENT OPERATIONS - NEW HOLLAND CANADA LTD.
P.O. Box 7300
Winnipeg, MB R3C 4E8

Tel.	204-477-2319
Fax	204-477-2325

Versatile Farm Equipment Operations - New Holland Canada Ltd. is involved in the manufacture of agricultural implements, including two wheel and four wheel drive tractors. The company has 700 employees at this location, a total of 800 across Canada, and 18,000 employees worldwide. Graduates most likely to be hired come from the following academic areas: Bachelor of Science (Computer Science), Bachelor of Engineering (Mechanical, Industrial Design, Industrial Production), Bachelor of Commerce/Business Administration (Accounting, Finance, Information Systems), Chartered Accountant, Certified Management Accountant, Certified General Accountant, Master of Business Administration, and Community College Diploma (Accounting, CAD/CAM/Autocad, Computer Science, Engineering Technician). Engineering graduates would occupy Industrial Engineer, and Manufacturing Engineering Analyst positions. Relevant work experience, vision, creativity, team player, and an interest in process improvements are all listed as desirable non-academic qualifications. Company benefits are rated above average. The potential for advancement is listed as being good. The average annual starting salary for recent graduates falls within the $32,000 to $36,000 range. The most suitable method for initial contact by those seeking employment is to mail a resume with a covering letter. Versatile Farm Equipment Operations - New Holland Canada Ltd. does hire summer students on a limited basis. *Contact:* Human Resources Manager.

VILLA PROVIDENCE SHEDIAC INC.
P.O. Box 340
Shediac, NB E0A 3G0

Tel.	506-532-4484
Fax	506-532-8189

Villa Providence Shediac Inc. operates a nursing home, employing approximately 210 people. Graduates most likely to be hired come from the following academic areas: Bachelor of Science (Nursing, Physical Therapy), and Community College Diploma (Nursing RN/RNA). Applicants should be able and like to work in an environment of physically and mentally handicapped people. Company benefits are rated above average. The potential for advancement is listed as average. The average starting salary depends upon the work classification, qualifications, experience, and number of hours worked. The most suitable method for initial contact by those seeking employment is to mail a resume with a covering letter. Villa Providence Shediac Inc. does hire summer students for student project work. *Contacts:* Yvon Girouard, Human Resources Director or Anita Belliveau, Human Resources Coordinator.

VISTAR TELECOMMUNICATIONS INC.
427 Laurier Avenue West, Suite 1410
Ottawa, ON K1G 3J4

Tel.	613-230-4848
Fax	613-230-4940
Email	jobs@vistar.ca
Website	www.vistar.ca

Vistar Telecommunications Inc. engages in technical innovation and systems development in the field of wireless and satellite communications and the integration of satellite and terrestrial communications networks. Vistar is a recognized leader in mobility systems and products, advanced multimedia, consumer infotainment, and consulting in marketing research. The company offers uniqueness in its products with technological, and cost advantage. Vistar employs approximately 60 individuals. Graduates most likely to be hired come from the following academic areas: Bachelor of Engineering (Electrical, Telecommunications), Master of Engineering (Electrical, Electronics), Doctorate of Engineering (Electrical, Electronics), and Community College Diploma (Electrical Technician, Engineering Technician). Graduates would occupy Hardware and Software Engineer positions, such as Satellite Systems Engineer, Digital Signal Processing Software Engineer, RF Engineer, and Hardware Designer. Team player and dedication are both listed as desirable non-academic qualifications. Company benefits are rated as excellent. The potential for advancement is listed as being good. The average annual starting salary falls within the $45,000 to $50,000 range. The most suitable method for initial contact by those seeking employment is to mail, fax or e-mail a resume with a covering letter. Vistar Telecommunications Inc. does hire summer students. *Contact:* Dr. R.W. Breithaupt, Vice President, Technology.

VITANA CORPORATION
5470 Canotek Road, Unit 26
Gloucester, ON K1J 9H3

Tel.	613-749-4445
Fax	613-749-4087
Email	hr@vitana.com
Website	www.vitana.com

Founded in 1992, Vitana Corporation uses the latest technology to design, manufacture and market design kits, which in turn are used by other engineers in the design of their products. Vitana works extensively with semi-conductor manufacturers, showing-off the features of their chips. The company has targeted companies offering chip solutions in the following areas: USB, FireWire (IEEE 1394) CMOS Imagers, video/image processing, graphics, data communications, bus architectures, DSP, input/output and motion control. Vitana's work begins with hardware and software design, through to manufacturing and distribution of its kits worldwide. Vitana employs a total of 27 people. Graduates most likely to be hired come from the following academic areas: Bachelor of Science (Computer Science), Bachelor of Engineering (Electrical, Computer Systems), Certified Management Accountant, Certified General Accountant, and Community College Diploma (Computer Science, Electronics Technician, Engineering Technician). Graduates would occupy Computer Engineer, Electrical Engineer, Junior Technician, and Senior Technician positions. Team player, quick learner, and enjoy challenges are listed as desirable non-academic qualifications. Company benefits are rated above average. The potential for advancement is listed as being good. The average annual starting salary falls within the $45,000 to $50,000 range. The most suitable method for initial contact by those seeking employment is to mail a resume with a covering letter. Vitana Corporation does hire students for summer and co-op work terms. *Contacts:* Marc Bisson, Director of Operations or Brigette Yachon, Director of Engineering Services.

VOLVO CANADA LTD.
175 Gordon Baker Road
Toronto, ON M2H 2N7

Tel. 416-493-3700
Fax 416-493-8754

Volvo Canada Ltd. employs 65 people at this location and a total of 250 people across Canada in the wholesale of automobiles for the Canadian market. Graduates most likely to be hired come from the following academic areas: Bachelor of Arts (Economics), Bachelor of Commerce/Business Administration (Accounting, Finance, Human Resources, Information Systems, Marketing, Public Administration), Master of Business Administration (Accounting, Finance, Human Resources, Marketing), Community College Diploma (Accounting, Administration, Advertising, Business, Financial Planning, Human Resources, Marketing/Sales, Secretarial), and High School Diploma. Graduates would occupy Accounting and Field Service positions, relating to dealer support. Company benefits are rated as excellent. The average annual starting salary falls within the $30,000 to $35,000 range, and is dependent upon the position being considered. The most suitable method for initial contact by those seeking employment is to mail a resume with a covering letter. *Contact:* Anne Lake, Human Resources Administrator.

VON METRO TORONTO
3190 Steeles Avenue East, Suite 300
Markham, ON L3R 1G9

Tel. 416-499-2009
Fax 416-499-8460

The VON provides community nursing and related health services to clients, either through CCAC referrals or direct, private fee for service. The VON employs approximately 300 people at this location, and a total of 3,000 people across Canada. Graduates most likely to be hired come from the following academic areas: Bachelor of Science (Nursing, Nutritional Sciences, Physical Therapy, Speech Pathology), Bachelor of Commerce/Business Administration (Accounting, Finance, Human Resources, Information Systems, Marketing, Public Administration), Chartered Accountant, Master of Business Administration (Accounting, Human Resources), Master of Science (Nurse Practitioner), Community College Diploma (Administration, Business, Human Resources, Marketing/Sales, Customer Service, Public Relations, Fundraising, Dietician, Massage Therapy, Nursing RN/RNA, Community Nursing), and High School Diploma. Graduates would occupy Nursing, Dietician, Physiotherapist, Volunteer, Hospice/Palliative, Occupational Health and Safety, Training and Development, Information Systems, Programming, Secretarial, Customer Service, Fundraising, Public Relations, Accounting, Records Management, and Purchasing positions. Creative, dedicated, highly professional, accurate, enthusiastic, continuous learner, self-motivated, problem solving skills, previous work experience, possess clinical work habits, confidence, and excellent interpersonal and communication skills are all listed as desirable non-academic qualifications. Company benefits are rated above average. The potential for advancement is listed as average. The average annual starting salary falls within the $20,000 to $25,000 range. The most suitable methods for initial contact by those seeking employment are to mail or fax a resume with a covering letter. The VON does hire summer students, applications should be made prior to May 1st. *Contact:* Elizabeth Macnab, Director, Human Resources Development.

VOYAGEUR INSURANCE COMPANY
44 Peel Centre Drive, Suite 403
Brampton, ON L6T 4M8

Tel. 905-791-8700
Fax 905-791-4600

The Voyageur Insurance Company employs more than 100 people in the selling of travel insurance through retail travel agencies and airlines, as well as providing claims service to policyholders. Also, Voyageur provides a 24 Hour Assistance "Hotline" to all policyholders while travelling. Graduates most likely to be hired come from the following academic areas: Bachelor of Arts (General, Psychology), Bachelor of Science (Computer Science, Nursing), Bachelor of Engineering (Computer Systems), Bachelor of Commerce/Business Administration (Accounting, Finance, Information Systems, Marketing), Chartered Accountant (Finance), Certified Management Accountant (Finance), Certified General Accountant (Finance), Master of Business Administration (Accounting, Finance, Information Systems, Marketing, Public Administration), and Community College Diploma (Accounting, Administration, Advertising,

Business, Insurance, Marketing, Purchasing/Logistics, Secretarial, Graphic Arts, Human Resources, Travel/Tourism, Computer, Emergency/Paramedic, RN/RNA). Graduates would occupy Programmer/ Analyst, Project Accountant, Assistant Coordinator, Claims Examiner, Outside Sales Manager, Inside Sales Assistant, Human Resource and Clerical positions. Customer service oriented, organized, and excellent interpersonal and communication skills are listed as desirable non-academic qualifications. Company benefits are rated as excellent. The potential for advancement is listed as being good. The average annual starting salary falls within the $15,000 to $20,000 range. The most suitable method for initial contact by those seeking employment is to mail a resume with a covering letter. Voyageur Insurance Company does hire summer students. *Contacts:* Sherry Duffy, Manager, Human Resources or Janet Eves, Human Resources Assistant.

WABASH ALLOYS ONTARIO
7496 Torbram Road
Mississauga, ON L4T 4G9

Tel. 905-672-5569

Wabash Alloys Ontario is involved in the recycling of aluminium scrap for distribution to automotive industry diecasters. Wabash is the largest organization in the world involved in the recycling of aluminium, employing more than 100 people at this location. Graduates most likely to be hired come from the following academic areas: Bachelor of Science (Metallurgy), Bachelor of Engineering (Industrial), Bachelor of Commerce/Business Administration (Marketing), and Community College Diploma (Metallurgy). Graduates would occupy Technicians, Management Trainees, Marketing Trainee, and General Accounting positions. Company benefits are rated as excellent. The potential for advancement is listed as average. The average annual starting salary falls within the $30,000 to $35,000 range. The most suitable method for initial contact by those seeking employment is to mail a resume with a covering letter. *Contacts:* Peter Black, Vice President, Administration or Greg Fuller, Vice President, Manufacturing.

WACKENHUT OF CANADA LIMITED
332 Consumers Road
Toronto, ON M2J 1P8

Tel. 416-493-8119
Fax 416-493-6683

Wackenhut of Canada Limited is an international security firm providing guard services, alarm equipment and response services, patrols and inspections, access systems, canine security, and upscale security services. Wackenhut's clients range from condominiums, to factories and parks. There are 350 employees at this location, a total of 1,000 in Canada, and a total of 50,000 employees worldwide. Graduates most likely to be hired come from the following academic areas: Community College Diploma (Accounting, Administration, Business, Marketing/Sales,

Secretarial, Security/Enforcement, Private Investigations) and High School Diploma. Graduates would occupy Security Officer, Private Investigator, Patrol Driver, Supervisor, Dispatcher, and Office Staff positions. Dedication, responsible, clean record, flexible, and able to work shift work are all listed as desirable non-academic qualifications. Company benefits are rated as industry standard, and include dental, medical and pension benefits. The potential for advancement is listed as excellent. The average annual starting salary falls within the $20,000 to $25,000 range. The most suitable method for initial contact by those seeking employment is to complete an application at this location. Wackenhut of Canada Limited does hire summer students. *Contact:* Tara H. Slade, Office Administrator.

WALBAR CANADA
1303 Aerowood Drive
Mississauga, ON L4W 2P6

Tel. 905-602-4041
Fax 905-625-8360

Walbar Canada manufactures turbine components, compressor airfoil and turbine parts for aircraft gas turbine engines and is a wholly-owned subsidiary of Walbar. In order to ensure precision manufacture, Walbar employs a range of equipment including CNC machine tools, Heat Treat and Coating Process, and E.D.M. (Electrical Discharge Machining). Walbar Canada employs approximately 200 people. Graduates most likely to be hired come from the following academic areas: Bachelor of Science (Computer Science), Bachelor of Engineering (Mechanical, Industrial Design), Bachelor of Commerce/Business Administration (Accounting, Finance, Information Systems, Marketing), Certified Management Accountant (Finance), Master of Business Administration (Accounting, Finance, Information Systems, Marketing), Master of Engineering (Industrial Design, Mechanical), and Community College Diploma (Accounting, Marketing/Sales, Purchasing/Logistics, Human Resources, Electrician, Engineering Technician, Industrial Design, Mechanic). Graduates are hired to occupy Manufacturing Engineer, Process Engineer, Industrial Engineer, Maintenance Mechanic, Electrician, and Finance positions. An ability to handle multiple tasks, work under pressure towards deadlines, computer skills and good interpersonal and communication skills are all listed as desirable non-academic qualifications. Company benefits are rated above average. The potential for advancement is listed as being good. The most suitable method for initial contact by those seeking employment is to mail a resume with a covering letter. *Contacts:* Director, Human Resources or Ramla Passi, Human Resources Administrator.

WANDLYN INNS LTD.
P.O. Box 430
Fredericton, NB E3B 5P8

Tel. 506-452-0550
Fax 506-452-8894

Wandlyn Inns Ltd. operates a chain of motor inns, including dining, lounge and convention facilities. The company is also involved in real estate sales and development. Wandlyn Inns Ltd. employs 50 people at this location and approximately 1,200 people across Canada. Graduates most likely to be hired come from the following academic areas: Bachelor of Commerce/Business Administration (Accounting, Information Systems, Marketing), and Community College Diploma (Accounting, Business, Purchasing/Logistics, Secretarial, Travel/Tourism). Graduates would occupy Clerical and Management Trainee positions. Hard working, an ability to deal with the public, strong personality, and a professional appearance are all listed as desirable non-academic qualifications. Company benefits are rated as excellent. The potential for advancement is listed as being good. The average annual starting salary varies with the position being considered and the qualifications of the applicant. The most suitable method for initial contact by those seeking employment is to mail a resume with a covering letter. Wandlyn Inns. Ltd. does hire students for seasonal and part time employment. *Contacts:* Rick Draper, Director of Operations or Doug French, Comptroller.

WANG GLOBAL
150 Middlefield Road
Toronto, ON M1S 4L6

Tel. 416-298-9400
Fax 416-412-4834
Email .... canada@wang.com
Website .... www.wang.com

Wang Global is headquartered in Billerica, Massachusetts and has subsidiaries in over 40 countries, including Canada. A leading international network and desktop integration and services company, Wang Global provides a comprehensive range of information technology (IT) services for today's network-centric business environments. Wang Global is focussed on improving the reliability, availability and performance of companies' IT infrastructures, thus freeing those customers to concentrate on their core business. Wang Global is the second largest independent network and desktop integration services company in Canada (IDC, May 1998). It has approximately 400 employees nationwide working from 30 direct service locations, plus over 100 service partner locations, thus providing coast to coast coverage. Wang Global employs a total of 20,000 people worldwide. Wang Global's strategic relationships and alliances allow it to offer best-of-breed IT solutions to customers. Key global alliances include Microsoft, Cisco, and Dell. Other alliances include: Intel, Novell, Olivetti Computers Worldwide, HP, IBM/Lotus, SUN, 3Com, Cabletron, Netscape, Compaq, Motorola, Bay Networks, NEC Technologies, and Viewsonic, as well as other industry leaders. Wang Global's commitment to quality service and customer satisfaction is backed by ISO9002 certification in Canada. The company's depth and breadth of expertise is ensured by superior technical personnel who keep current with rapidly changing technology through frequent accredited training.

Wang Global invests heavily to ensure it has the latest equipment and most up-to-date skill sets. Additionally, Wang Global has a worldwide internal electronic computing environment to give staff online access to the latest technical and marketing materials. Graduates most likely to be hired are Information Systems and Computer Science graduates with a Community College Diploma. Graduates would occupy Field Technician Trainee positions. Good customer service skills, ability to work independently, and previous work experience are listed as desirable non-academic qualifications. Company benefits are rated above average. The potential for advancement is listed as being good. The average annual starting salary falls within the $30,000 to $35,000 range. The most suitable method for initial contact by those seeking employment is to mail a resume with a covering letter. Wang Global does hire summer and co-op work term students. *Contact:* Human Resources.

WARNER-LAMBERT CANADA INC.
2200 Eglinton Avenue East
Toronto, ON M1L 2N3

Tel. 416-288-2200

Warner-Lambert employs more than 500 people across Canada in 4 divisions: Warner Welcome - OTC Products, Parke Davis - Pharmaceutical, Adams Brands - Confectionery, and Consumer Health Division - OTC Products. Graduates most likely to be hired come from the following areas: Bachelor of Arts (Psychology, Sociology), Bachelor of Science (General, Biology, Chemistry, Computer, Mathematics, Microbiology, Nursing, Pharmacy, Physics), Bachelor of Engineering (Chemical, Computer Systems, Electrical, Industrial, Materials Science), Bachelor of Education (General, Adult, Physical), Bachelor of Commerce/Business Administration (Accounting, Finance, Information Systems, Marketing, Public Administration), Chartered Accountant, Certified Management Accountant, Certified General Accountant, Master of Business Administration, Master of Arts (Psychology, Sociology), Master of Science (General, Biology, Chemistry, Computer, Mathematics, Microbiology, Nursing, Pharmacy, Physics), Master of Engineering (Chemical, Computer Systems, Electrical, Industrial, Materials Science), Master of Education (General, Adult, Physical), and Community College Diploma (Accounting, Graphic Arts, Human Resources, Journalism, Television/Radio Arts, Architecture/Drafting, Computer Science, Electronics Technician, Engineering Technician, Mechanic, Animal Health, Food/Nutrition, Laboratory Technician, Nursing RN/RNA, Radiology Technician, Respiratory Technician). Company benefits and the potential for advancement are both rated as excellent. The average annual starting salary is dependent upon the position being considered. Job hunters should research thoroughly and be creative when contacting Warner-Lambert, request an annual report and attempt to set-up an informational interview with the appropriate department. Summer students are hired for Sales and Marketing positions. Warner-Lambert is an equal opportunity employer. *Contact:* Joyce Spencer, Human Resources.

WEB OFFSET PUBLICATIONS LTD.
1800 Ironstone Manor
Pickering, ON L1W 3J9

Tel. 905-831-3000
Fax 905-831-3266

Web Offset Publications Ltd. is a commercial publication printer employing more than 100 people. Very few post-secondary graduates are hired. Those most likely to be hired come from the following academic areas: Bachelor of Arts (General), Bachelor of Commerce/Business Administration (General, Finance), Certified General Accountant, and Community College Diploma (Accounting, Administration). These graduates would occupy Clerk positions in the Accounting Department. High School graduates are also hired for printing press operations, and would occupy Press Helper positions. Company benefits are rated above average. The potential for advancement is listed as being good. The average annual starting salary falls within the $15,000 to $20,000 range. The most suitable method for initial contact by graduates seeking employment is to mail a resume with a covering letter. Web Offset Publications Ltd. does hire summer students for the period between May and August. *Contact:* Human Resources.

WENDY'S RESTAURANTS OF CANADA
6715 Airport Road
Suite 301
Mississauga, ON L4V 1X2

Tel. 905-677-7023
Fax 905-677-5297

Wendy's Restaurants of Canada is a major "quick-service" restaurant chain with over 250 locations across Canada and growing. Each location employs between 35 and 50 people, while Wendy's employs a total of 6,000 people in Canada. Graduates most likely to be hired come from the following academic areas: Bachelor of Arts (General), Bachelor of Commerce/Business Administration, and Community College Diploma (Hotel/Food Administration, Tourism). Graduates are hired as Restaurant Management Trainees. The applicant should maintain a positive attitude, possess excellent interpersonal skills and an eagerness to work. Company benefits and the potential for advancement are both rated as excellent. The average annual starting salary for management positions falls within the $25,000 to $30,000 range. The most suitable methods for initial contact by those seeking employment are to mail or fax a resume with a covering letter. Wendy's Restaurants of Canada does hire summer students, in certain cases. Application for summer and part-time hourly employment should be made in person to the Manager at the desired restaurant location. *Contacts:* Julie Seguin, HR Manager Eastern Canada; Liz Volk, HR Manager Central Canada; Dirk Nagy, HR Manager Western Canada or Sandra Lennon, Director of Human Resources.

WESCO
475 Hood Road
Markham, ON L3R 0S8

Tel. 905-475-7400
Fax 905-475-0294

Wesco is an international company involved in the distribution of electrical and related industrial supply products through 250 plus branches in Canada and the United States. There are more than 500 employees at this location. Graduates most likely to be hired come from the following academic areas: Bachelor of Arts (General, Economics, English, Political Science, Psychology, Recreation Studies, Sociology), Bachelor of Science (General), Bachelor of Engineering (General, Electrical), Bachelor of Commerce/Business Administration (General, Marketing). Graduates would move into entry level assignments in Warehousing, Counter, and Inside Sales with the objective of accelerating their development into Sales and Management. Assertive, task oriented, superior interpersonal skills, and an ability to work under a minimum amount of supervision are all listed as desirable non-academic qualifications. Company benefits and the potential for advancement are both rated as excellent. The average annual starting salary falls within the $20,000 to $25,000 range. The most suitable method for initial contact by those seeking employment is to mail a resume with a covering letter. Wesco does hire summer students. *Contact:* Douglas D. Dodge, Director, Human Resources.

WEST END SYSTEMS CORP.
39 Winner's Circle Drive
Arnprior, ON K7S 3G9

Tel. 613-623-9600
Fax 613-623-0989
Email .... bob_kedrosky@westendsys.com
Website .... www.westendsys.com/

West End Systems Corp. is a leader in the telecommunications industry, providing business-smart, innovative solutions to cable TV operators. As a member of the Newbridge family of companies, West End Systems is uniquely positioned to deliver fully managed voice, data and LAN service access for wireline and HFC networks. Graduates most likely to be hired come from the following academic areas: Bachelor of Science (Computer Science, Mathematics), Bachelor of Engineering (Electrical, Telecommunications), and Master of Engineering (Electrical). West End offers an attractive compensation package and ample room for employees to demonstrate their full range of creative and technical capabilities. Correspondingly, company benefits are rated above average and the potential for advancement is listed as excellent. The average annual starting salary falls within the $40,000 to $45,000 range. The most suitable methods for initial contact by those seeking employment are to mail, fax or e-mail a resume with a covering letter, or apply through the company's website at www.westendsys.com/. West End Systems Corp. does hire co-op work term students. *Contact:* Bob Kedrosky, Manager, Human Resources.

WEST PARK HOSPITAL
82 Buttonwood Avenue
Toronto, ON M6M 2J5

Tel.	416-243-3645
Fax	416-243-3422
Email	hr@westpark.org
Website	www.westpark.org

The West Park Hospital is a designated Greater Toronto Area rehabilitation and local complex continuing care facility with approximately 320 beds, employing approximately 800 persons. The hospital operates with a program management organizational structure and responds to the needs of its communities with evolving, innovative programs based on best practice research. Interdisciplinary teams are to be found in the following service areas: Respiratory, Amputee, Neurological and Geriatric Rehabilitation, Mycobacterial Lung Disease, Prosthetics, Special Care, Multiple Sclerosis, Adult Physically Disabled, Ambulatory Care, Post Polio, Seniors Mental Health, Acquired Brain Injuries, and Transitional Living. Graduates most likely to be hired come from the following academic areas: Bachelor of Arts (Journalism, Psychology, Recreation Studies, Sociology/Social Work), Bachelor of Science (Computer Science, Audiology, Nursing, Nutritional Sciences, Occupational Therapy, Pharmacy, Physio/Physical Therapy, Psychology, Speech Pathology), Bachelor of Education (Adult), Bachelor of Commerce/Business Administration (Accounting, Finance, Human Resources, Information Systems, Marketing), Certified General Accountant, Master of Science (Nursing), Master of Education, Community College Diploma (Accounting, Administration, Communications/Public Relations, Facility Management, Human Resources, Information Systems, Purchasing/Logistics, Secretarial, Journalism, Recreation Studies, Social Work/DSW, Computer Science, Health/Home Care Aide, Nursing RN/RNA, Respiratory Therapy), and High School Diploma. Graduates would occupy Physiotherapist, Occupational Therapist, RN, RDN, Respiratory Therapist, Recreation Therapist, Social Worker, Therapeutic Dietitian, Advanced Practice Nurse, Marketing Representative, Public Relations, Human Resources, Secretary, Personal Care Attendant, Organizational and Personal Development Consultant, Research Assistant, Information Analyst, Computer Support Specialist, Support Assistant, and Client Care Attendant positions. Excellent interpersonal and organizational skills, reliable work habits, strong customer service skills, able to work in a transdisciplinary team environment, and previous work experience in a hospital setting are all listed as desirable non-academic qualifications. Employee benefits and the potential for advancement are both rated as excellent. The most suitable methods for initial contact by those seeking employment are to mail, fax or e-mail a resume with a covering letter, or by applying in person at the hospital. The West Park Hospital does hire summer students. *Contact:* Employee Relations Department.

WESTBURNE INC.
505 rue Locke, bureau 200
Montreal, QC H4T 1X7

Tel.	514-342-5181
Fax	514-342-6347
Email	claude.marier@westburne.ca

Westburne Inc. is a leading integrated wholesale distributor of electrical, plumbing, HVAC and industrial supplies to contractors in the residential, commercial and industrial construction industries, as well as to industrial and commercial enterprises, utilities and public sector institutions across North America. The company currently has 5,200 employees in North America - a third of whom are in sales - serving over 100,000 customers in a network of branches extending from northern British Columbia to Newfoundland, and throughout the United States. Graduates most likely to be hired come from the following academic areas: Bachelor of Science (Computer Science), Bachelor of Engineering (General, Industrial), Bachelor of Commerce/Business Administration (Accounting, Finance, Information Systems, Marketing), Certified Management Accountant, Certified General Accountant, Master of Business Administration (Finance, Marketing), and Community College Diploma (Administration, Business, Marketing/Sales, Purchasing/Logistics, Human Resources, Electronics, HVAC Systems). Graduates are hired to occupy Sales Representative, and Branch Management Trainee positions. Initiative, creativity, a team spirit, and good interpersonal and communication skills are all listed as desirable non-academic qualifications. Company benefits are rated as industry standard. The potential for advancement is listed as excellent. The average annual starting salary falls within the $25,000 to $30,000 range. The most suitable method for initial contact by those seeking employment is to mail a resume with a covering letter. Westburne Inc. does hire summer and co-op work term students. *Contact:* Human Resources.

WESTBURNE INDUSTRIAL ENTERPRISES LTD. (NEDCO DIVISION)
5600 Keaton Crescent
Mississauga, ON L5G 3R3

Tel.	905-712-4004
Fax	905-568-2980

Westburne is Canada's largest distributor of electrical, plumbing and HVAC/R products. In Ontario, Westburne has 94 branches and 1,450 employees. There are approximately 375 employees at this location, the Nedco Division. Westburne's corporate office (see previous listing) is located in Montreal and its stock is traded on the Toronto and Montreal Stock Exchanges (Westburne Inc.). The company employs 5,500 staff across North America. Graduates most likely to be hired come from the following academic areas: Bachelor of Arts (General), Bachelor of Engineering (Electrical, Automation/Robotics, Telecommunications), Bachelor of Commerce/

Business Administration, Chartered Accountant, Certified Management Accountant, Certified General Accountant, Master of Business Administration, and Community College Diploma (Accounting, Administration, Business, Human Resources, Marketing/Sales, Purchasing/Logistics, Secretarial, Computer Science, HVAC Systems). Graduates would occupy Outside/Inside Sales, Counter, Warehouse, Purchasing, Quotations and Office Administration positions, as well as Head Office positions in Accounting (Receivable and Payable), Finance, Credit, Information Systems, Total Quality Management, Human Resources, and Payroll and Administration. Related distribution experience in the electrical, plumbing, waterworks, HVAC/R, wire and cable, drives and automation, lighting and telecommunications industries is preferred. Company benefits and the potential for advancement are both rated as excellent. The average annual starting salary is dependent upon the position being considered. The most suitable method for initial contact by those seeking employment is to mail a resume with a covering letter. Westburne Inc. does hire summer students. *Contact:* Lynn Campbell, Human Resources Administration Manager.

WESTBURY HOWARD JOHNSON PLAZA HOTEL
475 Yonge Street
Toronto, ON M4Y 1X7

Tel. 416-924-0611
Fax 416-924-1413

The Westbury Howard Johnson Plaza Hotel is a full service hotel employing between more than 100 people in the provision of hotel accommodation, and food and beverage services. Graduates most likely to be hired come from the following academic areas: Bachelor of Arts (General/Social Sciences), Bachelor of Commerce/Business Administration (Hotel/Food Administration), and Community College Diploma (Hospitality). Graduates would occupy Clerk, Supervisor and Manager (based upon experience) positions. Service oriented, and excellent problem solving, interpersonal and communication skills are listed as desirable non-academic qualifications. Company benefits and the potential for advancement are both rated as excellent. The average annual starting salary falls within the $20,000 to $25,000 range. The most suitable method for initial contact by those seeking employment is to mail a resume with a covering letter. The Westbury Howard Johnson Plaza Hotel does employ summer students as Waiters, Front Desk Clerks and Room Cleaners. *Contact:* Lasia Dubick, Administrative Assistant.

WESTCOAST ENERGY INC.
1333 West Georgia Street
Vancouver, BC V6E 3K9

Tel. 604-691-5814
Fax 604-691-5868
Website .... www.westcoastenergy.com

Westcoast Energy Inc. was established in 1957 and is British Columbia's only major natural gas processing and pipeline company. Canadian owned and operated, Westcoast's extensive facilities supply gas to domestic and U.S. markets. The company employs approximately 5,900 people. Graduates most likely to be hired come from the following academic areas: Bachelor of Engineering (Chemical, Systems, Environmental, Electrical, Mechanical), Bachelor of Commerce/Business Administration (Accounting, Finance), Chartered Accountant (Finance), Certified Management Accountant (Finance), Certified General Accountant (Finance), Master of Business Administration (Accounting, Finance), Community College Diploma (Accounting, Secretarial, Human Resources, Electronics Technician, Engineering Technician, Industrial Design), and High School Diploma. At the head office location, graduates would occupy positions in Engineering/Drafting, Administration, Accounting/Finance, and Data Processing. In field operations, with locations throughout northern British Columbia, graduates would occupy positions in Telecommunications, Measurement and Engineering Technologies, Instrument and Electrical Technologies, Millwrights, Heavy Duty Mechanics, Pipefitting, Steam Engineering, Welding, and Gas Processing. Company benefits are rated as excellent. The potential for advancement is listed as being good. The average annual starting salary falls within the $30,000 to $35,000 range. The most suitable method for initial contact by those seeking employment is to mail a resume with a covering letter. Westcoast Energy Inc. does hire summer and co-op work term students, primarily engineering and technology students. *Contact:* Joleen Beaven, Administrative Assistant.

WEYERHAEUSER CANADA LTD.
P.O. Box 800
Kamloops, BC V2C 5M7

Tel. 250-372-2217
Fax 250-828-7580

Weyerhaeuser Canada Ltd. employs more than 2,500 people in the manufacturing of pulp, paper, and lumber. Graduates most likely to be hired come from the the following academic areas: Bachelor of Science (Forestry), Bachelor of Engineering (Chemical, Electrical, Mechanical), Bachelor of Commerce/Business Administration (Finance), and Chartered Accountant (Finance). Graduates are hired to occupy Project Engineer, Electrical/Instrumentation Engineer, Process Engineer, Professional Forester, and Corporate/Divisional Financial Manager positions. Team player, results oriented, and good problem solving, communication and coaching skills are all listed as desirable non-academic qualifications. Company benefits are rated as excellent. The potential for advancement is listed as being good. The average annual starting salary falls within the $30,000 to $35,000 range. The most suitable method for initial contact by those seeking employment is to mail a resume with a covering letter. *Contacts:* Vinotha Naidu, Pensions and Benefits Coordinator or Mike Rushby, Vice President, Human Resources.

WHISTLER AND BLACKCOMB MOUNTAINS

4545 Blackcomb Way
Whistler, BC V0N 1B4

Tel. 604-932-3141
Fax 604-938-7527
Email .... bschr@intrawest.com
Website .... www.blackcomb.com

Whistler and Blackcomb Mountains is a major ski resort based in Whistler, British Columbia. Operational activities include retail, mountain operations, sales and marketing, food and beverage, finance, human resources, etc. The number of employees varies with the season. Graduates most likely to be hired come from the following academic areas: Bachelor of Arts (Recreation Studies), Bachelor of Education (Children), Bachelor of Commerce/Business Administration (Finance, Human Resources, Information Systems, Marketing), Community College Diploma (Accounting, Human Resources, Marketing/Sales, Secretarial, Graphic Arts, Recreation Studies), and High School Diploma. Graduates would occupy Kids Camp Child Care Worker, Accounts Payable/Receivable Clerk, Sales and Marketing, Graphic Designer, Receptionist, Administrative Assistant, Lift Maintenance Mechanic, Data Entry Clerk, Computer User Support, Human Resources, and Food and Beverage positions. Friendly, outgoing, team player, presentable, and excellent customer service skills are all listed as desirable non-academic qualifications. Company benefits are rated as excellent. The potential for advancement is listed as being good. The most suitable methods for initial contact by those seeking employment is by calling the Job Line at (604) 938-7367, or through e-mail at bschr@intrawest.com. Whistler and Blackcomb Mountains does hire students for the summer season (June 17 to September 4), and the winter season (November 22 to May 22). In addition, there are also a limited number of year round positions available. *Contact:* Human Resources.

WHITE ROSE CRAFTS & NURSERY SALES LIMITED

4038 Highway #7
Unionville, ON L3R 2L5

Tel. 905-477-3330
Fax 905-477-9432

White Rose Crafts & Nursery Sales Limited is the largest retailer of crafts and nursery related items in Canada. The company's stores are open seven days a week, every day except for Christmas and New Years. White Rose employs 130 people at this location, and a total of 2,500 people in Canada. Graduates most likely to be hired come from Bachelor of Science (Horticulture) and Bachelor of Commerce/ Business Administration (Marketing) programs. Graduates would occupy Staff Specialist or Department Management positions. An excellent command of the English language, an ability to deal with the public, punctuality, and a professional personal appearance are all listed as desirable non-academic qualifications. Company benefits and the potential for advancement are both rated as excellent. The average annual starting salary falls within the $25,000 to $30,000 range. The most suitable method for initial contact by those seeking employment is to mail a resume with a covering letter. White Rose Crafts & Nursery Sales Limited does hire summer and co-op students, as well as requiring additional staff in the spring. *Contact:* Nora Leung, Human Resources.

WHITEHORSE, CITY OF

2121 - 2nd Avenue
Whitehorse, YT Y1A 1C2

Tel. 403-668-8617
Fax 403-668-8384

The City of Whitehorse provides municipal government services (including fire suppression and transit) to a population base of approximately 23,000 people, spread over a wide geographical area. The City maintains a permanent workforce of approximately 200 people, plus a casual or seasonal workforce that will range between 10 and 50 employees. Graduates most likely to be hired come from the following academic areas: Bachelor of Arts (Geography, Recreation Studies, Urban Geography), Bachelor of Science (Biology, Computer Science, Environmental, Geography), Bachelor of Engineering (Civil, Resources/Environmental), Bachelor of Commerce/Business Administration (Accounting, Finance, Human Resources, Information Systems, Public Administration), Master of Business Administration (Accounting, Finance, Human Resources, Information Systems, Public Administration), Master of Engineering (Civil), Community College Diploma (Accounting, Administration, Business, Facility Management, Human Resources, Logistics, Secretarial, Recreation Studies, Travel/Tourism, Architecture/Drafting, CAD/CAM/Autocad, Computer Science, HVAC Systems), and High School Diploma. Graduates would occupy Planning, Engineering, Parks and Recreation, Community Services, Municipal Services, Human Resources, Accounting, and Administration positions. Previous work experience, good computer skills (word processing and spreadsheet applications), excellent oral and written communication skills, and good organization and interpersonal skills are all listed as desirable non-academic qualifications. Company benefits are rated as excellent. The potential for advancement is listed as being good. The average annual salary for a mid-range position falls within the $40,000 to $45,000 range. The most suitable methods for initial contact by those seeking employment are to mail a resume with a covering letter, or by responding to advertised positions. The City of Whitehorse does hire summer students, primarily for positions in the planning, engineering and recreation fields. *Contacts:* John Pereira, Personnel Officer, Human Resources Department or Roxane Larouche, Personnel Officer, Human Resources Department.

WIC, Q107/CHOG

5255 Yonge Street
Suite 3000
Toronto, ON M2N 6P4

Tel. 416-221-0107
Fax 416-512-4810

WIC owns and operates radio stations Q107 and CHOG. There are more than 50 employees at this location. Operational activities include on-air announcing, news production, creative writing, programming music, promotions, trafficking of commercials, engineering, computer operations, research, sale of airtime, accounting, human resources, reception and secretarial. Graduates most likely to be hired come from the following academic areas: Bachelor of Arts (General, Journalism, Music), Bachelor of Science (Computer Science), Bachelor of Commerce/Business Administration (Accounting, Finance, Marketing), Chartered Accountant, Certified Management Accountant, Certified General Accountant (1 or 2 accounting positions only), Master of Business Administration (Marketing), Community College Diploma (Accounting, Advertising, Business, Marketing/Sales, Secretarial, Television/Radio Arts), and High School Diploma. For broadcasting positions, talent and experience are the first and foremost qualifications overriding education in most cases. Company benefits are rated above average. The potential for advancement is listed as average. The average starting salary ranges widely with the position being considered, experience and talent, and is commission based for certain positions. The most suitable method for initial contact by those seeking employment is to mail a resume with a covering letter. WIC - Q107/CHOG does hire summer students. *Contact:* Human Resources Director.

WIC TELEVISION, ALBERTA AND PREMIUM TELEVISION

5325 Allard Way
Edmonton, AB T6H 5B8

Tel. 403-438-8476
Fax 403-438-8438

WIC Television, Alberta and Premium Television operates ITV in Edmonton, RDTV in Red Deer, CISA in Lethbridge, CICT in Calgary, and pay and specialty television services, and television production services. The company employs approximately 400 people. Graduates most likely to be hired come from the following academic areas: Bachelor of Laws (Corporate/Contract), Bachelor of Commerce/Business Administration (Accounting, Finance), Chartered Accountant, Certified Management Accountant, Certified General Accountant, and Community College Diploma (Accounting, Administration, Communications, Human Resources, Marketing/Sales, Secretarial, Graphic Arts, Journalism, Television/Radio Arts, Computer Science, Electronics Technician, Engineering Technician). Graduates would occupy Accounting Clerk, Accounts Payable Clerk, Secretary, VTR Technician, VTR Editor, Audio Technician, Post Audio Technician, Maintenance Technician, Camera Operators (E.N.G., Studio, E.F.P.), News Reporter, Producer, Writer, Traffic Secretary, Editor, Television Host/Anchor, Computer Systems Technician, Television Assistant, and Labourer positions. Company benefits are rated as industry stand-ard. The potential for advancement is listed as average. The average annual starting salary falls within the $25,000 to $30,000 range. The most suitable method for initial contact by those seeking employment is to mail a resume with a covering letter. WIC Television, Alberta and Premium Television does hire summer students. *Contact:* Fraser Hiltz, Manager, Human Resources.

WIC, WESTERN INTERNATIONAL COMMUNICATIONS LTD.

505 Burrard Street, Suite 1960
Vancouver, BC V7X 1M6

Tel. 604-687-2844
Fax 604-687-4118

WIC, Western International Communications Ltd. is an integrated Canadian communications, broadcast and entertainment company with its head office in Vancouver. WIC is the only Canadian broadcasting company operating in television, pay television, radio and satellite network services. WIC owns eight television and 12 radio stations across Canada and is a shareholder in the CTV Television Network. WIC employs 40 people at this location, and a total of 2,000 people across Canada. Graduates most likely to be hired come from the following academic areas: Bachelor of Arts (English, Journalism), Bachelor of Science (Physics), Bachelor of Engineering (Computer Systems, Telecommunications), Bachelor of Laws, Bachelor of Commerce/Business Administration (Accounting, Finance, Human Resources, Information Systems, Marketing, Public Administration), Chartered Accountant, Master of Business Administration (Accounting, Finance, Human Resources, Information Systems, Marketing, Public Administration), and Community College Diploma (Accounting, Administration, Advertising, Business, Communications, Marketing, Secretarial, Journalism, Legal Assistant, Television/Radio Arts). At the WIC Head Office, graduates would occupy Lawyer, Accountant, Public Relations, Secretarial, and Legal Assistant positions. At Station locations, graduates would occupy Journalist, Promotions, and Writer positions. Previous work experience, a willingness to learn, and good references are listed as desirable non-academic qualifications. The most suitable method for initial contact by those seeking employment is to mail a resume with a covering letter (contact head office for a list of stations). WIC employs summer students at some of the Television and Radio Station subsidiaries (contact station location). *Contact:* Human Resources.

WINNERS APPAREL LTD.

6715 Airport Road, Suite 500
Mississauga, ON L4V 1Y2

Tel. 905-405-8000
Fax 905-405-7581

Winners Apparel Ltd. is a clothing retail chain employing 180 people at this location and a total of 2,800 people across Canada. Graduates most likely to be hired come from the following academic areas: Bachelor of Commerce/Business Administration (Accounting, Finance), Certified Management Accountant, Certified General Accountant, and Community College Diploma (CAD/CAM/Autocad). Graduates would occupy Clerk, and occasionally, Coordinator positions. Previous related work experience, team player, and strong communication skills are listed as desirable non-academic qualifications. Company benefits are rated above average. The potential for advancement is listed as excellent. The average annual starting salary falls within the $20,000 to $25,000 range, varying with the position being considered. The most suitable methods for initial contact by those seeking employment are to mail or fax a resume with a covering letter. Winners Apparel Ltd. occasionally hires summer students. *Contact:* Human Resources, Recruitment.

WOMEN'S COLLEGE HOSPITAL
60 Grosvenor Street
Toronto, ON M5S 1B6

Tel.	416-323-6400
Fax	416-323-6177

Women's College Hospital is a general teaching hospital with a focus on women's health, family and community medicine, dermatology, and perinatal services. The hospital employs more than 1,000 people. Graduates most likely to be hired come from the following academic areas: Bachelor of Science (Nursing, Health Sciences, Occupational Therapy, Physiotherapy), Bachelor of Engineering (Mechanical, Electrical), Certified Management Accountant, and Community College Diploma (Nursing RN/RNA, Laboratory Technician, Radiology, Respiratory Therapy, Health Records/Administration). Graduates would occupy Registered Nurse, Health Records Technician, Respiratory Therapist, Radiology Technician, and Accounting Clerk positions. Team player, and excellent communication and interpersonal skills are listed as desirable non-academic qualifications. Employee benefits are rated as excellent. The average annual starting salary falls within the $30,000 to $35,000 range. The most suitable method for initial contact by those seeking employment is to mail a resume with a covering letter. *Contacts:* Camille Sherwood or Vicki Murray.

XEROX RESEARCH CENTRE OF CANADA
2660 Speakman Drive
Mississauga, ON L5K 2L1

Tel.	905-823-7091
Fax	905-822-7022
Email	corina_cluteman@xn.xerox.com

The Xerox Research Centre of Canada is involved in fundamental studies in materials science, synthesis and materials processing technology, and the development of materials for novel imaging processes. The Research Centre employs 150 people, with Xerox employing a total of 4,000 people across Canada and 90,000 worldwide. Graduates most likely to be hired come from the following academic areas: Bachelor of Science (Chemistry, Physics),

Bachelor of Engineering (Chemical, Industrial Chemistry, Materials Science), Master of Science (Chemistry, Physics), Master of Engineering (Chemical), and Doctorate (Chemistry, Physics, Chemical Engineering). Graduates would occupy Technical and Research positions. Team player, and good communication and interpersonal skills are listed as desirable non-academic qualifications. Company benefits are rated as excellent. The potential for advancement is listed as being good. The average annual starting salary falls within the $30,000 to $55,000 range, and is primarily dependent upon degree equivalence. The most suitable method for initial contact by those seeking employment is to mail a resume with a covering letter. The Xerox Research Centre of Canada does hire summer students. *Contact:* Corina Cluteman, Human Resources Specialist.

YANKE GROUP OF COMPANIES
2815 Lorne Avenue
Saskatoon, SK S7J 0S5

Tel.	306-955-4221
Fax	306-955-5663

Yanke Group of Companies is a worldwide multi-model carrier. This includes dry van, multi-modal/rail, refrigerated/heated, deck, expedited, freight carrier, ocean and freight forwarding, and logistics management services. The company employs 115 people at this location and a total of 650 people Canada wide. Graduates most likely to be hired are those with a Degree, Diploma or Professional Accreditation specializing in the following areas: Administration, Finance, Accounting, Human Resources, Information Systems, Operations/Logistics, Safety/Loss Prevention, Sales/Marketing, and Maintenance. Leadership abilities, transportation industry experience, and managerial and supervisory experience are listed as desirable non-academic qualifications. The ideal candidate can typically be described as a risk taker who is innovative, responsible, reliable and possesses a high level of energy. Company benefits and the potential for advancement are both rated as excellent. The average annual starting salary ranges widely, depending on the degree of responsibility, the level of authority and the complexity of the tasks to be undertaken as described in the work description. The most suitable method for initial contact by those seeking employment with the corporation is to mail a resume and references, under a cover letter. Yanke Group of Companies does hire summer students on an "as required" basis. *Contact:* Human Resources Department.

YELLOWKNIFE, CITY OF
P.O. Box 580
Yellowknife, NT X1A 2N4

Tel.	867-920-5600
Fax	867-669-3463
Email	cityhr@city.yellowknife.nt.ca
Website	www.city.yellowknife.nt.ca

Yellowknife, the capital city of the Northwest Territories has a population of over 18,000, and has continued to grow as a mining, transportation, communications and administrative centre. The City of Yellowknife employs approximately 150 people in the provision of Municipal Government services. Graduates most likely to be hired come from the following academic areas: Bachelor of Arts (General, Criminology, Recreation Studies, Urban Geography/ Planning), Bachelor of Science (General, Computer Science), Bachelor of Engineering (General, Civil, Computer Systems, Environmental/Resources), Bachelor of Commerce/Business Administration (General, Accounting, Finance, Human Resources, Information Systems, Public Administration), Master of Arts (Recreation), Master of Library Science, and Community College Diploma (Administration, Business, Facility Management, Human Resources, Information Systems, Purchasing/Logistics, Secretarial, CAD/CAM/Autocad, Computer Science, Engineering Technician, Ambulance/Emergency Care). Graduates would occupy Clerk, Technician, Secretarial, Facility Maintenance, Engineering, Municipal Enforcement, Emergency Services, Recreation Programming, Urban Planner, and Development Officer positions. Previous work experience, flexibility, team player, public relations skills and dedication are all listed as desirable non-academic qualifications. Company benefits are rated as excellent. The potential for advancement is listed as being good. The average annual starting salary falls within the $30,000 to $35,000 range. The most suitable method for initial contact by those seeking employment is to fax a resume with a covering letter. The City of Yellowknife does hire summer and co-op work term students. *Contacts:* Sheila Dunn, Human Resources Director or Kelly Arychuk, Human Resources Officer.

YORK SOUTH ASSOCIATION FOR COMMUNITY LIVING
101 Edward Avenue
Richmond Hill, ON L4C 5E5

Tel. 905-884-9110
Fax 905-737-3284

York South Association for Community Living employs approximately 125 people in the provision of residential and adult life skills programmes for people with developmental delays. Graduates most likely to be hired come from the following academic areas: Bachelor of Arts (Psychology, Recreation Studies), and Bachelor of Science (Psychology). Graduates are hired as Community Support Workers or Community Support Facilitators. Applicants should have a positive and pleasant personality, a good sense of humour and good team work skills. Applicants should also be willing to work shifts (weekends as well) with people who have developmental delays or physical handicaps. Company benefits are rated above average. The potential for advancement is listed as being good. The average annual starting salary falls within the $25,000 to $26,000 range. The most suitable methods for initial contact by those seeking employment are to mail or fax a resume with a covering letter. York South

Association for Community Living does hire summer and co-op work term students. *Contacts:* Erica Nielson, Administrative Assistant; Ms. Pat Card, Team Manager, Richmond Hill or Debbie Lewis, Team Manager, Markham.

YWCA OF CALGARY
320 - 5th Avenue SE
Calgary, AB T2G 0E5

Tel. 403-263-1550
Fax 403-263-4681

YWCA of Calgary provides services for women and families, including housing, employment, health and fitness, and educational services. The YWCA employs more than 100 people. Graduates most likely to be hired come from the following academic areas: Bachelor of Arts (English, Psychology, Recreation Studies, Sociology), Bachelor of Science (Computer Science), Bachelor of Education (General, Early Childhood), Bachelor of Commerce/Business Administration (Accounting, Finance, Marketing), Community College Diploma (Accounting, Administration, Communications, Marketing/Sales, Recreation Studies, Massage Therapy, Social Work), and High School Diploma. Graduates would occupy Counsellor, Clerk, Teacher, and Accountant positions. Team player, and good communication and supervisory skills are listed as desirable non-academic qualifications. Company benefits are rated as excellent. The potential for advancement is listed as being good. The average annual starting salary falls within the $15,000 to $20,000 range. The most suitable method for initial contact by those seeking employment is to mail a resume with a covering letter. The YWCA of Calgary does hire summer students. *Contact:* Verla Dowell, Executive Assistant.

ZEIDLER ROBERTS PARTNERSHIP/ ARCHITECTS
315 Queen Street West
Toronto, ON M5V 2X2

Tel. 416-596-8300
Fax 416-596-1408

Zeidler Roberts Partnership/Architects is a full-service international architectural practice with offices in Toronto (head office), Baltimore, West Palm Beach, London, Berlin and Hong Kong. There are 85 employees at this location and a total of 130 worldwide. Involved in all aspects of building design, the firm lists an impressive portfolio of very significant buildings across Canada and around the world, including Canada Place-Vancouver, Toronto Eaton Centre, Media Park-Cologne, Queen's Quay Terminal, and Ontario Place, to name a few. A demanding office, with high expectations, but always seeking exceptional new talent, graduates most likely to be hired come from the following academic areas: Bachelor of Arts (Urban Geography/Planning), Bachelor of Engineering (Architectural/Building), Bachelor of Architecture/Landscape Architecture, and Community College Diploma (Graphic Arts, Architecture/

Drafting, CAD/CAM/Autocad). Graduates would occupy entry level Design, entry level Technical Document Preparation, and entry level Construction Administration positions. Additional academic and non-academic qualifications desired include: second language with preference to French, German, Russian, Mandarin Chinese, Spanish and Arabic, an ability and desire to travel, excellent verbal presentation skills, solid design and technical background, Autocad 12, and additional computer skills in word processing, spreadsheet, 3D computer graphic and manual graphic applications. Company benefits are rated as industry standard. The potential for advancement is listed as average. The average annual starting salary falls within the $20,000 to $25,000 range. The most suitable method for initial contact by those seeking employment is to mail a resume and sample portfolio (non-returnable - 81/2 x 11). Interviews are by appointment only, written references. Zeidler Roberts Partnership/Architects does hire summer students, these are limited to architectural and related fields (model building, drafting and general office duties). *Contact:* David Jefferies, BES, B.Arch., OAA, Director of Administration.

ZENON ENVIRONMENTAL INC.

845 Harrington Court
Burlington, ON L7N 3P3

Tel. 905-639-6320
Fax 905-639-1812

Zenon Environmental Inc. is a world leader in providing advanced technology products and services in water purification, process separation and wastewater treatment and recycling. The company employs 200 people at this location, a total of 275 in Canada and 300 people worldwide. Graduates most likely to be hired come from the following academic areas: Bachelor of Science (Chemistry), Bachelor of Engineering (Chemical, Industrial Chemistry, Membrane Technology, Civil, Electrical, Mechanical, Industrial Design, Industrial Production, Resources/Environmental, Water Resources), Bachelor of Commerce/Business Administration (Accounting, Finance, Human Resources, Information Systems, Marketing, Public Administration), Doctorate (Chemistry), and Community College Diploma (Architecture/Drafting, CAD/CAM/Autocad, Electronics Technician, Engineering Technician). Graduates would occupy Environmental Technician, Engineer (All Types), Laboratory Technician, Chemist, Sales, Marketing, Finance, Administration, Accounting, Field Service Representative, and Mechanical Technician positions. Company benefits are rated above average. The potential for advancement is listed as being good. The average annual starting salary falls within the $25,000 to $30,000 range. The most suitable methods for initial contact by those seeking employment are to mail or fax a resume with a covering letter. Zenon Environmental Inc. does hire summer students. *Contacts:* Kathryn Toms, Human Resources Assistant or Susan Podilchak, Human Resources Manager.

ZIFF ENERGY GROUP

1117 Macleod Trail SE
Calgary, AB T2G 2M8

Tel. 403-265-0600
Fax 403-261-4631
Email .... ziff@ziffenergy.com
Website .... www.ziffenergy.com

With more than 40 employees, Ziff Energy Group is the largest energy consulting organization in Canada with offices in Calgary and Houston. Ziff offers a unique combination of corporate analysis, natural gas strategies and regulatory support for North American and international energy companies, government agencies and investors. The company's expertise and innovative approaches produce practical solutions for greater profitability for its customers. Graduates most likely to be hired come from the following academic areas: Bachelor of Arts (Economics), Bachelor of Science (Geology), Bachelor of Engineering (General, Computer Science, Geological Engineering), Bachelor of Commerce/Business Administration (General, Accounting, Information Systems), Certified General Accountant, and Community College Diploma (Computer Science). Company benefits are rated above average. The potential for advancement is listed as being good. The most suitable methods for initial contact by those seeking employment are to mail or fax a resume with a covering letter. Ziff Energy Group does hire summer students. *Contact:* Human Resources.

ZTR CONTROL SYSTEMS INC.

P.O. Box 2543, Station B
London, ON N6A 4G9

Tel. 519-452-1999
Fax 519-452-7764
Email .... hr@ztr.com
Website .... www.ztr.com

With offices located in Canada and the USA, ZTR Control Systems is involved in the design and development of monitoring and control system solutions for a number of different industries. The company has had a special focus on the railway, power generation and wastewater treatment sectors. ZTR integrates internally developed technologies with rugged off-the-shelf components when designing or enhancing control system solutions. Current products utilize PLC's and embedded microprocessors as the heart of the system. A graphical PC based application utilizing remote communications technology can also be implemented to provide customers with global access to their sites. ZTR Control Systems is currently marketing and supporting products in Canada, the United States, and abroad. Graduates most likely to be hired come from the following academic areas: Bachelor of Science (Computer Science), Bachelor of Engineering (Electrical, Mechanical, Automation/Robotics, Computer Systems), and Community College Diploma (Computer Science, Electronics Technician). Graduates would occupy Electronics Technologist, Electronics Technician,

Electrical Engineer, Controls Engineer, Applications Engineering, and Software Developer positions. Co-op experience, leadership skills, team player, excellent written and verbal communication skills, and an understanding of basic business values such as honesty and trust are all listed as desirable non-academic qualifications. Company benefits are rated above average. The potential for advancement is listed as being excellent. The average annual starting salary falls within the $40,000 to $45,000 range. The most suitable methods for initial contact by those seeking employment are to mail, fax or e-mail a resume with a covering letter. ZTR Control Systems Inc. does hire summer and co-op work term students. *Contact:* Patricia Rossi, Human Resources Manager.

ZURICH CANADA
400 Univerisity Avenue
Toronto, ON M5G 1S7

Tel. 416-586-3062
Fax 416-586-3082

Zurich Canada is a property/casualty insurance company. Zurich Canada employs 800 people at this location and a total of 2,200 people across Canada. Graduates most likely to be hired come from the following academic areas: Bachelor of Science (Actuarial, Computer Science, Physical Therapy), Bachelor of Engineering (Civil, Mechanical), Bachelor of Commerce/Business Administration (Accounting, Finance, Human Resources, Information Systems), Certified Management Accountant, Certified General Accountant, and Community College Diploma (Accounting, Administration, Business, Communications, Facility Management, Financial Planning, Human Resources, Insurance). Graduates would occupy Clerk, Trainee, Assistant, Programmer, and Recruiter positions. Customer service skills, work experience, and time management skills are listed as desirable non-academic qualifications. Company benefits are rated as industry standard. The potential for advancement is listed as average. The average annual starting salary for entry level positions falls within the $15,000 to $20,000 range. The most suitable method for initial contact by those seeking employment is to mail a resume with a covering letter. Zurich Canada does hire summer students. *Contact:* Norma Moyle, Human Resources Manager.

ZURICH LIFE INSURANCE COMPANY OF CANADA
400 University Avenue
Toronto, ON M5G 1S7

Tel. 416-586-3000

Zurich Life Insurance Company of Canada is a life insurance company providing individual and group policies, retirement programs/policies, and investment services. Zurich Life employs more than 250 people. Graduates most likely to be hired come from the following academic areas: Bachelor of Arts (Psychology), Bachelor of Science (Actuarial, Biology, Computer Science, Nursing, Nutritional Sciences), Bachelor of Commerce/Business Administration (Human Resources, Information Systems), and Community College Diploma (Human Resources, Computer Science, Emergency Technician, Nursing RN/RNA). Graduates would occupy entry level positions as Underwriters, Programmer Analyst, Claims Examiners, Dental Claims Examiners, Administrative and Secretarial positions. Enthusiasm, articulate, professional, intelligent, team player and a good work ethic are all listed as desirable non-academic qualifications. Company benefits are rated above average. The potential for advancement is listed as being good. The average annual starting salary falls within the $25,000 to $30,000 range. The most suitable method for initial contact by those seeking employment is to mail a resume with a covering letter. Zurich Life Insurance Company of Canada does hire summer students. *Contact:* Human Resources Manager.

Industry Index

BUSINESS: ACCOUNTING

BUSINESS: ADVERTISING

BUSINESS: LAW

BUSINESS: CONSULTING SERVICES

COMMUNICATIONS: BROADCASTING

COMMUNICATIONS: CABLE

COMMUNICATIONS: PRINTING

COMMUNICATIONS: BOOK, MUSIC, VIDEO PUBLISHING

COMMUNICATIONS: MAGAZINE, NEWSPAPER, INFORMATION PUBLISHING

CONSUMER PRODUCTS AND SERVICES: AGRICULTURE

CONSUMER PRODUCTS AND SERVICES: AUTOMOBILE

CONSUMER PRODUCTS AND SERVICES: BEVERAGES

CONSUMER PRODUCTS AND SERVICES: ENTERTAINMENT

CONSUMER PRODUCTS AND SERVICES: FOOD PRODUCTS

CONSUMER PRODUCTS AND SERVICES: HOUSEHOLD GOODS

FINANCIAL SERVICES: FINANCIAL MANAGEMENT

FINANCIAL SERVICES: INVESTMENT FUNDS

FINANCIAL SERVICES: LIFE INSURANCE

FINANCIAL SERVICES: MISCELLANEOUS

FINANCIAL SERVICES: PROPERTY AND CASUALTY INSURANCE

FINANCIAL SERVICES: TRUST AND SAVINGS AND LOANS

GOVERNMENT AND NON-PROFIT

GOVERNMENT: EDUCATION

GOVERNMENT: FEDERAL DEPARTMENTS AND AGENCIES

GOVERNMENT: MUNICIPAL

GOVERNMENT: PROVINCIAL DEPARTMENTS AND AGENCIES

HIGH TECHNOLOGY: BIOTECHNOLOGY AND PHARMACEUTICALS

HIGH TECHNOLOGY: COMPUTER HARDWARE AND SOFTWARE

HIGH TECHNOLOGY: COMMUNICATIONS AND TRANSPORTATION

HIGH TECHNOLOGY: ELECTRONICS

HEALTH SERVICES

INDUSTRIAL PRODUCTS: BUSINESS EQUIPMENT AND FORMS

INDUSTRIAL PRODUCTS: CHEMICALS, PLASTICS, AND PAPER

INDUSTRIAL PRODUCTS: ELECTRICAL PRODUCTS

INDUSTRIAL PRODUCTS: ENGINEERING, ARCHITECTURE, AND CONSTRUCTION

INDUSTRIAL PRODUCTS: MACHINERY

MERCHANDISING: HOSPITALITY, LODGING, FOOD, AND RENTAL

MERCHANDISING: RETAIL

MERCHANDISING: WHOLESALE

OIL AND GAS

OIL AND GAS PIPELINE

REAL ESTATE, PROPERTY MANAGEMENT, AND LAND DEVELOPMENT

TRANSPORTATION

UTILITIES: HYDRO, GAS, AND WATER

UTILITIES: TELEPHONE

Geographic Index

ALBERTA

BRITISH COLUMBIA

NORTHWEST TERRITORIES

ONTARIO

PRINCE EDWARD ISLAND

QUEBEC

SASKATCHEWAN

YUKON

Co-Op Work Index

Summer Job Index

Alphabetical Index

Talent Available

Market yourself to over 1,000 recruiters and search firms across Canada.

C anada's best advertising service for job-seekers is now better than ever. Now your Talent Available listing also reaches recruiters and employers immediately via our popular site on the world wide web.

For only $30 plus GST, you'll be featured in a 50 word listing that brings your skills and experience to the attention of personnel managers, executive recruiters, search firms and human resource directors across Canada. Your listing will:

✔ Appear immediately on our Talent Available web site (http://www.mediacorp2.com/ta) for three months from the date we receive your listing;

✔ Be published in the next consolidation of Talent Available listings in the national newspaper *Canada Employment Weekly*; **and**

✔ Be included in a special reprint of Talent Available listings mailed to over 1,000 recruitment agencies across Canada.

Talent Available provides you with a golden opportunity to tell hiring decision-makers about yourself and how to get in touch with you.

Here's what some customers say:

"I placed two listings in your Talent Available service and received well over 40 calls from recruiters. Ten of the calls resulted in face-to-face interviews! It's a great idea."
-CK, Toronto, ON

"I just wanted to say Thanks to you guys at Canada Employment Weekly! Since graduating in 1994, I've only had three businesses interested in my resume. The third was as a result of your online Talent Available. Thanks again."
-LD, Hamilton, ON

Complete details and an online listing form are available at:

http://www.mediacorp2.com/ta

Or call us at (416) 964-6069 and we'll send you a listing form.

Sample Listing:

EXPERIENCED MARKETING MANAGER seeks challenging position with a customer-driven consumer products company. B.Comm. in Marketing from Dalhousie University with five years experience developing marketing plans for large pharmaceutical company. Successfully launched three new products and boosted sales of existing lines by targeting new consumers. I'm familiar with all aspects of promotion and have good knowledge of retail distribution system in Canada. Computer literate and ready to take on a new challenge. Willing to relocate. Call Steve at (902) 555-1212 or email me at anyone@anywhere.com.

Canada Employment Weekly, 15 Madison Avenue, Toronto, Ontario M5R 2S2
Tel. (416) 964-6069 • Fax (416) 964-3202

Welcome to the Future of Job Searching...

Get your copy of CEW before it comes off the press!

CEW Express is the fast new online edition of Canada Employment Weekly.

✔ **Full text** of every career ad in the upcoming newsprint edition.

✔ **Hypertext links to employers' websites** so you can research hot prospects instantly.

✔ **All new positions every week.** We work hard indexing every position so you don't waste a moment reading outdated information.

✔ **Ads are indexed by occupation.** You'll see all the vacancies in your field across Canada at once.

✔ **You can also review articles** from the upcoming newsprint edition, plus articles and career ads from recent issues.

✔ **A 12 week subscription to CEW *Express* costs $49** plus tax, whether you live in Kapuskasing or Kathmandu.

A new edition appears on our subscriber site every Tuesday afternoon at 4:30 pm – a full day before the newsprint edition hits the newsstands.

To view some sample issues, point your browser to **http://www.mediacorp2.com** and follow the directions. If you like what you see, complete the secure online subscription form. You'll receive a password that lets you access current issues for the duration of your subscription.

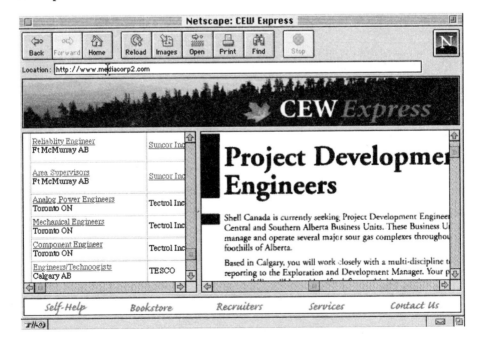

COMMENTS & CHANGES

Please correct / add the following information in the next edition of The Career Directory:

_____

_____

_____

_____

_____

_____

_____

_____

_____

_____

_____

_____

_____

_____
NAME OF EMPLOYER

_____
SUBMITTED BY (OPTIONAL)

_____
DATE   TELEPHONE

Mail completed form to: The Career Directory, Mediacorp Canada Inc., 15 Madison Avenue, Toronto, ON M5R 2S2. Or fax to (416) 964-3202. You can also email corrections to: ry@mediacorp2.com.

THE CAREER DIRECTORY

1999 EDITION

This directory is sold at major bookstores across Canada. You can also order directly from the publisher:

- ❑ Telephone. To order by credit card, please call 1-800-361-2580 or (416) 964-6069.
- ❑ Fax. Fax your credit card order to (416) 964-3202.
- ❑ Mail. Send this form and your cheque or money order (payable to "Mediacorp Canada Inc.") to the address below.

Total charges per copy ordered are:

Shipped to	Directory	Shipping	GST	Total
Canada	$24.95	$6.00	$2.17	$33.12
USA	24.95	10.09	0.00	35.04
Overseas	24.95	18.64	0.00	43.59

Charges shown are for delivery by first-class airmail. Shipments in Canada are sent via two-day Expressmail. FedEx delivery is also available on rush orders. All orders are shipped on the same or next business day.

ORDER FORM

GST # 134051515

THE CAREER DIRECTORY
1999 EDITION

Number of copies ordered: ☐

Method of Payment:
- ❑ Visa
- ❑ MasterCard
- ❑ Amex
- ❑ Cheque

NAME _____

ADDRESS _____

CITY _____ PROV. _____ POST. CODE _____

COUNTRY _____

TELEPHONE _____

CREDIT CARD NUMBER _____

EXPIRY DATE ____ / ____   SIGNATURE _____

Send or fax to

THE CAREER DIRECTORY
15 MADISON AVENUE, TORONTO, ONTARIO M5R 2S2
TEL. (416) 964-6069 • FAX (416) 964-3202